Quantum Mind

Also by Arnold Mindell

Dreambody
Working With the Dreaming Body
River's Way
The Dreambody in Relationships
Riding the Horse Backwards
City Shadows
Coma, Key to Awakening
Working on Yourself Alone
The Year I
The Leader as Martial Artist
The Shaman's Body
Sitting in the Fire

Quantum Mind

The Edge Between Physics and Psychology

ARNOLD MINDELL, PH.D.

LAO TSE PRESS, PORTLAND, OREGON

Distributed to the trade by Words Distributing Company, 7900 Edgewater Drive, Oakland, CA 94621.

Printed in the United States of America

Cover art: Hubble Space Telescope Observations of Comet Hyakutake (1996 B2). Used with permission from NASA and AURA/STScI.
Book design: Kate Jobe

Publisher's Cataloging-in-Publication
(Provided by Quality Books, Inc.)

Mindell, Arnold, 1940
    Quantum Mind : the edge between physics and
psychology / Arnold Mindell. -- 1 st ed.
    p. cm.
    Includes bibliographical references and index.
    LCCN: 99-66088
    ISBN: 1-887078-64-9

    1. Physics--philosophy. 2. Physics--Psychological aspects.
3. Quantum physics. 4. Consciousness.
5. Mind and body. I. Title

QC6.M56 2000   530'.01
                        QB199-1560

Contents

SECTION III
TAOISM IN RELATIVITY

SECTION IV
PSYCHOLOGY IS SENTIENT PHYSICS

List of Illustrations and Tables

Notation Example: "1.1 Alice's tree" indicates Chapter 1, figure number 1, and the title of illustration

Foreword

Waking up terrified one morning, I realized why I had to write *Quantum Mind: The Edge Between Physics and Psychology*. I was afraid of dying. I did not know what would happen to me when I lose my physical form.

Every other night for several years, I had been awakened with questions about what grand mystery lies behind our physical form. Who are we, where did we come from? Why are we here? What happens after death? What is the basis of physics and how does it connect to the psychology of dreams and with spiritual traditions? How is my personal fate connected to the fate of our planet, our solar system?

To ponder these questions, I followed my dreams, reflected on theoretical physics, and considered the thousands of experiences I have had over the past thirty years while working around the world as a therapist with individuals and large groups of people in normal and altered states of consciousness.

To answer my deepest questions, I pondered what I knew about psychology, shamanism, and physics. Then I had an insight. To find answers to my questions, psychology, shamanism, and physics had to come together in a new kind of unified field theory. What an impossible job! How could I do that?

In the chapters that follow, I share my discoveries about how dream-like states of consciousness are the basic substance of the universe. Matter is created from dreaming. These states are basic to moving in and out of the physical form, they are basic not only to shamanism and psychology, but also explain mathematics and physics.

Today, after five years of working on this book, physics, the science of matter, appears to me as an "emperor without clothes," a leader who is not quite up to the task of leading. Chemistry, biology, medicine, psychology, and other sciences cluster around physics as the most central, influential science. Yet the basis and explanation of the laws of physics are still unknown.

In this work, physics appears as if it were a building sitting flat on the ground, without a foundation under it. That is why physicists wonder about the ability and significance of mathematics that can describe new events before they have been observed. I shall be showing that, although physics works, in the sense of giving us a way to make computers and spaceships, we need psychology and shamanism to explain math and why physics works.

It turns out that physics and mathematics are based on what psychology and shamanism always knew; everyone's capacity to become aware of subtle, dreamlike events. *Quantum Mind* is about our awareness process and its mysterious power to participate in creating reality. I discuss the subtle manner in which nature interacts with herself in the background of our perception, creating the observable world.

I call the realm of psychology, shamanism, and physics—where things exist before they are seen—the sentient realm. The psychologist C.G. Jung called it the collective unconscious. The Nobel Prize–winning physicist David Bohm named it the realm of unbroken wholeness. Another Nobel Prize–winning physicist, Werner Heisenberg, called it the world of tendencies, of the quantum wave function. Indigenous people call the same world— where things exist before they are seen—the world of dreaming. Enlightenment in Buddhism is connected with knowing this realm. I claim this realm is the basis for unifying physics and mythology.

But oh! Once I discovered how to gain access to this dreamtime realm behind the physical universe, how to step out of time with the help of physics and shamanism, how could I formulate these new ideas in such a manner as to allow both the general reader and also the trained scientist to follow? This was a challenge I promised myself to meet.

I taught courses on physics to students at the process work centers in Portland, Oregon, London, and Zurich and felt encouraged to go further. I examined the fundamentals of mathematics and discovered, not only how math is a manifestation of our psychology, but also how the math of quantum mechanics is a treasure-house of codes. The math of quantum physics taught me details about consciousness I had intuited, but never

seen formulated! Math and physics contain hidden codes of consciousness.

My wife and partner, Amy, who is a trained therapist without much
background in mathematics or physics, helped me formulate scientific
ideas in a way that could be understood by the general reader. Every
chapter, every new thought, has been discussed with her, although she is
not responsible for the remaining difficulties in the text. I put the math
that was not absolutely needed into the footnotes or the Appendix so that
the scientifically-oriented reader can check out where my ideas come
from.

Amy showed me that my problem in explaining physics to her was
not due to inadequacies in her science background or my teaching ability,
but to problems originating in the sixteenth century, when spirit, mind,
and matter were separated from one another.

Amy wondered about how this present book was connected with my
last, *The Shaman's Body*, where I investigated the world of Carlos Castaneda's shaman, don Juan Matus. I showed how don Juan's teachings
about how to move through altered states of consciousness are crucial to
the foundations of psychology. Only after beginning this present book,
did I reconsider shamanistic teachings and realize that they were encoded
in quantum theory and relativity.

I am indebted to Marie Louise von Franz for having introduced me to
her own work, as well as that of C.G. Jung and Wolfgang Pauli, on synchronicity. I am indebted to my teachers at the Jung Institute in Zurich,
Switzerland, and the Union Institute in Cincinnati, Ohio, to my professors at the Massachusetts Institute of Technology in Cambridge, and to
shamans from Kenya, Canada, Australia, Brazil, and the United States for
insightful peak experiences. My colleagues from the process work centers
around the world have awakened me to special methods of approaching
social issues. I use these methods here to understand symmetry principles in physics.

I am thankful to the support given to me at different points in this
work by the physicists Fred Alan Wolf and Amit Goswami. I am also
endebted to Sharon Sessions for checking out much of the physics in this
book. I am very grateful for the feedback of Dawn Menken, Jan Dworkin,
Kate Jobe, Nicholas Ironmonger, Max Schupbach, and Steve Fenwick of
Portland, Oregon, who read early versions of this manuscript. David
Jones brought my attention to Cushing's work on quantum physics at the
right moment. Great conversations with Joe Goodbread were enlightening

about relativity. I am also grateful to him for helping with the final text. Carl Mindell's recommendations were invaluable in making the text more readable. Michael and Justine Toms of New Dimensions Radio were immensely supportive and helped connect me to Peter Beren, to whom I am indebted for help with editing and for having revealed to me what it was that I had written. I am also endebted to Peter for editorial comments.

Lily Vassiliou performed the immense task of understanding and transcribing the original audio recordings of my lectures on dreams, quantum physics, and relativity. Leslie Heizer gave me great suggestions about the structure of the book and helped create its final version. Margaret Ryan was amazingly helpful with the logic and structure of this work. Mary McAuley was a great help with editing. Kate Jobe of Lao Tse Press in Portland, Oregon, has supported this work with incredible insights and comments every step of the way.

Amy Mindell told me to turn my lectures on physics and psychology into a book. She helped outline some of the exercises in the book and taught courses with me on physics and psychology in the United States and Europe.

I am especially indebted to the spirits, singers, dancers, and Brazilian healers of the Amazon and their religious ritual, the Santo Daime ceremony. Using the sacred vine, Ayahuasca, to combine Native American with African and Christian traditions, the Santo Daime rituals revealed horrendous visions of a symmetrical universe during one of their jungle ceremonies. They allowed me to bring paper and pencil to record the insights into psychology and physics given by the great spirit.

It was in the Amazon in a trance state that I realized that the conflicts between my inner physicist, inner psychologist, and shaman could be resolved by getting these inner figures to collaborate in writing the following book.

Yachats, Oregon
1999

After the present text went to press the author and publisher noted the existence of an internet discussion list hosted by the University of Arizona, with the name, "Quantum-Mind." The material in the present book is not meant to either agree or disagree with the contents of that interesting internet discussion group. We wish to simply note its existence and availability.

November 1999

I

Consciousness in Math

1 | Physics in Wonderland

To us... the only acceptable point of view appears to be the one that recognizes both sides of reality—the quantitative and the qualitative, the physical and the psychic—as compatible with each other and which can embrace them simultaneously... It would be most satisfactory if physics and psyche (i.e., matter and mind) could be seen as complementary aspects of the same reality.

—Wolfgang Pauli, Nobel Prize–winning physicist, in dialogue with his close friend, psychologist, C.G. Jung.

"Think globally, act locally." "The world is a global village." "We are entering the global economy" —these now common phrases only hint at the essential truth of our existence. While you are probably most familiar with only that small portion of the earth which encompasses your personal life, your true home is not just the world, but the whole universe. As a therapist and scientist, I wish to take you on a journey through this universe, on its paths of reason and magic, math and myth. We shall explore math with meditation, quantum mechanics with shamanism, and relativity through a deeper understanding of human relationships. By the end of this journey, you will discover that the most elementary substance of the physical world is dreamlike. Perhaps best of all, you shall sense through the dream and bodywork, relationship and group work, just how the living, beating universal heart and mind may work, and exactly how you are a part of it.

--------~~\/\/\/\~~--------

Like Alice in the fairy tale, *Alice in Wonderland*, we shall be traveling through various worlds. In that tale, Alice found an underground

dreamworld where objects talked. Above the ground, was everyday reality. Until now, if you wanted to get beneath the surface of things you had
to do something with psychology which focused on underground things,
so to speak. Physics centered itself mainly on the world above the
ground. Only Alice and Aboriginal shamans bridged the gap between the
worlds, moving through life knowing every moment was a mixture of
both reason and magic.

In the fairy tale, Alice begins her journey at the surface above ground
and explores a different world below. There she finds an imaginary land
where matter is alive and animals and trees talk. In this underground
wonderland beneath physical reality, houses, even door handles have
voices. Alice's mother, living at the surface reality, is an everyday person
who thinks her daughter is strange and stranger still.

Here is what happened. One day, Alice and a friend hear a rabbit constantly complaining that time flies. Fascinated by that talking rabbit, Alice
and her friend run after the mysterious animal, who leads them to a hole
in the roots of a great tree. The two girls go close enough to the hole to
convince the friend that the spaces beyond are far too unknown to
explore. Courageously, Alice dives into the hole after the rabbit. As she
spirals down, down, down, into the unknown darkness, space bends and
time expands. She embarks on an awesome journey. She finds that the
world deep underneath the tree's roots is full of sentient beings, that is,
they are capable of perceiving and communicating things not generally
recognized by people who live on the surface.

Alice's rabbit reminds me of a subatomic particle—a tiny, almost
invisible thing that physicists study. The hole in the tree is like the place
where the particle, as such, disappears and can no longer be seen. Most
physicists, in fact, most of us, are like Alice's friend. We run up to the
hole, see the rabbit, but do not follow it by jumping in.

Not jumping into Wonderland is one of the main reasons why the roots
of matter remain a mystery to science today. In other words, most scientists stay in the ordinary world of clocks and measuring sticks and decide
to think about—instead of experience—the roots of the tree, the dreamland source from which particles and all of matter arise. Alice, however,
dives into the hole. Like courageous shamans everywhere, she sees the
edge, hesitates, and then jumps out of time, space, and ordinary reality
into Wonderland, the dreamworld we shall call lucid or sentient physics.

Standing safely on the ground above the hole, the outside observer
steps back in shock and wonders, "What guides Alice in Wonderland?
What gives her the courage to go in there? What will she find?" This book
is a guide through that land, our universe. Buddhist meditators, Aboriginal peoples, and shamans have all been there before. It is now time to
bring these worlds together.

AT THE EDGE OF PHYSICS

From the viewpoint of a therapist, physics has been at the edge of Alice's hole since the discoveries of quantum mechanics in the 1920s. The growing edge of physics is to investigate not only the world above ground, but also the underground world of the rabbit, that is, the roots from which experimental observations arise. Investigating the underground home and behavior of matter as described in quantum mechanics and relativity involves two viewpoints, the everyday world of cosmopolitan reality and the world of dreaming.

Following the rabbit involves a shift in viewpoint, a paradigm shift, specifically, a shift from observer to participant. As long as you remain like a conventional physicist, you only photograph or catch glimpses of how the rabbit or particle appears above the ground. You remain in everyday states of consciousness. But to understand and experience matter, you must enter dreamlike experiences, altered states of consciousness where space and time are less significant than they are in ordinary reality. You will have to explore the roots of your perceptions. You must learn lucid dreaming. Then you, like physicists of the future, will be able to do experiments and have experiences that allow you not only to stay above ground, but also to understand the roots of perception, the roots of physics, and the basic nature of the universe. You will be combining areas of knowledge usually kept separate: shamanism, psychology, and physics.

Today's physicists stand outside the entrance to Wonderland. They use concepts from ordinary reality such as "space," "time," "atom," and "particle," and even though they know that in the quantum world, space, time, and objects are all entangled, they stay on the surface of reality. The terms of everyday reality are imprecise in describing the dreamworld. In the quantum world—like in Wonderland—clear-cut meanings no longer exist for such concepts as subject and object, location and separability, future and past. Instead, the patterns and rules for events in the quantum world are described by mathematical formulae which have now become the most fundamental description of matter in physics. The main mathematical formula of the quantum world is called the "quantum wave equation." This formula describes what happens to elementary particles and is full of imaginary numbers that cannot be directly measured or seen in everyday reality. You cannot see or measure the patterns of the wave equation directly.

The root of matter in physics, the so-called quantum wave equation, is like the roots of Alice's tree. Above ground you can see the tree the roots generate, but not the roots themselves. Most of us, like Alice's friend, hesitate to experience the Wonderland of quantum states, the "underground roots" of reality. It is simply less familiar than everyday reality. Physicists are reluctant to say anything definitive about these great roots, and focus instead on measurements made in ordinary reality, which can be seen and substantiated. The following picture gives you a summary of the two realities as expressed by the tale of Wonderland.

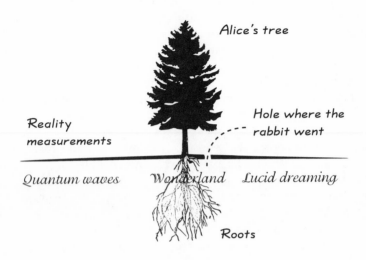

1.1 Alice's tree

A NEW GUIDE: THE "SECRET" CODE

Recently a second school of physicists has come into being which suggests that experiences like Alice's Wonderland are needed to understand the basis and implications of relativity and quantum mechanics. This new school studies "consciousness." Since the early 1920s, physicists have known that consciousness plays a central role in physics, but no one knew exactly what that role is, or where it enters the equations of matter.

By studying the dreamlike roots of physics, we shall explore the basics of perception and find out how consciousness enters physics. With the help of psychology, the mathematics behind physics (such as the wave function that describes quantum objects) will appear to contain a secret code which guides us through the underground labyrinth of dreaming as we explore how consciousness creates matter and what we call, "the real world."

This code will reveal how our individual psychology is universal, in fact, how our individual psychology is fundamentally physics. We shall explore the role that consciousness plays in creating dreams and how it organizes attention and observations. These explorations enable us to develop ideas about the origins of the universe and predict the future of physics, psychology, and shamanism.

PHYSICS IN WONDERLAND

Alice in Wonderland is a metaphor about where physics stands today; some physicists want to stay above ground, others want to explore the origins of consciousness in wonderland beneath the ground. The fairy tale does not tell us how to solve the conflict between these two schools of physics any more than it resolves the problem between Alice and her friend who wants to stay at the surface. A Zen story suggests how the two schools of physics can meet[1]:

> Long ago, two monks from different Zen schools met on a bridge going over a deep river. One monk asked the other how deep the river was and, instead of getting a verbal answer, was thrown into the water. The monk who asked about the depth of the water was thrown in and enlightened.

In other words, to know how deep the river is, you must experience its depth. This monk's enlightenment was freedom from the bridge, freedom from the everyday reality that stands outside of experience and asks for a measurement of, say, five meters in depth. Anyone who can swim knows that the experience of depth and the verbal description of the depth in terms of numbers are very different.

The conflict between those who stick to everyday experimental measurements and those who experience—instead of experiment—will never be solved just by throwing the one seeking real measurements into the water. Our Zen story is deeper than that. It reveals that apprehending enlightenment means simultaneously knowing the depth of the river by using a measuring stick and by using one's own experience. The depth of the river has both a measurable quantitative aspect and an experiential quality. In short, we need to realize that at any moment, we live in more than one world.

CONSCIOUSNESS IN PHYSICS

The quantitative and experiential views of the river are two descriptions of one nature. These two views are found to a certain extent in all the sciences and arts but are most clearly divided in physics. Since the beginnings of quantum theory in the 1920s, the need for putting these views together has been intuited by many noted physicists. The Nobel Prize–winning physicist Werner Heisenberg knew measurement and experience belonged together and spoke about a "consciousness" behind symmetries and other laws of nature.[2] His colleague, often referred to as the father of the wave equation, Erwin Schroedinger, deplored the "ghastly silence" in physics, how physics remains quiet about the topics nearest and dearest to us. He referred often to the philosophies of India, to the importance of recognizing that some universal intelligence like a god or a soul lies behind the universe.[3] John von Neuman, one of the most respected mathematical physicists of this century, claimed in the early 1930s that human consciousness somehow entered the laws of physics and determined the outcome of experiments. How consciousness worked in the physics of matter was not clear to him.

Collaborating with the seminal psychologist C.G. Jung, Wolfgang Pauli said in the 1950s[4]:

> To us... the only acceptable point of view appears to be the one that recognizes both sides of reality—the quantitative and the qualitative, the physical and the psychic—as compatible with each other, and which can embrace them simultaneously... It would be most satisfactory of all if physics and psyche (i.e., matter and mind) could be seen as complementary aspects of the same reality.

Bringing physics, psychology, and the collective traditional wisdom of humankind known as shamanism, together is both the challenge and commitment of this book. Since Descartes, quantitative, "objective" thinking in physics has been accepted as the standard. Physics itself occupies a fundamental position and is a sort of leader among the sciences. In my opinion, this is no longer acceptable today. While the paradigms and concepts of physics are powerful, physics is not sufficiently fundamental. The foundation of physics lies in the nature of the observer, the processes of lucid dreaming, or sentient awareness. To know more about that, physics must be allied with psychology and shamanism.

Two Worlds, One Bridge over Water

For millennia, shamans have tied the sciences of physics and psychology together by working in the real world and the dream world at the same time. Today's scientific thinking splits these worlds apart. Physicists call everyday reality the "classical" reality and use terms such as space, time, matter, and observer, which by consent are used by most people. Psychology calls the second world the realm of direct, personal experience, dreaming, deep feeling, psyche, and personal growth. This world consists of such subjective experiences as emotions, telepathy, and so forth.

Perhaps without quite realizing it, Einstein, on the first page of *The Meaning of Relativity*, a book that transformed science and prepared us to explore elementary particles and outer space, differentiates these two worlds[5] (the italics are mine):

> By the aid of language different individuals can, to a certain extent, compare their experiences. Then it turns out that certain *sense perceptions of different individuals correspond to each other, while for other sense perceptions no such correspondence can be established.*

Here Einstein begins a discussion of perception and experience. He points out that some of our perceptions correspond to one another while others do not.

Let's call the differing perceptions of individuals that correspond with one another "consensus reality" or "CR" for short. Let's call perceptions that do not collectively correspond "non-consensus reality" or "NCR" for short. For example, most people will agree that a given river is about five feet deep. But most will not agree on the idea that there are demons, monsters, or mermaids in that water. Monsters and mermaids are part of NCR. Einstein continues:

> *We are accustomed to regard as real those sense perceptions which are common to different individuals,* and which therefore are, in a measure, impersonal. The natural sciences, and in particular, the most fundamental of them, physics, deal with such sense perceptions.

Einstein believes that physics is the most fundamental science. He further clarifies what he means by "real." For him, and for most physicists, "real" means perceptions that people consent to as being common. "Real" for him means impersonal: consensus reality is the only real one. Only the study of impersonal sense-perceptions is authorized by science. Thus my term, consensus reality (or CR), implies not only a general collective agreement of modern international culture, but also scientific authorization.

How a person or a group defines the term "real" is not an objective fact, but a matter of opinion. Problems begin to arise when we use the term "real" as if it were the absolute truth. Making one experience real and the other "not real" because they have little "correspondence" with the perceptions of others makes them insignificant. Some perceptions are considered the important ones while other perceptions are marginalized, that is, set aside and given second-class status, so to speak.

As a result of implicit value judgments, as Einstein stated above, social psychology and psychology in general—which deal with non-consensual perceptions—are often considered less fundamental than physics. The result is a physics that splits itself off from parts of nature and from parts of human perception. Einstein implies that space and time are real and that other perceptions such as dreams, love, and pain are less fundamental or, at least, less real. He says that science deals only with "real" experience.

If Einstein were alive today, I would ask him to help physics become more relativistic. I would suggest introducing into physics two new terms to distinguish and value two fundamentally different realities—consensus reality or CR for the reality that has consent, and non-consensus reality or NCR for the reality that has been neglected by the present, scientific worldview.

I suggest that it is more relativistic and, therefore, more essentially true to the core of the universal human experience to speak of consensus reality instead of calling it the "real world." CR is impersonal; it has authorization and is considered fundamental in a given time and culture. NCR is another reality, the one that seems from the CR viewpoint to be more "individual," subjective and less fundamental; it has less consent and less mainstream cultural authorization.

In *Quantum Mind*, CR refers mainly to the reality of physics, the classical, everyday cosmopolitan reality of everyday life in which terms such as space, time, size, age, particle, and, even, person have fairly well-defined and collectively consented-upon meanings.

We should remember that neither consensus perception nor non-consensus perception is more real than the other. The depth of the river measured as five feet deep and the experience of the river containing monsters are both real. Neither of the two realities, CR and NCR, is absolute. In other words, even though Alice's friend and Albert Einstein's physics shy away from non-consensus reality, we are still not justified in ignoring the nature of Wonderland.

According to Einstein, in *The Meaning of Relativity*, "the only justification for our concepts and system of concepts is that they serve to represent the complex of our experiences; beyond this they have no legitimacy." We should be clear today that CR, or the consensus reality studied by physics, does not "represent the complex of our experiences" and therefore is not quite as "legitimate"—to use Einstein's words—as many think.

Without personal NCR experiences such as pain, love, and dreaming, physics will never be complete. In fact, *Quantum Mind* shows how some of the unanswered questions of physics may be answered by studying such universal human non-consensus events.

How did the universe begin? What was here before matter? To answer these fundamental questions, we need to perform a paradigm shift. We must enter the non-consensus Wonderland on which physics is built. This paradigm will no longer allow us, for example, to simply describe a rock in terms corresponding to everyone else's ideas about rocks. In the new paradigm, the rock will still have its CR, that is, its consensus reality physical characteristics: it will still be hard, rough, heavy, and so forth. However, in the new paradigm, the rock now will also have an NCR "feeling" such as beauty.

For example, Native American jewelers say they can see powers or forms within the rock asking to be sculpted and revealed. In the new paradigm, the rock will still be a rock but will also have new dimensions as experiment and experience come together. We shall explore in what way the rock itself is sentient, that is, how it too is a subtle communicator with a specific form of awareness.

We all bridge consensus and non-consensus realities daily. There is a traditional saying that Buddhists can see a friend through all stages of their life, as a baby, a teenager, and an old person simultaneously. Like these Buddhists, whenever we look at someone, we have both a CR appreciation of their real body and a sort of intuitive or NCR sense of things they have not yet spoken about.

SHORT HISTORY OF NON-CONSENSUS REALITY

Today's tendency to ignore the qualitative aspects of the world has a long history. Before the sixteenth century, physics and psychology were still one and the same "science"—alchemy. For example, metal was not just metal. Metal was a piece of matter as we know it today but, in addition, it contained a "metallic spirit" or soul.[6]

Indigenous people have always combined the fields of psychology, physics, group work, and bodywork in shamanism or what today some call aboriginal science. Shamanism was—and still is—used to heal individuals and couples and even, in some cultures, to change the weather through fantasy and incantations. Indigenous peoples have always interacted with matter through consensus and non-consensus realities. The earth was composed of the physical world but also the NCR experience native people called "Mother Earth." In the heart of the universal human experience, we were not only independent observers but also part of an earth which itself was full of sentient beings. The ocean and the sky were called Grandmother and Grandfather. Through shamanism, or traditional wisdom, psychology and physics were one indigenous science.

Favoring CR as the fundamental reality destroys the NCR sense of feeling connectedness to the world as a whole. Valuing CR over NCR began during the 1500s when Europeans began to speak about particles without souls. Physics and spirituality split, and religion was left with the job of tending to the spirit. We were no longer participants in nature but became "objective observers"—although at night we were still touched directly by the gods.

A great deal of clarity came from the deliberation and rational separation of mind from matter. But much of our inherent sense of communing with nature was lost. Instead, an "observer" appeared who was supposed to be able to stand above and beyond the world of events. Even today, the observer in modern physics is an impersonal being, more of a mechanical instrument than a human being with feelings. The scientist in an observer capacity focuses only on "reality," that is, the consensus reality agreed on by the majority of human beings in a given culture, in a given time and space, which can be measured with physical instruments. This observer is some sort of physical robot such as an electron counter, without a beating heart and an ocean of blood running through the veins. The observer does everything possible to remain objective and keeps feelings out of the picture; participating in the world being observed is deemed to be "bad" science.

Yet times change and consciousness and cultures continue to evolve. Modern physics has shown that, indeed, this observer does participate. As previously mentioned, the central unanswered questions today are about how this participation occurs.

When I studied physics in the sixties, you dared not speak about your interests in dreams and their connection with matter, or in synchronicities and the like. Today, these studies form the cutting edges of psychology and physics. History teaches us that consensus reality is not absolute. It continually evolves. And, with this process of evolution, our understanding of physics and psychology transforms as well.

MY BACKGROUND

My personal relationship to consciousness studies began when I arrived in Zurich from the United States, on June 13, 1961, a week after C.G. Jung had died. Wolfgang Pauli, the Nobel laureate in physics with whom Jung had collaborated on the connections between psychology and physics, had died a few years earlier. I was a twenty-one-year-old American going to Zurich as an exchange student from the United States. I had never heard of Jung, the famous Swiss psychiatrist. I only knew I was trying to follow the path of Albert Einstein, who had lived in Zurich and had studied at the ETH (the Eidgenosische Technische Hochschule), a well-known science university, the Swiss equivalent of MIT.

I met many psychology, physics, and engineering students in Zurich. I also met a new side of myself, a nighttime full of wild dreams. One of my student friends, who was already in Jungian analysis, listened to these dreams and promptly sent me to sign up for my own analysis. Little did I know at the time how much Jung's ideas would help me understand physics.

My first dream upon embarking into analysis was about Jung and physics. In this dream Jung said to me, "Well, Arny, don't you know what your job in life is?" And I said, "No, I don't know!" Jung said to me, "Well, the job that you have in your life is to find the connections between psychology and physics."

I did not know much about psychology at that time. I was just a student of physics and its applications. Nor did I think that dreams were very important, and I told my analyst so. I said to her, "Well, this dream of Jung is only a dream! Why talk about dreams? I've got plenty of real problems, believe me!"

My analyst said, "Dreams can be important, and that dream might be your personal myth." I was rebellious from the beginning. I said to her, "That dream—a personal myth? Prove it! After all, why should I have to study dreams to find out about myself? Why not just look at my life, at my physical reality?"

I was a firm believer in consensus reality. My analyst was very quick and told me that she could not see dreams in matter, but that my dream said that I should connect psychology to physics. "Doing that is your job," she said.

I was too stubborn to agree with that interpretation, although, looking back, it seems correct. In any case, I set about to complete my studies. While continuing my analysis, I finished my studies at MIT and at the ETH in Zurich and completed the diploma program at the Jung Institute in Zurich, as well as a doctorate in psychology in Ohio. After becoming a training analyst at the Jung Institute, I founded process-oriented psychology and co-founded centers for process-oriented psychology in many places around the world.

Process work, as this psychology is often called, is a wide-spectrum approach to people that includes working with bodily symptoms, psychotic and comatose states, relationships, large groups, and social issues.[7]

In a way, I have been waiting thirty-seven years to study the unification of physics and psychology. This unification brought me back to the storehouse of humanity's traditional wisdom, shamanism. I resisted looking into the connections between psychology, quantum mechanics, and relativity because I not only loved physics, I also detested it! I loved it for its far-out mathematical spaces and because it investigated the structure of the universe. But I disliked it because it was so abstract, so without feeling.

Soon after going into psychology I again became dissatisfied. Psychology—the study of the psyche—was not grounded in the body, in matter. I wondered how my dreams were connected to my bodily experiences. Dream work, in my view, needed new impulses! Since Freud's subconscious, Jung's collective unconscious, J.L. Moreno's psychodrama, and Fritz Perls' Gestalt psychology, research seemed to have reached a plateau.

My own work revealed how dreams become evident in the body as uncontrollable body sensations and subtle communication signals. I expanded this work into relationships and psychotic states. Then I began to work with large-group conflicts.[8]

Today, I realize that individual awareness and individuation cannot be separated from community awareness and the solution to social issues. For me today, consciousness means being aware of the various parts of yourself as well as being aware of yourself as an interacting part of a larger community. In any case, while I worked on bringing the body into psychology, I dropped my overt focus on physics.

In the meantime, physics evolved. Since the 1960s, physics has expanded its theories of the universe into daring new spaces, including its connection with psychology and spirituality. If we judge by the recent spate of popular books on physics, the fields of psychology and physics seem to be approaching one another at a faster rate than ever before.[9]

While some physicists are about to "jump into the water," considering whether quantum objects have consciousness, psychologists are pondering psychosomatic symptoms and, like Jung, the way in which dreams mirror outer events in what he called synchronicity. Brain-mind research and psychoimmunology hold great promise in understanding mood swings, while computer science is investigating the nature of consciousness through mathematical models.

Physics looks more like Alice's Wonderland as theorists create new ideas that are increasingly abstract, far from the CR of everyday life, ideas that can no longer be tested experimentally. The new criteria for the validity of theories in physics are how they fit together, that is, whether they are consistent with one another. At best, theories are checked against other theories. Theories in physics are also judged on whether they are "simple," "beautiful," and "symmetrical," as well as useful. Simplicity, beauty, and symmetry are psychological values, feeling values, showing that psychology and consciousness play a crucial role in physics.

The recent literature on consciousness in physics indicates to me that in the future, psychology and physics, medicine and philosophy will be taught as one discipline with many branches. But don't test my speculation by taking a poll among physicists or psychologists. Some think the human mind is not sufficiently developed to understand the world of quantum state events, let alone its connections with psychology![10] The new science will probe the universe by returning to the indigenous wisdom of our ancestors, valuing our deepest experiences. Since we are stardust, we know the universe, inside and out.

THE STRUCTURE OF THIS BOOK

Grounded in an appreciation of indigenous wisdom, *Quantum Mind* is divided into four parts, which explore mathematics, quantum physics, relativity, and psychology.

Part I explores how mathematics reflects meditation, that is, our human perceptual processes. No previous training in mathematics is needed. I take both a practical and an experiential approach to the study of elementary math and begin to relate it to physics.

Part II reviews quantum physics and its link with the psychology of altered states of consciousness. Here the reader will find discussions about elementary particles and their relationship to perception, dreams, and mythology. Of special interest in this section is how the code of consciousness appears in the mathematics of physics.

Part III discusses psychological patterns behind Einstein's theory of relativity and Hawking's concepts about the structure and origin of the universe. I connect what physicists call curvature and gravity with what therapists call trance states and complexes.

Part IV re-envisions psychology to encompass what we have learned about consciousness from math and physics in the preceding three parts. Part IV is the beginning of a new psychophysical approach to individual and group process psychology. This part forms a shaman's guide to the universe. Here physics creates new patterns for working with psychosomatic healing and relationships. With the help of psychology, physics leads us to new insights into death and the ecological fate of the earth. Of special interest is the application of symmetry principles to community and ecology.

To make this text as participatory as possible, I have included exercises in most chapters, as well as occasional comments and questions from learners. It is my belief that everyone, not only the "experts," is capable of participating in, exploring, and developing cutting-edge theories and experiencing the unification of shamanism, psychology, and physics.

It is my firm belief that each of us is, potentially, a "modern shaman." That means we must be able to personally experience the theories and ideas in these sciences. Only then can we participate in the future of physics and psychology. They depend upon our exploration of the mysteries of shamanistic perception and the ability to move between worlds. When this exploration is complete, we shall use the shaman's awareness not only to transform personal and community life, but also to co-create the physical universe. This is the essence of modern shamanism, which is also a journey home, to a true understanding of the nature of the universe and our proper place in it—modern shamanism is our natural birthright.

NOTES

1. The great translator of Zen into Western terms, Daisetz Suzuki, tells us in his *Zen and Japanese Culture* about these two monks meeting on the bridge, page 7.

2. Ken Wilber, a leading transpersonal psychology theorist, notes in his *Quantum Questions* a conversation recorded by the physicist Werner Heisenberg, which took place between him and two other physicists, Wolfgang Pauli and Niels Bohr. Heisenberg asked, "Was it utterly absurd to seek behind the ordering structure of this world a 'consciousness' whose 'intentions' were these very structures?" (page 35) Niels Bohr answered by quoting Fredrich von Schiller's "The Sentences of Confucius," which says that truth dwells in the depths (page 35).

3. The father of wave mechanics, Erwin Schroedinger, speaks in *What Is Life?*: "This life of yours which you are living is not merely a piece of the entire existence, but is, in a certain sense, 'total'; only this whole is not so constituted that it can be surveyed in one single glance. This, as we know, is what the Brahmins express in that sacred, mystic formula which is yet really so

simple and so clear: 'Tat tvam asi,' this is you. Or, again, in such words as 'I am in the East and in the West, I am below and above, I am this whole world.'"

4.   Pauli's quote can be found in *The Interpretation of Nature and the Psyche*, 1955.

5.   I will go into detail about imaginary experiences involved with mathematics in Chapters 3 through 7.

6.   We have the psychologist C.G. Jung to thank for elucidating this point in great detail. See, for example, the volume of his collected works called *Psychology and Alchemy*.

7.   For an overview of process work see Amy and Arny Mindell's *Riding the Horse Backwards,* where we report on seminars given at the Esalen Institute in Big Sur, California.

8.   I explore group work in Part IV.

9.   I am thinking about such popular new books on physics as Fritz Capra's *Tao of Physics,* Gary Zukav's *The Dancing Wu Li Masters,* Fred Alan Wolf's *The Dreaming Universe,* and Amit Goswami's *The Self-Aware Universe.* These books hint at the fact that the mysterious, long-denied spirit is trying to come back into physics.

10. Not everyone is so optimistic about the future of science. In *The Cosmic Code,* for example, physicist Heinz Pagel suggests that the human brain may not have evolved enough to understand quantum reality. Experimental physicist Leon Lederman wonders "whether the human brain will ever be prepared for the mysteries of quantum physics." See Lederman's *God Particle,* page 157.

2 | Counting and Discounting

Our science education has taken from us the qualitative feelings we once had for our natural world. This must be reversed.

—Rupert Sheldrake, noted biologist, in conversation with the spiritual teacher Matthew Fox and New Dimensions Radio interviewer Michael Toms, on New Dimensions Radio Ukiah, CA[1]

Physics cannot tell us about the spirit of rivers, but it can tell us how fast, how turbulent, and how high the water may be at a given moment. Physics is based on everyday life measurements, on numbers and counting. By counting, we can tell how many stars are visible in the sky or how many pencils are on our tabletop.

Although physics is based on counting and counting is one of the simplest things we do, it possesses encoded secrets. With the help of psychology and by exploring our experience of counting, we shall begin to unravel the entangled mystery of reality. In this chapter we will investigate what happens when we use our minds to count.

WHAT HAPPENS WHEN YOU COUNT

Counting is both math and psychology, as we can see in the dual meanings of such terms as reckoning, recounting, accounting, and enumerating. For example, the word "counting" is connected to "recounting," that is, sharing memories. Other terms for numbers also relate to the mental processes they represent. Think about the words "cipher" and "decipher." They are connected with the awareness procedure involved in understanding something.

To see what happens when you count, try reckoning the number of people in your family or imagine being a sheep farmer and counting the number of sheep you own. Most young children and some of us adults count by using our fingers. But what are you doing by using your fingers to count? You are using an awareness procedure that "matches" the individuals in the family, or sheep in the herd, with the fingers on your hands. Because of matching, each finger represents an individual person or sheep. You use a new finger whenever a new person or sheep is born, and subtract one if someone dies. This seems simple, and it is, but we may have forgotten something, namely, the process of "matching."

The awareness experience of counting matches the individuals in a family or the sheep in a herd with a standard group of things—like fingers or pebbles. Mathematics studies processes such as counting and creates general concepts such as matching, numbers, adding, and subtracting, which can be used to describe the general nature of just about any counting procedure.

Abstractions like "matching," "adding," and "subtracting" are important because such abstractions are tools that can be used with any objects or items whatsoever. The abstractions and methods of math—such as arithmetic, geometry, and calculus—allow us to count not only the number of people in our family, whom we can see, but also many other kinds of things that we cannot see, such as the numbers of things happening in faraway stars or the number of things occurring within the smallest atoms. Abstractions also help create machines like computers, which can count and add for us.

Nevertheless, the essentials of math, like matching, are subject to the processes of general awareness. As such, they belong to the domain of psychology. By studying such abstract mathematical procedures with the help of psychology, by studying how we experience things like counting, we will be able to understand why some of our calculations are, by their inherent nature, incomplete.

MY FIRST PROBLEM WITH ABSTRACT MATHEMATICS

As a teenager, I had a love-hate relationship with math because my teacher focused only on its abstract aspects. So, my first response to mathematics was to become a rebel. In seventh grade my algebra teacher, whom we shall call Ms. Gladstone, was a good teacher, but she gave us too much abstract homework. A friend of mine and I decided to rebel. Our rebellion was trendy, it matched the spirit of the time; we were all "rebels without causes." Since Ms. Gladstone lived nearby, we decided to help her understand our point of view by creating stink bombs that were destined for her home.

One day after class my friend and I worked a little chemistry and created a stink bomb, that is, what we used to call a sulfur bomb. It was not supposed to hurt anyone, only produce a terrible odor. We planted the stink bomb underneath Ms. Gladstone's house. I was not a bad kid, and I didn't really mean to hurt anyone, I just wanted to leave a stink in the air. Anyway, we hid at the edge of the street, trying to flatten ourselves on the road by squeezing against the curb. We lit a match to the long wire fuse that led to the bomb, which was under her house.

When the flame finally got to the bomb, it fizzled and never quite popped. The bomb was a dud. Oh, well, we were just beginning chemists. However, the bomb did leave a bad smell in the air. Nobody got hurt, but the white side of Ms. Gladstone's house got a little dirty. For beginning chemists it was a glorious sight, and the two of us young gangsters were thrilled.

Ms. Gladstone was not happy. She came to the window, threw it open, and let out a yell that cursed the gods. Worse yet, she called the police, who came and asked, "Who did it?" The police peered sternly at both of us, gave us a lecture, and let us go. No charges were pressed against us. I went home and had to tell my mother, who gave me a lecture on learning to speak more directly with my teachers.

Next day, I went to see Ms. Gladstone and told her about my unhappiness with the homework. Our relationship improved and, better yet, there was less homework! I don't know if I changed, but Ms. Gladstone did. She made math seem like more fun.

MATH SHOULD BE FUN

Looking back, I now see that the original problem between my mathematics teacher and me was that math was essentially not a fun experience for me. It sounded too abstract. I couldn't relate. Ms. Gladstone herself had learned that math was something quantitative and abstract, something which had to be worked at, and that is how she taught it. Even though she tried to make it more fun, I still picked up the general attitude that math was just a tool that can be used to keep your checking account or can be used to do physics. But math is more than a tool: it is based on a highly personal experience.

The fundamentals of mathematics can be fun. Understanding the elements of math is no more difficult than understanding meditation. In fact, it is through the meditation process that we will rediscover math together.

Another reason why mathematics frequently scares people is that terms like trigonometry, calculus, matrix, and non-Euclidean geometry sound utterly foreign and inscrutable. Some mathematicians even seem to want math to be that way. They want it to be pure and abstract, unblemished by the feelings of human beings. In any case, this abstractness contributes to making nonscientists (and also many scientists) feel intellectually inferior.

There is another reason why many non-specialists have trouble with math and science. Terms used by math and physics have different meanings from their everyday usage. For example, concepts in math such as "closure" and "field" or words in physics, like "attraction," "charge," and "energy," all have very specific scientific meanings that differ from their everyday usage.

Ultimately, math is connected to how we perceive. Our method of awareness and perception is encoded in mathematics. In other words, psychology, physics, and math are inherently connected.[2]

COUNTING DEPENDS ON CULTURE

Let's go back to the experience of counting. For example, let's say there are five stones on the ground. Two are red and three are blue. The stones on the ground are all quite similar in appearance except for coloring. If I ask an adult how many stones are on the ground, the adult, like most people, will count them all, one by one, and say, "five."

2.1 Stones on the ground

Children, however, are different. A young child would probably answer the same question, not by counting the total number of stones, but by counting the number of dark ones and then the number of light ones. Children up to eight years of age usually say there are three dark ones and two light ones.[3]

There is a difference between the adult method of counting and the child's method. Which method is the right one? The adult account, which says five stones, or the child's account, which say three dark and two light stones? Is the difference merely categorical?

No. Counting involves choice. It involves the psychology of the observer. We count what fascinates us. Kids, for example, may be more interested in the colors of the stones, not in their overall sum. Their perceptions work differently. They are less inhibited by the acculturation process that affects adults, and which demands we say that the total number of stones is five, not three dark and two light ones. Conclusion? What you count depends on who you are!

PERCEPTION AND MARGINALIZATION

Pretend you are a sheep farmer. Imagine watching your sheep going out in the morning. They pass through a gate as you stand there trying to tell how many sheep are leaving. How do you know how many sheep go out? You count them. How do you count them? You might stand at the gate and count each sheep as it goes out to the pasture. Let's say you count five sheep.

As in the example of the stones, a child might count differently. He or she might say there are two brown sheep and three black ones. Now "two brown and three black sheep" is different from "five sheep." Both ways of counting refer to different experiential criteria. If black and brown sheep have equal value in the market, then the number 5 is an important total number because it describes wealth, although it ignores the differences between the sheep.

The perception of 5 marginalizes the difference between the sheep. By counting up to 5, you are saying that the total number of sheep is more important to you—or to the farmer—than the differences between the sheep.

On the other hand, the child may have special feelings for the black sheep and may not be concerned with their market value. The child may experience that the sheep are sentient beings, even beings hoping to be counted. For these reasons, perhaps, the child notices three black ones and two that are not black, but brown. The child's method of counting marginalizes the adult interest in the total number, while the adult perception discounts or marginalizes the subjective feelings the child may have about specific sheep.

Each method of counting is exact according to its basic assumptions, but those assumptions are usually ignored when we state the final sum. This reminds me of a comment I heard while traveling in India. When a mother is asked how many children she has, she might answer, "two sons," even if she has five children, three of whom are daughters.

In other words, what we count—and how we count—reflects how we think or perceive. It reflects our relationship with what we are observing. Thus, the simple experience of counting depends on many presumably objective factors. Our awareness determines what we count and what we ignore or marginalize—that is, what we consider to be of secondary significance.

AGGREGATES AND MATCHING

Back to the sheep. How do we, as either adults or children, remember and share with others our accounting of how many sheep have left our pasture? We might look for stones on the ground to represent the number we want to communicate. As a sheep goes out, we could take a stone and put it aside to help us remember. As another sheep goes out, we can take a second stone and put it aside as well. Eventually, we have five stones in a pile. A child might also use stones but is more likely to have two groupings—one pile of three for the black sheep and one pile of two for the brown ones.

The piles of stones look simple in one sense, and they are. But what have we really done in making piles of stones to represent the sheep that went out to the pasture?

Separability. First, we assumed that the sheep are an aggregate, a group that can be counted.

The word "aggregate" comes from the Greek for "to herd together." An aggregate is a bunch of like things that remain separated enough to count. Stones are a typical aggregate. Each is separate and has an individual identity.

Psychology. Next, we assumed that the aggregate, or the group of sheep we perceive, is the one that needs to be counted. We now know that age, culture, and personal psychology influenced our perceptual choices.

Thus in the process of counting, not only are we assuming that the things we are counting can be separated, but also, we are choosing which groupings to focus on. Most of the time, without our even being aware, counting, by its very nature, assumes and chooses. Culture and psychology play a significant role in deciding what we count.

Standardization. In counting sheep, we make a third assumption as well. We assumed that we could use a standard aggregate or group, namely, the stones, to measure another aggregate, the sheep. The standard aggregate that we use depends on who we are and the people we want to inform about how many sheep we have. We can use sticks, stones, fingers, or other objects. Our final choice of standard aggregates or signs will demonstrate something about the collective nature of our community.

Matching. By using any standard aggregate, we are also assuming that we can use the standard aggregate as a sign representing another aggregate. That is, we can use fingers, let us say, to represent the sheep aggregate. We match one aggregate—the sheep that go out to the pasture—against another aggregate—the fingers or stones. We must remember that the stones represent the sheep but are very different from them.

So, by counting sheep we assumed that they are *separable* into parts. Then we assumed that the parts we choose are the important ones, that they form an *aggregate*. Then we assumed that we can use a *standard* aggregate, the stones, to represent sheep, and finally, that we can match each sheep that goes out to pasture with a stone.

Every time we count anything, whether we are counting sheep, atoms, or stars, we are assuming that what we are counting is separable, that it is independent of our psychology, and that it can be standardized and represented by something else. If we think about these assumptions, we know they are not always true, that our assumptions are only approximations. They are only partially true.

The conclusion is that what we count is always in some sense an approximation of what we are counting.

DEVELOPING NUMBER SYSTEMS

Let's think about standardization. Which standard is the right one to use? Who chooses the right one? Our forebears, the hunters and gatherers of early human history, probably counted, at first, like our sheep farmer. They needed some sort of method for remembering their sheep and sharing this number with their neighbors, so they developed standardization procedures. It was inconvenient to haul around a lot of stones, so, over time, people started to develop less cumbersome kinds of memory procedures such as cutting notches in a stick, using fingers, or creating little machines like the Chinese abacus.

What ways of counting and remembering would you use if you were tired of using the stones and wanted to share your information with others? Your fingers? Cutting marks into a stick is good, but your arms, legs, and fingers are more convenient than either stones or sticks. You might even use the joints on your fingers, or limbs, as the standard aggregate.

Which limbs, joints, or fingers would you use? You could use your head and two arms to count up to 3, fingers for counting 1 to 10, fingers and toes together to count up to 20, and the joints on the toes and fingers for higher numbers. This is exactly what our ancestors did, as we can see today in names such as "digit," which means "individual integer" and comes from the Latin for finger. Today, digit means number, but also finger or toe. In other words, some of our general, standard aggregates or counting systems are based on the human body.

WHEN WE COUNT, WE DISCOUNT AS WELL

Some of the elements we discount or miss through counting are discussed next.

Group Diversity. By choosing a particular aggregate to constitute the sheep, we marginalize the importance of other possible groupings, such as the brown and black sheep within the chosen aggregate.

Individual Diversity. By choosing to count each sheep in a given group, we marginalize the differences between the individual sheep within any one group. That is, individual differences are secondary, or ignored. For instance, to say that all citizens of the United States are "Americans" is true, but remember the aggregate "Americans" ignores the diversity of American nations such as Mexico, Brazil, Chile, Canada, etc. Also marginalized are the individual subcultures living within the

United States. And even if we agree to count all the people in all the different subcultures of all the nations in the Americas as Americans, we still marginalize the individuals within any given subculture, since they are assumed to all be alike.

Process Experience. By using standards such as stones or fingers, we forget we are dealing with sheep. We say "five went out," but we no longer have any feeling for the process involved in individual sheep moving out, the rate at which they moved, or the feeling we had about them as individual, potentially sentient beings. The number 5 conveys none of these experiential dimensions.

Non-Anthropoid Identity. Anthropoid means human-like. Using the body as a standard, we can represent five sheep by the sign of five fingers. The five sheep now match aspects of the human body. The sign of five fingers now identifies sheep with our human anatomy or form.

It turns out that the counting system of 10 is the most universal numerical system in use today. By using this and other systems related to the human body (such as 3 and 20) we inadvertently assume that the human form is a standard measure for the world. We may forget that we use ourselves to measure the world; nevertheless we have unconscious anthropomorphic assumptions, that is, we assume the world can be represented in terms of ourselves— in terms of human beings.

The point of this discussion is to bring home the fact that each time we count, we use numbers and forget or devalue many aspects of the "sheep process." When we count, we may think what we are doing is objective, yet we also discount many aspects of nature, including our own psychology.

The moral of the story is that when we use numbers, we are involved in a marginalization process that overlooks feeling choices, experiences, and human identification with events. Mathematics involves many subtle moments of awareness that we have forgotten.

Everything we count involves our psychology. Politicians and advertisers—in fact, everyone—use numbers that emphasize certain pieces of information and totally ignore other pieces of information. *Numbers are not simply quantities:* they represent the psychology of the person or group doing the counting!

One of the students in my class on mathematics seemed very frustrated with what I have just said. She moved restlessly in her chair and then blurted out that what we have lost by counting is clear, but "what have we won?"

The only answer that satisfied her was that by using numbers, we have won the ability to use a symbolic shorthand notation that can be shared with others. When we want to describe how many sheep went through the gate to the pasture and all we are interested in is the total number of what our culture considers to be the important aggregate of sheep, all we need do is raise five fingers on one of our hands. We win a shorthand method of communication.

Scarcely waiting for the first student to be satisfied, another student asked to speak up, saying she was a sheep farmer! "I work on a sheep farm. The first time I worked on the farm I was deeply disturbed by the fact that each animal has a tag in its ear that is color-coded and has a number. I agree with you. When you count, you do lose the sheep. I have to tag the sheep on the ear, and each time, I cry because I lose contact with the animal."

What could I say? I confessed that if I had known she were a sheep farmer, I would have asked her to teach this class on math. She understood the point better than I did. By describing a process, by saying anything about nature, you lose a certain degree of contact with it!

This insight, which we have come to from mathematics, is also basic to Taoism, the ancient Chinese spiritual belief that the flow of nature is what we must follow. The very first lesson of the *Tao Te Ching* says:

> *The Tao which can be said is not the eternal Tao!*

If we substitute the word "process" for "Tao," we come up with "The process which can be said is not the whole process." We lose contact with the direct experiences of events the moment we count, describe, or talk about them. Now, there is no way around talking about processes. But it is important to remember that when we describe something in terms of something else, we lose the essence of the first something.

A description of what you see and feel is different from what you see and feel. A map is not the road. When we gain the ability to share our understanding of experiences with others, we are in danger of losing contact with direct experience.

That is why, when the Zen monk (see Chapter 1) asked how deep the river was, his friend, a monk from another school, threw him into the water.

FROM THE TAO TO CONSENSUS REALITY

Our need to share experiences with others is so important to us that we often give up our individual experience. Telling a neighbor, "I have five sheep to sell," makes doing business much easier than speaking of each animal.

How do we do business? In conducting business, all we have to do is put up five fingers. We developed a system of counting with our fingers, the system of digits.

The use of five fingers, or the numerical symbol written as 5, to represent the count of five was decided on by cultural consensus. We consented consciously or unconsciously to describe events in a certain way. By using a standard aggregate like the fingers, we created a consensus reality. No one ever asked us directly, and no one even asks indirectly because most have forgotten. Yet we agree unconsciously, because we are taught or programmed to agree. We are told that in "reality" we own five sheep. But just because we use numbers to refer to an aspect of reality does not mean that nature complies.

Consensus reality (CR) marginalizes many aspects of nature. For example, CR discounts all the things we left out in counting. Clearly, the processes we describe as reality are not the complete processes! Numbers, whether they are used to count the people in dreams or used to calculate in quantum mechanics or relativity, can never be complete descriptions. They represent only the counter's personal psychology interacting with a given consensual reality. Uncertainty is built into consensus reality because "the map is not the experience of the road."

By creating a common reality, we share a certain worldview with our family, friends, group, subculture, culture, nation, and world, as our nation is part of the global economy. Around the world, numbers and words form a basic aspect of consensus reality, which means that around the globe we have lost contact with the Tao which cannot be said.

The basic limitations of consensus reality are an unspoken, unacknowledged part of our everyday experience and our minds are conditioned to believe that consensus reality is absolutely "real." A more total view of reality would include what is consented to plus what is experienced, but not consented to. In other words, what we count plus what we discount.

SYMPTOMS

Let me give another example of counting and discounting. When you go to see your doctor and describe a symptom—say a stomachache—you might use words that she understands, like stomach, intestine, and acid. You recount that you have a fever of 103°F. You tell the doctor that your thermometer said you were ill, but you probably don't include your experience of the fever or stomachache. You don't tell her about the fiery nature of the symptom or the fact that your stomach hurts only when you have a conflict with someone.

You and your doctor implicitly agree that your medical reality is CR, which is described in part by the numbers on your thermometer, and that reality says you have a stomach with acid in it. But all this is only consensus reality: you implicitly agree with your doctor to marginalize or discount your individual experiences, for example, the fiery nature of the symptom, which is part of a non-consensus reality (NCR).

Marginalizing NCR experiences is precisely why so many symptoms cannot be healed. Patients and doctors do not talk about the total process, only the CR aspects of it. Medicine, like physics, is defined by CR descriptors. In our culture, psychology is assigned the discounted subjective and personal language of individual NCR experiences.

In your doctor's worldview, your state is fairly cut-and-dried. If you have a temperature of 103°F, you are sick. That's all she needs to know.

But you may be consulting the wrong doctor. You might need someone who not only gives you something to reduce your temperature but also is interested in hearing about the fire of the fever. You may need help with that fire. If you are a calm, quiet person, maybe you don't want to simply put the fire out with cold milk or an antacid. You may need to become fierier yourself! You may need someone to tell you to stop keeping it cool! You may need someone interested in the subjective aspect of NCR experiences.

Many chronic symptoms do not clear up because only the CR part of the process is being focused on. In other words, *counting and discounting can be matters of life and death.* The Tao which can be said is not the eternal Tao, and the processes we focus on each day may not be the fundamental ones. The important aspect may be the river of actual experience, not just the numbers that describe its depth and breadth.

Thus, the point of this chapter is to become aware of our daily process, minute by minute, of counting and discounting. Such awareness can be a matter of life and death.

NOTES

1.   *New Dimensions* tapes can be ordered by writing to P.O. Box, 569, Ukiah, CA 95482-0569.

2.   An exception to this is the work of Ed Close, whose work is based on the work of G. Spencer Brown's calculus for indicating perceptual ordering procedures (see Bibliography).

3.   This difference in perception has been pointed out by child psychologist Piaget, who says that recognizing one-to-one correspondences occurs around the age of four years and that counting and calculating follow shortly thereafter.

3 | The Tao of Mathematics

*From an inner center the psyche seems to move out-
ward, in the sense of an extroversion, into the physical
world.*

—Wolfgang Pauli, noted physicist

As we have seen, math can be viewed as a living awareness process. This means, in part, it is a subjective psychological process. In this and the following chapters, I shall suggest some of the many possible meanings hidden within and behind numbers.

NUMBER BASES

Mathematicians call the fundamental numbers we use to count, before repeating them to count to higher numbers, a "number base." The numbers 1 through 10 are the most popular number base in use today. When we get to 10, we must start using 1 and 2 again to get the higher numbers (11, 12, etc.).

Just as cultures develop different kinds of consensus realities, throughout history, people also developed different counting systems and number bases. Today, our global systems are based on the number 10.

Other cultures used number systems based on 2 or 3. Many Native American tribes also used the base counting system of 10, probably in connection with the total number of fingers on most people's hands. Some native groups from the eastern U.S. used the base of 20, possibly reflecting the total number of fingers and toes.

An Australian Aboriginal person in one of my classes on number bases told me that when his people were asked to count, they'd say, "one, two, three, four, all the rest." Others told me that the native population of Queensland counted "one, two, two-and-one, two-twos, and much." Native people in central Africa had systems based on 3.[1] The native people of Tierra del Fuego had a number base of 3, and some South American tribes used 4.

The number base of 3, that is, 1, 2, and 3, is probably linked to experiences of the head, which people used to count as 1, and two arms, which represented the number 2, and the head and two arms, for 3. The number base of 4 apparently referred to using two arms and two legs; 5 was four fingers and the thumb. The number base of 5 can still be seen in languages where the word for "five" is "hand."[2]

Number bases reveal fundamental aspects of human psychology, that is, the consensus reality of a given group. Some peoples identified themselves with their head and arms, others with all four limbs, some with their hands, fingers, and toes, and so forth. I am less interested in the psychological meaning of how we identify ourselves than in the more general fact—that our psychology, culture, and consensus reality are linked to these types of choices. All peoples used the body as their common standard aggregate, although some stressed the fundamental nature of the head and arms, others stressed the crucial nature of the limbs, and others focused on the fingers and joints.

Counting unconsciously matches outer events with our bodies. Counting has always been a bodily experience! What we see and how we describe and measure the world are unconsciously experienced in terms of our own bodies.

THE NUMBER 1 REPRESENTS AN INTERACTIVE AWARENESS PROCESS

I became interested in Central African thinking during my travels a few years ago. Consider the system of the Pygmy group in Central Africa. This system is similar to the one used by the people of Tierra del Fuego in South America and the natives of Queensland. All three groups use a system based on the number 3.

The Pygmies, for example, call the number 1 by the sound "ahh." Let's write that as "*a*." They call the number 2 as "*oa*," and 3 as "*ua*."[3] All the rest of the numbers are combinations of these three. For example, 4 is *oa-oa* (2 + 2), 5 is *oa-oa-a* (2 + 2 + 1), and 6 is *oa-oa-oa*.

Notice that the number 1, that is, *a*, appears in the other two base numbers *oa* and *ua*. All three numbers share this "oneness." We can ask, what is this "oneness"? What do all numbers in a number base share?

As stated earlier, counting involves the process of choosing an aggregate to focus on, matching that aggregate with another, choosing a standard aggregate, and separating a discrete unit from the entire aggregate.

Thus the "*a*," which appears in the first number, one, and all the other numbers (*oa* and *ua*), convey a subliminal awareness of unfolding a discrete entity from an otherwise undifferentiated mass. The "*a*" is not just a symbol representing only a quantity "*a*" (or the number 1). It is a consensus reality term for that psychological process of choosing certain things to count and marginalizing others.

The number system and our counting procedures are codes for how we perceive reality. Just as DNA is a code that determines how our body grows, unfolds, and works as a system, math is a code of our minds.

The awareness involved in the psychological interactions between the observer and the observed is a common factor that is hidden or contained within all numbers. Remember the sheep and stones from Chapter 2. What we count depends in part on what is being counted. As observers, we make choices based on our psychology and the nature of what we are looking at. The feelings we have when we observe things, the interactional process behind counting, can be thought of as one of the elements behind what we observe or count on as the real world. Consciousness, as well as a form of unconsciousness, is involved in reckoning.

We normally think of counting as something that we do consciously, not something that happens unconsciously, an experience that reflects our culture, our consensus reality, and our orientation toward the universe. Nevertheless, from the viewpoint of our inner psychology, observational awareness processes generate reality.

Ancient Chinese ideas about the number 1 show that the first number symbolizes not only a quantity and an interactional process, but a generative power as well. The three-thousand-year-old *I Ching's* (The Book of Changes) first hexagram is "The Creative" (from a root word meaning "head")[4]:

> Great indeed is the sublimity of the Creative, to which all beings owe their beginning and which permeates all heaven... The clouds pass and the rain does its work and all individual beings flow into their forms.

Number 1, here the first hexagram, is associated not only with a quantity but also with a generative process, a creative "flow" that unfolds individual beings and numbers into their separate forms. Within the number 1 lies the idea of natural change—of life's process—which begins in a state of cloudiness and unfolds into a myriad of separate forms.[5]

Within the concept of the number 1 lie three ideas: a creative Tao that unfolds the rest of the numbers, an interactional process between the observer and the observed, and a consensual term for an abstract quantity, 1.

Since *"a"* or 1 is found in all the other numbers—in the Pygmy system, *a, oa,* and *ua*—we can say that each individual number has *"a"* or 1 within it, that is, each number has a creative generative nature as well as a quantitative and an interactional component.

In this way, numbers are both real and imaginary, although we tend to forget their implicit generative and interactional nature. Furthermore, we also forget that individual numbers symbolize aspects of an entire process, not just an entirety. The basic point is that aspects of daily events are marginalized by using abstractions to represent them.

In any case, the Pygmy system's *"a"* is a symbol for the awareness process that unfolds discrete numbers, an experience that is found again in the other unfolded parts or numbers. (Remember that *a* = 1, *oa* = 2, and *ua* = 3.)

COUNTING AND DREAMING

Waking up in the night, you might remember your dreams. Noticing your dreaming experience, you automatically enter into a recounting process while recalling what you dreamed.

Here is how. Something in the night caught your attention, it interacted with you in some way, and you decide to call this something the first fragment of what you dreamed. Say you dreamed about a man you believe could be called "Tom." You are not sure it was Tom, but through some subliminal awareness process that marginalizes some aspects of your dream and chooses others to focus on, you suspect your dream concerned Tom.

Counting and recounting give a consensus reality version of what happened in the dream process by using a consensus aggregate from your personal experience—the names of people, such as Tom—to describe a subjective experience that is itself only "Tom-like."

For most of us, the sense of the ongoing dreaming process is lost in the recounting of the dream. We forget the experience of dreaming, of generating figures like Tom. Instead we speak of the *a, oa,* or *ua.* Only the *"a"* in these numbers reminds us of the background interactional awareness process.

A PERSONAL EXAMPLE

While standing in front of one of my classes on number theory, I recounted an inner meditation:

While standing here, I will try to be wide-awake and meditate. I notice a feeling... I notice... I am excited, enthusiastic about math. When I hear myself recount to you what I am feeling right now, I realize that I have given you an outer or consensus reality accounting of the entire aggregate of my experience. I called it "excitement."

If I check back in with the details of my feeling experience, the first thing I notice is that my heart rate is rapid. Then I notice that my arms have a lot of energy in them; in fact, they want to move. Now I notice them rising, as if by themselves. I will go with that. They want to fly in the air. I notice I raise my arms and am sort of flapping my wings. I remind myself of the image of a child, excited by a new idea!

But I was supposed to be a teacher, not a child flying in the air with excitement. Both my students and I allowed me to "stop the world" and enter into non-consensus reality (NCR), and to recount the experience I then called "excitement."

The number 1—in my case the heartbeat—was an interactional awareness process between my mind and my body that was trying to unfold itself. Behind the number 1 was the awareness of choosing to feel the details of my excitement, noticing the pounding of my heart, which I called my "heart rate," matching my pounding heart with the collective term of consensus reality, "heart rate," and so on.

Then I returned my attention to the inner experience of the process itself, and noticed that the counting process was self-generating. I merely had to notice it. The process moved from my heart rate to what I called the motions in my hands. Let's call that motion "number 2." The process unfolded itself further. I noticed my hands flapping, and this process reminded me of an excited child. The child might be called "number 3" in the process.

Each of these terms—heart rate, hand, and child—may be viewed as "numbers" representing the first, second, and third elements of the process. Each number is a quantity, each expresses aspects of a consensus reality description of the true, inner experience, each arises through an interaction between the observed and the observer, each contains a self-generating element. Each number has a 1 or an "*a*" in the midst of it, so to speak.

We are not talking about the way you learned mathematics in school. We are talking about the experience of numbers as descriptions of a process. And this process is the process of awareness itself.

The following table combines Pygmy math with process thinking and modern mathematical symbols.

ABORIGINAL MATH	PROCESS THINKING	MODERN MATH
Number	**Discrete Elements**	**Number**
a	Process of noticing a first discrete element, giving it a CR name	1
oa	Process of noticing a second discrete element, giving it a CR name	2
ua	Process of noticing a third discrete element, giving it a CR name	3

In recounting my experience, I use words such as "heart rate," "arm motions," and "child" to account for my experience. But I know, and you know as well from your own experiences, that these words are only CR formulations of strong subjective and personal NCR processes and experiences I can hardly find the words to formulate.

In general, whether we are speaking about dreams or physical objects, each number is a "recounting" that uses a consensus reality term (such as heart or hands) to represent a quantity, and to represent also the interactional awareness process that notices a distinct event in the midst of other discretely unfolding events.

Thus the "*a*" that is implicit in all other numbers is my experience of a self-generating process with which I interact and which I name in consensual terms so that I can give you a sense of what I am experiencing. In brief, I am like an excited child!

Once again, we find that the numbers that can be counted, or the words that can be said, are not the real process which is happening. This reminds me of something Einstein supposedly once said:

> Not everything that counts can be counted, and not everything that can be counted counts.

THE FUTURE OF SCIENCE

This elementary survey of the processes behind numbers gives a general perspective into mathematics and physics. Pretend that you lived at the time when numbers were being discovered or invented. Imagine you lived thousands of years ago. If you were in touch with the basic awareness processes behind observation, you might have made the following predictions about the future of humankind.

Since you realized that the counting system was not accounting for the entire process, you might have speculated (and would have been correct) that the mathematics of the future would have to develop further to include many of the non-consensual or non-consensus reality awareness experiences marginalized by the present number system.

How might such NCR experiences reappear? You might have guessed that the "real" numbers you were using would have to be made more complex to incorporate imaginary and other non-consensus experiences. Perhaps you would have said that each number such as 3 would have to be accompanied in some manner by an imaginary number, perhaps something like "3i." In retrospect, you would have been correct, for in the seventeenth century a new set of numbers called "complex and imaginary numbers" did come into being.

You would have foreseen the history of mathematics; you would have understood that, at first, people would be fascinated by the use of numbers that can be applied to creating "real" (CR) things. You might have guessed that, later, the discounted experiences would appear as uncertainties in so-called real measurements, that is, as inaccuracies in our way of counting events, whether these events concerned whole particles or whole universes. You might even have guessed Heisenberg's "uncertainty principle," which was discovered in the twentieth century.

If you moved forward to the beginning of the third millennium, you might guess further and suspect that science will discover or rediscover what we always knew: that personal psychology and culture play a role in mathematics and physics. And that physics and psychology and philosophy must somehow flow together again.

Thinking only in terms of the CR aspects of numbers submerges our relationship to what we observe; it submerges all of the personal experiences and psychological assumptions involved in counting. Therefore the physics of today, which is based on CR measurements and counting, represents only part of nature. Remaining only with CR descriptions makes us forget that many of our uncertainties about nature come from sensory experiences we marginalized.

After all, just because we are interested in discrete entities because they can be counted, and just because we may not be interested in the other processes involved in this accounting, does not mean that discrete entities exist in nature independent of the processes producing them or independent of the observer. Thus, what we count is only symbolic of what is happening. Counting does not represent the full reality of what is being counted.

The ancient Chinese work, the *Tao Te Ching*, also tells us that the Tao which moves through each event creating our experience of all events is different from the so-called definitive CR description of the event: The Tao which can be said is not the real Tao.

NOTES

1. See page 8 in the excellent book *An Introduction to the History of Mathematics*, by Howard Eves.

2. See Frank Swetz's *From Five Fingers to Infinity* for an entertaining introduction to the history of math.

3. Remember that I am taking Africans' counting out of the context of their lives and therefore will never be able to fully understand it. Yet, because their system is in so many ways similar to systems in other places of the world, perhaps I can sense something about their psychology and the feeling behind this system.

4. See Richard Wilhelm's translation of the *I Ching*, page 370.

5. My Jungian teacher, a collaborator of Jung's, Marie Louise von Franz, speaks about number 1 as symbolic of a "one continuum" in her book *Number and Time*. The one continuum runs through all the other numbers. In her formulation, the number 1 symbolizes the one world, or the alchemist's *Unus Mundus*, the world beyond all duality. The one continuum is what I am referring to as the generative Tao behind the interactional awareness process we identify as counting.

4 | The Math of Dreaming

Counting what goes forwards, goes backwards
—From the *I Ching,* or Book of Changes

As we saw as we began our journey, the mathematical pattern we use in observing the world within and around us is not objective. It occurs as we observe the things around us. Math arises, so to speak, as we interact with the Tao. Math is a code. It might be called the code of creation. Mathematical description is symbolic, it approximates the world we experience and observe. Hidden within this code lies the influence of our personal psychology, our culture, and the historical epoch in which we live.

Counting is an interactional process between the observed and the observer. This interaction is a rapid, automatic awareness and a dynamic process. As a result, not only do numbers represent consensus reality characteristics of events, they also symbolize the awareness behind the observation process. In this chapter, I will show how math not only tells us about "real" events—like the sheep leaving the gate—but also tells us about the structure of our "noticing," that is, the awareness processes that exist like shadows behind each moment of observation.[1]

INNER WORK WITH NUMBERS

To experience the significance of numbers and how they arise from awareness processes, I suggest that you try the following simple experiment.

This experiment will take approximately two minutes. Make yourself as comfortable as possible. Let out a breath. When you are ready, ask yourself, "What am I am doing right now?" Make a note of the terms you use to answer the question. Perhaps you noted reading or sitting or pondering.

Now ask yourself a second question. What else is happening to me in this moment that is not described by the words I wrote down? Take a moment to sense your response to this question.

Are you feeling something that has not been described, are you making some kind of small motions, are you hearing something inside your head or from the outer environment? Are you visualizing something?

To go further, ask yourself to allow this new experience to progress, ask it to unfold. Let it "generate itself." Experiment. Just try. If you are not used to following your inner processes, this step may be new. Experiment with it, be patient with yourself as you let your process unfold.

You may need to pay attention to experiences you normally do not notice. Let your feelings, your visualizations, your little motions, or inner sounds, just progress. Just feel, look, listen, move. Take the time. Let things unfold in whatever manner they want to. Then remember the results. Write them down.

This is the end of the experiment.

Focusing on your experiences and then becoming aware of new components of experience is an inner math experience, the mathematical process of adding. Counting and unfolding can be both a psychological and physical process.

The first thing you noticed was that you were sitting, or meditating, or lying down, or whatever you called what you were doing. That was the "aggregate," the metaphorical "pile of stones" you were going to count. Then, when you noticed your first experience, that was a metaphorical number 1, or "*a*" in the Pygmy system. The events that followed were 2, or "*oa*", and so forth. Numbers "count" or differentiate parts of the original aggregate.

This exercise allowed you to experience how the numbers 1 and 2 arise as a result of differentiation, that is, as a result of the interaction between your inner perceptions and the rest of your experience. And you may have noticed how the numbers themselves are, in a manner of speaking, self-generating. Because you could notice what was happening yourself, we might say that math is a bodily experience as well as an abstract science.

ANOTHER EXAMPLE

Let's think about a second example. What am I doing now?

> As I pause a moment to notice what is happening, I become aware that I am sitting. Now, when I ask myself, "How does my sitting unfold?" I notice a visual experience or image forming. In my mind's eye, it looks something like a lake.

> I want to let this visual experience unfold by asking again, "What else is happening and not yet included in the visual experience of the lake?"

> I sense something like an "uneasiness" in the lake and suddenly see a round circle coming up from underneath the water. There is something more about that round circle that is trying to happen and is not yet clear to me... it makes me hesitate. What will I see next?

> As I continue to focus my awareness, I notice the round circle rising into the air and I can no longer describe one thing at a time, but am in the midst of a process that is unfolding itself further. A round face appears in the circle that is now in the sky, the face smiles down on me and seems encouraging.

Now, I am no longer in the midst of that experiment, but find myself thinking about it. I wonder why is that face so encouraging? I take a moment to ponder and I realize that I was shy about doing this work publicly and needed encouragement in doing this experiment.

Conducting the experiment of "sitting" and experiencing a visual image is a CR description of an aggregate I might call my inner work. Let's call the sitting experience the "pile of stones" I am unfolding. The description of this experience did not as yet include the experience of the image of the lake, the next number, so to speak, the number 1. Number 1, the lake experience, unfolded from the aggregate of sitting. The number 1 could not quite encompass the feeling of uneasiness in the lake image; that was a purely NCR experience.

The circle was a second element that differentiated itself from the lake. The face, a third element. Then I noticed that I was in the midst of an encouragement process that is only implied in the other terms—vision, lake, circle, sky, face, smiling, and so forth.

"*A, oa, ua, oa-oa*"—or in modern mathematical terms, 1, 2 3, 4—and so on describe only the CR aspects of the process that was occurring. Remember that words and numbers are only momentary consensus descriptions in which subjective, non-consensus aspects are no longer explicitly present.

Likewise, all the descriptive terms we use to describe the inner or outer world—terms such as volume, speed, self, other, inner, outer, process, particles, and archetypes—are just CR representations which, at best, symbolize the dynamics and sensations that lie in the NCR background.

An interesting aspect of my experiment is that my dreaming process created inner meaning for me. It pointed out that I needed encouragement. How was this meaning created? In a way, it was unfolding through my sitting experience. The meaning was implicit, apparently waiting to unfold, to explicate itself. The process provided its own explanation.

Is process always its own explanation? Is life its own solution? Yes, when processes are allowed to unfold! In psychology, as we have just seen, given a chance, dreaming or dreamlike experiences and unconscious experiences that we sense but cannot yet express in objective terms are part of a creative process within us always and continuously waiting to unfold. When they do unfold, they become self-explanatory.[2]

AMY'S BABY

Let's look more closely at how events unfold themselves by looking at a second example of the arithmetic of dreaming. I want to give another example of unfolding processes, one from a class where I was demonstrating these ideas with my partner and wife, Amy. During one of these classes, Amy said she would help demonstrate the unfolding process implicit in numbers.

Arny: Amy, what are you experiencing right now?

Amy: I notice I am excited, sitting here in front of this class, I see a lot of people. It's good to be here… Arny, I am not having a visualization like you had, but a sort of body feeling instead, a sort of rocking, a slight rocking back and forth…

[While editing this transcript I notice that Amy frequently uses the phrase, "sort of," which expresses the fact that she knows the term rocking does not describe the entire process—that there are non-consensus reality (NCR) experiences whose unfolding awaits her understanding.]

Arny: Okay, working with visualizations is one kind of process, body motions are another kind of dreaming process. Let's go further. You mentioned you noticed something like rocking back and forth. Sounds like you are working on the body experience called "rocking" while I was working mainly visually with lakes and circles. Fine. Now, as you give room for that rocking back and forth to unfold, what happens next?

Amy: [Focuses on her rocking and seems to begin moving slowly back and forth while she is sitting.] I feel… a sort of light rocking. Then [she laughs] I start to feel like a baby. I hear a little child's voice that sounds like it comes out of me, calling "Oochy, Woochy..." [Amy's voice sounds much younger] Like a little baby... I sort of feel like a little child, an infant and I want to jump around and play with a ball... being really playful and... somehow lighthearted.... Well, that is surprising!

(To the class) Amy's "*a*" is the rocking, the second experience, let's call it "*oa*," is the feeling of being a baby, and "*ua*" is sound and play from the child, "Oochy, Woochy."

Arny: Amy, would you like to go further?

Amy: [Laughs] It just seemed to stop there.

Arny: Fine, thanks. [Addressing the students] She's come to an edge, a barrier to further counting and unfolding. So let's all stop here, too. We can go back to Amy later.

Amy: That is a great place for me to stop too, it is so wonderful to discover the child within.

THE EDGES TO PROCESS

I use the term "edges" to describe the borders or barriers that exist to the eternal and continual flow of inner processes. In speaking, when we can no longer say something, we have reached a communication edge. An edge is a kind of threshold. For example, when I unfolded my lake processes, just getting into the process in the first place was an "edge." I felt a bit hesitant and had to get over that to even approach the unfolding of my inner processes. Every time you get into direct experience of a process, you step over your edges.

The shaman don Juan calls moving over edges into direct experience "stopping the world." By crossing over the edges created by culture and, even, your individual psychology, you begin to unfold process itself, you stop the world. You enter into the unconscious, into what don Juan calls the "nagual."

Just as logs or rocks in a river give form to the river, edges give form to your inner processes. Edges are neither good nor bad; they simply divide us into different worlds. We know this because at one point or another, we feel we cannot go more deeply into an experience, insight, thought, or feeling. We have reached an edge.

Edges are so much a basic part of our perceptual experience, we may assume that they also structure mathematics.

EDGES AND NUMBER BASES

In Chapter 3, I mentioned that the major number bases around the world are 2, 3, 5, 10, and 20. In the West, the governing number base is 10. After you reach the number 10 you must start repeating, 10 plus 1 is 11, and so forth. That is why in early English, the word "eleven" meant "one over," that is, 1 and 10. The number base for the Pygmy system is 3. Thus, when you get to the number 3, you must start again, so to speak. (*A, oa, ua* and then comes *oa-oa, oa-oa-a,* and so on.)

In part, these number bases are apparently connected with our anatomy. Number bases are a kind of body language which says, for example, that a group of sheep, when unfolded or counted, reminds me of twice the number of fingers on one hand.

In a way, number bases represent basic human experiences in which aspects of the body become standard aggregates that are matched against the aggregate, entities or objects that are being counted. Using math as a universal human experience, we can say that there is a widespread implicit consensus on using human anatomy to describe the world. As you do, I understand the world in terms of my friends and myself. We become aware of the world in terms of our own bodies.

Chapter 3 discusses how number bases are connected to our perceptual systems because numbers themselves involve psychological choices and filtering of information. Number bases are connected to our bodies and to our cultures, because the particular size of the number base is culturally determined. Since there are limits to our bodies, limits to the number of arms, legs, heads, and joints, number bases are limited as well.

The small size of the number base is connected with limitations to what we easily count, what we can perceive and remember. We can think of numbers bases as "body bases."

Let's think about limitations in terms of edges. Anything outside a body base is outside the edge of "me." In the same manner, anything more than 10 is "more of me" and is measured in terms of more than my own body, more than the basic human me, so to speak. The way in which we count or recount and talk about the world is in many additions of "me."

Eleven sheep are, quantitatively speaking, one set of all my fingers plus one more finger. Thirty sheep are three sets of my fingers, and so forth.

The number base is an example of an anthropic principle, a principle which says the universe becomes understandable in human-like terms. As humans, we understand the universe in terms of ourselves. In a way, when we count, we are saying, "Me, me, me, and many more of me!" What is beyond me and my size and form is measured in basic terms of me. The edge is the limit of me. When we get to that edge, we go back into ourselves and just say everything is more of me.

Before we go further with Amy's experience, let's summarize these ideas about number bases and their relationship to the edge concept and to the Pygmy and modern systems of math. Look at some of the details of the summary in the following diagram.

On the left side of the chart, we see the process of meditation, that is, of dreaming and counting. Under the column called "Process Theory," we see the various discrete elements of meditation and counting. Under the column "Pygmy Math," we see the Pygmy system of counting. This corresponds to the processes of counting, as well as the unfolding inner experience, as I have been demonstrating. I consider recounting, that is, telling the story of our inner experiences, to be a form of arithmetic, a form of dreaming—of unfolding and relating our inner and outer experiences to others.

On the far right we have the idea of modern measurable quantities of consensus reality. Modern numerical thinking focuses mainly on the CR aspects of number—the fixed quantity disassociated from any experiential attributes. It reflects a fixed or "state-oriented" worldview, in contrast to a process-oriented one.

NUMBER BASES AND EDGES

Meditation	Process Theory	Pygmy Math	Modern Math
DREAMING COUNTING	Process appears in first element	a	1
	Second element of process	oa	2
	Third element of process	ua	3

EDGE AND NUMBER BASE

Many, beyond me		$oa\text{-}oa$	4

As we move from top left to bottom in the diagram, we begin with what may be called meditating, with noticing the first perceptions. Then we enumerate them and reach the edge of the personal world when we get to the third element. Beyond the edge is the world of "beyond me."

Cultures with a number base of 3 said that after 1, 2, and 3 comes "the many." The Chinese called this world of "beyond me" the world of the 10,000 things.

What we experience as "the many" is the outer world, the "not me," the division between local and non-local—and our response is to return to the familiar and repeat the process again.

In psychology this repetition is sometimes referred to as "perseveration." In essence, perseveration is our response to reaching the edge of our process. Process is self-amplifying; when it meets an edge, it meets a door in our minds. When our process gets to this door, it keeps knocking on it, saying "Open up, let me in." This repeats itself again and again until someone or something lets it in. The process first appears visually in dreaming; then the same process might appear in a bodily experience or in a disease symptom. Then it might appear in the way you move, and finally, the edge appears, as if it were someone close to you who will not let you in, so to speak.

Processes "persevere." How many times have you listened to a friend repeat the same story? How many times have you told the same story from your own childhood? That story is recounted, in part, because you may have reached an edge that you have not been able to get over. I used to recount fights I had as a child because I was at an edge of standing for and embracing myself. My self-perception did not include self-support. Today, I am thankful that I have gone over that edge of mine and that my identity is changing a bit.

If you carefully observe a friend of yours or view yourself on video-tape, you will notice that you both repeat yourselves a lot. For example, when a client arrives for the first session, I notice that a few of her words, her posture, and her tone of voice predict some of what happens next. The way she identifies or dis-identifies herself repeats itself in many ways.

She might say, "I am a polite person" and "Other people are so insensitive, not me." These two elements—what constitutes the "me" (a polite person) and what constitutes "not me" (others are insensitive)—repeats itself again and again in the content of discussion and body signals. For example, my new client might make one polite gesture, such as smiling, and another gesture she does not identify with, such as raising her voice. If you ask her to describe what she hears, she will say her voice sounds very "insensitive."

Insensitivity is beyond her edge. Although she sounds insensitive, she is not identifying with that process. That is why she may talk a lot about insensitive people. Repetition at the edge!

CONCLUSION: ARITHMETIC DESCRIBES PSYCHOLOGY AND PHYSICS

Once you know several elements of a person's process, you know their number base, so to speak, and you can describe or predict a great deal of the person. If you know how someone identifies herself, you will be able to predict when she repeats herself and about what. In fact, most of our dreams are also about events that happen "beyond me."[3] Number bases are incredible.

In psychological terms, number bases reflect our personal identity. Edges form in our dreaming and thinking, when we feel certain processes are too far away from what we know, too unfamiliar, too distant from our identities. Edges protect us in a way, from the unknown, from the unfamiliar.

In Amy's case, the "*a*" is the rocking motion; "*oa*," the second element of her process, is the feeling of the baby; and "*ua*" is the perception of its voice. When she gets to "*ua*" (or 3), her process—the baby's voice—stops for the moment. Her process seems to have reached an edge, a barrier. It is as if her counting, recounting, dreaming, or unfolding stops. She reaches the child, the edge of how she identifies herself.[4] We stopped at that point. Let's get back to that.

GETTING OVER THE EDGE TO THE WORLD

Let us return to the process we began with Amy.

The atmosphere in the class was full of good humor from Amy's work with her "child." Everyone was talking at once. With some effort, I raised my voice to speak above the ensuing babble.

> Arny: Amy, getting back to your process, are you still there? [Amy says she wants to work further on her process.] We left off with you rocking and speaking like a child. Now I want to ask you if you can imagine taking that playfulness from your rocking motion into the world? Can you imagine yourself as a playful woman or child all the time?
>
> Amy: [Amy brushes her hair back.] I think if I were freer, I would be more… I think I would hug people more and sort of play… but I don't know how to get more involved… somehow with people…
>
> One of the students piped up and asked Amy if her incomplete sentences are an indication of the existence of an edge in a process.
>
> Amy: Edge? [Amy bursts out laughing and the group breaks out laughing as well.] …Wow, I'll say, being so playful in the world is an edge! I think I could… yes! This is an edge… Hmmm, I notice that I am nervous… my body is beginning to shake, it's rocking again…
>
> Everyone grows silent as Amy begins to focus on her movement process again. She is standing at the front of the class when she begins and now slowly moves out into the group of people, surprising some, bumping into people in the class. She roars with laughter and people clap as she goes over her edge and hugs some of the people around her. After a few minutes of playing, she speaks again.
>
> Amy: What an unusual class on mathematics! Looking back, I did not know what the rocking motion was going to create when it

began. Only as I unfolded it did it become clear. It is important, this childlike spontaneity and affection. Thanks to everyone.

Amy said that her process initially emerged through the rocking motion, which was then further articulated or counted via the image of the child and then the sound of the baby. Soon we got to the edge of her identity, which was bringing the process of playfulness out into the world and being publicly affectionate. In terms of our discussion in this chapter, as long as she was within her number base, she could dream about that child, discover its process, count or recount it.

We have many kinds of edges. The biggest edge is usually exposing your inner process out in the world, or in Amy's case, being a child in public with others. The big edge occurs at the edge of your number base, so to speak, at the edge of how your have identified yourself, at the edge of "me." At this edge, you tend to get "blocked." This is what most people mean when they say they are "stuck" in their lives.

Dreaming, thinking to yourself about things, and having deep experiences are important, but it usually takes us a long time to live them in the world. That is, to integrate our inner experiences with our outer realities and to essentially change our entire identity as it manifests itself in everyday life.

BACKWARDS-MOVING NUMBERS

As a modern shaman, and we are all potentially modern shamans, heirs to both scientific and traditional wisdom, it is crucial to unfold your process, to be free, to live it out in everyday life. But doing so tends to make us forget where we have come from. We forget the dreaming process that unfolded our lives. This may be why an ancient Chinese saying states: "Counting what goes forwards, goes backwards."[5]

This sounds very mysterious, and in a way, it is. In some sense, the ancient Taoists were always in an altered state of consciousness. They knew what they were talking about, but others often had difficulty understanding them.

Let's ask the question raised by the Taoists. How can counting that which goes forward, go backwards? Curiously, this same idea can be found in Egyptian hieroglyphics and in many indigenous number systems.

We shall never know exactly what was meant in statements that may go back almost three thousand years, but it is fun to guess. For example, in Amy's experience, we could say she unfolded her playfulness. Her state of undifferentiated wholeness, her rocking, unfolded or explicated itself in terms of 1, 2, 3, and so forth. She changed her identity and moved forward.

Yet, according to the ancient Chinese, she is going backward even as she goes forward. How? From the viewpoint of the original Tao that had not been said, from the viewpoint of dreaming, going forward means going backward, it means leaving her dreaming world. Explicating, the unfolding of things, is progress only from one viewpoint—the viewpoint of modern therapists or physicists who want to explain things in concrete and measurable terms.

In terms of the ancient Tao that cannot be said, Amy and all the rest of us leave the state of oneness, we lose something of life's mystery as we go forward in time. This loss is positive from the viewpoint of the unfolding unconscious experience, yet from the Tao's viewpoint it is also going backwards. Knowing something consciously is both a progression and a regression.

Thus, a complete process really requires us to go forward, unfold things explicitly, and then go backward to the essential source of all things, to go back to dreaming.

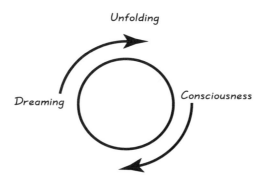

4.1 The process swing of awareness between the Tao which can be said and can't be said

The differentiation between going forward in counting and, at the same time, going backwards from the Tao which cannot be said, from the sentient experiences we usually identify with dreaming, is a baseline point, not just for the understanding of Taoism, but also for modern physics. The reality that can be described in terms of everyday life marginalizes our ever-present imaginal, non-local, non-temporal realities. CR is not NCR experience, sentient experience.

So, even as you and I and Amy go forward, we must be aware of backing away from the essential ground of all being. Remember the Tao which cannot be said, our deepest sentient experiences, and the fact that we go back, again and again, to the original unity from which everything comes.

This original unity has always had many names: Mother Earth, Yahweh, God, the Great Spirit, matter, the Universe, the Ground of All Being, the Void, the Clear White Light, the Source. The Tao, the source of processes inside and outside ourselves, has always been thought of as something divine, something which was the creator of all things. The Tao is not just something to use, but something creative—some might even say to worship. It is the essence of all non-consensual experiences, the essence of the original state from which everything we know unfolds, that bring us and all other forms into being. In a way, this essence is the most powerful, universal force we know of; it includes all other psychological, spiritual, and physical forces. Poets describe it as the thing that has us in its hands, which brings us to birth and leads us through death.

Thus "counting what goes forwards, goes backwards." After every meditation, after every occasion of inner work, I go back and say thank you to that mysterious something, thank you to the universal power that creates the Tao and math of dreaming.

NOTES

1. In process-oriented psychology, I call the awareness process from which observation arises, "dreaming," which is a combination of meditating, musing, and imagining experiences that most people ignore. I use the term "dreaming" as a basic, usually unconscious form of awareness, which precedes consciousness.

2. Jung's theory that a dream is its own interpretation is a process-oriented view. Process (dreaming) is its own solution. David Finkelstein's concept of process and David Bohm's ideas about the unfolding universe are attempts to base physics on process concepts. My *River's Way* discusses more about process concepts in psychology and physics.

3. Dreams happen over the edge, as I point out in my popular *Working With the Dreaming Body*.

4. Being a child is an edge for most adults.

5. See Part II, Chapter II of the Richard Wilhelm edition of the *I Ching*.

5 | Co-creating Our Universe

Useful as it is under everyday circumstances to say that the world exists 'out there' independent of us, that view can no longer be upheld. There is a strange sense in which this is a 'participatory' universe.

—John Wheeler, Nobel Prize-winning theoretical physicist

We have been studying how math encodes our awareness, our very bodies, and how each time we count, in some sense we co-create the "objective" (CR) universe. Math describes what happens when our attention interacts with the Tao, with universal NCR energies around us, unfolding reality. Math is not only the code of how our minds work. In later chapters math will appear also as the pattern behind the physical world.

Math can be used consciously or unconsciously to describe outer events such as the movement of sheep and to describe inner events, such as the flow of our fantasy processes. Numbers are descriptions of the unfolding of events from undifferentiated aggregates, that is, "outer" or "inner" situations. Thus the same mathematical laws which hold for psychology hold for material reality as well.

The flow of our perceptions is differentiated by edges, which appear in the patterns of numbers called number bases that symbolize the limits of our personal identities. Just as a river flows along until it meets an obstacle like a fallen tree, a branch, or a rock, the flow of our perception is blocked at edges. In Chapter 4 we saw that edges create perceptual barriers. The more encompassing our identities, the fewer obstructions to the river of experience.

Also in Chapter 4 we saw how events and numbers evolve as the result of interactions between the observer and the observed, as in the case of the sheep farmer and the sheep. In this chapter, we shall ponder the details of this interaction and how our personal psychology influences outer physical events.

For example, do our feelings about the grains of sand falling through the small opening of an hourglass influence the rate at which the sand falls? Some of us might believe that there is no interaction between ourselves and the sand particles. But if we begin to measure the rate of falling with greater and greater accuracy, if we begin to get down to measuring the smallest fragments of sand and time, it gets difficult, if not impossible, to clearly determine whether our feelings interact with the falling, individual sand particles. To avoid the influence of our subjective feelings, we can use a camera to take objective photographs. But then, what camera and what speed should we choose, and how do we interpret little blurs in the resulting pictures? One person will say the blurs represent particles of sand, the next might say a blur came from a grain of dust. In addition, we must realize, our feelings influence our accounting procedures in many different ways.

If we remember the awareness processes involved in what is counted and the nature of our number bases, we must admit that our feelings are always involved in the interaction between what we see and who we are. Do our edges, which set up blocks to perception, also influence the course of events themselves? Can we separate events from the observer at the macro level of large objects? To answer these questions, let's return to inner work.

THE EDGE TO GETTING INTO THE PROCESS

If we feel that certain events should not be happening or are too unfamiliar, a barrier to them arises so that they appear to us as "not me," or as "other." This is where edges arise. When we reach an edge, we know from inner work that our "internal" processes become blocked and repeat themselves. At the edge we feel uncomfortable, events seem to be against us, and they may frighten or even, shock us.

There are a number of edges or barriers to perception. One of the first edges we meet in inner work is involved in making the decision to notice what is happening. I call this first edge the "Edge to Getting into the Process." This first edge is noticing or observing an aggregate (an outer event or inner experience). In psychology, this is the edge to self-reflection, that is, using our attention to focus on our experiences.

Overall, we cling to everyday consensus reality. Thus, noticing a new thought, fantasy, feeling, or body sensation is an edge for all of us during those times when we are not interested in our so-called inner life. As long as this edge remains uncrossed, much of what goes on in non-consensus reality (NCR) remains unknown. This first edge creates projections, because if we do not notice events in ourselves, we "project" outside and the unknown remains unimportant or "not me." Amy told me, for example, that if she had not noticed the "child" in her own rocking motions, she would just have continued to be fascinated by the childlike spontaneity of others.

The "Edge to Getting into the Process" marginalizes body experiences as well; they become unimportant to us. This edge is linked with the experience of psychosomatic symptoms. You choose not to focus on your body's signals, and then, when these signals get stronger or when you get sick, your illness surprises you as if it had not been there before, present in your inner signals. The surprise is due to your edge, to the marginalized importance of the initial body experience.[1]

In physics, this edge appears when we need to make a decision about what to observe. For example, we might choose to observe an electron. Since the idea of a particle going through a hole in a wall seems more familiar to us than a particle going through a wall without a hole, we are likely to experiment with the first situation—the hole in the wall—not the second—the wall without a hole. As a result, we may be very surprised at another point to find out that electrons can, indeed, move through apparently impenetrable barriers: this is the so-called tunneling effect. Events that surprise us show that we had a previously unknown edge to the processes involved. We chose not to focus on these signals and are shocked when they actually manifest in our objective realities.

THE EDGE TO SIGNIFICANCE

There is a second edge to processes, which I call the "Edge to the Significance of the Process." For example, in her experience with her process, Amy giggled several times before she said the word "baby." If the content or symbols of the process are very different from how we see ourselves, we tend to marginalize their significance. Edges are like fences around our homes. They are intended to keep out the unknown. For example, most adults tend to ignore dreams in which children appear. Thus, there are edges not only to getting into processes but also to noticing the significance of what is being observed or dreamed.

In physics, this second edge appears in the tendency of observers to disregard the possible significance of individual, one-time observations and to regard instead a statistical collection or an average of similar observations. Scientists tend to believe there is no significance in spontaneous, unrepeatable observations. Repeatable observations have the validation of consensus. One-time events may be manifestations of NCR phenomena.

For example, physicists do not try to determine the significance of an individual outcome of an electron going through an opening, but only the statistical average outcome of such an event, repeated many times. We should remember that physicists, like almost everyone else in our objective, scientifically oriented culture, believe that only the repeatable statistical outcome of events is meaningful. Everything else is deemed meaningless, pure chance.

In any case, science places more emphasis on the use rather than the meaning of events. For example, during World War II this second edge may have been fundamental to our ignoring the dangers of atomic energy while focusing only on the race to make the bomb. Each perception, each discovery, each new event has meaning. Ignoring this meaning is equivalent to waiving ethical responsibility for our discoveries.

It is easy to criticize physicists, thinking they are exclusively rational and, by disregarding other more humanistic concerns, unethical. But we should recall that, in a way, mainstream physics merely reflects the current belief systems of the prevailing current of influence of our contemporary culture (the mainstream). You and I not only tend to ignore perceptions that seem different from our everyday interests but also ignore the significance of these perceptions, once we get over the first edge to even experiencing them!

THE EDGE TO LIVING PROCESS

There's a type of edge we might call the "Edge to Living Process in our Personal Life." This edge is more than just not noticing its presence inside or outside of ourselves or taking its meaning seriously. For example, you may sense and then discover something new about yourself—for example, believe you need to be more spontaneous—but then have an edge to letting this process manifest itself in your behavior and body in relationships. You may have gotten over the edge to noticing your perception, you may have gotten around your sense that it was not significant, but then you may get stuck at the edge of living it with those closest to you.

For example, I had an edge to getting into the process I mentioned earlier where I perceived a lake image in my inner reality. Then, once I saw the lake and thought the process was significant, I had an edge to living the process that arose, to living that smiling face that came out of the circle in the lake. I was shy about the encouragement image that emerged out of the process. I understood the meaning of the process, thought it was significant, but was shy about feeling and expressing it personally in my outer (CR) reality.

This "Edge to Living Processes" in our immediate lives finds its expression in physics in the belief that what we discover or observe is irrelevant to our personal development. Discoveries in physics are thought to be limited to the "objective" world of matter. For example, scientists think that matter's laws are irrelevant to their personal behavior at home. They split matter from psyche and think physics is interesting, but it is "not me."

Physicists discovered that little pieces of matter, "quantum objects," like electrons and photons, are "entangled." You cannot always separate them from one another. If this entanglement were taken seriously and its philosophical consequences deeply applied by the scientists who discovered and used this idea in their scientific work, if they thought, "I am matter," physicists would be more romantic, they would feel more entangled with other people and with all of nature. They would take their intuitions seriously and develop their "non-local" sense of what is happening at a distance. They would be more telepathic.

Of course, some scientists take what they discover very personally. Heisenberg and Pauli, Bohr and Schroedinger, the modern physicists who were instrumental in discovering the uncertainty principle, the wave equation, and the principle of complementarity in physics, all developed personal belief systems connected with the ancient Indian philosophy, expressed in the *Upanishads*, about the uncertainty and wholeness of the universe.[2]

THE EDGE TO THE UNIVERSE

There is also the "Edge to the Universe." This fourth edge is the edge that tends to separate our identity from the world beyond our own family or group. We think the world or the universe is unfamiliar, too unknown, "not me." That group, that country, that side of the planet Earth, the moon, Jupiter, the sun, the universe, those things we feel are "not me."

In psychology and physics, this edge is connected to the location of the so-called observer. We normally think of the observer in us as located essentially in our bodies. If the edge to the universe did not exist, we might experience the observer in us as the universe viewing itself. In dreams, we frequently experience a sort of "mountaintop" view, or the view of the world from outside of the Earth. The eye of the dream, so to speak, is a sort of universal view of what is happening.

In most religions this edge appears in the belief that the gods and goddesses are "not I." Most people in the West have trouble considering the possibility that the gods and goddesses of ancient myths and traditional wisdom symbolize their own transcendental experiences or states of being.

In psychology, the tendency to focus more readily on personal issues, rather than on transpersonal experiences, is also connected with this edge. In physics, the belief that the important observer is located in a particular locality at a particular time as a machine or a person, is another form of this edge. If this edge did not exist, we would be more open to the idea that the "observer" can actually be located outside of our bodies.

Physics would be different indeed, if it assumed that the observer function belonged to something like the mind of the universe, which observes itself through us and through all other sentient beings. As we shall see in later chapters, the assumption that the sentient NCR abilities of the observer function can be viewed as being located throughout universal space can help us understand certain seemingly perplexing aspects of modern physics.

As things stand today, physics is surprised when confronted with the non-locality and interconnections of objects and events that we assume to be separated.[3] In the past, however, according to shamanic or traditional, indigenous wisdom, everything was interconnected and part of the same family. The sky was "grandfather," the sea "grandmother," and the earth "mother." In native traditions, everything was "me" or, at least, part of my family.

In brief, perceptual edges appear when processes feel too foreign. Once you cross the first edge and decide to get into process, you encounter a second edge and pause again, because the content of what is arising is too strange for you. Once you get beyond the edge to the content, you meet another barrier, living the significance of this process with the immediate world around you, feeling it in your body, using it in relationships, and manifesting new perceptions in your everyday "objective" reality.

A fourth threshold is reached when you arrive at letting your perceptual process connect you with the universe, living processes outside your immediate community. There is a lot more to this psychological threshold—its link with the fear of death, with the dissolution of our personal selves in psychosis, and with a xenophobic fear of fate—but for the moment, I want to remain focused on physics, not the psychological implications of this universal edge.

There are experimental indications that simply choosing an experiment about a quantum object such as an electron or photon determines, in part, the outcome of the experiment.[4] This means, in a sense, we co-create the universe. Who we are determines what appears in our perceptions, in our psychology, and in our physical world.

All this has been known for centuries by shamans and by teachers of perception. Remember Aldous Huxley's thoughts, expressed in his research on mescaline in *The Doors of Perception,* that our personality and awareness actually restricts and ultimately determines our perceptions.[5]

Figure 5.1 summarizes the connections between number bases and edges.

NUMBER BASES, PROCESS, AND EDGES TO PERCEPTION

	PROCESS THEORY	PYGMY MATH	MODERN MATH
	EDGE TO PROCESS		
	Process appears in first element of perception	*a*	1
D R E A M I N G	**EDGE TO CONTENT**		
	Content appears in second element of process	*oa*	2
	Content appears in third element of process	*ua*	3
	EDGE TO PERSONAL WORLD		
	Manifesting content in body behavior and in personal relationships	Many	Higher numbers
	EDGE TO THE UNIVERSE		
	Relating to the world beyond one's self and family as one's own		Higher numbers

5.1 Number bases, process, and edges to perception

RELATING TO THE UNIVERSE

Often at this point in my classes on physics and psychology, students raise many questions. When asked about the "Edge to the Universe," Amy said that the fourth edge was about the universe being familiar and a place to live her internal processes. For her, that was a very important edge. She asked, how could the universe be her home in everyday life? How could she live her spontaneous self anywhere, anytime? Until now, she said she had identified with being shy in public. She said she was a bit shy about being spontaneous with friends. This was an edge to her personal world. Being free and edgeless in public, anywhere, anytime? "That's not me," she laughed and stated her convictions and her desire to remain behind her barrier.

I said I knew what she meant. It took me thirty-four years, for example, to live through the edge I had against physics because, although I studied it, I did not identify with being a scientist. I was a therapist and had "edged out" all perceptions dealing with physics. The fourth edge was the big one for her. It is the big one for most people.

The "Edge to the Universe" also appears in our feelings of surprise that our perceptions, which we assume belong only to us or our immediate vicinity, are not only linked with outer immediate events but sometimes appear to be connected to events at a distance. Jung called these linkages of events "synchronicities." We are often surprised when synchronicities occur because we are used to thinking in terms of matter being in a given, spatial locality instead of being everywhere at once and present in all dimensions of the "river of time."

Since the dawn of time, traditional or shamanic wisdom has expressed the individual's basic relationship with the universe in terms of a dialogue with the world of the gods. Since the Renaissance, physicists no longer conceptualized the universe in terms of deities, but in terms of energy and the space-time continuum. Psychologists refer to each individual's inner experiences and outer observations in terms of the "psyche." Before the Renaissance, indigenous peoples from around the world believed that a divine being was, in essence, the power behind all events. Indigenous peoples identified their goddesses and gods as the creators of fate.

A prayer from the Yoruba of West Africa shows how counting and fate are connected:

> Death counting continually, counting continually, does not count me! Fire counting continually, counting continually, does not count me![6]

This prayer continues relating how the spirits of Emptiness, Wealth, and Day, as well as Death and Fire, count in the same manner. The Jungian psychologist, Marie Louise von Franz, says that these deities symbolized psychic energy as the source of consciousness. The spirit of Death, for example, is an energy that counts or unfolds fate, just as aging or time unfolds our personal processes.

In the Yoruba prayer, the universe is represented by intelligent, omnipresent energies or deities, named Day, Death, Fire, and so on. They are the spirits that count. They are the universe that calculates, that reckons what occurs. They unfold our personal processes and all of existence, one step at a time, one number at a time.

Myths from ancient India speak similarly of the god, Brahma, who creates the universe by dreaming it into existence. The Australian Aborigines also say that various deities—in this case from the animal realm—dream up the world.

Traditional stories from indigenous cultures around the world speak of deities creating and unfolding the world in order to know themselves, to create a mirror image of themselves.[7] In these stories human beings reflect a universal intelligence trying to know itself. The universe is seen as an intelligence that is striving for consciousness through the unfolding of events in what we know as the outer world or "objective" reality. Jung in his article "Answer To Job" (found in his *Collected Works*) tells us that God, in essence, needs humanity and the unfolding of human life, to become conscious.

This is what physicists like John Wheeler have discovered. An observer today is partially responsible for generating the reality of even the beginning of the universe! A symbolic picture of the universe looking at itself can be seen below. This is a sketch of Wheeler's 1979 lecture about Einstein, in which Wheeler showed the universe as a sort of being with a tail and an eye. The tail represents the early stages of the universe that is later promoted to concrete reality by means of its own self-consciousness, which itself depends on that unfolding reality.[8]

5.2 The universe looking at itself

We not only influence the course of events; we are an inextricable part of them. From time immemorial, people have felt intelligent, divine energies manifesting themselves, working mysteriously behind fate. In the 1400s in western Europe, Christians saw God as a mathematician who "architected" the universe using His Divine Compass.[9]

Myths remind us that we are not only observers who count things, but also, products of universal processes, swept more or less helplessly along by fate, or a more universal counting process. To counteract the feeling of impotence that comes with living in a universe that is "not us," we need "seers" to make up for our own lack of overview; we need helpers, magicians, priestesses, and shamans to intervene on our behalf. Just as we count some things and do not count others, indigenous wisdom considers that we, too, can be counted or not counted or noticed by nature. In our own minds, we are a number as far as the universe is concerned. This is probably where such slang expressions about death as "your number is up" come from.

People have always believed that they can influence the universe in the form of intervening spirits. This assumption lies behind a universal spiritual tendency to pray to higher beings for help. We have always hoped meditation, prayer, shamanistic intervention, and direct contact with deities could influence the flow of time.

The gods do not create the universe alone, independent of humans. We, too, have access to godlike energies, if only in the minor sense of having a limited co-creative capacity. People have always had non-consensus experiences that led them to believe they could gather the attention of the universe through prayer, or their dreams, that is, through unusual or altered states of consciousness.

Our unique perceptions, our own apparently personal NCR experiences, are dialogues with the universe. Here is an exercise that demonstrates this co-creative principle.

AN EXERCISE IN NCR COUNTING AND EDGES

If working with your own inner process by yourself is new or unfamiliar for you, try this exercise with a friend. Otherwise, find a quiet place where you will not be disturbed. Get into a comfortable position, close your eyes, and prepare to focus on your inner world.

1. Ask yourself: What is happening? What do you notice? Make a note of what comes up.

2. Do you notice something new—like a thought, a feeling, a body sensation, a movement, a sound—that you have not noticed until now?

3. Invite yourself to notice and then follow your experience; notice how the process you are noticing unfolds, more or less just by observing and feeling it.

4. Your next job is to notice where your process hesitates or stops. In other words, notice your edge. That's all, notice the edge.

Which edge are you at? Are you at the edge of "Getting into Process, noticing and following the flow of your experiences"? Then you have arrived at the first edge.

Or are you at the second edge of "Discounting the Content"? Do you feel the potential significance is unimportant, too fantastic, too unusual, unknown, or inappropriate for you? Then you are at the second edge. To get over this edge, consider the possibility that what you are experiencing is significant and allow your process more time.

If your process unfolds further, check and see if you have reached the "Edge to Bringing This Experience into Your Bodily Awareness"; your relationships, family, and group.

The purpose of the exercise is to notice edges, not to pressure yourself to unfold your process.

In this work, noticing your edges is not to be confused with pushing yourself over them. When you get to an edge, try saying to yourself, "Oh, I am stopped. Do I want to go further or not? Does the process want to go on, or not? Can I imagine living this process in my relationships? In the world?"

Simply notice how your attitude toward experience inhibits or allows your inner process to unfold.

This is an awareness exercise. Notice where and when you come up against an edge. Then consider what your edges are and how these edges influence the relationship between you, yourself, as the observer and the processes you are observing. How would you describe this relationship? Notice how you co-create and define this inner reality.

THE WORLD EDGE

Whether you can live and express your inner process in the outer world in any given moment depends on such external factors as your personal and professional identity, the culture you live in, the times, and the world scene. The world participates, so to speak, in helping or hindering you from crossing edges.

Let's say, for example, that you had the inner process of speaking out as a social activist. In some countries activism can be life threatening. There is a lot that cannot be said or done because if it was, you might be jailed or executed.

Whether or not you can get over an edge is, ultimately, not up to you alone. We are changed, and our essence and experience is influenced by, observation and counting, so to speak, just as much as we, ourselves, observe, count, and influence processes when we are looking at our inner worlds. It is not just up to us to move over the edge and identify our processes as part of the universe. The universe plays a role in what seem to be our edges.

In other words, edges and personal development are interactive processes. They arise in connection with the observer and the observed.

With awareness and personal effort, we can open up and expand our identities. We can get over the obstinate tendency to favor consensus reality and get into the flow of our process experiences. Once in process, we can get over the shyness and the fear of the unknown. But there are also edges that some of us may never get over. Some people get stuck for years at certain edges, never feeling they are able to do certain things, such as speak out in public, be social activists, love themselves, become leaders, become introverted monks. They always seem to get blocked by a barrier or at an edge, thinking that their processes are their own and do not belong to the universe.

Non-Locality in Psychology

One of the reasons for this blocking is that personal change is not just personal but connected with global transformation. If your identity changes, the world around you changes as well. The third and fourth edges involve system changes, interactions between what may have seemed personal and inner and what seemed like the universe or outer reality.

Here is the point where the concept of non-locality meets psychology. When we come to the edge of the world, the limits of our number base, we enter the area where personal and collective psychology can no longer be differentiated. Our identity and role in the world partially determines which edges we can cross and which we cannot. This is where personal development and cultural processes are intertwined. Our edge, our sense of freedom, is intimately linked with the external world that surrounds us. It influences us and we influence it.

This is why the use of force rarely helps at the fourth edge; pushing ourselves to change may not be useful because it ignores the relationship between us as observers and the processes at hand. To change ourselves changes in the external world must occur as well.

Throughout history, people have always used magicians, shamans, astrologers, and dream interpreters to get over "The Edge to the Universe" and make manifest inner changes in the outer world. These facilitators help by making the unknown more familiar. When physicists experience the universe as too foreign or unknown, they turn to experiments, they poke it, speed it up, weigh it, and measure it as minutely as possible to get to know it. Experiments facilitate the process of making the universe more familiar. Physicists are experiential, empirical, and also try—like some therapists—to be sensory (bodily) grounded.

Part of our personal destiny as humans is not only to work on our personal lives but to move over "The Edge to the Universe" until it becomes more familiar to us. I see this development in the thousands of people I am in contact with, worldwide. My personal contact with these people makes me predict that our view of the planet Earth and the universe will become even more human-like, aware and alive, than even the present Gaia Hypothesis suggests. We shall not only imagine and experience aliens and extra-terrestrial, human-like beings, but also feel that everything in the universe is part of our extended family.

We are all taking part in the development of a new science, a new perspective, which includes indigenous wisdom, psychology, and modern science. This new perspective integrates psychology and physics and will allow what has until now been called "physics" to focus on the significance of singular, one-time events, including NCR processes as well as probabilistic and statistical averages. This means we are living in the age of a new, scientific shamanism where gateways open to both traditional wisdom and inner worlds as well as science's objective, measurable truth.

The conclusions of our journey so far can be summarized as follows. Our awareness process enters math and physics in the following ways of counting, observing, and perceiving:

- Choosing the aggregate to be accounted for (i.e., the sheep).
- Deciding which subaggregates of the whole will be focused on (i.e., all sheep).
- Discounting other aggregates and sub-aggregates (i.e., brown sheep).
- Anthropic matching, or comparing these aggregates with aspects of human life or the human body and using numbers as signs, such as 1 for the head, 2 for the two arms, 3 for the head and arms, and so forth to represent the aggregates.
- Structuring aggregate processes according to edges, that is, our personal edges and the edges of our culture. These edges appear in number bases and limit how we identify ourselves and what we consciously perceive.

The processes of counting and recounting are demonstrations of the intimate, semi-conscious relationship processes that continuously co-create the universe. More than 4 billion inner worlds exist on the one objective world we call Earth. These billions of interacting inner and outer worlds, counting and recounting, co-create the universe.

NOTES

1. The connections between symptoms and edges are elucidated in detail in my book on working with symptoms, *Working With the Dreaming Body*.

2. The discussions between these leading physicists can be found in Heisenberg's fascinating *Philosophy and Physics*.

3. I discuss non-locality in Chapter 19 of this book in terms of Bell's Theorem.

4. According to the work of particle physicists B. Mistra and George Sudarshan, the decay of an unstable particle like a radioactive nucleus can be suppressed by the act of observation. Such "quantum eraser" experiments suggest that particles react to the possibility that they will be observed at a later date. David Darling's popular *Zen Physics* (page 135) discusses these experiments and the newest work in this area, of physicist Raymond Chiao.

5. Aldous Huxley describes his own perceptual experiences using mescaline in *The Doors of Perception*.

6. von Franz discusses the Yoruba in her *Number and Time*, pages 217-219.

7. See Robert Lawlor's well-illustrated book, *Voices of the First Day: Inner Traditions*.

8. This illustration comes from John Wheeler's representation in his article, "Beyond the Black Hole," written to celebrate Albert Einstein.

9. This and other wonderful references to geometry can be found in Robert Lawlor's *Sacred Geometry*.

6 | Number Fields and Divine Games

God is a mathematician, and the universe begins to look more like a great thought than a great machine.

—Sir James Jeans, a well-known psychologist from the early 20th century, in his *Mysterious Universe*

Up to now, our journey has shown how numbers arise from interactive perception processes between the observer and the observed, becoming consensus reality representations of events. Numbers are structured by our perceptual processes. They have bases that create cycles such as 1 to 10, which repeat as counting proceeds. In a way, periodic, cyclical repetition is built into our perception system and connected with edges.

In this chapter we will explore how the series of numbers 1, 2, 3, and 4... forms a sort of map or, as mathematicians say, a "field." I shall show how this field maps out how our unconscious minds work. Arithmetic will turn out to be the game rules of this field. I am excited about showing how arithmetic, adding, subtracting, and squaring correspond to psychological processes.

NUMBERS AS FIELDS

Before we think about the "fields" of math, physics, and psychology, let's review the everyday usage of the term field. Most of us think of a field as a portion of land set aside for a particular use, such as pasture to support livestock or an area to grow crops or mine elements like coal or diamonds.

The idea of a field is also used in sports. We speak of a playing field, a football or baseball field that defines the space on which the game is played. The word "field" can also be applied to a sphere of intellectual activity or a career. For example, someone might say, "I'm in the field of psychology."

These different uses all have something in common: fields involve given spheres and set patterns of behavior. For example, in playing the game of football on a football field, players are allowed to do certain things, but not others. There are rules for game fields. Players must play within the boundaries of the field; if they go out of bounds, the game's events are invalid. The field's boundaries and structures tell everyone exactly where the ball is relative to the goal.

Fields organize and structure given areas. They can be physical, as with a football field or a wheat field, or they can be imaginary, as with a "field of study." On a wheat field, you can grow wheat, but not play football. In a given field of study, you can study certain subjects and progress to the top of the field.

The magnetic field is a typical physical field. It describes how magnetic forces extend throughout the space around a magnet. The field is strongest near the magnet; it has a many lines of force there. The field is weakest far away in space; it has fewer lines of force. See below.

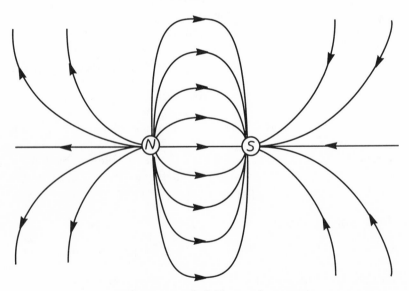

6.1 Electromagnetic field around a magnet

Magnetism is an invisible force field that influences little pieces of iron, which are pulled and pushed about near the magnet. Like magnetic fields, the gravity field of the earth cannot be seen, yet we all feel it pulling us down when we try to jump in the air. Gravity makes people relate to the earth as iron filings must relate to the magnet.

Field concepts are not new. Since ancient times the Tao was understood to pattern everyday life. Ancient Chinese thought of the Tao as a field with lines of force, which were called "dragon lines." This spiritual, psychophysical field was imagined to exert forces not only on the health and state of mind of people, but also on the geology and geography of the earth. These dragon lines looked very similar to the magnetic field lines above.

FIELDS IN MATH

Mathematicians also use the field concept.[1] The field of numbers is also a kind of game field. Specific rules apply here, the simplest of which are addition and subtraction.

For example, consider the field of the real positive series of numbers, that is, 1, 2, 3, 4, 5, 6, 7, 8, etc. When we add to any number, we still come up with a number in the real number series. So, we can play the game of addition with real positive numbers, since we still stay on the field. Addition and subtraction are descriptions of what we can do on the number field. These rules describe the way numbers can be related to one another.

In adding, we amplify the size of one number with the size of another number; we move further out along the series of positive numbers. In subtracting, we can do the reverse, that is, diminish our position by another number, and go in the opposite direction in the series of numbers.

Did you ever think about multiplication? It is an extension of the addition process. For example, instead of adding the number 5 four times, that is, instead of $5 + 5 + 5 + 5 = 20$, multiplication allows us a shorthand method of describing this as $5 \times 4 = 20$. Multiplication is a faster way of adding the same number to itself a number of times.

Division is the reverse of multiplication. Division is like cutting a pie into pieces. Division takes a number and breaks it down into parts. For example, $20 \div 5 = 4$ takes 20 and breaks it into five parts. Each part has the value of 4. Division splits something up, it asks about the equal parts of a number.

RULES OF THE NUMBER FIELD

Remember that only those games or processes can occur on a given field which fit its rules. What are the number field's rules? Here they come:

1. **Closure**. The first rule of the number field is the rule of all fields: whatever happens on this field must stay on the field to be valid. Anything that occurs outside the field is out of bounds; it will not be

counted as being a valid part of the game. Without the "closure" rule, the idea of a field would have little meaning. This gives the field boundaries or, as mathematicians say, closure.

2.   **Addition and subtraction.** A second rule specific to the number field is that we must be able to add and subtract at any time, day or night, and, of course, still stay within the field's boundaries.

Now let's investigate this rule. Will the unending sequence of real positive numbers 1, 2, 3, 4, etc., fulfill the second rule of the number field? No! Why not? Because, although we can add any two numbers and their sum will always be another number on this field, we cannot subtract any two numbers and still get a number on the field. For example, if we subtract 4 from 3, we get -1, a negative number, and that is not in the series of positive numbers.

So, to get a number field that obeys the rule that we can add and subtract and still remain on the field, we have to allow negative numbers to be on the field. Thus, we have to extend our number system from only positive numbers to include negative numbers to have a number field that works for adding and subtraction. The new set of numbers that are a field is thus:

$$-4, -3, -2, -1, 0, +1, +2, +3, +4$$

6.2 The real number field has positive and negative numbers

The real number field has closure if we add and subtract.[2] But does the field still have closure if we also multiply and divide? To do this, we have to include the ideas of fractions. If we extend the number field to include not only real whole numbers but also fractions, we can not only add and subtract but even multiply and divide and remain enclosed within the field.

In summary, the doubly unending set of positive and negative integers (and all fractions in between) can be called a number field because it fulfills the basic rules of the number game: the field has closure; we can move about on the game field with addition, subtraction, multiplication, and division and still stay on the field. Any of these arithmetic operations can be performed within that field with any two numbers and we will still be playing on that field.

CLOSURE AND WORLDS

Fields in mathematics have closure—we can move about in any way we want with certain rules like adding and subtracting, and still remain in that field. Closure means the field is a sort of world unto itself.

Every field is unique. We can play on the real number field by adding and subtracting, multiplying and dividing. In snowfields we can ski. In water fields we can swim. In crop fields, we can grow food. But don't try to swim the breaststroke in snow.

Fields are worlds in which processes evolve and in which we can travel around according to certain rules. The rules for skiing are that we need skis and snow. Then we can cross-country ski, snow plow, use a snow board, parallel ski, or telemark. But we can't swim there.

ADDITION AND AMPLIFICATION

The number field, like numbers themselves, describes consensus experiences, but it also patterns non-consensus experiences. The number field could just as well be called a "process field" because the same mathematical operations determine both consensus reality events and also psychological experiences, as we have seen in the past chapters.

We could just as well say that a number field is a field of awareness on which movements in awareness analogous to adding, subtracting, multiplying, and dividing take place.

The mathematical operation of adding is analogous to the psychological process of amplifying, making experiences stronger or more intense. There are many different words for this addition process in the area of awareness: we can add to, strengthen, extend, intensify, or enlarge experiences.

Everyone has an inner psychological pattern for adding because everyone inherently knows how to intensify or amplify an experience. We are, in my opinion, all born mathematicians. All you have to do to "add" is to ask yourself what is happening to you right now. Then ask yourself to "add" to what is happening, intensify it, and just about everyone seems to understand.

SUBTRACTION, DEBT, GOSSIP, AND PROJECTION

The mathematical operation of subtraction is analogous to the psychological process of making things less, that is, reducing the "value" or intensity of an experience. We can, for example, take something away from an experience merely by considering it worthless. Try it by trying to reduce the value of an experience you are having right now.

Minus is a powerful and subtle concept. The concept of minus numbers came into existence somewhere between 1400 and 1600 A.D. No one knows exactly who first conceived of these numbers.[2] But it took from the beginning of the human race to at least the 1400s to ask and answer what happens if you take 7 from 5. Why is this?

One of the students in my classes said that it took so long to develop the minus concept because no one had checkbooks. She made everyone laugh, but she was also very intuitive because the issues of money, or its lack, apparently led to the concept of minus. It seems that the bankers of Florence and Venice said, "You can take more than you have! We are happy to charge you for that debt."

Let's think about debt in psychological terms. What is a psychological debt? Think about it. In a way, if you talk about somebody you are borrowing from them. If you gossip about someone, you owe that person you gossiped about a debt.   What have you borrowed from them?

If you gossip about someone, if you praise or criticize them, you are borrowing an aspect of their personality you do not own in yourself on a conscious level. Psychologists call this form of borrowing a "projection." You have an edge against recognizing their praiseworthy or critical aspects as belonging to you, yourself. It is as if you cannot afford to be so good or so bad as they are. So instead you gossip, you borrow good and bad qualities from them.

A minus number in mathematics is like a projection in psychology, a spiritual debt. By gossiping and projecting, we are living off of someone else's energy. We increase the size of our personality but have not yet paid for it. Paying would mean expanding the size of your identity by identifying with those about whom you formerly gossiped.

Gossip is only one place we notice projection. The things we dream about are also projections. That is why gossiping about the people and objects we dream about is one of the oldest and most fundamental methods of dreamwork. Each dream borrows in the same manner as gossip.

Some indigenous groups of people like the Senoi, a tribe on the Malay Peninsula, know about this debt because they developed a ritual in which the dreamer must give a person a present if they were in the dreamer's dream. The Senoi understood paying for projections. If we were smarter, we would all realize we owe everyone we dream and gossip about something, we are indebted to them. We have borrowed a piece that we must eventually "own" as being our own life!

Let's say you dream and gossip about the Dalai Lama. You may say, he is a great person. You owe it to him and to yourself to realize that, in a way, you too are the Dalai Lama. If you withdraw your projection, you "pay back your debt," so to speak. That is why some psychologists say that you "own" your personality by increasing your identity.

SQUARING AND SELF-AMPLIFYING

There is a particularly interesting type of multiplication called squaring that gives us tips about how to work with our own minds. Squaring will be very important later, when we study imaginary numbers and quantum physics. So follow now, if you can.

To square something, you multiply it by itself or you add it as many times as it is itself. Four squared means, $4 \times 4 = 16$ (or $4 + 4 + 4 + 4$). Three squared, that is, 3×3, means $3 + 3 + 3 = 9$.

Squaring is that particular kind of addition or amplification that adds a thing to itself according to its own nature. For example, to square the number 3, you add it to itself three times. In this way, 3 is the seed or, rather, the root of 9. Mathematicians say 3 is the square root of 9. The number 3 is sort of underground, so to speak, as far as the number 9 is concerned.

Squaring has a geometrical significance, as the word "square" indicates. For example, 4 feet squared not only means 16 square feet, it also signifies mapping out an area by moving 4 feet in one direction and then 4 in a perpendicular direction. Four feet by itself is just a line moving 4 feet in one direction, in one dimension.

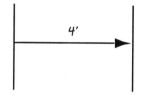

6.3 Four feet lays out a one-dimensional line.

Four feet is a line in one direction, it is one-dimensional. But 4 feet squared is two-dimensional, its represents an area. Squaring 4 demarcates an area of 16 square feet.

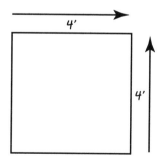

6.4 Four squared is two-dimensional.

The analogies between mathematics and psychology encourage us to look for a psychological aspect to every mathematical operation. After all, if numbers are an awareness field, everything done on that field must be related in some way with our awareness.

Since squaring is that special mathematical operation in which you take a number and multiply it by itself, squaring adds or intensifies itself according to its own pattern. It generates itself according to itself, so to speak.

The analogy to squaring in psychology is the self-generating nature of experiences, which amplify themselves according to their own pattern. Amy's inner child, for example, amplified or multiplied itself according to its own pattern. You might ask, How could the figure of the child amplify itself? Didn't Amy do that? The answer is, yes, Amy was at the controls of her process and allowed it to intensify itself, but her process was the motor. She was only the driver.

Mental processes are like breathing. We can control them, but when we are not at the controls, when we are sleeping, they are still at work. It is as if the gods were counting, although we too can count. Process is self-generating, although we can take part in its operation. Experiences unfold by themselves, they have a tendency to reach consciousness, and they are like underground roots that try to unfold into trees above ground.

Thus, the child tends to create its own "area." This is what Amy might call her childlike nature. In other words, the child makes an area for itself in her life.

Squaring (e.g., 4 × 4) is different than any old multiplication (like 4 × 3), just as the process of self-amplification is different from amplifying something yourself. For example, Amy can be a child and let the child itself self-amplify, or, she says to herself, "I should amplify the significance of that child in my life." The latter process is different from self-amplification. If she simply amplified the child, she might act like a child. That is, she acts like an adult, playing a child.

But if she lets the child self-amplify—that is, square itself—her child process unfolds itself in its own way. Remember that the word "child" is a CR term for the energy of a process that self-amplifies. Process evolves itself; it creates its own area. This is why people have always believed that in some way dreams come true. Dreams do not come true exactly as they are remembered, but they do try to realize themselves in our awareness in everyday life. They are part of self-generating processes.

At this point in a class on the subject of fields, students wanted to know how the squaring experience might work in practice. Amy decided to talk about herself. She explained that if she investigated the child in her earlier process, she would ask herself about the spaces it made in her everyday life. Just thinking about that make her crack up with laughter. She said, "If the child were to make space for itself, it would do it differently than I would! A child works at things in a childlike way. I would have to think like a child. When I do that, I see a very irrational, childlike picture of the child reacting to people in a childlike manner, like burping, crying, putting its nose in people's faces! That's so funny, I can't wait to try it! This is very different than asking myself, what does the child mean in life?"

I gave another example. I said to the students that if you have fantasies about a dog, a person, a house, or a group, you can unfold them yourself by adding to them, that is, by the process of ordinary amplification. You might bring in new ideas about them, associate them to other experiences, and so forth.

However, squaring is different. Say you dream about a singer. If you let this dream figure square itself, you drop your viewpoint and let it make its own area. Singing then makes a time and space for itself. If you dreamed of a tree, the job would be to investigate the tree's method of unfolding itself. How would a tree amplify the experience of being a tree? A tree might stand up and put out its branches (my hands) and swing with the wind. The idea is that I have the sense that the tree itself is doing the self-amplification, it is not me doing the fantasy work. It is like shamanism. You relax, shape-shift until you genuinely feel yourself experiencing the tree, and then you let the figure unfold itself.

At this point in our journey, I invite you to experiment with yourself, letting your inner experiences, your feelings, your most unusual and unpredictable movements, or the images and figures in your dreams square themselves. Take the time and try it.

SHAPE-SHIFTING AND SQUARING EXPERIMENT

Begin by recalling a recent dream. Now, choose a figure out of the dream—like a person, a tree, or whatever.

Now consider that this figure is the root of a process, it is the beginning of its own area. Shape-shift. Imagine being this figure and let it square itself. Advise yourself to let this dream figure unfold itself. Now give yourself some time, and let the dream figure square itself. That's a mathematical dreamwork experience of self-amplification. It is a form of shamanic shape-shifting.

FINDING THE SQUARE ROOT

Now let's go in the opposite direction and explore getting the square root of numbers. If 4 squared is 16 (since $4 \times 4 = 16$), what is the square root of 16? In other words, which number, when multiplied by itself, makes 16? The answer, of course, is 4; 4 is the square root of 16. The square root of a number is like its seed, its essence, which creates it. The essence of 16 is 4; the essence of 9 is 3, and so on.

Psychologically speaking, the square root of an area in your everyday life, where, say, you are very spontaneous, naïve, and full of energy, could be symbolized by a child. In other words, the dreamlike experience symbolized by the child is the root of an area of life that is very spontaneous.

We could say that elements of our dreams, fantasies, and body experiences are square roots of whole areas of our lives which we usually marginalize or else are about to develop.

If squaring is a psychological operation that can be consciously controlled or an autonomous process that occurs to us in everyday life, taking the square root of something is finding its source. In finding the square root, we can willfully go back to the source of an experience in everyday life or let it happen autonomously, merely by falling asleep.

Getting the square root of things is a useful psychological practice. Try it. Think about the area that just unfolded from a dream in the earlier exercise on squaring, but now go backwards. Notice how the dream is the root of that area.

Or try thinking about another area of your life you would like to know more about. Take a minute and really feel or think about and describe this area of your life. Now, instead of waiting to dream about this area, guess about its square root, its essence. Don't wait to go to sleep to dream. Find the square root of this area now. Find a symbol which, when squared, would give rise to that area. Find its root, its key.

INTENTIONAL AND UNINTENTIONAL AMPLIFICATION

We often talk about operations in mathematics such as finding the square root, squaring, and amplifying or adding as if we can do them when we want. Obviously you can add, subtract, make squares, and take square roots any time you want.

But this chapter has shown that mathematics is not just a set of operations we can perform consciously when we choose to do so. Mathematics also happens unconsciously or unintentionally. It is the basic pattern of amplification and reduction, projection and squaring or shape-shifting.

The operation of squaring, for example, can be performed consciously, or dream figures can work on themselves. They make areas for themselves in our lives without our conscious control. Our inner world unfolds itself.

Look back over your life, noticing how things that were beginning in their root form years ago have become realities. Look at dreams you had years ago—if you remember dreams—and see how they are unfolding themselves even as you live today.

You can assist this process of unfolding, you can co-create your universe by letting these processes square themselves, or just sit back. Life unfolds itself as well. One way or another, a root essence is unfolding you into being who you are and doing what you are doing. Knowing yourself means knowing this root.

Thus, physical or psychological processes follow the same mathematical patterns of unfolding. Mathematics describes patterns you can use intentionally to co-create your reality, and math also describes the unintentional unfolding you experience as life and death.

In retrospect, it seems as if life were a field with a few basic game rules for unfolding such as adding and squaring. In the midst of everyday life, you barely realize that some form of mathematical pattern is behind it all. Sometimes you play in the divine number game, sometimes you are played.

NOTES

1. Jagjit Singh discusses the history of fields in an easy-to-understand manner in his *Great Ideas of Modern Mathematics: Their Nature and Use.*

    Fields are defined in math as a set of entities subject to two binary operations, usually thought of as addition and multiplication. When this set of entities is added or subtracted, the set is "commutative," that is, $a + b = b + a$. Addition is commutative for real positive numbers, but subtraction is not, since $a - b$ is not always the same as $b - a$. For example, $10 - 1 = 9$, but $1 - 10 = -9$.

2. The number zero is an identity element of the set for addition, since you can add it and it leaves things unaltered. Furthermore, 1 is an identity element when we come to multiplying and dividing numbers.

7 | Awareness of Imaginary Numbers

The next great era of awakening of human intellect may well produce a method of understanding the qualitative content of equations. Today we cannot.

—Richard Feynman, Nobel Prize–winning physicist

As we have continued on our journey through number fields, we have discovered that numbers describe awareness interactions between an observer and the things she observes, whether these things are in her outer or inner world. We studied fields in Chapter 6 and saw that that all positive and negative numbers together create a "field" because they have closure. In other words, you can add, subtract, multiply, and divide and still stay on the same field. We found that math describes not only the way in which outer events may be counted, but also how our minds intensify and amplify events, create space, and unfold experiences.

In this chapter we are going to add another dimension to the real number field, the dimension of *imaginary numbers*. For some readers, this will mean encountering for the first time a kind of number they have never heard about before, the complex number, which is a combination of real and imaginary numbers.

IMAGINARY NUMBERS

Had we lived several thousands of years ago, we would surely have predicted the discovery of imaginary numbers because real numbers are only consensus reality versions of what we are experiencing when we observe and count. If we lived long ago and realized that numbers symbolize overt processes but also subtle processes that are not directly identified, we would probably have thought that we needed a new description of events which included real numbers and also something like "imaginary" numbers to describe both the CR and NCR aspects of events.

It turns out, after the development of "imaginary numbers" in the sixteenth and seventeenth centuries, that these numbers are not as imaginary as mathematicians originally thought, yet these numbers do give us insight into NCR aspects of nature and, of course, into our own natures. Furthermore, it is very important for us to explore these numbers because they form the basic description of quantum physics and relativity. Modern physics cannot exist without imaginary numbers.

Numbers and their systems gradually developed over many thousands of years. First came the ideas of counting and numbers; then came modern concepts such as "real positive and negative numbers," zero, and fractions. "Rational" and "irrational" numbers followed.[1]

We can see from the terms, rational and irrational, that the discovery of numbers was confounded from the beginning by the question of where these amazing symbols came from and what they were. When imaginary numbers were developed during the European Renaissance by Gottfried Leibniz and others to solve problems in mathematics, the concept of imaginary numbers was also considered ethereal. Imaginary numbers were likened to ghosts; they were present, yet could not be seen.

Let me introduce imaginary numbers. Remember how the series of positive, real numbers, 1, 2, 3, 4... was not a big enough number field to include subtraction because numbers such as 5 - 7 (= -2) could not be found on the positive number field. If we add negative numbers, we then have a more complete field: -4, -3, -2, -1, 0, +1, +2, +3, +4 etc. On this larger field we can now play with subtraction, as well as addition, multiplication, and division. The negative numbers added a new dimension to the positive numbers.

It was soon realized that a new dimension was needed, in addition to the real and negative numbers. Why? Because now you could add, subtract, and divide and still be on the number field, but you could not take the square root of a negative number and stay on that field. No one knew what the square root of -4 was. Mathematicians knew that 2 is the square root of 4 (that is, $\sqrt{4} = 2$), but what is the square root of -4? What number times itself gives us -4? To solve this problem, mathematicians thought of adding imaginary numbers to the real numbers.

The formal way to write imaginary numbers is to put the letter "i" next to a real number. For example, if 4 is the real number, it becomes denoted as an imaginary number by writing it as $4i$.

The "*i*" has the following meaning: it stands for the square root of -1 (that is, $\sqrt{-1}$). Another way of saying the same thing is that the square root of -1 is abbreviated by the letter "*i*." Thus $\sqrt{-1} = i$.

For example, if b is a real number, then its corresponding imaginary number can be written as *ib*, which is the abbreviated form for $(\sqrt{-1})b$.

The first mathematicians who developed and used imaginary numbers in the seventeenth century believed that imaginary numbers were unreal and impossible. How can a negative number have a square root? The brave man who first published a formula that included the enigmatic imaginary numbers was a sixteenth-century Italian mathematician, Jerome Cardan. However, he was in great doubt about his work and claimed that the numbers were meaningless, fictitious, and imaginary.[2]

What are imaginary numbers, really? Remember that real numbers encode but marginalize NCR experiences. Many of the specific and observable properties of the things we count are not taken into consideration by the act of simply counting. Because of the process of marginalization, real numbers will never be sufficient to completely describe events, so we need something like imaginary or non-consensus qualities in math, as well as consensual quantities like 1, 2, and 3. While useful, imaginary numbers also point back to the magical properties people often associate with numbers.

NUMBER MAGIC

Today, although most people know little about the non-consensus reality properties of numbers, many still believe, as in centuries past, that numbers have magical properties. Just as we use special geometries to make buildings, such as high, pointed roofs, and crosses, stars, and circles to represent spiritual ideas, ancient and some modern people believed in the magical power of individual numbers. For example, the number 1 is believed to represent unity, and many people identify the number 2 with the devil or the "binarius," 3 with fate (or the trinity in the Christian world), 4 with wholeness, and so forth.[3]

These beliefs are partially connected to the quantitative properties of numbers. For example, the number 1 does not get bigger by multiplying by itself, nor is it reduced by division by itself. Conclusion: the number 1 has godlike properties. It is eternal, unchanging. It is a "one and only." I have spoken of 1 as representing process itself, something that is always present, a constant like the inevitability of change. One is the first "prime" number.

A prime number has no factors except itself and unity. For example, 6 is not a prime, since its can be factored into (or produced by the multiplication of) 2×3. That is, the number 6 has factors other than itself, namely,

2 and 3. Other primes besides 1 are 2, 3, 5, 7, 11 and so on, and -2, -3, -5 and so on.

Let's think about the number 2. Two is a prime number because it can only be factored into 2×1. The number 2 is interesting because it yields the same number when added or squared, that is, $2 + 2 = 2 \times 2 = 4$. You can see how we might project all sorts of magical or otherwise fascinating qualities into numbers like 2. Other numbers when added to themselves produce different results than when they are squared. But not 2.

$$2 + 2 = 2 \times 2!$$

Three is a prime that is the sum total of the preceding digits ($3 = 1 + 2$). Four is the first nonprime numeral, the first square.

Many individuals and cultures believed that the numerical qualities of the dates of birthdays and the letters of names were not merely chance happenings but meaningful events that were imbued with magical significance. If you were born on the second of January, for example, the meaning of your life would be connected with the numbers 2 and 1. If your name is AMY, then your life would be connected to the numerical equivalents for the letters A, M, and Y, that is, 1, 8, and 25, and their qualities.

These imagined qualities of numbers are meaningful for many people, yet there is no consensus in our culture on the symbolic meaning of numbers. Some people consider them to have no meaning whatsoever. Thus, numbers have both consensus and non-consensus aspects. Scientists focus only on the quantitative, CR-oriented aspect of numbers and believe their non-consensus qualities are irrelevant to understanding reality. In fact, scientists have always hoped that numbers as a whole, regardless of what they are called, form a system that is logical and airtight, keeping irrational inconsistencies out.

In 1931, the logician Kurt Goedel proved (or reminded those who had forgotten) that consensus reality definitions of numbers and formulas are not airtight and cannot be used to prove their own validity through deductive reasoning. Goedel showed that there are unavoidable contradictions in mathematics; certain statements can neither be proved nor disproved.[4] Thus we cannot be certain that the science of mathematics does not lead to contradictions, or that numbers are free of magic.

As it stands, arithmetic may always be stuck with inconsistencies. We might suspect that Goedel's theorem would have discouraged scientists who hoped to devise a set of axioms from which all phenomena can be deduced.[5] The opposite seems to me to be the case. The majority of scientists today act as if a final theorem might be discovered from which all physical events can be reasonably deduced in terms of mathematics.

The only corollary to Goedel's theorem that I know of in psychology is the unwritten rule in some therapists' minds—like my own mind—that the human race is not consistent. True, arithmetic operations lend more consistency than appears at first glance to dreams and altered states of consciousness, but this consistency is more of a guideline than an inflexible law.

PRIMARY AND SECONDARY QUALITIES OF MATTER

At about the same time that imaginary numbers were being discovered or invented, Gallileo, in 1623, made a distinction between "primary" and "secondary" qualities of matter.[6] He called primary qualities of matter those which were measurable and describable by real numbers (such as 4 ounces, 10 miles, 60 seconds). He said secondary qualities (such as love and color) could not be reduced to empirical measurements and, according to Gallileo, were outside the realm of science.

From the viewpoint of our present discussion, it looks like Gallileo's primary and secondary qualities are similar to my use of consensus and non-consensus realities and terms of Albert Einstein, quoted in the first chapter from his book on relativity:

> ...certain sense perceptions of different individuals correspond to each other, while for other sense perceptions no such correspondence can be established.[7]

Gallileo lived at a turning point in Western civilization, at the time when quantitative characteristics were just being separated from feelings about matter. The history of Western civilization shows that science went in the direction predicted by Gallileo and rejected the qualities of NCR experiences. Scientists decided then, and still believe today, that the imaginary numbers were something like Gallileo's secondary qualities; they had no immediate physical meaning and were not the domain of science.

This resistance was due in part to the growing division during the European Renaissance between matter and soul, between physical and non-physical domains. Imaginary numbers appeared just then, when physics and math were desperately trying to divorce themselves from religion and the mysteries of alchemy, that combination of chemistry and meditation, psychology and physics. That divorce has been valuable, but it is time for a reunion. The history of imaginary numbers shows hints about how this reunion will take place.

THE MATHEMATICS OF IMAGINARY NUMBERS

The history of the development of imaginary numbers is quite interesting because it follows the path of constantly trying (and not quite succeeding) to do away with nature's "secondary qualities." In the seventeenth century, the mathematicians John Wallis (1616-1703) and Gottfried Leibniz (1646-1716), among others, were pondering the square root of negative numbers. They knew that if you have a square with area 1, the square root would be 1, too.

Let's rethink imaginary numbers. These men figured that if you want to find the square root of 4, they knew it was 2. Why? Because, as I have said before, if you square 2 you get 4, that is, $2 \times 2 = 4$.

What times itself would result in a negative number? No one had an answer. Thus mathematicians concluded that something must be missing in their real number field, since there was nothing on that field which would give them the square roots of negative numbers. They knew they needed a new type of number field that was an expanded version of the real number field because nothing in the real number field led to the square root of -1! Prove it for yourself.

The square root of +9 is   3.
of   +3   is   1.732...
of   +2   is   1.414...
of   +1   is   1.000...
of   +0.5   is   0.707...
The square root of +0.2 is   0.447...
of   +0.01   is   0.100...
of   -1.0   is   ???
What is the square root of -1???? Nothing in real number field...
... -5 -4 -3 -2 -1   0 +1 +2 +3 +4 +5...

After some deliberation about its possibly mystical nature, mathematicians finally agreed to repress the mysticism associated with *i* and define it in purely technical terms as the square root of -1.

In other words, they split off their feelings about leaving the "real" number field and entering into a new realm they called "imaginary" by creating, instead, a practical set of definitions. From the purely logical or mathematical perspective, they could not find the roots of negative numbers, so they made one up by attributing a mathematical property, $\sqrt{-1}$, to one letter of the alphabet! The result was and is today that the square root of -1 is designated by the letter *i*, that is:

$$\sqrt{-1} = i$$

This designation is interesting, but its true value comes out when you make the following definition. If you multiply the imaginary number times itself, you get a real number, that is:

$$i \times i = -1$$

thus

$$\sqrt{-1} = i$$

This definition means that there is a connection between real and imaginary numbers. This definition is meant to be logical and self-explanatory. And this definition is amazing! It gives science a new dimension.

Real numbers can be directly counted, imaginary ones cannot. You know what 5 refers to. It is smaller than 6 and more than 4. But what is the relationship of $5i$ to 5? It is neither bigger nor smaller than 5, nor is it equal to 5! You can count five sheep and call that 5. But $5i$ has no direct, measurable significance.

The first inventors of imaginary numbers thought the numbers were mystical, since they could not be seen in reality. The inventors hoped that they were simply logical or mental constructions, whatever that means. Leibniz, however, knew differently. He not only defined the imaginary number as $i \times i = -1$, but described it as the "Holy Ghost" of mathematics, perhaps because its physical significance could not be immediately grasped. The imaginary number was a ghost for him; the Holy Ghost, a spirit behind material reality. For Leibniz, imaginary numbers were "a fine and wonderful refuge of the divine spirit—almost an amphibian between being and non-being...."

For Italian mathematician Rafael Bombelli in 1575, imaginary numbers were "wild thoughts." Leonhard Euler (1701-83) said, "such numbers, which by their nature are impossible and ordinary are called imaginary or fancied numbers, because they exist only in the imagination."[5]

It was as if invisible spaces re-entered science, never to be withdrawn again! Imaginary numbers are ghosts because they cannot be directly measured in consensus reality. Only their squared natures are measurable, since i squared ($i \times i$) equals -1, which is a real number, while i is not. Thus, to this day, some four hundred years later, no one knows exactly to what imaginary numbers refer.

ON THE PSYCHOLOGICAL PROCESSES OF "I"

In the last chapters, we journeyed through the psychological significance of negative numbers, which, like debts, are something you owe someone. Remember the Florentine and Venetian banks and their concept of debt and how a projection is like a debt because you borrow something in projecting which you must eventually pay for by owning.

Carrying this analogy of negative numbers and projections further, we could say that the square root of a negative number is the square root of a projection. But what on earth is the root of a projection? The root of a projection is a dreamlike experience. If I get all upset and always say that certain people are "bad," I may be projecting a part of myself. The root of my projection might be found in a dream of mine where a "bad figure" appears. This bad guy, of course, is me.

Likewise, *i* is the square root, or dreamlike root, of a negative number. In this sense, *i* is ghostlike, as Leibniz said. It is something invisible like a dream symbol, which, when squared, unfolds itself into an area of life.

In other words, *i* is like a more or less holy ghost. It is divine in a sense; it has the autonomous power of dreams to unfold or square itself into an area of everyday life. A psychological analogy of the imaginary number *i* is a dream image which, on awakening, amplifies itself to the point where you think it is real.

For example, I vividly remember a friend of mine dreaming that his partner was having an affair with someone else. On awakening, he asked his partner if it was true, and even when she said it was not, he continued to believe it.

The dreaming process unfolds further as projections, which are a kind of debt in reality, analogous to the way in which the imaginary number *i*, now standing for a dream, squares itself in the formula $i \times i = -1$.

My friend was mistaken about his partner; he owed her something! But in dreaming, that is, in non-consensus reality, he was not mistaken. In my friend's dreaming, she was having a relationship with another person—a man who my friend said was more feeling and more responsive to her than my friend was. My friend was jealous of "the other man," for that imaginary figure had all the feeling my friend did not have in everyday life.

In other words, we can think of the imaginary numbers as analogous to figures in NCR: the imaginary numbers are real but only in a non-consensus way. They are not true in terms of the criteria of consensus reality, where things can be measured, photographed, and weighed. They are dreamlike.

The dreaming process—imaginary as it is—squares itself and makes projections in everyday life. Dreams may or may not be real in CR terms, but they are certainly one hundred percent real in NCR terms!

We know that dreams do not happen only at night. They happen during the day as well, in the form of subtle non-consensual perceptions. For example, what we call a projection is always preceded by glances, fleeting thoughts, subtle feelings about the object or person on whom we have a "projection." These subtle feelings and thoughts, glances and flirts are the square root experience of the projection. They happen so rapidly that they belong to the realm of dreaming, to the realm of our sentient abilities to perceive things in subtle and generally unrecognized ways.

COMPLEX NUMBERS

When added to the real number field, imaginary numbers increase their descriptive abilities. The resulting mixture of real and imaginary numbers is called *complex numbers*. Complex numbers are a combination of real and imaginary numbers. For example, $3 + 4i$ is a complex number.

Complex numbers can be written in a general way as *a* + *ib* where *a* and *b* are any real numbers. In other words, *a* and *ib* are the real and imaginary parts of complex numbers.

Just as all real numbers together create the real number field, complex numbers add a new dimension, an imaginary dimension to this field. We can draw this complex field in the form of a map or graph. Just as our ordinary maps have two directions or axes, namely, the east-west and north-south directions, complex numbers have a real and an imaginary axis. See the picture below.

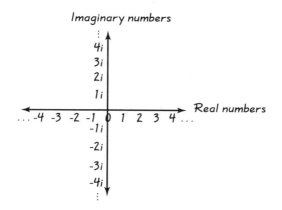

7.1 The complex number field or map

Now, even though this field is new to some readers, we can still play on it. Just think of it as a map. For example, let us find out where the complex number 3 + 2*i* is located. To find this number, count to the right three units on the real number axis, then go up two units on the imaginary number axis, and there you have 3 + 2*i*. I marked it with a dot as indicated in Figure 7.2.

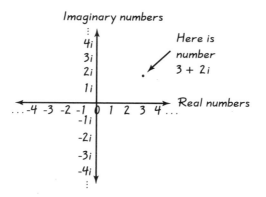

7.2 Location of the complex number 3 + 2i

The complex field is indeed a mathematical field because it has closure. You can test this if you want, by adding or subtracting any complex number you can think of. The result will be that you always stay on the complex number field. It has closure. You could not find the square root of a negative number on the real field because there were no imaginary numbers there! Now we have a more complete field, one of the most complete in mathematics. In fact, complex numbers include all real and imaginary numbers.

AWARENESS FIELDS

Some people do not like graphs, planes, or fields like those above. For them, graphs are no fun. But I like them because I think of this graph not just as a quantitative description of our ability to count real and imaginary quantities and qualities, but also as a field that tells us something about ourselves. Since numbers are descriptions of various aspects of our observational behavior, we could call the complex number field in mathematics an "observation" or "awareness" field.

The complex number field represents the idea that whatever we see has both real and imaginary (or non-consensus) characteristics. Furthermore, all of these characteristics of the complex field including real and imaginary numbers obey the very same rules of adding, subtracting, multiplying, and dividing, that is, the various types of amplification.

Consider, for example, a particular tree. Let's say, we think the tree is a wonderful birch tree and that it has a very motherly appearance. Around the world, people have felt that big green trees are motherly. Can you imagine such a tree?

In any case, the word "tree" has both real and also non-consensus characteristics, since there may be some people who do not feel that the big green tree is motherly. OK, motherliness is non-consensual.

My perception of the tree is that it is a motherly birch. This perception is the psychological analogy to $a + ib$. The real number "a" would then represent consensus reality aspects of the tree—its birch type, its size (say 8 feet high), its age (say ten years), and so forth. The imaginary number ib would then refer to sentient perceptions, to the feeling we get in response to that tree, the fact that we feel it is a motherly tree.

Remember that a and b in the complex number "$a + ib$" are real numbers and that ib is the imaginary component of that the complex number. Analogously speaking, the real number b in $a + ib$ is the term motherly, which is a consensus term describing non-consensus responses to that birch tree.

We can put this information about complex numbers into pictorial form—see Figure 7.3 on the next page.

The real or CR part of the birch tree (its height etc.)

The CR description of an NCR part of the tree, like its motherliness

$a + ib$ = Complex number: Awareness of the birch tree

The imaginary or NCR dimension sign

7.3 Real plus imaginary, or CR and NCR aspects of perception

Normally, we do not notice the various parts of our perception. We just see a tree and like it. Complex numbers, however, help us understand and differentiate some of the remarkable properties of our perception. The part of our awareness that is consensual we call observation. The part that is non-consensual I call sentient awareness.

Saying that the tree is a birch and motherly is a way of representing a particular awareness of the birch tree, just as, in mathematics, applying the formula $a + ib$ is a way of representing a particular complex number. Thus the awareness of the tree as being a birch and motherly, by analogy, can be represented by a particular complex number (which combines a real and imaginary number) in an overall NCR space.

Remember, mathematicians do not (yet) think this way. They do not ascribe any significance to the imaginary numbers. Indeed, Gallileo asked that we banish "secondary" qualities of matter like motherliness, love, and beauty because we cannot measure them (in consensus reality).

Today, mathematicians say that imaginary numbers are pure thought and do not refer to anything special. Yet, we can see how real numbers form an awareness field describing CR aspects of events, and how the complex field of real plus imaginary numbers is symbolic of an awareness field that describes CR and NCR events.

Each particular point on the complex plane is thus symbolic of an awareness that has both real and imaginary characteristics—like the real birch tree that is so many feet high and also motherly for you. Each person, object, or phenomenon we interact with, each event we notice, has real, consensual and imaginary, non-consensual aspects. The analogy in math is the complex number that combines real and imaginary numbers.

Whether we are waking or sleeping, the things we notice have both CR and NCR characteristics. Our new, differentiated awareness field still has closure, since we can dream, be awake, add or amplify, multiply, square, and do anything with our awareness we like and are still on the field of awareness as long as we use CR terms to describe real and imaginary experiences. We can say that our awareness field is a CR description of the universe or rather, of our relationship to the universe.

THE HIERARCHY OF NUMBERS

Let's look at some more details of complex numbers. Note, for example, that while there are similarities between the complex numbers and real numbers, there are differences as well. Remember, you can say that 5 is larger than 3, but you cannot say that a complex number, such as $5 + 5i$, is smaller or larger than any other complex number, for example, $3 + 3i$. The concept of size is a consensus reality concept. We cannot measure $5i$ or $3i$!

In the real number field you can compare size and quantity. The complex number field with imaginary numbers is a matter of imagination, of immeasurable, subjective quantities. Likewise, we cannot say that a tree that reminds you of the feeling of motherliness is more or less powerful for you than for someone else who says the same tree is simply beautiful. There is no consensus on the "size" of these terms.

Yet, in dreaming, we definitely notice an increase or decrease in value and sense of importance. Trees in dreams can be amazing, catastrophic, wonderful, exciting, horrendous, "huge" or insignificant. What was in reality a normal, possibly insignificant tree can become huge in the course of dreaming. It can be blown up out of proportion.

In any case, we now have a hierarchy of numbers.[8] Complex numbers, such as $a + ib$, include both real and imaginary numbers, a and ib. Real numbers can be considered to be complex numbers without imaginary components, b. And imaginary numbers are complex numbers without any real number component, a.

Complex numbers are analogies of all our most general types of experience, which is a combination of both real and imaginary qualities. From now on, I will refer to complex experiences simply as "experience" and mean awareness of real and imaginary quantities and qualities, a mixture of everyday reality and fantasy or dreaming, of CR and NCR characteristics.

In other words, whatever we call real is a special case of a more complex reality where the imaginary is missing or marginalized by the viewer. In general, whenever anyone speaks of dreaming or fantasy, we should think of that special state of consciousness which is not recognized by mainstream, scientific thinking today as significant to observations—unless or until that dreaming state squares or unfolds itself so that it can be viewed as real.

Complex numbers represent a paradigm that includes not only how our meditative awareness processes unfold, but also how we observe everything.

NOTES

1. "Rational" numbers (that is, any number that can be expressed as a ratio of two integers, such as 1 and 2) came along shortly thereafter, followed by "irrational" numbers (that is, any number that cannot be expressed as the ratio of two integers, such as the square root of 2, or the number pi). The rational and irrational numbers together are called the set of real numbers.

2. In his *One Two Three... Infinity* (page 42) the twentieth-century astronomer George Gamow notes these remarks by Jerome Cardan.

3. See Marie Louise von Franz's *Numbers and Time* (Chapters 4–7) for more information on number symbolism.

4. No axiomatic mathematical system is powerful enough to prove its own consistency. Such proof requires additional axioms from outside the system. See Kurt Goedel's paper, "On Formally Undecidable Propositions" (pages 711–715 in *From Frege to Goedel, a Source Book in Mathematical Logic, 1879-1931,* edited by Jean van Heijenoort. Also, see Frank J. Swetz's work, *From Five Fingers to Infinity: A Journey through the History of Mathematics,* for a simple discussion of Goedel's work.

5. See Carl B. Boyer's *A History of Mathematics* (pages 611 and following) for further discussion.

6. The physicist David Darling reveals this statement about Gallileo, which shocked me at first in *Zen Physics*, page 123. I was amazed because process-oriented psychology, which I have been so involved in developing over the years, is based on primary and secondary processes, that is, processes we identify and disidentify with. In understanding people, both are needed.

7. See Albert Einstein's *The Meaning of Relativity,* page 1.

8. All numbers are complex numbers, thus complex numbers are at the top of a hierarchy. Complex numbers are the sum of real and imaginary numbers. Imaginary numbers are real numbers multiplied by $\sqrt{-1}$. And real numbers are either rational or irrational.

8 | Conjugation Means Lucid Dreaming

If you keep the mind sufficiently active while the tendency to enter REM sleep is strong, you feel your body fall asleep, but you, that is to say, your consciousness, remains awake. The next thing you know, you will find yourself in the dreamworld, fully lucid.

—Stephen LaBerge, dream researcher, in *Lucid Dreaming*

As we continue our journey, we have seen that the math of complex numbers can help us ponder how consciousness enters the observation process. Math can also help us observe how our awareness influences the subatomic world and everything around us. Math is like a secret code for the interactions between observer and observed, and learning to decode the mystery is an exciting adventure. We shall find in it not only everyday reality, but also the pattern for lucid dreaming, that is, staying awake in your dreams.

Remember the idea of the complex field? It is a kind of map. Just as your home can be located on a map if you know its position east, west, north, or south of the center of your city or town, complex numbers can be located on a complex number field if one axis is real and the other imaginary. For example, in Figure 7.2 in Chapter 7, the complex number $2 + 3i$ is located two units to the right on the real number axis and three units up on the imaginary number axis.

CONJUGATES AND MIRROR IMAGES

In general, any complex number $a + ib$ can be represented on the complex number field.

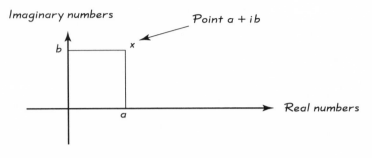

8.1 Number a + ib *on the complex plane*

Now let's go further. I want to show how the point *a + ib* can be reflected on this map, that is, on the complex plane. Imagine the complex plane to be a room we are looking into from above. From above, the real axis is a line representing a wall covered by a mirror.

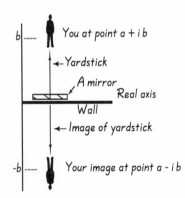

As you look at yourself from above, your reflected image seems to look back at you from below, that is, from the other side of the mirror.

8.2 Your reflection

If you were standing at point *a + ib* looking at the mirror on the wall, you would see yourself as an image in the mirror. Your image would appear to you as if it were to be standing at point *a - ib*, on the other side of the mirror, behind the wall. If you are standing 3 meters from the mirror, b is 3 meters, and -b, where your image is, is -3 meters, that is, behind the mirror. Your mirror image is more or less the same as yourself, except it is standing at *-b* instead of *+b*.[1]

Now, back to the complex plane. In the same way that you are standing at point $a + ib$, you see your image in a mirror, standing at $a - ib$. The point $a - ib$ is a reflection, so to speak, of $a + ib$.

Mathematics calls this mirror image of a complex number a "conjugate." In other words, if we reverse the sign before the "i" in the complex number $a + ib$, we have its conjugate, $a - ib$. Two *complex numbers are conjugates if they differ only in the sign of their imaginary parts.* For example, $4 + 3i$ and $4 - 3i$ are conjugates.

In a way, this sounds simple, and it is. But it is very important, because mathematicians do many things with these simple conjugates, and physicists use them to understand reality. Before we jump to that view of the world, let's look first at the details of complex numbers.

One conjugate number reflects the other. Figure 8.3 shows that point $a + ib$ reflects its conjugate, point $a - ib$.

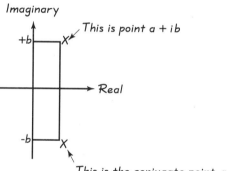

8.3 Complex conjugates are reflections.

A complex number's reflection is its conjugate. They are the same, except for a change in sign around the imaginary component ib.

THE PSYCHOLOGY OF REFLECTION AND CONJUGATION

Now let's think about psychological analogies to complex numbers and their conjugates. In Chapter 7 we saw that our perception, like a complex number, is composed of both consensus reality and non-consensus reality qualities. Our awareness field, including everything we notice, such as a tree, has both real and imaginary qualities. For example, we may see a tree both as a birch tree (CR quality) and as a motherly tree (NCR quality).

Let's consider what the conjugate or reflection of an NCR experience might be. We have many ways of reflecting. For example, we can repeat back the words of another person. We can also mirror her movements by repeating them. When we reflect, the other person can hear or see what she is doing. If someone's words and gestures occur unconsciously, reflecting these signals can enable the other person to become conscious of what has occurred.

Repetition and reflection help the other person become conscious. Reflection is a basic element in creating consciousness, which in this instance means understanding that all the unconscious gestures, feelings, and thoughts that emerge from us are either reflected by someone else or self-reflections. What were these gestures and feelings before they were conscious? Just semi-conscious, imaginary, dreamlike experiences for the person who was having them.

In a way, everything you do is reflected by things around you. It is like being in the mountains and calling out your own name. You can hear an echo, that is, an auditory reflection, coming back to you. It is as if the mountains are calling out your name. Reflections help us know that we are here.

A less well-known mirroring happens spontaneously when we wake up in the morning. If we are careful and use our awareness during the waking-up process, we will notice that we not only remember dreams, but reflect them as well. In a way, dreaming goes on even after we are awake. After breakfast, we usually forget the dreaming part of ourselves, yet it continues throughout the day, as we can discover by investigating slips of the tongue, accidental gestures, and sudden fantasies.

Pretend, for example, that you dreamed someone was critical of you. If you pay attention as you awaken, you may notice or hear that you are criticizing yourself. This might make you feel upset or depressed. Nobody likes criticism. Suddenly you understand your dream! The critical person in the dream is a critical part of yourself you are not aware of.

It is as if the dream figure of that critical person is reflected in the semi-conscious state in the form of your own self-criticism! Using mathematics as a metaphor for psychology, we can say that complex conjugates represent two forms of dreaming: one is done *without awareness* and the other *with awareness*. One conjugate represents *sentient experiences that happen to us as in dreaming*, while the other conjugate represents *those same sentient experiences reflected by our more lucid selves*.

In summary, there are two dreaming or sentient states. Let's call the first state *dreaming* and the other *lucid dreaming*. As we move forward on our journey, we will visit conjugates again, deepening our understanding of the psychological processes of complex numbers.

CONJUGATION PRODUCES REAL NUMBERS

Here, we shall focus on another marvelous quality of complex numbers. When you multiply a complex number by its conjugate, the result is an entirely real number, "R."[2,3,4] If we multiply the number $a + ib$ by $a - ib$, the result is $a^2 + b^2$. a^2 and b^2 are real numbers without any imaginary sign, "i," in front of them. For example, $(3 + 4i) \times (3 - 4i) = 3^2 + 4^2 = 25$. This real number, 25, has no imaginary qualities.

The amazing, important point for physics and for psychology is that *a complex number times its conjugate produces a real number without any imaginary qualities to it.*[5] At first, this sentence may sound abstract, but it contains a vital concept for physics and psychology. Multiplying a complex number by its conjugate produces reality, just as lucid reflection of dreaming promotes consciousness.

Earlier in this journey, we discovered that squaring a number makes an area for it. The number 3 is the square "root" of 9, that is, 9 is the area represented by 3. Multiplying complex numbers by their conjugates is like squaring in many ways.[6] We could say that multiplication of a number by its conjugate makes an area in everyday life for that number.

Since a complex number represents a dreamlike experience, multiplying a complex number by its conjugate represents the experience of actively, lucidly dreaming a dream into everyday life. Lucid dreaming *generates* consensus reality.

Unlike real numbers, complex numbers cannot be measured directly because they have imaginary numbers in them. Similarly, although we cannot measure dreamlike sentient experiences directly and know exactly what the dreamer senses, we can see the overall effect of dreaming in the unconscious gestures and signals people make. Although we cannot prove what we have dreamed to someone else, we can show them the effects of dreams in any given moment by dancing, or sharing ideas. If you reflect some of your own unconscious motions, you might create an amazing dance. If you find yourself unconsciously moving your fingers to a certain rhythm, and if you reflect this rhythm, you might sing a wonderful song.

Likewise, although physicists cannot directly measure complex numbers such as $a + ib$, the results of conjugation can be measured, because conjugation produces real numbers. When we conjugate, the imaginary components fall away. If I want to understand a dream (let's call it $a + ib$), I can wake up slowly and carefully, noticing how the nighttime dreaming is reflected as I am waking up. By following how the dream experiences "self-amplify," by watching how they "square themselves," creating an area in everyday life, I can discover the "real" meaning of what was previously dreamlike.

Lucid dreaming amplifies ordinary dreams. It differs from dreaming in that the lucid dreamer is aware of being lucid, whereas in the ordinary dreamlike state, the dreamer is usually not aware that she can become lucid and unfold dreaming.

Thus, *multiplying a complex number by its reflection* to get a real number has a psychological analogy: *letting a dreamlike experience generate reality by lucidly dreaming* to find its significance in everyday reality.

Lucid, wakeful dreaming amplifies dreaming and transforms unconscious actions into conscious, "real" actions. Lucid dreaming unfolds dreams into reality. It is a form of conjugation, a key psychological tool for unfolding NCR processes. Lucid dreaming is also a shamanistic method that can be applied to psychosomatic experiences.

If you like, you can try an experiment with lucid dreaming now. Discover a motion you are experiencing, or tending to experience, in your body just now. Reflect it by doing it again, reflecting it as closely as possible. Take a few minutes. The only tip you need is to keep your attention on the dreamlike quality of the motion, until it clarifies, or realizes, itself.

COMPLEX NUMBERS IN PHYSICS

As we travel onward into the worlds of shamanism, psychology, and physics, we will explore complex numbers again. For now let's relax for a few minutes and fantasize forward in time, skipping hundreds of years from the discovery of complex numbers in the fifteenth century to the quantum physics of the twentieth century.

Conjugation is a key not only to the psychology of consciousness but to the physics of observation. In physics, material objects such as electrons are described by what are called "wave functions," which are simply complex numbers. The wave function describes the patterns of the electron's behavior, how the electron behaves.

We have seen that an object such as a birch tree has both real and imaginary aspects—it is a birch and also "motherly." Thus, we have discovered that all observation is partly real, partly dreaming. By analogy, electrons, which can be described by complex numbers, are also partly real, partly imaginary. We cannot see everything about the electron. Some of its characteristics are uncertain. Physicists cannot measure an electron's entire behavior, since they cannot measure complex numbers.

The physicists have a basic formula, the wave function, complex numbers that describe matter. Physicists need these partially imaginary complex numbers to describe matter. But a problem appears here! The measurable reality of matter cannot be described by imaginary numbers—the numbers that describe reality must be real, and imaginary numbers have no reality in everyday life. So, the physicists decided to use the special property of complex numbers: when conjugated, complex numbers become real. Conjugating complex numbers eliminates the imaginary aspects that can't be measured.

If one number of the wave function, say $3 - 4i$, is conjugated, the imaginary numbers disappear in the result, which is 25. This real number "hides" the imaginary. It no longer shows the roots of 25. It hides the fact that it was the result of multiplying $(3 + 4i) \times (3 - 4i)$. In a way, we can say that real numbers hide their complex number background and the process of reflection. By analogy we might also say that reality has a hidden dreaming background!

The physicists can test and measure the product of conjugation, that is, a real number such as 25. At one point, the physicists made a decision not to worry about the meaning of the reflection process needed to produce real numbers, namely, $(3 + 4i) \times (3 - 4i)$. After all, they did not know what complex numbers like $3 + 4i$ refer to in everyday, consensus reality. Complex numbers and the process of conjugation that gives rise to real results have never been understood. Now, we have a metaphor for comprehending their significance.

Complex numbers have analogies in the realm of sentient, NCR perception. Furthermore, their conjugation creates real numbers through the process of lucidity and reflection. Knowing this gives us a hint about the significance of what happens in quantum physics.

We shall see that electrons and their wave functions are like dreams in the sense that, when reflected or amplified, that is, conjugated, they unfold into the reality of measurements of subatomic particles. This amplification is analogous to how conjugation unfolds dreams into everyday life.

In other words, sentient experiences are basic to understanding reality, both in psychology and in physics. Sentient experience is basic to the process of observation. It gives us a hint about the essence of and keys to matter, to the universe in which we all live and breathe.

Until now, physics has used math as a tool and has not focused on the meaning of its math. Thus, physics inadvertently ignored sentient experience. Most of us are like physicists. You and I constantly repress our complex numbers, dreamlike fantasies, our feeling experiences, and our reflection processes. Either we have no one to discuss them with, or we forget them if they seem to make no sense. We often try to get around the imaginary realm and orient all our experiences to consensus reality.

We look only for the most probable meaning of something, its real number value. Metaphorically speaking, looking only at the real value of an experience gives us answers in reality, but ignores the sentient dreamlike experience and process of reflection behind reality. As we saw at the beginning of our journey, consensus reality is like a tree with roots in the non-consensus or sentient realm.

For example, let's say you tell me that you had a dream about a tree. If I ask you, "What does that mean in consensus reality?" you are going to have to give me its most probable "real" meaning. My question about the tree marginalizes the experience of reflection and conjugation. Instead, I could ask you to unfold that dream tree lucidly by re-imagining it and following its unfolding in terms of images and other experiences.

Unfolding is different from questioning or interpreting. Unfolding by lucidly dreaming values the irrational, the experiences that produce consciousness. The experience of unfolding or conjugation gives us a sense of how dreaming underlies all of reality. Asking only what the dream "means" taps into its CR attributes and ignores its awesome roots. In contrast, conjugation, or lucid dreaming, focuses on NCR experiences of being a tree. Such experiences are as close as we may ever get to the roots of reality.

Understandably, physics focuses mainly on CR and real numbers. After all, physics defines itself as the study of consensual perceptions. But science has forgotten that its definition is self-limiting and inadvertently marginalizes psychological experience. Physics avoids studying non-consensual aspects of observation, such as the personality of the observer or the feelings the object of observation evokes. Physics loses track of its mathematics, its complex numbers, its wave functions, and the dreamlike reality in back of CR. However, the study of the dreamlike realms is not lost: traditional shamanism and psychology pick up where today's physics ends.

We have seen that the patterns found in the psychology of perception and in shamanic experience are consistent with patterns found in math, and now in physics. This consistency points to the unified field, the dreamlike substance of experience, which is basic to life, to psychology and physics, to electrons and their observers, to all of us as we live and grow. This field is basic to unfolding 1, 2, 3, and infinity.

As we move further, we will discover in greater detail how lucid dreaming is encoded within. The same lucid dreaming that generates consciousness and reality in psychology gives us a basis for understanding the invisible realm of quantum objects and the world we live in—the basic substance of the universe.

NOTES

1.   To check this out, imagine that you place a measuring stick on the floor, between your feet and the mirror. If you stand in the room at point $a + ib$ and look straight down at the tip of your feet, you will see, at first, the mark on the stick that reads 100 centimeters. As you keep your eye on the measuring stick and let your gaze move toward the mirror, you count 95, 94, 93, and so forth until you are at 1 centimeter and, finally, the wall.

Then, if the mirror is so good that you scarcely notice it is there, there will appear to be another measuring stick in the mirror. This stick is a reflection of the one at your feet and reads backward, in the opposite direction.

As you let your gaze follow that measuring stick, you count 1 centimeter, then 2, 3, 4, and so forth and, finally, 100 centimeters. Then, if you look up, you see your own self in the mirror looking you in the eye! The mirror image of yourself looks exactly like you—except that you are at +100 centimeters while your double is at -100 centimeters.

There are other differences between you and your double. For the moment, however, let's think only about the fact that you are at +100 while the double is at -100.

2.   Footnotes 2, 3, and 4 discuss more amazing characteristics of complex numbers. You can express the geometry of complex numbers in trigonometric fashion, that is, in terms of angles.

Let's say θ is the angle between R and x, as shown below in Figure 8.4 (*tan* means tangent, *cos* means cosine; also, tan (θ) means the tangent of θ).

The laws of trigonometry tell us that $\tan(\theta) = y/x$ and thus that $x = R\cos(\theta)$, $y = R\sin(\theta)$.
Finally, it turns out that complex number z can be rewritten in terms of angles as $z = R[\cos(\theta) + i\sin(\theta)]$.

8.4 Complex number expressed in terms of angles

To read more about complex numbers, see Ruel V. Churchill's *Complex Variables and Applications* and Hans Schwerdtfeger's *Geometry of Complex Numbers*.

Mathematicians call the $[\cos(\theta) + i\sin(\theta)]$ the "angular factor" of the complex number and denote it by $e^{i\theta}$ because of the laws of algebra and trigonometry. e is a number that can be used to abbreviate long trigonometric explanations and make calculations simple. This happens in part because a feature of exponentials is that for two angles (one angle, θ_1, and another θ_2) we have

$$e^{i\theta_1}e^{i\theta_2} = e^{i(\theta_1 + \theta_2)}$$

thus the formula, $z = R[(\cos(\theta) + i\sin(\theta)] = Re^{i\theta}$.

3.   The above equation $z = R[(\cos(\theta) + i\sin(\theta)] = Re^{i\theta}$ means nothing less than the fact that z has a periodic behavior, since as θ increases, $\cos(\theta)$ and $i\sin(\theta)$ go through periodic, wave-like changes. In other words, there are two waves: one is real, and the other "imaginary," or out of phase by 90 degrees with the real one. See Figure 8.5 on the following page.

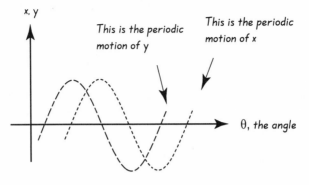

8.5 Periodic motion of x and y

Exponentials are easier to deal with than sines and cosines. Thus complex numbers in the form of $e^{i(\theta_1 + \theta_2)}$ are used all the time in physics to represent oscillations. Only the real part of z is used to represent oscillations that can be measured, such as the swing of a pendulum. The imaginary element is neglected.

For a good elementary discussion of math and waves for scientists, see Feynman's *Lectures on Physics,* Volume I, Chapter 23, page 1.

Another interesting aspect of real and imaginary numbers is that the real and imaginary aspects of z are like two different dimensions of reality, traveling together, but not quite together. In general, if the real and imaginary axes rotate, we can see that the imaginary number axis Y always lags the real axis X by a 90-degree angle, as shown below in Figure 8.6.

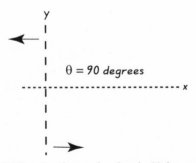

8.6 Rotating the complex plane by 90 degrees

We can say by analogy that the imaginary world is always in another dimension from the real one, or, vice versa, that as θ gets bigger, the X and Y axes look like two waves—one in front and the other just behind—as if they were drums with an echo going "boom boom," pause, "boom boom," pause, "boom boom," and so on. Pictorially two waves out of phase with one another are shown in the wave picture above this one. This is analogous to the rhythm or music in back of our experience.

I will show in a later chapter that quantum physics uses the periodic behavior of complex numbers (the wave equation) to describe an invisible state of a material system. The state of a physical system, such as a little ball, an elementary particle, or a person, can be represented by a complex number at every point in space and time.

4. If we draw a line R from the center to $a + ib$, it looks like an access route between this complex number and the center of the complex plane. See Figure 8.7 below.

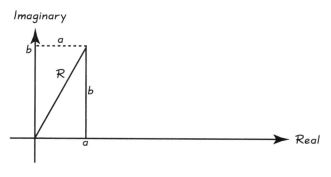

8.7 Line R on the complex plane

How long is R? R is the long part of a triangle of which a and b are the other two sides. R is the long side, b is the vertical, and a is the horizontal side.

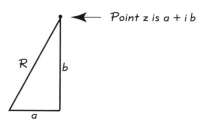

8.8 R is part of a right triangle.

The Greek scientist Euclid borrowed information from the Babylonians and discovered how you could measure R if you knew the lengths a and b. It turns out that if there are two sides of a triangle which are perpendicular, Euclid's formula tells us that the square of the long side, R, is the sum of the squares of the smaller sides. That is,

$$R^2 = a^2 + b^2$$

which is Euclid's formula for right triangles.

Thus, multiplying a complex number by its conjugate gives us R, the distance of the point from the center.

5.   Let's multiply $a + ib$ times $a - ib$. You get

$$a^2 - iab + iab - i^2b$$

If you remember that $i^2 = -1$, and notice that $+iab$ and $-iab$ cancel each other in subtraction, you are left with

$$(a + ib) \times (a - ib) = a^2 + b^2$$

$(a + ib)(a - ib)$ is what mathematicians call the absolute square of $(a+ib)$. For example, if we let a be 3 and b be 4, then the absolute square of the complex number $3 + 4i = (3 + 4i) \times (4 - 4i) = 32 + 42$ or $9 + 16$ or 25. This is a real number without any imaginary numbers mixed in.

6.   Mathematically, the process of conjugation is similar to squaring but just a bit different. Squaring complex numbers produces more such numbers, whereas conjugating and getting the absolute value gives us real numbers!

     This is how. If we square an imaginary number such as $a + ib$, we multiply it by itself and what remains is a complex number, that is, a combination of real and imaginary numbers because:

$$(a + ib) \times (a + ib) = (a + ib) \times (a + ib) = a^2 + 2iab - b^2$$

To get the absolute value of the complex number $a + ib$, however, we must conjugate it, or multiply it by its conjugate:

$$(a + ib) \times (a - ib) = a^2 - iab + iab + -i^2b^2$$

But since $i^2 = -1$, we get

$$(a + ib) \times (a - ib) = a^2 + b^2$$

as in note 1. Thus, getting the absolute value of a number is similar to squaring the number, except that the absolute value has no imaginary numbers in it. Unlike conjugation, squaring the complex number, $(a + ib)$, gives us

$$a^2 + 2iab - b^2$$

whereas the absolute value that comes from conjugation is $a^2 + b^2$, which is a real number because it has no i's in it.

9 | The One World in Pauli's Dream

It (the imaginary number) makes the instinctive or impulsive, the intellectual or rational, the spiritual or supernatural, of which you spoke, into the unified or monadic whole that the numbers without the i cannot represent.

—Inner vision of a music teacher from a vision of Wolfgang Pauli

Let's take a breath and look back at where we have traveled on our journey up to this point. After we review the familiar terrain, we shall go further into complex numbers with the help of a dream-fantasy of Wolfgang Pauli, Nobel Prize–winning physicist.

REVIEW

Math is a personal experience as well as an abstract tool. Every time you dream or work with your fantasies you are doing math, just as when you count how many sheep you have in your pasture.

Counting is an abstraction of an interactional awareness process that involves noticing, marginalizing, marking, and unfolding. Counting matches events with a given standard aggregate such as fingers.

Consensus reality (CR) refers to a given community's "reality," expressed with an agreed-upon verbal and nonverbal language, including numbers and gestures.

Number bases are the basic numbers needed to create higher numbers. Number bases depend on the structure of our awareness and on our cultures.

Early on in our exploration, we saw that the first human mathematical systems worldwide had number bases of 2, 3, and 4. This primary reality might be linked to the fact that we are able to notice and differentiate between 2, 3, and 4 objects. Around 5, we lose the ability to perceive specific quantities, seeing only groups or clusters that we speak of as "lots" or "many." You can experiment with this for yourself by looking at the clusters of a's, x's, u's, p's, 0's and ^'s below. How many of each type do you see in each cluster?

x   ^ ^ ^ ^ ^ ^   a a

u u u u u u u   00000000   x x x

x x x x   p p   v v v

00   x x x x x

9.1 How many individual parts do you see in each cluster?

Most of us can recognize one element, two elements, three, and four, but when we get to more than four, we reach an awareness block and have to count the elements. Our number concept is based in part on our awareness processes.

Adding is a process of unfolding or amplifying an element with another element.

Minus numbers were created to resolve the mysteries of debts and can be linked to the psychology of "unowned" experiences, such as projections.

Multiplication is an abbreviated form of adding a number a given number of times.

Squaring adds a number to itself according to the number.

The psychological process of squaring (multiplying a number by itself) encompasses self-creative processes with generative, procreative, self-propagating experiences such as moods, which get worse or better by themselves. Much of our human experience is generated outside of our conscious control; it multiplies or squares itself, so to speak.

The **imaginary number**, i, is defined mathematically as the square root of minus one, that is, as $\sqrt{-1}$. Imaginary numbers represent non-rational, non-consensus experiences. The imaginary number was created or discovered because real numbers cannot be used to find the square root of numbers with a minus sign in front of them.

Imaginary numbers cannot be measured in reality, whereas "real" numbers can be. Leibniz called imaginary numbers "a fine and wonderful refuge of the divine spirit—almost an amphibian between being and non-being...."

Among the psychological analogies to imaginary numbers are the figures and symbols we find in dreams. These figures are both real and not real. In spiritual language, they are the home of the spirit. Dream symbols are analogies of imaginary numbers in that they are the roots of unconscious areas in everyday life. For example, the root of an attack of rage might be seen in a dream as a bear.

Complex numbers, including both real and imaginary numbers, are the most complete numbers. They include all the other numbers.

Observations that include both CR and NCR experiences are the psychological analogy of complex numbers.

Every observation is analogous to a complex number in the sense that it includes both real (objective, consensual) and imaginary (subjective, non-consensual) perceptions.

The complex number field is a numerical map including all real and imaginary numbers, an area within which all mathematical operations can take place. The complex field is a mathematical analogy of the field of awareness that includes both CR and NCR experiences and in which processes may unfold, that is, where we can add, reduce, generate, self-amplify, and so on.

Conjugation is the mathematical operation of multiplying a complex number by its reflection. The result of conjugation is always a real number.

A psychological analogy to conjugation is lucidly dreaming a dream into reality. In this process, an unconscious process, such as a dream, generates an insight or interpretation through being reflected by a lucid dreamer.

The psychological process of conjugation, or lucid dreaming, includes two separable aspects. One is the NCR aspect of unfolding experience (analogous to the complex number being multiplied by its reflection). The other is the final result of that process (or operation) that can be shared with others—an insight or interpretation analogous to the real number. It is possible to forget or marginalize the conjugation process by focusing only on the real result, the insight or interpretation.

CORRESPONDENCES BETWEEN MATH AND PSYCHOLOGY

If we generalize on what we have discovered so far, we may begin to suspect that all mathematical concepts, regardless of how abstract they may seem, correspond to psychological experiences or principles. We have already seen a few such correspondences (summarized below).

9.2 Correspondences between psychology and mathematics

PAULI'S DREAMLIKE MUSIC TEACHER

All these correspondences might lead us to think that scientists must dream about math not only in relation to their personal problems, but also as an expression of natural patterns. I know this is true for myself, and I have met other scientists who told me they keep paper and a pencil near their beds in order to get insight into their work from their dreams. Physicist Richard Feynman worked on his dreams this way. One of my professors at the Massachusetts Institute of Technology, Norbert Wiener, the father of cybernetics, said that he developed the art of almost sleeping even when talking to someone, in order to connect with his dreams. I sometimes saw him in the corridors, mumbling to himself and asking others exactly what city he was in. I thought he wanted to forget Cambridge, Massachusetts, but that was not true. I once met him in Zurich, Switzerland, and he was still asking the same question. He was close to dreaming, and brought me closer to dreaming than I realized!

Although many scientists do not speak much about their inner life or about the psychological nature of physics or math, they dream about these things. Fred Alan Wolf, in *The Dreaming Universe*, tells us about the inner life of Wolfgang Pauli. I am also grateful to C.G. Jung and Marie Louise von Franz, with whom Pauli worked closely, for information about Pauli's crucial dreamlike experience involving imaginary numbers.

Pauli worked closely with Jung in the areas of synchronicity and parapsychology. Before his untimely death from throat cancer in 1958, Pauli was passionately interested in how psychology and physics fit together.

He knew that physics was incomplete without psychology and that psychology without physics lacked firm footing in the material world. Pauli wrote to Jung (*Letters*): "As physics strives after completeness, your analytical psychology longs for a home." We can see today that psychology needs a home, one that bridges CR and NCR experience, the same home that can house physics.

Pauli had a dreamlike fantasy about how physics was striving for completeness. In his fantasy, an inner piano teacher instructed him about not only mathematical but also spiritual bases of imaginary numbers and physics.

In Pauli's dreaming, his inner music instructor has a magic ring with the symbol "i" on it, a ring from which voices can speak. At one point in their discussion, she gives him the following lesson.[1] (I have inserted footnotes in the following transcript to explain what Pauli may have been referring to.)

Pauli: At that moment the lady slipped a ring from her finger which I had not seen yet. She let it float in the air and taught me.

She: I suppose you know the ring from your school mathematics. It is the ring i.

Pauli: [I nodded and I spoke the words] The *i* makes the void and the unit into a couple. At the same time it is the operation of rotating a quarter of the whole ring.[2]

She: It makes the instinctive or impulsive, the intellectual or rational, the spiritual or supernatural, of which you spoke, into the unified or monadic whole that the numbers without the *i* cannot represent.

Pauli: The ring with the *i* is the unity beyond particle and wave and at the same time the operation that generates either of these.[3]

She: It is the atom, the indivisible, in Latin...

Pauli: [With these words she looked at me significantly, but it seemed to me unnecessary to speak Cicero's word for the atom out loud.] It turns time into a static image.[4]

She: It is the marriage and it is at the same time the realm of the middle, which you can never reach alone but only in pairs.

Pauli: [There was a pause, we waited for something. Then the voice of the master speaks, transformed, from the center of the ring to the lady.]

Master: Remain merciful.

Pauli: [Now I knew I could go out of the room into normal time and normal everyday space. When I was outside, I noticed that I was wearing my coat and hat. From afar I heard a C-major chord of four tones, CEGC, apparently played by the lady herself when she was on her own again.]

THE MARRIAGE IN PAULI'S DREAM

Pauli's teacher stays "inside" as he leaves and goes into the world at the end of his fantasy. The teacher is a musician who plays the notes that Pauli can differentiate as the chord CEGC, much as matter manifests itself in ways that physicists must decode. She creates harmony, probably a feeling Pauli needed.

Since the teacher comes from within, it seems to me that she must be the music and the teacher, both the feelings and their own instruction about how to live them. Similarly, if we feel what sort of atmosphere lies within us, we can feel its tempo and the inner instructions it gives us about how to express itself.

Pauli's teacher is our own inner atmosphere that we feel but usually do not communicate with or express. She is the sentient realm of dreaming, the "inside" we must get to know. The sentient realm is a teacher of feelings.

Pauli's teacher wears a ring. Rings often represent a commitment to something or someone. Her ring has the symbol *i* on it. At the end of the fantasy, the ring speaks as the voice of the master, telling Pauli, "Remain merciful."

The teacher tells Pauli that the *i* represents the connection between the material and the supernatural. Pauli realizes that the *i* generates reality and yet is beyond the particles and waves it generates. Both he and his teacher feel that i is the "atom," the basis of reality. It represents the indivisible, the one world of experience, which was split off by our rational minds into concepts such as matter and psyche. The i represents the non-dualistic, unitarian, or sentient, dreamlike source of reality.

Throughout history, people have spoken about the gods dreaming up the world. Leibniz spoke of a divine spirit having "refuge" in the symbol i. This dreamlike world is the source from which duality arises. It is the same world from which our instinctive or impulsive motions arise and also the world from which our intellectual or rational ideas come. The sentient experiences we have, the inner atmosphere that can barely be formulated in words is the realm of the i which connects "the spiritual or supernatural" with everyday reality.

Pauli's inner teacher tells him, "It is the marriage and it is at the same time the realm of the middle, which you can never reach alone but only in pairs." In his fantasy, Pauli uses the mathematics of complex numbers to explain the psychophysical or sentient background that generates the world of everyday reality, of time and space. His teacher is telling him that it is impossible to understand this realm from a purely intellectual viewpoint, unless we use paradoxical thinking, such as "it is true and not true" or "meaningful and meaningless." Physicists talk about the quantum world in terms of duality—of wave and particle, energy and time—because any one CR description is insufficient. None of the terms we can use to describe the sentient, NCR realm suffice.

The master/mind gives the final lesson, "Remain merciful." This seems to relieve Pauli and send him back into reality. "Remaining merciful" is a lesson coming from the center of the ring with i on it. It is the lesson that we remain open-minded, compassionate toward both rational, physical reality and non-rational, non-consensus events.

Pauli's teachers are reminding all of us to love and not to marginalize either the apparently physical world and its events or the dreaming universe and its imaginary, barely formulated NCR experiences. Both realities are important. The teacher asks us to have mercy on both.

DREAMWORK EXPERIMENT WITH COMPLEX NUMBERS

We can experiment with the idea of mercy towards our own experiences, our inner worlds, and inner teachers. The following experiment provides a way to explore our inner world on its own terms.

1. **Choose a dream**: Pick a dream or fantasy to meditate upon. You may choose any dream or fantasy that interests you, recent or older.

2. **Choose part of the dream**: The next step is to consider the most interesting part of the dream. This might be a weird or scary part such as a wild animal, or a passionate part such as a love scene, or a magical

element. It must be a part that fascinates you and which you want to explore.

3. **Try interpreting**: Next, try interpreting this part or figure in the dream—try to make it "real" by guessing at its meaning. Make a mental note of this interpretation, or write it down.

4. **Shape-shift**: Now, experiment with shape-shifting. Instead of being yourself as you are in everyday consensus reality, try feeling your way into the part of the dream you are interested in. Get to its essence, the experience of the image or images, the experience behind the images from which they came. Here, you will be experimenting with entering the imaginary realm, the space and time of what fascinated you in the dream.

5. **Track**: Experiment with being merciful, open and kind to your inner experiences. Try taking them as seriously as you do everyday life. Open up to them. Bring them out; express them in the manner they wish to be expressed.

Now you are in the complex realm of experience, in dreaming. Stay in the complex realm and use your attention and your awareness to track and lucidly follow what is happening. Marry this realm with your focused attention.

Let the experience unfold itself. Perhaps you will find yourself feeling or behaving differently in this dreaming than you do in everyday reality, doing things you don't ordinarily do. Go ahead. Try getting to know and interacting with the various parts of your dreamlike experience.

6. **Come back**: Stay with this experience and allow it to unfold or generate itself, follow it, until you come back to everyday life and your normal state of consciousness. Keep going until you, like Pauli, are ready to walk "outside," remembering or still hearing what happened "within."

Remember your experiences. Remember what it was like to experience the "monadic" (to use Pauli's term), that is, the simple, indivisible, non-dual world of complex numbers directly. Is this a world you are often in, but which you ignore? Have mercy on it.

What changes in your everyday life is your dreamlike experience trying to generate in reality? You may want to be merciful and let them happen.

What was the difference between the interpretation you gave the dream and the experience you now have of being in that world, allowing the dream to unfold itself? How close was your interpretation of the dream to your experience of dreaming lucidly?

You have now had an experience of the unitary realm of complex numbers and the manner in which they try to generate consensus reality. You experienced your inner process that is both a teacher of expressiveness and the expression itself.

This is the realm Pauli's inner teachers are telling him (and us) to remain open to—the complex plane, the non-rational realms of awareness. The mastermind of the ring says, "Remain merciful," be a partner to your dreaming, follow it in a lucid manner. When we are merciful towards our inner experiences, we discover how they are attempting to generate reality. We enter into the one world of NCR experience, the universal spirit behind life and death, the real and the imaginary, the physical and the supernatural. If you are merciful and compassionate with irrational experiences, you will not separate the pair, will not split off reality from dreaming. If we follow our inner experiences closely, we experience in person how reality is generated from dreaming.

If you experienced how dreaming generates reality, how the imaginary gives birth to new motions, feelings, and intellectual insights, you have found your own music teacher, learned her lesson, and can go back into the CR world as well.

NOTES

1. This transcript is from Fred Alan Wolf's *The Dreaming Universe*, page 294.

2. Pauli probably means that the "void" was the imaginary (i.e., i), which is coupled with the unit (that is, the number 1), since $i = 1i$. If you multiply all the numbers on the complex plane by the imaginary number i, the plane rotates counterclockwise, one quarter of a turn.

3. Pauli means that the mathematics of quantum mechanics, which I discuss in the next chapters, requires the imaginary number i. It "generates" the particle and wave through the process of conjugation, that is, $(+i) \times (-i) = 1$.

4. We shall never know his associations, but it seems to me that Pauli meant that imaginary numbers turn "time into a static image" in the sense that quantum objects become real, fixed measurements when observed.

10 | The History of Nature's Death

I rightly conclude that my essence consists in this alone, that I am a thinking thing... And although perhaps... I have a body... I am truly distinct from my body, and can exist without it.

—Descartes in *Meditations*

We may never have definitive answers to questions such as, "Where did Pauli's dream come from?" "Why did he need to hear about 'mercifulness,' from his 'master'?" "Why did he have a music teacher in his dreaming world?"

As we saw when we looked at Pauli's dream, everyone has an inner music teacher because our inner life is trying to instruct us in how to express it. Through meditation, we can experience how dreams try to realize themselves, just as through observation the quantum world in physics comes into consensus reality and can be measured. In fact, as Pauli's dream indicates, the patterns behind psychological and material reality are the same.

The idea that the same patterns are behind how dreams and material energies express themselves is new for modern physics. This statement will be doubted, debated, tested, and probably accepted. Such doubts about the connection between dreams and reality were not always present. Before the European Renaissance, spirituality and science were intimately connected in alchemy. History divided spirit from matter as quantitative, consensual, CR characteristics of life took precedence over NCR qualities.

Pauli, one of most respected quantum physicists, represents the conflict between spirit and matter that takes place in all the "hard" sciences. The conflict between spirit and matter comes from the assumption that CR measurements are the important "reality." If we look at philosophies from around the world, we see that this reality is only one version of numerous possible consensus realities. Hindu philosophies, for example, view the "reality" of everyday life as "Maya," that is, illusion. Likewise, shamanic teachers such as Castaneda's don Juan Matus see real people as "phantoms" because they are not grounded in the world of dreaming. What Western reality calls a dreamer, don Juan calls a "real person." In other words, Western thinking about what constitutes consensus reality has been reversed at other times and in other parts of the world.

History indicates that the present Western view of reality is a relatively recent formulation, dating back only as far as the sixteenth century. It was then that a gradual consensus to ignore experiences such as magic, spirits, and witchcraft emerged. History tells us not only about a renaissance or "rebirth" from the "dark ages," and about the rise of great technologies and ideas such as Newtonian physics, but also about a painful marginalization of the spirit. In history, as in all stories and recountings, there is no single, objective version. The version of history I present comes not only from my own experiences and readings, but from my education and the period of time I live in.

The discoveries and insights of modern physics, as well as the narrow vision about what is real, are based on the premise that perceptions that cannot be tested can be ignored. As a result, experiences that were an integral part of Western consciousness before the 1500s, such as hearing messages from animals, plants, and spirits, were gradually marginalized.

Up until the sixteenth century in Europe, people believed in the earth as a nurturing mother, and explained the growth of plants and what we now call parapsychological phenomena as a result of divine mystery.[1] Mother Nature was seen as kind, but also respected for her ability to produce plagues and storms and her potential to be wild, unpredictable, and dangerous.

Witches were called on to intervene between ordinary people and nature, but witches were also believed to be connected with the devil or demons. Witches were upsetting to the religious authorities that saw witchcraft as heretical. Gradually, the growth of the scientific view depotentiated the Church's power over the practice of magic, but the wider acceptance of science also collaborated in keeping down the magical nature of individuals who, like nature herself, seemed uncontrollable.

THE SCIENTIFIC REVOLUTION

The "Age of the Scientific Revolution" shifted the focus away from the unseen powers of the Earth and promised security from Her "wildness." But science also split us off from the Earth.

According to Carolyn Merchant,

...the new world-view... by reconceptualizing reality as a machine rather than a living organism, sanctioned the domination of both nature and women. The contributions of such founding 'fathers' of modern science as Francis Bacon, William Harvey, Rene Descartes, Thomas Hobbes and Isaac Newton must be reevaluated.[2]

Merchant shows that the rise of science, the devaluation of women and nature, and the rise of the patriarchy were all part of the same movement.

As part of a new breed of scientists trying to break with witchcraft and religion, Francis Bacon proposed that the only valid knowledge was based on analytical reasoning. Copernicus, another founder of the scientific revolution, shocked his contemporaries by asserting that the Earth was not the center of the universe and the human being was no longer the central element of God's creation. He thus challenged dogma that had been accepted for more than a thousand years in Europe. The ruling religious paradigm at that time said that God, rather than the animistic powers respected in witchcraft, had structured the cosmos. God was the spirit of matter whose ways could not be doubted, much less tested, and the cosmos was perfect and unchanging. Copernicus posed his theory as a hypothesis and did not publish it until the year of his death (1534) because he feared a reaction from the Church.

Today, the logical, consensus-bound, mechanical observer in physics, who vows not to explore anything that cannot be measured, continues to reflect this four-hundred-year-old reaction against the unpredictability of Mother Earth's wildness and the oppression of religious dogma that forbids doubt.

Yet, before we all become rebels, we must remember that today's rational, testable consensus reality was marginalized in the Europe of the 1500s. At that time, scientists both feared and fought the governing religious powers for the freedom to doubt, debate, and test the theories and principles of nature. Scientists claimed that just because something was believed to be true, that belief did not make it "true."

It took Tycho Brahe's sighting of the new star of 1572 and the great comet of 1577 to show humankind that the heavens were indeed capable of change. Many scientists concurred with the perspective expressed by Johannes Kepler (1571-1630), who wrote to a friend in 1605:

My aim is to show that the celestial machine is to be likened not to a divine organism but to a clockwork.[3]

DEFINITION OF PHYSICS: DON'T SPEAK ABOUT WHAT CAN'T BE TESTED

Scientists defined their field for five hundred years as the freedom to doubt and test. That is why the majority of quantum physicists today follow Heisenberg's philosophy of: "if you can't test it, don't talk about it." Although Heisenberg was referring to the difficulty of measuring quantum-level events, this philosophy is basic to all of science. If we apply this basic philosophy to complex numbers, it implies that if we cannot measure imaginary numbers, we should not try to talk about their possible significance. If something cannot be tested, it is not "real" and therefore not significant.

The definition of reality in physics implies that testable reality constitutes absolute reality. This definition has proven to be both a great strength and a great weakness in physics. Its strength is that, from this perspective, the multitude of religious views about the nature of the universe becomes relativized. What one person, group, or subgroup believes is seen as a belief, not the final answer. There is no final view of what is in heaven but instead, many views to be tested, checked, and discovered. New aspects of nature can be revealed through experimentation.

The weakness of the scientific viewpoint is that it inhibits the investigation of those aspects of reality (such as imaginary numbers) that cannot be directly measured in a CR, repeatable manner.

The reality explored by physics is a consensus reality in which observations are discussed only if they can be measured in terms of real numbers, photographed, recorded, or agreed upon by the majority as existing. This bias toward consensus reality pervades the other sciences as well. For example, parapsychology claims that ghosts are real because they can be photographed. Parapsychology thus supports the mainstream scientific measurement paradigm: if something can be photographed, it is real; otherwise, it is not.

From this perspective, the only ghost I ever saw could never be shown to anybody because I was too afraid to get a camera to take its picture! The dictum "don't talk about it if you can't measure it" implies that the ghost did not exist. A conventional physicist would suggest not talking about the ghost unless my experience could be tested. An honest physicist would not assert that ghosts do not exist, but he would marginalize the importance of the experience by claiming that it is not in the realm of science. Thus, NCR experiences are cast out of physics.

The one-sided view of reality that characterizes today's physics has influenced psychiatric diagnosis as well. A client who says, "I saw a spirit once and it had meaning for my everyday life whether or not it was real" will encounter a less severe judgment, because of the dangling disclaimer, than a client who says, "Spirits are around all the time, and have been bothering me for years." If someone hears voices coming from trees and does not interpret the experience metaphorically (i.e., "that tree must be my own inner mother") this person would probably be considered to have symptoms of an illness with a biological basis.

Concepts of reality are political. Every group—any group—claims that some things are real while others are not. For example, the Church Council of Avignon, France, in A.D. 323, passed a law that banned water nixies. Until A.D. 323 you could worship a clay image of a water nixie placed near a river or lake. After that date, water nixies could no longer officially exist.

The conflict between religion and physics is portrayed in the story of Gallileo, who wanted to test the speed of falling bodies and the appearance of the moon. He constructed a telescope with a large lens. When he looked through it, he saw that the moon had craters in it. Gallileo invited the Medicis (a leading family in Italy) to look through his telescope. "Come on by and look through my telescope, you're going to really enjoy it!"

"No!" they said, "You cannot look at God! You must not do that!" Gallileo said "OK, but at least come look at my slide over here, the slide with a ball on one end. I want to test how long it takes for the ball to roll down that slide."

But the Medicis said again, "No, you cannot do that either, you cannot test God, we don't agree with that." The Medicis' reaction contained many beliefs. They believed that there could be only one experience of God, the one accepted by religious authorities. They thought material reality was the work of God, who is perfect and cannot be tested, measured, or even looked at. The official view was that your personal ideas and experiences of God were not acceptable if you felt something about God which religious authorities did not agree with; your feelings were simply wrong. Of course, behind this belief was a deeper passion, the desire to guard the concept of God as an NCR deity beyond testing.

The new, emerging paradigm wanted to doubt and test everything. Gallileo wanted to separate God from matter, if possible. To guard his freedom to explore nature in 1623, Gallileo precisely defined the distinction between physics and spirituality, between what he called matter's "primary" and "secondary" qualities. He identified the primary qualities as those measurable in terms of real numbers, such as 4 ounces and 10 miles. He said that secondary qualities such as love and color, which could not be reduced to empirical measurements, were outside the realm of science.

Thus, over time, the governing social and cultural consensus about the divine nature of reality slowly gave way to the Renaissance view that the cosmos was a machine composed of elementary parts or gears. The Renaissance championed the freedom to test and think but also marginalized imaginary experience as unreal. In a way, the new science was different because it tested the universe and divided its study from religion.

But in another way, the new science was not different. The new science, as well as the mainstream religion, marginalized individual, sentient experience and expression and favored collective views about nature and the divine. In a way, the new science simply replaced the domination of one view—that of a living, sentient Earth—with another—that of a mechanical, testable world. Both the religious and the scientific views repressed direct, personal experience, each for their own reasons.

Between the sixteenth and seventeenth centuries, scientists were split between the two views. They practiced physics but used religious metaphors. For example, Isaac Newton was not only a great physicist, but also perhaps the last great magician. He made great discoveries in math and physics such as calculus and the laws of mechanics, but also practiced magic and alchemy.

Today's scientists are still equally split. Einstein, for example, doubted probabilistic interpretations of quantum physics, saying, "God does not play with dice." He identified matter with God, not unlike religious leaders before the Renaissance. In other words, physicists still connect the world of nature to the experience of God while saying that God's existence cannot be proven.

Although this split still underlies science today, if we look at popular books integrating modern physics with quasi-religious frameworks and terms, such as Capra's *The Tao of Physics*, Wolf's *The Spiritual Universe*, and Leon Lederman's, *The God Particle*, we sense a change in the air. Five hundred years after the Renaissance, we are flirting with a rapprochement between science and religion, a marriage of shamanic perspective and objective measurements.[4]

THE PHYSICS OF SLAVERY

Pauli's inner life, which recommended mercy, was probably different from that of Francis Bacon, who had little tolerance for irrational events. Bacon was merciless when he said:

> Nature had to be hounded in her wanderings. She had to be bound in service. She had to be made a slave. Nature had to be put in constraint and the scientific goals were to torture nature's secrets out of her.[5]

Bacon's sexism, racism, and dislike of the Earth were products of times in which sexism and slavery were standard practice. Yet, even today, marginalized groups are thought of as barbaric, primitive, animal-like, and impure, and liberal democracies still exert economic prejudices that "bind in service" and make economic "slaves" of non-mainstream groups. Sexism and racism cannot be divorced either from ecological destruction or theoretical physics, which both operate under the same premise of marginalization.

The concept of enslavement of nature is behind the terms and definitions used by physics today. For example, work is a form of energy.[6] In the symbols of physics, $E = W$, where work is defined as the force applied over distance, that is, $W = F \times D$. Although human slavery was eventually officially abolished, machines using energy and doing work became the new slaves, pulling and pushing weights through distances. Today, most mainstream people no longer think about slavery, yet nature is treated as a slave as machines do hard labor.

The essence of all forms of slavery is the belief that the slave is the "other"—not I. The slave is considered to have no feelings and therefore can be used without being related to as a spiritual being. If we think of the slave as someone with no sentient capacities, we feel justified in doing whatever we want to her—she will not notice. Nature was and is viewed as an energy source to be tapped and applied to human needs. Water-power, coal, oil, minerals, and other naturally occurring substances are no longer mysteries to be worshipped but resources to be used or enslaved. Most people consider thoughts such as "the earth suffers if we dig in it" to be unproven, ridiculous, or antiquated.

Even today, astronomers such as Nicolai Kardashev of the former Soviet Union categorize civilizations according to how much energy they use. His ideas are used frequently by modern physicists, who, together with governments, plan the future for the planet. Kardashev defined a "type I civilization" as one that controls energy resources for the entire planet. According to this view, our present civilization is type I. The more advanced type II will control the power of the sun, and type III, the entire universe—and will even manipulate space-time as well.

What is disturbing about this perspective is the assumption of entitle-ment and the philosophy of acquisition as ownership. This perspective assumes that humans are entitled to do anything with the universe and measures civilization in terms of how much control it has over nature.

During the Renaissance the experience of "relationship" to nature as a spirit was replaced by the idea of using "it." Since nature was considered to have special powers, women with similar special powers, i.e., what was considered witchcraft, could be studied but also had to be con-demned. Bacon said,

> ...the use and practice of such arts is to be condemned, yet from the speculation and consideration of them... a useful light may be gained, not only for a true judgment of the offenses of persons charged with such practices, but likewise for the further disclosing of the secrets of nature...[7]

During these times, thousands of women were burned after being accused of being witches. It was acceptable to torture nature and women as well as people of color. Bacon was not only a scientist but also an attor-ney general in England. Science and politics were one.

When I studied physics, nobody mentioned these historical facts. I doubt that my teachers knew them. If I had known these things when I was studying physics and its application, I would have taken a different path. Perhaps I went into psychology to retrieve the feelings I felt were missing in the hard sciences. Today we are on the verge of bringing together physics, psychology, and shamanism into a new and inclusive worldview.

History is not only a description of the past but also an unconscious part of the present. It influences everyone. We need to remember that even today, new discoveries in physics are not usually aimed at helping us improve our relationship to Mother Earth. Perhaps that is why we attempt to put people on other planets but are stumped when it comes to working out personal relationship problems and group issues. These deal with the spirit and with feeling, a marginalized part of life that needs greater understanding. Many scientists admit, as Einstein did, that it is easier to solve equations than to deal with people.

But a science that supports ignorance of personal issues creates a politics unconscious of ethics, a politics that gives the most powerful guns to people who know the least about nature or other human beings. If we are to oppose this marginalization, physicists must not only ask, "What is the next particle to be discovered?" but also, "What is the next step in relating to nature?" Likewise, therapists must ask not only "What does this inner experience mean for me now?" but also, "How is it connected to my body and to the environment around me?"

THE MOTIVATION BEHIND PHYSICS

Not all motivations underlying scientific development are devoid of feeling. Many are emotionally based. For example, Newton's ideas are inextricably connected to the second European plague. He was a twenty-one-year-old living in Oxford in 1665 when the second plague struck Europe, leaving behind immense suffering.

Imagine this. The year is 1665 and Newton is a university student. In his first year of studies, Oxford closes to save its students, remembering that in 1350 the school lost two-thirds of its students to the plague. Newton suffered from these events. His subsequent discoveries were linked with this horrendous experience. He studied nature in part to bring her under control for the benefit of all human beings.

When we recall science's distrust of nature, we should remember all the events of the Renaissance period. People died young and saw nature as a devastating problem. The consensus approach was to try to control events such as the plague. Most people act the same today. If you get a tumor, you may be thrilled to have someone give you radiation treatment or chemotherapy to control the forces of nature in your body.

Can we control nature? Yes and no. We can control the flu and the plague, yet new diseases such as acquired immunodeficiency syndrome (AIDS) appear. Today the average duration of a human life in the West is about 74 years. During Newton's time it was about 38 years. But a longer life does not necessarily mean less suffering for all.

THE BODY AS A CLOCK

Descartes believed that experiences of chimeras, spirits, and monsters were figments of the individual imagination. For him and others, the universe and the body were machines. Non-mechanical individual experiences were unimportant in illness. He said, "in my thought a sick man is like a clock that is broken whereas a healthy man is a well made clock."[8]

He was not altogether wrong. Much about the body, such as eating and exercising, is mechanical and clocklike. If you don't eat properly and regularly, your body-machine suffers. The belief that the body works causally, like a clock, remains a popular concept today. We have machines that save us labor, but our lack of energy-expending labor results in weight gain for us. Then, paradoxically, many people try to lose weight using machines once again, machines that work according to the Newtonian message given by the media: "Exercise, use energy, you'll burn fat and lose weight." Newton would be pleased! If you use an exercise machine, you will be healthy. Another Newtonian message is: "If you eat too much cholesterol, your veins will clog up." According to this view, your mind is not important in health, just your body.

Descartes expressed the same concept when he said, "Whatever you think in your mind has no influence on your body, and whatever happens in your body has nothing to do with your mind."[9]

The consensus today is that if the body does not behave regularly, have steady temperatures, menstrual periods at the right time, and so forth, the body is sick. It is not seen as dreaming something meaningful, but as pathological. Every time we say we are "sick," we are like Bacon and Descartes, putting our body's wisdom down and treating ourselves like broken clocks. But the body isn't only a machine. It is a human, feeling, irrational being, it is you!

Today a new wave of therapists and doctors believe the mind influences the body. Farther along in our study together, I will speak about a new approach to the body, which works with symptoms as processes that are neither good nor bad, but simply true and meaningful.

LEIBNIZ'S "VIS VIVA"

Isaac Newton showed that if you throw an object into the air, you can see the path it makes while falling to the ground. Newton said the reason the object fell was the force of "gravity." Though he did not know what gravity was, he said that it was a force that pulled the ball to the earth and could be measured.

Leibniz disagreed and said that the force pulling the object down is not just a force *outside* of the object. As indigenous peoples said before him, Leibniz asserted that there was a living force, a "vis viva" within all objects which makes them behave as they do.[10] Leibniz defined this living force as mv^2 where m is mass of an object and v its velocity.[11] For him, this living force was proportional to kinetic energy.

While Newton said the forces on the outside controlled the fate of lifeless objects, Leibniz insisted there were living energies inside every material thing. He said the inner force, the "vis viva" in matter made it move. For him, matter and spirit could not be separated; matter was sentient. It moved by itself, so to speak. The world was still alive for him. Leibniz was also the one who said that imaginary numbers were the refuge for the divine spirit.

In the debate between Newton and Leibniz, history has decided in favor of Newton. Yet, today, more than three hundred years later, Einstein's relativity theory says that every material object has an energy which is inherent within it, an energy that depends on its mass, m. In fact, $E = mc^2$ where m is the mass of an object and c is the speed of light. Energy is locked up in matter. In other words, Leibniz's living force in matter intuited Einstein's understanding of matter's energy.

Newton's idea of lifeless matter still prevails in science, since energy is defined mechanically. Yet, Leibniz's "vis viva" hovers in the background, behind the new tendency of scientists on the cutting edge of physics who are exploring where consciousness enters matter. As we saw earlier, Pauli suspected that psychology would play a fundamental role in understanding the problems of observation in quantum physics. He said redefining "reality" would be crucial to understanding the interaction between the observer and the observed.

THE PRESENT POINT IN HISTORY

One of the main points of this book is that matter is sentient and that this subtle, generally unrecognized consciousness is encoded in the math physics uses. Matter is neither alive nor dead; everything is alive as far as our NCR experiences are concerned. This view, seen within the perspective of history, is part of the chain of philosophies linking physics and psychology with shamanism, alchemy, and perennial philosophy.

Physics is an aspect of everyone's psychology. Every human being is a physicist. Each of us is matter; therefore every experience we have of ourselves is part of physics. Moreover, everything we touch has both NCR and CR qualities. Awareness of experience links us not just to matter, but to the experiential reality that gives rise to both psychology and physics. This awareness makes us modern shamans, alert to the unified whole behind all aspects of experience.

In the modern shaman's way of thinking, sentient awareness, not matter, is the central feature of science, the basic substance of the universe. In this new paradigm, non-consensus experience is the fundamental "material" or reality, and consensus reality and measurability result from it. If we become modern shamans, reincorporating NCR experiences into science, the multitude of experiences that were mercilessly cast out of the scientific paradigm at the time of the Renaissance may reappear in everyone's awareness. In this way, the style of using nature as if she had no feelings transforms into relating to Her as if she were another human being.

NOTES

1. See Carolyn Merchant's excellent history, *The Death of Nature*. I am thankful to Fritz Capra whose *Tao of Physics* brought Merchant's work to my attention.

2. Ibid., page xvii.

3. Ibid., pages 128 to129.

4. An interesting text on this rapprochement from the perspective of theology is Brian Hines' *God's Whisper, Creation's Thunder*.

5. Merchant, op. cit., page 169.

6. See, for example, Michio Kaku's fascinating futuristic predictions in his *Hyperspace*.

7. Merchant, op. cit., page 168.

8. Sommers, 1978.

9. Ibid.

10. Merchant, op. cit., page 279.

11. It is fascinating that what Leibniz call the spirit of matter, physics calls ($mv^2/2$), that is, kinetic energy.

11 | Calculus and Enlightenment

Mathematics has been an integral part of man's intellectual training and heritage for at least twenty-five hundred years. During this long period of time, however, no general agreement has been reached as to the nature of the subject, nor has any universally acceptable definition been given for it.

—Carl Boyer in *The History of the Calculus*

I love dancing. To learn a new dance, I have to learn the steps, take a step or two in one direction, and then take another step in another direction. Counting helps. It tells me how many steps I have taken. But the steps are not the dance. At a certain moment the steps become irrelevant, and I find my body dancing.

Arithmetic, numbers, and counting are important in learning how to dance and describing it to others. But the numbers are not the dance. Likewise, to describe the twirls and whirls in nature, we need something new, beyond mere counting, that can describe movement and flow. We need calculus. Some of us may have learned that calculus is complicated, serious, and difficult. I want to show you that calculus is not only a lot of fun, but that it can lead to enlightenment.

VELOCITY AND CHANGE

Calculus is a Latin word for counting and is related to the word for stones and pebbles, probably because we all learned to count by marking off small rocks. Calculus is a branch of mathematics originally developed by Leibniz, Newton, and others in the 1600s to describe change better than ordinary math was able to at that time. Ordinary counting procedures did not deal well with speed and acceleration. Arithmetic can deal with the steps we need to get from one place to the next, but not with the *fluid motion* that occurs between.

It took mathematicians from about 1660 to 1830 to develop and understand the basic ideas behind calculus.[1] On our journey together, rather than studying the historical development of calculus to understand its essentials, we will develop it together, from scratch.

Let's be empirical for a moment. Think about motion and speed. Speed and velocity are CR measures of how fast you can move across a certain distance. If I walk at a speed of 3 miles an hour, I will be able to walk 3 miles in 1 hour.

From one perspective, this is simple. Yet, it's not simple because the speed, 3 miles an hour, only says that in 1 hour I can go 3 miles. The speed describes only the beginning and the end of a generic trip extending for 3 miles! Three miles an hour, or 3 mph for short, does not say what I was doing within that distance of 3 miles. I might have been moving faster or slower than 3 miles per hour. Speed only tells us that if I went at a steady a rate of 3 mph, it would take me an hour to go 3 miles. In between, a lot of things could happen. I might stop for a rest along the way, and still make the average speed of 3 mph if I hustle along rapidly after resting.

To demonstrate to my students the difference between the average speed between two points and the momentary velocity at a given point I usually take a little walk in the classroom. I speak to the students in the following way.

"Watch me taking a walk in this room. It is crowded here, but let's say, I start at the wall near the blackboard where I am now standing, and walk to the center of the room. Count my steps. How many steps would you say I took?"

A student will say something like "You took twelve steps to the center." Then I ask, "How fast I was going?" They say, "Not too fast... About 3 miles an hour." Usually someone asks what all this has to do with psychology and physics or shamanism and I have to encourage them to wait while we stay in CR for a while.

I ask my students how they know I was going about 3 mph. "How can you say that I went 3 miles an hour when I only walked a few feet? I did not walk 3 miles, nor did I walk for a whole hour! How can you say it would take an hour to walk 3 miles, just by watching me walk a few feet in a few seconds?" The students answer correctly that they are "extrapolating" from my present motion, they were averaging, guessing.

The word "average" means I was going at an average speed of 3 miles an hour over those few feet. I then ask the students to watch me again while I walk toward the center of the room and back, but this time not at a steady pace. Instead, I stop in the middle, scratch my nose, and then speed up as I walk to the center of the room and back.

Then I say to the class that they could say that on the average I was still going 3 miles an hour, but that "3 miles an hour" is a poor description of what actually happened. It is not an accurate description of my velocity. After all, I stopped in the middle and scratched my nose. Averages leave out all the interesting details of the journey.

IN THE LIMIT

Average velocity is a weak description of my speed while walking. "Three miles per hour" does not tell us the speed at every point on my walk, but only the average speed from the beginning to end of my walk. *If I want a better description, I will need to find a way to measure my velocity at every point.* Most of us are less concerned with velocity than we are with the experience of traveling. But physicists, and police, need to measure speed!

It took Western scientists until 1650 to discover how to measure velocity at every point in space and time. Newton and Leibniz wanted to measure the shifting realm of change in motion and came up with a radical idea, which they called *the limit*. The idea of the limit is central to calculus, and, because all of physics is based on calculus, the idea of the limit is central to all of physics.

I tell my classes that in order to understand the concept of the limit, we have to go back to the details of the walk. Let's say that the distance between the wall and the center of the room is about 30 feet. I suggest that if we use a consensual measure of time, such as the clock on the classroom wall, we can time my walk. Then I walk those 30 feet again, and notice, together with everyone in the class, that it takes me 5 seconds.

With this new information about time, we can calculate my velocity. If we divide the distance of 30 feet by the time of 5 seconds, we get a velocity of 6 feet per second. We now have the average velocity between two points, but we still need to know more. If we are going to be specific, we need to figure out how to measure my velocity at any single point. This is the same question Newton had to answer.

I imagine that Newton created something like the following experiment. He probably thought, "Let a person walk and we will measure his speed at a given point by getting a good watch and measuring how much time it took him to move for a couple of seconds. Then let's reduce the time. Let's allow him to move for only a very brief period of time, such as half a second. Then we can find his speed again, within the smaller periods of time and within a shorter distance. All we have to do is to divide how far he went by this "half a second" and discover his average speed.

11.1 A short walk

Then Newton had a breakthrough. He must have thought, why confine ourselves to what we can measure today? Why think only about our clocks and measuring sticks, which are not all that accurate? Let's pretend our measuring instruments are much better and can measure tiny distances and times like one millionth of an inch or a trillionth of a second. Imagine a split-second walk!

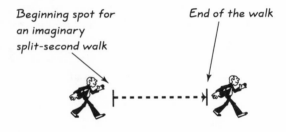

11.2 Tiny walk

Why confine ourselves to a split second? Why not go on with the thought experiment, take it to its limit? Let's imagine measuring the distance someone moves in an infinitesimally small amount of time approaching zero, because in that tiny amount of time, we are getting extremely close to his speed at *a given point* in space and time, which is our goal.

11.3 Infinitesimally short walk

During that infinitesimally small amount of time, the person will not have moved far. Though the split second is brief, we can still say that he moved some distance, and, as long as no one really tries to measure the exact distance, we can say that we are measuring the distance moved and time taken at a single point. Since velocity is distance divided by time, we have the velocity more or less at a given point.

Now, you might be a very accurate reader or a physicist and say, you can't do that. One billionth of an inch is still a distance between two points and not a single point. I imagine that Newton would have said, "We are not finished with the experiment. Let's take the experiment to the limit in time, the limit at which the amount of time approaches zero. When we get closer to zero time traveled, we shall just about be at the single point."

Mathematicians do not worry about whether you can really measure something; they just try to be as reasonable as possible. So Newton developed the idea of velocity at a point: the velocity is the space that was traveled divided by time, *as the amount of time* needed for that little trip *approaches zero.* Let's say it again.

In the limit, as the distance and time between two points gets very small and approaches zero, the distance divided by the time is the velocity at any given single point.

This limit concept allowed Newton to say that velocity at a given point could be found by dividing distance by the time, as the time involved, in the limit, approached zero. (See note 2 for Newton's exact expression.)

You may be wondering why am I spending so much time talking about this detail. Most physicists and mathematicians are happy with it. We have defined velocity at a point: it is the ratio of distance to time as the amount of time under consideration approaches zero. We have given some hints about how to measure the velocity approximately—use a good measuring stick and clock, and do the best you can. What more can you want?

But there is still something that we can wonder about. I want to know more about what happens exactly *when we switch from moving between two places to moving fluidly at a given point.* We know today that measuring little distances is a problem. As we get to instantaneous and exact positions, we have to measure things the size of atoms, which no one can even see. We cannot measure well when things are so small. Physical reality inhibits us.

In other words, there is no such thing as a point! The point is a consensus reality concept, a figment of the mathematical imagination. *Points do not exist in physical reality.* What we once considered a single point actually contains millions of atoms.

Nevertheless, pure mathematical thinking is not bound to measurement as physics is. Math can roam freely in the realm of ideas. And math suggests that there is something like a velocity at a given "point" even though we know that in consensus reality, the best we can do is get the average velocity between two points when the time involved is extremely small. The concept of *velocity at a point is a dream, not a reality.*

Leibniz and Newton squeezed their way out of this impasse by saying that as the time we are using to measure gets smaller and smaller, in the limit as the amount of time becomes less and less and approaches zero, a brand new world emerges. What kind of world? A world in which one no longer has to measure anything between two points but is concerned only with fluid motion at the point itself. Newton called the fluid motion or velocity at a given point the "fluxion," which means "flowing" or "flow."[3] Newton made a transition from a world of larger steps to smaller steps, then to tiny steps, and finally to fluid motion—fluxion.

Later, mathematicians changed Newton's term, "fluxion," to "derivative." This change in names means that students of calculus no longer hear the term "fluxion" and are in danger of forgetting that derivatives apply to the world of flow. To be exact, the fluxion or derivative is defined at that mysterious point where the world of traveling step by step merges with the world of continuous change.

The derivative is the essence of calculus, the mathematical description of movement that is crucial to all of science, especially physics. At this point, you have already learned the heart of calculus. We just need to remember that the fluxion, later called a derivative, is the rate of change of anything (such as distance) at a given point in terms of anything else (such as time).

STATE AND PROCESS WORLDVIEWS

In summary, by creating derivatives or fluxions, that is, velocity at a given point, we have shifted worldviews. As we measure shorter distances and smaller times, suddenly the whole world shifts. We move from the realm of material measurability and consensus reality into the realm of pure thought and flow.

Velocity is a mathematical concept describing the momentary rate of change of distance. But this concept can never be measured with complete accuracy at a given point in consensus reality.

We have moved from *a fixed or state orientation* of assessment of discrete steps measured accurately in terms of distances and times to *an immeasurable world with a process orientation.*

State and process present two very different orientations and types of awareness. State orientation requires stepping out of the flow and making a judgment about, or measurement of, where you are at a point. State orientations require us to notice, "Now I'm here, now I'm here, now I'm here."

Let's think again about dancing. To learn to dance, you learn the particular steps, one at a time. That is the world of fixed, state orientations. But once you know those steps, you can truly dance, and dancing is different from repeating the proper steps. In dancing you forget the steps and just flow; the steps more or less disappear as you enter another orientation. Your awareness is no longer on the steps. Now you have another awareness, the awareness of a dancer!

The state orientation and the process experience are two different worlds. One requires stopping and judging from the outside, so to speak, while the other is immersion in the flow. These two worlds approach each other in the limit, in that mysterious space between the measurable and the immeasurable. This is probably why Newton called his differentials and derivatives fluxions—because of their inherent fluidity.[4]

As we have seen on our journey so far, the concepts of math correspond in many ways with psychological ideas. Thus, it is not surprising that there are psychological analogies to mathematical concepts such as the fluxion.

THE PATH OF CRUMBS

I call the state orientation in psychology, which depends on precise, step-by-step observations, the "path of crumbs." When a therapist is using this orientation, she tracks a client's process from point to point, following the path of crumbs—one little bit at a time.[5] This perspective can be very helpful in becoming aware of how dreams, moods, and feelings appear on a moment-to-moment basis.

Following the path of crumbs, tracking something an inch at a time, is not the same as swinging with the flow as someone moves through their dance, their process. Following somebody from the outside by utilizing the path of crumbs is dramatically different from joining them in the flow.

The process orientation (like Newton's fluxion) can be approached by beginning the path of crumbs in consensus reality—the state-oriented viewpoint. Then, by taking the state orientation to the limit as we track each step as minutely as possible, we suddenly cross the border between the worlds, enter the realm of fluxion, the realm of pure change, where no states are involved.

Calculus allows you to step out of consensus reality by entering the flow. It is like stepping out of the CR world, where you can measure and track everything by saying, "now this, now that," and moving into pure process, where you are aware only of movement, flux.

STEPPING IN AND OUT OF TIME

At this point in my classes, students usually ask for an example of the difference between states and processes. I'll share one example of such a demonstration with you.

I began by asking if anyone had a dream in the last few weeks. A woman, whom I'll call Jan, said she had dreamed of "riding on a bus that was going fast. We were going to Mexico on a windy mountain road. Mexico reminds me of the shaman, don Juan, Castaneda's wizard who teaches him amazing things. Maybe I am on a bus in shamanism land?"

We can look at Jan's interpretation "being on a bus in shamanism land" as an "average speed" description of the entire trip she was on, but this description lacks detail. At this point, I suggest that we just follow her process for a moment, and that I meditate with her, wherever she is in the moment. I begin by focusing with her on her momentary experience, that is, I follow the path of crumbs, and assist her awareness by repeating back to her what I see from one moment to the next.

> "I notice now you are standing up. Now, all you have to do is the same, observe, check in with yourself, maybe with your body, and tell me what you experience physically just now."

> Jan said, "I notice my heart is beating fast and I'm hot. Hmm, actually, shivering… and there's a tremble.

> I say, "Trembling. I notice a little bit of that tremble in your arms, are they shaking? I notice they are beginning to move, sideways, now up and down." I was trying to follow her by using ministeps, going from point to point, state to state. I noticed that her shoulders moved up, then down.

> Jan mumbled, apparently a little nervous, "Yeah, it's trembling! Everything in me wants to move, OK, I will let the movement happen. I have to close my eyes. Now I notice it's in my shoulders, there is a little jump in my shoulders!"

> I noticed she was following those individual steps or states at this moment, and I said, "Do I notice you smiling?"

> Immediately she responded with, "I am at an impasse, an edge! I'm embarrassed…" I said I understood, after all, since nobody wants to climb aboard an unknown process without knowing where it is going, especially in front of others. Jan did not respond to my comment but went on. "But the trembling, the shoulders… it's strong actually… If I just get into it… hmmm…"

> At this point she seemed to have decided to follow her body motions and let them unfold. "Shoulders trembling… But… the thing that's really interesting is when the movement just does itself!"

Jan stopped speaking at this point, closed her eyes, and started hopping up and down. She almost looked as if she were jumping on something with springs that was giving her a bounce into the air. Suddenly she sprang high into the air and almost reached the ceiling in the classroom. She let out a wild howl and landed on her feet, squarely on the floor. She laughed and also looked a bit shocked.

"Gee, it's... embarrassing... it's like, let's see... I am a little altered!" Roaring with laughter she cried out "Oh god!" and began to leap again. The class, which had been relatively quiet, now broke out in good-humored laughter, amazed at her leaping. Jan jumped up and down and stopped after a few minutes, catching her breath. After she caught her breath, she said that she realized something. "I lead myself around with my head instead of experiencing the fun that is inside of me!"

She went right back to her movement and jumped so high, she fell right into the lap of her partner, sitting next to her. She was thrilled and said, after recuperating from the excitement, "If I trust my process, I have a happy landing."

When the class quieted down, I ask Jan how she formulated the difference between the dream of the bus going fast in shamanism land and her present experience. She said, "The difference is life itself. Yes! That's it! This transition is a transition into a wild state and back! Moving from step to step helped me become aware of my process. The weird moment happened when the steps suddenly merge into the process. That is the difference between states and process, it's the experience of life. Don Juan... hmmm, yes, shamanism. It's like feeling something real deep, a flow, and then being moved by it instead of thinking about it from the outside."

In other words, you can connect to your continuous dreaming process in NCR by following the path of crumbs, noticing events as they occur one after another, but this is still the world of physics, the world of measurable reality. It's fine, but it is very different from Newton's fluxion, the differential. Physics helps by measuring and tracking events. It notices and observes from the outside.

Flow awareness, symbolized by the fluxion in calculus, is very different. It refers to movement—the dance, we could say—and corresponds to flow awareness. Words can only approach this awareness. Their precision, their state-oriented nature tells you a lot, but words cannot describe the merging experience of being in the flow of your process.

The flow description requires more than arithmetic. You need calculus. You need more than talking about things, noticing things as they move from point to point. You need a movement-oriented psychology, a process orientation.

We can talk about where Jan was and what she experienced. We can say she moved her shoulders up, she moved her shoulders down, trembled and sprang in the air. These are verbal, measurable CR terms. But when she gets into the flow, she is suddenly in another world. From the viewpoint of her inner experience, she is no longer in the world of steps. She is dancing or being danced. Her awareness is sentient, sensitive to motion and emotion not generally recognized by her consensus mind.

At this point Jan said, "In my dream—I did not tell you all of it—the bus was going fast to Mexico. It was on that winding road. I did not say before, but the bus was about to go off the cliff when somebody in the bus looked at his watch and said, `What time is it?' And at that moment I came out of the dream."

The unknown is truly awesome. I commented that, for better or worse, time, a CR interest, kept Jan away from the cliff. "You were at the edge; in your dream you stopped. You went back to state-oriented thinking and measurement of little times and spaces. That brings you out of dreaming. That is the difference between noticing and flowing, between measuring and fluxions. Jan agreed and said, "Yes, and today I went over the cliff, and back. My body answered my own question, about the meaning of calculus in everyday life."

This flow awareness in mathematics and life may best be described by Taoism, which has a term for the sentient experience of being danced. The best term for this dance may be the Tao that cannot be spoken. Taoism also labels the steps of the dance, or the measurable differentiations as the Tao that can be spoken, i.e., the numbers that can be reported.

When we count, we break up a particular process by reporting on it, by breaking it into segments. What we gain is a consensus reality we can all share; we gain awareness of where we are at a certain point. But what we lose by counting and measuring and describing things in consensus reality is the fluxion, the flux, the unique sense of process, and the NCR sense of dreaming.

We all have access at different times to this state of flow. I love working as a therapist because I frequently have flow experiences. I also remember accessing a similar state as a child, when I was fighting. I would measure and check on my opponents and myself. But then, when I was in the midst of the fray, I lost track of my tracking, and what happened was uncanny, it was dreaming. Today, I know the same sense while I am skiing. I began by learning how to ski. Then the flow of the mountain became my experience.

You become immersed in this flow whenever you are totally involved in life, when you are dancing, fighting, loving, eating, learning, writing, or cooking. These experiences cannot be properly described; they are awesome. They make you feel well, make you feel as if you were tuned into something greater than yourself. In a way, you step out of ordinary time.

At this point, you may want to try the following exercise that reveals the transition from state to process-oriented thinking, from steps to flow.

STREAM-ENTERING EXERCISE

Find a comfortable position. Then experiment by asking yourself the following questions.

1. **The Dream**. Focus on a dream that feels significant to you. Ask yourself, "Where do I think this dream is taking me? What is the direction it wants me to take in everyday life?" If you can't guess this, don't worry about it. If you have a guess, make a note of it.

   For example, Jan is heading toward shamanism. You might be heading toward self-confidence, more feeling, more thinking, or toward a specific project.

   Pick any dream, even a dream of twenty years ago is fine.

2. **The Path of Crumbs**. Now ask yourself, "What do I notice in my body?" Just take note of any sensations that draw your awareness and follow them, one after another. Be brief and precise.

   Use this path of crumbs. Observe to yourself, "I notice this and that." Try not to be too prejudiced about what you're saying. Just say what you're noticing. Report on the small changes you notice.

3. **Process**. Now, notice how reporting on these little tiny bits and pieces of process merges gradually into experiencing the process directly. Follow it; amplify it, letting it unfold. If you get stuck, watch for edges, go back to the last step, and gently encourage yourself to go on.

   If you stop and think about the process in the midst of it, that's OK. Think about it, but then ask yourself gently to go back into experiencing it.

4. **Notice the differences**. After the process has completed itself and you feel you are back in everyday reality, ask yourself, "What is the difference between the experience of streaming process and reporting or thinking about it?"

   What is the somatic difference, what happened to you physically? What was the moment like in which you switched from a state to a process-orientation?

Starting with space and time, with exact observations, allows you to value and then briefly leave time and space. In the New World, space and time are mixed, combined. This is the world of traditional shamans. When we enter this world of flow, we know how to step out of reality. Some have called this state "being dead in life." This state is behind many stories from Tibetan and Zen Buddhism. The spiritual goal is stepping out of time, getting into the flow and being aware of its presence. Soto Zen calls this "stream entering." Many psychologies, including process-oriented psychology, also value and study this experience. Transpersonal and gestalt psychology and Jung's active imagination are about flow.

As we explore together, we see that entering the stream is a perennial goal. This time, you got there by studying calculus. Calculus takes us into the flow experience by showing us how to take our measurements and observations to the limit. Here we find the place where physics meets math, where psychology meets shamanism, where the steps and states of consensus reality melt into the stream of life. Traditional awareness practices are one way to get into that flow, calculus is another. Calculus is like shamanism. It leads us into the world of traditional and modern shamans, tells us exactly how to enter this new world: if we go to "the limit," we reach the point of switching into the world of flow.

NOTES

1. Those interested in detailed development of calculus will enjoy Carl Boyer's *The History of the Calculus.*

2. Let's call distance by the letter "s." Consider two points on a straight line, X and x. Let's call the distance between these two points s = X - x, or in picture form X<- - - - s - - - ->x

    Let's call that distance s by the name "X - x," or call it "delta s," which is a Greek symbol mathematicians use (Δ or delta just means a little change in something).

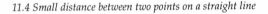

11.4 Small distance between two points on a straight line

Let's say our clock says 2 minutes after 5 PM when you begin your walk at X, and 3 minutes after 5 as you get to point x. In general, let's call the difference in time between one measurement and the other Δt. Remember, Δ is shorthand for "a little change." Thus, in general, we need Δt of time to move through a distance of Δs, or in picture form: X<- - - -Δs - - - ->x. Thus it takes Δt to go Δs from X to x.

Now let's think about speed and velocity. If we say velocity is how fast you are going at each point along the way, we can now measure velocity by saying that your speed is the amount of distance—like delta s—you cover in a certain time—like delta t.

Now we know what the velocity means between two points: it is the time you need to get from one to the other. If the points are far apart, we can get the average. Say that, at some point P between a and c, you average out that you went 2 + 4 or 6 feet in two seconds (see below), which means 3 feet per second on the average. But we know, if we measured things more accurately, that 3 feet per second is an average, not a fact about your speed at point P!

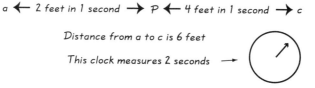

11.5 Time and distance for a short walk

But we need to know more than averages. We want to really get specific and know, what does the velocity at a given single point mean? How can we say that you are going 3 feet per second or 3 miles an hour at a single point? This is the question Newton had to solve.

He figured that your velocity at a given point P between x and X could be approximated by starting with the velocity between two points near P. A little distance, say 2 inches around point P, would look like the following.

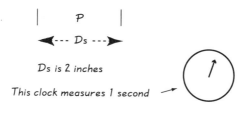

11.6 Time and distance for a shorter walk

Let's say our stopwatch says it takes Δt time, which is just a little time, like .one tenth of 1 second, to move through these 2 inches, which we are calling Δs. The velocity at P is then Δs over Δt, that is, 2 inches divided by one tenth of a second. In other words,

velocity = Δs divided by Δt, which is
2 inches for every 0.1 seconds,
or in shorthand:
$v = \Delta s / \Delta t = 20$ inches per second

If you calculate this out, 2 inches in a tenth of a second amounts to 1.136 miles an hour, which is pretty slow for a person. The 1.136 miles an hour means only that if I continued at the same exact rate over 1.136 miles as I was going during those 2 inches, I would go 1.136 miles in 1 hour.

(Here is how you calculate that: If we multiply top and bottom by 10, we find we were going 20 inches per second. If we multiply by 60, we find we were going 1200 inches a minute, or 72,000 inches per hour, that is, 6000 feet per hour or 1.136 U.S. miles an hour—since a U.S. mile is 5320 ft.!)

3. In other words, v is a fluxion, which is defined as
   Lim $\Delta s = ds/dt = v$
   $\Delta t \to 0$
   (where the term "lim" refers to the limit of Δs as Δt goes to zero)

Newton's name for

$$\text{Lim } \Delta s = ds/dt = v$$
$$\Delta t \to 0$$

was "fluxion." Later, fluxion was changed by mathematicians who called it a "derivative," the derivative of s relative to t in our example. Sometimes ds/dt is written simply as an s with a dot over it. This change in names is a shame because students of calculus no longer hear the term "fluxion" and forget that ds/dt is really a fluxion—another world that meets this one at the limit when the deltas get very small.

ds/dt is the core of differential and integral calculus, which are crucial in the physics of everything that moves.

4.   As described in note 3, a fluxion is two differentials, such as space and time, divided by one another, that is, ds/dt.

5.   Remember "Hansel and Gretel," that old fairy tale collected by the Brothers Grimm? Hansel, the little boy, and Gretel, the girl, found their way home from the terrible witch's candy house at night by leaving a path of crumbs as they went from their home into the forest where the witch lived. When they ran away at night from the witch, they followed the path of crumbs.

II

SENTIENT QUANTUM MECHANICS

12 | Newtonian Laws and Shamanism

Whence arises all that order and beauty we see in the world?

—Isaac Newton

t this point on our journey, we will temporarily depart from the spiritual domain of math to begin our study of physics, which could not exist in its present form without the language of math. Once calculus was invented, physicists were able to use Newton's concept of the fluxion, and for the first time velocity, acceleration, and the rates of change of any quantity relative to other quantities could be described by physics. The worlds of modern technology and science were born.

Newton experimented with how objects moved and used discoveries in calculus to formulate the laws of motion on which most of our consensus reality worldview has been based since the 1600s. In this chapter, we will explore Newton's laws and their connection to shamanism. In the following chapters we will discover how quantum mechanics evolved from Newton's laws.

ACCELERATION

Measuring the time it takes to go a certain distance is simple until we try to measure that time and that distance around a given point. We have just discovered that velocity at a given point (that is, the distance traveled divided by the time taken at a given point) is a fluxion.[1] In general, this fluxion or derivative can be written as follows (change means increase or decrease):

$$\frac{\text{Change in distance}}{\text{Change in time}} = \text{Velocity}$$

For example, we might be moving at 3 miles an hour at a given point. But we know we can change velocity as well. Sometimes you go slowly, sometimes fast. The rate of increase of speed or velocity is called acceleration.

Acceleration describes a change in velocity. Acceleration is defined as:

$$\frac{\text{Change in velocity}}{\text{Change in time}} = \text{Acceleration}$$

We know from our body sense that acceleration always involves force. It takes force to stop quickly or to speed up. In a car, acceleration pins us to our seats and deceleration throws us forward; that is why we need safety belts. On the other hand, if there is no acceleration, that is, if the velocity is constant, there are very few forces acting on us. If the car is not moving (going zero velocity) or is rolling along at a constant velocity, we do not feel pinned back in our seats or thrown forward. Again, acceleration, or changes in velocity, involves forces.[2]

NEWTON'S FIRST LAW OF MOTION

Now we are ready to study the laws of motion. After Newton developed calculus he used to it to describe the laws of motion, which he believed governed all moving objects. His three laws are still used today to determine everything from the amount of gas we need to drive our cars to predicting the orbits of planets. Even exercise machines are based on Newtonian physics. Newton wrote his first law of motion as follows:

Law I: An object remains at rest or in a state of uniform motion in a straight line unless acted on by an external force.

Consider an object such as a ball. The first law of motion says that it will not roll on a horizontal or flat floor unless we push it. The first law also says that if the ball were rolling on the ground by itself, and if, for some unknown reason, there were no friction from the ground, it would roll forever at the same speed and direction if some external force did not stop it.

This first law implies that objects have no minds of their own. As far as Newton and his laws were concerned, the planets (or a ball) have no inner lives and therefore no input into their fate. If nothing intervenes from the outside, they will continue exactly as they are. Quantum physics has changed this belief a bit, but we will explore that later in our journey.

THE SECOND LAW OF MOTION

The second law of motion says that if you push something that is at rest, it not only moves (which is predicted by the first law), but it accelerates according to the strength of the shove. Formulated more accurately, the second law says that the acceleration produced by a force on an object is proportional to the strength of that force. In other words, for the same mass, stronger forces make greater accelerations. We could also say that for given forces, the acceleration depends on the mass of the object. A given force applied to a massive object will result in less acceleration than the same force applied to a less massive one. This second law may be stated as follows:

Law II: Force = Mass × Acceleration or (if f is force, m is mass and a is acceleration)

$$f = m \times a$$

The second law of motion says that a push with a force *f* will accelerate a ball at the rate of *a*. In general, this laws says that if you apply force to any mass, whether it is has the form of a person, a teacup, a rock, or a ball, you produce an acceleration. Whether matter is alive or dead, it obeys the second law of motion that $f = m \times a$. And whether it is alive or dead, it resists change, it has inertia. According to this law, *all matter is stubborn and will not change velocity without a push.*

THE THIRD LAW OF MOTION

Now, let's examine Newton's third law of motion, which says that for every action there is an equal and opposite reaction.

Law III: For every action there is a reaction.

We can think of this third law of motion as the car-crash law. The first law tells us that things don't accelerate if we don't push them. The second law tells us how they accelerate, and the third law says that if you bang into my car with your car we both get dents! It tells us that if two objects collide, they do so with equal and opposite reactions.

NEWTON'S PSYCHOLOGY

Are these laws always true? If we study our car accidents, we can say yes, we know these laws to be true. But are they psychologically correct? Many would say yes. The third law, for example, could be called the law of abuse and retribution: If you hurt me, I get hurt and will hurt you back.

But this law is not always true for all people. A bang from you will not always dent me. Under what circumstances do I not get dented?

When I ask this question in my class, there are often many opinions about the answers. There is usually someone who says, "If you were an Aikido expert, you would not get dented from a bang."

This is true. If I move fluidly and respond by going with your motion, if I see you coming and am centered inside myself, if I know that I have you in me, and even agree in part with you, then it is likely that you will stop and not hurt me. Or, I will be so detached that when you hit me your punch will not cause me pain. There will be no resistance and you may fall over as I roll backwards.

Now you might say, "Well, OK, I see how the third law is not always true for people. But matter has no life of its own." I would then say, "Let's be exact and put your statement in as part of the third law."

In other words, the car-crash law is not correct for objects with consciousness. The laws of Newtonian physics *assume that particles have no spirit in them.*

For example, Newton's third law does not hold for very sensitive people. I have seen such people get bruises even when nothing has touched them. Some people get bruises just talking about people who hate them. I remember a particularly dramatic example of this when the hand of a young woman I was working with started to bleed when she thought she was Christ—yet nothing punctured her skin that I could see. She was like shamans who draw things out of people's bodies without making a wound, much less a dent.

The third law—and for that matter, all the laws of physics—are most applicable to objects without any spirit in them.

Remember the debate between Leibniz and Newton? Leibniz thought that there was a spirit in objects. Objects had an inner force he called "vis viva." Newton disagreed. Until now, history has favored Newton.

Thus today, consensus reality is Newtonian. The governing political mentality defines people, objects, and forces as if they had no inner life. Newtonian physics has become a political platform that says, "If you give others a good push, they are going to change!" But as some of you know from your personal experience as social activists, a push doesn't always lead to change. Change needs to happen from the inside as well.

We are at the mercy of forces more powerful than our own only when we have no inner life. The past does not entirely determine the present. Karma is not entirely correct. Past dents and smashes do not entirely determine the present life.

You cannot force change to occur in another person. You cannot make a dent in everyone just because you want to. You cannot force someone to understand and agree with your viewpoint as Newtonian laws suggest. By the same thinking, you cannot totally enslave someone only by making her a slave. You cannot imprison someone with walls alone, and you cannot entirely kill someone by putting a bullet through his head or placing him in an electric chair. A person's spirit continues on in others!

People are not lifeless objects. Dealing with people as if we had no spirit hurts the person exerting the pressure, the oppressor, almost as much as it hurts the "oppressed." In a car crash, both vehicles are dented. The oppressor in a Newtonian world becomes a machine—an empty, dead object in a realm where everything else is spiritless and can be pushed around.[3]

INNER WORK

As we move along, we are studying physics and psychology simultaneously. We have seen the ways in which the world is an interwoven whole and how our awareness creates reality. Thus, to understand matter, we need to know ourselves. The following questions help us explore how we operate both in accordance with Newton's laws of motion, and also how we choose at times to respond in non-Newtonian ways.

Experiment with the following:

- When did you last feel that some outer force, fate, people, nature, or time itself was oppressing you? Were you oppressed by someone, by a group, by social pressure? Is this happening now?
- How did you, or do you, react? Did you try to push back, make a dent and change the other, or succumb to it and get dented yourself?
- Should you have pushed back more and protected yourself? In other words, do you need to be more Newtonian?
- Was there or is there now an alternative to either pushing back or giving in?
- Imagine yourself being the main figures in the scene you are thinking about, both the oppressor and the oppressed. (If you have trouble imagining yourself as an oppressor, remember another time in your life, recently or in the past, when you tried to accelerate the pace of something but were met with resistance. How were you trying to press when your push was contested?)
- Now imagine again that you are both the oppressor and the oppressed, and experiment with the fantasy of facilitating the interaction instead of being only the victim or the persecutor.
- If you do not reach a resolution, pretend you can feel and speak with the Great Spirit and ask it for the way through the impasse.

This is one way to become free of Newtonian forces pushing and pulling you about.

MYSTERIES IN PHYSICS

Learning to do something besides push may be hard for some of us, some of the time. Similarly, it was and still is hard for physicists to make the transition from Newtonian physics to quantum physics and relativity.

For example, Newton's physics was based on standard, consensual concepts, and CR terms, such as object and force. The new physics needs a new language, since the ideas of object and force are no longer as clear as they were in Newton's time. We need a new vocabulary reflecting a world beyond action and reaction. Although we have a newer physics, newer concepts are still based on Newtonian terms and the older worldview.

We have discovered together that calculus describes the laws of how physical bodies move through space. Calculus carries the secret of how to move from point to point into flow, from the steps to the dance. Calculus describes the dance of movement processes that cannot be measured exactly in terms of changes in distance and time. Change at a given point is a process concept. It cannot be precisely measured; it can only be experienced. In a way, there is an uncertainty principle built into the mathematical patterns that attempt to describe physical phenomena, since the physically measured values of things in flux will never be sufficiently precise.

Added to this uncertainty is the limitation that is inherent in all counting; all enumeration: the description of an event is not the event itself. Counting marginalizes the psychological procedures of matching events.

Even though our descriptive systems and terms imply interactions between the observer and the observed, and even though we know calculus speaks about a world of flow instead of a world of broken-up states, we think of events as if they happened without human involvement, without human consciousness.

Let's think more about the formula $f = m \times a$. Exactly what do we mean by the "force" or the "object" the force accelerates? What is an object with mass? Newton assumed that mass was a measure of inertia. An object with lots of mass resists acceleration more stubbornly than a smaller mass.

But the idea of an object with mass is not so simple. Think about a rubber ball. Try defining the ball. Does it include the atoms that are coming or going from it all the time? Does it include dust and dirt? The ball is constantly changing. Over time, even its color changes, since rubber deteriorates. There is uncertainty about what a ball is, so its mass is a bit vague as well.

Even if we managed to stop the dust and the color changes in the ball, we would still be unable to stop its mass from changing. In the early part of the twentieth century, Einstein predicted that the mass of the ball changes. Mass, he discovered, depends on its speed relative to the observer. According to Einstein, just throwing a ball into the air changes its mass according to the speed it is traveling.[4]

Since energy is the capacity to push things about, a ball gains energy simply because it is thrown into the air. Einstein said that if the ball's energy changes, its mass changes as well. Not by much, but it does change. If the ball is heated, it gains energy again and the mass gets heavier. Energy and mass are intertwined. According to the theory of relativity, there is no essential distinction between mass and energy. Energy has mass and mass represents energy.

The point here is that today's physicists are far less certain than ever about what a ball really is. Our old CR view—Newton's view—on the nature of an object's mass, its weight and size, has changed. Nothing is totally certain any longer.

FORCES

At this point, let's reconsider forces. Newton believed that forces are transmitted when one "object" pushes directly on another object, such as when my foot kicks a ball. Newton also imagined forces transmitted over distances, such as the moon's gravity pulling on the earth, or the earth's gravitational pull on you, which gives you the sensation of weight. Newton did not know what the force of gravity was. He simply assumed it held us down to the Earth. He reasoned that gravity acted on matter everywhere like a magnet acts on pieces of metal as a force pushing them about.

Today, more than 250 years after Newton's death, physicists are still unsure about what constitutes gravity or even magnetism. Some think electromagnetism is due to bombardments of virtual, that is, invisible, imaginary particles—ghosts, so to speak. In quantum electrodynamics, forces are even stranger. They are "virtual," invisible particles that bump into other things. The concept of force acting on something at a distance is being replaced by the concept of imaginary events. There is speculation that gravity, too, is not only a force, but also a virtual particle. What used to be called forces are now particles, communicating in the quantum realm. Forces are communications in an invisible realm.

Our notions about mass and objects are also shaky. What Newton thought was a law, namely, that $f = m \times a$, turns out to be somewhat true for large, slow objects as long as you don't try to measure them too accurately. If you don't ask too many questions about mass, don't go too fast, or don't break things down into smaller and smaller parts, in other words, if you stay within the consensus reality of today, then $f = m \times a$.

THE GOOD IN THE OLD PARADIGM

Thus we now know:

1. Laws formulated as mathematical statements such as $f = m \times a$ are only approximations because calculus (which describes acceleration) is about the world of process, not discrete measurement.

2. Mathematics marginalizes the interaction between the object and the observer.

3. The concepts of object, mass, energy, force, and particle are limited.

If we agree that terms such as particle and force are not quite correct, why do we continue to use them? Some people say that these terms are convenient consensual terms, since everyone has a sense of what they mean. But why stick to terms if they are no longer accurate? Perhaps we are hypnotized. Physics is at an impasse in its worldview because the world is at an impasse. We are approaching a time when a new paradigm must occur. However, before we launch into that view, let me first speak in favor of the old one.

The old terms are retained in physics for various reasons. One is that many aspects of matter behave as if matter were lifeless, at least most of the time. Another reason for retaining the old worldview of particles and forces is that the Newtonian paradigm is still needed. We cannot give something up psychologically if we have not used it completely.

Some of us need the old Newtonian paradigm, the third law, which says "a dent for a dent." We need the old paradigm to fight back. Newtonian thinking is an important paradigm. If someone unfairly applies forces against us, excusing them will not prevent them from doing it again. We need to think in terms of "for every action there is a reaction" in order for important personal and social changes to occur. Too much of the time, we do not react to situations we feel are harmful.

In other words, Newtonian physics is a type of mechanics and psychology that is useful in some ways, especially in the framework where we need to react more and in the framework where objects seem momentarily without life.

SHAMANISM AND THE NEW WORLDVIEW

In biological frameworks, however, where objects are alive, the laws of Newtonian physics are only partially correct. In fact, the Newtonian laws are inapplicable when we are dealing with the NCR or non-consensual experiences of objects, since in these perceptions objects have both real and imaginary properties.

Despite its remarkable discoveries, which we shall explore soon, the newer physics, which continues to use older terms such as object, force, mass, and particle, is part of the old worldview. Quantum mechanics and relativity theory only hint at a new worldview. They themselves are based on old concepts even though physicists know that these are not quite correct.

As we move into a new worldview, our perception changes and becomes more fluid and diverse. Relativity enters our psychology. We will be able to value the depth of the river by measuring it in meters and also understand the river by jumping in. Both measurements in meters and direct experience in terms of the river's flow will be valid experiences.

This will bring our present worldview back into correspondence with shamanism, which assumes that the "objects" or people you are trying to change have a spirit and life of their own. In the viewpoint of the traditional and the modern shaman, "matter" is assumed to be alive. Everything is sentient and can feel. The shaman deals with the real world not only by pushing, but also through relating to it as if it were human-like and had a soul. Shamanism assumes that a ball is both the ball most people see and also a potentially sacred object. In fact, the modern shaman assumes that the world is full of mysterious events, massive and inexplicable powers that cannot be explained or resisted by the methods of everyday reality.[5]

While the average person in all of us lives in a Newtonian world, pushing against mysterious forces that bother him or her, hoping that one day these forces will be explained as viruses, complexes, or ecological problems, the modern shaman is different. Instead of fighting these forces with materialistic explanations, she stops trying to change what cannot be grasped and steps out of time into the realm of complex numbers to find solutions.

Can the shamanic path be understood in terms of the physics of today? Absolutely. The so-called laws of physics are described by math, by calculus. The theory of calculus not only patterns the step-by-step measurements of change as events move from point to point, but also leads the way to flux, that is, pure experience beyond measurement. Calculus, together with arithmetic and complex numbers, hints at the non-dualistic world beyond matter and psyche, the real and the imaginary. From the viewpoint of this non-dualistic world, today's concepts of mass, force, and object are themselves in flux. They are changing spirits of the times, capable of flowing into one another.

The modern shaman lives in the world hinted at by math. She loves and respects everyday life in terms of force and change, energy and time, but also knows that this life is a mysterious process whose essence is beyond both life and death. The modern shamans challenges us to develop a new worldview that does not simply favor altered states of consciousness over "Newtonianism" but sees both perceptions as aspects of one and the same world. This new way of looking at things is the long-awaited paradigm shift into a unified worldview.

NOTES

1. The velocity or the time it takes to move a given distance at a given point, in the terms of mathematicians, is $v = ds/dt$.

2. How did Newton deal with acceleration? Remember the chapter on calculus. He described acceleration as follows. He called measurable changes in velocity (like from zero to 20) by Δv, and reasoned that in the limit (as we enter the stream, so to speak), the change in velocity at a point can be expressed by the acceleration, which is $a = dv/dt$.

    More exactly, he said that in the limit as the amount of time in a measurement goes to zero, that is, in the limit as the change in time becomes zero, the acceleration can be measured as the change in velocity divided by the time which has elapsed. In mathematical terms,

    $$\lim_{\Delta t \to 0} \Delta v/\Delta t = a = dv/dt$$

    If he knew the velocity and time, v and t, at different points, he could calculate the average acceleration, since acceleration, a, or the change in velocity divided by time at a given point, or during the trip in your cart, (see below) is:

    $$a = (v_1 - v_2)/(t_1 - t_2)$$

    According to our discoveries in calculus, this can now be written mathematically (imagining that the time gets small at a given point, that is, as t_1 approaches t_2 or as $\Delta t \to 0$. Thus $dv/dt = a$ is the instantaneously experienced acceleration, a, that is the rate at which things speed up or slow down.

    In other words, if you are traveling in a cart on a sidewalk between points 1 and 2, the following distances, times, and velocities at given points can be used to describe your motion. See Figure 12.1.

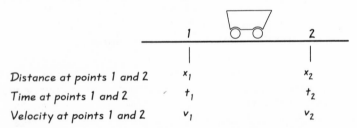

12.1 Cart traveling between two points

Why do we need all these measurements of times and spaces? Distances do not tell you enough about your cart. Times alone are not enough. Velocities tell you more! But even velocities are not enough. We need to know your acceleration, the rate of change of velocity (just as velocity is the rate of change of distance).

Now we have more information about the cart at point x. We know where your car is, when it is there, its speed, and we also know whether it is accelerating or not when it changes speeds. Of course, we do not know who is driving it, we do not know the spiritual atmosphere in that cart, we don't really feel its process. All these things are marginalized by our mathematics, at least temporarily. We can track how your cart is moving. Let's use an extreme example and say that the cart travels in a straight line for a while but then drops off a cliff. Watch out! Cliff ahead! Oops, the cart is falling!

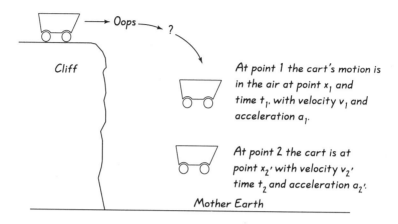

12.2 Cart went off the edge

If you were not so terrified while you were falling, you could still measure your height above the ground, at points 1 and 2.

We can draw all this out. Let's pretend that in one second you fell a foot, in two you fell 2 feet, in three you fell 3 feet. Your path, mapped out on distance and time, would look like the following Figure 12.3.

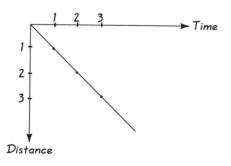

12.3 Speculated distance fallen measured against time

In Figure 12.3 the distance you fell at a given moment is a linear graph if we plot feet against seconds. This is a relationship between the space and the time of your movement. Thus speed at any moment, or dx/dt, or the distance traveled per unit of time, is constant. Distance changes and time changes, but the rate stays the same. You fall with the same speed. This is what people thought before Gallileo.

But in reality, your position changes faster than the linear diagram 12.3 shows. In fact, as your clock ticks off 1 second, you can be measured to fall about 16 feet. In 2 seconds, it turns out that you fall about 64 feet. In 3 seconds you will fall about 144 feet. As time goes on, x goes further and faster! (and then the air begins to drag on you and keep you from going much faster).

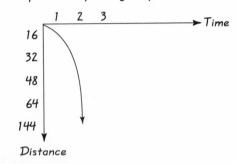

Real path of any falling body

12.4 *Actual distance your cart falls measured against time*

The above (Figure 12.4) is described by the equation $x = 16t^2$ where x is feet and t is time. Try it out. One second put into that equation gives 16 feet, 2 seconds squared makes 4, 4 times 16 equals 64, and so on. This is close to what you will measure. Since $v = dx/dt$, according to calculus, velocity is a function of time, or $v = 32t$. Since $a = dv/dt$, $a = 32$ feet per second, the acceleration created by gravity on the earth's surface.

3.   This may be why Aldous Huxley once said, "if we evolved a race of Isaac Newtons, that would not be progress. For the price Newton had to pay for being a supreme intellect was that he was incapable of friendship, love, fatherhood, and many other desirable things. As a man he was a failure, as a monster he was superb." Huxley's quote can be found in John Keynes' article, "Newton, the Man," in *The World of Mathematics*, Volume I.

4.   Relativity predicts the formula for the change in mass that is due to the speed it travels relative to the observer as $m = m_0\sqrt{[1 - v^2/c^2]}$ where "$\sqrt{}$" means square root, "c" is the speed of light, and "m_0", the so-called rest mass.

5.   In the first chapter of *Shaman's Body*, I discuss the philosophy of don Juan, which like Taoists, assumes that whatever is happening is mysterious, inexplicable powers are at work, and no one, scientist or mystic, can do anything other than align with these powers.

13 | The Theory of Theories

If it is true that the earth is round and that God can see everybody, does that mean He (surrounds the earth and) is like a circle?

—A three-year-old child, from Dora Kalf's *Sandplay*

Newton's causal laws ruled supreme and undisturbed from the 1600s until the beginning of the twentieth century, in part because of mainstream, collective thinking. In this chapter, we will explore together how the laws of physics reflect changes in collective awareness.

We have seen that Newton's laws deal adequately with large objects when the speeds involved are well below the speed of light. Furthermore, we saw that calculus, which expresses the laws of motion, can never measure with complete accuracy. There is no way to track a process with the accuracy suggested by math. Calculus implies that uncertainty is connected to all physical motion processes.

Physicists working in the field of quantum mechanics came to similar conclusions about uncertainty between 1905 and 1927, not by analyzing mathematics but by investigating the behavior of atoms and subatomic particles. The formulation of quantum mechanics that has achieved the greatest recognition today is the Copenhagen or "indeterministic" interpretation of experimental events. Other formulations such as the "causal" theory of David Bohm offer different explanations of the same events but are less developed at present.

The unsolved mysteries in subatomic physics will come as no great surprise to us, since we have seen that even Newton's concepts of force, mass, and particle, which were based on macroscopic aspects of consensus reality, not on events with subatomic dimensions, are uncertain.

QUANTUM MECHANICS

Until around 1900 and before quantum mechanics, matter was considered to be an aggregate of imagined particles. Each particle in Newtonian mechanics is more a mathematical concept than a reality. A Newtonian particle has a mass and a position in space and time associated to it, yet the particle has no extension in space, no volume.

Atomic research brought about a new attitude toward particles. It was found that the properties of particles, such as their position in space and time, needed to be understood in terms of probable positions. Subatomic particles were no longer simple points at well-defined positions, but rather entities that had a certain probability of being found at a given position at a given time.

Moreover, their energies could not have just any value but were quantized, that is, energy was absorbed and emitted from atoms in little chunks. Only certain amounts, or "quanta," as Einstein called them, were allowed. For example, if an atom was heated, its energy, manifesting in the radiation it emitted, was found to have only certain colors or frequencies and not others. Since around 1905, the energy of matter has been considered quantized.

Physicists still believed Newton's laws of motion; they were just thought to hold true only for macroscopic matter. The equation $f = m \times a$, describes large objects well enough—f is said to be a force, m is mass, a is acceleration, and all of these are understood in terms of everyday life. But physicists no longer agreed on the meaning of the mathematical equations that describe atomic phenomena. These equations, which we will explore together soon, turned out to be full of imaginary numbers.

New formulas, called wave equations, were developed to explain the unexpected behavior of particles in the subatomic world. The "new" wave equations had been used previously to describe all kinds of waves, such as water waves in oceans or lakes. Yet, in part because of the imaginary numbers, no one knows exactly what the waves in the wave equation for atomic events refer to.

There is still no agreement about how the macroscopic world of observation emerges from wave equations. Murray Gell-Mann expressed the physicists' discontent about the present status of quantum mechanics:

> Quantum mechanics [is] that mysterious, confusing discipline, which none of us really understands but which we know how to use. It works perfectly, as far as we can tell, in describing physical reality, but it is a 'counter-intuitive discipline', as the social scientist

would say. Quantum mechanics is not a theory, but rather a framework within which we believe any correct theory must fit. (1981)

Nobel Prize winner Richard Feynman (1965, pp. 127-128) adds, "I can safely say that nobody understands quantum mechanics." I remember the great teachings of Richard Feynman, who began his lectures in physics by saying, "We will not be able to understand what it is that is happening with matter." He meant that the mathematical formula (the wave equations) which describes the basic structure of matter, cannot be measured directly, nor can the particles these waves describe be measured exactly.

The ongoing discussion about the theory of quantum physics reminds me of a story I heard when I was a student at MIT in the early 1960s, a story that depicts the current state of affairs in quantum research. Herman Weyl, a well-known mathematician in the 1930s, had a party and invited Albert Einstein and Niels Bohr. These two physicists were not in agreement about the interpretation of quantum mechanics. Weyl gave the party because he hoped to have the two schools of physics come together. But Einstein and his students stayed on one side of the room, while Niels Bohr and his students remained on the other. They had two separate parties in one room.

Today things are not much better. Some physicists agree with Einstein that quantum mechanics is wrong, it is too uncertain or even incorrect because its laws are not consistent in relation to the observable world. Other physicists say that uncertainty and inconsistency are basic to nature.

This conflict is well known in psychology as well. Some psychologists say that there is nothing mysterious about people, while others say that people are mysterious and can never be understood.

These debates are useful because they remind us that our theories and interpretations of mathematics are incomplete. We can safely say that theories are not truths. Theories are mental constructs about processes that cannot be entirely grasped with CR formulations. As new things are revealed to us through discovery, theories transform.

PARTICLES AND WAVES

In 1690, when Newton was writing *Principia*, which formulates his ideas about math and physics, the European Renaissance was in full swing. Newton thought of particles as irreducible bits of matter with a specific known location in time.

Even before the advent of quantum theory, some physicists doubted Newton's theories. For example, David Bohm tells the story of two mathematical physicists, William Hamilton and Jacob Jacobi, who said, forty years before quantum theory, that instead of using Newton's law of motion, written as $f = m \times a$, we could just as well think of particles as waves! They showed how the everyday events described by Newton's particles could just as easily be described as waves.

In other words, we do not have to think of a particle moving through a specific path. Other mathematical formulas also described the motion of particles, and the new formulas had wavelike qualities. Hamilton and Jacobi said that what seems to be a particle on its own trajectory could just as well be considered the point on a wave crest. For example, instead of a piece of wood being moved forward by its own momentum, we could imagine that piece of wood being moved forward as the wave it rides on moves forward as well.

These two men came up with a wave-particle description of matter, but no one paid attention to it. No one knew what the waves could refer to. It seemed absurd to scientists at that time that a particle could be an aspect of a wave. How could you have a wave description of a particle? The quantum physical experiments, which showed that particles sometimes behaved like waves, had not yet been performed. Hamilton and Jacobi themselves thought that the particle-wave duality shown in their mathematical equations was just an accidental freak of math, an anomaly. It could not be true.

The moral of this story is that if mathematics describes an aspect of physical, consensus reality that has not yet been discovered, this aspect will eventually appear. In other words, math is a fundamental form of physics. As we have seen, math describes both consensus and non-consensual realities, all of which are intertwined. If we continue along this line of thinking, we can see that physical reality is one aspect of a general unified reality implied by mathematics. This is no surprise because math, like other imaginings and formulas describing the world, emerges from our deepest experiences. As we have seen, math is a manifestation of how our perception unfolds from a unified world beyond duality, from the Tao that cannot be said. We would even be justified in calling mathematics the most fundamental of all sciences.

THE CHILD AND PHYSICIST

How we make theories is in a deep sense like child's play. Theory making is a matter of 1, 2, and 3, of lines, circles, and squares. It depends on the momentary dreams, experiences, and images of ourselves and the world around us. For example, if you ask a child who is about 3 years old to make a picture of herself, what will she draw? The first picture a child makes of herself looks like a circle with a face. There are no arms or hands, no legs or feet yet, just a big circle with eyes and a mouth.

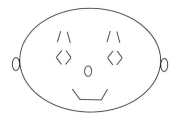

13.1 Child's theory of herself: no arms or legs

Such pictures are theories because the child has knowledge and experience of herself, and she is making a picture of her experience. Her theory says, "That's what I look like!" She draws her experience of herself, of eyes that see, of a mouth that eats, of a more or less symmetrical face.

What happened to her arms and legs, those four limbs we can see? Her theory, so to speak, marginalizes these limbs, in part because they are not yet part of her awareness, they are not under her control—not like her eyes, nose, and mouth. Only *we* think she has arms and legs, and indeed in CR she does. But in her reality, she is but a circle moving through life.

As the child grows older, she changes the picture. She now draws a body with arms and legs, and she adds a neck below her face. There are new aspects to her theory of herself.

13.2 More advanced picture theory

The body is not very big yet, and the legs and feet are very present, because those features correspond to the child's experience.

Theoretical physics does the same thing by making theories, not about people, but about matter. In the 1500s Leibniz thought that there was consciousness in matter. Like Leibniz, some people thought there was a soul in the particles. In a way, matter had a face and an inner life.

13.3 Picture of an elementary particle for Leibniz

Shortly thereafter, by the mid-1700s, that picture changed a bit: the soul was taken out of matter and reserved for people. European science reached a consensus that there was no soul in matter, since you could not measure it. This was the Renaissance theory of matter:

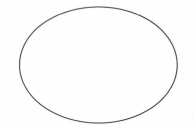

13.4 Renaissance picture of particles for Newton and others

The image of matter changed again near the turn of the twentieth century. The elementary particles that had lost their faces gained a nucleus and a few electrons that traveled around the outside of the circle.

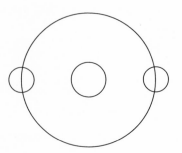

13.5 An atom, about 1900: nucleus with electrons moving around it

Today, again at the turn of a century, the view is that the atom can no longer be imagined as a circle with particles in it. In fact, it is like nothing we know in ordinary reality. Most physicists say it cannot be imagined at all. It is part of a network of relationships. The forces that hold it together are not even forces; they may be exchanges of ghostlike things. Some physicists visualize atoms as forming cloud-like patterns more or less located in a given area. The darkest area is most likely to have an atom or a subatomic particle in it.

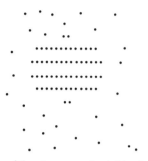

13.6 Imagination of the atom as an invisible cloud, 1925-2000

Scientists at the cutting edge of physics today say that these views are insufficient to describe the reality of matter. As we will explore over the next chapters, it seems as if particles have an elementary form of awareness. Physics will soon imagine the particle as a face again, giving us the impression that the spirit is returning to matter.

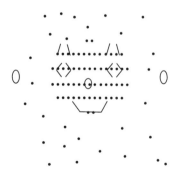

13.7 The consciousness of matter, 2010?

What will happen to our view in the year 2100? We might guess that it will return to being a circle again, an all-encompassing, godlike, NCR awareness. My guess is that awareness itself will be substance-like and will be understood as the essence of matter.

The one point of agreement, which has remained since 1550, is the theory that matter is composed of elementary, finite particles. Although these infinitesimal particles may be difficult to measure and imagine, and although it may even be theoretically incorrect to imagine them in CR because they cannot be tested, we still try to imagine them. The images we have resemble how we see ourselves; they look similar to the child's picture of herself.

The word "theory" comes from the Greek word "theos," for god, or "theoria," which means to speculate. Our images of our worlds and ourselves are speculations: they are religious belief systems. They are psychologically correct for those who believe in them because these beliefs describe not only outer events but also inner processes.

Theories are fragile. Theories express changing inner experiences that we find more or less validated by the CR reality of experimentation with matter. Theories are psychological. They describe how CR events are mirrored by inner experiences. Theories, especially in their mathematical formulation, marginalize phenomena that we are unable or not yet ready to observe.

Theories are not "objective" facts. At best, they are helpful explanations of the universe we experience. We go astray if we think of them as unchanging, objective CR facts unrelated to our own personal and cultural development.[1]

The problem, of course, is that because our theories match certain inner processes, we get attached and cannot let the theories go. Psychologists have the same problem. People who had painful early childhood experiences favor abuse, shock, and trauma theories; those who are searching for transcendence of everyday reality describe the world as if its social problems were not very important. Therapists coming from privileged backgrounds are rarely interested in large-group ethnic conflicts. All these theories are useful at one time or another. The problem occurs when we get attached to one theory and negate its interconnectedness with all the others.

OUR CURRENT IMAGE OF MATTER

As science has matured, its images of matter have changed. Today physicists believe that a quantum object like an electron can be observed at point A and later at point B, but that it cannot be observed in between without totally disturbing its course.

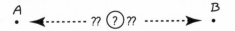

13.8 An electron moving through space, measured at A and B

The situation is something like dreaming. In the evening you go to sleep at point A, and in the morning you wake up at point B and remember the image of what we call a dream. We can observe you at A before you went to bed and at B, when you wake up, but where were you in between?

What do we mean when we say you were dreaming? What happened in the time between when you went to sleep at point A and when you woke up at point B? You can use the consensus term "dream," but that is only what you recall at point B—only what you can count or recount.

A　　　　　　　　　　　　　　　　　　　　　　*B*

13.9 You move through the night from A to B
and in the morning report at B on what happened.

By analogy, the electron is also in an altered state like dreaming until it is measured or "awakens" at point B through observation. We can take this analogy between people and particles further. Particles can be anyplace before they are measured, and people, too, can be anyplace, anytime they dream at night.

The future image of matter may reflect this theme of waking up and becoming conscious. When the electron is not measured or observed by a CR observer, it is as if the electron were dreaming. The physics of today cannot track the electron during its dreaming, but future physics may be able to if it expands to include psychology. Then physics will track the electron at all times with the help of sentient lucid dreamers.

13.10 2010-?: Image of matter connected to observation and
sentient, lucid awareness

THE SOUL IN TODAY'S PHYSICS

The Copenhagen interpretation of quantum mechanics (Bohr, Born, Heisenberg, and others) shared by most physicists today teaches that the world around us is a semi-material fog of probabilities, full of "tendencies for things to happen." Bohr suggested that to describe subatomic events, we need two consensus reality points of view, two measurements of special qualities of any material event. He called these two views "complementary." The complementarity principle says that, to understand the quantum world, we need two or more classical descriptions (classical means consensus reality) of the same event. For example, a particle upon measurement appears at one moment to be wavelike and, at another, to have particle-like characteristics. Both wave and particle are complementary descriptions of the same quantum object.

In this interpretation, quantum mechanics is a complete mathematical description of matter.[2] Together with this description goes a warning: do not discuss or even try to imagine the CR idea of "particle" between measurements. Discuss only what can be tested. What happened between measurements is not considered the realm of physics.

This last statement, which lies in the background of science and implies that you are not allowed to think of things you cannot test, is strongly debated by physicists such as David Bohm. However, if you met privately with the physicists who support the Copenhagen interpretation of physics, they might admit that they do not believe the official view. For example, Richard Feynman wrote (Feynman and others, 1965) that he believed in the Copenhagen approach to quantum theory. In private, however, he said that he didn't really think it was correct. Einstein also said he did not believe in Bohr's ideas.

The old split between Einstein and Bohr remains. Many physicists suspect that there is more to the material universe than is described in physics. Some admit to the possibility of a soul in matter. They suspect that the Renaissance marginalization of NCR processes was an error. In a way, they are going back to the three-year-old's original image of herself as a face with consciousness—without arms or legs, which give it self-motivated action.

Courageous physicists such as Stephen Hawking, Fred Alan Wolf, Roger Penrose, Amit Goswami, and many others are stepping out of the present frameworks, trying to find out how consciousness enters physics. For example, Goswami says that consciousness creates events.[3] Some neurophysiologists say the reverse—that consciousness emerges from matter. Other scientists suspect that if consciousness has an effect on matter, it must be separate from it.

The only thing we can say for certain is that we are standing at a border between a mechanical view of the world and a new view in which matter possesses sentient powers, not totally unlike human beings. This new view requires both CR facts and knowledge of the timeless universe. This emerging viewpoint must satisfy two constraints, the CR world of repeatable facts and figures and the NCR world of sentient psychology and spirituality. The budding trend in physics which sees matter as having something like a soul may well be paralleled by a more sentient psychology, leading to a philosophy of life, a new biology and Western medicine based on awareness in both everyday time and dreaming.

NOTES

1. Theorist Cushing warns about our tendency to formulate theories and facts. He quotes several "one and only" statements from Bohr, Einstein, and Heisenberg (*Quantum Mechanics* 1994, Chapter 3) showing how these men, and all of us, confuse our theories as facts in consensus reality.

2. Quantum mechanics is complete and expressed in terms of what are called state vectors, wave functions or probability amplitudes.

3. More precisely, Amit Goswami, in *The Self-Aware Universe,* says that consciousness creates events by collapsing the wave function. Other physicists such as Zukav, Capra, and Wolf have hinted at the same. The highly respected mathematical physicist John Neuman said, as early as 1932, that consciousness exists in quantum mechanics, yet no one knows exactly where.

14 | The Double Slit Experiment

Anyone who is not shocked by quantum theory has not understood it.

—Niels Bohr

In order to delve further into where consciousness enters physics, we are going to take a side road into the nature of quantum objects. Then we will return to our sentient psychology based on both everyday time and dreaming.

When physicists want to find out what matter is, they test a small piece of it. When you get down to things as small as elementary particles, isolating and studying them is difficult because they are too small to see even with high-powered microscopes. If you are dealing with electrons, you need to do new experiments with new equipment. You need an electron gun that emits electrons and a counter that clicks when the electrons hit a target. You can propel the electrons through a cloud chamber and see the tracks they leave, or you can count them when they hit a counter. But you never will see electrons directly.

In this chapter I want to discuss what happens to electrons when they zoom through tiny holes, because when we understand what happens to electrons under these conditions, we will be able to understand some of the deepest aspects of quantum mechanics. Then we shall be able to delve further into where consciousness enters physics.

THE DOUBLE SLIT EXPERIMENT

Let's think now about the double slit experiment, which shows us most clearly the nature of all quantum objects. Imagine an ordinary square room with a gate in the middle of it. Electrons will be shot from a gun through one or two openings in the gate. The electrons are propelled through the slits in the gate and hit a screen at the other end of the room.

An electron gun doesn't look like the guns we see in ordinary reality. It is basically a hot wire like the one you find in light bulbs. Our hot wire acts like a gun in the sense of shooting out electrons. We shoot them at a screen covered with electron counters. These counters are sensitive to electrical charge. The counters, which are placed all around the screen, make clicking sounds and record or count how many electrons land at a given point on the screen.

It turns out that how many slits are open affects the final appearance of the electrons at the screen. Let's begin with only one slit open in the gate.

Imagine shooting electrons through the gate with one slit in it. Pretend the other slit is closed (see Fig. 14.1). Furthermore, to make things easier, let's pretend I am an electron. I'm getting really hot where the gun (hot wire) is, and I can't wait to be ejected through the slit in the gate. The gun is heating me up and soon I'm going to have enough energy to shoot right through the slit in the gate in the center of the room and land on the screen.

Remember that there is only one door I can get through. The other door is closed. It's a very limited world, but it could be fun so I'm going to see what happens. I shoot across the room and hit the screen on the wall. I arrive at the screen at a particular point and am counted by an electron counter, which goes "click."

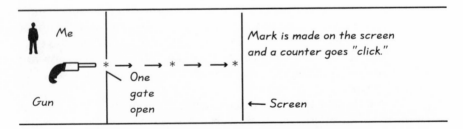

14.1 Room with gate on the left and screen on the right

To continue the experiment, you can heat up that gun and send more of my friends through the gate. After you're done shooting, what results will you find on the other side of the gate? You will find that we electrons behave more or less like a bunch of pebbles being thrown. In other words, my friends and I go through the slit, and most of the time we hit the screen in the center. Of course, there are times when some of us go further from the center of the screen, a few times we hit the screen still further out, and on rare occasions one of us hits the screen at the top or bottom (Fig. 14.2).

Most of the time, though, we hit the screen at its center, right in front of the open slit through which we passed. The result is that our pattern of dispersion creates a probability curve, which looks like a vertical bell, with a peak at the center.

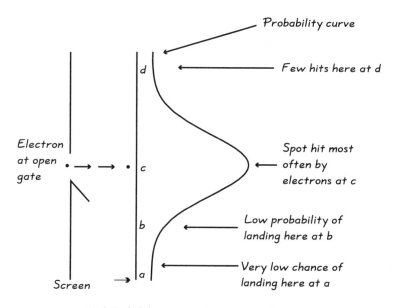

14.2 *Probability curve when one gate is open*

When physicists saw electrons moving through a single slit and producing this probability curve, they were happy. They said, "Well, electrons act like ordinary particles. They are like pebbles or paint spray. You spray the paint and it goes right through the slit, and on the other side you get more paint in the middle where we expect most paint particles to arrive." They saw fewer electrons, or less "paint" at the two edges of the screen. With one slit open, there are no blank spots, only varying dispersions.

Physicists said, "We expected the results we saw. Now let's see what happens if we are more generous to the electrons and open a second slit in the gate." Imagine the same room, but with two open slits in the gate. This time when my friends and I cross that unknown area between the open slit in the gate and the screen, we land on the screen in an unexpected way. We do not land as if we were two sprays of paint propelled through two slits to produce two bell-shaped curves.

No. Instead, at certain points on the screen, there are blanks—that is, almost no electrons are counted. Our bell-shaped probability curve changed into the regular wavy marks you see on the right side of the diagram below. What happened?

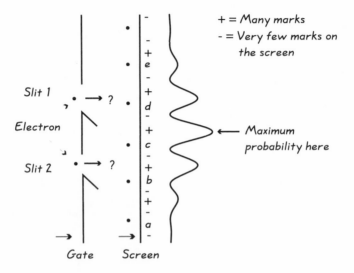

14.3 *Probability curve when two gates are open shows that electrons act like waves which cancel or interfere with one another.*

The new curve is very different. There are still more marks in the center than at any other point. However, at other points that would be covered with electrons when only one slit in the gate is open, there is almost nothing at all. There are lots of electron marks at the peaks of the curve, but next to these marks, where the minus signs are, not many electrons arrived. How could this have happened? Why is it that when there are two slits that give me and my electron friends two possibilities when we arrive at the screen, sometimes we don't land anyplace at all?

Scientists have been trying to figure out this yes/no pattern since the 1920s, and there are many ideas about it. One answer that students in my classes give to this question is, "Choices make electrons crazy!" Another is that electrons "want to stick together because they get lonely." These are great theories, but these and similar ideas are non-consensus explanations that are difficult to test. We cannot test whether electrons make choices or like to huddle together without communicating with them, which no one has done in a repeatable manner to date. This does not mean that electrons do not want to stick together, or that two choices do not make them crazier than one. Either possibility may be as close to the truth as anybody knows. We just cannot test these ideas.

Quantum objects like electrons live in their own world, which is normally inaccessible to us in consensus reality. If we try to track electrons, we disturb them so much that the picture we get is no longer what they would be doing on their own, undisturbed. The CR question of what exactly happens to an electron cannot be answered because of our observation. The very energy needed to look at electrons, the light beam we use to see them, bounces them to uncertain regions of the universe!

Thus we don't know exactly, in terms of time and space, what is going on between the electron gun and the screen. We only know where the electrons started and that they finally made a "click" at the screen. All we know is the result, which is the behavior of electrons at the screen. We know that this behavior depends on whether we open one or two slits. The results indicate that, for some unknown reason, the electrons behave as if they were waves when there are two slits present, but as particles when only one slit is open.

INTERFERENCE AND WAVE MECHANICS

Why do we say that the electrons behave like waves? Because their yes/no pattern on the screen is periodic. We all know what it means for things to be "periodic in time." They oscillate from day to night, from winter to spring to summer to fall. Periodic in space means wavelike, like waves in water. If we think of a wavy line, we see high crests and low troughs. The electrons' behavior on the screen after going through two slits seems periodic and reminds us of waves.

All waves have an interesting quality that scientists call interference. When two waves meet, they add where their high spots coincide and subtract or cancel in other places, where a high spot of one wave meets a low spot of another wave. This adding up and cancellation is called "interference." Intersecting waves of water, for example, get very big in some places and interfere with one another at other places, where they appear small.

In my imagination when the father of wave mechanics, Erwin Schroedinger, looked at the pattern of electrons on the screen, he said, "There is a yes/no type of behavior at the screen. That reminds me of the way known waves behave when two or more interact—they interfere with one another. We see these interferences happen in sound and water all the time. Let's call quantum mechanics 'wave mechanics.'" The electrons, like the known waves of sound or water, interfere with one another. They leave a yes/no pattern where they add to and subtract from one another.

You can test for interference in your kitchen sink or bathtub. Fill the sink with water. Wait until it settles down so that the surface is smooth, then let a drop of water from the faucet fall into the sink and watch the waves spread out in a concentric pattern. Now drop a second bit of water a few inches away from the first drop and watch its waves spread out from this second location. Finally, notice what happens in the middle of the water's surface when, at the same time, you drop two drops from different locations into your sink. The waves from the two locations merge in some places, making a bigger wave, and cancel or subtract in other places, making it look like no waves are present there. The result is a beautiful interweaving tapestry of criss-crossed waves. The pattern is due to interference.

Physicists theorized that electrons going through two slits must be "matter waves." Niels Bohr called them "probability waves." Heisenberg said that you cannot test or see the probability waves—all you can see is the wavelike appearance of quantum objects on a screen when they have two slits to go through. Therefore, we cannot call electrons or other quantum objects matter waves—or any waves at all—because we cannot see what is happening while the electrons are in flight. We only see the wavelike results on the screen. The most we can say is that these results could have been caused by waves. Undaunted, Schroedinger said that whether he could actually see the waves or not, he might as well use the basic formulas for the visible motion of water and sound to describe the invisible electron.

The resulting equation for quantum objects of all kinds was called the "wave equation," even though no one has ever been able to see the waves themselves. Physicists use wave equations because the math fits the resulting picture on the screen so well. The math matches the tracks left on the screen by electrons and has been very helpful in showing the patterns of all other subatomic particles under varying conditions. In other words, whether we call this branch of physics wave mechanics, quantum mechanics, or quantum physics, it has been quite successful at describing the patterns of subatomic particles.

The wave equation doesn't answer the question many have about the underlying reality of quantum objects. What are they after they leave the gun and before they appear on the screen? Some physicists still think that matter is some sort of vibration or wave pattern, while others hold to the more consensual concept of particles. Almost everyone agrees, however, that matter is composed of quantum objects that have both wavelike and particle-like characteristics, depending on the experiment done with them. Which aspect of matter appears, wave or particle, depends on the decision of the observer (i.e., to use one or two slits). We must remember that both "wave" and "particle" are consensus reality descriptions of an invisible world. Both descriptions together are considered "complementary"; both CR terms are needed to approximate the measurable qualities and quantities of matter.

FROM PHYSICS TO MATH

Physicists use math to symbolize the basic, underlying average patterns emerging from the interaction between quantum objects like electrons and the observer. The resulting mathematical formula is the general pattern governing what happens in any given event connecting observer and observed. We saw this concept early in our journey, when we discovered that numbers are a description of the interaction between the counter and the counted.

Let's pretend that electrons left another design on the screen. Instead of a periodic, wavelike appearance, let's imagine they left a pattern like the one below.

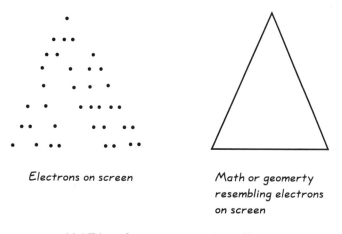

Electrons on screen

Math or geomerty
resembling electrons
on screen

14.4 Triangular pattern approximated by a triangle

If the results on the screen had been triangular, we would call the pattern a triangle because the triangle approximates the average pattern behind all the dots. Instead of wave mechanics, we would have triangle mechanics. The equations we would then use in quantum physics would be descriptive of triangles, not waves—even if physicists never saw a triangle flying through the air.

Some physicists, including Bohr, became upset about the invisibility of the wave equation. They warned fellow physicists, "Be careful, friends, get those wave images out of your heads. Math is only descriptive of the images we see on the screen and says nothing definitive about the electrons themselves while in flight. *You cannot discuss what you cannot test.* If you can't test it in midair, don't call it anything." Since the electron is always in midair, exactly what we mean by the term "electron" is a grand mystery.

DREAMS AND PARTICLES

The wave/particle description of matter observed in consensus reality and its mysterious, unknowable nature outside of CR are not as foreign to our understanding as we might think at first. Psychologists know this problem well; they must often face paradoxical experiences whose essence is unknown.

The invisible trajectory of particles through the slits closely resembles the path we experience in dreaming. In fact, the patterns of quantum objects are very much like the symbols of dreams. Consider this. The dream you remember in the morning is analogous to the tracks of electrons that are counted on the screen. The term "dream" is like the term "electron": both are CR terms for something essentially unknown, things that move through the night, so to speak, land on our memory screen, and get counted and recounted in terms of the images they produce.

Just as the description of events on the screen is not necessarily the same as the events occurring before observation, the images and feelings you report from dreaming are not really equivalent to the dreaming process itself. Dreaming is barely verbalizable. It is an unknown you can only sentiently experience.

Wave functions are codes that pattern the behavior of electrons on the screen, in the same way that dream symbols, when amplified, describe our behavior in everyday reality. Just as wave functions are symbolic of what happens to the electron when it is not yet observed, we might say that dream symbols are formulas of the quality of dreaming before waking up.

The wave function in physics turns out to be a complex number because these numbers are the best for describing wavelike, periodic phenomena.[1] Complex numbers, as we remember from Chapter 8, have both real and imaginary aspects and cannot be measured directly. The same is true of dreams: they contain both CR solutions of everyday problems and also NCR experiences—emotions with unconscious, spiritual, romantic, and ghostlike qualities. Like quantum objects, dreaming cannot be directly measured. Thus both wave functions and dream symbols describe the non-consensus domains that I have been referring to as NCR experience.

An interesting aspect of the wave function of quantum objects is that it predicts that quantum objects such as our electrons, before being observed, can be anyplace in the world. Their complex numbers may refer to any place, any time in consensus reality. Likewise, in dreaming you can be at any place or time in the real world as well.

Wave functions describing matter are considered by physicists to be the most fundamental description of matter. Many who work with dreams and dreamlike processes assume the same—that dreams contain the keys to human behavior.

INTERFERENCE AND PSYCHOLOGY

Other connections between dreams and particles can be understood by examining interference in psychology. Interference, that is, the periodic amplification or cancellation of experience, is a well-known psychological principle.

Let's think about children for a moment. Take just about any child on the way to the school. Let's say that the school is analogous to the screen in our electron experiment. If a child can get to school by only one route, chances are good she will go that way. But if you give your child two ways to go to school, what happens? She may never get there! Why? Because she cannot decide, and may get distracted. What does distracted mean? What do we mean by "she can't decide?"

Psychological interference happens when two different internal processes happen simultaneously. You have likely seen interference in yourself and your friends. When you have two processes going on at the same time, you look like a kid on the way to school. Given one choice, the kid goes that way. Given two, he may blank out altogether and do nothing. That blanking out is due to the interference of two processes.

Here is another simple example of psychological interference. Imagine that we are sitting in a restaurant engaging in conversation while waiting for our lunch. I am starving. I do not intentionally want my hunger to interfere with our chat, but I cannot help myself if it does. My stomach is growling about hunger. I try to ignore it and concentrate on our conversation, but I can't listen well. My stomach is also talking to me, saying it wants lunch. In CR, I try to act like I am listening to you, but I am distracted by my stomach's signals.

The result? At certain moments there is nothing on the screen—my face looks blank. You think I am "absentminded." I don't really listen to you, and you become uncomfortable talking to me, sensing that I'm not really there. I don't know what I am saying or thinking. I don't quite notice that my hunger interferes with the process of talking.

Wavelike interference in physics is analogous to what we call "blanking out" in colloquial speech, or "incongruence" in psychological terms. Just as the particle has two possible slits through which it can pass, we can have two processes occurring simultaneously. We usually identify with one opening or slit, which we call our conscious mind, for example, my interest in conversing. The other slit refers to unintentional processes like my stomach's hunger.

These unintentional processes interfere, sometimes producing blanking out while at other times producing great energy and happiness, especially when the conversation turns to food! Then the intentional chat becomes congruent with the unintentional stomach signals, and my processes add themselves together, producing a huge wave of enthusi-asm. All the parts of me finally say, "It's time to eat!"

Nature might perhaps operate in the same manner. Perhaps electrons going through two slits become "incongruent." They cancel each other; they "blank out." Given the possibility of two processes, two slits, they become confused and incongruent.

One of the main goals of therapy is to help our two processes become more congruent, to harmonize with one another. But this goal can never be permanently reached, because as soon as we become congruent, another unintentional process appears from somewhere and we experi-ence absentmindedness again. Interference is as basic to human nature as it is to quantum objects.

We see interference in our dreams whenever two or more figures are in conflict or harmony. Just as wave functions are capable of describing no interference on the screen when one slit is open and interference from quantum objects when two slits are open, so dreams can describe two dif-ferent figures or processes as friends or enemies, that is, adding to one another or canceling one another out.

Of course, there are also times when we are one slit, one process—con-gruent beings, so to speak. During these periods we are simpler, one-pointed individuals. We are less in conflict and have one simple process. We eat when we are hungry and sleep when we are tired. There is, momentarily, only one congruent process occurring. This congruency may occur by itself or through inner work connecting us to our dreaming process.

In any case, if we use the analogy of experiments with quantum objects, the process of dreaming can be like the single or double slit exper-iment. When we are a single slit, we have a simple, singular process. In the situation of the double slit we are incongruent and experience inter-ference and blanking out.

A fascinating characteristic of quantum objects is that the decision about which experiment to make, using one or two slits, influences the final outcome, which is particle-like or wavelike. The appearance of mat-ter depends on the human decision to make one kind of experiment ver-sus another. Whether we see waves or particles depends on our focus!

Dreams, too, are known to depend strongly on the focus of the "observer." Dreamers who are in tune with their inner life experience a minimum of interference, or blanking out. When we are congruent, and also interested in dreaming, we can see an unbelievable array of dazzling relationships and attempted harmonies in our dreams. The observer is crucial in the outcome of events in both quantum and dreaming realms.

COLLAPSE OF THE WAVE FUNCTION AND WAKING UP

At this point, we are reaching an exciting connection between quantum objects, such as electrons, and dreaming. We will explore this connection further in the next chapter, but for now, let's think about the following.

Dreaming is analogous to the invisible period when quantum objects are not being observed. In a dream, your presence can be anyplace at any time. However, when you are waking up, the awareness of your waking mind lands you in one spot in space and time. No one knows exactly how this "collapse" into a particular spot on earth takes place. Just as there is no theory explaining how you wake up in one spot, there is no agreement in physics as to how observation "collapses the wave function" so that a quantum object appears more or less located in one particular spot.[2]

As we have seen, the mathematics of wave functions describes the images quantum objects make when observed and recorded on the screen. The equations for wavelike phenomena use complex numbers because these numbers (discussed in Chapters 7 and 8) simplify calculations. We have also seen that the wave function—like dreaming—cannot be measured directly. It is a general pattern for events happening in non-consensus realities. To get from the domain of quantum objects before they are observed to the observation of an electron on the screen, that is, from electrons which can be at any time or place, to observed electrons on a counter, mathematics mechanically "collapses" the wave function through conjugation.

We discovered earlier that conjugation is the mathematics corresponding to observation. Conjugation takes the wave function, which has the form of a complex number $(a + ib)$ and multiplies it by its reflection $(a - ib)$. Conjugation generates real numbers $(a^2 + b^2)$. Physics interprets these real numbers as the probability of finding a quantum object at a particular point on the screen.

Conjugation of the wave function is the necessary mathematics for describing observation, the transition between an invisible particle in complex number space to a real particle and countable number in classical, consensus reality.[3] Conjugation "collapses" the wave function in the sense of enabling a particle that is anywhere before observation to collapse into being at a particular spot. Physicists know they need to "conjugate" but have not been able to explain why this mathematics gives the correct answers in consensus, physical reality. This is why I have said that physics is like a house without a foundation.

Thus far, we know that the process of conjugation, which involves the multiplication of a complex number by its reflection, is analogous to the process of lucid dreaming, and of awakening. Dreaming is comparable to a complex number with real and imaginary characteristics. Lucid dreaming mirrors dreaming. When lucid dreaming is applied to dreaming, the two "conjugate," and the linked processes generate insights and awakenings, as well as signals and unconscious expressions which can be observed in everyday life.[4]

In other words, dreaming is sentient experience that underlies our consensus observations of reality, of matter. The collapse of the wave function in physics is analogous to the process of awakening in psychology. The core of observation in physics and of waking reality in psychology is unfolding or reflecting an invisible experience. We have seen that, in mathematics, conjugation refers to multiplying a complex number by its reflection. In psychology conjugation is the pattern of conjoining dreaming and its reflection, lucid dreaming, thereby generating consensus reality and everyday consciousness.

Until now, physics has been unable to give significance to the process of conjugation because of its imaginary numbers. It has simply been known that conjugation produced real values and was very useful in calculating real events.

Many physicists have suspected a new or missing principle involved in the mathematics representing observation, a principle that would explain how the math of conjugation works. I would like to suggest the following additional principle required by quantum mechanics to explain what happens on observation, in the collapse of the wave function. This new principle is *the tendency for nature to reflect upon herself*, to be aware, to lucidly notice otherwise invisible events. Nature is a lucid dreamer, a generator of everyday reality. In other words, what we call an observation is a manifestation of an unconscious tendency in us, a tendency in which nature is trying to look at herself.

There are so many analogies between dreaming and wave functions that it is tempting to equate the two as reflections of the same basic nonconsensus, underlying experience of reality. The NCR process of dreaming seems to be an expression of that one, non-dualistic world, the domain from which complex numbers arise.

We can use sentient experience, that is, dreaming, to understand aspects of complex numbers, and vice versa. Both dreaming and complex numbers give us insights into the one world, the invisible or unspeakable in quantum mechanics and in psychology.

The reflections we find in the math of quantum physics have analogies in psychology in the reflective tendency of human nature to pay attention to certain things, to reflect upon them. These reflections in the math of quantum physics seem to point to self-reflection and lucidity in nature herself, which generates reality from deep feelings, hunches, and dreams—that is, from sentient experience.

NOTES

1. See the next note for the mathematics of the electron's non-locality before observation.

2. The general equation or pattern for the particle relates the tendency of its being found at a position x at a certain time, t. If we call this tendency the wave function then Ψ depends on or is a function of x and t.

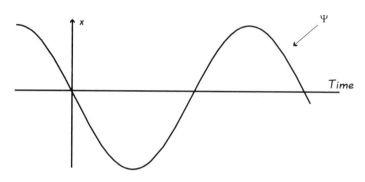

14.5 A wave pattern

Since the dependency is sometimes wavelike, we can use a general wave equation. The most general one has the form

$$\frac{\partial^2 \Psi}{\partial x^2} = k\frac{\partial^2 \Psi}{\partial t^2}$$

which simply says that Ψ, the tendency to be at point x on the screen at time t, depends on x and t in a periodic manner. (Thanks to Leibniz and Newton for creating calculus and differentials!)

The wave equation in quantum mechanics is called a partial differential equation and can be written for one particle, in one dimension as

$$-\frac{h^2}{2m}\frac{\partial^2 \Psi}{\partial x^2} = ih\frac{\partial \Psi}{\partial t}$$

The wave equation for one particle with no external forces.

One of the solutions to the wave equation can be written as

$$\Psi = A e^{i(\omega t - kx)}$$

or any addition or superposition of these Ψ's. Notice the imaginary number i in the above. Hence, Ψ is a complex number. The reader will remember this solution from Chapter 8, on complex numbers, which can be used to represent harmonics, and music. (Complex math is the mathematics of choice for systems with oscillations because of the ease with which such movements can be calculated and expressed.) See Chapter 8, notes 2 and 3.

In any case, the wave function Ψ has a wavelike solution, which can be generally written by the exponential form

$$A e^{i(\omega t - kx)}$$

Exponentials make differential equations very simple. If you put them in, the complicated-looking equation becomes algebraic, since the differential of an exponential function simply brings down the exponent as a simple multiplier:

$$\frac{d}{dt} e^{i\omega t} = i\omega e^{i\omega t}$$

The second derivative does the same thing, it brings down another $i\omega$. Thus, differentiation of exponentials turns out to be multiplication.

In the case of quantum mechanics, the ω is the frequency of the wave connected to a classical energy idea, $E = h\omega$ (h is Planck's constant and $h = 2\Pi h$). A wave number, k, describes the momentum or push of the electron, by $p = hk$. If we knew the exact wave number k, we would know the momentum of a quantum object.

A fascinating aspect of the wave equation, which is sometimes called the amplitude, is that the absolute square of Ψ can be gotten by conjugating and gives the probability of finding a particle at point x and time t.

Notice that the wave function for an electron without any external forces says that it is equally likely to be found anywhere in the universe! That means we are uncertain before measurement about where the particle is. The absolute value, however, gets rid of the imaginary factors. Thus the probability f for the particle does not vary with time or space. The particle has a definite energy. That is why we sometimes say that an atom in a definite energy level is in a stationary state.

The quantum wave function and quantum mechanics are described in greater detail in the Appendix.

3.   The mathematical expression for the results of conjugation is the absolute real value of a complex number. Physics interprets this number as representing the probability of finding the particle at a certain point on the screen.

4.   See Chapter 8.

15 | Conjugation and Dreamtime

An independent reality in the ordinary sense can be ascribed neither to the phenomena nor to the agencies of observation.

—Niels Bohr, in *Atomic Theory and the Description of Nature*

Questions that have plagued physics since the discovery of quantum mechanics in the 1920s are still with us today. Does it make sense to even speak of an electron or its path if the electron cannot be measured without disturbance? How does an electron whose track we cannot follow turn into a measured click from an electron counter? How does an electron move across an unknown region, dematerialize, so to speak, and appear again as an electron when measured by an electron counter?

These questions may not be answerable in the terms of physics because physics cannot track the "electron" during its mysterious flights. Until now, psychology has been the "science" responsible for understanding this invisible area of life. By studying psychology, we can get a hint about how to understand the physics of non-consensual, untestable processes. Through exploring principles of psychology, we will be able to investigate the acts of perception that underlie quantum mechanics and the mysterious collapse of the wave function.

TRACKING AND UNFOLDING

Psychology and medicine must deal with invisible processes that are exceedingly real for people. Let's think together about headaches. We know that a headache involves the head. We know it often begins with a sensation of tension. We know how to suppress the pain it causes. Yet, it is very difficult to define what this pain is, and even more difficult to measure it, although pain is often much too real when you feel it. Pain is an NCR phenomenon.

Many years of working with psychosomatic effects such as headaches has taught me that if and when the experience of the headache is tracked sentiently, it often disappears. To track an NCR process such as a headache, you need to be patient and use your attention. Since most of us are trained to pay attention only to the signals that are considered meaningful for consensus reality, such NCR tracking is rare. For example, when I told my students I had a headache, most people listened to my words but did not notice what my body was doing when I mentioned my pain. They heard what I said, but did not notice the grinding of my jaws when I spoke about how the headache felt. The jaw signal had no immediate consensus reality meaning.

When I spoke about the headache, my body signaled subtle messages about the headache, messages the students were not used to looking for. As I mentioned the headache, I unwittingly tensed the muscles in the back of my neck, slightly drawing my head in while crunching my jaws together.

These body processes were aspects of my headache, yet they are likely to go unnoticed because there is no consensus about the significance and meaning of these signals. There is no standard meaning for tightening the muscles in the back of my neck, or crunching my jaws together. Other signals, such as smiling, formulating words, and shaking hands, are CR signals. They have given cultural meanings, which vary depending on the community and region of the world.

To track a headache, you have to pay attention to subtle signals. I once tracked a headache during one of my classes. I began by noticing my tendency to crunch my teeth together, tighten my neck, and so forth. By paying attention, I experienced these things more fully. When I tracked my headache, it evolved, turning into sensations beyond words... a surging stream moving up through the top of my head into the air, which, in my inner vision, seemed like a geyser. I laughed when I suddenly realized that the headache's streaming geyser represented my excitement, my "outpouring" about my work. I jumped in the air with enthusiasm about what I was teaching, and as soon as I let out my enthusiasm, my headache disappeared.

WHERE PSYCHOLOGY, MATH, AND PHYSICS MEET

Between the beginning and end states of having a headache was an NCR process appearing as a tightening of the neck and grinding of the teeth. The beginning and end states of the headache experience are CR states, analogous to the beginning state of the electron leaving the gun and its final measurement at the screen. In physics, however, there is no known method of following the electron's flight through the space of complex numbers that describe its existence between CR states.

The idea of unfolding processes in the NCR domain is likely to be foreign to the physicist or layperson who has never tracked herself in this manner. Let's explore tracking or "unfolding" processes in greater detail to elucidate the process.

In all types of observation, you can marginalize certain experiences. We have seen this in what we have already explored in mathematics. Counting one event can discount other aspects of that event. This kind of counting is like asking yourself what a headache is in consensus reality. When you do this, you count what can be counted in CR, but you are in danger of marginalizing NCR experiences.

Another method of marginalizing experience occurs when you start thinking about the meaning of a fantasy while in the midst of fantasizing. Thinking about it stops the fantasy. This state of affairs is similar to physics. If you try to measure the state of an electron while it is in flight, the electron behaves like a CR concept, with either wavelike or particle-like characteristics.

Following processes through the NCR domain without stopping them or transforming them into CR events involves a special tracking ability that does not marginalize signals because their meaning is unknown. In the example of my headache, if we skip the tracking process, we neglect the NCR or imaginary quality of the muscles and streaming experience and guess, instead, at its probable significance or cause. We might say, for example, that headaches come from psychological tension, and try to relax.

However, if we track a process like my headache, we follow NCR processes such as the geyser and come up with insights. In my case, the headache was due to a blocking of my enthusiasm. The mathematical analogy to this unfolding headache would be to follow the NCR processes through the domain of imaginary numbers until they generate a real number result. I have referred to this generative process mathematically as conjugation. Figure 15.1 summarizes analogous processes in the sciences.

STAGES OF UNFOLDING SENTIENT EXPERIENCE INTO REALITY

NCR ⟶	*NCR* ⟶	*CR*
I. Conjugating ⟶	*II. Tracking* ⟶	*III. CR Reality*

IN PSYCHOLOGY: Unfolding non-consensus experience generates everyday reality. For example:

(Headache) (Reflection) Noticing a headache reflects ⟶	unfolds NCR and generates experiences which result in ⟶	CR observable change and insights

IN MATHEMATICS: Conjugating a complex number results in real numbers. For example:

$(a + ib)(a - ib)$ =	$a^2 - iab + iab + b^2$ =	$a^2 + b^2$
Complex conjugates with imaginary numbers	when multiplied, result in	real numbers because $i^2 = -1$ and because $+ iab - iab = 0$

IN PHYSICS: Observing a quantum object marginalizes imaginary numbers and leaves us with a real number result, an "observation."

Intention to observe a quantum state ⟶	generates and collapses the wave function, creating an ⟶	Observation or CR measurement on the screen

15.1 Unfolding sentient experience into reality

Notice that the intention to observe something in physics is an NCR process that requires the patterns of math and psychology to understand. Furthermore, the unfolding process in math results in a canceling out of imaginary numbers in the CR result. In fact, this process is called taking the "absolute" or real value of a number which means valuing only its measurable quality.[1]

It is also interesting to notice that tracking NCR experiences in psychology moves through stages I and II. This allows NCR experiences to generate themselves through lucid reflection. However, we can also ignore the unfolding of processes, that is, we can ignore stage II and focus only on the CR result by asking questions that relate to consensus reality. For example, the answers to questions such as "Why do you have a headache?" or "When did the headache begin?" easily marginalize the tracking process.

NCR aspects of a headache such as its pain are like the NCR aspects of quantum objects like electrons; you can notice their effects but cannot see their path if you use your ordinary measuring apparatus. Nevertheless, although the electron's path may be an enigma, an electron counter makes a click when the electron arrives, just as your sense of pain occurs when a headache is around. Everyone consents to the concepts of pain and clicks. But we should not fool ourselves into thinking that an electron is only a particle or that a headache is only a psychological tension. These are purely consensus reality terms. Greater understanding of both can be had only through tracking NCR experiences.

CONJUGATION AND MARRIAGE

The term conjugating means uniting things, for example, fusing cells or individuals for reproduction in biology. "Conjugal" is often used in connection with marriage. These uses of this term are related to its core sense, which means bringing two partners together.

The mathematical process of conjugation summarized in Figure 15.1 requires us to couple one complex number with its conjugate, or "spouse." Remember that the first part of a complex number $(a + ib)$ represents the NCR experience (or quantum object), while the second part or "partner" $(a - ib)$ mirrors the first. Conjugation marries an experience with its reflection.

The idea of "marriage" is important here because we rarely marry our experiences—that is, we usually do not notice them, much less reflect or love them. Most of the time, we want to ignore experiences that seem odd to us. The conjugate or mirror of our experiences, on the other hand, reflects them with a positive attitude. Instead of ignoring sentient, NCR experiences, conjugation reflects and tracks them.

CONJUGATION AND THE SECOND ATTENTION

Castaneda's shaman, don Juan, calls this kind of attention to subtle, sentient, generally unrecognized NCR experiences "second attention." Second attention is the skill we need to allow sentient experience to unfold. The first attention is our focus on everyday, CR, observable experiences, that is, "reality." The second attention involves interest in and compassion for NCR experiences. We need this special awareness to hold NCR experiences in our focus and allow them to unfold, even when we do not know their meaning. To conjugate unknown processes, some combination of belief, respect, ruthlessness, courage, and cuddling is necessary. These feelings are different from the ones needed for ordinary meditation procedures that simply notice experiences.

Conventional education trains our first attention, which adapts us to a given consensus reality. We are taught to ignore our second attention, which is attuned to socially marginalized experiences such as somatic sensations, flickering fantasies, and moods. The first attention is related to consensual events, to time and space, and the second to generally unrecognized feelings and intuitions.

Physics is a master of the first attention, favoring testable, consented-on terms and results. Clinical psychology and shamanism have been the areas that focus on NCR experiences. The training of traditional shaman warriors depends on developing the second attention for the purposes of healing, telepathic communication, and creating community through sharing spiritual experience.

Processes unfold themselves and generate solutions if and when some form of the second attention is used. In the same manner, lucid dreaming unfolds dreamlike phenomena. Lucid dreaming, that is, the intention to reflect on an experience, can be voluntary or involuntary. We can choose to be lucid and reflect on our experience, or reflection can happen automatically, without our having been aware of even doing it. Normally, we are aware of wanting to reflect on something. But frequently, reflection happens to us. We don't "do" it consciously.

In the same manner, we think we observe something, but if we have practiced meditation or have worked with our perceptions, we can catch ourselves intending to observe something before we even turn toward it. In a way, it is as if a piece of nature operates in us, choosing to observe something, causing us to want to observe it.

Many biological and psychological processes occur automatically, like conjugation. Our body reflects on itself. By having feedback signals, the body has a dreamlike NCR ability to be self-correcting. Pantanjali, one of the earliest yoga masters, said, "Yoga teaches yoga." A core statement in Eriksonian hypnosis is, "Your unconscious mind will solve your problems without any help from your conscious mind." These suggestions indicate that the sense of conjugation, that is, of reflecting, conjoining, or paying attention to dreaming, may occur automatically as well as voluntarily.

We can explore conjugating with awareness in many simple ways. When you slip and do something that seems foolish to you, instead of hating yourself for the error, try honoring the unknown in your nature that made the "mistake." Love and encourage the mistake to unfold further. If a friend says one thing but does another, encourage her to befriend the "other." The attitude of the second attention will inhibit you from criticizing your own and others' "unconsciousness" and encourage you instead to enter into it more deeply. Instead of neglecting body symptoms and accidents, welcome them! If you climb aboard such energies, life is richer for all. Help create and unfold symptoms; don't just experience them in a non-lucid manner. When dreams befuddle you, immerse yourself in the dreaming process.

The mathematics of quantum mechanics gives us the subtle details of how the unfolding of NCR processes through the act of conjugation takes place. When I have a headache and use my attention to enable the process to generate itself, I value experiences by holding a generous and positive mirror to them.

I would like to suggest that the mathematics of physics, which depends on conjugation, describes how real, observable reality is created through the collapses of the wave function in the same way that our second attention generates results "realizable" in CR by tracking NCR processes. In Figure 15.1, the state of the electron is unfolded through the reflection in the mind of the observer. The electron appears as a CR phenomenon that can be measured, *because of* the normally marginalized, non-consensual, reflective interaction with the observer.[2] When the non-consensual, reflective interaction with the observer is marginalized (and normally it is), the electron does not appear as a CR phenomenon that can be measured.

The electron becomes a measurable, CR phenomenon at the screen in terms of real numbers and probabilities, whereas in its unobserved state it is dreamlike. In this state it cannot be observed, but it can be sentiently experienced.

Uncertainty in the CR definition or state of the electron is due in part to a one-dimensional CR focus on its appearance at a counter. There will always be an uncertainty in all our CR measurements because as observers, we marginalize the sentient relationship or reflective process behind observation. From the viewpoint of non-consensual realty, without reflective processes, CR measurements could not be made. Because our normal state of consciousness marginalizes sentient, reflective processes, we become uncertain about the nature of reality.

In conjugating, our attention surfs the NCR process and "co-creates" the electron, so to speak. The important point is that reality rests on interactions between the observer and the observed at levels of experience we do not always normally notice.

Psychologically speaking, focusing on the real number resulting from conjugation is just as important as focusing on conjugating. The process of conjugation and the final result are simply two phases of how reality is created. By asking CR questions about the body, for example, you can discover its chemistry and discuss diet, heredity, and so forth. You can get interesting information without pressing anyone to use their second attention. You leave people on firm land and do not enter terra incognito. CR questions allow you to arrive at the screen in the double slit experiment without tracking the mystery. Conjugation, however, follows processes through unknown, almost unspeakable territory. It is different from the psychological technique of mirroring in which an act is simply repeated. Through conjugating, we experience the unspeakable on its own terms—we enter the dreaming world between the electron gun and the counter.

ELECTRONS IN DREAMTIME

Many people believe that little pieces of firm matter, such as elementary particles, are the basis of reality and physics. But in the areas we have been exploring, the basic substance of the universe (according to the mathematical formalism of quantum mechanics and the interpretation of *Quantum Mind*) is sentient experience—subtle experience and our tendency to observe and reflect it. Remember Pauli's inner teacher, who said about the imaginary number *i*, "it is the marriage and it is at the same time the realm of the middle, which you can never reach alone but only in pairs."

Through pairing, through the relationship to the fundamental sentient, dreamtime aspect of matter, to the realm symbolized by complex numbers, we participate in what Pauli's teacher calls the "realm of the middle," which is flux, process, the indivisible "atom." Pauli said, "The ring with the *i* is the unity beyond particle and wave and at the same time the operation that generates either of these." His teacher responded, "It is the atom, the indivisible..."[3]

I like to use the Australian Aboriginal term, "dreamtime," to describe electrons in their NCR phases, when they are not being measured. Dreamtime connotes sentient experience of process, in contrast to measurable experience. Dreamtime becomes particle-like when recalled and observed in CR. Aboriginal myths say that the foundation of reality is dreamtime. This dreamtime is the most elementary constituent of our universe, the mysterious psychophysical Tao that cannot be said. Dreamtime generates itself to create consensus reality, our everyday world.

For example, "geyser" is a dreamtime name for experiences unfolding into everyday reality as my headache. Likewise, the NCR reality of the wave function is dreamtime. Dreamtime is the basic reality for many peoples of the world. It is the sounds of the wind, the roar of the surf, the silence in the mountains. Dreamtime was once honored as the greatest of all spiritual deities, the creator of life and death. Calling this realm dreamtime, instead of naming it the NCR experience of an electron or a headache, is an attempt to honor nature.

EXERCISE: CONJUGATING DREAMTIME

If you would like to experiment more with this idea of conjugating dreamtime, try the following experiment.

1. **Choose a particular somatic experience you'd like to know more about.**

2. **What is your CR explanation of that body experience?** For example if you have a stomachache, you might explain it in various ways: "I ate too much for breakfast," "I am a tense person," "My mother had a

touchy stomach," and so on. These descriptions are analogous to the mathematical focus only on the real numbers. The CR explanation ignores the background of conjugation.

3. **Now use your special, second attention.** Value sentient, subtle experience and notice or conjugate the experience. If you are working alone, notice an irrational aspect of the somatic process. Use your second attention, value the experience, and let it unfold.

    Just follow the process. If and when it gets irrational, check on your edges, your barriers to further unfolding. Are you at the edge of getting into the process, examining its unusual content, or letting the process arrive in CR? Whatever your edges are, gently go back and check, allowing the process to unfold to completion.

    Perhaps you will have feelings, see pictures, or make small movements. Perhaps you will hear sounds. Just follow these irrational things until they seem to come to their own conclusion. Be patient, and take your time. If you get stuck with a body experience, make a picture out of it.

4. **Now compare your NCR tracking experience and its explanation of your body condition with your CR explanation.** What did your "real number," that is, your CR explanation, leave out, if anything?

DEMONSTRATION

The following demonstration is a verbatim transcription from one of my classes about conjugating dreamtime. It may help make the example of how to unfold a body experience more clear.

Arny: I will try to demonstrate this experiment with someone. Dawn, your hand is up. What sort of body experience would you choose to work on given a chance?

Dawn: [Stands up in a meditative posture and speaks] In the moment my eyes are so heavy, I would choose that... My eyes can hardly keep open... they feel sort of like... [Closing her eyes]

Arny: Can you explain your heavy eyes?

Dawn: Well, they are probably heavy because I haven't been sleeping much recently [laughs].

Arny: Yeah! That's a really good reason! If you don't sleep much at night then you're normally tired in the daytime. That would be a fine explanation and the recommendation would be to sleep more! Would you like to know more about that energy of closing your eyes? Would you be interested in conjugating this experience?

Dawn: Yes. How do I focus on that? It's not just my eyes that are heavy, but my whole body could just drop.

Arny: [To the rest of the class] I will reflect what Dawn is doing, by simple comments. I notice her dropping down. [The class makes room in the middle for Dawn to unfold her experience.] I see you dropping, this body experience, dropping down.

[At this point, I mirrored her body language and experience. I too began to feel into her situation, and felt heavy. I half-closed my eyes and, empathizing and mirroring Dawn's experience, began to sink slowly to the floor.]

Dawn: You want me to go into this falling sensation more?

Arny: I have no idea. Follow your process. [I said very little, but just went into the "heaviness" process. Suddenly Dawn dropped to the floor, and just as spontaneously sat up.]

Dawn: [After a pause, with a smile on her face] Ummmm that falling is good!

[Dawn started to stand, then collapsed, got up and seemed to enjoy falling to the floor again. After a few moments she mumbled that she felt like her energy was moving her about in a relaxed manner, doing whatever it felt liked. She continued to roll about.]

Dawn: …not stopping at anything anymore… wow, this is awesome, it feels great! It feels like being open to whatever happens and just letting it take you instead of always holding back. I got an idea, I got the idea! Living life like that for me would be wonderful. Yeah! Like letting go and going with things…

Arny: [To the class] Dawn said her eyes were going down because she's tired, because she hasn't slept. That is the CR explanation of her body experience. But conjugating the process brings out other aspects of what appears to be tiredness, namely, just letting go and no longer trying to control or organize life.

Dawn: Yeah, I am tired of trying to organize everything. No more energy for that!

This demonstration shows us what happens when we conjugate dreamtime. When we focus only on the CR aspects of life, we miss dreamtime and that mysterious pulse of life that makes existence worth living. Focusing only on CR marginalizes a big part of who you are. Connecting to NCR processes is a sniff of dreamtime, a meaningful experience whose details can hardly be shared with others.

If you notice NCR processes and conjugate them, you heal a deep wound created hundreds of years ago when NCR experiences and altered states of consciousness were marginalized. You become partners, or lovers, with dreamtime, with your dreaming body and the dreaming world. And you get a sentient hint about what the math behind quantum mechanics is about.

NOTES

1. Conjugation of $a + ib$ creates a real number, $a^2 + b^2$. Let's call this number $a^2 + b^2 = c^2$. The pictorial form of this equation can be seen in the diagram below.

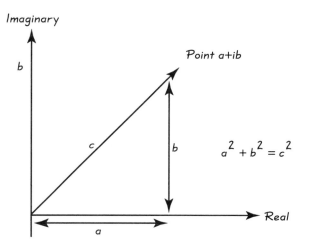

15.2 Finding the absolute square of $a + ib$

2. The mathematical processes of arriving at a real number can be understood by considering one particular real number, let's say, 12. To get to the number 12, we can multiply 3×4 or 2×6, or add $6 + 6$, and so forth. Each method of getting to 12 is different.

    The number 12 is a specific number, unlike a general number such as $a^2 + b^2$. The number 12 can be understood as a fact or measurement unto itself, or it can be understood as having evolved from the complex conjugation or unfolding process where all the imaginary numbers 'i' are involved, or it can be understood simply as the result of applying the formula for the absolute square.

    Thus $a^2 + b^2$ can be seen simply as a real number, or it can be understood as the result of having been unfolded using complex numbers. If it is understood as simply real, the imaginary, non-consensus process unfolded by using the second attention is hidden. This is like saying that a stone appears real and hard because we marginalized all the sensations we have about that stone, such as its aura or beauty. When unfolded, the total result in CR is that the stone is simply being hard.

    The real number is what CR measuring instruments can account for. But the process of arriving at a measurement can be completed in one of two ways. If it is experienced and followed with attention, we "conjugate." Or it can be found simply by marginalizing the imaginary path.

3. This transcript is from Fred Wolf's *The Dreaming Universe*, page 294. See discussion in Chapter 9 of this quote.

16 | Uncertainty and Relationships

If you want your children to be brilliant, tell them fairy tales.

—Albert Einstein

At this point, we have seen that the mathematics of quantum physics reveals the patterns behind psychological and spiritual methods of unfolding dreamtime. Since the beginning of history, the job of tracking events in dreamtime has belonged to the shamans. To conjugate, they stepped through the veil of consensus reality, culture, language, and personal identity to experience sentient, barely verbalizable realities, and to take their experiences back to this world in order to transform everyday life. Once outside of time and space, the shaman is free to do uncanny things such as turning up in two places at one time, moving backward and forward in time, and developing the telepathic ability to guess the future. Today, physicists believe that particles can do almost the same.

By exploring this sentient world and discussing how uncertainty arises in physics, we shall discover some of the central connections between physics and relationships.

MELUSINA AND THE MAN WHO DOUBTED HER

Developing the second attention for NCR events seems so central to life that we should expect to find this awareness suggested by the tales and stories passed down by our ancestors. There are many myths and stories about dreamtime, the problems associated with focusing on it, and how this focus resolves problems and uncertainty in everyday reality. One such tale is the French story of Melusina.[1]

> Once upon a time there was a man called Raymond, who was searching for his bride-to-be. He was sitting by a river when out of the water there suddenly emerged a beautiful maiden! Bedazzled, the man ardently proclaimed his love for the maiden and asked her to marry him.
>
> She said, "I'll marry you but whatever you do, don't look for me on Saturdays." Raymond said to himself, "Well, there must be something very interesting happening on Saturdays. She's a great woman from Sunday to Friday. She's predictable, she has a nice character, but what is she doing on Saturdays?"
>
> One Saturday he broke the rule and looked in on Melusina. What did he see? A mermaid! She screamed and disappeared and he never saw her again. He probably said to himself, "That was some woman. She was beautiful but she had a fish tail!"

This story speaks about the part of everyone that lives partially in the water—an imaginary part, a soul part, something eternal, wavelike, and fluid, symbolized by Melusina. Our story says that if you view this part with a disbelieving attitude, symbolized by Raymond, you doubt this part of yourself and this doubt chases it away. The disappearance of Melusina speaks about the doubt and uncertainty that arise from lack of relationship to the imaginary NCR aspect of life. It speaks about a loss of the wavelike essence of life, the river spirit, and process.

Among other things, this tale discusses what it means to be human. Are we only fixed ordinary bodies in time and space, playing out our roles in society, or are we also fluid beings, part of the river, flowing on and on to the sea? This tale, which preceded the discoveries of modern physics, points to a general principle later rediscovered by physicists. Most of the time, our consensus reality viewpoint focuses on time, space, and social norms. But sometimes—in our tale, on Saturdays—the CR viewpoint is shocked by the part of us that is able to live in water, a part that experiences dreams and altered states of consciousness. We not only have bodies, but dreamlike bodies whose experiences cannot be understood in terms of pathology but which can be comprehended only within the flow of experience. The general principle in physics that goes along with this experience is that particles do not exist. Instead, they are more like waves of probability, tendencies for things to exist.

That part of us which lives in the river experience is symbolized by the mermaid, Melusina, who suffers and disappears if we look at her doubtfully or with disrespect. We feel lifeless and depressed if we marginalize our dreaming experiences, sensations, fantasies, and dreamlike movements.

HEISENBERG AND UNCERTAINTY

The moral of the Melusina story is that if you look at your dreamlike body experiences and sensations without love, you lose contact with dreamtime and even banish it. Doubt and lack of relationship to these experiences create uncertainty about their nature. On the other hand, by developing an understanding of dreamtime, we can train ourselves to pay attention to it and conjugate, letting our processes come to life.

The importance of this story in the present context is not simply its psychological significance. This story reveals more general patterns about observability and uncertainty.

Melusina asks Raymond not to view her on Saturdays because she probably realizes he has a conventional attitude and will marginalize the significance of anything he sees that is not part of consensus reality. If what he sees is not logical or rational, he inadvertently chases it away through marginalizing its potential significance.

Likewise, a physicist who feels that only consensual "realties" and observations of matter are significant, marginalizes its dreaming background. Both the fairy tale figure of Raymond and the modern physicist-observer of today unconsciously use the same CR attitude, which perceives only that reality which corresponds to the generally agreed-upon one.

When Raymond tries to track Melusina, he loses track of her. Likewise, the physicist who tries to track subatomic particles loses them as well. These results can be summed up as follows, in what physics calls the uncertainty principle:

We cannot track a subatomic particle by any method whatsoever (in consensual reality).

The statement within parentheses is mine. It is not usually included with the rest of the statement in physics.

What would happen if there were more relationship between the hero and the heroine in our fairy tale? What would happen if there were more relationship between the physicist and matter? If the CR attitude were relaxed, and a more loving, second attention used, we would be in a new realm of physics. But before we move into that realm of physics, let's go back to psychology.

It is always interesting when I ask my students if they can tell me why people are uncertain. Where does uncertainty come from? Some students say that uncertainty comes from new ideas emerging inside of us, which are in conflict with our identities and belief systems. Some say that we need uncertainty to know what certainty is. Others bring up the multicultural factors of disenfranchisement—where different voices have not been heard or appreciated—which makes everyone uncertain of the overall state of society. We can look at our tale of Melusina and see that it tells us that uncertainty comes from not being in contact with the river spirit, not loving our dreamtime experiences.

In physics the uncertainty principle says we cannot know all the details about the state of physical systems; we cannot measure the impetus, that is, the momentum, of a particle with certainty because the energy of our measurements disturbs the particle, altering its position in space.

Momentum—technically, mass times velocity—is the push something has because of its mass and velocity. A pencil going 3 miles an hour is easier to stop than a car rolling at the same speed because of the greater mass of the car.

Werner Heisenberg, a friend of Pauli's since their school days in Munich in the early 1920s and a parent of quantum mechanics, is credited with the discovery of the uncertainty principle, often called the indeterminacy principle. This principle says that there is no way yet thought of for measuring the details of the path of an electron without totally disturbing its appearance at the screen. (See note 2 for Feynman's ingenious method of showing that uncertainty cannot be disproved.)

Formulated in a general way, the uncertainty principle in physics tells us that it is not possible to track a subatomic particle precisely by any method whatsoever in consensual reality. In other words, no instrument can be built in this universe that measures the path of what is happening without disturbing the final picture. In a way, the uncertainty principle protects nature. You cannot grasp what is here with rational, CR methods. It is forbidden!

Heisenberg pointed out that if you know a lot about one aspect of an electron, such as its position, you lose track of another aspect, its velocity. And, if you want to pinpoint its velocity, you lose track of its exact position. You cannot know everything about both aspects simultaneously. Heisenberg said that uncertainty is a fact of nature.

This uncertainty can be formulated mathematically. Think of the particle's position as a point, x, in space, and its velocity as v. Let's call Δx the uncertainty about its position. If we call momentum "p," and define momentum as mass times velocity, then Δp is the uncertainty in its momentum. Now, the uncertainty principle has a mathematical form:

$$\Delta x \geq \frac{h}{\Delta p}$$

where h is a very small constant called Planck's constant.[3] This formula says that the uncertainty in position is equal to h divided by the uncertainty in momentum. Said more simply, the more you know about x, the less you can know about p. Vice versa, the more you know about p, the less you can know about x.

COMPLEMENTARITY

Niels Bohr looked at the uncertainty formula and realized that it suggested a second principle, which he called "complementarity." He noticed that p and x were two "complementary variables" involved in the uncertainty principle. In Heisenberg's formulation ($\Delta x = h/\Delta p$, where x and p are position and momentum, respectively), x and p are complementary in the sense that if you know a lot about one, you cannot know much about the other. This is a sort of seesaw effect: if x is up, p is down.

If you know a lot about a particle's position, you don't know much about a particle's push, velocity or momentum. At this point, Bohr said, "Hmmm, looks very interesting. If you know one, you lose the other. The two quantities, position and momentum, are 'complementary.' You need both to describe matter." Bohr then took a look at the other equations of physics to find out if there might possibly be other quantities with such complementary characteristics.

It turned out that there are other quantities that are related in complementary fashion through the equations of physics. The one set of quantities already mentioned is position and momentum. Another complementary set is energy and time. This discovery led Bohr to the generalization that two complementary (CR) variables are always needed to describe anything in the quantum world. Furthermore, if one is certain, the other is not.

THE IMPLICATIONS OF UNCERTAINTY

Uncertainty and complementarity lead to some interesting, strange, and wonderful possibilities. To explain these possibilities, we will first do some simple mathematical thinking. Consider, for example, energy and time. If e is energy and t is time, then the uncertainty in energy, Δe, and variation in time, Δt, are related, according to the Heisenberg uncertainty principle. That is,

$$\Delta e \times \Delta t \geq h$$

This equation says that the product of the uncertainty in energy times the uncertainty in time is equal to that little number, h.

16.1 Energy and time on a seesaw are complementary. If you know a great deal about one, you know little about the other.

Let's see what this means in terms of practical measurements. Let's say you do an experiment as quickly as you can, which takes you 3 seconds. Knowing this, you can predict—from the uncertainty formula for energy—that your measurement of energy will have an uncertainty to it (namely, $h/3$). (See note 4.)

On the other hand, if you measure things more quickly, let's say, in 0.3 seconds, then Δt is smaller and Δe gets larger. (It is now $h/0.3$ and this number is bigger because h divided by a smaller number gives a larger result!) The quicker we are with time, the less certain we are about energy. This means that the range of possibilities for possible energy gets larger as the time you use to measure things gets smaller.

But wait. How can a measurement in energy be uncertain? Isn't energy always the same; isn't it a constant? And if energy is a constant, how can there be any uncertainty about it? The uncertainty principle is the answer.

Quantum mechanics breaks the old energy law a little bit by allowing uncertainty, or deviations in energy, for very short periods of time. It is still true that energy can neither be created nor destroyed in a closed system over long periods of time. But the uncertainty principle tells us that deviations in energy may still occur if—and only if—they occur rapidly.

Let's think about it this way. You can speed on the highway—break the law and go 100 miles an hour without getting caught—if you do this for a split second, because then the police cannot catch or measure you. The same holds for energy. If the energy gets really big for very brief time periods, you cannot measure it. Big deviations in energy are allowed if energy deviates only for a split second, since no one would have enough time to measure it. No one can prove that the law of energy conservation was broken.

Uncertainty allows you to break the energy law for a very brief time. But that hole in the energy law is big enough for a lot of spooks to get through.

Physicists crept right through this hole, too, and let their fantasies go wild. If there is the possibility of breaking the energy law for short times, we could have great deviations in energy and allow ourselves to fantasize about quick explosions and creations that no one could measure. The uncertainty principle allowed physicists to fantasize about NCR events.

One of the most amazing fantasies occurred during the sixties and seventies, during the time when quantum electrodynamics was created. Physicists fantasized ghostlike energies called "virtual particles." These particles, they fantasized, might be created with all that wild, uncertain energy for very brief periods of time and no one would be able to check on them.[5] Virtual particles are ghostlike speculations, which might occur without anyone ever noticing. Virtual particles are used to explain all sorts of things in physics, but that is a story we will explore in greater detail later.

The point for now is that uncertainty allows spooks back into physics. A virtual particle could exist for a very brief time and then disappear and no one could tell it had ever been there. Ghosts, virtual particles, or anything else could be present (in NCR) because no one can prove the opposite. The uncertainty principle says that we cannot prove that spooks do not exist. An electron could even have a wavelike tail, just like Melusina, and no one could disprove it.

The complementarity principle and the uncertainty principle leave open the possibility of highly non-consensual—if not downright weird—processes. These principles say that the physical universe can never be known independent of the observer's measurements and choices about what she observes. And these principles say that you can imagine anything you like, within limits, like the creation of lots of energy and particles with mass within the limits of a very brief period of time.

PSYCHOLOGY AND COMPLEMENTARITY

In any case, our choices about what to measure (in CR) fall into two distinct or "complementary" categories of observation. Observations carried out in one category, such as position or time, always preclude the possibility of simultaneously accurately observing the complementary category, such as momentum or energy.

The exact implications of complementarity are not yet entirely clear and have given rise to much speculation. For example, Pauli extended Bohr's complementarity law further by adding other sorts of complementarities such as magnetic or electromagnetic fields and the instruments needed to measure them. Object and observer are complementary.

If we extrapolate from Pauli's thinking, we could say that physics needs two more complementary variables: consensus reality and non-consensus reality. We have seen that you can make predictions and measurements in CR, but the more you do that, the less contact you have with NCR, or the experience of the flow of whatever you are measuring. My formulation of the uncertainty principle is that CR and NCR are complementary.

We could also say that the more you focus on consensus reality, the less contact you have with the dreaming process and the more you focus on dreaming, the less you know about CR.[6] This lack of contact with one whole aspect of reality makes us uncertain.

CAN WE GET AROUND UNCERTAINTY?

You may be wondering, "Who really cares if there is uncertainty in an electron's energy, time, position, and momentum or whether it has one or two tails? Be content with what you know. Accept the situation. If there is one slit for it to go through, an electron behaves like a particle; if it has two possible slits, it behaves like a wave. Call it dreamtime or anything else between measurements, but stop asking so many questions about that poor little thing!"

But most of us are like Melusina's partner. Many of us are like physicists who want to know about nature, about how to define matter. We are not always in the mood to simply admire her and believe in her. Sometimes, we, too, take a peek at Melusina on Saturday—especially after she said, "Do not look!"

Asking questions reveals things; we have already found that uncertainty is inherent not only in physics, but in mathematics. Uncertainty is connected to the aspect of awareness that marginalizes NCR. We saw that a similar marginalization process is inherent in calculus, and here we find it again in measurements of quantum objects.

We are forced to suspect, from the study of math and from the fairy tale about Melusina, that *uncertainty principles are more fundamental than physics itself, that they are created by one-sided CR attitudes.* Uncertainty is due to the way we use our awareness and to our tendency to validate a description of the world to which everyone consents. In other words, the uncertainty in describing and determining the state of the world around us is a product of our one-sided consensus reality orientation to descriptions of the world.[7] As long as we stay in only one reality, uncertainty seems like a general principle. Uncertainty arises from psychological attachment to CR that marginalizes sentient experiences. And uncertainty can also arise from wandering only in dreamtime.

Our fairy tale illustrated uncertainty as a relationship problem. If we poke around too much, things get uncertain and we don't know where Melusina is. In other words, we lose track of our fantasy worlds, or our process. The tale hints at a new kind of relationship beyond the observer/observed contact of today. Another kind of contact with matter would involve partnership.

Today's physics tells us that uncertainty allows the possible existence of virtual particles, ghosts, dreams, gods, or a maiden with a tail. All of these NCR experiences are allowed by physics—for short periods of time. Today's physics goes up to the river of experience and stops there. Scientists say, "Matter may have a tail, but we can't test it." But if physics changes as I predict it will, if it goes back to its authentic purpose, which was to comprehend the nature of the experienced as well as the measurable world, physicists will not only observe the river but also enter it.

Then we shall have a new science, which explores, like Alice in Wonderland, the other side of matter, its non-consensus reality. The new physics will unravel new principles about NCR events typical of shamanism and magic. As science places its focus on the stream and swims with its essence, it will investigate the realm of experience of complex numbers and virtual particles.

If physics changes as I predict it will, new methods for experiencing the river, the world of Melusina, will arise. A new, more advanced sha-manism will begin. At this point, the old physics, and its uncertainty principle, will become nothing more than a warning sign that says: If you relate only from the CR viewpoint to the universe, you injure Her feelings and create more uncertainty than is necessary. In the new worldview, we will all have the capacity to relate as modern shamans to the ongoing stream of experience.

NOTES

1.   From *French Legends, Tales, and Fairy Stories* (Oxford Myths and Legends), by Barbara Leonie Picard, and Joan Kiddell-Monroe (Illustrator). Melusina's theme is widespread. Versions of this story come from Northern Africa, South America, old Europe, and China.

2.   To understand the meaning of uncertainty in quantum physics, let's think about an experiment inspired by Richard Feynman in *The Feynman Lectures on Physics* (Volume II, Chapter 1, page 1). The point of the experiment is to be contrary, to doubt Heisenberg and to try and prove that his uncertainty prin-ciple is a mistake. In other words, we want to try to determine the position and momentum of an electron with certainty.

   Let us say that the mark "*" represents an electron in the diagram below. Let's say we know an electron is present if an electron counter at the screen makes a "click." A counter is symbolized by a bracket,]. An electron gun on the left is shooting electrons. The electrons go through a gate with two slits in it. The gate on the left is a little different from the gate we studied in Chapter 14. The circles above and below the slits in the gate represent rollers, wheels that enable the gate to jiggle up and down if it is bumped by the electrons going through the slits.

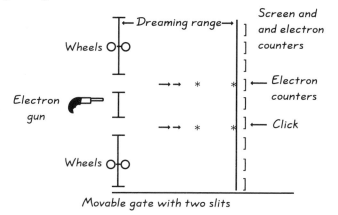

16.2 New jiggle experiment which failed to disprove uncertainty

Will this experiment give us certainty about the electron's momentum and position? Let's see. If an electron hits the upper gate, it bumps the gate upward a bit; if an electron hits the lower gate, it bumps it downward a bit. In each case we can measure the bump (the momentum) by how much the gate jiggled and rolled up or down.

If we know the weight of the gate system and its velocity once hit, we can calculate the momentum of the electron at a given position and get around the uncertainty principle. (If M is the mass of the gate and V its speed, and m the mass of the electron and v is unknown speed, then because of the rule that momentum is conserved, $MV = mv$, we know the momentum of a particle by measuring the velocity of the gate.)

We can determine the momentum of the electron because of the bump it gave the gates. And we know its position because if the electron hits the upper slit, the gate goes up, and if the electron hit the lower slit, it pushes the gate down. So there we have it. We beat the uncertainty principle.

Right? No, wrong. We skipped a little problem. If the gate wiggled, then we no longer know the exact position of the gate, and when the next electron goes through, the slit's position will be altered. We may have measured the position and momentum for one electron, but the experiment has been changed because the setup for the next measurement is jiggled! The slight movements of the gate change the patterns on the screen. It turns out that the gate's movements cancel out the wave effect.

Thus, if we track the electron's position with great precision, we destroy the experiment and no longer get the wave effect, no matter how well we make that system. Scientists have tried with many other experiments to outsmart the uncertainty principle but failed. You can get better wheels, a lighter gate that rolls better, but the jiggling cancels out the waves.

Experimental results verify this by showing that the particles no longer act like waves after they go through the two slits in the gate with rollers. Locating the momentum and position of an electron en route makes it behave like an ordinary particle as far as observations at the screen are concerned. The moral of the story is that when we too look closely, the electron turns into a particle and loses its wavelike nature.

3. The symbol h represents a general, special, natural constant which, as far as we know, never changes. The constant h is approximately equal to 6.63×10^{-34} joule-seconds. Thus, for a given momentum, we can be sure only that a particle landed in the region Δx!

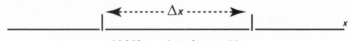

16.3 Uncertainty about position

4. Since $\Delta e \times \Delta t \geq h$, if we need 3 seconds, then we find that
    $\Delta e \times 3 \geq h$, or $\Delta e \geq h/3$.

5. A little extra energy for a split second would allow us to have a little extra mass because of the famous equation $e = mc^2$, which we will discuss in Chapter 33.

6. We could say, along with Jung, that conscious and unconscious realms are complementary. To understand a dream, you have to know the conscious situation of the dreamer. Jung spoke of complementarity in his "Structure and Dynamics of the Psyche" (*Collected Works*, Volume VIII).

7. We find uncertainty even in the mathematical descriptions of the wave. In Chapter 15 we saw that the concept of particle can be represented by something called a "wave packet" in quantum mechanics. The mathematical concept of a "real" particle is a mini wave packet, a millionth or a billionth of a centimeter in diameter. The particle is not an exact thing but a bunch of waves that pile up into a lump. It is fascinating that even in this "lump" description, it is impossible to determine the momentum of a particle because we would need to identify the lump by one particular wave frequency. And there is no single frequency for a wave packet.

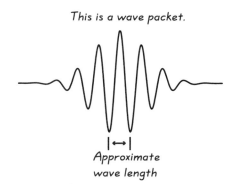

$|\leftarrow x \rightarrow|$ = Wave length

16.4 *The wave length of a wave*

For example, a single wave has a given wave length, x. But the wave packet in Figure 16.5 below has no single wavelength.

This is a wave packet.

$|\leftrightarrow|$
Approximate
wave length

16.5 *Uncertainty in the frequency of wave packets*

Wave packets are interesting because, as a clump of waves, they approximate the nature of particles as they move about in space and time.

17 | Quantum Flirts

The next great era of awakening of human intellect may well produce a method of understanding the qualitative content of equations. Today we cannot see... whether Schroedinger's equation contains frogs, musical composers, or morality—or whether it does not.

—Richard Feynman

If physics steps over the edge into the river, it enters the flow and interacts with matter in a new relationship. In this chapter, we will explore how the relationship between the observer and the observed is a sentient interaction that is encoded in the mathematical patterns of quantum physics and has been known for centuries by Buddhist meditators and Aboriginal Australians.

There are various subtle levels in the relationship process between the observer and the observed. In today's physics the entire observational process is classical. This means that both the observer and the observed are conceived of as separated in space and time, even though we know that the observer's decisions about which experiment to perform influence the final observations.

As we explore further, we shall find that the observer and the observed are like two trees above the ground. As long as we stand on the ground, the two trees look separate. But as soon as we dig beneath the ground, we find that the roots of the trees are so intertwined that the observer and observed can no longer be separated.

We will investigate this underground root pattern in terms of subtle NCR perceptual processes patterned in the math of physics. From this viewpoint, observation becomes a mutual, dyadic process. We will also begin to look at various levels of the observer/observed relationship and some of the many worlds in which we all coexist.

WAVES FORWARD AND BACKWARD IN TIME

The wave function in physics, which is our most basic description of matter, is written in terms of imaginary numbers. As we discovered in Chapters 7 and 8, imaginary numbers can be understood as describing NCR events.

Let's quickly review what we know about complex numbers. Remember that the conjugate of a complex number is almost the same as the original number, except that the sign in front of the imaginary number has changed. For example, the conjugate of the number $3 + 4i$ is $3 - 4i$. Furthermore, conjugates are mirror images of one another. Also, when we conjugate, that is, multiply an imaginary or complex number by its conjugate, we produce real numbers. For example, $3 + 4i \times 3 - 4i$ gives us the real number 25. (You can check this by remembering that $3 \times 3 = 9$, and $+ 12i - 12i = 0$, $i \times i = -1$, and $4 \times 4 = 16$.)

Complex numbers are needed to describe the quantum wave equation, the basic and most fundamental pattern describing quantum events such as the behavior of electrons and other elementary particles. Until now, physicists have tried to avoid interpreting the complex numbers in the quantum wave equation, since the numbers are not directly measurable, and, according to the Copenhagen interpretation of physics, what you cannot measure in CR you cannot discuss.

But times change. Today we have a chance to understand complex numbers as analogies to NCR processes such as dreaming and its reflection. In the 1980s, John G. Cramer, an innovative theoretical physicist working at the University of Washington in Seattle, described another analogy to the complex numbers in the wave equation.[1] In the process of conjugation, he saw the process of observation and imagined two interconnecting events, one moving forward and the other backward in time.[2]

Cramer saw that each conjugate could be understood as traveling "imaginary waves," all points of which are potential places where measurements might occur.[2] Even though he knew that, as a physicist, he could not describe the reality of these imaginary waves as something substantial, he said they were potentials for measurement, since potentials cannot be directly measured. He could not help imagining these potentials, which we have been discussing as another non-consensus reality, which all of us experience in a sentient fashion.

Before Cramer, physicists had ignored the possible significance of the reflected or "backward-moving" waves, since they did not have a known counterpart in everyday life. Cramer realized that, although these waves cannot be measured in reality without disturbing them, they can be used to guess at some of the possible mechanisms behind observation in quantum mechanics. They can be used to guess about the so-called collapse of the wave equation, which is spread throughout space and time into a particular spot in consensus reality.[3]

Cramer uses the analogy of two electronic machines, such as two fax machines, communicating with one another, to understand the conjugation process, which collapses the wave function from a vague ethereal fog into a particular point. The first fax machine, machine 1, emits an "offer" signal, such as a "beep beep," to machine 2, which sends back an "echo wave," or another "beep beep," indicating that machine 2 is there and ready for more communication. The echo reflects the offer in time.[4]

In other words, the first wave can be thought of as a signal saying "hello," and the second wave (the conjugate wave) is the "go ahead and transmit" signal. Cramer uses this analogy to give us a sense of what he calls the "quantum handshake," which is his fantasy of the NCR processes occurring beneath the surface of what we call observation.

FLIRTS IN DREAMTIME

Analogies from psychology may be closer to the mathematical patterns of quantum mechanics than the analogy of electronic machines, whose interactions can only be tracked in CR. Psychological interactions can also be tracked in NCR with the use of the second attention.

Let's say you are walking on a path in the trees. A particular tree catches your attention, but, to tell the truth, you cannot tell which came first, your looking at the tree or a "flirtlike" attraction coming to you from the tree, which is more or less asking to be looked at. Which came first, your observation of the tree or its call to you to look at it?[5]

Although we normally marginalize these NCR experiences, we can, with the use of our memory, that is, by reflecting backward in time after the observation took place, recall that this flirt occurred.

If you are trained in meditation and observation, if you are quick, you can notice a sort of flirt "coming at you" at the same time or even before you decide to look at the tree. Your sense of looking at the tree goes forward in time, but the sense of its having "flirted" with you is experienced as coming from the opposite direction.

You cannot clearly delineate which signal came first or second. You cannot prove going forward and backward in space or time in CR terms, but your experience tells you retrospectively that the tree flirted with you! The Australian Aborigine David Mowlajarai puts it this way:

> It doesn't matter where we walk about, it's there! When we walk by a tree, that tree has this power—Wayrrull. We can see that tree because its Wayrrull, its power, contacts our eye. Wayrrull lets that tree talk to us. It tells us its story, that tree. The Wayrrull lets us hear. Out of the Wayrrull we get understanding. We learn from it.

It guides us... That's my job, help'n' people remember. Help 'm remember the mystery.[6]

Mowlajarai says, "We can see that tree because its Wayrrull, its power, contacts our eye." I call this "power" of the tree making contact with our eye a "quantum flirt." The NCR flirt may have no common consensus from anyone else who is around, but for the person moving through the forest or on city streets, such NCR awareness of quantum flirts can be a matter of life and death.

Quantum flirts have two components. One is the NCR experience of intending to observe, which seems prior to the actual observation. This signal is experienced as going forward in time. The other component is the sense that the object is "asking" to be seen. If we are quick, we can sense this "Wayrrull power"; otherwise, we can notice it retrospectively, once an observation has taken place.

While the CR concepts of the observer and the observed are separated in our classical understanding of nature, the complex and imaginary numbers in the mathematics of quantum physics place the observer and the observed in one inseparable system, which corresponds in many ways with the NCR experience of observation. In this experience, the observer senses the observed flirting with him and may recall a flirt (which is not testable), that is, an NCR signal from the object, before a CR observation takes place. After the flirt, the intention to observe occurs and an observation takes place.

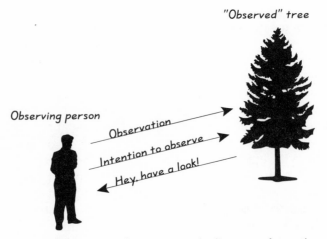

17.1 NCR quantum flirting process leading to an observation

The timing of which signal was experienced as coming first is an NCR experience. Such timing cannot be described or measured definitively in ordinary time. If we are talking about communication between two people, both may experience the other as having originated the communication, and both may even think the other caused it.

Many people have had the experience of walking down the street and feeling that someone is looking at them. Let's imagine that you are walking down the street, and I am in front of you. I sense some signal from behind me, or perhaps I begin to think about you for no apparent reason. If I do not marginalize my experience, but follow it, I might turn around and see you. From my perspective, I received a signal from behind me, and then I turned around toward you.

As far as you are concerned, however, the first signals of communication may have come from my back! We can only say that we flirted with one another, so to speak. We cannot say, in an absolute manner, who sent which signal first. Did you see me first, or did I fantasize about you first? Although we cannot say who did what first, we know that the moment of observation occurred when I turned and we saw each other. But as far as our experience is concerned, the NCR flirting occurred first—before a CR observation took place.

As soon as we saw each other, CR occurred: we observed each other in everyday reality. Someone could have photographed us looking at one another, but no photograph could have been taken of my sensing you behind me.

Most of the time, we marginalize NCR flirting experiences, and focus only on the CR observation. But the pattern behind observation in the math of quantum mechanics is based on such marginalized NCR experiences, flirts in dreamtime. In quantum mechanics we find the conjugation, which is a sort of code behind consensus reality created through the unfolding of dreamtime experiences. While the observer and the observed are CR concepts, sentient communicators are NCR concepts and cannot be definitively separated in terms of time or space.

While physics speaks of an observer/observed dichotomy, we can also see from the examples in psychology and physics that observation is based on a mutual, dyadic sentient process. I use the term "quantum flirt" because interactions happen so rapidly, so sentiently, that they cannot be reproduced without destroying the atmosphere or dreamtime in which they are experienced.

WHO OBSERVES WHOM?

Since we cannot tell which wave or flirt precedes, that is, whose tendency or intention to look came first, we have no way of knowing who first made the decision to observe. There is no clear causality at the sentient NCR level of experience; there is no way of telling which signal came first and which second, since the idea of time is a CR idea. At the NCR level, two parties are mutually involved in the act of observation. There are no single, simple categories of observed and observer, except from the viewpoint of consensus reality, when people consent on making measurements.

The quantum flirts help us get a sense of the meaning of the mathematics needed to describe the collapse of the wave function. For example, if I spontaneously phone you in the morning, my call lies in the realm of consensus reality. You can record it if you like. But what if I say that I felt you calling me for help before I called you? And what if you insist that you thought of me calling just before you heard the telephone ring? Although such NCR experiences are universal, they are not testable in CR.

If I do not marginalize my experience, I realize that my experience of you is an NCR experience and that something about your essence is not located in time or space. You are neither clearly outside nor inside of me, before nor after me, dead nor alive. Rather, you and I both participate in dreaming as well as in consensus reality. In NCR, we cannot clearly differentiate you from me. In NCR we are one.

Quantum flirts give us, as observers, permission to identify ourselves at the sentient level with the so-called observed object. Both the observer and the observed are sentient dreamers participating in an observation that in CR seems to have been initiated by the observer.

CONSCIOUSNESS IN MATTER

The ability to sense someone looking at us before we look at them is almost universal. The Australian teacher mentioned earlier calls this flirt by the term "Wayrrull," a power coming from a tree—or any part of nature—that catches our eyes and makes us look at it.

The Australian Aborigines believe not only that trees interact with us, but also that dreaming creates the Earth. They feel that what we call "matter" flirts with us and with itself as well. The belief in the link between what we call the material world of objects and the world of people is the basis for traditional shamanistic lifestyles. This belief is why aboriginal people wait for dreams before undertaking a venture such as a hunt. Reality is created by dreaming.[7]

The language of some aboriginal peoples, such as the Hopi, does not contain the words for time, the past or the future. There is no movement in creation from past to future, but only a passage from dreaming to waking reality and back again. One of my Jungian teachers, Marie Louise von Franz, points out that the Hopi speak of "that which is manifest" and "that which is beginning to manifest," corresponding approximately to our consensual and non-consensual realities. For these people, real objects are part of the past—they have manifested. The creator of all manifestation is called "'a'ne himu," a "Powerful Something."[8]

The consensus reality of aboriginal people is based on dreaming and consciousness, in contrast to time and space.[9] The first thing people do upon awakening in some Australian groups is to sing a song based on their dreams so that the animals and birds hear the dreams and assist the dreamer in daily hunting and gathering. In this worldview, each substance (animal, plant, and mineral) has its own dreaming. Aboriginal peoples abolish or, rather, reduce CR uncertainty by tracking NCR experiences.

Western-oriented observers who remain only in consensus reality marginalize NCR experiences and may feel that they are able to observe an object whenever they choose to do so. In NCR dreaming experiences, however, the observer and the observed may both experience each other as trying to "catch" the attention of the other. From this viewpoint, the physics of observation takes place because of dreaming.

We need to consider the possibility that what we call matter is capable of flirting in NCR, thereby participating in CR observations. This means that an object may choose to be observed just as much as an observer may choose to make the experiment.

In other words, an electron getting ready to approach the screen in a quantum physicist's slit experiment may "want" to be counted and send NCR flirting signals just as the observer herself begins to catch herself pondering the possibility of making the experiment. The experiment finally occurs only because of this background flirt and with or without awareness of it!

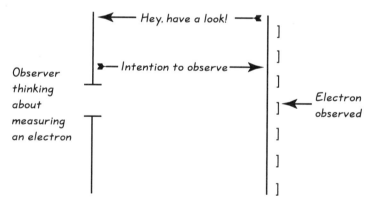

17.2 Quantum flirting process in the slit experiment

SENTIENT PERCEPTION LEADING TO OBSERVATION

If the electron sends us signals, then everything is flirting with everything else in the observable world, and the world becomes a network of interactions as much as a place full of parts and people.

While consciousness depends on awareness of CR signals, sentient experience of NCR flirts is more like lucid dreaming, reflecting and looking (back) at things that call to us. This involves attention and awareness of NCR experiences, or what the physicist might call quantum processes, occurring in the non-measurable realm. Thus, total awareness involves both consciousness and sentience.

SENTIENT FLASHES IN BUDDHISM

The reader familiar with meditation will pose questions such as, "Who meditates?" "When do 'I' appear in the overall observational situation?" "Where is the ego in sentient observations?" The answer from at least twenty-five hundred years of Buddhist study of perception is that sentient perception occurs before there is an observing "I." According to Buddhist tradition, there is no coherent "I" but only a sense of "I" that "arises and dissolves."[10] Brian Lancaster, a researcher who synthesizes Buddhist thinking and neuroscience, points out that, as in all spiritual traditions, training is needed to notice this subtle perception and that "nothing is permanent, and least of all the 'I.'"

Buddhist meditators have long experienced various levels of perception preceding everyday observations. In fact, according to Lama Anagarika Govinda (1975), there are many different "classes of consciousness," or as Rhys David (1914) called them, "moments or flashes of consciousness."

If you are trained in the arts of noticing what I have been calling NCR sentient experience, you can notice that something in you is able to sense many experiences, although "you" are not involved. Such NCR experiences "come to you." If they are strong enough, they catch your attention, and then the process we have been calling observation arises. The "I" enters the perceptual process only at the moment "you" decide to notice something that, in a way, your perception has already noticed.[11]

In other words, in the beginning of the perception of an observation, there is no "I" that perceives, but rather, an object was seen. Lancaster gives a delightful example of various differentiated sentient experiences preceding what we have called observation.[12] Observation itself occurs only at the end of a number of differentiable, perceptual experiences.

In the extended sense, all objects participate in the act of observation. There is a "flash" or a "flirt" followed by lucid approach to the object, then—still in dreaming—a decision to look, and finally an everyday, conscious observation. From the NCR viewpoint, there is no such thing as an inanimate object. A term such as "inanimate" refers only to the final act of observation and ignores the roots of CR, the flashes and rapid flirts or subtle perceptions and NCR experiences.

Most people assume that only humans have consciousness. But the NCR interpretation of the mathematics of conjugating the wave function to create reality allows us to consider the idea that the sentient roots of consciousness arise not in any one observer or object, but in the relationship between the observer and the observed.

Our present CR concepts of observation or consciousness will never be defined in a satisfactory manner by either psychologists or physicists with reference only to consensus reality. Psychology, meditation, shamanism, and neuroscience show how consciousness enters physics. Anthropology and the history of meditation teach that we cannot define consciousness as a reality concept because its roots lie in sentient experience. Perceptual experience explains the mystery of the collapse of the wave function in quantum physics: Dreamlike events reflect and become real.

The creation of reality happens unintentionally. This creation can be marginalized or tracked lucidly by noticing how quantum flirts unfold. In either case, the collapse of the wave function occurs because of the quantum flirt relationship between the parts of the universe.

NOTES

1. Cramer wrote a paper in 1986 and reviewed it two years later, in the *International Journal of Theoretic Physics* (1988).

2. The wave function in physics has the mathematical form $a + ib$ and is analogous to our NCR experiences. This form can represent a wave running forward in time, whereas $a - ib$ would represent waves where time runs backwards. When a solution to the wave equation is written as $Y = a + ib = |Y| e^{i(kx + wt)}$, we have the case of waves going forward in time (see below). If it is written in the form $Y = e^{i(kx - wt)}$, waves go backward in time.

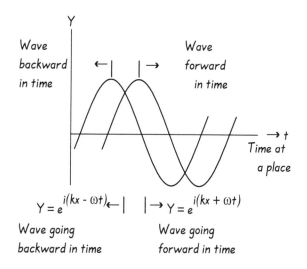

17.3 *Waves going forward and backward in time*

A signal going backward in time is an NCR experience like a "regression," which goes backward in time, forcing us to review traumatic situations.

3. Cramer's work has gone largely unnoticed until recently. Excellent introductions to Cramer's ideas can be found in the works of physicists Fred Alan Wolf and John Gribbin. See Fred Alan Wolf's imaginative *The Dreaming Universe* and John Gribbin's *Schroedinger's Kittens* (pages 238 and following).

4. Mathematically, the original (imaginary) wave emitted by machine 1 has the form $a + ib$; this is the "offer wave." The conjugate ($a - ib$) of the original wave is the "echo wave," similar in form and content to the original wave except that the conjugate is going backward in time.

5. Physically blinded at the age of eight, Jacques Lusseryran, in *And There Was Light: Autobiography of Jacques Lusseryran, Blind Hero of the French Resistance* (1998, Parabola Books, New York), developed an amazing sight that describes what I have been referring to as reflection and sentient awareness. He says, for example, that after the accident causing his blindness, "Now my ears heard the sounds almost before they were there.... Often I seemed to hear people speak before they began talking" (page 23). To know a table was under his hands, "To find out, my fingers had to bear down, and the amazing thing is that the pressure was answered by the table at once. Being blind I thought I should have to go out to meet things, but I found that they came to me instead... I didn't know if I was touching it (an apple) or it was touching me. As I became part of the apple, the apple became part of me... everything was an exchange of pressures... I spent hours leaning against objects and letting them lean against me"(page 27).

6. Salome Schwartz (1996) brought this to my attention through her dissertation, *Shifting the Assemblage Point: Transformation in Therapy and Everyday Life* page 3.

7. See Robert Lawlor, pages 38 and 39.

8. Marie Louise von Franz, in *Time: Rhythm and Repose*.

9. Lawlor, op. cit.

10. Brian Lancaster, *Cognitive Science and Buddhist Abhidhamma Tradition*.

11. Lancaster (op. cit.) takes some of his information from the erudite work of S. Z. Aung, *Compendium of Philosophy*, (1972, page 126), revised and edited by Mrs. Rhys David, London, Pauli Text Society, 1910.

12. Lancaster (op. cit.). Buddhist meditators recognized that every observation consists of no less than seventeen differentiable moments, grouped into different stages. Following an initial disturbance, which occupies moments one to three, there is a subliminal experience that something is occurring. A sensation can be said to arise in moment five. Then a visual perception arises, for example, but the object is not yet recognized. This state is "characterized by a sense of contact between the sense organ and the sense object, and might be thought of as a consciousness that arises intimating that a formed entity has stimulated the eye." This is followed by further stages called "receiving," "examining," and others referring to the tendency to react, and, finally, by the

sense of a stream of consciousness, of a "running of the mind…. Many of such moments arise in one flash of lightning, and the whole process "happens in an infinitesimal part of time."

18 | Parallel Worlds

Could the solution to the dilemma of indeterminism be a universe in which all possible outcomes of an experiment actually occur?... Although this proposal leads to a bizarre world view, it may be the most satisfying answer yet advanced.

—Bryce S. DeWitt, in *Physics Today,* Volume 23, No. 9, 1970

Although you can sentiently experience NCR flashes of perception and interchanges with objects before observation, the fact remains that, at present, it is impossible to measure these non-consensus interactions in CR terms. Thus, you cannot tell which flirt came first, that of the so-called observer or that of the observed. This inability to differentiate the causality of sentient experiences means that, as far as the CR observers are concerned, they are theoretically symmetrical, that is, reversible. The rules or laws of physics remain unchanged if the role of the sentient observer in an observational process is switched with the role of observed! This symmetry may be connected with the symmetries of microphysics and spiritual beliefs that at some level we are both the other and ourselves.

We might say that the experiences, results, and observations in psychology and physics remain the same at the NCR levels when your sentient impulse to participate in an observation is replaced mathematically by the observed's impulse to participate in that same observation.[1] This replaceability, or symmetry, is one of many kinds of symmetries in nature. For example, a ball is symmetrical if we can turn it any way and it still seems the same. Nature is egalitarian. She does not care how you rotate that ball in space; it always looks the same. In the same vein, there is symmetry in the field of gravity: all objects, regardless of how heavy they are, fall at the same rate. As far as the rate of a falling object is concerned, nature is egalitarian. Replace one object with another, and the rate of fall is the same. This simple fact about the symmetry of gravity fields was crucial to Einstein in his discoveries of relativity.

A basic observational symmetry exists in psychology and physics at the NCR level. Nature does not differentiate between the observer and the observed at the sentient level in the mathematics of physics. The physics of quantum phenomena and the psychology of dreams are based on symmetry between the observer and the observed. While this particular symmetry may be new to physics and psychology, it is not new to spiritual thinkers who suggest that at some deep level, "you are me and I am you." We shall come back to these symmetries in Chapter 36, when we begin to discuss the kind of psychology that can be developed from understanding math and physics.

At this point in our journey, we will investigate another quality of observation, namely, the existence of simultaneously occurring, parallel worlds and states of consciousness.

EXPERIMENTING WITH ATTENTION AND DIFFERENT WORLDS

To introduce the idea of parallel worlds, let's begin with an awareness experiment to bring the idea of the quantum flirt closer to personal experience.

Let's consider how we observe things. In my classes on physics and psychology, I use a piece of wood to talk about observation. Imagine, if you can, that you are seated with the rest of the students in the class. I am standing with a piece of wood in my hand. I'll talk directly to you like I do to my classes, and we'll go together through what happened one time when I talked with a group about observation.

"Consider this piece of wood, which is a breadboard, or chopping block. I'm going to put this block of wood in front of you and we're going to enter into a quantum physical experiment with it."

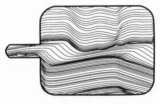

18.1 Wooden cutting board

"You can use this experiment at any time if you run into a problem and want an answer. It's easy. You don't have to go deeply into altered states of dreaming to reduce your uncertainty in life. This experiment will also help you understand the physics of quantum flirts and prepare a basis for understanding the theory of parallel worlds. Who wants to experiment with me?"

John, a scientist in the class, came forward. "I'd like to experiment with you. What do I have to do?"

I told him he need not do much. I said, "Just follow yourself and see what answers come up when I ask questions. My first question is simply, what do you notice when you look at the cutting board?"

John: It's a piece of wood.

Arny: A piece of wood, good, that's the consensus reality viewpoint. Most people will agree that it is a piece of wood. In fact, those of you who know something about trees will see certain things in the grain of the wood. You might think, the piece of wood comes from a certain type of tree, it is so many years old, it's a birch tree or a pine tree, and so on. Let's say that these are consensus reality views, or facts. It is a piece of Douglas fir made into a chopping block.

Now, I want to arrive at other views so I'm going to ask John a question. John, look at that piece of wood. Is there any place on the wood that flirts with you, any place catching your attention?

John: The part at the top of the cutting board where the grain is wavy, that catches my eye. I like those waves.

Arny: Good, focus on those waves, notice the flirt coming to you from that piece of wood, notice the wavy spot, and focus on it. That is, try to reflect the flirt. Give your focus time, let it unfold. Take a look at the waves and the grain and tell me what it does to you, what you see. Let an image, feeling, movement, sound, or whatever come to mind about it.

John: It's sort of like ocean waves or... I don't see an image... but hear a sound like, waooon... waoon... I feel like I'm moving rapidly on a soft wave.

Arny: There is the image and sound of a soft ocean wave that occurs in connection with those waves in the wood. That is very interesting. Can you go further with your perception, your experience of that soft waviness?

John: [After hesitating a few moments] Yes, it feels very much like I normally feel, sort of heartful and kind.

At this point he turned from the piece of wood and looked at me, as if the experience were completed. I thanked him for what he had seen so far, and asked him to look again at the same section of the wood that he had just looked at. I said, "Give yourself a second chance, allow yourself to see a second set of images coming from that same section. This may be more difficult, but see if you can allow yourself to see something else in this area. What comes to you? Use your attention, your second attention to whatever occurs to you."

John: ... Let's see... Oh... those lines are not just ocean waves; they have changed a bit, now they seem to be whizzing quickly, something fast... I sort of see... it doesn't make any sense! OK... I'll use my second attention and try to appreciate this nonsense... I see... it's weird, I see the edges of dozens of sheets of metal, thin sheets of metal with a lot of sharp edges all lined up. In my fantasy they're making a buzzing sound.

Arny: I noticed you just made very little, quick chopping motions with your fingers and hands connected to that "buzz."

At this point, John, who was amazed that his hands had made this quick motion, replied, "It's like a... it's ridiculous! It's like those sheets of metal are zooming, rapidly in succession, flipping, they sound like a gun firing quickly... or, a very fast, exact sort of thing putting holes in something." John meditated on these rapid motions and let them unfold a bit further.

After a minute he exclaimed, "I got it! The sound is coming from a very exact chopping sword, a precise, chop, chop, chop. Oh... wow... this is new for me, hmm, yes, I love and need that precision." He thought quietly to himself about all this and continued excitedly, "My normal sense of life is soft and wavy, everyone says I am so kind. I need that precision and rapidness. Maybe that's why I get sharp headaches—they are really cutting!"

I complimented him, saying that I was thankful for the manner in which he seemed able to unfold perceptions and fantasy. I reminded him that the first time he looked at the wood, he just saw it as a chopping block, the second time, as soft wavy lines, and this time, as sharp, precise chopping images.

I asked him a further question. "Can you see both the fast, precise sword you just saw now, as well as your vision of the soft, wavy ocean and also your image of the wood as a cutting block? Can you see all three images at the same time? Look at the board and try to see both the soft and the precise states together, and the board too."

John said, "Oh... that's not easy! I can sort of see a soft flow of something and also.... sharpness and.... oh yeah, I see the wood too. Wow, that's interesting. I feel dizzy. What is happening?"

I assured him that his own inner process would explain best what was happening. He said he was also interested in my views, and so I continued, explaining that we had seen both CR and NCR realities at the same time. Usually we see only one or the other. John went back to his place, and I went on with my lecture.

PARALLEL WORLDS

Let's call the first view of the board, in which John saw a piece of Douglas fir and a chopping block, the view of consensus reality. The next view of the wavy ocean came from something in the board that flirted with John. Something caught his eye. Is that wavy ocean a projection of John's psychology? Yes, he described himself as being soft. Is that wavy vision really there in the wood? Of course. With a little awareness, we can all see the waves in the grain.

At first, we have a piece of consensus reality, a piece of wood. Then we have a dreaming process in which John related to the wood and found what we might call his "ordinary personality" represented by the ocean waves he saw. In the last vision, a secondary process seemed to occur. John used his second attention and ability to conjugate and unfold to see the view of the whizzing, sharp metal and the sword.

When I asked him to see all these things together, John developed an overview, a metaview that included the wood, the softness, and the sharpness. All of these visions—the wood, the soft sea waves, and the sharp metal—are parallel worlds, so to speak, each existing at the same time in John's relationship with that wood.

The first thing we normally describe when asked about a chopping block is its CR description: it is a breadboard, or wood from a particular kind of tree. Most of the time, John and the rest of us see only wood, not waves or sharp metal. Why is this?

At this point in my classes, a student usually says something like, "That is simple. We see the wood because it's a piece of wood and not a wave or a sword!"

This student is right, but if, and only if, he adds "it's a piece of wood in CR." In other realities, in NCR, it is whatever we perceive it to be. To be more precise, we should say that we all agree in consensus reality to call that board a piece of wood. One of the reasons John does not see waves or sharp metal edges all the time is that when he looks at the wood, his education and history press him to agree with others and see consensus reality. Most of us look at objects and are trained to marginalize our other views, the other worlds such as the softness and sharpness experiences. They seem irrelevant to us.

Calling that piece of wood a breadboard has a horrendous effect on everyone. When you say to yourself, "I must use my cutting board," you have made a useful CR statement, but you have also effectively repressed your relationship to the material world around you. Consensus reality views of objects and yourself marginalize your dreaming experiences.

Consensus reality not only marginalizes people because of age, gender, and racial, ethnic, cultural, and sexual orientations; it also marginalizes dreamtime experiences. CR represses the power of matter, the soul of matter, its flirting ability! When you go down the street and you look at another person or you see a streetlight, you need to remember that "person" and "streetlight" are CR views that may marginalize the NCR qualities of that person or light.

From the NCR viewpoint, we kill parts of ourselves and the world around us when we ignore our sentient experiences. The world is a combination of parallel realities, all of which are present, all the time.

If you marginalize the many NCR experiences you have, you will become uncertain about what you are viewing, about objects, about space and time, about the future, and about life itself. If you use only a CR viewpoint about yourself, you are cutting off half your life. For example, when you look in the mirror, if you use only a consensus viewpoint about what you look like, you reject yourself, regardless of whether you think you are conventionally good or bad looking! Either view may marginalize and hurt you in part because it represses other viewpoints, other worlds, other aspects of yourself, other spirits, masks, and demons within your being. Consensus judgments are not wrong; they are just one of many worlds.

The cutting block is not just a piece of wood. It is also an unknown being, participating with you in dreaming and creating its own and your reality. One day that piece of wood might suddenly come to life. For John, it might become a sword and suddenly drop off the table and slice an apple in two. Perhaps it will fall from a counter and chop a wasp in half on the floor just when John feels unable to be a swordsman in his life. It might seem to John as if the cutting board had a life of its own.

In fact, everything that flirts with you is not only a CR object—it has magic as well. The concept of parallel worlds, of quantum flirts from NCR realties, gives explanation and meaning to parapsychological events, to synchronicities. But the pattern for such events is encoded in your relationship to the objects and world around you. You cannot understand unusual events with the use of the CR aspect of physics. But with the addition of this observation experiment, you can see that the wooden board is a part of John's world, or he is a part of its world. If you are smart, you will relate to the world around you and respect its powers. You will offer respect and compassion to that piece of wood and other so-called pieces of dead matter around you!

In the class with John, one student asked why it seemed more difficult for John to see the second image of the sharp pieces of metal. Another student answered that he apparently became identified with the first view, with its softness. I added that John had become identified with the first view because the wavy sea was closer to his identity; that is why he saw the sea before the sword. Like most of us, he tends to see only that part of himself he knows about in the wood and to marginalize other experiences, such as the sharpness. But everything we see flirts with us, as if trying to say, "Hi there, I am me and I am a part of you. Have a good look."

Another student, looking confused, asked timidly if John's precise metal sheets and sword were really there or if they were projections.

I said that, as far as we can know, the answer depends on what is meant by "really there." Really is a consensus reality term. It implies that there are no other realities. One CR answer would be, "The sword is there depending on how many people agree on it being there."

On the other hand, CR is only one reality. If John sees precision in nature, then it is there for him. It is the reality he participates in; it describes a part of his relationship to nature. From the most relativistic viewpoint, that sword is neither in him nor in nature, but in both. Even if everyone else says he is crazy, wrong, a fool, or a liar, we cannot assume that the waves and the sharp stuff were not there. Each of us may see a different side of the wood because of the specific nature of our relationship to that wood. The point is that all worlds are present all the time. Yet, the only thing we agree upon in CR is that the breadboard is a piece of wood.

PARALLEL WORLD VIEW EXERCISE

At this point, you may want to experiment personally with the parallel world view exercise that John did with the breadboard.

1. **Look at a piece of wood, or choose a part of the room you are in.** Pick a part of the room that flirts with you, that catches your attention. Watch for a flirt from the walls, the ceilings, or the curtains. First, ask yourself, "What's the consensus reality view of what I'm looking at?"

2. **Then notice what it is about the object you are looking at that flirts with you.** Keep looking at the object you're attracted to, and let an image appear in your mind. Describe that image to yourself.

3. **Now, be patient. Keep looking at the same thing and allow yourself to form a different, second image.** Be patient with yourself until this happens.

   Hold your attention to this new image and process it for a couple minutes. Let it unfold. Be patient. Seeing takes time, and unfolding what you are seeing takes patience, so give yourself time to focus on the events that arise. You may have prejudices that hinder your seeing the second image, so just try, even if it seems irrational and unusual. Focus on it, and let things arise in connection with it until the unfolded result has some meaning for you.

4. **Finally, switch from one view to another, to another.** Can you see them all at the same time?

You and your environment are constantly dreaming together. It is as if you and nature are artist-partners. You are both the artwork and the artist in one.

EVERETT AND DEWITT'S THEORY OF MANY WORLDS

The relationship between observer and observed, between John and the piece of Douglas fir, occurs in many worlds simultaneously. In one world, John is John and the wood is Douglas fir. In another, John and the wood are soft waves. In a third world, they are both fierce, sword-bearing warriors.

A many-worlds experience is about the relationship between an observer and the observed. Only in one of these worlds is that wood a piece of Douglas fir, in the observable world of physics. If physicists leave the shore and get into the river, many sides of nature, that is, many worlds, appear. Using your second attention is like being Alice, going through the hole into Wonderland.

Many-worlds experiences are one of the psychological patterns behind the many-worlds theory in physics, which was developed to explain the collapse of the wave function. Hugh Everett and Bryce DeWitt developed the "parallel world theory" in the 1970s to understand the mathematics of quantum physics.[2]

According to this theory, as soon as you look at something, its appearance breaks up into an infinite number of other possibilities, all of which come into being at the same time. All these other possibilities exist simultaneously in parallel worlds. These worlds are all present and real. They are what DeWitt calls "branches" of the total reality.

The many-worlds version of quantum physics states that the observer becomes a part of the observed by noticing and remembering what she experiences. If we consider non-consensus events such as John's visions, the theory becomes easier to understand. Each world represents a specific aspect of the observer-observed relationship.

According to the many-worlds theory, a quantum system is capable of being observed in many possible states. When an observation occurs, a system such as an electron or a piece of wood breaks up into all of possible states connected to the observer's companion states. In other words, many states arise, and in each one there is a particular observer-observed relationship.

This theory is analogous to John looking at the piece of wood. When he sees it, he enters into several simultaneous relationship states. He and the Douglas fir are one state. He and waves of the ocean are another state, and he and the warrior's sword are yet a third state.[3]

According to DeWitt's thinking, we collapse all the other worlds that come into being at any given moment by focusing, holding, remembering, and believing that the only view of events is the one we now see, whichever it is.

Analogously, we could say that as soon as you enter into relationship with that view of the world you are focusing on, a particular event comes out of all the potentials because of the interactive nature of the observer and the observed. At that point, you marginalize all the other views.

If you spend all year observing a quantum object such as an electron, over time you will see a whole ensemble of possible worlds in connection with the electron. Whenever you look at something, many worlds arise. If you are not careful, you will marginalize them by focusing only on one.

A MORE COMPLETE QUANTUM THEORY

The many-worlds theory of DeWitt and Everett is the skeleton of a more complete quantum mechanics that includes NCR observer/observed experiences.

Psychology supports that aspect of physics that assumes that the relationship between an observer and the observed has many possible dimensions. Psychology adds to physics the idea that the particular dimension or world that appears at a given moment is not just a matter of chance or statistics, but is linked to a number of subtle factors including the viewpoint of consensus reality and the psychology and physics of the observer and the observed.

Briefly said, *what is seen depends on the relationship between observer and object.* This relationship is connected with:

- The observer's momentary consensus reality
- How the observer identifies herself
- How she uses her second attention
- The particular nature of all involved parties and their mutually interactive relationships

In the moment of observation, these factors determine which experience or observation occurs and which others tend to be marginalized as insignificant or nonexistent worlds.

What does all this mean for you as an individual? As a lucid witness, you can see various worlds more or less simultaneously if you are sensitive to quantum flirts. The above exercise may have given you the sense that if you are uncertain about an observation, uncertainty arises in part because you are focusing only on one possible world.

Awareness practice connects you not only to yourself, but also to quantum physics, psychology, the future of science, and to the whole universe. Using your awareness at any moment seems to have an unlimited number of benefits, and no known side effects except greater certainty.

NOTES

1. In the sentient world of complex numbers, quantum mechanics, and spiritu-
    ality, we are entangled, even though in the CR world of everyday reality, it
    may be important and relevant to everyone to clearly distinguish who is
    doing what with whom.

2. See DeWitt, Everett, and Graham, *The Many-Worlds Interpretation of Quantum
    Mechanics*, 1973.

3. This parallel-world theory and its perceptual analogy are closely connected
    with other theories of physics. Physicists familiar with statistical mechanics
    may suspect, as I do, that DeWitt got his idea of parallel worlds from the
    ideas of Willard Gibbs, a mathematician and statistician who lived in the
    1800s.

    Gibbs said that any one event could be understood in two ways. It can be
    understood as an average taken from repeating the same event again and
    again. Or the event can be understood by imagining it to be one of many
    (parallel) events just like it, all lined up, all occurring at the same time. The
    average over these many possible systems of like events is an average taken
    over the entire "ensemble" of events.

    For example, we could measure the average behavior of one atom with an
    electron coming from it, if we watched the single atom over time. Or, using
    the ensemble idea, we could think of that atom as one member of a huge
    ensemble consisting of thousands of atoms, all of the same kind, each with an
    electron about to be emitted. Some electrons are getting ready to be emitted
    from their atom, some are being emitted, and some have already been emit-
    ted from the atom.

    In other words, each atom is a system, one of an ensemble, one of many
    parallel worlds. Like systems in different physical states, each comprises a
    parallel world. To understand your observation of one atom, you can com-
    prehend it as a possible single event within an ensemble of other, like events.
    Gibbs' notion of ensembles seems to be an early predecessor of parallel world
    theories.

18.2 A Gibbsian ensemble of boxes with electrons coming out

The weak point in Gibbs' ensemble theory is that it seems as if those many
worlds or states of the system we are observing have nothing to do with us.
The strong point is that any event is understood as one of many possible
events all occurring simultaneously.

19 | Non-locality and the Universal Mind

...This life of yours which you are living is not merely a piece of the entire existence, but is, in a certain sense, the "whole," only this whole is not so constituted that it can be surveyed in one single glance. This, as we know, is what the Brahmins express in that sacred, mystic formula which is yet really so simple and so clear: "Tat tvam asi," this is you. Or, again, in such words as "I am in the east and in the west, I am below and above, I am this whole world.

—Erwin Schroedinger in *What Is Life?*

Everett and DeWitt's many-worlds theory was meant to solve problems connected with observation in physics and also to explain the surprising interconnectedness between quantum events at the subatomic level. As we move farther along our journey into modern shamanism, we will explore another link between quantum physics and spiritual philosophies by discussing what physicists call quantum entanglement and non-locality. We shall explore how these features of the quantum world connect us to the psychology of human relationships, and to a universal mind.

THE BELL EXPERIMENT

The experiment that demonstrates quantum entanglement, or interconnectedness, is sometimes called the "unity of the world" or the Bell experiment. This experiment showed that the photons from a given source of light are interconnected.

Like all other quantum phenomena, light sometimes acts as particles and sometimes as waves. Imagine, for example, a neon lamp giving off light. A pair of light photons emerges from the neon lamp, with the photons radiating away from one another. One photon goes in one direction and the other goes in the opposite direction. An amazing experiment conducted with these photons showed that whatever happened to one particle seemed to be connected to what happened to the other particle, regardless of how far apart they were or how long they had been separated.[1]

Results show that the measurements of the motion of one particle are inextricably connected with those of the other, even after they have been separated for a while and at great distances. To be more exact, measurements of the spin of particle A in one location give us information about the spin of its twin particle B, which is in another location and time. If I throw two balls, one to the right and the other to the left, with my two arms, after 10 minutes, measurements of the spin of one will not tell us much about the spin of the other. How can two separated quantum objects be connected if there is nothing imaginable connecting them?

Subatomic particles such as photons are not really like little balls that spin. In fact, the concept "spin," like the concept "particle," is a CR term that is useful in describing spinlike characteristics of quantum objects, which are not balls at all. The concept of spin simply indicates an intrinsic angular momentum of a particle, which, like the angular momentum of a spinning ball, resists being stopped.

If the measurement of the spin of *A* shows that its momentum is directed upward, we can guess that the spin of *B* will be directed downward. If we find that *A*'s spin is downward, we can guess that *B*'s will be upward. *A* + *B* compensate each other in a way; they are connected; their total spin is balanced.

Now, let's think about this phenomenon more personally. Let's assume that you and I are twin photons leaving the neon lamp at the same time (see below). Let's say you move with the speed of light to Moscow while I'm shining in the direction of Los Angeles.

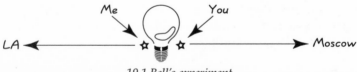

19.1 Bell's experiment

Now let's say that people in Los Angeles and Moscow look at our heads. At a given moment, if they find my head looking down, people can guess, correctly, that your head will be up in Moscow. If someone checks this out in Moscow, indeed, your head will be found to be looking up! If people in LA see my head looking up, then Muscovites will find yours looking down. Bell's experiment shows that the two of us, through some unknown means, remain connected through time and space.

This is the essence of Bell's experiment that we need to know about at present. The results show that two quantum entities, which were originally part of the same system, remain interconnected in the most inexplicable manner. They are considered to be "entangled," which means that if one photon in the system is spinning in one direction, the other must spin in the opposite direction so that their total "spin" is balanced.[2]

The experiment shows that if you know the movements of one entangled photon, you know those of the other. The analogy to this entanglement on the human level may be more than metaphorical. Since we human beings come from the same source, whether we call it the Earth, or a god, or something else, and since many of us experience ourselves as coming from the same family, we are also "paired." The closer our relationship, or the more we feel we come from the same source, the more we seem to be linked in connections that seem beyond the laws of chance. The experience of being linked is an NCR phenomenon and, like the entire sense of interconnectedness, is difficult to substantiate in a CR manner.

Nevertheless, many people feel linked in paranormal ways. I have often seen that if one person in a group knows what is happening inside herself, she knows a great deal about what is happening or going to happen in others around her. The reverse is true as well. If you know me, you know yourself. In a way, many people have always felt connected, just like the photons in Bell's experiments. We seem to know each other. Our relationships are symmetrical in the sense that we compensate each other's behavior. Theoretically, this compensation exists regardless of how far we are separated from one another in space or time. Another way of saying this is that there is no locality, or that "non-locality" exists.

If we look further at our particles, it turns out that if you know the behavior of one particle in, say, 2001, you will know what that particle is going to do in the year 2025! Stranger yet, if you know what one particle did in the year 2025, you can go backward in time and you will know what the other particle did in 1920. Furthermore, the connection between the two entangled photons is just as strong when they are at opposite ends of the Earth as it would be if they were 10 feet apart.

Are there hidden forces that connect the particles? No one knows. For the moment, the reasons for the interaction remain unexplained in quantum physics. Some people imagine the photons connected through signals that go faster than light—so-called tachyonic signals. A tachyon is a particle that can go faster than the speed of light and disobey relativity theory, which says that nothing can go faster than the speed of light. The word tachyon means fast.

If tachyons existed and could go faster than the speed of light, then they could go backward in time so that the future could influence the present and the behavior of a particle in 2022 could influence another in 1970.

Some physicists think that there may be a tachyonic communication between the photons—that the one in Moscow signals forward and backward in time to the one in LA—thereby explaining how one photon "knows" what the other is doing. But this tachyonic theory is forbidden by one of the results of the theory of relativity developed by Albert Einstein. Relativity says that nothing measurable can go faster than the speed of light.

All we can say at present is that the locality or spatial separation of the particles is no longer a meaningful concept. Particles no longer have a separate locality. There is no simple analogy for this "non-locality" of entangled quantum objects in everyday life, except that none of us lives in a separate reality. Saying that the spin of one particle tells us about another particle is something like saying that if you know something about me, we can understand my partner, regardless of where he or she is, regardless of the time difference or the spatial separation. If I know something about my behavior, I know something about yours as well. At the level of our deepest, most sentient, subtle experiences, we are entangled. How does this occur?

BOHM'S UNBROKEN WHOLENESS

If signals cannot go faster than the speed of light, then how do they connect? This question stimulated a lot of speculation such as Everett and DeWitt's many-worlds explanation of quantum mechanics. David Bohm came up with another NCR concept.[3] He suggested that we not begin with a theory of the world in which separate particles and separate states are the basis of everything. He said we should develop a new theory in physics that assumes from the beginning that the world is a field of unbroken wholeness. In this theory, quantum events—like the relationship of the twin photons—are interconnected from the beginning. Bohm began with unbroken wholeness and tried to redevelop quantum mechanics and relativity.

Bohm tried to show how everyday reality unfolds from this interconnected wholeness. Rather than saying, "Let's put the noodles and the peas in the water, cook it, and get soup," Bohm postulated that the great soup in which all things are mixed is the crucial reality, and this unfolds itself, so to speak, into individual noodles, peas, electrons, and people.

Bohm began discussing the idea of unbroken wholeness by first reconsidering the nature of movement. He differentiated state-oriented thinking from process-oriented thinking:

> Whenever one "thinks" of anything, it seems to be apprehended either as static, or as a series of static images. Yet, in the actual experience of movement, one "senses" an unbroken, undivided process of flow, to which the series of static images is thought to be related as a series of "still" photographs might be related to the actuality of a speeding car.

...Thought itself is in an actual process of movement. That is to say, one can feel a sense of flow in the "stream of consciousness" not dissimilar to the sense of flow in the movement of matter in general. May not thought itself thus be a part of reality as a whole?[4]

Bohm is comparing non-consensus experiences such as the "stream of consciousness," with the "movement of matter." He is speaking about a new, process-oriented basis for physics. Perhaps because Bohm did not succeed in developing the mathematical background of his theory to include relativity before he died, his ideas have not been popular among physicists today. Another reason for avoiding Bohm's theory, however, may be psychological. Physics in its present form is built on the state-oriented paradigm of consensus reality. Bohm's theory is a process paradigm. While the state orientation is based on parts and particles, the basic elements of reality in the process paradigm are change and flow.[5] Process orientations and philosophy exist in Western thinking, but the main philosophers in this area have been from Asia.

CAUSAL AND NONCAUSAL CONNECTIONS IN PSYCHOLOGY

The essential new quality implied by the Bell experiment in quantum theory is non-locality, which means that a system cannot be explained by reference to the interaction of its parts in a given locality. Non-locality implies that a system's most subtle properties depend on the whole.

There are dramatic differences between systems whose world depends on unbroken wholeness and systems whose behavior can be understood through connections between interacting parts. We know this not only from physics, but also in the psychology of relationships. Some aspects of relationships can be understood in terms of cause and effect, and some need the concept of synchronicity, or as Jung defined it, "meaningful coincidence." Victor Mansfield and Marvin Spiegelman suggested a parallel between the interconnection between photons in the Bell experiments and the interconnections between people in Jung's concept of synchronicity.[6]

Let's think about communication between people. Consider the visible signals of two people speaking with one another, signals that have been recorded on a videotape machine. The signals of one person seen on videotape may be linked to the signals of a second person in various ways.

First, the signals of the two people may be linked in a causal manner. How we respond to others depends on what they are doing, and what they do is in part a response to what we do. In this case, we have two people, two separate entities, in visible and causally linked communication.

To think further about communication between people, let's say that two people, Bob and Sharon, come to you for help, and you decide to videotape their interaction so you can study it with them at another point. Let's say Bob feels inferior when Sharon feels superior. Let's imagine that they are a polite, ordinary couple; when she feels elated, he becomes too shy to talk about feeling inferior. So they go on acting as if nothing is bothering them.

Now, imagine their nonverbal body signals. When Bob tries to act happy and asks Sharon how she is doing, Sharon's head goes up and she says proudly, "I am fine, how are you?" When Bob sees her proud signals, his voice hesitates, his head droops, his chest caves in, and his shoulders go down. Nevertheless, he answers as perkily as he can, "It's nice to see you today." Still with her head in the air, Sharon says that she thinks it's great to see Bob, too. He tries to smile, yet more and more, his nonverbal signals show that he is unhappy.

Their signals seem, at this point, causally connected. You can see how the signals he does not consciously identify with—his tone of voice, drooping head, sunken chest, and so forth—are linked causally to the motion of her head, her air of superiority. Furthermore, you can see how, the more depressed he looks, the higher her nose goes into the air. If you videotaped this interaction, you would see that her "superiority" signals came a split second before his depressed reaction. It looks like her signal of superiority causes his depression.

We can identify a causal communication sequence: her signals seem to cause his. In therapy it is extremely important to point out how the signals of one partner are causally linked to the signals and psychology of the other partner. Causal thinking can be helpful. It has a local orientation and an individual focus. It can help us see how the behavior of one person is linked to that of another. What happens in one person can be understood by reference to the other person. If one head goes up, the other reacts and goes down. Both partners become responsible for events. In working with them, you might say something like, "Bob, you look depressed when Sharon looks so proud!"

Now, let's say that you study the same videotape even more precisely than the first time and you notice that it is difficult, if not impossible, to determine who did what first. You first have to answer, what is a signal? When does a signal begin or end? In fact, the more exact your observations of Sharon and Bob's head motions become, the more you must ask what constitutes a signal. Do we have to consider sudden intuitions you cannot see on videotape? Must you include your own state of mind or their preverbal signals that preceded the motions of their heads? Do you have to determine which impulses came before which body gestures? His head went down after hers went up, but he clenched his jaws before her head went up. Why? Imagine we asked Bob, and he said he was trying to hide a certain unhappiness he had when he saw Sharon.

In other words, the origin of the macroscopic, CR signals involving head motions is uncertain. Could his depression have caused her sense of superiority, or was it the other way round? We cannot always determine the causality of the situation because in psychology, only some events—like the direction of a head up or down—are consensual signals. Other signals belong to NCR, and we have no consensus about their existence. These sentient impulses, or subliminal feelings, cannot be easily seen on our video playback.

We encountered NCR signals in the quantum flirt phenomena of entangled photons, which are interconnected outside of time and space. We can speak of Bob and Sharon as entangled in an analogous manner, interconnected sentiently, beyond time and space. People flirt with one another in more ways than one.

Thus, one possible explanation for the interconnection between people or photons is that signals travel faster than the speed of light; another is Bohm's interpretation, which implies that people and photons are connected in a sentient universe of unbroken wholeness. In another explanation, people and photons flirt with each other in NCR. In the sentient world, quantum flirts occur in a non-local manner.

COMPENSATIONS IN LARGE HUMAN SYSTEMS

Interconnections are familiar to most people because of the phenomenon of compensation in relationships: one person balances the other, as if their total spin must be zero. If one is unhappy, the other tries to be happier. If one is of one opinion, often the other has a compensating idea.

The same holds true in large groups. Marginalized groups speak up not only because they are unhappy, but also because of the overall wholeness of the community. The tendency for a community to be whole and diverse, and for each individual in the group to be seen by the entire group as a significant individual, creates an awesome sense of entanglement and NCR connection between all members of the group.[7]

There are many situations in relationships where the members of a couple behave as if they were part of a system that has non-causal connections, where the principles of interconnectedness and symmetry seem to evoke reactions and experiences that balance one another. This may be why you are possessed by certain thoughts and observations at a given moment. The idea of compensation explains why certain events appear to flirt with you at a given moment, and why other events do not. Compensation suggests that what you experience is needed to balance what others observe.

If you work with people using only the causal perspective, you learn a great deal, but something is missing. You need the sense of that mysterious interconnection where you are entangled as well. Only then do you sense the subtle background to community and relationships.

Do we always balance, complement, or compensate the other, making situations whole? Is this a general psychological rule? We may never be able to answer this question, since to answer it completely would require us to experiment with NCR experiences in a CR context. And we can't do that, because non-consensus experiences avoid tracking in time and space. However, we can certainly say that symmetry and balancing principles hold between many NCR experiences of entangled interactions. We can think either that we are connected by some phenomenon that moves beyond the speed of light or that we are entangled because of the unbroken wholeness we share together. Since most human minds tend to be more or less self-balancing, perhaps some form of human-like universal mind connects us.

In any case, if we picture the psychological borders of Sharon as a circle, we can imagine the realm of what we refer to as Bob as another circle. The two people are separate but also overlap. The overlapping area is the area of unbroken wholeness, the area of entanglement, the area where we cannot speak clearly about you or me, but only about us. Here is where we flirt with one another in NCR.

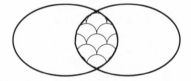

19.2 Entangled people: how "we" overlap

In the "us" area, we cannot say who has influenced whom. We can only say that signals are difficult to differentiate as far as locality and time are concerned. In one area, the signals of two people can be separated, but in the "us" area, the signals are entangled. There is no way of saying whether the sense of superiority or inferiority came first.

Signals such as the motions of the head that pass between us are separable and distinguishable; yet NCR exchanges, such as sudden intuitions and feelings, flickering of the eyes, or tightening of the jaws, are not easily separable. There will never be a consensus about the timing of these latter signals or their interconnection.

Thus, both inseparability and separability are present in every relationship. Inseparability is what we mean by "us"; it is both you and I. This "us" is something like a body with hands, feet, and torso, which can be separated, but with blood running through the veins, which cannot be localized as if it belonged to only one place.

Think about your own body for a moment. Your feet, for example, are different, yet they are not separate. When you walk, each foot knows what the other has done because a mind and nervous system connect them. The separate identities of people in relationship are like the limbs of their couple's body, of the "us" in a relationship. If we extend this analogy, then all separable people and beings are the limbs, channels for a greater body, for the body politic, the corporation, mass, aggregate, or group. As individuals, we are both separate from the whole and, at the same time, inseparable aspects of this same whole.

If we stay with psychology for a moment, we must ask what this means in practice. In the non-consensus view, the sense of inferiority that arose in Bob was coincident with a sense of superiority arising in Sharon. The senses of superiority and inferiority are like two aspects of one being, two roles in the overall relationship. Both senses are polarities in a shared field. They are like two political parties—anyone can belong to either party.

From the viewpoint of consensus reality, the couple has separable and inseparable system aspects; it is a whole, like a quantum system, which appears in the form of constantly entangled, non-causally connected NCR and CR signals from quantum objects. NCR signals are experiences such as body signals, dreams, and synchronicities, or "meaningful coincidences."

In the psychological view, human systems have both separable and inseparable aspects. In the feeling realm there are different identities and intentions; there are different parts whose NCR experiences are entangled, as in dreaming. Yet in CR we are not able to consistently and exactly differentiate which part belongs to which person. Exactly who did what, whom is to be blamed or praised, is never completely certain. At best, we can only speak in consensus reality of a relationship field with roles in it.

We cannot be certain if the field around us is a loaded atmosphere that comes before the roles such as depression and superiority, or if these roles created the field. Was the field of the couple there first, or was it the individual people? Such time-oriented questions are intriguing, but they deal only with consensual time, and can only be answered by the individuals involved.

Focusing on the separable individual psychology of the people involved in a relationship is an important and useful CR viewpoint. From this perspective, we can say that Bob is depressed because of his work, or that Sharon feels superior because of her background. But the system or relationship field, the atmosphere between the people, is just as important. Blame and responsibility are associated with individuals only in individual psychology when signals are separable. But there is no blame or causality that we can associate with one person or another in the NCR field. From the viewpoint of the overall field of a relationship, there is a dialogue, an interaction, or streaming, between what in CR appears to be inferiority and superiority.

UNIVERSAL MIND AND SYSTEMS THEORY

At this point, let's return to physics, where we can say that the manner in which particles compensate one another is a sort of symmetry or balancing. The balancing symmetry in the particles' behavior makes the idea of locality inapplicable. The manner in which the particles reflect and flirt with one another is due to their entanglement in the realm of unbroken wholeness. Particles are coupled, or interrelated. They compensate one another as if something like a worldwide field connects them.

Both people and particles exist in fields that have a system's character, something like a system's "intelligence" of its own, a tendency toward balance, wholeness, and self-compensation.

System ideas in the sciences have been recently forwarded by Fritz Capra. He quotes Immanuel Kant as one of the first philosophers (1790) to use the term "self-organizing" to explain the nature of living organisms: "We must think of each part (of such systems) as an organ that produces the other parts (so that each reciprocally produces the other). Because of this, (the organism) will be both organized and a self organizing being."[8]

This concept is similar to the self-organization hypothesis suggested by James Lovelock in *The Ages of Gaia*. Lovelock's Gaia hypothesis suggests evidence for the coevolution of living organisms, the Earth's climate, and its crust. The whole Earth strives to maintain itself. More recently, holistic biologist Rupert Sheldrake postulated the idea of a nonphysical "morphogenetic" field, which generates system intelligence, as the causal agent in the development and maintenance of biological form.[9]

Lovelock uses the term "Gaia," which comes from the Greek word meaning "mother earth," an anthropic and mythological concept suggesting that a human-like mind encompasses everything. Lovelock suggests—without saying exactly how—that our world has an anthropic nature, a human-like form.

If we put together the apparently intelligent, entangled human system with the Gaia hypothesis, we extend Lovelock's theory to include the entire field of relationships between all interacting, sentient beings. The world we live in now takes on a special quality. It becomes a unified whole filled with flirting partners; everything is flirting with everything else. The world itself is a human-like, self-organizing mind.

What are the organizing principles of this mind? This question lies, perhaps, at the very basis of theoretical physics; it is the core of theology and basic to psychology as well. From our previous discoveries, we can say that one of the principles of this universal mind is its symmetry. On the level of quantum objects, this symmetry manifests as balance, that is, as the "conservation of spin." In psychology, this symmetry manifests in the way we tend to compensate for one another's behavior, not necessarily in the moment, but certainly over time. Another aspect of this symmetry is the NCR principle of the reflecting quality of the quantum flirt, the tendency for partners to interact mutually in such a manner that we do not know which originated the signal exchange in the NCR realm. Such flirting phenomena give rise to the sense of non-locality.

Still another aspect of the symmetry of the universal mind can be called "equal access to all our parts in time." Let me explain. We all know what it feels like to be ourselves. I am Arny, and I identify myself in a certain way. But I dream a lot about Amy and flirt with her, too. In quantum flirting, I cannot tell the location of her or my signals. I cannot say if she is inside or outside me; she is both. Yet I am Arny enough to have an overview of the situation. In this view, I can see that I am sometimes Arny, but that I also sometimes identify myself as being like Amy. This potential for me to be both myself and the other, my ability to have an overview that sees both Arny and Amy, is a personal, NCR experience of what the universal mind must be like. But since Amy has these same capacities, the universal mind is in both of us.

Extrapolating from these thoughts, we can say, in general, that I am me, but I am also you; in fact, I am all the things I notice and that notice me. Also, I am a universal mind and operate according to symmetry principles. I tend to know all parts of myself, and to want them to know and communicate with each other, to value one another, and to compensate each other. A symmetry manifests itself in a tendency toward inner democracy, that is, toward treating the different parts of myself as equally important; no part is "first" and no part "second" in an absolute sense.

Most—if not all—people have this NCR tendency toward self-knowledge and balance either within themselves or in relation to the world as a whole. This self-balancing tendency is not found just between people around the world, but in one form or another in all psychologies and spiritual traditions. At some deep level, we all have all things within us.

These general considerations make it seem most likely that there is a sort of universal mind we all take part in, a gigantic human-like being, an "anthropos," a field in which we all live and manifest as our individual tendencies toward completeness in time. This universal mind appears not only as an aspect of individual people, but also as a balancing mechanism in our relationships and communities, as well as in the so-called material world around us. Until now, this interconnectedness has defied the sense of linear time and locality and has been called by many names, such as deja vu, synchronicity, and god.

The anthropos or universal mind is a basic pattern behind all observable events, and is a hypothetical basis for physics and psychology. We need such a hypothesis to explain the Bell experiment and interconnections between people. Marginalizing the sense of the universal mind gives us a sense of uprootedness. The sense of coming home, which many people find near death, is a rediscovery of our place in the universe, in the universal mind.

In my book, *Coma: Key to Awakening,* which I wrote with Amy after we witnessed the incredible awakening of a client who had been in a coma just before dying, I show how near-death experiences bring a rapid transformation of individual identity from the separate self toward the universal mind. Many people, perhaps every person, experience this NCR interconnectedness near death.

Besides symmetry, compensation, and non-locality, the universal mind must have a kind of "closure" to it. In Chapters 7 and 8 we discovered how closure in math refers to the fact that whatever happens in a number field must remain in the field. Closure means that all events remain on a field where events occur with specific rules. All CR and NCR perceptions are on our field of perception. This means that whatever we experience, whatever happens to you, to me, whatever happens between us or between everything else, happens in one and the same field. The perceptions of all events and interactions occur in one and the field. This "closed" field is our awareness field, since anything we experience unfolds as a CR or NCR experience in that field, amplifying, reducing, and squaring itself, reflecting upon itself. In other words, the universal mind has characteristics analogous to the field of complex numbers, which describe events that can be measured or experienced in NCR.

We may never be able to test in consensual terms the hypothesis of unbroken wholeness, the anthropos, or the universal mind, since we are each aspects of the universe. We can never do an experiment on the universe as a whole of which we are a part. Thus, we cannot create any CR proof of a statement about the entire universe, at least in consensus reality. On the other hand, we cannot disprove these theories in CR either.

We can only judge such theories on the basis of their being consistent with one another and their ability to give explanations and some meaning to life as a whole. For example, the universal mind theory is consistent with mythology. Until now, the universal mind has been projected on goddesses and gods. This same projection is found in the Gaia hypothesis. There is a long history of the images of human-like figures such as Gaia, which personify the universe. Such huge, human-like beings or anthropos figures, as they are referred to in mythology, are widespread. We have the Mother Earth or Great Spirit of Native Americans. Medieval Christians thought of the universe as Christ. Earlier, Germanic peoples imagined Ymir and Wotan to be the universe; Pan Ku was the universe in Chinese stories, Purusha in India.

In Chapter 26, on sacred geometry, we will see that such anthropos myths speak of the gods as having created the world to know themselves. They are often portrayed with symmetrical qualities.[10] They are consistent with the symmetry and balance found behind the reflective interaction in what I have called the quantum flirt, the math behind observation in quantum physics. The universal mind is consistent with the Gaia hypothesis, and with the psychology of interpersonal interactions. We could almost say that the divine spirit is a symmetry principle.

EVOLUTION OF THE UNIVERSAL MIND?

When we explore mythology, we discover a history of the universal mind not found in physics or psychology. According to anthropos myths, the great spirit we imagine ourselves to be part of is constantly dying and being reborn. In mythology, when the gigantic anthropos figures periodically die, they go to pieces, and from their dismembered parts the world is recreated. Their hair becomes the grass, their blood the rivers, their bones the trees.

When She goes to pieces, what we call our world, our culture, goes to pieces as well. This "going to pieces" implies that our NCR sense of togetherness comes apart. We then find ourselves isolated from one another, and become separated parts of the CR world. When the great spirit of the anthropos dies, we find ourselves in the midst of isolation and separation as individuals, couples, families, cultures, and worlds. When the universal mind falls into pieces, each of us, and each part of it, is wrenched away from the whole we belong to. Our sentient basis to community is broken into parts, and we become isolated, lonely human beings.

The mythic tragedy of death and dismemberment of these anthropos figures is experienced by us as individuals as the end of the world of unbroken wholeness. Broken wholeness then remains as the world. This is our present consensus reality where the trees, rivers, people, and other beings have little connection to one another. Our relationship field and the NCR experiences of oneness are marginalized.

Myths tell us that our present world has forgotten that the trees were once the bones, the rivers the blood, animals and people the cells of one being. In our broken modern world, we marginalize the experience of interconnectedness and ignore the quantum flirts and dreaming upon which the everyday world rests.

Perhaps this forgetfulness is why many people seem surprised at the beginning of the third millennium to rediscover through physics that photons are entangled. We have forgotten our own non-consensus, sentient experiences of being an inseparable part of a whole. You and I need to rediscover that everything we see is significant, that our awareness is needed to make the universe whole and conscious of itself.

Separation, however, is not all bad. It is also a pleasure to clarify and differentiate, to discover and know things in detail. The Western world has been mastering differentiation for centuries. But the recent Western interest in shamanism and the second attention seems to indicate that the anthropos is about to be recreated. Perhaps this is why ecologists and eco-psychologists have been asking us to identify more with the universal mind and to experience the Earth as our body.[11]

Perhaps the dismemberment of the universal mind is about to reverse itself. In that case, we find ourselves in the process of rediscovering unbroken wholeness. Bohm's hypothesis is an aspect of this rediscovery. The many-worlds theory of Everett and DeWitt is another. The Gaia hypothesis and the concept of a universal mind are yet other signs of rediscovery.

We live in a time when the universal mind is growing back together again. In the future, we can expect not only more differentiation of the world into parts, but also more insight into how all sentient beings are interconnected. As the inevitable renewal of a universal mind concept occurs, we shall know more about the mythic, NCR mind of the anthropos, God's mind, and the rules of the games She plays.

Our brief journey through math and quantum physics in these first nineteen chapters indicates that NCR awareness is patterned in part by the mathematical game rules of Her mind. Her NCR game rules include addition, subtraction, and closure. Furthermore, the rules govern reflection, quantum flirts, compensation, symmetry, and non-locality. Most, perhaps all, of our NCR perceptions are organized by the patterns of Her mind. Finally, the tendency to marginalize and create edges to certain experiences is the human part of the divine game.

Her mastermind may not be invulnerable to our consensual attitudes towards her. She goes to pieces, becomes crazy, or falls apart during periods in which our sense of NCR interconnectedness is frail or ignored. Marginalization of Her underlying unity may indeed be our particularly human role in creating or destroying the universe.

NOTES

1.   Bell's theorem (1964) proved that the chances for spin correlation for local hidden variables were constrained and exceeded by the quantum theoretical spin correlation function. This implies that quantum phenomena are inherently non-local, although it leaves open the possibility of non-local hidden variable theories as alternatives to quantum theory. Since the experimental verification of Alain Aspect in 1982, physicists are in general agreement about non-locality.

2. According to physicist Charles Card from the University of Victoria, British Columbia, "If there is a general lesson to be learned from non-local phenomena, it is that the primacy of conservation or symmetry principles over space-time localization in quantum mechanics may indicate that in nature, symmetry is ontologically prior to space and time. This conclusion is amply reinforced by theoretical particle physics in which the use of symmetry properties to characterize elementary particles prevails by necessity." See Card, page 41.

   The conservation principle says the total momentum of the system of two photons must remain the same. This is a symmetrical principle, since you can exchange you for me and the system remains unchanged. If one looks right, the other will be looking left.

3. See David Bohm's *Wholeness and the Implicate Order*, 1980.

4. Ibid., page ix.

5. William Keepin discusses Bohm's creative work further in a most interesting manner in *Revision* magazine, 1993.

   We should note that Menas Kafatos and Robert Nadeau, in *Conscious Universe*, 1990, show how the universe has a global locality in which its parts create a whole. This universal, undivided wholeness demonstrated by Bell occurs at all levels from atoms to galaxies and affects quantum properties such as spin. Kafatos and Nadeau argue that the universe must have a consciousness and that this has to be greater than any single part. Physics, in dealing with only observable parts of the universe, is unable to conceive of it as a whole. Yet this is crucial, for the whole influences the parts.

6. Mansfield and Spiegelman, in their essay "Quantum Mechanics and Jungian Psychology," connect non-locality to Jung's idea of synchronicity. According to Mansfield, "I suggest these correlations are perfect examples of non causal 'constant and experimentally reproducible phenomena'—examples of Jung's broader notion of synchronicity as 'general acausal orderedness." Also see Mansfield's fascinating book, *Synchronicity, Science and Soul-Making: Understanding Jungian Synchronicity through Physics, Buddhism, and Philosophy.*

7. See my *Sitting in the Fire*, written in the heat of community fire, for more information on managing group tensions.

8. Kant, 1790, 1987, page 253. I am thankful to Capra for this quote and for pointing to the systems theory and its importance in drawing the sciences together. See his *The Web of Life*, 1996, page 23.

9. See holistic biologist and theorist Rupert Sheldrake's easy to read *A New Science of Life*.

10. For more on the psychology of the anthropos, see my *The Year I*, 1985, which tells about the field in back of community life.

11. Eco-psychology will be discussed in greater detail in Chapter 42.

III

TAOISM IN RELATIVITY

20 | The Psychology of Relativity

*I want to know how God created this world. I am not
interested in this or that phenomenon. I want to know
His thoughts, the rest are details.*

—Albert Einstein

Most of us, like Einstein, ask big questions we cannot answer.
How was the universe created? What is it made of? How
large is it? What is the meaning and purpose of human
life? Where do we go when we're dead? How do universal laws connect with our behavior with others and ourselves?

To answer such questions, psychologists study dreams, near-
death experiences, and spiritual beliefs. Shamans go into altered
states and physicists do experiments with elementary particles.
Astrophysicists and cosmologists study the universe, questioning the
nature of its space and time, age and size, linearity and curvature.
They question the validity of the frameworks from which we observe
things. Their experiments deal with the observation of planets, with
enormous spaces, times, and energies, with the entire universe.
Experimental verifications for astronomical theories take place by
observing events such as the way light bends as it speeds by massive
stars.

Quantum physicists deal with questions about the nature of matter and the universe by developing quantum theories, while astrophysicists develop and extend the theory of relativity. In Section II
we considered how quantum theories are connected to math, psychology, and shamanism. In Section III we will focus on Einstein's
theory of relativity and its connections with quantum physics and

the psychology of altered states of consciousness. We'll begin by looking at the psychological background and implications of relativity.[1]

AN OVERVIEW OF RELATIVITY

The word "relativity" comes from relationship. Relativity theory in physics describes the relationships between different frames of reference. The theory has important implications for dealing with our frame of mind, our relationships, and the nature of reality. Each mental and physical framework has a specific view associated with it.

For example, one physical frame of reference might be the ground you stand on while watching a train go by. A second frame of reference might be you on the train moving over the tracks on that ground.

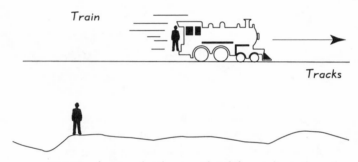

20.1 Two frameworks: the ground and the moving train

As far as the person in the train is concerned, if the train is steady and quiet, the train could be at a standstill and the world outside the train could be seen as moving.   Have you ever wondered whether the train is moving and the earth still, or whether the train is still and the earth moving by it? This experience points to the fact that there is no such thing as a one and only, correct and absolute frame of reference. Each view is relative to the other.

Physics says that since no framework is absolute, the basic laws must be formulated to fit all frames of reference and must have the same validity and basic form in all reference frames. In other words, the same laws of motion must apply for the person standing on the ground as for the person riding in a train going at a constant speed relative to the ground.

It turns out, as we will later see in detail, that Newtonian laws did not hold in the same way in all frameworks. The rules governing Newton's ideas about electricity and magnetism give very different answers when applied to events occurring from the viewpoints of the person standing on the ground and the one traveling inside the train.

Einstein, with his special theories of relativity, explained how to relate what happens in one framework to what is happening in another, how to relate the viewpoint of the person on the train to the viewpoint of the person on the ground. It turns out that if relative velocities are great, i.e., if the train is moving very fast, the concepts of space and time must change for the physical laws to be the same in all frameworks. Relativity will change our sense of consensus reality and make us reconsider its absoluteness. But let's not jump ahead too quickly.

The point is that relativity is the story of how space and time can no longer be understood as they are in daily life. In relativity, basic CR dimensions such as space and time are no longer absolute and independent from one another, as they are in everyday life, but vary from one framework to another. A measuring stick that seems to us to be one meter long while we are traveling in a moving rocket ship seems less than one meter long to someone standing on the ground measuring the stick with a telescope.

In the physics of relativity, a new spacelike dimension had to be created to replace the old, separate ideas of time and space because time and space varied depending on the frame of reference. The new spacelike dimension is called "space-time," which is a combination of what used to be called space and time.

Einstein showed that for the laws of physics to remain the same in all frameworks, events themselves have to be seen "relativistically," which means that the shape, size, and mass of things depend on the relative speed and direction of events. For example, someone walking two meters on the train will be seen by a person on the ground as having moved a distance that is a bit less than two meters. How much different? This depends on the speed of the train relative to the ground.

Relativity says that nothing, or almost nothing, is absolute. Only the speed of light does not change from framework to framework. We shall see that, regardless of how you measure the speed of light, it has a tendency to be the same. Even if you run alongside a light beam almost as fast as it is going, no matter how close you get to that beam, today's physics suggests that you will always measure the same speed of light. Relativity is full of wonders. Everything is relative but the speed of light.

Space and time can vary; space shrinks and time slows down—from the viewpoint of a person on the ground, the clock on the train runs more slowly. Why haven't we noticed all this? One reason is that none of these weird things shows up until the relative velocities get near the speed of light. The speed of the train relative to the ground may be fast, but is only a fraction of the speed of light. That is why even if we on the ground could get a quick look at the clock on the train, we would not see space and time bending and shrinking.

Another reason we do not notice such things is that we usually marginalize our own non-consensus experiences. Most of us have felt times when time seemed very fast, or unreasonably slow. Because our speed in CR is usually within the range of 0 to 600 miles an hour (the latter on airplanes)—instead of 186,000 miles a second, the speed of light—and because we tend to marginalize NCR experiences, some people are shocked to consider that space and time depend on the framework of the observer.

ASPECTS OF RELATIVITY IN OTHER THEORIES

The relativity theories of Einstein are not the first we have seen. Aspects of relativity theories appeared in the study of quantum mechanics in the many-worlds theory, which said that many different viewpoints or worlds can exist simultaneously. The observed event is not the only event but one among many that are also present, although marginalized through observation.

We have also seen that observations are not absolute, but depend on the decisions about which measurements to make.   Furthermore, from the discussion of quantum flirting, we saw that the very idea of an observer who initiates the observation is relative, since both the observer and the observed "flirt" with one another in an inseparable manner. CR and NCR are relative frameworks.

The study of mathematics in the early part of our journey also included relativistic ideas. We found that numbers and counting depend on the psychology of the observer and the relationship between the observer and the observed. Mathematics too is only valid relative to the psychological framework of a given observer. What one counts depends on who one is!

INTERCONNECTING PSYCHOLOGICAL FRAMEWORKS

In psychology we must often deal with relativity because of the differences between frames of reference within any one person and between people of different ages, cultures, races, and so forth. Each culture has its own framework, and within any one given individual there are at least two frameworks from which to view the world. There is consensus reality, or CR, and altered states of consciousness, or NCR, in which experiences seem irrational to those in CR. We marginalize viewpoints in ourselves and in others as well.

All over the world, the main framework of consciousness is connected to spatial and temporal ideas, to clocks and measuring sticks, rigid spaces that can be separated from one another and times that progress forward in a linear fashion.

There is a general consensus that an hour and a meter are the same the world over. In non-consensus experience, in another framework, a square room can become curved and time can be warped, as we know from being in altered states of consciousness linked to dreaming, drug use, or physical injury.

Despite relativity, many psychologists think that the framework of everyday reality is more important than dreaming. If someone is in an altered state for a long time, something is considered to be wrong with the person; his or her framework is considered disturbed, not "normal."

Instead of considering people in all frameworks as being in equally valid states of consciousness, the statistical majority is considered "normal." In contrast to such psychological prejudices, our journey thus far has suggested instead that the rules for CR are the same for NCR, in the same manner as the processes of addition, subtraction, multiplication, and division hold not only for real numbers, but for imaginary numbers as well.

The psychological processes of amplification, marginalization, and repression occur in all frameworks. Moreover, just as the speed of light is the same in all frameworks in physics, the concept of awareness seems to hold in each framework in psychology. There is a potential for awareness in all states, even in psychotic and near-death situations.[2] Furthermore, since the same basic patterns (such as arithmetic) can be found in psychology as well as in math, physics, and shamanism, math and psychology should eventually be seen as different frameworks, or viewpoints, of the same art or science.

A crucial aspect of relativity in physics is that no one framework is absolute. Relativity theory is a natural democracy in a world that tends to be one-sided. Since no one viewpoint is sufficient to describe the world, all viewpoints have equal importance and are significant, relative to one another. In physics, relativity describes the details of how the varying frameworks relate to one another.

Yet, just as most people stress the value of everyday reality over the reality of dreaming, physics too places more importance on the classical (CR) setting involving everyday language and state-oriented terms such as matter and particle than it does on the NCR aspect of quantum objects. In other words, physics emphasizes consensus reality and marginalizes the NCR events of the quantum world described by complex numbers. This is most likely why Bohm's theory of starting with unbroken wholeness has not had the popularity of other theories that begin with parts and particles. Future physics will need a broader concept of relativity, one that includes the equal validity of all states of consciousness, not just CR states.

ON THE PSYCHOLOGY OF RELATIVITY

We shall see in the next chapters that light, or rather, the speed of light plays a crucial role in relativity because this speed is the only thing that remains constant in all frameworks. Everything is relative in relativity theory, except the speed of light.

To get a feeling for the speed of light, let's think about light. Some people do not realize that light actually has a speed because it goes so fast. But it is not instantaneous. It takes time to go from one place to another.

Until recent times, people thought light was infinitely fast—and that we are able to see because light comes out of our eyes! A Greek myth about the goddess Aphrodite explains that she took fire from the heart of the Universe and lit the fire in our eyes at birth. In this ancient theory, our eyes transmit light into the world. In other words, we see things by sending light out toward the objects being viewed.

This idea has been updated by today's physics, which explains that we see by virtue of the light that reflects off objects into our eyes. No light comes out of the eye itself.

Yet the myth is not totally incorrect, even though it cannot be substantiated in terms of consensus reality. This myth is one of the patterns of non-consensus reality. Aphrodite, goddess of love, is said to have fashioned the human eye with love to hold the eye's various constituents together. The idea of the quantum "flirt" rejuvenates the ancient myth of the loving, radiant eye. In the quantum flirt, the NCR process behind observation, signals can be seen as transmitted from the observer to the observed and back again before an observation takes place. In NCR reality, CR observations can take place only because of Aphrodite. All observations are based on aphrodisiacs, in a way—tendencies not to increase sexual desire, but to relate!

The idea of sight occurring because there is light within us is a myth: it may be a NCR experience, but it is not a CR fact. Do we have light coming from our eyes? The answer is both yes and no: yes in NCR and no in CR.

In fact, all myths are correct from the viewpoint of the personal experience of the people who believe them. All lies, myths, legends, fairy tales, and historical viewpoints are correct for those who have experienced them. But something that is true in NCR is not necessarily also true in consensus reality. Truth is a matter of framework! Likewise, because something is true in consensus reality, such as a diagnosis that says you are ill, does not necessarily mean that this "diagnostic truth" is true in your experience.

It is both true that light originates from our eyes in NCR and not true in CR; it does not move infinitely fast in human time. How long do you think it takes the light of the sun to get to the Earth? When I ask this question in my class, I get various answers. One exchange went like this:

Richard: Eight and a half minutes!

Arny: That's right! He remembers his physics! It takes eight and a half minutes to get here.

Jan: It seems long, the sun's distance is further away than most of us realize.

Arny: That's right! It's a long way off!

Joe: Especially in Oregon, where it rains so much!

Arny: The sun is far away and if you put clouds in between, it seems even further. But seriously, the sun that we see when we look at it out there in space is not the real sun. What we see is the sun that was out there eight minutes ago. Sound like Taoism? Lao Tse could easily have said, "The sun you can see is the not real sun!" Anything we see is not the real thing; it is the thing it was a split second ago.

If the sun burned out, we wouldn't know about it here until eight minutes later. One day the sun is going to burn out because it is constantly using up its energy. The sun is a big star. It's about a million times the mass of the Earth. But one day it will burn out.

The moment it burns out will be fascinating for the scientific part of us, if humans are still living at that time. If you were alive and the Earth were still around, this blackout would remain unknown until eight minutes after it happened. Since, according to Einstein, nothing goes faster than the speed of light, the last light rays will be reaching you eight minutes after the sun is extinguished. We can see only the past. In a way, there is no such thing as present.

What happens if a child comes along and says, "Einstein is wrong. I know things ahead of time. I dream about things before they happen, therefore something must travel faster than the speed of light."

Who is correct, the child or Einstein? Both are right. They are simply in different frameworks. What Einstein meant was that *nothing that you can measure in consensus reality travels faster than the speed of light.* Consensus reality defines itself, so to speak, in terms of what can be measured, reproduced, and shared with others. If there is no consensus about the child's precognition, physicists will say that the child is just plain lucky, because telepathy cannot be measured.

As physics becomes more relativistic in its basic outlook, there will be more room for the child's viewpoint, for dreaming, for precognition and altered states. There is already room in the mathematics of physics for such states, but not in experimental physics as long as the child's experiences cannot be measured. Physics need only include experience to understand itself better.

The math of relativity describes its basic dimensions of space-time in terms of imaginary numbers and therefore deals with things we cannot see or prove. This may be why relativity has inspired so many science fiction stories about going forward and backward in time. It gives room to explain the child's telepathy (an explanation I shall attempt later in Chapter 27, on synchronicity). The math also has inspired many astrophysicists to consider the possibility of hyperspaces and universes other than our own.

No Place of Absolute Rest

In the early 1900s, Einstein was a file clerk for the Swiss government. He had flunked his physics exams and couldn't get into the Swiss technical university (ETH). His teachers thought he was lazy and poor at math. Einstein wrote his first papers on quantum mechanics in 1905 and his first papers on relativity about ten years later. It was only after he published his ideas on relativity and quantum physics that he was finally hired by the ETH as a teacher.

Although Einstein was eventually awarded the Nobel Prize for his work on quantum mechanics, his work on relativity was ignored at first. People thought it was a mistake! No one could imagine a four-dimensional universe, and people wanted to reject its existence. The world believed Einstein only after experiments and observations of the way light behaves in the universe verified predictions from his theory.

One of Einstein's breakthrough notions in the special theory of relativity was that there is no place in the universe that is at absolute rest. Everything is in constant movement relative to everything else. Until Einstein came along, people assumed that there must be something that is absolutely at rest. In the eighteenth century, people speculated that a universal fog, or viscous fluid, called "ether," was at rest while everything else moved through it. For hundreds of years, people clung to a CR framework in which Earth was the fixed center of the universe. After a time, people realized that the Earth moved relative to the rest of the universe. Still, people thought that if the Earth was not fixed, the solar system was at rest. If the solar system was not fixed, then, it was hoped, the galaxy was. If the galaxy was moving, then at least the universe itself must be at rest.

Why do physicists need some absolute medium that is at rest? If something is at absolute rest, you can measure the velocity of other things relative to it. If the Earth is at absolute rest, the velocity of the train can have an absolute value. All trains then have a velocity relative to one framework, the solid earth. Everyone looks for something absolute from which to judge all other things.

But experiments proved that the ether was not at rest. In fact, it turned out that there was no ether at all, at least in consensus, measurable reality. Ether was a figment of everyone's imagination, especially the imagination of those developing theories of electricity and magnetism, like Clerk Maxwell. At the turn of the century, ether may have been a goddess—a precursor to something like an NCR universal mind. But she was not an objective fact.

Physicists were not alone in wanting things to be steady and absolutely fixed. Most of us feel similarly. We often feel that one thing is right and another absolutely wrong. We feel that fundamental truth must exist. Most of us feel we cannot live without something firm and fundamentally stable. This is why most of us are frequently convinced that our viewpoint is the correct one. We want to measure ourselves and everyone else from this viewpoint. Yet in CR, there is nothing absolute, not even what I am saying. Everything we say comes from one of many possible viewpoints.

Consider the speed measured by a traffic cop parked at a corner, whose radar measures your car going 60 miles an hour in a 55-mile-an-hour zone. If you were going 60 in a 55-mile-an-hour zone, she could give you a ticket. But you could argue in a court of law that you were not going 60 in any absolute manner but only 60 relative to the cop's standing radar meter. You could argue that your speed was really zero and that she and the rest of the world were moving too fast, that everything else was going 60 miles an hour. Slow down, world! From your viewpoint, you should be giving the rest of the world a speeding ticket. Could you be the only normal person? Are you not correct in this scientific evaluation of speeding?

If you made this argument in court, the judge would probably give you a ticket and wonder about your sanity. She would say that the Earth or the stars, or something like ether is at rest and that relative to that, you were going too fast. Most likely she would say, "Sorry, the Earth does not move, you are wrong."

If you hired Einstein as your lawyer, he could say, "You are right, your speed is relative, not absolute. The policewoman and you are in different frameworks; different times and spaces are involved. None is absolute."

What does speeding mean? What is velocity? If the cop were enlightened and relativistic, she might say, "Your relative speed is too fast relative to the viewpoint of society, of the consensus reality framework. You are being given a ticket—not because you are going too fast, but because you are going too fast relative to consensus reality. This ticket says there is a relationship issue for us all to think about. You need to know more about CR, and it could be that it, too, may need to hear more from you." The question of who must pay should be a negotiation between you and the world.

If you ever meet such a policewoman, you should really get out of your car on the spot and bow down to her, pay on the spot for the ticket, and thank her for the enlightenment. Such a person would awaken you to relationship, the basic problem of relativity. She would be awakening you not to the absolute measure of your being wrong (or right), but to the need for a greater, environmental, relationship consciousness.

Relativity questions are all absolute-sounding formulations of what is normal, what is healthy, what is too fast, who is best looking. Much of everyday life is based on CR evaluations that are one-sided and entrenched in the illusion of absolute values. How do we know that the temperature of your body, your moods, your blood pressure, your hair, your face, your skin color, and your size are not the normal ones? How do we know that everyone and everything else is not off? Who is the absolute measure of anything?

Einstein's relativity theory was not accepted at first because the world around him—like most of us—wanted time and space to be absolute and hoped for something at rest, stable, and firm. People hoped for standards from which all else could be measured. Alas, no cultural or individual consensus reality is absolute, and no one reality can be used as an absolute judge for others. There is only relationship, and this relationship between frameworks is what Einstein discovered.

Notes

1. I recommend the following books for those who want a broader background on the details of the physics of relativity than I will be able to give here.

    Robert Osserman's *Poetry of the Universe* was written by a mathematician. It's poetic and easy to read if you're interested in science. This book helps us understand where geometry came from and its connection with everyday life.

    Albert Einstein's *Relativity* is my favorite, but may be heavy if you haven't studied much science. It contains a minimal amount of mathematics. If you want to read how this unusual man really thought, read him directly.

    Roger Penrose's *The Emperor's New Mind* is for those of you who aren't shy about math. Penrose is a mathematical physicist who is also interested in the connection between psychology and physics.

    Larry Gonick and Art Huffman's *The Cartoon Guide to Physics* is easy and fun. When you have nothing to do, pull this book out to study physics and laugh.

2. I discuss extreme and altered states of consciousness and the evidence of existing awareness in all these states in *Working on Yourself Alone* and in *City Shadows*.

21 | The End of Illness

... the special theory of relativity has grown out of electro-dynamics and optics.

—Einstein, in *Relativity*

In this chapter, we will discover how Einstein developed the special theory of relativity and explore the paradoxes it resolved in the theories of electricity and magnetism. We will then be able to see how relativity theory will resolve similar problems in the theory of mental and physical diseases.

The special theory of relativity says that the laws of physics that are true for you while you are sitting in a train moving at a constant speed relative to the earth must be just as true for you when you are sitting quietly on the earth at rest.

"Isn't that obvious?" you may say to yourself. It is, and is not, so obvious. If you bounce a ball while you are on the train, it goes up and down. But for someone on the ground looking through the window at the ball as it goes up and down and the train rolls along, the motion of the ball is not simply up and down at all. Relative to the observer standing still on the ground, the ball appears not only to move up and down but to go forward as well. The ball's path for the person on the ground will look like the diagram on the bottom in Figure 21.1.

From the train

*a ball that seems to go up and down in
the framework of the train . . .*

From the ground

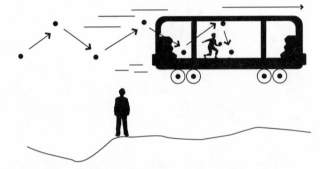

*can look like it goes up, down,, and sideways
to someone standing on the ground
watching the train go by.*

21.1 Bouncing ball from two viewpoints

If the laws that govern the way the ball is bouncing up and down are to remain the same in all frameworks, then these laws must compensate for the apparent differences in the ball's path.

In general, if many of us look at the same thing—whatever it is— whatever we say about it must be formulated as "from my framework, my viewpoint." For example, applied to psychology, relativity means that instead of saying, "the unconscious is incomprehensible and unknown," we need to say, "as long as I am in the framework of Western consensus reality, the unconscious is incomprehensible." A relativistic shaman would have to say, "the unconscious is not incomprehensible from the viewpoint of altered states of consciousness." A Taoist might say that from her non-dualistic viewpoint, there is no such thing as the unconscious. All these statements about the unconscious are correct only if they are relativistic, since their accuracy depends on a given framework. No one viewpoint is completely correct if stated as if it were a "fact" without reference to the framework it is coming from. The principle of relativity is needed to resolve differences of opinion attributable to different frameworks in psychology and physics.

MAGNETISM AND ELECTRICITY

Einstein used relativity to resolve basic problems in electricity and magnetism. Consider your comb. If you run the comb through your hair, it sparkles with electricity, and if you put it near your hair again, it tries to draw your hair away from your head. The difference in electrical charge between your hair and the comb attracts the hair to the comb. Although nobody knows exactly what it is, an electric charge can be represented schematically at a point by the letter q. Two positive or two negative charges repel one another, whereas a positive and a negative charge attract one another.

Electric charge has an effect on the things around it. The electric charge has a field of force around it and attracts or repels other charges. In physics, a field around an electric charge can be represented by a diagram like Figure 21.2.

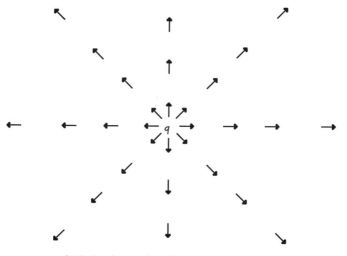

21.2 An electric force field around a charge q

The charge q at the center of the field creates a field represented by arrowheads, ← or →. There are more arrows near the center and fewer further away, which indicates that more electric force will be exerted on another charge near q than further away, where there are fewer arrowheads. The pull and push, the attraction and repulsion on other electric charges are greater near the center than further away. The further you go from the center, the weaker the field's "lines of force" become.

So, as you move your comb further and further away from your hair, the field around the comb gets weaker: it has less force to move your hair.

I have been speaking as if we knew what an electric field is, even though no one knows exactly. What is going through the air that acts at a distance? How does it do that? And why does it get weaker and weaker? Is it magic? Without creating answers at this point, physics simply assumes that fields exist, and that they can be measured by the forces they produce on objects. Physics uses many schemes, theories, and imaginary concepts such as "fields" because such schemes produce measurable results, like the amount of force exerted on your hair at a certain distance from the comb. Later in our journey, we shall improve on these theories.

MAGNETISM

Now let's think about magnets. If you put metal filings on the top of a sheet of paper and put a magnet underneath, the magnet organizes the metal filings into a certain shape. A magnet has its own field, which manifests by how it pulls little metal filings around.

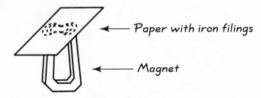

21.3 Magnet organizes metal filings on a sheet of paper.

Until the 1890s, people thought that the force created by the field of magnets and the force created by electric charge were independent. Then physicists discovered, by putting a metal wire in the midst of a magnetic field and moving the wire around, that the two forces, magnetism and electricity, were connected. When they waved the wire in the midst of the magnet's field, they discovered that electricity goes through the wire! They discovered a way to generate electricity, a method that changed our world.

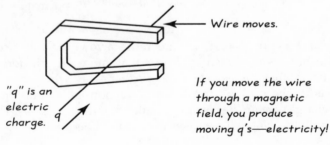

21.4 Generating electricity

This motion of wire through a magnet's field is how generators work. If the wire is wound around a wheel, and if water turns the wheel around in the midst of a magnet, the wire moves through a magnetic field and you get electric power from the wire. If your car's motor moves wires on the wheel that turns in your car's generator, which has a magnet in it, you get electricity for your lights and other equipment.

If there's an electric charge moving through a wire, electricity not only flows through the wire, but also creates a magnetic field around the wire. You can test this by using a compass. The magnetic needle will sense the magnetic field created by the moving electric wire, just as the compass senses the magnetic field of the Earth.

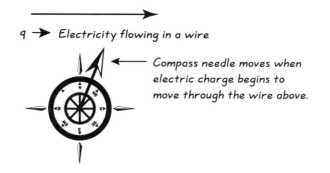

21.5 Compass needle (of stationary compass) is moved by the magnetic field created by electric charges moving through the wire.

From such experiments, we can see that electricity, (the movement of electric charge) and magnetism (which was needed to move the metal compass needle and metal filings) must be connected because they are able to create one another. A moving electric charge produces a magnetic field and a moving magnetic field produces an electric current.

Clerk Maxwell made this interconnection between electricity and magnetism and developed the laws of electricity and magnetism in the latter half of the 1800s. These laws are now called Maxwell's laws.

If you keep in mind how magnetism generates electricity and how electricity generates magnetism, you might enjoy experimenting with the following fascinating "thought" experiment.

Let's pretend that I am standing still on the ground with a compass in hand and I notice an electric charge go by in the air. Since I know moving electric charges create magnetic fields, it makes sense for me to expect that while I'm standing there on the ground, the needle of my compass will go zoom! And it does.

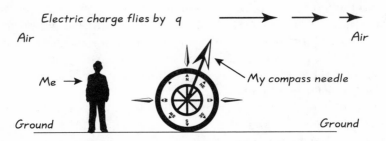

21.6 Electric charge goes by, my compass notices magnetism.

But what happens if you are not bound to the ground like I am but can fly through the air, alongside the electric charge? Relative to your position, that electric charge stands still because you and it are both traveling at the same speed. So, if you are carrying a compass and look at your compass, what will you see? Will it move because of the charge that is flying with you in the air?

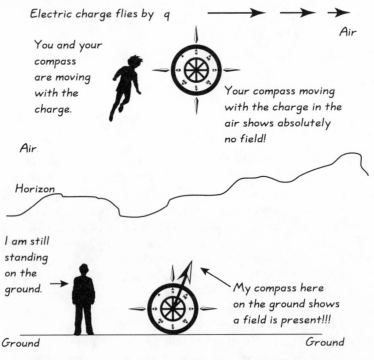

21.7 Your compass needle senses nothing if you fly with the charge—but my compass on the ground senses a magnetic field!

Nothing happens to your compass because the charge is not moving relative to you. Thus, that charge does not create a magnetic field for you, but the moving charge does impress my compass. Since I am standing on the road watching you and your electric charge zoom by, *the charge is moving relative to me* and creates a magnetic field, as far as I am concerned. My needle senses this and moves.

Thus, when you call down to me, "Hey, Arny my compass says there is no field," and I call back, "No, dear friend in the air, you are wrong, my compass says there is a magnetic field," the two of us have a relationship problem. You tell me that my compass is broken and I tell you that yours is incorrect because it shows no field. Is this just a problem of perception? No. If you could look down and read my needle, you would see that it moved, and if I could look up and read your compass needle, I would see that it did not move.

If the laws of physics are going to be the same in all areas and frameworks, both of us must be correct. But how could I measure something as fundamental as a magnetic field in a given area with a given moving charge, while you show no such measurement?

This was such a core problem that Maxwell was ready to throw away his equations, which described electricity and magnetism in one framework. He knew magnetism and electricity were connected, but he could not figure out how to solve the riddle of how two compasses could say different things. His results led to paradoxes. What a dilemma.

Then Einstein came along and said, "Relax, everything is fine. I will solve the riddle by the principle of relativity." Einstein showed that electricity and magnetism could not be described independent from frameworks in space and time. Space, time, and matter—which includes magnetism and electricity—are all *interdependent*. Before Einstein's relativity principle, people thought the forces of nature were independent of space and time, and that the forces had nothing to do with the framework of the observer. But Einstein said, "I will show you mathematically how to transform your velocities into relative velocities, change space and time into relative space and time—that is, relative to a given framework—and finally, I will show you how to relate the results in different frameworks. Then, dear Maxwell, your laws will hold everywhere."

What Einstein discovered, and what we can guess from the above experiment with compasses, is that forces like magnetism depend on velocities of objects relative to the observer and her measuring instruments. Results depend on the framework of the observer. In other words, the forces of nature are all connected to our observational frameworks, to the times and spaces of the world from which we observe things.

PATHOLOGY IS RELATIVE

We are exploring physics in part because its lessons have the potential to enrich our personal lives. Let's think for a moment about the psychological analogy to the problems of magnetism and electricity. What is the psychological equivalent of somebody moving with a charge who feels no forces, while another person watching that same charge from the ground thinks, "Wow, that's a very magnetic situation"?

You may know the answer from your experience with altered states of consciousness. The person flying in the air is in something like an altered state. Imagine someone who is in an altered state and who thinks he or she is God. As far as the rest of us are concerned, he or she is flying high, like that charge. Imagine further that, as far as she herself is concerned, she is normal. Nothing weird is happening; she is simply God.

If you were able to get into her state and fly with her through her process, you might begin to understand why she feels she is God and think that, as far as her state is concerned, she is God. In fact, when you can truly move with her in her world, the normal world looks strange and boring, and she looks fine, while the people on the ground look weird.

If you are not moving with her, you think her compass is off, she has lost her way, she doesn't notice that she is creating confusion around her. You might even call her psychotic. Others like you in your frame of mind think she is weird, too. But she feels she is normal and that you and your friends are nuts.

THE END OF ILLNESS

Let's think about another example that is totally internal to you and your body. Remember what it feels like to be tired. If you move with your own inner experience of that tiredness, if you step into it and go deep into yourself, you may suddenly feel at peace instead of tired. If you do not go with your experience, if you and your body are in separate frameworks, your body, like a compass, feels like it is dragging, it feels heavy and tired. You feel there is a problem and search for a solution: more sleep, perhaps, or more coffee.

As long as you sit in consensus reality and do not move with the flow of your process, it seems like the force of tiredness works on you. If, however, you let go of your grounded "reality" orientation, if you fly with your body process, you flow with your own nature and feel no resistance. In fact, everything is perfect.

In the first state, your "compass," that is, your inner body monitor, tells you that you have symptoms, you are crazy and sick. In the second state, your monitor is peaceful, you feel you are in the Tao and all is well. In the first state you maintain your position in consensus reality; in the second, you flow with dreaming. In other words, how you experience your body depends on your frame of reference.

Many relativistic effects occur in hospitals. One day you may find your body lying on the operating table after an accident, while "you" float near the ceiling above your body, experiencing no problems whatsoever. Meanwhile, you see the doctors and nurses below saying urgently, "This person is dying, save her." From your framework, they are wasting their time being upset. You know you will come back as soon as you are done with your out-of-body trip.

In other words, whether or not you are ill or crazy or even dying is a matter of relativity. Having a symptom is a matter of your state of consciousness. What appears to be an illness from one viewpoint is not an illness from another.

Even the experience of pain depends on your frame of consciousness. In one state your process causes you pain, while in another, when you go with the pain, there may be no forces at all causing pain. Instead, you feel creative and full of energy.

It's all about the relativity of frameworks. In one framework there is a magnetic field, in another, no magnetic field at all. Both viewpoints are correct. Neither viewpoint is the one and only truth. Don't assume one viewpoint is the right one. Don't let anyone convince you that one reality is real and another is unreal.

A psychological symptom, a "mental disease," or a "physical disease" exists only from the viewpoint of consensus reality. In dreaming, and in the midst of following your process, all can be healthy and well.

In other words, diseases are not absolutely real. They are seen as disturbances only from the CR viewpoint, which defines a normal body in terms of weight, size, temperature, and other factors. From the viewpoint of NCR, symptoms are processes you can follow like paths through the woods.

Some chronic symptoms, such as skin problems, allergies, and headaches, cannot be cured because they are symptoms only from the viewpoint of consensus reality. From the viewpoint of altered states of consciousness in which you follow their direction, these symptoms may not exist at all. Regardless of how far science progresses, as long as it retains only the CR viewpoint, many physical diseases will never be "cured." This may be why we still cannot cure the common cold, why people get old and die, why we cannot get rid of asthma. We don't only get colds—from another framework, we simply go through periods of shedding lots of tears, dripping water from the nose, and going internal, to bed and to sleep. Likewise, from another viewpoint we don't just get old and die—we transform into something besides the human form.

If Einstein were here now, he might say, "Yes, physical diseases exist only in one frame of reference, not in another." In one framework, in the altered state framework where you follow and conjugate experience, diseases do not exist. There is just a process moving along. In dreaming, your dream "thermometer," "compass," and everything else measures wellness. Relativity hints at a paradigm shift in how we think about illness and wellness.

Healing, too, has no absolute meaning. It is relative. You can be healed in reality and seen as sick in a dream. Similarly, you can be healed in a dream and still have symptoms in consensus reality.

You may think at this point, "Come on, Arny, if you put a cast on a broken leg it gets better. Or if you give somebody in a wild state some drugs, they calm down or at least feel better and are quieter. Who needs relativity?"

My answer would be that you can help a broken leg to heal with a cast, but you have not dealt with the force that broke leg in the first place. As far as dreams are concerned, this force may be the problem, and, if it is not dealt with, something else could be broken.

You can drug a hyperactive kid into docility. We can make a headache feel better with aspirin. Many people feel more comfortable in consensus reality by repressing their symptoms. But we must still be careful to notice which observer in which framework describes the body as hyperactive, painful, or broken. Such terms apply only to consensus reality, where we identify ourselves as physical bodies, as individuals, parents, doctors, and school systems.

Consensus reality is an important reality. But it is not the only one. And it may not even be the crucial one, as far as symptoms and other events are concerned. That is why, when the cast and the drugs are removed, the NCR origins of the problems are still present. From the viewpoint of dreaming, consensus reality is one-sided. Its absoluteness is incorrect, an illusion. We might even say, from the viewpoint of dreaming, that this one-sidedness is hurtful, a diseased attitude. Healers for centuries have been immersing themselves in dreaming to assist "ill" people not only to "heal" their symptoms but also to "heal" the one-sidedness of consensus reality. By reminding their clients of relativity, traditional shamans heal one-sidedness.

A holistic healing occurs in consensus reality not only through dealing with symptoms with CR procedures, but by going with the dreaming process, with the so-called symptoms as well. If you have a headache, for example, and it feels like a hammer is hitting you, get into hammering as well as taking an aspirin. In the paradigm shift hinted at by relativity, we need to deal with symptoms from the viewpoints of both CR and NCR frameworks.

Illnesses are like electricity and magnetism: they appear in one framework but not another. Pain, like magnetic fields, bothers us in part because of our lack of relationship to the dreaming framework. If you are ill, my recommendation is to treat your symptoms in terms of consensus reality, make yourself as comfortable as possible, and then congratulate your body for dreaming, leave your consensus reality mind, and get into the body process. Then you know that you are not only sick in CR, but a powerful dreamer as well. In this way, you put an end to illness.

22 | Shape-shifting and Hyperspaces

> *"The third gate of dreaming is reached when you find yourself in a dream, staring at someone else who is asleep. And that someone else turns out to be you,"* don Juan said.
>
> —Don Juan in Carlos Castaneda's
> *The Art of Dreaming*

At the core of Einstein's relativity theory are patterns for transforming events in one framework to those in another. At this point, we will begin to study the psychological analogy of these transformation patterns, namely, "shape-shifting," an anthropological term for shamanic methods of moving between realities.

Shape-shifting means changing identities and states of consciousness. Some form of shape-shifting is always involved in the resolution of psychological problems in therapeutic practice. Your personal development depends on being able to move from one framework or state of consciousness to another, seeing the same thing from different viewpoints, living in various worlds, one at a time. For example, in one world you may be in consensus reality where time goes forward, yet in another world, you may enjoy another kind of life in which time goes slower, backward, or even stops.

Let's explore together some of the special means for shape-shifting. To help us understand the details of the transitions between frameworks, I shall clarify what is meant by special terms such as framework, dimensions, spaces, and hyperspaces. We will be moving together not only through mathematical but also through shamanic and psychological domains.

DIFFERENT FRAMEWORKS

Einstein did not ask how to make the shamanistic transition from one state of consciousness to another, but he did ask how to connect observations made in one physical framework to those in another. Even as a child, Einstein asked himself amazing questions. He pondered whether he could see himself in a mirror if he were traveling along with the speed of light. He thought, if I am on Earth, I look into my mirror and see myself. The light that reflects my face on the mirror, and brings the mirror's image back to me, is light that travels at a certain velocity, let's say *c*. But if I travel at the speed of light, *c*, can I see myself? To see myself in my mirror, something unusual must happen because the light I need to see may no longer be able to catch up to me. To see myself in the mirror moving at the speed of light, something weird must happen... perhaps something warps space and time? Today, we know his suspicions are correct.

Remember our discussion in the preceding chapter about different physical frameworks in physics? Remember the person standing on the ground in one framework and the other person in the train in another framework? Another example of two different frameworks is two possible ways of viewing an event that takes place in a particle accelerator. Imagine a two-mile-long tube, which is used to accelerate particles. Imagine the particle accelerator curved into a circle—the kind physicists use to accelerate one particle and smash it into another to find out what the particles are made of. If you put a particle in one end of the accelerator, you can accelerate it around in a circular tube until it reaches two thirds of the speed of light.

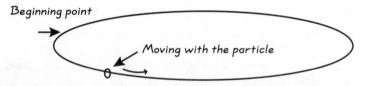

22.1 Particle accelerator (a two-mile-long circular tube)

Standing on the ground at the beginning of the accelerator tube, you are in a "grounded" framework. In that framework you are able to measure the particle, which weighs next to nothing. When the accelerator speeds up the particle, after a short time and about two miles travelled, the particle seems to you, measured from your framework on the ground, to weigh almost double what it did to begin with! From your viewpoint, it gained a lot of weight after traveling two miles. From your viewpoint the particle went two miles.

Now, let's switch frameworks and travel with the particle, much like we traveled on the train. How far do you think the particle went from its framework, from its own viewpoint? Only two or three inches! From its viewpoint—that is, from the viewpoint of someone traveling along with the speed of the particle—things are relatively quiet. In fact, it seems as if the particle went only a few inches and did not gain weight. It certainly did not go two miles!

Even though Einstein was only a child when he pondered what would happen when he went very fast with speeding particles, he was right. Unusual things happen with space and time when you approach the speed of light. Today we know that if you were able to fly along with the particle at a constant speed, you would be able to understand it better and see that, from its viewpoint, the world around it shrinks while you and it remain about the same weight and size. If you are moving with the particle, the outer world shrinks, although for those on the ground, the world remains the same and the particle changes.

Einstein considered the problem of how to relate measurements taken of the same event from different frameworks. He discovered how to relate the size of the particle measured while standing on the ground outside the accelerator to the size of the particle measured while traveling along with the particle in the accelerator. His answer was called the "Lorentz transformation," a mathematical formula that explains how things bend, bulge, and transform—how what seems like two miles in one framework is only a few inches in another. This transformation shows how the space and time of one framework relate to another, and how space and time expand and contract as you move between frameworks.

SHAPE-SHIFTING TRANSFORMATIONS

The math used to discover the Lorentz transformation is not very complicated,[1] but instead of focusing on it, let's focus on understanding the sense, meaning and psychology of this transformation. To do this, it may be helpful to consider the concept of shape-shifting.

We humans shape-shift in small ways by gaining and losing weight. We shape-shift psychologically by expanding or shrinking our identities in everyday life. Traditional shamans did a lot of shape-shifting, and that may be why they were sometimes called headshrinkers. Today, psychiatrists are still called "shrinks," after shamans who, I believe, reduced the size of people's heads… perhaps when people got pumped up or inflated.

In any case, every night we transform or "shape-shift." From the viewpoint of dreaming, CR images of the body shift, and our sense of time and space gets larger or smaller, heavier or lighter. Moreover, an event from everyday reality that seemed like nothing can suddenly become a gigantic nightmare in dreaming.

Before falling asleep most of us live in consensus reality. In this reality, we behave more or less like the majority of other women and men around us. However, in dreams we can become animals or spirits, fly and disappear. In dreaming we can shape-shift and become eagles or bears, snakes or plants. These transformations do not normally occur in everyday life.

Traditional shamans ritualize these events and become amazing beings by shape-shifting with the help of music, dance, and drugs, allowing themselves to be possessed by their guardian spirits. Gifted shamans can shift identities: personalities leave and reenter their human form. Most physicists do not become eagles and bears, gain and lose weight like the particles they are viewing; yet scientists must be able to understand how transformations take place. To understand relativity, you need to understand shape-shifting.

Psychology—like ordinary physics—has procedures in which the "observer" can be like the observer in physics, staying in her own framework while dealing with the results from another. Jung called the procedure of staying in your everyday life while communicating with dream figures "active imagination." Jung suggested that you "hold your own" while speaking to visions in NCR. One of my teachers, Barbara Hannah, who was one of Jung's students and colleagues, wrote an amazing book called *Active Imagination,* in which she emphasizes the importance of maintaining two viewpoints simultaneously. In the terms of our present discussion, we might say you must hold onto the framework and viewpoints of consensus reality and your everyday life while speaking with the figures of your dreams. If you can do this, an interesting dialogue may occur. If you slip into their reality, or they slip back into yours, you are merely dreaming, or thinking as you ordinarily do. Maintaining two viewpoints is crucial to active imagination.

The interpretation of dreams in psychology is another method of staying in your own framework while relating to dreams. In active imagination, you actually reach into the other framework while remaining in your own. In contrast, interpretation allows you to stay in the world of consensus reality while transforming the weirdness of dreams into your own terms. Interpretation translates dreams through finding their meaning in consensual everyday life.

Say you dream of a bear. One formula for interpreting the meaning of the bear is to assume that the bear is a part of you of which you are unconscious. In other words, during your everyday life you may behave a bit like a bear, but you are unconscious of it. The transformation you perform via the interpretation formula is changing your self-image, discovering that, in fact, the meaning of the dream bear is that you are bear-like in some aspects of your everyday behavior. This transformation allows you to tap into the bear's energy with greater awareness. We could say that although you appear to yourself to be a human being in ordinary reality, in a dream, your behavior appears to be that of a bear.

Another formula for shape-shifting is leaving CR and entering NCR by playing the bear. Kids do this all the time. Play allows you to shift from CR into NCR. Playing is different from interpreting, however, because in the process of interpretation you remain more or less like a person. But in playing, you can become the thing you are playing; you actually leave your normal frame of reference and identity for shorter or longer periods of time. Play is a crucial transformation between different states of consciousness, different frameworks. Play is important to your survival. Without play you can get very bored or depressed.

However, if you become a bear or think you are a bear for long periods of time, you may no longer be playing; chances are others will think you are crazy. Relatively speaking, CR is as weird or crazy as NCR. If you slip permanently into one state, if you go into dream states for long periods of time, you may actually become psychotic from the CR viewpoint. Psychosis is another means of transformation, one that is usually characterized by shifts that last a long time.

If you have an overview and realize that there are various states of consciousness, various frames of reference, you can "metacommunicate" about them. "Meta" means "about," and "communicate" means to inform. If you metacommunicate, you can talk about your states of consciousness. You have a view of your own views and can communicate about both CR and NCR states of consciousness.

To metacommunicate, you need to be detached enough from both viewpoints to move from one to the other without getting caught in either. If you have such detachment, you tend to laugh a great deal and can acknowledge or giggle about that part of yourself which is one-sidedly possessed by CR time and space, by business, nervousness, depression, or mania. You can also laugh at the part that is a devotee of dreaming.

From the meta view, both everyday life and dreaming are just states of consciousness, viewpoints, frameworks. This view is different from the viewpoint of CR, which contends that dreams are "reduced states of consciousness" of the everyday mind. From the meta viewpoint you sense that a dream is an ongoing experience which continues throughout the day.

In a dream, your face can transform into that of a deer, your bones into its skeleton. With a meta viewpoint, you can experience yourself walking down the street as a CR human being and simultaneously walking down that same street as a deer moving through the forest, sensing the trees and the other animals. You can be a person and also a magical being or anything else while carrying on your everyday life. When you gaze at the city or up into the mountains, stare at the sunset, or look into water, you feel special sensations that transport you into experiences that make everyday reality magical. If you have a metaposition, you sleep or awaken from the viewpoint of CR, but you may also live in a world where there is no sleeping or waking, where you simply feel like a deer even when you have business to do.

The metaposition in you knows you are neither a person nor a deer but a process with the capacity to continuously transform. From the metaposition you are aware that the transformations between frameworks in physics are pale images of the transformations you are capable of making in dreaming.

Thus far we have discovered the possibilities of staying in CR and interpreting dreams, of leaving CR and shape-shifting, and of achieving a metaposition, which means maintaining your awareness of CR and of dreaming at the same time.

To sum up, psychology has many possible methods of transformation between CR and NCR, including the following.

Active imagination means remaining in everyday reality, while communicating with the figures of dreams.

Interpretation views dreams as parts of you. Interpretation is analogous to multiplying a complex number by its reflection (or conjugate), which, you will remember from Chapter 8, gets rid of the imaginary numbers and leaves us with only a real number. Conjugation generates reality from NCR and can be used to ignore NCR. Likewise, interpretation takes the absolute value of a complex number, so to speak, marginalizes the imaginary components, and allows you to stay in consensus reality. Interpretation is like observation in physics: you sit in one reality and talk about the other, trying to understand the meaning of one world in terms of the other.

Psychosis moves from CR into NCR or altered states. In psychosis, you do not just go into an altered state and come back; instead, you leave CR and may not come back for long periods of time. There are no analogies to this transformation in physics unless we think of wandering into a black hole or the world of imaginary numbers, which, you will remember, has no everyday significance for physicists.

Death is yet another transformational process, a procedure in which your identity leaves your CR in life, usually at the end of life. Many religious practices, such as those described by Sogyal Rinpoche in his *Tibetan Book of Living and Dying*, view death as a transformation from your ordinary self into an altered state through the use of meditation on light, quietness, controlled breathing, and other methods. Altered states arising from these practices are described in terms of enlightenment, light, emptiness, silence, and quiet.

Sacred substances such as drugs and plants are often used in spiritual traditions to transform realities. Sacred plants, such as peyote or ayahuasca, enable temporary withdrawal from CR and entrance into altered states. Ritualized sexual practices, certain forms of yoga, and other methods achieve similar transformations.

Fluidity in relationships is a less known method of transformation, but similar transformations can occur in everyday life by simply learning to see things through the eyes of another person. The more fluid we are in our relationships, the more we can view the same event through our own viewpoint and also through the viewpoint of another person. Here, shape-shifting occurs not through being an eagle or bear, but through realizing that the role we are playing in life is only one of many possible roles.

I am using shape-shifting as the general category under which all psychological transformations take place because all of these helpful healing procedures alter our view and image of shapes, sizes, times, colors, movements, and other things. You may still use consensus reality terms to describe the differences, for example, between being a bear and being a woman, but the shape-shifting experiences I am referring to completely transform your framework, your feelings and your sense of time, space, and identity.

DIMENSIONS

Transformations in physics do not occur because of dreaming, drugs, or role-play, but because of changes in speed, that is, in velocities, accelerations, and forces. Einstein's "twin paradox," which was one of his thought experiments, illustrates this point. Einstein imagined two people, such as Peter and Paul, who are twin physicists. Paul takes a trip on a spaceship and travels at near the speed of light. When Paul gets home, he sees his twin brother Peter and notices that he has aged less than Peter has.

Paul went so fast that he slowed time down and aged less. He saved himself a couple of minutes, or years, by going very fast. It's just the opposite of the way we normally think. Everyone says, "Slow down and take it easy." Physics implies that you need not slow down to lead an interesting life. It says to forget that! Go for it! Get moving faster than others, you live longer! One of the amazing consequences of relativity is that time and space shrink if you go fast. In fact, just running, moving, driving, or flying allows you to slow down time, but the amount is so small you never notice it.

In physics, speed is measured in terms of the amount of space you move through during a given time. When we are thinking about space and time, we are thinking about dimensions. Dimensions describe frameworks, the universes in which our observations take place.

In science, the word dimension usually refers to the number of points or coordinates needed to locate something in a given space. In ordinary space, in the room where you are now if you are reading indoors, you need three coordinates to locate yourself: you need the dimensions of length, width, and height. To locate a point on a flat piece of paper, you need two dimensions, length and width. Then you can say, for example, the point is two inches up and two inches to the side.

CR frameworks usually involve three coordinates, the three dimensions of space. The frame of reference for the room you are in has three perpendicular directions. In a one-dimensional framework such as a straight line, all you need is one coordinate, length, to describe the location of an object. On a piece of paper you need two dimensions, and in a room you need three (Figure 22.2).

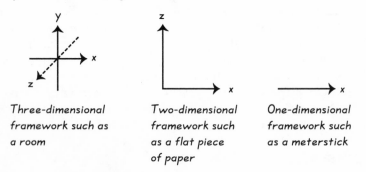

Three-dimensional framework such as a room

Two-dimensional framework such as a flat piece of paper

One-dimensional framework such as a meterstick

22.2 Three-, two-, and one-dimensional frameworks

Up until this point, we have been speaking about consensus reality dimensions, about spatial lengths for space in the room and the area on the paper. But NCR dimensions play important roles in our lives, and are also necessary to fully describe events. For example, to describe the room in which you are now sitting, you might say that it is comfortable or austere, big or small, in an old or a new building. Your room has CR dimensions such as length and width, as well as NCR dimensions such as big or small, old or new, austere or comfortable, which not everyone will agree to. Yet all these CR and NCR dimensions are needed to describe exactly where you are.

Physics would consider the word comfortable an NCR dimension, since comfort is not a measurable CR term. There will be no consent from everyone about whether something is comfortable or not. Remember the quote from Einstein in Chapter 1, where he said that science does not deal with such dimensions.[2] Space and time are CR dimensions: they can be measured.

We live in a many-dimensional CR and NCR space, although we usually marginalize our NCR experiences or don't discuss them with others, since there may be no general consent on our personal experience. Nevertheless, to truly describe anything we observe, we need more than space and time; we also need feeling descriptions, sentient NCR dimensions.

The number of variables that you need to describe an object and similar objects is the number of "dimensions." What dimensions do you need to describe yourself or other people? If you use CR dimensions, you need time and space, culture, age, religion, location, and the like. As a doctor, you need more dimensions to understand the body. For example, you also need temperature and weight. Therapists may ask about your relationship with your parents, about your sense of happiness, depression, your moods, and so forth.

Psychology, like physics, has preferred dimensions. There are one-dimensional psychologies, meaning that the world is seen in terms of a single dimension. You may be seen simply as normal or abnormal. We also have two-dimensional psychologies, which see everything in terms of the interactions between parents and children. Given the nature of the parent and the nature of the child, these psychologies describe a great deal about human behavior. Then there are three-dimensional psychologies, which add the analogy of height or depth. These are the transpersonal or depth psychologies, which deal with the superconscious or subconscious, as well as with the other dimensions. A fourth dimension in psychology deals with movement, time, and process. Process, like space-time, cannot quite be visualized; it has to do with flow, as we will discover later.

Mathematicians call a one-dimensional world a "one-space world" and a two-dimensional world a "two-space world." Three dimensions are "three-space," four dimensions are "four-space," and so on.

"Hyperspace" is a term that refers to any multidimensional space that has more than three dimensions. We can visualize one-, two-, and three-dimensional spaces as a straight line, a flat piece of paper, and a room with height. But it is very difficult, if not impossible, to visualize a four-dimensional space, a hyperspace. How shall we draw it? For example, a path through a room (a fourth dimension) can be drawn as a series of points on the floor of the room, each point representing a position in space at a different second. But how shall we portray the fourth dimension itself? We can only imply its existence by making a line through a three-dimensional space like a room.

To give us an approximate sense of the significance of a four-dimensional space, mathematicians and physicists try to reduce four-dimensional pictures such as space-time, which has three spatial dimensions and one temporal dimension, to three-dimensional pictures, by leaving out one of the spatial dimensions. One of the reasons relativity was resisted at first was because Einstein's new four-dimensional hyperspace was inconceivable.

Why are hyperspaces inconceivable? Why do we have trouble visualizing spaces that have more than three dimensions? There is no definitive answer, but it seems from our exploration of mathematics that our perception easily grasps only one, two, three, or possibly four dimensions at one time. This perceptual limitation may be the origin not only of the visibility of three-dimensional spaces, but also of number bases, which structure math by using standard aggregates such as the human form. With a bit of trouble, we can grasp more than three dimensions, but when we get to five, we are over the edge.

The few dimensions we commonly use can be easily conceived but do not tell us everything. Using two or three dimensions simplifies life, but marginalizes other experiences that remain hidden.

CREATING HIGHER AND HYPER-DIMENSIONS

The dimensions we use have political ramifications. When Einstein suggested a four-dimensional space-time, no one wanted to consider it. Physicists thought he was imagining things that were not real. Even recently, when Stephen Hawking spoke of "imaginary time" dimensions that describe the first moments of the universe, many thought he was far too speculative.

But Einstein and Hawking were not the first to use four dimensions to describe the world. Earlier peoples used four and more dimensions to describe the universe. The Chinese, native people of the Americas including the Inca and Mayans, and many pre-Christian societies used fourfold structures to describe the cosmos.[3] If four dimensions can be used to represent the "universe," anything less than four is missing something. In fact, any small number of dimensions leaves out others. For example, let's think about the psychological example of a two-space world.

Let's think about someone who is in a phase where she is thinking only about her negative parent and herself as a hurt child. All movements in this two-space world occur on a sort of flatland. We can think of the diagram below as a flat piece of paper on a flat table. There is length and width but no height. Any point on that flatland (like on a sheet of paper) can be located by speaking about the strength and weakness of the parent and child.

Any route from point 1 to point 2 in a two-space world remains on the piece of paper. In Figure 22.3, whatever you do, wherever you go, can be located in terms of the parent and child. Your state in flatland is simple: you are mature or infantile, growing up or regressive, an elder or child; a negative parent hates or loves you.

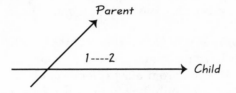

22.3 Movement in a two-dimensional world

People who think in two dimensions easily get stuck in life; they feel locked into a two-dimensional parent-child identity. They can move only within the dimensions of parenting and being a child. From an outside perspective, from a higher-dimensional world, we could say that they do not have access to other dimensions. This may be why people get depressed or search for something to elate them—they search for methods that go down or up.

If you use only two dimensions, there is no depth or height, so to speak. A priestess might be very helpful here. She might say, "Talk to your god. God is a third dimension." If such a person went to see a therapist, she or he might advise, "You are stuck in a two-space universe." A therapist might also add a third dimension by saying, "Follow your dreams because there you will find processes that move beyond your CR dimensions, the problems and the solutions in your world." In dreams, there is more than the child and the abusive parent. Perhaps there is a merciful queen, a frog, a goddess or a god. Perhaps there is nothingness, emptiness.

Until now, this third dimension was marginalized. It existed but was unnoticed. As the person changes, a new dimension is added to awareness. We can represent the addition of the new dimension as shown in Figure 22.4.

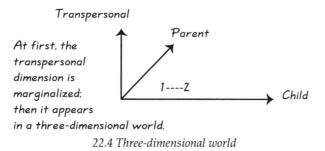

22.4 *Three-dimensional world*

The third, or transpersonal dreaming, dimension allows the client to leave the old world, to transcend flatland, to get up into the air or down into the ground, and to feel less confined. Now the client is in a three-space instead of a two-space. The moral of the story is that the number of dimensions we live in most of the time is usually fewer than we need. By adding dreamlike dimensions you can leave the human form, move into realities or frameworks that are very different, new and invigorating.

Were the spiritual, dream, or religious dimensions not present in CR before? They were present, but usually only dimly perceived or entirely marginalized. The dreamer may have been interested in transpersonal dimensions, but marginalized them. In other words, even before going to a priestess or therapist, you could find new dimensions, new realities, and change the shape of your life.

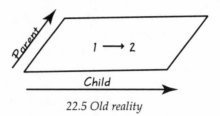

22.5 *Old reality*

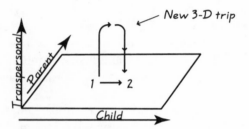

22.6 *New reality: a three-dimensional trip*

By comparing the two worlds in Figures 22.5 and 22.6 above, we see that dimensions are not really added by physicists, priestesses, or therapists, for these dimensions were already there. What happens in physics and psychology is that new dimensions and ways of being and thinking simply open up to us, ways that were present but marginalized.

Although we often live as flatlanders in two dimensions, we have three- and more- dimensional potential. Access to the third dimension is usually hidden in our moods, and in sudden inspirations that hint that there is a subconscious, an unconscious or transpersonal domain.

If you use only three dimensions, you can transcend everyday life; you have the capacity for a transcendental overview. But with only three dimensions, your views and insights may still be too fixed and static or inflexible. You may develop a marvelous philosophy and wonderful insights, but you have still not tapped your full potential. A fourth dimension may be missing.

Time is missing in the first three dimensions; process is missing. Without change, your lofty or deep views quickly turn static, even dogmatic or rigid. You may think you need to do this or that, become this or that, instead of simply becoming aware in the fourth dimension of events and situations moving from one to another. The fourth dimension gives you access to time, to process, to the Tao—the first hyperspace. This fourth dimension—let's call it process or change or Tao—can no longer be visualized geometrically in terms of a one-, two- or three-dimensional diagram. This may be why the Taoists' central message is that the Tao that can be said is not the eternal Tao. That is, the process that is described in terms of everyday realities and three dimensions is only a static reminder of how things flow.

Process is experience; it is the dimension of movement and difficult to verbalize. Time is hidden in our ordinary, fixed, three-dimensional or state-oriented vocabulary. For example, psychological concepts such as ego, id, shadow, or even the self have a static or fixed sense about them. Even the concept of physicist or observer, or shaman or client, is fixed. Yet we have seen from relativity that there is nothing fixed about anything. Although our concepts seem static, events are always transforming, transfiguring, transubstantiating—difficult though it may be to describe such processes in words.

Alchemy, the predecessor to physics and psychology, stressed transformations instead of fixed, solid states. We easily forget process and make fixed states out of ideas such as typology and personality, which become state or "thing" oriented, concrete in connotation. Taoists and Buddhists advise against believing in structured concepts and stress instead "no-self," "egolessness," and "emptiness." The central message of Taoism and Buddhism is that everything changes.

Four- and more-dimensional hyperspaces are crucial to living fully using CR dimensions, but following the heart is also crucial. For example, you need math to be a good physicist. But invisible dimensions such as intuition are crucial to making discoveries. Einstein was a great physicist but a lazy math student. He had amazing physical intuition about the nature of the universe. You can teach math, but not intuition.

Likewise, great musicians cannot always read musical notes. They play things "by ear." CR dimensions are important, but creativity is related to the fourth, process dimension.[4] In these hyperspaces you are free to be any age, or anything that is occurring; you are not attached to one form or description. You become fluid, unbound to one fixed state or object.

SOLUTIONS IN HYPERSPACE

I am using hyperspaces as a physicist and psychologist to mean worlds beyond three-dimensional reality. We need hyperspaces to solve problems. In psychology, the experience of process, of music, of creativity and flow, solves problems state-oriented interpretations cannot solve. A good interpretation hints at the fourth dimension and gives you a direction, but it can stop the process from happening. We can speak about dreamwork in terms of your everyday reality, but dreaming itself is a process that is both dreamlike and real (CR), a process that lives dreams in the times and spaces of the everyday world.

Similarly, physicists try to solve basic problems such as how to bring quantum theory and relativity together by adding new, hyperspace dimensions that go beyond the present three. Einstein solved many problems by adding the four-dimensional world that includes time. The addition of even more dimensions, such as the imaginary time of Stephen Hawking and the ten dimensions of recent mathematical physics, may enable us to unify physics.[5] Additional dimensions create worlds in which there is more space, greater freedom.

If you can't solve a problem in your CR world of three dimensions, adding another dimension works wonders. If you add transcendence and this does not work, immersion in process is a further possibility. There is a mathematical theorem that says any knot that cannot be untied in three dimensions can be untied by adding a fourth![6] Knots can be unraveled in the fourth dimension because there is "more room." This is impossible in three dimensions, but easy in the fourth. In fact, it turns out that the third dimension is the only dimension in which knots stay tangled.

The equivalence of this theorem in psychology would be that with greater awareness of the fourth dimension, of process, of the Tao, problems that seem impossible are no longer even problems: knots no longer exist and can be resolved. In other words, there is no such thing as a problem in three dimensions that cannot be solved with awareness of process. Once you use awareness of movement, you have already untied even the worst problem. We will delve more deeply into this area in Section II on psychology as sentient physics.

WHOLENESS AND SYMMETRY

Jung used symmetrical pictures, called mandalas, to describe completeness in people. He imagined psychological wholeness in a three-dimensional sense without time or process, as being balanced or whole at any given moment, having all your aspects balance one another. Yet, even wholeness is more complete when formulated with the time dimension. While few of us are balanced for more than a few minutes at any given phase in our lives, the truth of the symmetry principle of balance can be more readily seen over time. If you think about yourself over a period of several years, you may notice how you circle around different forms of behavior. At one time or another you may have been angry, then peaceful; conflictive, then harmonious; thinking, then feeling, active and passive, mature and infantile, and so on.

Symmetry, wholeness, and balance appear phenomenologically over time. Though we may not appear whole at any one moment, we are over time. Symmetry appears in four dimensions, whereas it may not be true at any given moment in three. To experience symmetry in psychology, we need a hyper-dimension, a process dimension.

This discussion of frameworks, shape-shifting, and dimensions leads us to a process-oriented meaning of wholeness, which is experienced as completeness over time. We could say that individuation, or becoming yourself, self-actualization, is a state-oriented concept asking for understanding in time.

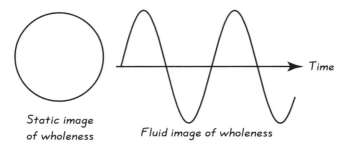

Static image
of wholeness   Fluid image of wholeness

22.7 Static and fluid images of wholeness

Just as wholeness is a guiding process that enables us to comprehend our own actions and tendencies over time, symmetry in physics is a guiding pattern that allows science to grasp the overall character of nature.[7] Symmetry in physics is often pictured in the form of a round ball. Rotate the ball in space, through the three spatial dimensions, and it remains the same. The spatial concepts of height, length, and width are interchangeable in describing it, since it is as high as it is long and wide. If we replace the width of the ball with its length or height, the description is unchanged. The ball is rotationally symmetrical because it remains the same as we rotate it through its various spatial dimensions.

The tendency for the laws of physics to have symmetrical characteristics means that no physical CR dimension can be more important than another. Many laws of physics remain unchanged if length, width, height, and time are interchanged—as with the ball just mentioned. Many aspects of elementary particles remain unchanged if we substitute forward-moving time with backward-moving time. Most laws of microphysics are symmetrical with respect to time.

CONCLUSIONS

What we can learn from the laws of symmetry and the ideas of dimensions, shape-shifting, and transformation of frameworks is that, if you shape-shift and experience additional dimensions, not only will your concepts of what it means to be human change, but physics will change as well. We can no longer be certain of our everyday concepts of object or particle. Everything is in process. Today, most people think of themselves as a person with a given identity, as a static body resisting change, process, and time. Likewise, we think of our physical world as more or less fixed.

If, instead, you have reconsidered that you are not something fixed in time, but rather a fluid in the midst of constant and eternal change, life becomes different. You are no longer only a three-dimensional body with a given past, needing solutions for problems in the future. Instead, you become a changing form, now a bear, now a person, finally process itself.

Relativity and psychology make it possible to understand one framework in terms of another, the train in terms of the ground, NCR in terms of CR. Yet each framework is only a framework: it is a state of mind, a state of matter. Implicit in all the transformations between frameworks is the possibility of constantly transforming instead of being a fixed object in a fixed state.

Einstein and psychoanalysis showed us how to understand one framework from the viewpoint of another but never really discussed the meaning of life from the viewpoint of the grand overview, the world of constant change. Physics tells us about the four-dimensional, hyperspace world, but not how to live there while remaining simultaneously aware of the more limited versions of reality. To understand how to live in higher-dimensional realities, we must turn to traditional shamans who can not only step back and forth between frameworks but also enter a constant process of shape-shifting. Learning to live in a higher-dimensional space and not just in one world or another is now the challenge for everyone. If we can travel between frameworks and fluidly shape-shift, we are on the path to becoming modern shamans who live in a multi-dimensional world.

From now on, being realistic has a new meaning. It signifies recognizing our ordinary human fate, and also moving to four- and higher-dimensional spaces, becoming whole, transcending time, life, and even death.

NOTES

1. See Chapter 5 of Einstein's *Relativity*.

2. Einstein differentiates these two worlds on page 1 of *The Meaning of Relativity*: "By the aid of language different individuals can, to a certain extent, compare their experiences. Then it turns out that certain sense perceptions of different individuals correspond to each other, while for other sense perceptions no such correspondence can be established.

    We are accustomed to regard as real those sense perceptions which are common to different individuals, and which therefore are, in a measure, impersonal. The natural sciences, and in particular, the most fundamental of them, physics, deal with such sense perceptions."

3. See Marie Louise von Franz, *Number and Time*, page 115 and following.

4. Thanks to my friend and colleague from Portland, Oregon, Adam Zwig, for this analogy.

5. Mathematically, it is easier to write the laws of nature in higher dimensions because interconnections are easier to see. See the excellent work of physicist Michio Kaku, *Hyperspace*, pages 11, 13, and following.

6. The proof of this knot theorem can be found in Kaku's previously named work, page 339.

7. See mathematician Eugene Wigner's timeless book, *Symmetry*, on the topic of its title.

23 | Einstein's Detachment from Time

People like us, who believe in physics, know that the distinction between past, present, and future is only a stubbornly persistent illusion.

—Albert Einstein

Some physicists, such as Stephen Hawking, say certain aspects of relativity theory, such as the constancy of the speed of light, are too difficult for the general public to comprehend.[1] But understanding how the speed of light is constant in all frameworks will be important to the comprehending nature of perception, the universe, and our minds.

At this point, let's first think for a bit about Einstein and consider how he was able to detach from the everyday concepts of space and time. After all, he lived in the same world the rest of us do. His consensus reality, his apartment in Zurich, was probably flat and square.

Consensus reality for most people is relatively flat. If your experience of traveling through space is steep as it is in the mountains, you usually take the flattest route possible. We all try to sleep in a more or less flat position, on a flat surface. Consensus reality is local in the sense that you know the space and time in your neighborhood. You know your road or street and the one next to you. Your apartment or house is probably fairly square or flat, which may be why an apartment is sometimes called a flat.

CR Is Slower Than the Speed of Light

Although many of us complain about the speed of everyday life, it is actually quite slow compared with the great speed at which light travels. With the advent of e-mail, letters go faster, but most of life is fairly leisurely. The fastest way most people travel is in an airplane. An extremely fast plane flies at the speed of sound, or about 300 meters per second, which is 1090 feet, or one-fifth of a mile, per second.

That seems fast, but if you think about the speed of light, the speed of sound is slow. In the same second it takes sound to go one-fifth of a mile, light goes 186,000 miles—light is about a million times faster than sound. The great speed of light is why people used to think light was instantaneous, that it took no time at all to go from place to place. Light is quick, but not instantaneous. Most things we do in our lifetimes crawl along at a terribly slow pace in comparison with the speed of light. We have almost no CR experience with such high speeds. High speeds, curved spaces, and gigantic non-local distances are very unusual for us in everyday life.

CR Time Is Anthropomorphic and Linear

Let's think further about our experience of space and time. Worldwide, life in consensus reality is very earthbound, highly social and human-oriented. With the exception of astronauts, few people get to the moon or out into space. Who ponders the problems of the galaxies besides astronomers and science fiction writers?

The time span familiar to us is our own age in years. We all have some sense of a century because we're caught in a particular century or in the transition between centuries. We have difficulty thinking backward beyond the time of our births or forward beyond our deaths. If you were born after 1960, can you imagine what the world was like in 1920? For most people, 1920 is another world. Now try to think about 1890, 1700, or 3000 BC. Those periods are like other dimensions altogether; they are mythic for us, imaginary, not real. History has an unreal character for us; only the time of our lives seems real.

Eighty years is approximately the span of a human life. If we think in terms of life cycles, seven lifetimes ago is when the European Renaissance began, when the Europeans discovered the Americas. Native American cultures have wider views of time than the span of one human life: they say we should make decisions based on the outcome of what occurs seven generations in the future. Imagine making a decision by thinking about what this decision will do to your area of the world five or six hundred years from now.

Now imagine considering what will happen 10,000 years from today because of what you are doing now, or what happened 5,000,000,000 years ago when the Earth came into being. Such times go beyond our anthropocentric considerations. These times are on the verge of having a non-consensual character, yet they are the times physics must deal with.

We normally think of time as going forward at a relentless rate. That is why we decide to do things at certain times. Yet many native peoples wait for the time to be right. Some people, such as the Hopi, do not even have a word for time, but speak instead of that which is manifesting or that which is manifest. There is no past, present, or future. Timing is important; it can be experienced as a relentless unfolding from one point to another, or as something that stops, pauses, expands, and shrinks according to the circumstances and the culture. Although we have a CR idea about time as unfolding in a forward-moving direction into the future, time may not be the most basic or fundamental substance. In some respects, our personal experience of time is more fundamental.

MOVEMENT

Relativity considers movements through time and through space, while movement in consensus reality usually refers only to movement through space. Most of us would agree that movement in CR means doing something like dancing in a room or walking, which are movements in space. Let's consider also moving in time. For example, imagine that I am a couch potato who sits still and watches television all the time. Am I moving in time? Yes, I am. When I go to bed at night, am I moving? I am moving in time. Most people say I'm not moving in space when I am sleeping—if we neglect my breathing and rolling around in bed. But even if I am still, I am still moving in time.

23.1 *Moving through time, not space*

Moving along the straight line going upward in Figure 23.1 is a graphic explanation of what we mean when we say, "time goes by" or "time flies." While movement in space requires kinesthetic ability, we do not notice movement in time unless we have awareness of the changing atmosphere inside us, awareness of process. At night you move anywhere you want in time—forward, backward, out of time, out of the body—but you must be aware of dreaming to notice this process.

While sitting still during the day, if you close your eyes and remain awake, you may experience your body as if it is moving. This is an experience of movement not in ordinary space, but in imaginary space. Yet you experience it as movement. This sort of movement is more like movement in time. Movement in time is linked to awareness of NCR characteristics, in contrast to movement in space, which requires only visual or kinesthetic abilities to be noticed.

Movement in time is not entirely separated from our kinesthetic sense. When waking from a dream or coming out of a fantasy, there will be no consent about where you were, but as far as everyone's clock is concerned, you moved in time. Time passes. There is both CR and NCR movement in time; furthermore, time has spatial characteristics. In other words, consensus reality dimensions such as space and time that we consider separate are mixed in our experience of process. We can tell that the CR ideas of space and time are interesting, but not perfect. There are all sorts of inconsistencies associated with them.

THE MICHELSON-MORLEY EXPERIMENT

Although Einstein lived in the everyday world of space and time, he, too, had the intuition that space and time were not absolute. They did not interest him all that much. That is probably why he decided to call his original paper "The Invariance Principle of Light" and not "The Relativity of Space and Time." Apparently, he was not as impressed with the relativity of times and spaces as he was with the invariance, that is, the constant nature, of the speed of light.

Einstein's invariance principle says that even if space and time vary as things go faster, the speed of light is constant and does not depend on the framework you are in. He arrived at this idea by thinking about an experiment done by Michelson and Morley in 1887.

The gist of this experiment can be understood by thinking of two people who are moving relative to one another. Imagine that a man stands on a bridge to measure the speed of light coming from the flashlight of a woman who is walking on the roof of a speeding train. The man on his bridge constitutes one frame of reference; the train on which the woman is walking is a second. If the woman with the flashlight doesn't duck beneath the bridge, she will hit her head.

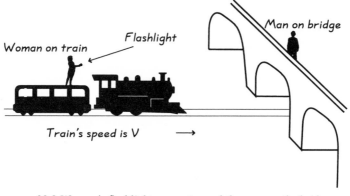

23.2 Woman's flashlight moves toward the man on the bridge.

From the CR perspective, the faster the train is moving, the more her head will hurt if she hits it on the bridge. If she walks on top of the train at a speed we can all call v relative to the train, and if the train is going at the speed we'll call V relative to the Earth, her speed relative to the Earth will be $V + v$, that is, her walking speed plus the train's speed.

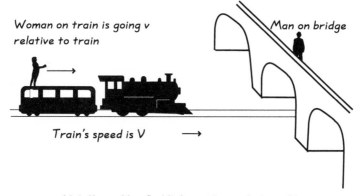

23.3 She and her flashlight go $V + v$ relative to him.

The velocity of the train plus the velocity of the woman walking on the train add together to make the total velocity at which the woman's head will hit the bridge. If she walks backward while the train is going forward, we would expect her head to hurt less because her backward velocity, v, would be subtracted from the train's velocity, V (resulting in $V - v$.)

Now, let's think about the man standing on the bridge. He is about to measure the speed of light coming out of her flashlight. At a given moment, she agreed to flash her light on so that he could begin to measure the time it takes the light to reach him. Let's pretend he has great measuring instruments so that he can measure the time between the moment she is supposed to have turned on the light until the moment he sees it. Let's say she turns the light on when the train moves by a certain lamppost. He sees the train do that and begins his measurements, and she flashes her light.

Let's say he is very thorough and decides to take a couple of measurements. He measures the time and the speed of light when she is standing still on top of her train, which is moving at V. And let's say he measures the speed of light again when she is walking on the train in his direction, so that her total velocity is $V + v$ relative to him. He even measures the time it takes for the light to get to him for a third time when she walks backward as the train goes forward. This third time her speed is $V - v$ relative to him.

What do you guess about his measurements? When is the speed of light the greatest? Most people guess that, since the woman is walking forward on the train toward the bridge, the light will reach the bridge faster than if she were standing still or going backward on the train. But this guess is based on consensus reality notions of time and space and turns out to be incorrect.

Experiments like this one, performed much more elaborately by Michelson and Morley (who did not use a train and a bridge, but an interferometer) showed that as far as the man on the bridge is concerned, the measured speed of light is the same, whether or not the woman on the train was moving.

In fact, whether the woman on the train is moving forward or backward, whether she is standing still or jumping, regardless of the velocity of the train or the velocity she has when she walks on top of it, the man on the bridge always measures the same speed of light.

We have seen that velocity is the amount of distance, D, something travels in the amount of time, T. If we call c the speed of light, then c equals D divided by T (that is, $c = D/T$). Thus, each time he measured and divided the distance she was from him as measured by the train's position on the track, each time he measured the time her light took to get to him, he found the velocity of light to be the same. But how could the velocity be the same if she and her flashlight were sometimes moving forward and sometimes backward on the train?

Physicists were shocked by the results of the Michelson-Morley experiment. How could this be possible? The results showed a major paradox. At this point, Einstein, who was very detached from our ordinary sense of time and space, came along. He developed his theory and said, "Take it easy. All you have to do is accept the experimental evidence. The velocity of light is always measured to be the same, namely, $c = D/T$. But D over T is a ratio. Thus, if the velocity, or rather the ratio, of distance over time remains the same, then *the commonplace ideas of time and space must be variable!"* The space and time between the man and the woman must shrink or expand depending on the velocity of the woman relative to the man.

For D/T to remain the same, then what he measures as a meter and a second in one of her frameworks (or velocities) must shrink or expand when she is in another framework (or another velocity). If we use the numbers 1 and 2 to represent the situations in which she goes slower and faster, then for D_1/T_1 to be equal to D_2/T_2, the measurement of distance D and time T must get bigger or smaller depending upon her velocity.

If the velocity of light is 300, then distance and time, or D/T, measured at one train velocity might be 600/2. But when the woman on the train is moving more slowly, D and T measured at the same place still have the same ratio of 300. Therefore, at a different train velocity, he may measure D/T to be $(602)/(2.006)$. In other words, the measurement of space and time change with changing velocities. For c to remain the same, D and T must expand. For example:

$$c = 300 = \frac{600}{2} = \frac{602}{2.006}$$

Time must expand and shrink for the velocity of light to remain the same. The velocity of light could not remain constant under varying train speeds unless the measurements of time and space vary. If the train speeds up, say from 50 to 100 miles per hour, then the measurement of distance and time on that train will vary as well.

The mind-boggling thing about the measurements of the velocity of light remaining the same is that the meaning of a minute is no longer a minute under all circumstances. A minute is no longer a fixed thing, a constant, but changes for the man on the bridge as the speed of the woman's moving system on the train changes. The one minute her watch shows will be different from his measurement of a minute.

Einstein did not worry about this, but simply figured that the times and spaces the man on the bridge measured depended on the speed of the train. Einstein figured that the faster the train travels, the more time gets varied or distorted. The woman's measurement of time relative to her train's framework, her "proper" time, is the same time the man measures on the bridge only if the train is not moving. With the increasing speed of the train, the time she measures on her train and the one he measures on the bridge become different. This means that if she is on a moving train and he is not, their watches tell different times, even if they were perfectly synchronized ahead of time. In fact, time becomes more strongly warped and slowed down, in his opinion, the faster her train goes.

You as a reader may be confused or amazed that the speed of light remains the same and that time and space get distorted. These events also surprised me when I first learned about them, but today I am even more amazed by Einstein than by the constancy of the speed of light. I am impressed by how he was able to detach from the concepts of space and time that the rest of his world and most of today's world consider fixed. Einstein was unconcerned; he was detached from the ideas of others, from the concept of standard dimensions. Instead, he believed in the experiment.

Dimensions such as space and time, which are firmly rooted in the consciousness of the Western world, are more difficult for some of us to detach from than for Einstein. He had never been a very conventional person—he said he was not attached to his own family, to his friends, or to his personal appearance. I recently saw a TV show which said that Einstein forgot to wear socks when becoming a U.S. citizen.[2]

Einstein was unconventional enough to realize that dimensions such as time and space are simply aids in understanding a consensus reality world; they are not absolutely real. He guessed correctly that the woman's watch would appear slower to the man on the bridge than it would to her on the train. In fact, if her train went very fast and then stopped, we might think something was wrong with her watch, because it would appear, to the man on the bridge, to have lost a few minutes. But there isn't anything wrong with her watch. Time was just distorted for him because of her speed relative to him. Thus, measurements from our clocks and rulers are not objective. Space and time are affected by the speed of events we are observing relative to us.

Why have we not noticed this before? We do not notice the distortion of time or space at low speeds, although infinitesimal changes in time and space do occur at low speeds. At high speeds, though, the distortion factor can be seconds, minutes, or years!

With the advent of relativity, the absolute rulership of time and space concepts crumbled. Since Einstein, space and time have fallen from their throne. The speed of light has taken their place as being absolute. The speed of light, called c by physicists, is constant in all frameworks, while a minute or a meter on the bridge is not at all the same minute or meter on the speeding train.

You can argue that in consensus reality a meter is simply a meter. But if your yardstick or meterstick starts to move really fast, the faster it goes—according to relativity—the more its length shrinks for someone standing still. In other words, your meterstick gets smaller as it goes faster, relative to me if I am standing still.

You may wonder at this point if the changes in a yardstick or a watch were real and actual, or whether they were a perceptual distortion. We have seen from our exploration of relativity that nothing is actual or real: there are only relative lengths and times. Do a meter and a minute on the train really get smaller or larger? For the person on the ground, yes. For the person on the train, no.

"Really" no longer has any meaning. Big and small are now reduced to relative concepts. In other words, there's no such thing as an absolute five feet or five minutes. There's no such thing as two days! These are all relative or apparent measurements. Our perceptions based on our measurements depend on how fast whatever we are looking at is moving relative to us.

Here we arrive at the basic psychological problem of detachment from our own viewpoints. When we use words like real and actual, we are assuming that there is a fixed reality instead of reality being a combination of observations, all of which are relative to one another. This is a very deep issue that is basic to our understanding of democracy, which we will explore further later on.

One of my students once asked, "In elementary school they taught us that a meter is the length of a certain material that is somewhere in Paris, under a specific temperature, at a specific longitude and latitude and a specific humidity. What happens if you take that meter-long stick and throw it into space at the speed of light? Does it become a different length?"

I answered, "It shrinks for us on the Earth. They told you a lie in school because it was too difficult to tell you the truth! They should have said that as long as that stick in Paris doesn't move in relation to where you are standing, then it is a meter in length. But if that meterstick starts to move, you will observe that it shrinks."

If you asked Einstein what the real length of a meterstick is, Einstein would have to say, "That question has no meaning. Length and time are relative concepts now; their absoluteness is done. They must be replaced by a new measure that is a mixture of the two. The new measure is called space-time. To calculate space-time, you must follow a recipe, given by a formula that is a matter of addition and multiplication, squares and square roots."[3]

Thus, while many things are relative, the speed of light is not, and the new measure of space-time, which is a mixture of space and time, takes the place of space and time. We will go more deeply into the concept of space-time in the next chapters.

For now, let's just notice that the speed of light is 3×10^{10} centimeters per second. In kilometers per second it is 300,000, and in miles per second it is 186,000. Remember that this measurement is of miles per second, not miles per hour. The speed of light, called c in the equations of physics, is indeed a large number.

LIGHT IN PSYCHOLOGY

The speed of light, 3×10^{10} centimeters per second, is a natural constant.[4] You may wonder why the 3 appears in that number. No one knows the reason for the particular values of the constants in nature. They just appear and remain a mystery for science.

But that does not inhibit us from speculating about the origin of the number 3 in the speed of light. To understand the reason for the number 3, we may need the psychology of math. Remember that in our study of numbers we spoke about how we perceive things. The structure of our awareness creates certain limits and number bases. For example, we can't easily notice more than three things together. We have inborn awareness limits. These limits are part of the dynamics that occur when we try to count something and share that with others.

In psychological terms, light is the major medium we use to see. Light symbolizes human awareness for most people around the world. Light is connected with other terms such as kindle, illuminate, weightless, easy, and fast. In comic books, a light bulb goes on over someone's head when new ideas pop up or understanding occurs. Light differentiates day from night. We think of light in connection with sunrise, with waking up and consciousness, just as we often think of the lights going out as signifying a time to sleep and be unconscious. The verb enlighten is linked with learning, teaching, informing, and communicating new information. One person's enlightenment often kindles another's. The moment of awareness happens quickly; it is spontaneous and very fast.

Thus the speed of light is a metaphor, in a way, for the speed of awareness, the time it takes us to awaken to something, to realize it, to get it, to perceive. Is there constancy for this speed in psychology, as there is in physics?

For example, could the speed of lucidity, of flirting, of sentient flashes in shamanism and psychology, be equal for everyone, regardless of their frame of reference, regardless of who they are or where they are coming from?

In the next chapters I will argue that we are all equally "bright," despite the concept that says some of us are faster or slower than others are. I will argue that non-consensual perceptions such as sentient awareness and lucidity are the same for all sentient beings. In other words, the constancy of the speed of light may be a more universal truth than even Einstein realized.

I had a dream about light the morning before giving the class from which this chapter was taken. In my dream I saw a bright meteor, not coming from the heavens toward the Earth, but starting from the Earth and going with the speed of light to the heavens. The meteor zoomed, at first, across the surface of the ocean in the Pacific Northwest of the United

States, where I live. The meteor zoomed along as fast as a bullet moving with the speed of light, flying over the water. I could not see the meteor, but I certainly could see the waves that came after it went by. I thought, "My god it's going to crash into the Oregon coast!"

But it didn't. It knew where it was going and it suddenly flew straight upward above the surface of the Earth. It went right up into the sky, then it went high into the universe and became a star in the cosmos streaking across the heavens!

Einstein apparently had a similar dream when he was a child.[5] The dream was something like the following: "I was going downhill on my toboggan in the snow. The rocks and trees began speeding by me, faster and faster. Then I was in the universe and the planets were speeding by me faster than the speed of light."

What are the meanings of such dreams? We may never know for certain, but I suspect that behind the constant speed of light may be cosmological principles even Einstein did not think of. We will explore together in the next chapter that the constancy of the speed of light is only one part of a larger principle, a principle related to enlightenment.

NOTES

1. Stephen Hawking, in *Black Holes and Baby Universes* (page 36), mentions that the public will have trouble understanding that two observers going at different velocities will measure different time intervals between the pair of events.

2. "Einstein: How I See the World," was shown several times on the program "Nova," PBS Home Video, distributed by Pacific Arts, 1997.

3. If x, y, and z are three dimensions of space, c is the speed of light, and t is time, then s for space-time can be found by taking the square root of the following sum: x squared, plus y squared plus z squared minus ct squared that is

    $$s^2 = x^2 + y^2 + z^2 - c^2 t^2$$

    In a way, c, the speed of light, is merely a way of showing how space and time relate.

4. This speed is the same, regardless of the framework, usually measured in the medium of a vacuum. We have already seen one other natural invariant in quantum physics, the so-called Planck's constant, which was the number 6.626×10^{-34} joule-seconds, the ratio of the energy of a quantum of energy to its frequency.

5. Thanks to Rob Sanducci for telling me one of Einstein's childhood dreams.

24 | Light and Lucidity

There is hardly a simpler law in physics than that according to which light is propagated in empty space.

—Einstein, in *Relativity*

Although Einstein is correct in the above quote, there is far more to light than appears in relativity theory. The ideas in this book show us that, even while modern physics bases its views in conventional reality, the concepts of physics also point to non-consensual domains that traditionally have been traversed only by dreamers and shamans. In this chapter, we will begin to explore beyond consensus reality ideas of space and time to understand the origins of our experience of light and its constancy.

To begin our exploration, we must ask the most basic questions: "What is light?" "Why is its speed constant?" and "What is its significance for us?"

To answer our questions, let's think about the wavelike nature of light. Like all quantum phenomena, light has both particle and wave characteristics. Moreover, all waves have at least two characteristics in common: their frequency and wavelength. The frequency of a wave is how many times it goes up and down in a second. The length of any wave, including light waves, is measured as the distance between two of its crests. If we call the length of a wave L and call its frequency f, then the speed at which it travels can be found from a simple formula, $L \times f = c$, if c is the speed of the wave—in our case, the speed of light.

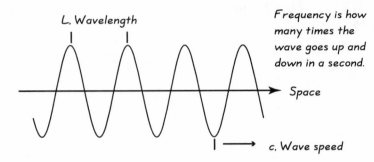

24.1 The wavelength of a wave times its frequency equals its speed.

What we call visible light is a small part of the entire electromagnetic spectrum of waves, all of which travel at the speed of light. Therefore all electromagnetic waves are connected by the formula $L = c/f$, where c is the speed of light.

As you can see from this formula for waves, long waves must have low frequencies and short waves must have higher frequencies. Radio and TV waves are longer than waves of visible light, and X-ray waves are shorter, as you can see from the diagram below.

1000 Meters   *10 Trillionths of a Meter*

10^3 10^{-11}

|----|----|----|----|----|----|---- |----|----|----|---- |----|----|----

10^3 10^2 10^1 10 10^{-1} 10^{-2} 10^{-3} 10^{-4} 10^{-5} 10^{-6} 10^{-7} 10^{-8} 10^{-9} 10^{-10}

/   /   \   \   \   /   /   /   \

AM   FM   UHF   Micro- Infra- Visible Ultra-   X   Gamma
radio   radio   radio   wave   red   light   violet   rays   rays

Radio   *Light*

24.2 Wavelengths of the electromagnetic spectrum: 1000 meters to
10 trillionths of a meter long (logarithmic scale)

THE INVARIANCE OF THE "SPEED" OF QUANTUM FLIRTS

As we can see in Figure 24.2, visible light is truly a very small portion of a communication spectrum that includes radio and TV waves, microwaves and X-rays. All of these waves are part of consensus reality; they have space and time associated with them and can be measured and picked up by our various instruments.

However, there are many kinds of communication that are non-consensual, which cannot be measured in time and space. In Chapters 17 and 18 on quantum flirts and parallel worlds, we discovered how the act of observation in quantum mechanics depends on the mathematical operation of conjugation in which one complex number is multiplied by its reflection. We have interpreted the process of conjugation in terms of non-consensual "flirts," or NCR "pre-signal" exchanges that are not measurable, unlike the measurable TV signals, radio waves, or X-rays.

The speed of all CR electromagnetic waves is c, the measurable speed of light. But the speed of quantum flirting cannot be measured; it can only be experienced. We shall never have a consensus on who sent which flirt first. You only know what you experience, namely, that you sense things flirting with you before you have a desire to observe them. You notice flickering thoughts about others just before you look at them. But it is difficult to catch these thoughts and photograph them or measure them in another manner.

In other words, although CR contact with another person or object is consensual, it is also based on an exchange of NCR flirts, an exchange of immeasurable signals. Even people who marginalize sentient events have experienced, at one time or another, telepathy, synchronicity, or other NCR communication exchanges. How many times have you thought of someone and in the next moment they call on the phone or you see them on the street? While most people experience quantum flirts, telepathy, clairvoyance, deja vu, and synchronicity, there will never be a consensus on the moment, meaning, or speed of the signals involved.

Likewise, the NCR properties of the signal exchanges hinted at in the conjugation of the wave functions in quantum physics are relational and cannot be pinned down in terms of time and space. In fact, the more we try to locate, photograph, and track NCR phenomena of any kind—including the behavior of quantum objects like photons between measurements—the more uncertain we become about them.

We cannot speak of an exact or certain velocity of an NCR signal, since velocity is a CR measurement. Yet there are space-like and time-like characteristics to such NCR experiences and signals, since we experience ourselves as being close to or far away from people, and see our timing as the same as or different from that of others. Likewise, CR velocity has an NCR analogy in our non-consensual feelings about whether something or someone is fast or slow. We can see the time-like and velocity-like nature of NCR signals in such terms as "precognition," "synchronicity," and "deja vu."

In any case, there is a general consensus that the speed of NCR signals such as quantum flirts and precognition is rapid, even instantaneous. Before physics, people thought the speed of light was instantaneous. But now we know it is limited—it is a large number, but it is finite.

Although we no longer think that light is instantaneous, we still experience NCR signals as taking no time at all. In our experience, they happen with a certain "click." Enlightenment itself, or "satori," is instantaneous. Likewise, most people experience sudden intuitions and the like as having an instantaneous nature. In other words, NCR quantum flirt communications occur at the highest imaginable speed, instantaneously.

We could say that the speed of quantum flirts is experienced as an imperceptible duration. Thus, the speed of NCR awareness processes behind CR observations such as time and light is *experienced* as a sort of invariant; that is, the speed does not change. Likewise, the speed of light that can be *measured* in relativity theory is also invariant, unchanging.

In other words, non-consensus quantum signals such as quantum flirts are like the consensus reality signal, light, in one important way. Both NCR and CR signals are invariant: they seem to be the same for all people in all frameworks. The NCR quantum flirt signals have the same imperceptible duration in all frameworks, whether we are dreaming or awake. Both NCR flirt signals and CR light signals have a speed experienced as being the same independent of the framework or the observer's state of mind.

It seems as if basic awareness processes in CR and NCR are experienced as occurring with invariant speeds, regardless of who is looking and what is being looked at, and regardless of the frame of reference.

NON-CONSENSUAL AWARENESS AND COMMUNICATION PROCESSES

Before we go further, let's put together the various awareness processes we have been considering.

Dreaming. The mathematical analogy to dreaming is the wave function, whose general form is $a + ib$. For CR observers, dreaming is a subliminal or "flash-like" awareness that exists without reflection.

Quantum flirts. Quantum flirts are the NCR signals behind observation; two dreaming signals reflect one another, link a potential observer with an observed. They are instantaneous in NCR, that is, without perceptible duration. In CR, these signals cannot be measured and thus may be slower or faster than the speed of light.

Conjugation. Mathematical physics expresses reflection of a signal with the operation of conjugation, which multiplies the quantum wave by its reflection, $(a + ib) \times (a - ib)$. In psychology, this reflection is the amplification needed to lucidly generate reality. This lucidity may occur spontaneously, or it can be produced with practice.

Consciousness. Consciousness, or the awareness of consensual signals, is rooted in dreaming and quantum flirts and created through the self-reflection of these NCR experiences. In physics, conjugation multiplies complex numbers to create real numbers.[1]

Consciousness is like observation; both are the result of self-generating NCR reflections and can be consented on. Dreaming and quantum flirts occur at a speed without perceptual duration, but the advent of consciousness occurs in time.

Lucidity. Lucidity is awareness of subliminal, "flash-like" dreaming. Without lucidity of dreamtime events, consciousness ordinarily marginalizes NCR events like quantum flirts. Thus consciousness has what physicists call "classical" spatial and temporal characteristics. If we ignore the dreaming background of consciousness, it occurs without lucidity.

The study of NCR signals and consciousness draws together the domains of relativity and quantum mechanics. Relativity tells us how observations depend on the speed of light and can change according to the speed of events, while quantum mechanics describes how observations depend on the NCR experiences that occur with instantaneous speeds. The analogy in NCR to the constant speed of light is the consistently instantaneous speed of quantum flirts.

Thus everything in the universe communicates with everything else with both CR and NCR velocities. We are involved in a truly remarkable, high-velocity communication system with everything and everyone!

THE SPEED OF DREAMS

The non-consensus analogy to ordinary light is the quantum flirt, which, like light, is part of a large spectrum of awareness processes such as dreaming, conjugation, and lucidity. The speed of the quantum flirt is the speed of dreaming, the basic speed of non-consensual awareness.

While it may take our CR conscious mind awhile to "see the light," it takes our non-consensual awareness no time at all. That is why we know everything instantly, and, at the same time, we may need a long time until we understand what we "know." If I have a dream, for example, in the dream I may understand something instantly, although it may take me several months to get the point in my waking life.

WHO IS FASTEST?

If the speeds of both non-consensus awareness and lucidity and light are. experienced to be the same for all individuals, all of us must have the same basic speed of awareness. The analogy to the constancy of the speed of light in psychology is that we all have the same speed of NCR awareness.

We are not discussing the time needed for personal change, the time needed to actually realize something in consensus reality. This change depends on many things—such as how we identify ourselves, who is measuring the time needed to learn something, and how far away from our everyday consciousness the new information is. While the time needed to get information into our everyday consciousness depends on the distance this information is from us, our identity, and who is measuring learning, our basic speed of awareness is independent of all these facts. This basic speed of awareness is the same for everyone.

AN EXAMPLE

Let's consider, for example, a common psychological problem: feeling inferior and suffering from internal criticism. Learning to love oneself may be easier for some people than for others for whom such love is "far away." If love is "far away" a person needs a "longer" time to learn self-love. The term "far away" is an NCR term. Although such a distance cannot be measured, we all have a sense of its meaning by knowing one another. For example, for some people, liking themselves is near at hand, while for others, it seems very distant.

Whether an NCR event such as loving yourself is close or far away, and whether it takes a little or a lot of time, are relative concepts. Consider the two people in Figure 24.3. Person 1 takes a longer time to learn to love herself than Person 2 does. We could say that Person 1 has more NCR distance to cover than Person 2 does.

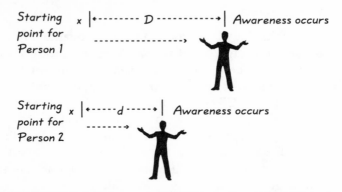

24.3 The relationship between NCR "distances" and times in learning

While the NCR speed of awareness is instantaneous, that is, while feelings of self-love travel at immeasurable speeds, the time it takes for our identities to accept the information depends on how "far away" from our overall identity these new things are.

If, at the starting point, the identity of Person 1 is further from the new thing to be learned than it is for Person 2, then, if the speed of awareness is the same, it will take Person 1 longer to get the same point than it takes Person 2. For example, it took me thirty-six years to write this book and to realize the meaning of the dream I had when I was 21—that I should put physics and psychology together! Was I slow on the uptake, or was the dream recommending something that was very far away from my identity? It was far away.

The basic ability and speed at which we reach consciousness starting with sentient experiences are the same for all people, but the distance between our conscious identity and the new learning varies.

I once saw a wonderful illustration of this concept. On a television show, the Dalai Lama said, "I'm not so good when it comes to mathematics and physics, not very good at all!" He roared with laughter and said he was very good at other things, "like religion!" He then explained the reason: "In my earlier incarnations I was closer to religion and had no connection to science and that is why this time around I am not so good at mathematics and physics. Ho, ho!"

He is "closer" to religion than math! Even though the speed of getting something is the same for all human beings, it takes the Dalai Lama longer to get math because it is farther (in the NCR sense of distance) from him than it is for a mathematician.

SOCIAL ACTIVISM AND PRIVILEGE

It is luck, a privilege, to have something like math close to you, a privilege that you may have inherited and not earned. Thus, if we say that someone else is less intelligent than we are, we are unconscious of our privilege, and of the relativity of space and time, and of our basic innate and equal capacities to dream. It is a privilege for the Dalai Lama to be close to religion. Is he better at religion than someone else? No, not basically; he is just closer to it.

If you have had experiences that allowed you to understand racism, sexism, or homophobia, is someone who is racist, sexist, or homophobic stupid? Yes, from the viewpoint of someone who is being hurt by them. But, on the other hand, they are not stupid; the whole spectrum of issues of color and sexuality, power and supremacy, may be farther from them than it is from you.

If you understand something, if you are close to it, you are privileged. You are lucky. But if you think others are stupid, you may not be all that bright yourself. Or I should say, you are bright, but the idea of relativity is farther away for you than for others. We are all equally capable of awareness and of learning, of enlightenment or seeing the light. The Dalai Lama would say that the time it takes to see the same light depends on your incarnation, your distance from it.

A social activist might argue that all this sounds good, but what happens when those who don't get it are in power and they're equally incapable of accelerating their own "getting it"?

We can find an answer to this question if we look at history. Throughout history, revolutionaries have believed that force hastens consciousness. Are they right? Yes and no. You can force people to behave or act as if they have learned something; if you can apply pressure, they can seem to change instantaneously. Moreover, you can force political correctness on someone. But "seeing the light" takes more time. It involves changing your entire picture of reality. It involves seeing the connections and relativity between frames of reference. Real understanding inevitably means opening up to what has been marginalized. Such opening takes more or less time, depending on how far or close the marginalized information is from you.

If you suffer from another person's stupidity, you naturally try to change the person. But real change comes when you realize that we are all equally fast, that the other person just appears slower or faster because of the distance she has to go to "get it." We are equal in our basic abilities, not in our momentary consciousness.

If you get this point about equality, you can go forward and try to change the world, knowing that you are like everyone else. You, like the people you want to change, also need a lot of time to get the point about equality of speed and the relativity of distance and time. A compassionate activist realizing the relativity of all things and the basic equality of abilities will begin a new kind of world.

If we could all get the point about relativity, we would be living in a different world. We are all very quick and smart; we all get it in a flash, an instant. Everyone understands everything in a split second, and at the same time, it takes some of us years to get certain things, to "get it" in everyday consciousness.

ENLIGHTENMENT IS THE PATH

Thich Nhat Hanh, a Vietnamese Buddhist priest, says that there is no path to enlightenment, but that enlightenment *is* the path. From the viewpoint of our present discussion, we could say that all of us are on the path every moment, getting the light and awareness we need. In other words, enlightenment is not a goal but a process.

We have seen that in daily life we are like photons: our paths are entangled with one another and with all things because of the quantum flirt. We are all moving with the same speed of light or faster than that speed through time, with the same speed of sentient awareness, dreaming together with everything else. In this sense, each path, each moment, is part of the process of enlightenment. Enlightenment is the path we are on when we lucidly reflect upon what we experience.

If we are all on the path of enlightenment, then why do we suffer so much? The answer is that pain itself is the enlightenment path, or the path of potential enlightenment, because pain is mostly an NCR signal, a quantum flirt looking for a lucid observer who will reflect it. Once conjugated, the signals of pain become meaningful events enriching everyday life. Pain is like everything we experience, an NCR path, a path that can be lucid, or, as Thich Nhat Hanh might say, enlightenment.

Every fantasy you have, every night you dream, every feeling you experience in your body is enlightenment, information traveling with the speed of light or faster, information moving with imperceptible duration. Who is sending that information to us? No one. All we can say is that we are part of a self-reflecting universe.

WE ALL MEET ON SENTIENT PATHS

Dreaming is the realm in which we interconnect, reflect, and share quantum flirts. We may not agree on our everyday view of things, but in dreaming we find a shared world.

Let's think for a moment about the psychological process of projection. Let's say that you experience me projecting something "good" onto you, something that you feel is not you. If you use your second attention, however, you can almost always notice that you flirted with me first. You took part in the process of projection. Perhaps the CR value of what I said about you is not quite accurate as far as you are concerned, but something in you flirted with me, giving me the possibility of projecting something onto you.

You may normally experience me as living in another framework, as being wrong about you, and see yourself as unworthy of my compliment. If you study your dreams, however, you may see that the "good" characteristic is really part of you. With your second attention, you can notice that, in fact, you send signals to me, asking for support of your good qualities. Your incredible qualities flirt with me, asking to be seen. Yet, without the second attention, you will barely notice how a flickering request for a compliment moves across your eyebrows, sending me signals that beg for a compliment. If you did, you would feel more understanding or, at least, more sympathy for my message. You would know you are with me in dreaming; you share those good qualities in NCR hyperspaces; you are no longer separate from them. In a way, if you are lucid, you notice in dreaming that you are the one who needs the compliment and also the one who sends it. In fact, in the dreaming world, you and I are inseparable in our viewpoints.

If you are lucid in the sentient realm, you experience the path you are on as enlightenment because you perceive the dreaming signals, those quantum flirts that happen with the speed of light or faster. You participate with me in a dreamworld that has space-like and time-like characteristics. In that world, your view of yourself and my view of you are the same.

The speed of sentient, NCR signal "exchanges" in that world is the speed of interconnectedness, our entanglement with one another, the speed of an NCR communication network that is our common ground. It is the speed of the mastermind of the universe, and of our own capacity to perceive as well.

This speed is so fast and constantly immeasurable that we shall never be able to say for sure who did what first. The constancy of this speed is one of the NCR, cosmological principles behind consensus reality. Without the speed of NCR signals, the physical universe would not exist, and there could be no psychology where individual life and community life intermingle.

We shall see in Chapter 25 that spaces and times of dreaming are the NCR analogies to the space-time of physics. Both dreaming and space-time are hyperspaces containing views shared by all viewpoints. Both are common grounds shared by people, in all frameworks and states of mind.

NOTE

1. Conjugation, you will recall, involved multiplying a complex number $(a + ib)$ times is reflection $(a - ib)$. If you do this and add and subtract all the needed terms you find the real number a squared plus b squared. Mathematically, this means:

$$(a + ib) \times (a - ib) = a^2 + iab - iab + b^2 = a^2 + b^2$$

25 | Space-time and the Secret River

Tao in the world is like valley streams flowing into rivers and seas.

—*Tao Te Ching* translated by Ellen Chen, Chapter 32

The mind-boggling, four-dimensional hyperspace of relativity called space-time is not only a mathematical procedure for calculating high speed and cosmic events but also a metaphorical description of shared individual and community processes. At this point, let's explore how studying the physics of space-time can lead to understanding human community processes and the experiential link between quantum mechanics and relativity.

To begin, let's look at some of the details of space-time. To explain the principles of relativity in his book, *Relativity,* Einstein used what he called thought experiments (Gedanken Experimenten), or pure thought, to imagine experiments without actually doing them. In the thought experiments, Einstein used vehicles such as trains, which were familiar to people in the early 1900s, to illustrate the principles. In one of these thought experiments, he imagined a train, with its cars going at a velocity V relative to the ground. One person was standing in a train car, while another person was standing on ground, watching the train go by.

Einstein tried to imagine what would happen to a stone if the person standing in a car of the moving train were to let the stone fall out the window of the car to the ground. He asked himself how the path of that stone would appear to the person on the train and also to someone on the ground looking at the train.

He reasoned that the stone would appear to drop straight down for the person on the train. For the person standing on the ground outside watching the train pass, the stone's path would appear not to simply fall straight down but to move forward in the direction of the train.

In Figure 25.1 below, you see a person in a train compartment, letting a stone fall out of the window. Notice that the stone appears to that person to fall straight to the ground as the ground speeds by underneath. (Let's pretend there is no wind resistance.)

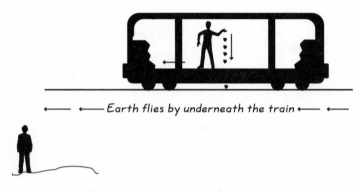

25.1 Dropped stone as seen from the train

However, in Figure 25.2, you can see that for the person on the ground, the stone's path seems to move forward and down.

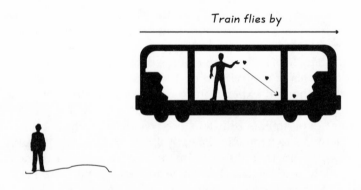

25.2 Dropped stone as seen from the ground

Now we have two viewpoints for the same event. Whose viewpoint is right? Both are. The stone's path from the time it left the person's hand to the time it hit the ground is a relative concept that depends on the viewpoint. There is no one path it took. Our views of life depend on our framework. Furthermore, if the train's velocity is great, the meaning of the length of a measuring stick or the duration of a second vary because space and time become distorted according to the formula of relativity.

If Einstein hadn't come along, the two observers would have a hard time talking about stone's trajectory. Einstein reasoned that there must be some characteristic of the stone's flight that remains unchanged, even if the measurements of time and space are different and even if time and space get distorted because of the relative motions of the frameworks. He knew from experiments that the speed of light bouncing off the stone would be the same, regardless of the point he viewed it from. But that did not tell him much about what characteristics of the stone remained the same.

Einstein thought that even though space and time are relative to the framework of the observer, a particular mixture of space and time called "space-time separation," or *s*, must be independent of the framework. He thought that when the velocity of the train is small, this mysterious "*s*," whatever that was, must just be the ordinary distance measured by someone on the embankment. For greater velocities, *s* must turn out to be very different from measurements obtained in both frameworks, since these measurements would be different. Instead of speaking about a stone dropped from a train, he thought the observers should find a "common ground," so to speak, a common "*s*."

He reasoned that this common ground would be very important, especially when scientists think about the huge differences in frameworks involved, for example, in space travel and interplanetary communication. Einstein was thinking not only about dropped stones, but also about the path of a falling star and the relative distances the different observers see it fall, let's say from your perspective on Earth and my perspective on the moon.

Instead of someone on the train or on the ground, let's speak about you and me on Earth and the moon. Say you ask me how far that falling star moved in the heavens between June 1 and June 15.

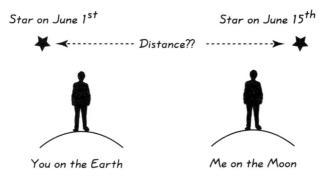

25.3 Measuring the distances a star has moved

How will you on Earth discuss the distance between these two points in space with me, who lives on the moon? On the moon I measure one distance and see one motion, while you on Earth measure another distance and see another motion. After all, what you see depends on the speed of the star relative to the position you are measuring from.

Einstein's answer was the "Lorentz transformation," which relates viewpoints from different frameworks and allows for the calculation of that common-ground measurement, namely, space-time symbolized by s, or "space-time separation." His formula is not complicated. It can be derived from the assumption of the constancy of the speed of light in all frameworks and from the fact that an event occurring in one framework must be the same event even when it is seen in another.[1]

Scientists believe Einstein's formula because there has been a great deal of experimental proof of the special theory of relativity, showing that his calculations were correct and that the spaces and times we measure of a given event do indeed get distorted and depend on the velocity of the framework we measure things from. Scientists have found that by finding s, which is a mixture of each person's measurements, we have a common ground that is the same in all frameworks.

"S" IS THE COMMON GROUND

But what is this common ground, this space-time? Einstein was never able to tell us exactly, except with a mathematical formula. It's up to us to explore what space-time really means.

To begin with, it is fascinating that the resulting mathematics for relativity (which the mathematical reader can see in the footnotes) requires complex numbers. Furthermore, that mathematics tells us that velocities greater than the speed of light are not allowed because the formula gives only imaginary results and they have no consensus reality meaning. Remember, when mathematics results in imaginary numbers, that is, unreal times and spaces, no one has ever been able to say what they mean.[2] The results of relativity cannot be directly measured in the case that something goes faster than the speed of light.

Today, when we ask if events can occur faster than the speed of light, we must answer both yes and no. Dreaming, quantum flirts, and other non-consensual events are outside of measurable time. When we go faster than the speed of light, Einstein's mathematics produces imaginary numbers. We know from our learning thus far that imaginary numbers cannot be measured. Imaginary numbers refer to events occurring in non-consensus realities, such as telepathy and synchronicity, whose outcomes depend on subjective judgments. Thus, from the viewpoint of consensus reality, nothing *measurable* goes faster than light.

SPACE-TIME SEPARATION

Let's take a closer look at Einstein's mathematics for space-time separation. The recipe to calculate space-time separation is basically a salad. In this salad you have different letters, such as x, y, z, c, and t, which are mixed together. The letters represent length, or x, width, or y, height, or z, the speed of light, or c, and time, t.

When you square these letters, that is, multiply them by themselves, then add together the squared distances and subtract the time factor squared, you have the right recipe for space-time. In other words, if x, y, and z are distances and t is time measured on earth, and if c is the speed of light, the formula for space-time, in words and symbols, is:

Space-time squared equals [width squared plus depth squared plus height squared] minus [distance traveled by light squared]

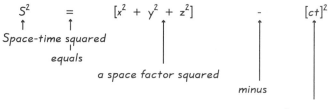

Space-time squared equals [width squared plus depth squared plus height squared] minus [distance traveled by light in time squared]

$$S^2 \quad = \quad [x^2 + y^2 + z^2] \quad - \quad [ct]^2$$

Space-time squared

equals

a space factor squared

minus

a time factor squared

25.4 Equation and aspects of space-time separation

In other words, if you take the dimensions of your local framework where you are, your measurement of width (x), breadth (y), height (z), and time (t), and if you take the constant, c, the speed of light, all you have to do is combine them with the above recipe to find s. The remarkable thing, which we have yet to explain, is that this s will no longer depend on which framework you look from! If you put in your measurements of width, breadth, height, and time, which will be very different from mine, which I got by looking from my viewpoint at the same event such as the falling star—we will get the same s. This is a great thing, because it allows us to share a given value and speak of that value instead of our own dimensions all the time.

Space-time s is that special mixture of space and time which is an invariant for a given event, that is, it is independent of the framework from which you are looking. It is no longer my description, or your description, of the event itself that is invariant, as we had thought before

Einstein. Now we know that space-time is a certain mixture of x, y, z, and t that is always the same.

When we look at the formula for space-time, we will see that it is four-dimensional: it has x, y, z, and t in it. In contrast, space has x, y, and z in it: space is three-dimensional. In other words, space-time separation, s—not space or time—is a hyper-dimension, a hyperspace, a world we might experience but not the one that is consensual. S will be the same experience for the person on the moon as for the person on Earth. And both can compute it using their own measurements of their individual spaces and times between the stars.

MINKOWSKI'S IMAGINARY TIME

Einstein's teacher, Minkowski, realized that Einstein's space-time was talking about another world and decided to portray this world as best he could by simplifying Einstein's equations for space-time. Minkowski took Einstein's four-dimensional formula and made it easier to see by making it like a two-dimensional picture, a triangle.[3] Minkowski's simplification was great, but to make things easier to see, he realized that the time dimension became imaginary, as we saw above.[4] Minkowski looked at Einstein's work and realized Einstein's equations had a new worldview in them, a space-time world where events were described in terms of "world lines."

The new, four-dimensional world of world lines is needed to see that relativity, in one way at least, is like the wave function in quantum mechanics. Both are represented mathematically by imaginary numbers. Remember that the wave function is a complex number—it is partly real, partly imaginary. And complex numbers, as we have seen, are connected to non-consensus experiences like dreaming, fantasies, hallucinations, feelings, and pain.

In other words, the imaginary numbers in relativity, as well as in quantum mechanics, represent non-consensual experiences. Complex numbers, or dreaming, connect quantum mechanics and relativity. It is as simple as that. Our non-consensus experiences pattern the manner in which we describe both the very smallest, subatomic realm and the most gigantic universe we live in.

The observers, or experiencers, you and I, are participants in an NCR relationship. From the viewpoint of my interpretation of quantum mechanics, you on the ground and I on the moon are both able to observe the falling star only because we are both attracted by that falling star. It is flirting with both of us. Thus we connect in a hyperspace, knowing something non-consensual is happening before we observe it. Now, according to relativity, when we observe it in our own frameworks, it is not our observations themselves that make up the common ground of our observation between us, but a mixture,[5] which is an imaginary number. In other words, in our non-consensual experiences, the space-time of relativity is indistinguishable from the quantum flirt we discussed earlier.[6]

SPACE-TIME AND INDIVIDUAL PROCESS

One analogy for space-time separation can be found in the work of an artist. If the artist is more or less ordinary, most of us see her as having specific talents and abilities that can be defined. But if she is exceptional, each of us begins to see something different in her work.

Let's think about Picasso. Let's say that he called one of his paintings "a woman." Let's say you and I agree about that. But exactly what the woman is doing, you and I and Picasso may never agree on. Something awesome happens in Picasso's art. While each of us has a different view of his abilities and exceptional nature, we will all share the same view that something awesome occurs in his painting. We do not have a consensus about exactly what he painted, but we do agree about the awesomeness of it all. We have a consensus about the power of non-consensus experience. It is as if Picasso has taken us out of the three dimensions of our ordinary lives and propelled us into a fourth dimension, a sort of space-time. We have a consensus on the awesome nature of this hyperspace, this "space-time," which is a combination of real things he does in the painting plus creative genius, which we cannot quite define. The total effect can no longer be defined in everyday reality!

An artist's talents are a combination of her consensus reality abilities and the imaginations she provokes, which results in a hypnotic, four-dimensional effect. While we can gain consensus that her total effect is amazing, we cannot say exactly how this takes place. We can only say that she brings us beyond our ordinary reality into a hyperspace. She sets us all into dreaming, and it is this dreaming experience that we share of her presence. Each of us sees her art in terms of a given space, but what happens after we look can only be described as dreaming. We are outside of ordinary time and space, in an experiential space, or hyperspace.

Another example of space-time dreaming involves the behavior of traditional sorcerers and shamans. I think in particular of the dancing madman, don Genaro, from the books of Carlos Castaneda. Imagine don Genaro. When someone comes to visit him and stands at his door, instead of saying hello or good-bye don Genaro goes into a creative, shamanic dance. Two different shaman apprentices visiting don Genaro may witness him differently. One might see the shaman dancing and think he has shape-shifted into being a small fluttering bird about to fly. The second apprentice sees him fluttering and dancing like an eagle. Both viewpoints come from their different psychological frameworks and are different—

just as a person on Earth and another on the moon see a falling star very differently.

Both apprentices experience don Genaro as dancing and birdlike and as hypnotic and having shamanic powers. The power of dreaming witnessed by two different observers is an analogy to space-time. The power of dreaming is the common ground, similar to the complex mathematics found in quantum flirts and in relativity. The power of dreaming has real qualities (the figure of don Genaro, dancing as a bird) and also imaginary qualities. These real and imaginary qualities, these complex numbers, so to speak, are a shared experience, a common ground associated with the different visualizations, an experience analogous to space-time.

The very term "shamanism" implies that we are in consensus about the fact that the shaman enters other realities, although we cannot exactly define them in terms of everyday life. The study of non-consensus experiences in shamanism gives us a hint about the invariant, constant quality shared by otherwise very different viewpoints.

We can ask, "What was don Genaro himself experiencing?" He might say that he experienced himself as stepping out of time and space, outside of consensus reality, and into the "nagual," the unknown, the Tao, the unconscious. He became congruent with all the various parts of himself and was just traveling through space, forward and backward in time, in the midst of a flow.

SPACE-TIME AND THE COMMON GROUND OF COMMUNITY

I have never met don Genaro, but I have experienced similar traditional shamans in Africa, Australia, and South America, often in group settings. I have always had the feeling that the spirit was moving the shamans I was witnessing. Their "acts of power" were numinous and mutually shared by all. Even though each viewer had his or her own separate experience of the shaman, we all shared what seemed to be ecstatic trances and healing.

These trances and "acts of power" were a form of space-time, a "common ground," for all who were present. The experiences took place in a hyperspace, in a magical and unifying atmosphere. In fact, this common ground is what creates and holds communities together.

I felt both awestruck by and at home with these shamans. I couldn't understand their languages, yet the shamans brought me into their most intimate spheres, into my own "home," through our experiencing the common numinosity of what the Native Americans call the Great Spirit, that secret river running deep beneath all communities.

In everyday life we are separated by our consensus reality frameworks, by our differences of opinion, education and social and class background. Each of us lives in her or his own world. Yet, in dreaming together, our separate frameworks fall together and we each share the same unifying reality hinted at by the space-time of relativity.

In most of the world's cosmopolitan cultures, consensus reality stresses mainstream dimensions of space and time as if they were absolute. We measure ourselves and one another in terms of our abilities and intelligence, our gender, race, sexual orientation, age, and so on. These separations lead to useful differentiation but also to marginalization—to racism, religious wars, sexism, homophobia, ageism, and loneliness.

Yet, during moments of dreaming together, these dimensions and separate viewpoints come together and we are no longer any one race, religion, gender, sexual orientation, or age, nor are we totally alone. In deep community experiences, we become some indescribable mixture of life and death, black and white, Moslem, Buddhist, Hindu, Jew, and Christian, male and female, gay and straight, old and young, you and me.

I remember a particularly moving community experience Amy and I went through together with a large group of Koreans, Japanese, Chinese, black Americans, Latinos, white Americans, and individuals of many other nationalities. We had all come together to work out devastating effects and resulting alienation between Asian countries created by World War II. The main focus of the group was working through the pain and antagonism attributable, in great part, to war atrocities. Open group discussions, arguments, and interactions among the various Asian nationalities took us all through amazing emotional clashes, insights, and partial resolutions. Many members of the group had trained themselves in the use of the second attention and could bring up and move through awesome feelings.

The conference went as well as could be expected under the circumstances. Many deep moments occurred; partial resolutions occurred under the most painful circumstances. As we were ending the group experience, a Korean participant, who had been particularly hurt by the events of the war, clearly and decisively proclaimed that he would never like the Japanese, no matter what agreements and excuses they gave for the historical events that had occurred. The Korean said emphatically that he would never feel anything again, would never laugh or cry, never shed a tear, not in this lifetime or the next, even if the Japanese did the best they could to work out the difficulties.

After the Korean spoke, there was a tense silence. After what seemed like a long time, though it may have been only a minute, a Japanese participant stood up on the opposite side of the room and said something briefly and softly in Japanese. Then, to the shock of everyone in that large group, the Japanese stood up, almost as a unit, and in one thrust threw themselves, face down, toward the ground, prostrating themselves with outstretched hands in a submissive bow to that Korean, apologizing and begging forgiveness for the atrocities committed by the Japanese against the Koreans.

Again there was silence. Then the Korean burst into tears and wept and wept, opening everyone's heart, ushering us all into that secret river running beneath community.

Each person who witnessed that incredible event had his or her own view of what happened. Yet something was common and shared. Everyone was deeply moved, transported, so to speak, into another reality. We all lived in that common hyperspace I refer to as dreaming together. Moments like those make the difficult, terrifying, and uncomfortable effort needed to sit in the fire of conflicting communities more than worthwhile.

The Koreans and Japanese moved us all into the domain of dreaming by using their second attention on non-consensus experiences, thoughts, and unspeakable feelings. They stepped out of everyday reality, through history, and into dreaming. Everyone will have their own viewpoint on what happened, but everyone will be in agreement that something unrepresentable occurred, something awesome and beyond everyday life.

Consensus reality vocabulary is useful in thinking about that process. We can use archetypal images, history; we can speak of social issues and global problems. These descriptions are the path to the river, but they are not the experience of the river itself. It is rare that groups go so deeply that they bring up forbidden feelings and move beyond everyday reality. When this occurs, the meaning of the spiritual term "Mother Earth" used by the Native Americans becomes clear. Mother Earth is the power of community, which collapses differences by bringing forward the interrelatedness between all things. The experience of Mother Earth is what makes us hope that the world will come together in the face of global alienation.

Mother Earth is a form of space-time. Psychology can learn a lot about Mother Earth from native peoples, but also from physics. The math of relativity tells us in no uncertain terms that space-time, the most universal domain in which everything happens, is a calculation that is always present wherever and whenever there is an observer. Just begin with the description of reality as you see it in your own terms, and soon enough new dimensions and a flowing process will appear. In this process realm the parts and particles of everyday reality flow together into a common river.

CONCLUSIONS

We have discovered in this chapter that space-time can be calculated from the spatial dimensions in which events occur, minus time factors. If the relative velocities involved are not great, space-time is simply everyday space and time. But at high velocities, viewpoints on events begin to differ. Under these circumstances, the only thing we all share is a four-dimensional combination of our spatial and time dimensions.

The analogy in psychology to high velocity in physics is when communities enter altered states of consciousness. In these states, the differences between our intense experience and ordinary selves are very great. Time and spatial distortions occur, and we all enter into a new realm, a hyperspace. Our own individual explanations of the resulting altered states differ because they depend upon our individual frameworks. Nevertheless, analogously to four-dimensional space-time, we still share that special reality in which something amazing flirts with all of us, a common heightened sense of dreamtime. In that moment, we feel we are transported into a special interconnectedness, as dreamtime becomes space-time.

Space-time, that non-consensus common ground native peoples called Mother Earth, is always present, though hidden, in the one-sided manner in which we see things. When we climb into our various consensus reality viewpoints on an issue, when we unveil hidden, irrational factors, a time-like characteristic of events, namely their process, begins. The moral of this story is that, if we have the courage to bring out personal experiences around a given issue, we can transform the world of separateness into a sense of connectedness.

The commonness, or as scientists say, "the invariance of space-time separation" gives hope to those of us who worry about facilitating the complexity of individual and large-group processes. Especially when we are bogged down by one-sided, non-relativistic views that separate and alienate us, and when we are in the midst of tension and trouble, it helps to remember modern physics. Physics states clearly that a common space-time measure and dreaming together are possible if someone goes over the edge of their individual experiences and enters the realm of dreaming. We need to remember that the secret river of community is inherent even in overwhelming enmity.

Physics can learn from psychology about the experiences that pattern space-time. Physics can learn that shamanic attention is needed to apprehend and understand the domain of imaginary numbers, the realm of sentient experience, as well as the four-dimensional space-time. What the shaman calls the unknown, the psychologist calls telepathy, synchronicity, and community, a process or flux the mathematician finds in calculus. Physicists of the future will realize that space-time in relativity and conjugation in quantum mechanics are where cosmic and microcosmic realms come together with sentient experience in psychology and shamanism. This realization is the beginning of a new world-view, the modern shamanism that senses the interconnected nature of all our "separate" realities.

NOTES

1. The basic concept behind Einstein's derivation of the Lorentz transformation
    is based on the idea that the velocity of light remains equal in all frameworks
    and that distance equals velocity times time. Here is the approximate deriva-
    tion. The distance traveled in one dimension of the speed of light is $x = ct$. Or,
    $x^2 - c^2t^2 = 0$. The appearance of the same event in any other framework, let's
    call it x′ and t′, must mean that $x'^2 - c^2t'^2 = 0$. If we consider the general case
    of propagation of light, which is not in perfectly straight lines, and are not
    forced to be Euclidean or reckon with the Pythagorean theorem where the
    hypotenuse is the square root of the sum of the squares of the sides, then, in
    three dimensions and in general,

    $$x'^2 + y'^2 + z'^2 - c^2t'^2 = x^2 + y^2 = z'^2 - c^2t'^2 = s^2$$

    where s is space-time separation.

    If we remember that $x = vt$, and set $y = z = 0$, the above equation gives us
    the Lorentz transformation for one dimension found below in Figure 25.5.
    (More information about this derivation can be found in Einstein's *The Mean-
    ing of Relativity*.)

    In general, the resulting Lorentz transformation from one framework to
    another, given the values on the ground, x, y, t, and z, gives the values in a
    framework moving relative to it with velocity v as x′, y′, z′, t′ (when $y = y'$,
    and $z = z'$) by

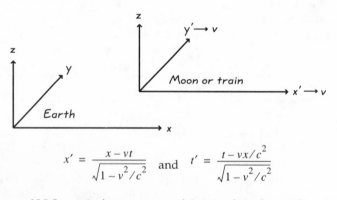

$$x' = \frac{x - vt}{\sqrt{1 - v^2/c^2}} \quad \text{and} \quad t' = \frac{t - vx/c^2}{\sqrt{1 - v^2/c^2}}$$

25.5 Connection between spaces and times in relative frameworks

The speed of the train (or the moon) relative to the Earth is

$$v = x/t$$

If we take a meterstick which measures a meter on the moving framework
such as the train or a star as seen from the ground, we get x′ there. How long
will that meter be for people measuring on the Earth? Since

$$x - vt = x'\sqrt{1 - v^2/c^2}$$

we see, if $x' = 1$ and $t = 0$, that

$$x = \sqrt{1 - v^2/c^2}$$

This shows that, for very small (let's say train) velocities, x is about 1 meter, too. But for very great velocities, when someone on the train measures 1 meter, someone on the Earth will think the meterstick shrank! You can see that if v gets bigger than c, then

$$x = \sqrt{1 - v^2/c^2} = \sqrt{\text{-number}} = i\sqrt{\text{number}}$$

since $i = \sqrt{-1}$ and we have imaginary values. Thus, nothing can go faster than the speed of light, according to present-day physics, because if it does, it cannot be measured in CR. Anything above the speed of light deals with imaginary worlds, with dreaming. Furthermore, from the above formula for t' in Figure 25.5,
at $x = 0$, we notice that as velocities increase, time for 1 second measured on the train will be measured by someone on the ground to be less than 1 second; time shrinks with increasing v since

$$t = \sqrt{1 - v^2/c^2}$$

2. Note 1 above shows how imaginary numbers result if v, which is x/t, is greater than c.

3. Before we go on and discover more about space-time, let's just think a bit more about it. This will not be complicated, but it might seem so if you have not been dealing with right triangles for awhile. I want to talk a little about triangles and try to show you how Einstein's math teacher, Hermann Minkowski, reevaluated and, in some senses, simplified Einstein's results.

    Minkowski looked at s and realized that it is something like the diagonal, or hypotenuse—the long line—of a right triangle.

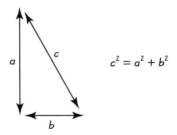

25.6 Euclidean formula for right triangles

Minkowski looked at the formula for the right triangle and thought that the equation for space-time looked similar:

$$s^2 = x^2 + y^2 + z^2 - c^2 t^2$$

If we simplify and let the space coordinates x, y, and z be represented by one spatial coordinate, say, x, then we have the form

$$s^2 = x^2 - c^2 t^2$$

This space-time formula looks a bit like

$$c^2 = a^2 + b^2$$

which is the formula for a right triangle where c is a distance.

Minkowski looked at this and thought, "Hmmm, that s or space-time is a four-dimensional measure (three spatial measures and one time measure), whereas that flat triangle is two-dimensional. How about reducing s to two dimensions, since s is hard to visualize in four dimensions. We have nothing like four-dimensional reality in our everyday world, which is basically three dimensions. Physicists of the future will want to visualize Einstein's work on relativity, but it's too weird if you can't visualize what he is talking about."

Since two or three dimensions are easier to conceive of, Minkowski decided to reduce the four-dimensional hyperspace, consisting of x, y, z, and t, to two dimensions. He approximated its nature by visualizing it as a flat triangle. This is like estimating the surface of a piece of earth that is bumpy. The curved surface is difficult to measure, so you approximate the surface by thinking of it as flat and by applying the formula for area, which is width times length.

In his effort to visualize the new, four-dimensional world, Minkowski simply renamed the spaces and times to put them on an equal footing. He called x_1 the spatial dimension ($x = x_1$) and x_4 the time dimension ($-ict = x_4$) and arrived at a simpler formula, which had the form of a right triangle:

$$s^2 = x_1^2 + x_4^2$$

The point of all this was to visualize a hyperspace in terms of ordinary reality. And yes, the above four-dimensional formula for space-time does, indeed, look like the formula for the diagonal of a right triangle! This makes s a sort of diagonal, if we can imagine a triangle in two dimensions.

Minkowski's mathematics simplifies by hiding the imaginary dimension of time. The new world of Minkowski is a combination of consensus reality spatial dimensions and temporal dimensions, but time has an imaginary number in front of it (since $-ict = x_4$)! In other words, it is difficult to visualize the time dimension!

But we already knew that from the beginning, without math: time has spatial qualities, but movement in time is very hard to imagine. We spatialize time in our thinking. (For example, if asked, "How long will it take you to get to where you are going in the next city by road?" you might say, "About 500 miles."

Minkowski called the dimension x by a new name. That is like calling you not by your name, but by "space 1." He renamed x, x_1! He called y by a new name, too: he said, call it space 2 or x_2. Likewise, z became x_3. Now what on earth, he thought, should he do with time, which has that uncomfortable minus sign in front of it, namely, $-c^2t^2$? He thought, let the time dimension become x_4.

That was really tricky because he hid the minus sign in the term $(-c^2t^2)$ by saying $x_4{}^2 = (-ict)^2$, and thus, $x_4 = -ict$, since the square root of minus one is i. (Remember Chapter 7?) With new names, space-time becomes a bit more familiar:

$$s^2 = x_1{}^2 + x_2{}^2 + x_3{}^2 + x_4{}^2$$

since $x = x_1$, $y = x_2$, $z = x_3$, and $-ict = x_4$, which reduces to

$$s^2 = x_1{}^2 + x_4{}^2$$

when y and z are zero.

4. But wait, what happened to time, $x_4 = \sqrt{-c^2t^2}$? Since the square root of a negative number like -1 is i, now we have $x_4 = ict$).

5. Calculating space-time: Pretend that, as far as you are concerned, y and z are not needed to measure the distance a planet moves along in one spatial dimension x. Then we can draw space-time as if it were a two-dimensional map, which we can easily visualize. Space-time can now be represented in two dimensions.

   Let us try, for example, to measure the space-time separation of a planet that went 250 miles in terms of space and 1 year in terms of local time.

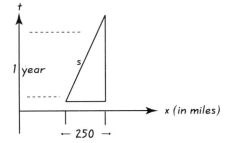

25.7 Space-time diagram measuring 250 miles and 1 year

Now, we could substitute these values into the formulas for x and t above and we can get s, the space-time separation a planet had moved in 1 year of

Earth time and 250 miles of Earth space. Likewise, we could even measure the velocity of the planet as it moves through time!

The reason for finding space-time separation is that this value *s* is the same, regardless of the viewpoint you measure it from.

If the planet remained still in space, it would still move in time—after all, it gets older!

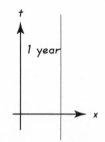

25.8 Movement in space-time when there is no movement in space

With only movement in time the planet makes a straight line in space-time, since *x*, *y*, and *z* do not change at all. Is there a velocity for movement in time? Surely there is. The velocity in time is then $c = s/t$. How can there be a velocity of things in time? The velocity is the speed of light. Thus, even if you do not move an inch from the viewpoint of a given reference frame, you are traveling at the speed of light through time.

The man on the moon measures x_1' and x_4'. Since

$$s^2 = x_1^2 + x_4^2 = x_1'^2 + x_4'^2$$

In diagram form, this equation looks like Figure 25.9.

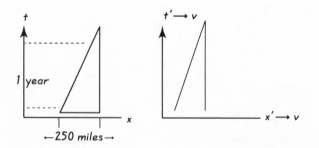

25.9 Relative measurements seen on the Earth and on a moving framework

I measure 250 miles and my time *t* is 1 year, yet *x'* and *t'* are different for the person on the train which is moving relative to the Earth.

6.   Space-time involves an imaginary time in the math of relativity. See note 3, where the time factors for every observer are a matter of the measurement of

time in their respective frameworks multiplied by the speed of light times the imaginary number, that is, *ict*. I am very grateful to a friend of mine, Joe Goodbread, for interesting discussions about connecting space-time and relativity.

26 | Sacred Geometry: The Structure of Darkness

In the beginning, was the great cosmic egg. Inside the egg was chaos, and floating in chaos was Pan Ku, the divine Embryo.

—Pan Ku myth (China, third century)

Ordinarily, when most of us think about space, we imagine an amorphous emptiness, like a room that can be filled with anything, such as people, plants, and objects. To measure space, we imagine laying out measuring sticks or the like in the three dimensions of space, which, like immense, straight tracks, stretch out toward infinity in all directions.

Einstein's first relativity theory, the special theory of relativity, changes our concept of linear, independent dimensions into four intertwined dimensions called space-time. His general theory of relativity goes further and changes our very notion of space from a linear, empty, nothingness into a curved, filled, substance. In the general theory of relativity, space, or rather space-time and its structure, geometry, are not empty and formless, but a mass-like form. In other words, the empty space we walk through as we walk down the street is not just an open void, but a substance.

This segment of our journey will begin by exploring space and geometry as a prelude to exploring the psychological connections between relativity and mythology. The message we shall discover together is that space is, in fact, who we are.

GEOMETRY

To understand space, let's consider geometry, the structure of space. For-
tunately, geometry is easier than algebra for most people to understand.
Geometry is pictorial; it has artistic form and seems less abstract than the
formulas of algebra. For example, consider the algebraic formula $c^2 = a^2 + b^2$, the Pythagorean equation for the longest side, the hypotenuse, of a
right triangle. This formula probably seems more complex to most of us
than its geometric equivalent, the picture of a right triangle.

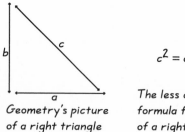

$$c^2 = a^2 + b^2$$

The less artistic algebraic
formula for the hypotenuse
of a right triangle

Geometry's picture
of a right triangle

26.1 Compare geometry and algebra.

In Figure 26.1, the formula can be described in terms of the map. The
map explains the formula in a pictorial manner. The formula says that to
find the distance between points 1 and 2, you have to find the distances *a*
and *b*, square them, add the squares, and take the square root of the sum.
Because geometry is a map, it plays a central role in describing not only
the physical universe but also the spiritual universe in religion and the
psychic realm of wholeness in psychology.

For example, one of the central spiritual and psychological formulas,
or geometrical structures, behind our behavior has been pictured in various religious traditions and in Jungian psychology as the circle, or the
mandala, a symmetrical diagram from India. Jung felt that the mandala
symbolized the goal of human behavior, wholeness or individuation, as
he called it. The mandala implies that we have many sides and must
develop them all equally. Mandalas have many shapes; they may be
round or square, starlike or oblong, but they are always symmetrical.

When a ball is symmetrical, you can rotate it in one direction or
another and its basic shape does not change. Squares are less symmetrical
than circles. You can rotate a circle or sphere any way you like and it
remains the same. You have to rotate a square exactly a quarter of a turn in
order for it to stay the same. Rectangles are still less symmetrical; you have
to rotate them 180 degrees for them to remain the same. This holds true for
crosses, too; if the "arms" are higher up than the base, the cross is symmetrical with respect to flipping it from right to left or from left to right. If you
do that, its shape looks the same. The shape changes, however, if you

stand it upside down. A six-pointed star is symmetrical if you turn it 60 degrees. You need to turn a five-pointed star a bit more to maintain symmetry.

26.2 Examples of symmetrical objects

Geometry has many symmetrical structures, which pictorialize the deep tendency we have to become complete, whole beings. Symmetries are also fundamental to the laws of physics. A little further along, we will explore together the origins of these symmetries.

HISTORY OF GEOMETRY

The term "geometry" means, literally, "earth measure" and comes from the Greek words "geo," for earth, and "metron," which means measure. The evolution of geometry and of our ideas of space, time, and the shape of the universe go back many thousands of years and are linked to measuring and partitioning land. When the early Babylonians and, later, the Greeks found that $c^2 = a^2 + b^2$, they were happy. Before that time, people were not able to accurately calculate the distance or c, the diagonal or hypotenuse between the corners of their property; they couldn't speak about the length of their barriers and fences or the size of their land.

Around three thousand years ago, Babylonians who lived where Egypt is today wanted to know how big the Earth is and how far it is from the sun. They used their formula $c^2 = a^2 + b^2$ as their starting point to take measurements. They stuck straight poles in the ground pointing up into the sky and noticed changes in the angle made by the sun's shadow as it hit the ground at various times of the day and year. From this, they were able to compute how far the sun is from the Earth. In fact, by observing the angle the sun made at different times of year and the way its shadow moved, the Babylonians guessed that the world was round, and they approximated its diameter as well.[1]

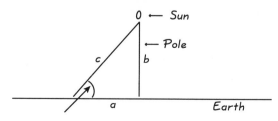

26.3 Angle made by sun on the Earth

Europeans thought they were first to discover that the Earth was round, but that is not quite true. The Babylonians knew much earlier, based on their geometrical theories. Many years later, about 300 BC, the Greeks began their studies of geometry and rediscovered facts already known by the Egyptians. The Greek philosopher Euclid wrote thirteen books, called *The Elements;* four of these books are about geometry. Euclid's work is often quoted as the first to reveal the laws of geometry, but we should remember that it was the Babylonians in northern Africa who were first—at about 1000 BC—in knowing, for example, the formula for finding the area of a square (take one of the sides and square it).[2] At least, credit is still given to the Africans for our numerals, which are "Arabic."

The Greeks are given credit for geometrical formulas—such as the hypotenuse being the square root of the sides of the triangle squared—because they proved the formula by using deductive reasoning. Until then, there was no such thing as "proof." The Babylonians were more empirical than deductive. They said, "If it works, it is right." The Europeans preferred deductive reasoning for their proofs. They said, "It must be logically consistent as well."

By the way, it turns out that two thousand years later, in 1931, the Austrian Kurt Goedel showed—deductively—that we cannot be certain that the logical propositions of mathematics are absolutely airtight. Goedel's theorem proves that no mathematical system can prove itself.[3] Since math is the basic description of physics, it follows that the theories of physics will never be entirely self-contained; they will never be able to reach "closure" as long as they depend on today's math. Math is, deductively speaking, inconsistent, and will always lead to paradoxes.

SACRED GEOMETRY

At the same time that logical formulas and geometries were being discovered in antiquity, a more mythological geometry was being considered as well. Sacred geometry is an aspect of mathematics that is not described in the history of math, but an aspect that will be important to us in the study of the universe.

At around 600 BC, while Pythagoras and many others were thinking reasonably and deductively, the Egyptians and East Indians were pondering where mathematics came from. The Egyptians speculated that math was created by the mythic spirit of the ocean, the great goddess Nun, who was also called "Unlimited Space." She is credited with creating "volume" and "differentiation."[4] We can see this same idea today if we think of the zero-point energy field in physics, which is the hypothetical vast sea of energy basic to the universe that gives constant birth to virtual particles. In other words, according to both modern physics and ancient sacred Egyptian geometry, parts, particles, and differentiation arise from the sea of nothingness.

These ideas about vast, creative, unlimited spaces are found in the psychology of individuals as well. I have worked with several people who were in "psychotic" states (I prefer the term "extreme states") who seem to know about sacred geometry without ever having studied it. One of these clients, with whom I worked while I was a student in Zurich, told me in no uncertain terms that I should realize that volume was created from the sea. While she was in an altered state, speculating about the nature of the universe, she said that the universe was first a great ocean. She called the ocean a huge "fluid full of potential," an immense undifferentiated "field." I knew that she was speaking about herself, and that she was about to recreate herself and her own world. I was fascinated by the fact that theories of the universe coming from her and other so-called schizophrenics not only have mythic counterparts such as the goddess Nun, but also mirror theories of modern physics. Only academicians separate theology, psychology, and physics. Ordinary people experience these supposedly separate areas as the ancients did, that is, as one and the same subject.

People who use mythology and physics in their fantasies are giving their version of the universal mind. The ancient theories and modern experiences indicate that we are living within a universal dreaming body. The Egyptian myth about the goddess Nun and one of its modern counterparts, physicist David Bohm's theory about the universe unfolding its particles and other structures from an original state of unbroken wholeness, are metaphors for our experience of creativity out of nothingness. All of us who have spent time meditating notice something like the goddess Nun each time some sort of creative power brings sudden insights, words, and concepts out of apparent emptiness. Likewise, apparently comatose people sometimes awaken spontaneously out of an apparent sea of nothingness with amazing insights.[5]

In an Egyptian text of about 700 BC, the creative, universal space goddess Nun says:

How to describe the indescribable?
How to show the unshowable?
How to express the unutterable?
How to seize the ungraspable instant?[6]

Here, Nun personifies our deepest tendency to describe, show, utter, grasp, and formulate the sentient experiences we can barely verbalize. She is the figure that takes the Tao, which cannot be said, the sentient background of reality, and realizes it in terms of structures.

According to ancient texts, Nun, the infinite source of the universe, was before space and time; she was yes and no, positive and negative.

The creator of geometry, she is the order-making potential in nature. She reminds us that space is not a dormant, passive, empty substance waiting for dimensions to create structure but rather, an intelligent being brimming with creative potential. In a way, the Africans knew this before Einstein.

According to mythology, Nun's magical powers and creativity reflect her impulse to know herself.[7] Therefore, one of the meanings of the myth of the goddess Nun might be that you don't always have to work to get enlightened. It is not up to you to get the answers you need. The universe uses you to get to know itself. All you need to do is go to sleep and dream. When the universe is ready, you will get to know yourself. When the time comes, you'll get the specific information you need in a given moment.

One of my professors at MIT, Norbert Wiener, used to do this very thing. When Professor Wiener, who was the father of the communications field called cybernetics, got bored or stuck figuring something out, he would fall asleep and have a dream. He told us in class one day that he put a notepad next to his bed and waited, and that in this way he found solutions. He was an amazingly brilliant and unusual teacher. He was totally "spaced out." Perhaps he was flirting with Nun. He would come to class or go to meetings and fall asleep during interactions with people, and suddenly awaken with insights. As I mentioned earlier, I remember him walking down the hallways of the buildings of MIT, asking where he was. I thought he was weird because I knew he lived in the area. But then I met him a few years later in Zurich and he was still confused about where he was. Although his location in physical space was tenuous, he was a genius at revealing new ideas and structures about communications.

In ancient India, there were also mythic and mathematical creators of the universe. The Hindus spoke of the Purusha, who suddenly created the world in the form of an icosahedron, a twenty-sided geometrical figure in which all the faces are equal.[8] According to the Hindus, our world was created by Purusha and is Purusha unfolding. In other words, the universe is a self-created, geometrical structure. In modern terms, we might say that mathematics is the structure of mind of a self-creating universe.

Purusha's number, 20, is not that surprising if we remember that our number bases are connected with our anatomy—ten fingers and ten toes. Purusha is a human-like world structure, an "anthropos" figure with a human-like form.

According to myths, our mathematics and the physical universe are not creations *ex nihilo*, out of nothing, but are created by the goddesses and gods who are themselves unlimited space. Since the universe is mathematical, the math we use seems human-like, in part because we are part of the universe. In other words, our human form is a manifestation of the deepest principles in the universe. This may be why the principles that fit us psychologically, such as symmetry and wholeness, also fit for the physical universe. Our theoretical systems reflect our natures.

It is fascinating that even today scientists are trying to use ten-dimensional hyperspaces to understand particles in string theory to unify physics. Why 10? Perhaps because deep within us, we suspect that we (and everything else as well) are reflections of a human-like universe.

SYMMETRIES: THE MIND OF NATURE

Around the tenth century, Christian mystics envisioned Christ as a part of the universal space consisting of four circles. Christ was pictured between the four circles with a compass in one hand. Christ was considered to be a geometer. He is drawing a circle with his compass, reenacting the creation of the universe from the chaos or the primeval state.[9] The circle in geometry is, here, the instrument of creation.

26.4 Christ in the Midst of Four Spheres

This theme also appears in Japanese Zen calligraphy, which shows creation through a progression from the circle to the triangle and finally to the square. [10]

26.5 From Japanese calligraphy showing creation from the circle through the triangle and finally to the square

What sort of a religion would you have if you went to your mosque, church, temple, or synagogue and saw a goddess standing there with a compass? When I asked this question in a class, one student burst out laughing with an answer: "All encompassing!" I responded with another question, "And do you know of any religions besides Christianity where the compass plays a sacred role?"

Most of the students knew that the Masonic orders use the compass and the square and that Native Americans have the four directions. Today, native peoples feel that space is holy, sacred; it is dreamtime. The compass and its directions are believed to be divine. The gods of the North, South, East, and West govern the four directions. In rituals, shamans and chiefs honor each of these spirits, giving homage to the living intelligence structuring the atmosphere in which we live.

During the Renaissance, the sciences tried to marginalize spiritual experience, yet the gods are still here. When physicists and astronomers talk about the universe today, they often refer to God, even if they do not believe in religion. Einstein's famous declaration and criticism of quantum physics, "I shall never believe that God plays dice with the world," shows that he thought God was a mathematician, a geometer who structured the universe in an exact manner. For him, the universe was an intelligent deity not unlike Purusha and Nun.[11]

EUCLIDIAN AND NON-EUCLIDIAN GEOMETRY

By the year 1900, most mathematicians and physicists were no longer in contact with the sacred powers behind math, or with a mathematics that is a description of the universe reflecting upon itself. In fact, the spaces of physics were very much like the square rooms of our consensus reality. The deductive reasoning of the Greeks became central to science. The goddesses and gods were temporarily marginalized.

The most common idea about space among physicists in 1900 was what mathematicians call "two-space" or "flatland" because it can be imagined as a piece of paper lying flat on a desk, with circles and squares drawn on it. The world of physics was Euclidean and supposed to consist of circles and triangles that can be measured with the theorems that many of us learned in school.

The Babylonian and Greek surveyors used the formulas for squares and triangles to measure the area of their property. To map the distance from one town to the next, of course, they could have walked off the distance in feet. But it would have been hard for them to measure the distance if there was a steep hill in the middle. Formulas provide generalizations that help you when you cannot go in a straight line to measure distance. To measure the distance a bird might fly between your town, *A*, and *C*, the next town, just use the formula for the right triangle.

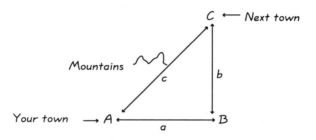

26.6 Measuring distance between A and C

If mountains are between *A* and *C* (Figure 26.6), all you need to know to find the distance *c* is the sum of a^2 and b^2 (assuming there are no hills there). You don't have to measure the distance *c* between *A* and *C* directly. Geometrical formulas tell you how to go places in space, and how far away they are, even when you cannot measure them directly.

It turns out that when we measure big distances such as the spaces between planets, we cannot use this Euclidean, or rather Pythagorean, formula for triangles. In fact, the formulas for distances, triangles, squares, and circles no longer hold. We need a new formula, the formula of non-Euclidean geometry, which deals with curves.

To understand some of the peculiarities that come from curved thinking, we can begin by using the more or less spherical Earth on which we live. If you take a plane trip around the world and go along the Equator, you will eventually end up in the same place you started. That is because we live on a sphere.

The fastest route between two points on this Earth via air travel is not a straight line, but a curved one. To get from Portland, Oregon, to Paris, France, you save about a thousand miles if you fly close to the ground, but you do not go straight to Paris. Instead, you must go at first toward the north, not east.

To get an idea about what it is like to travel in empty space, let's consider a trip out into space. If you start from where you are, say in Portland,

Oregon, and don't travel around the planet, but leave the Earth and go straight out into space, you will eventually return to Portland! Why? Because, according to our most modern theories of the universe, the universe is curved.

Another way of visualizing the curvature of space is to measure the straightness of a line shooting a beam of stones or their quantum equivalent, a beam of photons, between two points. If there was no gravity and no wind, you would expect the little stones or photons to go in a straight line. But our expectations turn out to be wrong. We hardly notice that we are wrong as long as we stay on the Earth, but even though we don't notice it, the path of the photons is not straight but curved.

This curvature is so small that no one noticed it until the early 1900s. Einstein showed that space is curved, and he even had a physical intuition about why this was the case. He said that the amount of matter in the neighborhood of a bunch of stones or photons bends their course! A beam of photons is light, of course. Another way of formulating the same thought is that it is not the beam of light that is bent, but space itself. From one viewpoint, matter or gravity bends space. Thus anything that should go in a straight line in the hypothetical Euclidean world can't in the universe we live in, because its space is bent.

Since the discovery of relativity, we have to conceive of space as a substance, a stuff that is bent and curved, depending on how much matter is around. If you are near a big planet, space is bent a lot. On Earth, space is not bent very much. This, in short, is the result of the general theory of relativity. We will be exploring this area further as we move into the next several chapters.

The special theory of relativity, which we discussed earlier, deals with relative frameworks whose relative motion is more or less straight and steady in space-time. The general theory deals with frameworks that are not moving at constant speeds but changing speeds—slowing down and speeding up, or accelerating.

While most physicists today accept the special theory of relativity, the general theory is mathematically complicated and is still being investigated. But the idea that space is bent and that the bending is connected with the amount of matter present is well accepted in the general theory.

The idea of space is already strange to some people, but what if we then add bent space? That is truly weird. It is an incredible concept that matter curves space, and only someone like Einstein could think it up. He realized that if we live in a universe where light bends, and if it is true that space is not just straight and flat, then there are no true triangles or circles. In our universe, triangles and circles are curved and can't be accurately drawn on a flat piece of paper. Furthermore, the ideas and formulas of Euclidean geometry many of us learned in school are correct only for your immediate neighborhood. For the universe at large we need a geometry that works with curves.

CURVATURE AND TRANCE

Euclidean geometry is to behavioral psychology as non-Euclidean geometry is to shamanism. In behavioral work, as in Euclidean geometry, you try to get linear causal connections. In shamanism, as in non-Euclidean geometry, you must work with non-linear, moving, bent spaces and altered states.

We all deviate a bit from everyday reality and consciousness every time we sleep, dance, fantasize, or have fun. In altered states of consciousness, such as trances, space and matter seem to bend and the idea of straight dimensions and a straight, linear life seems limiting. Once, some years ago when I took an LSD trip on the Oregon coast, I remember driving down the road with Amy and experiencing the very solid earth and the road in front of us curving upward, in front of the car, and then moving backward as it made a U turn in the air above us!

26.7 Highway 101 curved up into the air in front of us!

My point is that your sense of curvature of space and time depends upon your state of consciousness. Psychologists and shamans have always known the universe was a curved place to be. In other words, the shape of the space depends on the amount of mass nearby and on the state of consciousness you are in. What physics calls mass and the curvature of space, psychology calls the psyche and experience. The more intense the experience, the less directly we experience mass. What we experience is a sense of being drawn about; we sense curvature and gravity. We experience straight space in our ordinary lives, and four-dimensional or higher-dimensional hyperspaces such as space-time in altered states.

Dreaming may occur in hyperspaces, but it is also a down-to-earth, practical activity used to guide us through life. Native peoples all over the world have depended on guidance from their dreaming to catch game and to live everyday life. If we think of the environment only as linear space, predictable and measurable, or as emptiness waiting to be filled with our plans and programs, we ignore dreamlike effects of the environment such as "power spots." These are areas native and sensitive people recognize as having gravity, sacredness.

To know the environment, we have to trust altered states, which sense its intelligence. Then we experience the non-consensual aspects of space-time, the aspects we need to guide our lives in accordance with our deepest selves and the rest of the universe.

NON-EUCLIDEAN THINKING

Non-Euclidean geometry describes the curvature of space. We have seen that Euclid's geometry, with formulas such as $c^2 = a^2 + b^2$, holds only for a flat world. In your own local area, the earth seems flat. Small lakes seem flat. This sense of flatness is why Europeans, at the time of Columbus, still thought they would fall off the edge of the Earth if they sailed too far. In areas where the field is intense—that is, where there are huge planets and lots of matter, we must use non-Euclidean geometry. Remember the four dimensions of space-time, in which we must consider three spatial dimensions and one time dimension? Separations in space-time subtracted a time-like factor, let's call it b, from a space-like factor, let's call it a.[12] Thus, space-time separation, s, has the form $s^2 = a^2 - b^2$. Take a look at this. It almost looks like Euclid's formula, $s^2 = a^2 + b^2$.

Non-Euclidean geometry differs from the Euclidean by a minus sign, that is, $s^2 = (a^2 - b^2)$. If you want to find space-time separation you must find the square root of $(a^2 - b^2)$.

If space were not flat, we would have a formula that looks something like Euclid's except a minus sign is involved.[13] The minus sign has the effect of bending space-time. It curves it; it can no longer be entirely flat. Space needs another, imaginary dimension, as you can guess because imaginary numbers are involved.[14] It is this dimension which connects us back to non-consensual worlds, to sentient experience, to mythology and the things that make life worthwhile.

The non-Euclidean world is different from the Euclidean world of consensus reality. In non-Euclidean geometry, two lines that begin parallel to one another do not go on forever without meeting, as they do in flat space. The parallel lines eventually meet because space is curved. Physicists have tested the non-Euclidean formula by using telescopes, measuring how space bends by measuring how starlight that travels along straight lines in ordinary space bends when it moves around the sun. Our universe is curved around big planets.

Non-Euclidean geometry helps us estimate the size of the universe. The exact size of the universe will remain unknown for a while, since our telescopes are not powerful enough at present to see its entirety. But the latest estimate of the size of the universe is hundreds of billions of light years, which is hundreds of billions multiplied by the distance light travels in a year. That's a big number, but the important thing is that it is still finite.

A finite universe is another break in our intuitions. The Egyptians thought of Nun as unlimited space, and most people who are not physicists think the same way. Perhaps because of our dreaming about Nun, and perhaps because we are so limited by the spaces of our ordinary lives on Earth, most of us expect the universe to be infinite. But today's science implies that the physical universe that we live in is not infinitely big. The Big Bang theories tell us that the present universe is expanding but will also eventually contract.

What lies beyond the physical, visible universe is predicted by the theory of relativity. At first physicists thought that there was only one universe. Then, in the 1930s, people began to experiment with Einstein's math and found something Einstein hadn't spoken about. His math actually predicted small holes in the universe, "black holes," "discontinuities" in the mathematics that describes the four-dimensional universe.[15] These black holes have since been confirmed experimentally, and may lead to other universes.

Discontinuities in the general theory of relativity gave astronomers the sense that the equations of relativity indicated there must be holes in space-time, black holes, which may lead to other universes. Today, it is common opinion among physicists that if you go into a region of space-time where there is a black hole, that is, where there is an immense gravity field, then space will be bent into a funnel, or tube. Near black holes you meet discontinuities, not only in mathematics but also in your experience of physical reality. Weird things happen which, until now, only science fiction could imagine.

WHAT IS THE UNIVERSE?

Some theoreticians say that advances in the math of relativity predict that you can go through the black holes in our universe into other universes. How do we know this is possible? Has anyone actually set foot in another universe? How can you speak about it or measure it? After all, the experience of going through a black hole would be disastrous because, according to theory, our body mass increases as our velocity is accelerated under the influence of immense gravitational forces near the black hole. No one could survive such a situation in bodily form. In any case, no one I know has been through a black hole in the universe. And most people have trouble imagining one, much less several, universes.

At present, the math of physics predicts that the universe is more like a living, roundish pumpkin than a flat pancake. The pumpkin grows and shrinks in time. While it does, we float around inside it, the course of our lives determined by the thickness of the pumpkin material at every point. Where the material is very, thick, where the matter is very condensed, we find black holes, which seem to be tunnels to neighboring pumpkins.

And the face of the pumpkin? According to the myths of Purusha, Pan Ku, Nun, Christ, and Shiva, its mind is not entirely different from your own, dreaming constantly of reflecting upon itself, self-creating symmetrical and whole forms. In other words, the structure of the darkness you observe at night in your universe seems to be like the forms, structures, and symmetries you experience in yourself as you slowly grow into being more complete.

Thus it seems that this universe of ours is not entirely foreign. In fact, it is somehow familiar, a member of your family, a close relative of yours. Perhaps that is why native peoples called the universe by family names such as Father Sky and Mother Earth. In fact, the universe is your nearest and dearest relative, one you experience each time you tune in to your sentient experience, that hyperspace you call intuition.

According to our discussions of space-time in Chapter 25, this curved, pumpkin-like universe of ours is a common family ground, the one place we all come together. Mythic stories indicate that this ground is not mundane but the sacred space of Nun, Purusha, Christ, and Pan Ku. These gods personify the power used for centuries by shamans who went into other worlds to find visions and healing for their communities. These gods personify the power intuited by today's physicists who suspect infinite realms within black holes. These figures are your own universal deities, which create amazing forms and ideas just when you need them the most.

NOTES

1. Robert Osserman, in his marvelous and entertaining *Poetry of the Universe* (Chapter 1), goes into detail about how to measure the size of the Earth and its distance from the sun.

2. See the histories of math related by Robert Osserman and Uta Merzbach in *A History of Mathematics*.

3. Goedel showed that within a rigid, logical system such as the one developed for arithmetic, propositions could be formulated but cannot be demonstrated or decided upon within the logic or axioms of that system. Certain concise statements will always exist in these logical systems which can neither be proved nor disproved. In other words, there is no way of knowing if the axioms of arithmetic will not lead us into contradictions. This seems to doom any hope of mathematical certainty through the use of the most obvious methods. It seems that physics will never have a set of axioms from which all phenomena of the natural world can be deduced as long as physics sticks only to math in its present state. Yet scientists today still hope to find a way to assure themselves that there is a way of determining whether each of their

mathematical propositions is true, false, or undecidable. No one has yet succeeded in finding this way.

4. See, for example, Robert Lawlor's *Sacred Geometry*, a most amazing book in which he beautifully weaves together geometry with mythology.

5. See my *Coma, Key to Awakening*, which describes such awakenings.

6. See Lucie Lamy's *Egyptian Mysteries: New Light on Ancient Knowledge*, page 8.

7. See Lamy, op. cit., pages 8 and 14.

8. Lawlor, op. cit., pages 102 and following.

9. Lawlor, op. cit., page 11.

10. Lawlor, op. cit., page 13.

11. The quote is from Philipp Frank, *Einstein, His Life and Times* (1947), according to *Bartlett's Familiar Quotations*, edition 15, 1980.

12. Space-time separations could be written as:

$$s^2 = x_1^2 + x_2^2 + x_3^2 + x_4^2 \text{ or } s^2 = x^2 + y^2 + z^2 + (-ict)^2$$

13. If we forget the y and z dimensions, to simplify things, space-time separation becomes easier to understand. It becomes:

$$s^2 = x_1^2 + x_4^2 = x^2 - (ct)^2$$

14. The effect of the imaginary numbers in space-time connects the time dimension with a minus sign. If we put in actual values for a and b in the above formula, $s^2 = (a^2 - b^2)$, say a is 1 and b is 2, we get:

$$s = \sqrt{1-4} = i\sqrt{3}$$

because the square root of a negative number ends up being imaginary. If a is bigger than b, like 3 is bigger than 1, then you get a normal number like the square root of 2, which is about 1.4.

15. A mathematical discontinuity is like a very deep hole in a road. Mathematically, something becomes discontinuous when you try to divide a number like 2 by a number like 0. Dividing two numbers such as 2/1 is easy; the answer is 2. Likewise, 2/0.5 is 4. But 2/0? That is infinity. Numbers like 2/0 occur in the general theory of relativity as "discontinuities" and have given astronomers the sense that the equations of relativity indicated there must be holes in space-time, black holes.

27 | Jung's Last Dream: Synchronicity

I simply believe that some part of the human Self or Soul is not subject to the laws of space and time.

—Carl Jung

I first arrived in Zurich on June 13, 1961, six days after Jung had died. The Jungian circle was very sad, missing their analyst, teacher, best friend, grandfather, and neighbor. His students were talking about his last moments of life.

In the last dream he had before dying, Jung dreamed he was wandering through different spaces trying to find a mathematical formula with which to understand synchronicity. Apparently he was walking forward, but had a mirror in which he could look backward. There were triangles around.

What was Jung dreaming about? Was he dreaming about reflection, about triangles, Euclidean and non-Euclidean geometry, about the meaning of time and space? In this chapter, we will begin to explore these questions, and to discuss and update Jung's concept of synchronicity.

Before he died, Jung had been studying the common ground between psychology, physics, and the topic of synchronicity with Nobel Prize–winning physicist Wolfgang Pauli. In Volume 8 of his *Collected Works* (paragraph 845), Jung says synchronicity means "a meaningful coincidence of inner and outer." Here Jung uses ideas that we will eventually differentiate, such as "inner," "outer," "meaning," and "coincidence."

Jung said, "This principle of synchronicity suggests that there is an interconnection or a unity of causally unrelated events, and thus postulates the unitary aspect of being, which can very well be described as *Unus Mundus*" (the Latin meaning "one world"). In terms of our present discussion, synchronicity is a non-consensus experience wherein the observer feels that two events unrelated in consensus reality are related to one another in an NCR manner through meaning. The events give the observer the experience that there is a unity, that is, a "one world" implied by the interconnections.

Over the past thirty years, I have been through many phases in understanding the Unus Mundus and synchronicity. First, I had to immerse myself in the link between dreaming and the body. Then, I needed to study the connections between bodywork, relationship, and world tensions.

EINSTEIN AND JUNG

Jung gives Einstein credit for inspiring the idea of synchronicity—that is, the idea about the connection between events that seem separated and without causal connections in time and space. He says (in a letter to Dr. Carl Seelig, February 25, 1953, in his *Letters*):

> Professor Einstein was my guest on several occasions at dinner… these were very early days when Einstein was developing his first theory of relativity, (and) it was he who first started me off thinking about a possible relativity of time as well as space, and their psychic conditionality. More than thirty years later, this stimulus led to my relation with the physicist professor W. Pauli and to my thesis of psychic synchronicity.

Jung's ideas on synchronicity can be summarized (from his paper of that name found in paragraph 984 of his *Collected Works*). Using my own italics, Jung says that synchronicity is:

1. A coincidence of a *psychic* state with a simultaneous, *objective external* event.

2. A coincidence of a psychic state with an external event simultaneous in time but spatially removed.

3. A coincidence of a psychic state with an external event distant in time.

THE ROLE OF THE OBSERVER

My previous experience as a Jungian training analyst gives me a general sense of what Jung means. "Psychic state" implies a non-consensus experience such as a dream or sudden intuition. "Objective, external event" means consensus reality of time and space.

Since Jung was not yet thinking about concepts such as CR and NCR observers, he mixed CR and NCR observers, speaking of the NCR experiencer as if she were a CR observer. Only an NCR experiencer can judge the coincidence of a "psychic state" with "external," "objective," events, which are "spatially" distant or "distant in time." The psychic state is an NCR observation, while time and space come from a CR framework. Whether an NCR event is coincident with a CR event is a matter of one's NCR framework.

Today, if we include the NCR experiencer in these statements, synchronicity can be reformulated as NCR events that one or more participators experience as coming together with a CR event in space or time, or both. The connecting factor is an NCR sentient experience, or an NCR shared space-time experience of community. These NCR experiences are what Jung meant by the Unus Mundus.

Later, Jung spoke of synchronicity in the wider sense of "acausal orderedness," the manifestation of some pattern or underlying principle different from the consensual one of cause and effect. He put in this category sudden insights and creative acts, as well as "a priori factors such as the properties of natural numbers, the discontinuities of modern physics etc."[1]

Jung thought that synchronicity was only a particular instance of general connection between "psychic and physical processes where the observer is in the fortunate position of being able to recognize the *tertium comparationis* (the third position) which combines the other two."[2] The tertium comparationis would be a framework such as space-time, which views individual space and time frameworks as one, although they may see each other as apparently separate realities. Jung suspected that this third position must somehow be related to the fundamental unity the alchemists referred to as the Unus Mundus, which had some sort of transcendent existence underlying the duality of "psyche" and "matter."[3]

RELATIVITY IN SYNCHRONICITY

Let's begin again, this time with relativity, and investigate how it may help us differentiate the concepts of synchronicity, coincidence, and simultaneity. Einstein pondered the idea of simultaneity and concluded that it had no absolute significance. To reach this conclusion, he conducted the following thought experiment.

Einstein thought about one man in a car and another standing on the sidewalk. The man in the car is driving along and is reaching the midpoint between points A and B, at point M. As he is passing the midpoint, M, he waves hello to the man on the sidewalk.

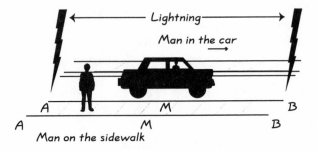

27.1 Suddenly there is lightning at points A and B!

Then lightning struck. The man standing on the ground says, "Wow! I saw two lightning bolts hit the earth at the same time at *A* and *B*! Wasn't that thrilling to see them both at the same time?" But the man in the car, even though he's at the same point *M*, says, "No! Lightning first hit point *B*!"

Who is right? They are both correct; their evaluation of when the lightning struck depends on the velocity of their frameworks. Here is how. Let's say the man in the car is driving forward at 50 miles an hour when he passes point *M*, where the other man is standing on the ground. Point *M* is an equal distance from both points *A* and *B*. Lightning suddenly strikes at point *B* and at point *A*.

The man in the car sees the lightning striking point *B* before he sees the lighting hit point *A*. The lightning at point *B* strikes first because, for him, the lightning at point *A* takes a little longer to get to him. He's traveling forward at 50 miles per hour, so the light from point *A* has to "catch up" to him first. So he sees the lightning at *B* as striking first. As far as he is concerned, the lightning did not strike *A* and *B* simultaneously.

For the man on the ground, lightning strikes *A* and *B* simultaneously because he is equidistant from *A* and *B*. The lightning from both points takes the same time to reach him, since he is not moving toward one point and away from the other.

The moral of the story is that *what is simultaneous for the man on the ground is not simultaneous for the man driving the car!* There is no such thing as absolute or objective simultaneity if people are not in the same framework.

SYNCHRONICITY? YES AND NO

The above thought experiment implies that whether or not two things are coincident is a matter of framework. Events judged as being coincident on Earth can be years apart when judged from another framework. Simultaneity does not exist in an absolute sense.

If we look at psychology, we will see that the same basic thinking holds for non-consensus events such as "meaning." Let's examine the meaning of "coincidence" in psychology.

Synchronicity implies, for example, that what happened in a dream and what happens in everyday reality are coincident or simultaneous for a given observer. Jung defined the term "synchronicity" to signify "meaningful coincidence" between events that do not seem to have a causal connection. Coincidence thus implies that *two events correspond to one another as far as their meaning is concerned for the individual who is experiencing both events.* However, coincidence, like simultaneity, is a purely relative term, that is, a matter of perceptual framework.[4]

Let's consider a specific example. Say you dream about a man kissing a child. The next morning, when you open the door to your apartment, you are shocked to see your next-door neighbor, who is not usually very affectionate, kissing his granddaughter on the cheek. You think to yourself, "Wow, that is a coincidence, a synchronicity," since it is more than a chance coming together of the two events—your dream of the man kissing a child and then your neighbor doing just that in reality. The "psychic" or dream event and the physical or "external" event occurring outside your door seem connected.

But for whom are they connected? Who is the observer? In this case, it is you. You are the one who experiences the events as a synchronicity. Your next-door neighbor may not experience anything but kissing his grandchild. For him, there may be no synchronicity at all. If you told him about your sense of a synchronicity, about your dream and about how he kissed his granddaughter, he might not understand you at all! In fact, he might not even know why you are excited. Your neighbor simply experienced a loving moment, so there is no synchronicity for him.

Synchronicity is valid only for the dreamer or others in agreement with the NCR evaluation of coincidence. But for those who are not in the dreamer's framework, there was no synchronicity because there was no coincidence. For them, synchronicity does not exist.

Our conclusion is thus that *synchronicity does not exist in consensus reality for observers in different NCR frameworks.* In general, synchronicity is a mixture of CR and NCR events and is therefore based in part upon the psychological framework of the experiencer.

The sense of "timing" and "meaning" are non-consensual evaluations. They are not objective in the consensus reality of the Western world. If you try to reproduce a synchronicity, you may find it difficult. It is difficult to "prove" the statistical validity of CR experiments on synchronicity. Jung tried such statistical experiments, which he reported in his paper on synchronicity. He concluded that synchronicities and coincidences occurred at a higher than expected rate only as long as he was excited about the work! When his excitement dissipated, the coincidences diminished.

Although meaning cannot be measured in objective, consensual terms, this does not mean that coincidences do not exist. Meaning can be a matter of life and death for those who experience it. By definition, synchronicity simply has no provable CR significance. The observation of a synchronistic occurrence, like Einstein's conclusion about simultaneity, depends on the observers' viewpoints and their frameworks. In other words, two events may appear to be meaningfully connected as far as you are concerned, yet these events may be irrelevant to me.

The two lightning bolts striking points A and B occur simultaneously in the non-moving framework of the man on the sidewalk, but not for the man in the moving framework of the car. Similarly, a synchronicity may appear to you but *not for me if I am in another psychological framework.* In general, synchronicity is neither objective nor absolute. This may be why synchronicity has never been proven. By definition in terms of frameworks, synchronicity cannot be proven as long as we define it as a coincidence of NCR and CR events.

Most of us who have been uncertain about our perceptions want to gain CR substantiation and try to "prove" parapsychological phenomena. These phenomena, like many types of synchronicities, may be true for you and anyone else in your framework, but they are not true for somebody who is not in your framework. They are not "real" in the sense of consensus reality!

Trying to prove parapsychological phenomena in a consensus reality framework doesn't prove or disprove anything. Synchronicity exists in dreaming, and for those whose state of consciousness is dreaming, everything is synchronicity. The world "agrees" with them. But for others, synchronicity will remain an amazing enigma as long as their observing mind remains in consensus reality. In the case of such observers, the world never shows signs of anything meaningful.

Someone else traveling in another framework, looking at the same events, might say, "Forget it. That is not synchronicity; that is only fantasy. It is not real. The events do not happen at the same time, in the same space, or with the same meaning."

Nothing happens in an absolute way at the same given time, in the same space, or with the same meaning. The whole idea of simultaneous interconnections is a relative matter of perception.

I prefer to redefine synchronicity as the non-consensus reality experience of a connection between two or more events, at least one of which occurs in consensus reality.[5]

Non-consensus events, including synchronicities, will be included in the physics and psychology of the future, as physics generalizes its relativistic conclusions so they apply not only to CR events but also to NCR states of mind, to dreamers and non-dreamers, to the person who dreamed of the man kissing the child and to the man who kissed the child. The consensus reality that physics focuses on is, ultimately, only a relative state. When physics incorporates this insight into its formalisms, it will be able to better understand one-time events without statistical significance. We have already seen hints of the beginning of this new physics in the interpretation of complex number spaces used in quantum physics.[6]

TIME TRAVEL

We have seen that meaningful occurrences and simultaneity are not absolute, and that space and time are relative. There is no absolute meaning to the concepts of the past or the future. What lies in the future for you in your framework can be the present for me. The past for you may not even exist for me. Only if we are all in the same NCR framework do we meet experientially in some form of synchronicity.

Although we may not agree on the significance or meaning of two events, we can step out of consensus reality time and space and, like the traditional shaman, practice traveling forward and backward in our own time sense. As we move further along on our journey, we will see how the future can change the present and how, as we become modern shamans, we can step into the present to change the past and the future.

Let's consider time travel in physics by thinking again about our man in the car going 50 miles an hour toward point B. Let's say he speeds up and goes so fast that he can reach B in 2 minutes. Now, let's pretend that he goes even faster and that he arrives there at the very moment lightning strikes. Now, let's imagine that it took him no time at all to get to B. He was moving even faster than the speed of light, so he got there before the lightning struck.

If he goes faster than the speed of light, he can arrive at B in less than zero minutes. In fact, he got there in -1 minute—before the lightning struck! If he went fast enough, he would go backward in time. If he went still more rapidly, he could get to B 15 years ago. This is hard for us to think about because it requires leaving CR.

No one else has to agree with him about how fast he is going or whether simultaneity is happening or not. No one can prove or disprove when he gets to B at these high speeds, since proofs of consensus reality depend on signals and, until now, no one has developed a consensus reality signal that can go faster than the speed of light.

Yet, even without consensus reality proof, this driver may know things before they happen. If he goes that fast, he will enter the world of dreaming. Going forward or backward in time is personally real in dreaming for him. This reality may lie outside of today's physics, but it still lies within the realm governed by the patterns of the complex numbers and imaginary mathematics of relativity.[7] Einstein said nothing consensual can go faster than light, but he did not say that NCR events must be limited to the CR velocity of light.

In other words, you can go backward in time. You can suddenly know things that happened in a certain locality hundreds of years ago. You may not be able to prove a dreamlike event such as going backward in time and seeing things happening hundreds of years ago in a déjà vu type synchronicity, but you can surely live through such an experience, as long as you understand that others who are not in your framework may not agree with you. *Your personal process is your own special time machine and your compass in space as well.*

A PERSONAL EXPERIMENT: TIME TRAVELING

At this point, you may want to experiment with your personal process and time travel. If you would like, I suggest trying the following imaginary thought experiment.

Most of us human beings are going to die one day, and most of us do not like thinking much about it. Yet, at one time or another, everybody has a suspicion that he or she is going to die from something. Think for a moment about how your imagine yourself near the end of life. Let's go forward in time in your personal experience and, in dreaming, imagine yourself at the end of life. Better yet, you may want to imagine dying of something, be it a particular disease, old age, an accident, or whatever. In a little while, I'm going to ask you to talk to yourself from that point at the end of your life.

Are you ready? Going forward in time is already unusual for some. And thinking about death is more complex. But this need not be gloomy or depressing. It may even be very useful in your everyday life, perhaps even fun. Let's go a little further now.

1. **Imagine yourself traveling into the future, as you are dying.** Imagine you are on your deathbed—or you're dying wherever you're dying. It's an unusual thing to fantasize, but it could be interesting, so try it!

   Take a look at yourself as if you were watching a picture or a movie. For some strange reason you can look into the future and you see yourself older than you are now. Go ahead and see yourself in that state.

   Most important, imagine what you are dying of. Envision yourself; hear your breath. Try to actually see what you are dying of. Is it old age, an illness, or an accident? Take a look at that, as if it's the future. It may feel a little scary to see what you might be dying of.

2. **When you're ready, see this figure of yourself, who is dying, and imagine that this figure has a message, a wise message for you.** Now imagine that this older, dying self is speaking to your present self.

Have this conversation as if it were happening in the future. Be your-self today, and simultaneously imagine yourself near death and listen to the older one's message.

3. **Now, let the older self give the younger one advice about life and how to live.** What did that dying figure do that was good in life? What did it do that was not so good?

    Is this older version of yourself satisfied with how life was? How would it have lived differently? Let it give you advice. Ask it about your present life. How should you be living your life now?

    If your future self could speak to your present self about reliving life, what would it advise about living life differently today? Listen to its advice.

4. **When you are done talking, thank the figure and time travel once again back to the present where you are right now.** When you feel ready, you may want to share the message with somebody else or to write it down. Make sure you feel yourself back in your body, and that you are able to put your feet solidly on the ground, still remembering the message of your future death.

THE MEANING OF TIME TRAVEL

Although physics does not work with the psychology of going backward in time, its mathematics has patterns for it, in part because we all have the pattern of time reversibility. The experiment we just did may have given you a hint about what it is like to go into the future to look backward in time to the present. Traditionally, psychology goes to the past to change the present. It tends to have us think about our parents and our childhood to understand our present behavior.

Along with visiting the past, it is also important to visit the future. We usually do this unconsciously through getting afraid and anxious. But we can also travel into the future consciously and with awareness. There we can focus on unfolding events, which can enrich the present. Your per-sonal NCR experience is real for you; in the past and future you can talk to death or to earlier incarnations. You can re-orient yourself in the present according to future and past time experiences, because in a way, future, past, and present are all collapsed in the moment, in an entangled bundle, unfolding themselves in time.

As we have explored imaginary numbers in quantum mechanics, the quantum flirt and its conjugation, and self-reflections, we have seen that past, present, and future are also entangled in dreaming. In dreaming, the future flirts with you now. In fact, the communication between quantum waves, which can be thought of as going into the future and past, pro-duces the present. This sounds complex because the concept of time is a

CR concept, not one derived from inner experience. But from the viewpoint of subjective experience, the idea of waves going forward and backward producing the present is not complex. The present moment in time is created by interactions between parts of yourself situated in the past or future—as far as your present identity is concerned.

In other words, the concepts of past and future, that is, the dimensions of time, are linked to how you identify yourself in the moment. In NCR experience, everything is here, right now. Thus, because of your psychology, or because of flirting at the quantum mechanical level, or because of time travel in relativity, *the way in which you identify yourself in the moment is linked to, or even created by, NCR interactions traveling backward and forward in time.*

A SACRED RITUAL

When Jung spoke about the Unus Mundus, the one world that lies behind synchronicity, he may have been intuiting the imaginary aspect of spacetime, the part of relativity that cannot be measured because events occur faster than the speed of light. This is the domain of complex numbers; it is also the sentient realm of flirts, which I have used to understand the quantum wave field.

What Jung called the Unus Mundus I refer to as dreaming together. In other words, the Unus Mundus, or one world, is the dreaming world where CR differentiations of space, time, and identity are no longer binding. It is the world of pure experience.

When we dream together, when we go into altered states together, we feel something numinous, something uncanny. But your vision of that uncanny thing will be totally different from my vision of it. The only thing we finally share is the awesomeness of the Tao. We do not share our sense of separateness in such shared synchronicities.

When Amy and I participated in sacred ceremonies using the sacred plant ayahuasca led by native people from deep within the Amazon jungle in Brazil, Amy went to the women's side of the ceremonial location, and I went to the men's area. Amy and I both had intense psychedelic experiences using the ritual psychotropic plant, and everyone else participating in the ritual also experienced intense visions.[8]

Yet, our individual visions were very different. I saw symmetries, while the man sitting next to me saw demons. Amy saw her grandmother. What we shared was not the content of the visions, not the images or a given meaning. Our personal dimensions and frameworks were too different. The thing we all shared was the sentient experience of immersion in dreaming. As we sat together in the intense heat of that jungle tent, encountering incredible visions, supported from the center of the group by the chanting of singers, one thing was clear: we were all involved in something that could never be formulated in words. The shaman leading us said that we were encountering God, each in her own way, and recommended paying attention, holding our focus to get through that awesome experience. The shaman was suggesting something like the second attention.

That collective experience drew us together. Everyone had his own particular insights and also a shared knowledge that the world we are part of is inexplicable, awesome, and inspiring. Near the end of the ceremony, all 120 of us stood up and danced a slow, rhythmical step to the rhythm of the drums and the hypnotic chanting. We shared dreaming, space-time, quantum flirts, the universe that we usually meet separately and alone in the night. Meeting that world together created a community of all beings.

These experiences were real for everyone there, and they are the kind of experiences that make life worthwhile. Yet, I no longer imagine that what we experienced can be made comprehensible to anyone who has not had similar world-unifying hyperspace experiences. We did not share the meaning or significance of the events, but the generalized sense that something numinous had occurred. We shared the sense that we were in the realm of the imaginary, not the world of CR terms any of us use to explain that realm. In that shared community realm, things balance; the universe feels symmetrical and mysteriously informs us as individuals about how to balance everyone else.

The experiences of that night gave me a global worldview. This view was an experience, not a theory we get from theoretical physics. That global worldview was an inner knowledge of how Egyptian visionaries saw the goddess Nun creating geometry, how European visionaries saw Christ constructing the world with a compass, and of how Indian visionaries saw the supreme Purusha creating a self-reflecting universe.

Thus the Unus Mundus, the background to synchronicity, is the world of complex numbers and mythology, the world of Jung's last dream, the realm of awesomeness that connects us.

NOTES

1. He continues, "...consequently, we would have to include constant and experimentally reproducible phenomena within the scope of our explained concept, though this does not seem to accord with the nature of the phenomena included in synchronicity narrowly understood.... I incline in fact to the view that synchronicity in the narrow sense is only a particular instance of general acausal orderedness—that, namely, of the equivalence of psychic and physical processes where the observer is in the fortunate position of being able to recognize the 'tertium comparationis.'" (C.G. Jung, *Collected Works*. Volume 8, "Synchronicity," paragraph 965).

2. Ibid., paragraph 965.

3.   Ibid., volume 14, paragraph 767 and following: "…all these preconditions for consensus reality are archetypal, that is… prelogical."

Jung says (in *The Portable Jung*, edited by Joseph Campbell, page 518) "Synchronisitic phenomena prove the simultaneous occurrence of meaningful equivalences in heterogeneous, causally unrelated processes; in other words, they prove that a content perceived by an observer can, at the same time, be represented by an outside event, without any causal connection. From this it follows that the psyche cannot be located in time, or that space is relative to the psyche…. Since psyche and matter are contained in one and the same world and moreover are in continuous contact with one another and ultimately rest on irrepresentable, transcendent factors, it is not only possible but fairly probable, even, that psyche and matter are two different aspects of one and the same thing."

4.   Jung's use of "meaning" in the concept of synchronicity (that is, meaningful coincidence) was linked to Richard Wilhelm's use of the term "Tao." Wilhelm translated the *I Ching* and used the word "meaning" for "Tao." Tao can be loosely translated as "the way," as "timing."

5.   I am dropping the idea that the events are non-causally related, since a non-consensus event—such as a dream or feeling of pain—cannot be causally related to consensus events—such as an automobile accident—because non-consensus events are, by definition, statistically unreproducible.

6.   The mathematically inclined reader who is interested in seeing how synchronicity might be found in the mathematical formalism of quantum mechanics should see the Appendix.

7.   The equations for the Lorentz transformation show how imaginary numbers appear when relative velocities are greater than those of the speed of light. The frameworks and equations are pictured in what follows:

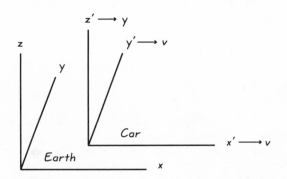

27.2 Frameworks and equations of the Lorentz transformation

Here we see that if the velocity v of the car goes fast enough, t' will become imaginary. For example, if the velocity of the car is greater than that of the speed of light, then v^2/c^2 becomes greater than one. Then at $x = 0$, the time (t) the person on the ground will measure for the one in the car will become imaginary (since the square root of $[1 - v^2/c^2]$ becomes the square root of a negative number, which results in imaginary numbers). Here we step out of linear time, and into dreaming, that is, into NCR reality.

8. Even though ayahuasca is non-addictive, I am aware that writing about drug experiences can be problematic for those with addictive tendencies. I want to point out that I do not favor the abuse of drugs, in great part because of their addictive qualities and the danger to health they present.

28 | Curvature and the Second Attention

According to the general theory of relativity, the geo-
metrical properties of space are not independent, but
they are determined by matter.

—Albert Einstein in *Relativity*

B efore moving more deeply into relativity theory, let's quickly review a few important ideas from our journey thus far. You may remember from the section on quantum physics that quantum flirts happen all the time, every time something catches your attention just before you pay attention and observe it. Quantum flirts are very rapid, easily marginalized NCR experiences basic to all observation. They come from your deepest, barely verbalizable sentient experience, and are flickering events apparently arising from the Unus Mundus. This one world is the world of dreaming: it is non-local (everywhere at one time), not temporal (linked with the past and future), and non-consensual (has no agreement with others who are not in your framework).

Synchronicities are non-consensual experiences that connect with outer events; they are quantum flirts that catch your attention and or the attention of others and seem to be mirrored in outer, CR events. For example, someone suddenly comes to mind, and then you see that person walking down the street. It is difficult to prove synchronicity, since it is mainly an NCR event for you; it's hard to prove you really thought of that someone first.

The closer you and everyone around you are to their sentient experience, the more shared synchronicities seem to happen all the time. To notice synchronicity in its constant sense, you need your second attention, awareness of weird things happening around you, awareness of how dreaming impinges on CR reality. In moments of such heightened awareness, many people feel that space is not empty but rather, an energetic, material-like, living substance that interconnects everything and everyone.

In synchronicity, reality seems dreamlike and space becomes something like the spirit we find described in the philosophies and shamanic experiences of people worldwide. Consensus reality space seems like an all-embracing substance in which the boundaries of our individual selves become difficult to define; you and I become non-local and non-temporal ourselves.

A most fascinating thing is that Einstein's general theory of relativity reveals many aspects of space as an "all-embracing substance." His space is not empty but a material-like, energetic substance. More precisely, in the general theory of relativity, the geometry of the universe takes on material qualities such as gravitational intensity. We shall see in this chapter how the curvature found in the universe's space is a metaphor for deviations in your attention, that is, for altered states of consciousness.

CURVATURE IS CONNECTED WITH CHANGING VELOCITY

Einstein knew that the special theory of relativity dealt with events that occur at constant velocities from the viewpoints of given frameworks. He knew he had to expand the special theory into a more general theory, which dealt with varying velocities. Trains or cars or rockets moving at constant velocity are a matter of the special theory. To generalize his theory of relativity, he considered velocities that change by speeding up and slowing down.

Here is approximately how Einstein arrived at the general theory of relativity. He realized that huge forces were needed to change the velocity of objects. Newton had described these forces in the seventeenth century. You probably remember Newton's law: force = mass × acceleration. A change in velocity means acceleration or deceleration, that is, speeding up or slowing down. For example, when taking off and landing in an airplane, you change velocity from zero to five hundred miles per hour and then back to zero again. Acceleration and deceleration create great forces, as you know because your body gets pushed back against the seat during take-off and thrust forward in your seat belt during landing.

Constant velocities do not have to deal with such forces, pushes and thrusts. When you are flying high and at a constant velocity, if the plane is quiet, you barely notice that you are flying. Any change in velocity, even changing the direction of velocity, involves force. You know that because to turn your car when it is driving in a straight line, you must exert force on the steering wheel. We all know from everyday experiences that force is required to effect changes in how matter moves through space.

In other words, curving around in space is connected with forces. Furthermore, forces can be connected with curving motions in space. Einstein reasoned that, since gravity is one of the big forces in the universe affecting all material objects, the force of gravity must somehow be connected with changes of velocity or curvature, or both. He knew that what Newton called gravity changed the velocity of objects and was related to the changes in direction in which planets move.

Einstein knew, of course, that gravity made the Earth rotate around the sun, and the moon around the Earth. So he leapt in his thinking and speculated about something very new. He thought that perhaps these very orbits, such as the orbit of the Earth around the sun, which everyone thought was due to gravity, could actually be due to the fact that space itself was bent, and the Earth could only travel in that way around the sun. He thought to himself that gravity was only a speculation, and that perhaps it did not exist; instead, what existed was curved space.

All of us may not have the same physical intuitions that Einstein had. So, instead of using your intuition to follow his, let's consider the following. Wherever there is a lot of mass—like in the space occupied by our sun—space is more curved than near a smaller planet, like Earth. In other words, mass and gravity are simply reflected in the curvature of space. You can think of mass or of curvature.

On or near the little planet Earth, space is not changed much, since Earth is a relatively small planet. If you try to go in a straight line and nothing much pushes you around, you will not have much trouble going straight. The Euclidean geometry you learned in school to calculate your path is more than sufficient. However, assuming you can stand the heat and radiation of the sun, you need non-Euclidean geometry to calculate the path you must take while traveling near the sun, since that path is strongly curved.

THE SIZE OF A SQUARE

The connection between Euclidean, or straight, and non-Euclidean, or curved, geometry can be understood by imagining the problems involved in constructing a perfect cube. If you could make all six sides or squares perfectly equal (which I cannot do in the diagram below) and place them perpendicular to one another, you would have a perfect cube.

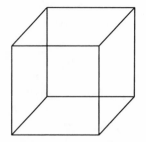

28.1 Six perfectly square sides create a cube.

Euclid said that the diagonal, d, of the cube (the line that goes from one corner, say point 1, to the other corner, say point 2) can be measured by finding the square root of $x^2 + y^2 + z^2$ (that is of the sum of the squares of the width, depth, and height.)

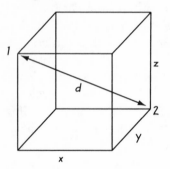

28.2 The diagonal, d, goes from point 1 to point 2.

Now let's say you have fantastic measuring instruments and you can find the actual length of the diagonal d by measurement. If you have such instruments, you will find out that Euclid was wrong. In fact, $x^2 + y^2 + z^2$ does *not* exactly equal d^2! The perfect cube we made does not follow the Euclidean formula because space is bent. On Earth, we almost never notice this because space is not bent much on a small planet like Earth. Near bigger planets it bends more. In other words, *in our universe $x^2 + y^2 + z^2$ does not equal c^2!*

To measure anything with accuracy in our universe, we need non-Euclidean geometry. On Earth, gravity isn't that strong; otherwise you would have noticed that a cube is not a cube. Anyplace where there is a lot of matter or gravity, like near the sun, space is bent more; in areas of the universe where there is very little matter, Euclidean geometry is a very good approximation of reality.

Near very dense stars, gravity is so intense that space-time is warped. In fact, space-time can be bent so much by these stars that the shape of space—or the pull of gravity—sucks everything back if it tries to get away from these areas. How do we know this? We can see what happens to things such as light. When light moves by a heavy planet, its rays bend instead of being straight. When the mass of a heavenly body is very dense, light rays are curved even more, and if the planet is extremely dense, the rays curve right into it and can't get away. In this case, we have a black hole. Space-time is so curved that light gets bent out of shape and curves back onto itself.

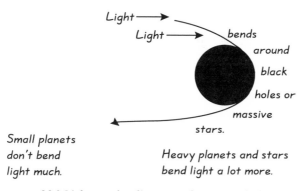

28.3 *Light rays bending around a massive body*

COLUMBUS DID NOT DISCOVER THAT THE EARTH WAS ROUND

Most people are surprised that space is curved and not straight. In consciousness, most people believe in linear, straight things and are surprised to discover anything that is not straight. Perhaps it is especially European civilization that needs to remember curves. Around the ninth century, Europeans went into the Dark Ages and forgot what they had learned either on their own or from Arabian civilizations. They forgot that early Egyptians knew the world was round. By the Middle Ages, Europeans believed that the Earth was basically flat. All the old information they had borrowed from Egypt had been burned or lost. That is why today, most people in the West believe that Columbus discovered that the Earth was round in 1492. According to the mathematician Osserman, however, on his boat, Columbus had a reprint of an old Egyptian text saying that the Earth was round![1]

One of the reasons that the Spanish resisted letting Columbus sail to the so-called New World was that gravity had not yet been discovered and people thought that if he sailed around the world he would fall off into space. In the minds of the Europeans, the "new" world was the Americas, and the "old" world was Europe, Asia, and Africa. But this emerging picture of the planet Earth was based on where the Europeans lived. They saw the world as composed of two circles.

New World   Old World

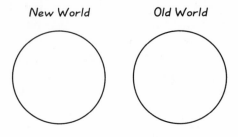

28.4 The world from a European perspective

If you look at the two circles, you will notice that the picture is Eurocentric. The "new" world was not new: Native Americans had always lived there. The New World was new only for Europeans; in this view of the planet, there was no understanding of relativity. The Eurocentric perspective also considers Asia to be the East. But it is east only relative to Europe. From the viewpoint of those of us living in Oregon, Asia is west. Today, from the viewpoint of India, the so-called Mideast is considered west Asia.

If you are a "western" person, and you are not aware of Eurocentric thinking, then Asia is considered to be even more mysterious. It becomes the "Far" East. But in fact there is nothing "far out" about the east, nothing more unusual than the "west."

How would those of us who have European or European-American heritage feel if Europeans and Americans were considered to be living in the "Far West"? Can you feel the difference? You feel yourself displaced from the center of the universe. You feel left out, marginalized, pushed to the side of everyone's focus.

In any case, after this diversion into the politics of relativity, let's get back to curvature. After Columbus discovered the Americas, people in Europe realized the world was round. But now came a horrendous problem. In a flat world, the shortest distance between two points is a straight line. But on a round surface, it is a curved line.

MEASUREMENTS ON THE GLOBE

To get more of a feeling for curvature, imagine drilling a hole through the Earth and going straight until you reach the other side. That drilled route would be the shortest way to the other side of the world. The fastest and shortest route above the Earth, however, is a curved route, like the one from Portland, Oregon, to Zurich, which is a great circle going up over the North Pole. This fastest, curved route is called a geodesic line; it is the shortest line on a curved surface lying entirely on that surface.

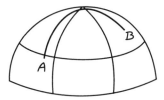

28.5 A–B is a geodesic line.

Consider the trip from Portland (at *A*) to Zurich (at *B*). If you think of going from Portland to Zurich, since the latitude in Portland is, say, 46 degrees, you might think that the shortest way to get to Zurich would be to go straight on the 46th latitude for most of the way. But this isn't the case. The shortest route is over the top of the globe, not because the Earth is crushed on the top, but because of geodesics. If you took the time and stepped off the distance with your feet, you would find that the shortest path on a globe from here to there follows a great arc whose center lies in the middle of the Earth. Better yet, to check the distance, you could stretch a wire around the Earth. Then you could prove that geodesics, rather than traveling straight ahead on a longitude or latitude, are the shortest routes on spheres.

Now let's leave the Earth and think about the space of the universe around us. If you could shoot up off the Earth like an astronaut and then drop down, you would be falling through space. But you would not fall in a straight line right down to the Earth; your fall would follow a curve. This is because the universe is curved near the Earth and because the shortest path through a curved space is a geodesic, which gets more curved the closer you get to the Earth, where the gravity is most intense.[2] Gravity curves space.

The universe is so curved that most astronomers believe that if you had really good eyes and looked out into space, you would eventually see your own back! Or, if you had a really long arm and you reached out as far as you could, your hand would arrive on your own shoulder! This almost sounds like psychology: wherever you look, you see yourself. If you reach out to others, it is you who is touched.

IMAGINARY GEOMETRY

Einstein knew he needed more than Euclidean geometry to describe the universe, but he did not know where to find it. Luckily he had good friends who taught him the mathematics he needed. He discovered that mathematicians had been thinking about curving space for a long time.

The Russian mathematician Nikolai Lobochevski (1793-1856) was one of the first to experiment mathematically with new spaces. He discovered that if he introduced imaginary numbers into geometry he could create what he called "imaginary geometry."

His geometry turns out to be what is called "hyperbolic geometry," but he didn't know it himself at the time. Today we know that he discovered a geometrical space that looks like a trumpet! In 1829, he discovered the first non-Euclidean geometry by breaking the straight Euclidean rule of his day, which said that parallel lines on a flat or square world can go on forever without meeting.

RIEMANN'S CURVES

Einstein then learned about the German mathematician Georg Friedrich Bernhard Riemann, who went further than Lobochevski with curvature. In 1854, he imagined that space could be curved. In fact, he developed the exact mathematics used later by Einstein for relativity.

Riemann had a short and incredible life. Apparently, it took him only six months to create his new geometry. Riemann did his own thought experiment by asking himself, "What happens if you put a torch above the Earth? If you hold the torch 50 miles above the Earth, and if there's a little bit of fog up there, how would the torch appear to us on Earth?" He thought there must be a halo in the fog, and he wondered if the halo would be a perfect circle. He also wondered about how to measure that circle. Could he use Euclid's formula to measure the perimeter of the circle? This formula is $2 \times \pi \times r$ where π (or "pi") is about 3.14 and r is the radius of the circle.

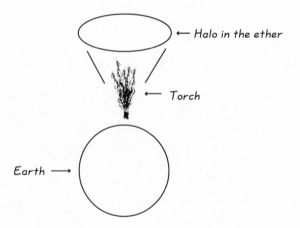

28.6 Riemann's thought experiment: If a torch 50 miles
above the Earth makes a halo, how big is it?

Riemann imagined himself walking off the halo in that ethereal fog to test whether the perimeter of the circle was really the Euclidean formula, $2 \times \pi \times r$. According to his thought experiment, the halo, if you could measure it, would not necessarily be a perfect circle.

I am amazed that Riemann had the courage and the ability to doubt that the perimeter of the circle would be $2\pi \times r$! That is like doubting that $2 + 2$ makes 4.

Riemann thought that if you actually measure something and it's not using Euclidean geometry, the difference between Euclidean geometry and the curviness of the new geometry should be called "curvature." The difference between a straight line and its curve in space was what he meant by curvature. Riemann knew nothing about whether space was really curved; he merely followed his intuitions. He figured that he could define curvature as the difference between a Euclidean straight line and the way things really were. He called this curvature g. He knew that little distances in Euclidean geometry, called ds, could be calculated according to his formula for the diagonal of a cube.[3]

His new formula for the real distance in space could then be this ds, changed by a factor of g. In other words, in the universe, distance is no longer simply ds, but $g \times ds$.[4] The measure g determines how curved the properties of the spaces of the new geometry would be. When there is no curvature, that is, in situations where relatively small massive bodies are involved, g can be approximated as 1 and the curved geometry becomes the normal, straight Euclidean geometry.

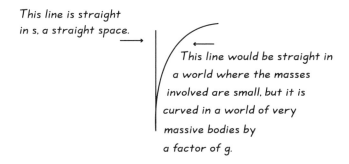

This line is straight in s, a straight space.

This line would be straight in a world where the masses involved are small, but it is curved in a world of very massive bodies by a factor of g.

28.7 Curvature is measured as deviation from the straight line.

Riemann recommended that we study all curved spaces in a similar and general manner. In this way, he prepared the mathematical tools for Einstein to use to write the curvature of the universe, to express the fact that space must be curved. The only difference between Einstein and Riemann is that Einstein had the intuition about why space was curved—namely, that gravity was responsible for curving space. Einstein had an uncanny physical intuition about why space was curved, whereas Riemann was more of a mathematician and simply imagined that this curvature was possible. Thanks to Einstein's Zurich friends who taught him math, he found Riemann's work and created the general theory of relativity.

PSYCHO-CURVES

Curvature is crucial to our universe and to physics. Like other principles from physics, it is not just a measure of what happens in geometry and in space-time, but is connected to our innermost experiences. We already saw in Chapter 11 on calculus that things which curve force us to leave the measurable realities and enter into the stream of experience. We also discussed in Chapter 25 that curvature is related to straight geometry as altered states and shamanism are to straight behavior changes in psychology.

Now we can say that the connection between straight lines and curves, between normal, linear life and altered states of consciousness, is "curvature." But what is a psychological analogy to curvature? Psychological curvature is a feeling measure of how things are warped and weird, strange and dreamlike. There are many analogies to curvature, but most of the terms are negative, such as warped or deformed, which are related to, "out of your mind," "nuts," "crazy," "wild," "insane," "cracked," "demented," "deranged," "unbalanced," "screwy," "mad," and the like. There are also positive connotations, such as "creative," "genius," "wizard," and "dreamy."

When I ask students how we measure curvature in psychology, there is usually a huge debate. They ask why being "straight" is consensual, why being weird is not agreed upon. Often, someone comments that the measure for a "curved" person is the inability to work on a problem in a linear manner. In other words, people who are unable to approach a problem in a linear or rational manner, but who approach problems in a nonlinear or feeling manner, tend to be marginalized.

Traditional shamans appreciate curved situations and use their second attention to measure or notice that something weird and "abnormal" is happening in the moment. Instead of marginalizing this moment, shamans follow their weird curviness. We are all trained in the linearity of consensus reality. In everyday life, when something deviates from linearity, you will avoid the "deviation"—unless you are a creative writer, dancer, musician, or shaman. Shamans use their second attention to check out the weird thing and hold on to that state, letting the dreaming unfold. This takes them out of linear time.

When you notice that something is curving, you're noticing deviation from consensus reality by the use of your second attention. Just as Riemann and Einstein measured curvature in the universe by the curvature value, g, you can use your second attention to notice when the world begins to curve away from linear reality.

The spiritual warrior's central task is to develop this second attention and to notice when curviness begins, get into it, and live in NCR reality. Deviation from the norm is where the spirit becomes evident. If you use your second attention, you have a chance of having an unpredictable and creative life. Otherwise, linear living bores you. Everyday CR is the standard against which we can measure our states of consciousness, but if you stick to the standard, you get depressed.

Much of medicine and conventional therapy is devoted to getting people back into linear time and straight directions, to crossing out the curved deviations and blocking the second attention with drugs that repress depression, mania, fantasy, dizziness, and the like. But if you use your second attention, you will notice that the "deviant" or "abnormal" life is only one reality. In other words, not only is the universe of Einstein and Riemann curved; everyday reality is altered as well. Just as curvature is omnipresent and changes from moment to moment in space-time depending on which planets are around, dreaming, too, is omnipresent and depends on global and universal NCR spaces.

You can use your second attention at any time to notice when something seems a little curved, weird, or strange. You can always ask yourself if what you're experiencing is exactly lined up with the thing you intend to do, or not quite. You can try it now if you like. Instead of following your linear track, practice stepping out of it. Follow the deviance. Appreciate it; use your second attention. Where is the deviation trying to take you?

The shaman don Juan calls the NCR world we live in the "nagual"; Jung called it the "unconscious"; others call it altered states of consciousness. Don Juan had his own measure of curvature. He was more like Einstein and said that those who live with altered states and the nagual are "real" people. The others, who live only in the straight, consensus of linear time, are "phantoms." In the shaman's terms, when you are a phantom, you don't notice synchronicities; you live only in a straight world. When you are real, you sense that the universe is curved and live accordingly. Most people are probably like conventional physicists, phantoms basing life on the CR dimensions of the universe.

To be most realistic, we need to develop awareness in both straight and curved spaces, to notice and follow both CR and NCR events.

NOTES

1. Osserman, *Poetry of the Universe*

2. If you follow the fall of an astronaut in space-time, this freefall would be like a spiral—instead of a straight line around the time axis—because of the space and time shrinking. The spiral gets tighter the closer he gets to the Earth.

3. If little distances are *ds*, then Euclid formula for the diagonal of a cube is

$$(ds)^2 = (dx)^2 + (dy)^2 + (dz)^2$$

4. Riemann developed what is known today as Riemannian space, where the numbers, symbolized by *g*, represent curvature and depend on the exact location and nature of space. That is, the *g*'s are functions of *x*, *y*, and *z* and time. He put *g*'s in front of Euclid's space, which was $x^2 + y^2 + z^2$ and wrote his new formula for distance *s* or rather, little distances (*ds*), as:

$$\begin{aligned} ds^2 = {} & g_{11}(dx)^2 + g_{12}(dxdy) + g_{13}(dxdz) \\ & + g_{21}(dydx) + g_{22}(dy)^2 + g_{23}(dydz) \\ & + g_{31}(dzdx) + g_{32}(dzdy) + g_{33}(dz)^2 \end{aligned}$$

Euclidean space turns out to be the special case where

$$g_{11} = g_{22} = g_{33} = 1$$

because in the Euclidean situation, all the other *g*'s are zero.

29 | Big Bangs and Black Holes

There are good reasons for predicting that black holes should exist, and the observational evidence points strongly to the presence of a number of black holes in our own galaxy and more in other galaxies.

—Stephen Hawking

All things, among themselves, possess an order; and this order is the form that makes the universe like God.

—Dante Alighieri

Riemann discovered curvature and the mathematics of the Einsteinian universe in the mid-1800s, but the Italian poet Dante (1265-1321), in his epic drama, *The Divine Comedy*, envisioned a similar structure of the universe six hundred years earlier.[1] In this chapter, we will investigate how a poet could see what a mathematician discovered six hundred years later.

Riemann's universe can be simplified and pictured as two separate hemispheres.

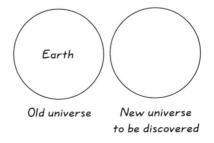

29.1 *The universe according to Riemann*

The simplified version of Riemann's four-dimensional universe can be understood as a sphere with two sides (Figure 29.1). On the left, Riemann's old universe is a known world with the Earth in its midst and a universe beyond. The circle around the Earth represents the outer limit of how far we can see with our best telescopes. The sphere to the right is the rest of Riemann's universe (again pictured in two dimensions); this is the new universe beyond what we can see today and therefore the one yet to be discovered. We will probably be able to see big chunks of this "new universe" in the next century with stronger telescopes than we now have.[2]

Dante also imagined a universe with two spheres (Figure 29.2). At the center of one sphere was the known world, the Earth. The outer perimeter of this world represented the farthest you could see at that time. If you went beyond the limits of the known world, you would enter the unknown world, the universe to the right. At the center of the new universe, you would discover a beaming light called "the Empyrean," surrounded by angels.

In *The Divine Comedy*, Dante's hero is led by his spirit guide, Beatrice, on an imaginary journey through Hell, Purgatory, and Paradise, finally arriving at the Empyrean, abode of the gods, source of pure light or fire. Together, Beatrice and the hero travel from his home on Earth to the outskirts of the visible universe, the perimeter of the sphere on the left. From there he peers over the edge and into the sphere of the Empyrean, the highest universe, sphere of fire.

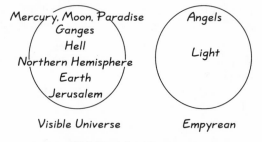

29.2 *Dante's universe*

Today's maps of the planet Earth are similar in at least one way. They often show two ovals representing the "new" world and the "old" world.

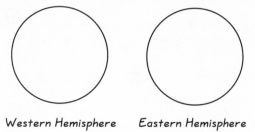

29.3 *The world today*

DIFFERENCES BETWEEN DANTE'S UNIVERSE AND RIEMANN'S

Just as Einstein thought that the universe was shaped by the masses of the bodies within it, Dante thought his universe was organized by the power of spirits such as Mercury, the moon, and the sun. For the thirteenth-century poet, these were not just planets, but deities, astrological powers that governed fate. To predict the future, astrologers of that time (like astrologers today) used the constellations. The patterns of the future were encoded in planetary constellations and used to predict the most appropriate timing for entering into relationships, having children, settling business transactions, and so forth.

Today, such thinking appears to be an NCR reflection of the theory that the stars have gravitational power that acts at a distance, curving the very shape of the universe, arranging the fate of any object in their vicinity. However, the theory of today's CR universe tells us very little about our personal fates, besides the fact that our sun will burn out in five million years.

Dante's universe was a map of where we move on our psychic journeys, through the sense of sin and failure, toward some fiery center of existence or enlightenment. What the modern scientist imagines to be a universe bent by massive bodies, organized at the beginning of time by a distant fiery center called the Big Bang, the poet saw as a domain through which all human beings must journey, seeking the highest wisdom with the help of spirit-allies such as Beatrice.

We can see the effect of the universe's NCR characteristics on today's astronomers, who still think of the most distant universe as a fiery big bang. This distant, unknown fiery center is the place of our origins. In an extended and metaphorical sense, that fiery center is the true place of our birth, our home. According to today's Big Bang theory, that home is also the place to which we shall all return, once the expansion of the present universe reverses.

HUBBLE'S LAW

Perhaps the biggest difference between Dante's view of the universe and the scientist's view today is that our present view sees the universe as expanding and contracting. The idea of an expanding and contracting universe had its origins in 1912, when the American astronomer Hubble added a new element to Riemann's hyperspheres and Einstein's 1905 theory of relativity. Both Einstein and Riemann had little foresight about the possible size of the universe. They did not expect it to change or expand. Their view of the universe was that it was an immense, unchanging, four-dimensional hyperspace.

Hubble discovered that our universe is not at all static. He looked at the universe with the newest telescopes of his time and discovered a "red

shift" in the light coming from luminous bodies, indicating that the farther away they were from the Earth, the faster they were receding.[3] Hubble realized that stars near us move away from us more slowly than stars
farther away. The farther away a star is, the greater the velocity at which
it recedes from us. Since observations indicated that everything is receding from everything else, Hubble's observations indicated that our universe itself was expanding.

Although it is difficult to imagine an expanding four-dimensional universe, we can get a glimpse of the hypersphere's motion by thinking of a
three-dimensional object like a balloon. As more air is added to the balloon, it gets larger. In the balloon universe, all the stars and we are like
points on the surface of the balloon. As the balloon expands, it gets bigger
and therefore each point moves farther away from all the other points.
The balloon is not a perfect analogy, but it gives us a hint about an
expanding universe.

BIG BANG

The discovery of the expanding universe provoked an inquiry into what
caused the universe to expand. Today, the answer to the expanding universe question is the Big Bang theory. Hubble's observations suggested
that the universe began with a bang and will expand until gravity contracts again. When the energy of the original explosion from the Big Bang
has expended itself, all the stars, all the matter comprising the universe,
will stop expanding and begin to recede. Then the force of gravity will
begin to contract the universe until it becomes very dense. This package
of matter will be so dense and full of mass that its gravitational force will
pull in anything, including photons of light, preventing them from escap-
ing. If photons of light cannot radiate or emanate from the condensed
massive universe, the resulting dense matter will become invisible. It will
become what is called a "black hole."

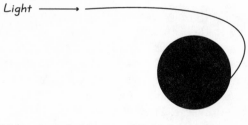

29.4 Light gets sucked in near a black hole and cannot escape.

Black holes cannot be seen because we need light to shine from or be
reflected from an object to see it. If gravity is so strong that light cannot

escape from an object, the light gets trapped there and the object becomes a black hole.

Stars expand because of the explosive atomic energy in their massive cores, but when this energy is burned out because the condensed fuel has been used up, the gravity of the star's parts begins to pull them together, and the star begins to collapse. Our sun will eventually burn itself out and condense into a ball with a radius of about two miles. According to the Big Bang theory, the whole universe, as we currently know it, will also condense into a volume about the size of the Earth.

At present, our universe is still expanding from an originally dense, contracted mass. As the matter of a star collapses and becomes a black hole, its core gets denser and hotter. When it gets super dense, its gravitational pull is great and light cannot get away. Then, it must cool down before light can escape or emanate again. When this occurs, the black hole starts to expand once again. This is, in brief, the theory of the Big Bang and the expanding universe.[4]

There have been many debates about this theory since it was introduced. Today the vast majority of physicists agree with the Big Bang theory, namely, that the universe began as a black hole of condensed matter that gave off a huge blast and created the expanding universe we know today.

According to physical theory, it looks as if we are now in an expansion phase, but that, at another point, the universe is going to collapse. According to science, we have another five billion years before this happens. After collapsing, our universe will then expand again.

The opposing theory to the Big Bang is the Continuous Creation theory. The problem with this theory is that creation must continuously happen in many places all over the universe to keep it in a steady state. This continuous creation would occur, theoretically, to ensure that the density of matter remains the same at great distances. No one has seen this to be the case; therefore most cosmologists think of a huge primordial fireball, a big bang, which is now expanding but will eventually collapse.

WHERE ASTRONOMY MEETS RELIGION AND PSYCHOLOGY

Some philosophers argue with physicists and astronomers, insisting that the creation of the universe should not be the realm of physics but of theology. After all, we cannot do an experiment to begin a universe—at least, not yet. Some people say this realm should be the realm of religion, since we will never be able to see the Big Bang itself. We can only see what happened shortly after the Big Bang, when the universe cooled off enough to radiate, begin its expansion, and show itself.

The physics of black holes constrains us from ever being able to see the beginning of the universe. The beginning of the universe, if there was one, would be invisible. Another way of saying this, in mathematical terms, is that the big bang happened in imaginary space and time, beyond the constructs of consensus reality, in a realm where events must have occurred and yet will never be able to be seen. If the universe began as a black hole, our ability to observe the universe has a theoretical limit in consensus reality. If we can never see the beginning of the universe in CR, then what?

According to theory, we can only see it in its cooling-off phase, since before that, radiation could not escape, thereby giving off information about what happened in the first instants. By looking through our telescopes and seeing light from distant events, we are seeing backward in time, since it takes time for the light from these events to reach us. For example, the sun we see today is the sun the way it was eight minutes back in time. Farther out, we're looking further back in time. As our telescopes get better, we will look even farther out and discover galaxies our instruments of today cannot see. Perhaps by the year 2010, we will be able to see back to just after the Big Bang, and we will know more about when time began.

To see way back in time, to the point where the cooling down of the contracted universe allowed information and light to escape, we need really good telescopes. Before that time, however, no matter how good our telescopes are, there is, in principle, no way of seeing far enough to know the beginning of the universe.

In the next few years, new telescopes will show us events that occurred just after the Big Bang; we shall see events that occurred at the time when the universe first began to radiate. Then we'll know more, but we may never have an experimental method that can see into a black hole; we may never know for sure whether the universe is infinite or finite.

To see the beginning of the universe, we have to see faster than the speed of light, and such velocities are forbidden by Einstein's theories. At speeds greater than the speed of light, his equations produce imaginary numbers, numbers that today's physics cannot interpret. Thus, the law that nothing can travel faster than the speed of light in consensus reality creates another uncertainty principle in our lives, because it says we will never have consensus on what began the universe.

However, we should remember that the limits of observability of consensus reality have never inhibited people from knowing, in non-consensus reality and dreaming, things that happen synchronistically before they occurred. You can dream that the sun burps, even before you get the message eight minutes later.

Dante wrote *The Divine Comedy* six hundred years before Riemann, seven hundred years before Einstein. He investigated the essence and origin of the universe and saw a map of the universe not unlike the one in use today. Therefore, we must suspect that dreaming poets see beyond the consensus reality signals constrained by the speed of light.

The mathematics of relativity and quantum mechanics allows for signals that travel faster than the speed of light; however, they exist in the realm of imaginary numbers. These numbers imply that there are both real, or CR, and also imaginary, or NCR, characteristics of the universe. The existence of these numbers implies that the beginning of the universe is not real, but imaginary. In other words, we can investigate the beginning of the universe with telescopes and with dreaming as well.

Osserman, the mathematician who pointed out the similarity in Dante's, Riemann's, and Einstein's visions of the universe, merely points to the structural similarity between the universes of the poet, the mathematician, and the physicist. Yet we must stress that the poet's dream of a structure was later re-imagined by Riemann's mathematics and Einstein's relativity.

In quantum mechanics we saw that the observer participates with the observed in a dreamlike flirt occurring in non-consensus reality. This dreaming is basic to observation. The same must be true in the consensus reality of astronomy as well. The image the universe reveals to us in CR is inseparable from what we dream about.

While pursuing the "real facts" about the beginning of the universe, we must take our imaginations about it seriously as well. Imaginary dimensions in our math make us reconsider the "one world" prefigured in mythology, delineated by the Egyptian goddess Nun and the Indian god Purusha. We need to connect Riemann's math, Einstein's speed of light, and Hubble's law, with mythology. The total universe we see and experience is a combination of mythology and consensus reality, of real and imaginary numbers. The universe is simultaneously a map of our potential human self and a map of potential space-time routes spaceships must follow.

How to Investigate Black Holes

The core of the Big Bang, that hypothetical blast of power from atomic reactions that sprayed out the galaxies and universe we observe today, is not unlike Dante's image of the Empyrean, abode of the gods from which everything originates.

We can scarcely avoid connecting the universe's Big Bang with the central, peak experiences and fiery moments in our psychological past, which—in popular culture, at least—are responsible for personal behavior today. In other words, the theories of physics are metaphors for causal theories about big blasts that create our psychology of today.

In the same way that Dante foresaw the Riemann-Einsteinian universe, dreaming can see into the Big Bang or any other black hole and beyond. Knowing what happened at or before the big bang would be like knowing what our previous incarnations were. We dream and know our future and past when this information becomes crucial to us, just as a starving hunter may dream where her prey is before she raises her bow and arrow.

Personal experiences of black holes might help to investigate how they connect to other universes, before these things are discovered or rather, rediscovered, in consensus reality by physics. To begin with, we must ask, "What are the NCR analogies in psychology to the Big Bang and black hole theory in physics?" What seems to create everything, what sucks you in when you approach it and threatens to never let you out if you get too close?

One answer is big complexes! Most people have at least one black hole. Certain topics upset everyone, put us into "complexes." Big issues disturb us so much that we lose our standpoint and feel overwhelmed or drowned. Stories from childhood, criticism, depression, the sense of abandonment, and abuse issues are "black holes." But black holes might also be the fiery powers of spiritual experience, creativity, near-death experiences, holes that suck us in, and where we might even gladly stay once entrapped in their power. These black holes, the gigantic mythic patterns of life, are dreamlike events whose stories explain our entire present behavior.

We can go into black holes with stories, dreams, and imagination. All indigenous communities have had shamans who were able to travel in trance states into the most unknown areas of life, into the complexes of individuals and the fate and origins of communities.

Amy and I have used an adaptation of the awareness procedure (discussed in Chapter 11 on calculus), to successfully communicate with people in one of the most formidable black holes, the comatose state. Comas have always been understood, especially in connection with near-death experiences, as transitions to other universes.[5] We should remember that, as far as the present consensus of the medical community is concerned, people in comatose states are essentially vegetables with whom communication is deemed impossible, just as black holes are supposed to be domains of space-time where communication is forbidden.

What we can learn from communication with people in comatose states is that these "black holes" are filled with incredible information and "peak experiences." Although not everyone emerges from these states with new discoveries about the origin and meaning of life, many do emerge, speaking of the key to life.

I have introduced Dante, shamans, dreamers, and comatose states in order to support the following theory: *we can experience what happened in the beginning of the universe and what is going on in black holes because of our own NCR abilities.*

Personal Experiment: Practice with Black Holes

The premise that physics is mapped out in our psychology is not only philosophical, but leads to empirical suggestions such as the following experiment, which you may want to try.

1. **Identify a Black Hole**. Take a moment and try recalling an issue that turns you on or off so much that it overwhelms you and sucks in all your consciousness. It should be something that curves everything in your neighborhood. Do you fear the loss of all your light, of all your consciousness? You may want to ask yourself, what is, or what has been, your greatest problem?

   You may have a list of such black hole areas, which may be sources of creativity as well as madness, new life as well as death. Consider just one of them now. Does it force you to obey its gravitational pull?

2. **Explore the Black Hole**. While physics suggests that we stay clear of black holes unless we want to leave this universe, the spiritual warrior feels summoned to explore, rather than to avoid, the black hole.

   Entering black holes is an ancient shamanic art.[6] To be a shaman, you have to enter now and, in a few minutes, be able to leave those deepest unknown spaces again, bringing help and information to yourself and others.

   In black holes there is very little ordinary light. So you need to take a little of your everyday consciousness in there. To find Dante's Empyrean, the highest heaven, the sphere of fire, you need to use your second attention.

   When you are ready, take a few minutes and actually identify and explore a black hole. Imagine or re-imagine it. Feel it, make images out of this feeling, make motions that remind you of it. Now use your awareness. Try saying to yourself, "Now I notice this feeling, now that feeling or vision," and follow your experiential process as it reveals itself to you. Track the pictures and feelings and the way not only into but also out of the black hole. Go into the black hole and wait for it to show itself. Use your second attention, and let it reveal its message to you.

3. **Get to the Core of Black Hole**. As you begin to track the black hole, go back in your imagination to what created it. What does the creation event look like, sound like, feel like? Is it fiery, wild, demonic, loving? Trust your experience, and make a note of it.

   If you get a feeling or visualization of what the essence of that black hole is, write it down, paint it, talk to it, know it. Ask yourself where else this core of energy appears in your life. Your poetic formulation of the origin of your black hole is a view into its essence.

As you meet this core, notice if it changes, or how you change. Are you a participant, an observer? Try accepting and getting to know this core. Have you always known it in some way, have you suspected its existence?

Knowing the experience of your core might give you a hint about what you expect to occur in your future. How do you feel about how you encountered your core? How did you deal with what you met there?

After getting to the core of that black hole, ask yourself how your present life would change if you were to not just suffer from that black hole, but identify a bit more with the energy of its creator.

This kind of individual work is important in our understanding of black holes. But black holes also influence groups and nations. Finding the core or creation of a culture is as important as individual work. In group life, black holes lie at the limits of the known universe, at the core of a group's problems, a culture or nation's identity. Black holes are filled with conflicts, hatred, and war, but also ecstatic religious experiences. The discussion of the group working through issues from World War II in Chapter 25 shows how, in the most troublesome places, ecstatic centering experiences, perhaps even new universes, can emerge.[7]

Physics does not allow us to go into black holes in a consensual manner, but shamanism contains many hints about how to do so. I have given only the barest details here about how to enter and leave black holes. The point is that with courage, compassion, understanding, and intelligent respect for the unknown, when the timing is right, you can enter into the mysteries of the universe and emerge with new information and wisdom.

At this point I am reminded of the awesome story and troubled times of the Native American group, the Oglala Sioux, described in John Neidhart's account, *Black Elk Speaks*. There, the visionary Black Elk tells the story of how he went into a trance and had visions to find the origins of the next universe, the new cultural form for the endangered Oglala people.

All individuals and cultures undergo transformations, life and death. In the future, our own solar system will come to an end, confronting all human beings with the question about what the future will bring. Whether our universe contracts, expands, or self-destructs, ultimately, may not be independent of our NCR relationship to it. The future of the entire universe may depend on the Dantes as well as the Einsteins, on how you and I deal with the core of our own black holes and peak experiences.

If we can learn to travel into these realms, we are on the path of a new universe, a new way of being in the world. At that point, we are no longer only contemporary physicists, but modern shamans, traveling fluidly between the consensus world and the mysterious unknown cores of our universe and ourselves.

NOTES

1. See Osserman's *Poetry of the Universe,* page 90 and following, and Dante's *The Divine Comedy,* page 343. *Divina Commedia* (*The Divine Comedy*), a literary masterpiece, is an epic poem written in Italian by Dante Alighieri. Finished just before the author's death in 1321, the narrative conceals an allegory of life on Earth and the pilgrim poet as a figure of Everyman. One of the greatest poems of the European Middle Ages, it has a beauty and humanity that transcend its times.

2. The reader wanting more information on images of the four-dimensional universe of Riemann should refer to Osserman's *Poetry of the Universe,* page 87.

3. The red shift is the relationship between the positions of spectral lines from light of near and distant stars and luminous bodies. The greater the distance, the greater the shift toward the longer wavelengths and lower frequencies at the red end of the spectrum.

    If v is the velocity of the recession of a galaxy that is at distance, d, from us, then $d = v \times T$, where T is sometimes called the age of the universe (although this age—$T = 8 \times 10^9$ years—should not, as far as I know, be taken literally).

4. When energy is burned off, there is less mass because of the famous energy-mass relationship, $e = mc^2$ (e is energy, m is mass, and c the speed of light). I shall discuss this equation in greater detail in Chapters 31 and 32. For the moment, let's just assume that gravity is very great in the beginning of the universe because of the density of the mass. But then it begins to cool off by burning off energy, thereby reducing the density of mass. With less energy, there is less mass; with less mass, there is less gravity and exploding things can get away again. Things can escape the black hole now; light particles and bits of matter get away. When this radiation occurs, space expands. I call this a yo-yo effect.

    The theory of the expansion and contraction of the universe is based upon there being enough matter and enough gravity eventually to pull the universe inwards during the contraction phase. The visible matter in the universe that we can see today is not enough to create such a gravitational effect, ending up in the "big crunch." Another form of matter, the so-called "black matter" or "missing matter," may make up the difference. This stuff is called black matter because, although its presence can be seen in the manner in which it bends light rays, it is invisible because it has no electric charge like the matter we can see. Without electric charge, this matter does not show up on our measuring instruments, but since its effects can be seen, we know it is there. Some physicists guess it may make up as much as 99% of the universe, thereby giving the universe enough "weight" or gravity to pull itself back together again.

    Without such black matter, the universe could not be pulled together and would expand forever, eventually chilling out and ending up as a bunch of low-energy particles. One way or another, the universe will change and, in many billions of years, will end either in a huge, expanded chill out, or evolve into a big crunch. I would guess that in billions of years, we will be able to create new hyperspace universes or be able to influence the evolution of the present one.

5.   See my *Coma, Key to Awakening,* and Amy Mindell's *Coma, A Healing Journey.*

6.   Such procedures are discussed in my book *The Shaman's Body.*

7.   In *Sitting in the Fire,* I discuss an ethnic conflict that threatened to escalate to violence. At the most threatening moment, an African-American man, aware of the dreaming background, began to wail because of the pain racism causes everyone. One by one, people began to embrace him, so the final, unexpected, and totally unpredictable result of entering into the most dismal point of humanity was a coming together, meeting in what many felt was a spiritual experience.

30 | A Person Is a Secret Path

(Einstein) had the revolutionary idea that gravity was not just a force that operated in a fixed background of space-time. Instead, gravity was a distortion of space-time, caused by the mass and energy in it.

—Stephen Hawking in *Black Holes and Baby Universes*

When Einstein developed the special and general theories of relativity, no one was thinking about black holes. Einstein was concerned with the speed of light and the nature of gravity. We have already seen that Einstein's general theory implies that matter bends space and time, but we have not yet considered some of the important details showing how he came to this conclusion. In this chapter we will briefly explore how he developed his theory, and will begin to explore its significance for a general theory in psychology.

As we now know, the special theory of relativity deals with trains, cars, and other objects that move only with constant velocities. Since many things do not move with constant velocity, Einstein wanted to generalize the special theory so that all possibilities were included.

Remember airplanes. We have seen that a constant velocity occurs when the plane is up in the air and you barely notice you are moving unless you look out the window. We also saw earlier that this constant velocity changes during takeoff and landing, when you are forced by the changes to think about the plane. On takeoff you feel a force on your body pressing you into the seat. When you land, the plane decelerates and throws you forward.

Acceleration and deceleration are zero when the velocity is constant. The changing velocity at the beginning and the end of plane trips makes us aware of huge forces not totally under our control. As we saw in Chapter 28, the general theory of relativity, unlike the special theory, deals with the effects of such changing velocities and therefore with the forces connected to these changes.

In psychology, the analogy to the special and general theories of relativity would be a "special theory of psychology," which deals only with ordinary consciousness, and a more "general theory," which deals with rapid changes, huge forces, and the warping of space and time into weird, altered states. At present, such a general theory of psychology, which deals with strongly altered, extreme, and psychotic states and near-death experiences, is less complete than the analogous general theory of relativity. Studying general relativity in physics may allow us to learn more about extreme and altered states in psychology.

EINSTEIN'S ELEVATOR EXPERIMENT

Let's begin by looking at a simplified version of how Einstein discovered the general theory of relativity. Einstein began with the following thought experiment. In his mind, Einstein saw a man standing in an elevator that had no windows and operated very quietly. Einstein imagined that the man in the elevator could not hear the elevator moving, nor could he see outside it. He can only feel pressure from the floor, the kind of pressure he normally associates with standing on firm ground, let's say on the Earth.

Looking at this man and elevator from the outside, Einstein imagined himself hanging in an area of space that was not affected by gravity. Einstein looked in from the outside, while hanging out in space, and imagined a huge crane pulling on that elevator, creating a force drawing it upward. The person in the elevator—who could not see outside—felt that pull, thinking it came from the ground. (Einstein calculated the force needed to accelerate the elevator in accordance with Newton's formula: Force = Mass × Acceleration. Given the mass of the man and the elevator, Einstein imagined what force the crane would need to match the accelerating potential of gravity.)

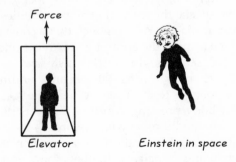

30.1 Einstein's elevator thought experiment

Einstein then went further in his imagination and pretended that he received a call from the man in the elevator, who said he felt that his weight kept him on the elevator floor. Einstein asked, "What kind of force is it?" The man said, "It's the force of gravity, of course!" But Einstein said, "It's not gravity! There is a big crane pulling on you!" But the man in the elevator said, "What? No, it feels like gravity!"

Einstein concluded that, as long as the man in the elevator could not see outside, he could not tell the difference between the force of gravity pulling him down and a force—like the force from the crane—pulling him up.

Einstein understood immediately from this thought experiment that the man inside the elevator cannot tell whether there is a big planet under him exerting a gravitational force pulling him to the floor, or whether there is a crane above him exerting a force accelerating him upward.

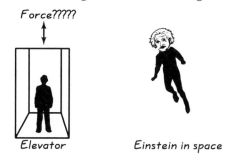

30.2 *The man in the elevator thinks a planet with gravity is near.*

To prove his point, the man in the elevator says to Einstein that he will drop his glasses and see what happens. He then said, "Look, they fell to the floor!" But Einstein said, "Sorry, that is due to the acceleration created by the crane!" Again, Einstein concluded that the man can't tell from the inside the difference between gravity and acceleration by some force.

Since the man cannot tell the difference between acceleration attributable to forces from a crane or from gravity, the force of gravity must in some way be equivalent to the force of the crane. Said a bit differently, gravity and acceleration are equivalent for the person in the elevator.

Einstein called this the "principle of equivalence"; the local effects of gravity are equivalent, at a given point in space-time, to the effects of an accelerating frame of reference.

He knew that his general theory of relativity had to include changing velocity—that is, acceleration—and therefore gravity as well. Why? Because gravity and acceleration have similar effects. Einstein realized that gravity has the same effect on matter as acceleration. Thus, the force of gravity and force of acceleration were indistinguishable. Since acceleration (and its forces) can be caused by changing direction—as you will remember from steering a car to the right or left—curvature in space and the effects of gravity are equivalent.

Einstein trusted his own thought experiments as much as, or even more than, the real measurements—which later confirmed his conclusions. He knew that whatever general relativity was going to do, it had to deal with this equivalence.

You might think, "So what if gravity and acceleration are equivalent?" "So what if Einstein was interested in gravity being part of relativity?" The answer to why this is relevant is that the equivalence principle connects gravity to curving space-time.

Here is approximately how. Remember, if s is distance traveled, t is the time involved, and v is velocity, then $v = s/t$. Acceleration, a, is the change in velocity; therefore a = change in s/t. Thus acceleration is equivalent to changes in space and time. In other words, the equivalence of gravity and acceleration implies that gravity, the most universal of all material forces, is equivalent to changes in space and time that can occur when these dimensions curve and warp.

SPACE-TIME AND THE NATURE OF GRAVITY

Until about 1910, gravity was just an idea; no one knew how it worked. Even today, it is still an enigma, and more research is needed. But at that time, people knew only that gravity was a universal force inherent in all matter that made masses attract one another.[1]

In fact, gravity is the most "democratic" force of all. It does not depend on the nature of matter, its color, its electric charge, its magnetic polarity, whether it is hard or soft, small or large. All the other forces in nature depend on the exact kind of matter involved. For example, magnetic forces work only on magnetic materials. But gravity is a general property of the whole universe that works on all kinds of matter. But what is it?

Scientists knew that all matter has a sort of "stubbornness" about it, called mass. The property of a piece of matter called mass speaks to the rest of the universe, saying something like, "Let me go on in a straight line or I will put up a resistance. I resist being pushed around and accelerated. Once I am moving on my path, I will stay on that path as long as you do not force me to do otherwise!"

That is approximately what mass would say if it could speak. In other words, all matter has mass: the greater the mass, the greater the resistance to acceleration and change. As to the nature of mass, all we can say is that it is stubborn and resists change. Mass has inertia, and we need force to accelerate mass. Big planets have a lot of mass, which means a lot of gravity, or its equivalent, a lot of curvature, around them.

To understand more about the connection between mass and curvature, let's go back to our images of the elevator experiment. This time, let's put a hole in the elevator so that bullets from a pistol can shoot through easily.

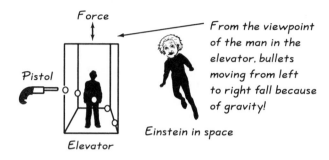

Force

Pistol

Elevator

From the viewpoint of the man in the elevator, bullets moving from left to right fall because of gravity!

Einstein in space

30.3 What's causing the bullets to fall?

When we shoot the pistol the bullets do not go straight, but seem to fall. Since there is a force pulling the elevator upward, the man in the elevator will see the bullets fall to the floor. For the man in the elevator, if the elevator weren't accelerating because of the crane, or if gravity was not acting on the elevator, the bullets would go straight across and hit the wall at the other side. But since the elevator is accelerating, the man in the elevator sees the bullets fall.

For Einstein, the whole elevator and, of course, the floor as well, seems to move up to meet the bullets, but for the man in the elevator it looks like the bullets go down. As far as this man is concerned, he knows from his past experiences that a ball, or a shooting bullet, falls because of gravity. But his past experiences are not the absolute truth!

From Einstein's viewpoint, the bullets try to go in a straight line because of their mass, and the floor rises to meet the bullets as a result of the accelerating force of the crane.

Light, which has both wavelike and particle-like properties, can be understood as a stream of bullet-like particles. Light will behave more or less like bullets—even though the difference between light and bullets is that light has no weight, no mass.

Einstein reasoned that, since light will try to go in a straight line, if the elevator is accelerating, light will appear to "fall" as it moves through an accelerated box, just as it would if it were near a huge planet which exerted gravitational forces on it. Even though it has no mass, the path of light would appear to fall or curve. Since we can speak of acceleration as changes in space and time (or as curved space-time), we can just as well say that light curves because space is curved inside and around that elevator. The reason for this is that, according to the principle of equivalence, the effects of gravity are the same as curves in space and time.

Gravity—or its equivalent, curved space-time—bends light. The principle of equivalence says that since gravity is equivalent to acceleration (i.e., curves in space-time), to have the effect of gravity, space itself must be curved near a big planet. In other words, what Newton thought was gravity, Einstein realized was curved space-time.

In this thinking, gravity is no longer the central force—it becomes instead a manifestation of curved space-time. Curvature is a mass-like property. The spaces around us bend at certain times and places, and the very space we live in has a substance-like effect on us!

The conclusion Einstein came to was that *light curves because of gravity, that is, because of the bending of space.*

You may feel that this whole concept is too far from your everyday experience to be believable. But you can trust your sense of dreaming more than you can trust everyday experience. You know that when things "get heavy," they seem to curve everything. But let's go back to physics before we go further into altered states.

It turns out that when scientists actually measured light near heavy planets, light was, indeed, bent by gravity. Astronomers waited for an eclipse of the sun and measured light from other stars bending in space near big planets. They found that Einstein's calculations were correct. It made a big stir in the scientific community when these astronomers verified that space-time bends.

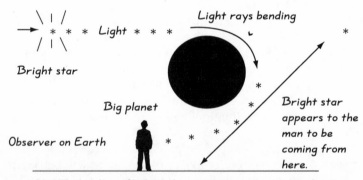

30.4 *The bending of light and space-time near a massive planet*

Because space around a heavy planet is curved, if light is emitted from the bright star in the upper left corner (Figure 30.4) and that light travels by the sun, the star will appear to an observer on Earth to be coming from the star on the right side, rather than from the star where it really is, on the upper left. Experiments have shown that light from such stars is bent when there's a heavy planet or star around, like the sun. The more gravity, the more the path of light is bent.

You will remember that a black hole is a star that has become so dense that light beams trying to escape are pulled right back in. Thus, if the heavy planet is not the sun, but the densest of all planets, namely, a black hole, then gravity bends space-time in such a way that it pulls light into itself.

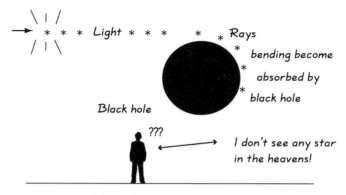

30.5 Because of the black hole, the observer sees no star at all!

Light tries to follow space; it travels in straight lines if space is straight. But if light curves, we can assume from the principle of equivalence that either space-time itself is curved or there is a big planet and lots of gravity nearby. As far as Einstein was concerned, gravity is simply bent space-time.

GRAVITY IS CURVATURE IN SPACE-TIME

Another way of saying this is that what we call gravity is a forceful effect coming from the otherwise hidden curvature in space-time. In short, that is the general theory of relativity without the mathematics associated with it.

You can think of space-time like you think of your mattress. The space around a black hole would be something like what happens to your mattress when you stand on it with one foot. The rest of mattress is more or less flat, but near your foot, that is, near the black hole, the mattress sinks. If you are heavy enough, you put a hole in the mattress.

The space around stars is also pushed in. Unless a star is very massive, like a black hole, the indentation is not all that serious. Euclidean geometry for flat space works pretty well where there is little mass. But if you were moving near a black hole, you would be like an ant near the great dent in your mattress. You suddenly experience a great change in your normal path; your velocity changes and your begin to fall into the hole.

Curved space accelerates things as if it were gravity. In other words, what we call matter is a consensus reality term which is equivalent to curvature in space-time in the theory of relativity.[2] According to Einstein, gravity was a property of geometry. What was matter from one viewpoint was the space-time's curvature from another.

In consensus reality, mass is associated with gravity and has nothing to do with the shape of space. The CR concept of gravity begins to lessen in significance as far as relativity is concerned, just as the concept of a particle began to lose its meaning in quantum mechanics, as we saw earlier.

The calculations we can make from the mathematics of Riemann and Einstein tell us exactly how much light bends when it moves around a heavy planet. Since experiments verify these calculations, the general theory of relativity is accepted today as a great advance over Newtonian formulas, which do not allow us to make accurate predictions about light. The mathematics of relativity shows that the shape of the universe's space-time at any one spot depends on the amount of matter everywhere.

In Western thinking since the Renaissance, space has been seen as a vacuum, an absence, a void with no shape and no meaning. Since the advent of relativity, this concept has changed. Space-time becomes a sort of material substance, and the concepts of matter and gravity are replaced by curvatures in space-time. In this new world view, geometry cannot be divorced from substance. In Einstein's general theory of relativity, space is no longer an abstract concept, but becomes the substance-like place we all live in.

EXAMPLES OF CURVATURE AND GRAVITY

To make all this easier to understand in everyday life, let's imagine that we can see cars zooming around on a racetrack—an analogy inspired by astronomers Alan and Hilary Wright. You think, "Wow! Those cars zoom around in a circle and must have great drivers. Or perhaps they have some sort of magical wire holding them to the center of the circle." But the closer you get, the more you see that there are no drivers; moreover, there is nothing connecting the cars to the track! What you see is that the track itself is curved in such a manner that the cars can only take the path around a circle.

The interplanetary equivalent of the motion of these cars is the motion of light, bullets, particles, meteors, and everything else flying through space-time. Everything is on a curved trajectory, just as the cars can only move around the curves of their circular racetrack. And everything curves, not because of some magical force such as gravity but, in relativity theory, because space-time is bent. We don't need gravity to account for the fact that things are moving in a curved manner, any more than we need a secret driver or a magic wire to account for the way in which the cars travel. The cars can only go round a circle because the track is curved, not because of gravity or other forces.

In other words, the Earth is not going around the sun just because the sun exerts a great deal of gravitational attraction on the Earth. Space itself is bent; the Earth can only take this particular curved path around the sun. If someone insists that the path is caused by the gravity of planets, that is fine, but that is only one viewpoint.

Four-dimensional space-time bending can only be approximated by examples of mattresses and cars on racetracks because there is no exact analogy in our three-dimensional world.[3] But there are many NCR examples.

THE NCR EXPERIENCE OF RELATIVITY

Where did Einstein get the courage to think that space was curved, even though everyday experience seemed to forbid this? It was a physical intuition, which I believe came from his sentient experience.

The analogy of the general theory of relativity in psychology implies that there are two viewpoints for each event. One viewpoint is that we are moved about by the forces of our personal psychology, our complexes, abuse issues, history, myths, personal physiology, health, cultures, society, history, and so on. The other viewpoint in a general theory implies that our path in life is due to a universal Tao, to the nature of the universe.

In other words, we have two viewpoints. One is that personal, interpersonal, and collective forces and fields create our path in life. The other viewpoint is that our path is a momentary expression of nature's way, of a universal field through which our personal existence is passing, a field created in conjunction with all the other paths of the universe.

In a way, we are not just objects interacting with other material objects gravitationally or psychologically, but expressions of a path, or perhaps invitations to a particular path. Whoever comes near us must, like the Earth moving about the sun (or the sun moving about the Earth) move along a path which is us. *We ourselves, and everything else, are not just objects but also secret, unseen paths for everything around us.* Others may experience this as an aura or an attraction or repulsion, yet from the most detached viewpoint, we are just an invitation to a path.

As individuals or objects we influence and curve space-time. The fate of anyone or anything in your neighborhood is to fall into the dent that is you, just as you fall into theirs. When others get near us, their paths merge with ours, and everyone must change their way. When we are near them, our paths must change. Likewise, from Einstein's viewpoint, every piece of matter creates a sort of invitation to traverse a certain path. Each object is a path invitation. The older I get, the more I share Einstein's thinking, that what looks like forces pushing you around are, from another viewpoint, simply the Tao.

NOTES

1. Newton's gravitational theory was that every particle of matter attracts every other particle with a force that is directly proportional to the product of the masses, and the inverse square of the distance between them. If 1 and 2 refer to the masses, *f* is the force between the masses of the two particles, and *r* refers to the distance between them and *G* is gravitational constant, then

$$f = \frac{(Gm_1 \times m_2)}{r^2}$$

2. The mathematically oriented reader may enjoy Einstein's discussion in *Relativity* (page 55 and following). Also see Pauli's criticism of Einstein's approximations in Wolfgang Pauli, *The Theory of Relativity.*

    Einstein used the math developed by Riemann. In note 4 of Chapter 28, you find the equations for distance involving *g*, the curvature factor. Einstein generalized this *g* by putting mass and energy together to create what a "energy-momentum tensor," describing the mass-energy of a body. His curvature factor *g* became a geometry tensor representing the bending of space in a particular region. He made approximations and suggested that his geometry tensor, that is, the curvature of space-time, had a very simple connection with the energy-momentum tensor. This meant that the shape of space, so to speak, was decided upon by the amount of matter there.

3. The car analogy is interesting but like all analogies, not perfect. The more cars there are on the track, that is, the more matter in the universe, the sharper the curves in the track. With still more cars, we eventually reach the state of a black hole, where the cars must spiral inward toward the center, eventually disappearing altogether.

31 | Peak Experiences: How the Universe Began

The universe does not exist "out there" independent of us. We are inescapably involved in bringing about that which appears to be happening. We are not only observers. We are participators. In some strange sense this is a participatory Universe.

—Physicist John Wheeler

At this point on our journey, we will begin to see how the theories of relativity and the Big Bang are metaphors for peak experiences. The study of these experiences may even illuminate the origin of the universe.

Einstein said that gravity is an effect of space-time curvature. From the viewpoint of relativity, the most basic substance is the field, space-time, the four-dimensional space we live in. Non-physicists might wonder why anyone would care about the difference between gravitational forces, acceleration, and the curvature of space. One reason to wonder is psychological. The difference between force and curvature is the difference between having something pushing you around and finding out that what is pushing you is actually the Tao, the way, the path you should be on.

Say you have a problem. Let's say that you suffer from dizziness, seeing double, dreaming, or similar experiences for long periods of time. One type of doctor or therapist says that your problem is due to a brain injury. Another says it's linked to the trauma you suffered in childhood. Still another helper might say, "You are having the beginning of an out-of-the-body experience attributable to alien abduction." A parapsychologist might add, "A ghost did it." A psychiatrist says, "It is a mental illness, caused by an imbalance in your body chemistry."

FORCES OR THE TAO?

Asking which of these views is right is like asking if there are material forces or if it is just the Tao disturbing you. This question is similar to asking if the forces at hand are due to a nearby planet whose gravity is affecting you or if your dizziness is just a manifestation of the curvature of space-time. While material explanations deal with objects and parts such as chemicals, ghosts, or personal psychology, geometrical explanations include the astrological moment in space and time, or simply the Tao.

Remember Einstein's thought experiment with the person in the elevator? The person inside the elevator is just like you and will probably experience things from her own framework and give her explanation in terms of her "planet." But from a more general viewpoint, the explanation in terms of forces is replaceable by a description of the universe in terms of space-time curvature.

Thus all doctors and therapists have an ethical dilemma about how to view your situation. Is your personal mind-body problem due to your physical chemistry, or is the problem a matter of the Tao? Each explanation represents a paradigm, a belief system and a feeling about life.

TAOISM AND CURVATURE

For the Taoist, "the Tao that can be said" is chemistry, the father, the mother, or the ghost. However, "the Tao that cannot be said" has nothing to do with the forces creating illness. In fact, there was nothing wrong with you in the first place: what happened was your Tao. The result of this thinking is that you can learn to let go of your normal viewpoint and open up to being the events themselves. Let's say you are dizzy. Instead of dealing with low blood pressure, spirits creating altered states of consciousness, or brain problems, as a Taoist you have the option of adjusting to the curves of fate, or even becoming them. This would mean that you become dizzy instead of remaining your normal self. You are the path, rather than being an immovable object tossed about on the path.

People have always thought of the Tao as the curvature of space-time, the geometry in which we live. The Chinese described the Tao as a field of waves moving through the environment, as "dragon lines."[1] Australian Aboriginal drawings of dreamtime show similar representations of fields and curves in space.[2]

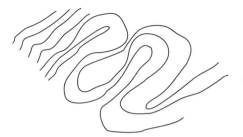

31.1 Chinese Taoist dragon lines and Aboriginal Australian dreamtime lines

If asked to comment on the theory of relativity, the Taoists and Aboriginal people might very well agree with Einstein that the field we live in, the Tao or dreamtime, is curved, and that is why light, consciousness, and everything else seems to be altered. For the Taoist, times and spaces change in a more or less unpredictable manner and the goal of life is to learn to live with curved fields, rather than to go against them.

In a materialistic frame of mind, you don't care about the Tao or dreamtime. You want causal explanations and a linear life. In a materialist framework, you believe that a virus causes your flu. You look for allopathic vaccinations, alternative medical cures, or folk remedies to heal you. But the vast majority of human problems have no simple causes. For example, why you often get the flu may require an understanding of your relationship to the Tao, the manner in which you meet, resist, or go with life's events.

The explanations that suit you are a matter of the times. Sometimes you want to know that your problems are due to social situations, familial genetics, pathology, not enough vitamin C, or that they were caused by your father or mother. While these consensus reality explanations are useful, most people tend to get depressed by the continuous use of CR explanations, which take the awesomeness and spirit out of life. The Taoist view is complementary to the material one. The material view gets you to change things at a material level, and the Taoist viewpoint detaches from a given cause and relates to the vision of yourself as part of an incredible, spiritual universe.

WHICH EXPLANATION WORKS BEST?

Let's say that your primary identity is everything that you refer to as yourself. Secondary identities are projected onto others, onto the horrible and amazing people and things around you.

As long as you are a self with a primary identity such as Arny Mindell, you experience life as pushing you around. You think something like, "Oh! I am Arny Mindell, and I am having a hard day. I got malaria in Brazil and it is bothering me, and certain people are irritating me," and so on. In the moment, malaria, irritating people, and so forth, are my secondary processes.

As long as I am connected with my primary identity, the rest of the world is "not me." It is a "secondary process," a force working against or for me. I experience accelerations, gravity, people, illness, and everything else as foreign and invasive as long as I am not moving along with that secondary process.

When I go over the edges of my primary process, my identity, I find myself identifying with being the forces around me: I am the Tao, so to speak. If I get over my edge to my identity, if I can relax Arny Mindell and let in the troubles around me, then I become malaria, a powerful, mind-altering force that keeps me inward, drowsy. When I do this, I suddenly find myself no longer on the linear path of time. Instead, space-time curves backward to the time when I got malaria—the time when I had powerful hallucinations and spiritual experiences with the native people of the Amazon. Instead of feeling feverish with malaria, the experiences I had a year ago then become my Tao.

As long as I stay in the materialistic paradigm, my body's problems seem like an opponent, a force called malaria, until I let go, give in to tiredness, and become the state of consciousness coming from malaria, an NCR path recalling Amazon experiences. What looks like illness from one viewpoint is a deep, mind-altering experience trying to unfold from another viewpoint. When you are what you notice, there are only fields—there are no longer causes.

Which identity you have in the moment answers the question: "What determines whether you feel there are (or are not) forces working on you?"

PEAK EXPERIENCES AND THE WAY THE PATH IS MOVING

As you identify with the field around you, with the Tao or the geometry of the universe, other questions arise: "What is this universe?" "Where is it going?" "How did it get started?" "Who am I?"

In physics, the answer is that the universe manifests more or less as a meaningless, particular calculation of space-time: *the universe manifests as a path and each path is just a path leading into or out of a black hole. All paths originated in the Big Bang.*

We have seen already that the Big Bang theory and the black hole concept are related to our psychology. In order to understand the original black hole, from which everything emanated at the beginning of the universe, we need to explore the NCR significance of big bangs.

Let's re-investigate the Big Bang again, this time from the viewpoint of peak experiences. In Chapter 29, we learned that most astrophysicists believe the universe began with the Big Bang, one massive, spatial curvature of a condensed universe, about the size of the Earth, which exploded and unfolded into the present expanding universe of stars and planets, each moving away from each other at rates that increase the farther they are from one another.

According to the Big Bang theory, matter condensed, became massive, cooled off, and then exploded. The aboriginal idea about how the world was created is not altogether different. Many peoples think that in the beginning there was some sort of earth maker from which everything emanated.

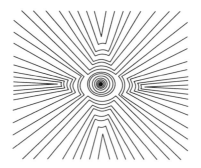

31.2 An approximation of Aboriginal paintings[3]

The Muslim, Jewish, and Christian traditions also see the beginning in terms of a prime, singular act, personified by God, the creator. We saw in Chapter 18 that something like a universal mind has been believed to have created the universe through reflecting upon itself. In the form of Brahman, Shiva, Pan Ku, Nun, Christ, and Wotan, this being reflected upon itself and the universe came into being as a reflection of itself. In these theories, curiosity was the motivating force of the creator. In other words, questioning yourself, wondering, exploring life, and self-reflection give rise to new and creative solutions to life.

Now let's see how dreamtime and its reflection (attributable to flirting or curiosity) appear in physics. You remember the mathematics of quantum physics: imaginary numbers are used for wave functions and conjugation, that is, the multiplication of an imaginary number by its reflection produces the real, measurable numbers of everyday reality. In Chapter 26, on relativity, we saw that imaginary numbers also play a significant role in calculating space-time. To be more specific, the time factor is imaginary in relativity; this factor is "ict," where c is the speed of light and t is time.[4]

You can see in note 4 that physicists do not normally have to deal with this imaginary factor if the time factor is smaller than the space factor. This mathematical jargon means that for events in which there is a lot of movement in space over short times, the numbers for space-time are real, and imaginary numbers do not appear in the calculations. Such large movements in space are the normal domain in which relativity has been applied.

Stephen Hawking decided to apply relativity theory to the origin of the universe, that is, a situation in which events did not have much spatial movement because the universe was so condensed. In this situation, space-time turns out to be imaginary because of the cramped, condensed, and collapsed condition of the universe. Hawking decided to deal with imaginary numbers and the resulting imaginary time and dimensions, which arise in such a situation as the beginning of the universe. He came up with a very speculative but interesting theory.[5]

Hawking saw from calculations such as the ones you can find in note 4, which come from Einstein's theory of relativity, that space-time becomes imaginary when the spatial distances involved are less significant than the temporal ones. We might find such a situation in the beginning of the universe, or we can imagine such a situation in everyday life as well. For example, the calculation for space-time becomes a real number if we consider the space-time separation of New York at 1:00 P.M. and London at 1:08 P.M. Here, the spatial dimension of about 5000 miles of space-time is more significant than the temporal one, which is only 7 minutes. However, if we calculate space-time separation between New York at 1:00 P.M. and New York a minute later, at 1:01 P.M., the spatial dimension is zero and the temporal one is 1 minute, and space-time turns out to be imaginary.[6]

For physicists, such imaginary results mean that we have traveled in time but not space and therefore that the spatial factor is not real and not significant. Hawking played with such considerations about space-time to try to figure out what might have happened at the beginning of the universe. He considered that the time factor in Minkowski's and Einstein's space-time theory had an imaginary number in front of it (ict). In the beginning of the universe there was not much space involved because the universe was so condensed; therefore Hawking saw that space-time was essentially imaginary because it was mainly time.

Then Hawking had a brainstorm. He thought, why not let time intervals in those very first split seconds of time be imaginary? After all, no one will ever be able to measure such intervals because they are too small. He figured the time factors involved in the split seconds of the beginning of the universe were very, very small; in fact, they were of the order of 10^{-43} seconds. If no one can measure such little things, why not change time as we know it today into "imaginary time," whatever that means. He did not speculate about its meaning; he only said, let time be imaginary. Then, if time is imaginary, it turns out that the time factor $-ict$ is now $+ct$.[7]

Can you follow Hawking? By replacing time with a speculative imaginary time for the first split second, space-time comes out to be a real number! Hawking assumed that time intervals in those very first split seconds of time are imaginary, since no one could measure them, and then space-time became real because the imaginary numbers were squared and no longer appeared in the equations. Once space-time was real, the beginning of the universe was a reality. That is the essence of Hawking's theory of imaginary time.

To review, Hawking thought that if no one can measure such times, then they might as well be imaginary as far as physics is concerned. No one can prove that they weren't imaginary; thus we can use the idea of imaginary time, which allows for a real universe to begin.

Hawking's assumption reminds me of our previous discussion of quantum flirting, in which we interpreted the imaginary numbers in the math of observation as an NCR flirt. Calling the origins of observation a quantum flirt gives us an NCR experiential basis of observation. Quantum flirts, or reflected signals, are conjugated and generate consensus reality. Hawking's assumption of an imaginary time existing at the first split second at the beginning of the universe is similar. He presumes that an imaginary time occurred before the primal act of the universe creating itself.

Many physicists find great problems in making sense of and verifying Hawking's theory. But psychologically, we can say that his explanation for what happened in the beginning of the universe is similar to my explanation for the creation of everyday reality; imaginary numbers and their associated NCR experiences are basic to the creations of reality, of the universe.

The imaginary time in the beginning of the universe uses imaginary numbers and deals with NCR experiences. From the viewpoint of NCR, or dreamtime, when spatial dimensions are less significant than temporal ones, we travel in time. The imaginary numbers that occur in the calculation for space-time in this case are patterns for NCR experiences such as time travel, which, although non-consensual, is still possible for us. After all, everyone knows sensations such as "time flies" or "time is dragging." Time travel is like dreaming, being in the flow of things, stepping out of linear time.[8]

In other words, Hawking's view of evolution can be understood in the terms of our present discussion as follows: the universe began with dreaming, with imaginary time and with the universe reflecting upon itself.[9] The universe has an NCR process, which became curious and therefore self-reflected. That's how the real world came into being.

According to Aboriginal people, when the great deities dreamed, when dreaming was conjugated, the universe came into being. Dreamtime preceded everything. In dreamtime, the universe can be considered to have reflected upon itself, and this self-reflection created the real universe in something like a big bang.

For physicists, the imaginary results we find for space-time at the beginning of the universe mean only that we traveled in time but not space, and therefore the space-time factor is not real and not significant. But if we consider with Hawking that time was imaginary, then we can consider dreamtime to have created the universe.

My point is not to prove or disprove physics, but to show that whatever we discover in physics has been part of our perennial philosophies and religions. Briefly said, in the beginning of the universe, some form of NCR universal mind, in one mythic form or another, reflected and generated the universe. An original, non-consensual reflective act created the real physical world. Before the self-reflection, there was just dreaming, just imaginary numbers in a timeless, spaceless something. Curiosity and self-reflection generated reality from dreaming.

PSYCHOLOGICAL PEAK EXPERIENCES

Whether or not you followed the technical details of the last few paragraphs, you know from personal experience that dreaming and curiosity precede moments of creativity. You know that you can ponder basic questions about life for months or years. Then suddenly, a sort of big bang occurs, a peak experience, a huge blast, which organizes, or seems to reorganize, all of life. During this big bang, the world seems to collapse; you may have a near-death experience or a mind-blowing experience and suddenly see the meaning and core of everything.

PERSONAL EXPERIMENT: THE BIG BANG

If you would like a personal NCR experience of the big bang, you may want to try the following inner work exercise.

1. **Recall a peak or most amazing experience.** You might think you've never had one, but go back over your lifetime and think about some really big, ultimately maximal experience, be it a wonderful or terrible one.

    Chose one example of such an experience. When and where did it occur? How old were you? Who was there? What was it like? In what way were you dreaming before and during this peak experience? How long did it last? What events in reality unfolded after that experience?

    What was time like in that experience? Describe this imaginary time for yourself. Did travel in real space play any role in your experience? When and how did you reenter consensus reality after that peak experience? Was the world condensed or collapsed, more intense?

2. **Experiment with yourself and see if your mind and your body will let you feel that peak experience again.** Can you remember the feeling of that peak experience?

If you can, experiment with expressing the feeling of that experience in movement, with your hands and feet. Give it some sort of movement expression, even if it is a small movement expression. Absolute stillness can also be a movement, but try to move it in some way.

3. **Consider in what way that peak experience organized or is now organizing your life.**

How has it been central in your life? How has it touched upon your everyday work, if at all? How is this peak experience connected with your goals, if at all? Does this peak experience somehow influence your relationships? In what manner did it organize the period of life before the peak experience?

How do you suspect it might organize your future? Are you still somehow searching for that peak experience? Play with the idea of organizing your future. Guess or decide what you're going to be doing, based on this peak experience.

4. **In what way is this peak experience connected to body experiences or fears of body problems today?**

Is this peak experience in some way connected with your body problems? Choose one of your body problems. How would your peak experience influence that problem, if at all?

AFTER THE EXPERIMENT

I have done this experiment with students in my classes on physics and psychology. We speak about the experiences afterwards. The following is a list of peak experiences that people have mentioned over the years.

Childhood Experiences. Many people, especially creative artists, associate their life's work with a "big bang." Peak experiences are often associated with blasts from childhood experiences, and from trauma. These are black-hole types of phenomena.

Callings. Many peak experiences were felt to be callings defining one's task in life.

Near-Death Experiences. Feeling you are near death, out of the body, seeing the whole of life in a nutshell, noticing light, love, or detachment, is considered a peak experience. Sometimes, out-of-the-body experiences occur in meditation. Then you see your "real" body from outside "yourself."

God Experiences. Thinking or feeling or dreaming that a goddess or god is speaking to you is a common peak experience.

Love. Some people talk about falling in love as one of the biggest experiences of their lives—feeling swept off your feet.

Satori. Moments of enlightenment, catching on, "satori," sudden insights into the nature of life are often associated with peak experiences. One of my students put it this way, "I was with a guru in India and had an enlightenment, I had a true awakening, a Shakti-pat."

Unity Experiences. Being at one with the earth and the stars. Some experiences connect us to feeling we are one with a rock, an animal, or the universe. Many experiences deal with having the sense that all things fit together, or that they balance one another and create a unity.

Creativity. Being very creative, doing something artistic or intellectual can be a peak experience.

Giving birth. Giving birth, having a child, is a wonderful and/or horrendous peak experience for some women.

Killing or Rescuing. Having rescued someone or having killed somebody in a fight or during a war can be a central experience. One of my students said, "I worked on a time when I was in a car that killed two people. It was horrible, but in a strange way, it was also the most amazing event of my life."

Psychotic Experiences. One student said, "I thought back to a time when I almost went crazy, when voices were bugging me and I could not tell if I was dreaming or awake."

In our discussions, we have discovered that psychotic or near-psychotic experiences are very common peak experiences demonstrating the conflict between reality and imagination. Most peak experiences seemed at least a bit crazy in the sense of combining reality with the feeling that the other world is equally significant. This is like the Big Bang, which manifests at the moment when the imaginary world becomes real, when dreaming manifests in everyday consciousness.

CONCLUSIONS

Peak experiences are blasts awakening us to the core things in life. They come from extreme and dreamlike altered states of consciousness and can link us to everything in the universe, to the meaning or origin of life. These experiences come from a deep, NCR search and curiosity about one's self.

Peak experiences are psychological analogies to big bangs in the sense that when the experiences cool off a bit, they unfold for years afterwards in terms of our everyday lives. Their meaning does not appear right away, but only in time.

Before the big bang occurs, you may be in a black hole—light does not come out of your life. You may feel blocked, bored, collapsed. But big bangs then occur. They may come at any age, when you are ten, thirty, forty, or eighty years old. Peak experiences deal with reflections of the other world in this one, with imaginary time, with dreamtime. Only after such a big bang does the real world return.

Just as the Big Bang organizes the universe, peak experiences organize much of your life, both before the experience occurred and afterwards, even today. To check on this, just ask yourself if your peak experience gives you a hint about the answer to the following questions: "What do you really want to do on this planet?" "Why are you here?" The most satisfactory answers to these questions may be formulated in terms of these peak experiences.

Physics, astronomy, and theology answer big questions about life and the universe in different ways, but the questions are the same: "What is life about?" Again and again, you may ask yourself, "Why am I doing what I am doing?" "What is pushing me into this?" "Where did I come from?" "Where do we all go?"

In physics, the answer to these questions is space-time's "world line" on which you travel. The world line is the course or path of your life. You normally think only of today and tomorrow, try to explain things in terms of mythology, abuse, inheritance, chemistry, or world history. But if you look at the larger picture, you see you are part of a world line, created by a big bang.

What I am calling peak experiences, shamans called the results of prayer and vision quests. A basic part of all aboriginal cultures has been to seek such experiences, to go on vision quests and then unravel, with the help of a shaman, the meaning of the events on that quest. In this way, people have always tried to get onto the paths implicit in peak experiences, to re-orient their personal and community lives.

Your peak experience can be understood similarly as a method for orienting you to the Tao, a way to feel "in line" instead of feeling pushed and pulled by life. Peak experiences are "core" experiences that are central to the curved nature of your everyday world. The peak experience manifests in unexpected events, in the meaning of life you may have forgotten.

Such peak experiences and vision quests give you a hint not only about personal life but also about the beginning of the universe. A general theory of psychology that goes along with the general theory of relativity is a theory about where material forms came from and where we are all going. My theory is that the universe began with dreaming and curiosity about dreaming. Self-reflection led to a peak experience, a sudden explosive awakening.

When the universe reflected upon itself in NCR processes, it discovered itself, just as we discover aspects of our essence through each peak experience. What we perceive in consensus reality as a collapse may be, in an NCR universe, a way for the universe to re-center itself, to self-reflect.

Perhaps the universe collapsed in a depression, condensing into a ball, doubting and wondering about the meaning of its own incredible vastness and diversity. Self-reflection about its own nature revealed what we are discovering today: the mathematics of self-reflection, of self-curiosity.

Since all the material forms around us, our friends, city, solar system and stars in the sky, arrived here after having traveled on a world line originating with self-reflection and the Big Bang, everything is theoretically participating with us in wondering about its true nature. We are all on the road, together, to discovering the unity that is all of us.

NOTES

1.   See Figures 56 and 57 of Rawson and Legeza's *Tao* (1979), where the dragon lines appear as vortices in the clouds, energies that could be harnessed.

2.   See, for example, page 125 in Peter Sutton's, *Dreamings: The Art of Aboriginal Australia* (1988), "Witchedy Grub Dreamings."

3.   From Figure 150 of Sutton's *Dreamings*.

4.   In Chapter 26, we discussed the details of space-time separation, the distance measured in the four-dimensional universe, which can be written in the general four dimensions of space-time as:

$$s^2 = x_1{}^2 + x_2{}^2 + x_3{}^2 + x_4{}^2$$

or in terms of the spatial coordinates x, y, and z and the time coordinate t, as:

$$s^2 = x^2 + y^2 + z^2 + (-ict)^2$$

We can simplify things if we think of motions, for the moment, only in the x direction. Then y and z dimensions no longer need to appear in our equation, and to simplify things, space-time separation becomes:

$$s^2 = x_1{}^2 + x_4{}^2$$

But since the fourth dimension is ict, we finally have the simplified equation for space-time separation, which is:

$$s^2 = x^2 - (ct)^2$$

In other words, the effect of the imaginary numbers in space-time means that the time dimension has a minus sign in front of it. Moreover, sometimes, space-time separation itself becomes imaginary. If we put in actual values for x and ct in the above formula, say x is 1 and ct is 2, then you would get:

$$s = \sqrt{(1-4)} = i\sqrt{3}$$

because the square root of a negative number is imaginary. If x is bigger than ct, like $x = 2$ and $ct = 1$, then you get a real number, square root of $4 - 1$, or 3, and the square root of 3 is about 1.4, a real number.

5. Hawking's theory is expressed in admirably simple terms by physicist Paul Davies in *About Time, Einstein's Unfinished Revolution* (1995), pages 190 to 192.

6. If we are dealing with a time dimension of 1 minute and a spatial difference of zero, then $s^2 = x^2 - (ct)^2$, $x = 0$, and s is the square root of a negative number and thus imaginary.

7. If we substitute an imaginary time factor for time t, then $-ict$ becomes $ic \times it$, which turns out to be $+ct$ since $i \times i = -1$.

8. You know non-linear time already from Chapter 4, where I quoted an ancient passage from the *I Ching*, which said, "*Counting what goes forwards, goes backwards.*" This statement refers to the NCR experience of going forwards in CR time, getting older, watching things manifest, unfolding from sentient seeds while simultaneously being aware that in NCR, you are retreating from the sentient roots of reality.

   In the grand view, time is not as useful a concept because it is not relative to the NCR sense of events unfolding from a given root. In CR terms, the experience of imaginary time refers to stepping out of linear time, being able to fantasize, imagine, dream, going backwards or forwards and out of time.

9. I use the term self-reflection here to express the mathematical idea of note 4 where an imaginary time (it) takes the place of t, making the calculation at the beginning of the universe:

$$s = \sqrt{-(ct)^2} = \sqrt{-(cit)(cit)} = \sqrt{(-ict)(+ict)} = ct$$

The time terms $-ict$ and $+ict$ are effectively squared or self-reflected in the beginning of the universe.

32 | Hunting Energy

In the beginning God created the heaven and the earth.
—*Genesis* 1:1

But no one was there to see it.

—Physicist Steven Weinberg, in *The First Three Minutes*, comments on the beginning of creation

I have been wondering about God since I was first introduced to religion at the age of four or five. I didn't know much about synagogues or churches. My parents took me to a synagogue and I saw everybody standing, swaying back and forth, and praying. I asked my mother, "What are they doing?" My mother said, "They're praying." I asked, "Do all people pray?" My mother said, "Let's go and find out!"

So we went to a church in the neighborhood and there people were doing the same thing, praying. Again I asked, "Why do people pray?" And my mother said, "Because all of us are uncertain; we need more contact with God." I could not understand why people had to go into such a big house in order to pray to God. I thought God was everywhere.

As I grew older, I forgot this problem about human uncertainty and the search for God, yet I must have unconsciously continued my search, for it has always been important for me to find that God was everywhere. Later, when I became interested in physics to find out more about the goddesses and gods, I called them nature.

In these final chapters on relativity, we will ponder ideas about the nature of the gods and how they may be hidden in what physics calls energy. My hope is that by discovering more about energy, we shall have less uncertainty and more contact with infinity.

THE PHYSICIST AND THE SHAMAN

A central aspect of relativity is that it reduces the significance of consensual concepts such as space, time, force, and gravity and replaces them in part with a four-dimensional space-time, the field we call the universe. Space-time combines our ordinary experience of the world with dreaming and in a way is a new dimension. It is a prototype of the common factor in all-human experience—the common ground shared by all material forms. What physics calls space-time, native people experience as "Mother Earth," the sacred omnipresent power of the unfolding universe.

Today physicists are refining Einstein's theory of relativity by trying to increase its four dimensions to five or even ten, in order to unify quantum mechanics with relativity. The old concepts of time and space are farther away than ever before.[1] In the not-too-distant future, physics will agree with psychology that all material and spiritual forms interconnect in a hyperspace not unlike the present concept of space-time.

As space and time become less significant in the scientific worldview, the old ideas about inert, spiritless matter are disappearing as well. Renaissance concepts of soulless matter are being replaced by quantum views of matter. Instead of a box with a bunch of fixed, independent "things" in it, today we see matter as an energetic activity of entangled, inseparable elements. Invisible particles of matter are replaced by energetic fields, which create everyday reality upon observation. In our attempt to understand matter, energy, and the universe, it seems as if we are going back to sacred geometry and the power of invisible but self-aware gods who create order and number out of nothingness.

One of the main differences between the spirits of sacred geometry and the fields of physics is that sacred geometry checks itself by experience, not experiment. Another difference between the realms of sacred geometry and the multidimensional spaces and energies of modern physics is the observer's focus. While the shaman uses her second attention to perceive reality, the physicist avoids attending to non-consensual events and focuses only upon consensus reality.

Like the physicist, the average person today is not necessarily prepared to use second attention. While it may be true that following the second attention increases your sense of liberation from the mundane aspects of consensus reality, you usually do not focus upon non-consensual events until forced to by illness, depression, or near-death experiences. A crisis in awareness occurs when the energy of life is no longer at your disposal. When your energy is no longer under your control, you realize that your concepts of time, space, and everyday life are no longer useful, and you must enter into imaginary spaces like space-time and travel with the use of your second attention instead of your rational mind.

ENERGY

To understand more about surviving and traversing irrational spaces and energies, let's think about the concept of energy, which bridges both the realm of the physicist and that of the shaman. Energy implies potential action, vitality, vigor, activity, and potency in both NCR and CR realms. While energy in psychology refers to the vitality and potential power of experience, energy in physics is more concrete.

To begin with, energy in physics can be understood in terms of mechanical or electric power. Physics defines energy in terms of work. The term energy is connected to the Greek word "ergos," which means work. Although energy is invisible, it is evident as the capacity to do work. Thus energy is defined as the capacity to do work, and work is measured by the amount of force needed to move a particle through a distance. To measure energy, you measure work. Work is a form of energy.

Energy = Work = Force × Distance = F × D

Consider the woman in Figure 32.1. She exerts a force to pull a weight, by means of a pulley, through a certain distance, which can be measured with a yardstick. She is lifting a weight with a force, *F*, from the ground to a distance, *D*, in the air.

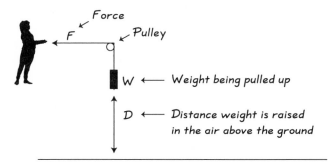

Work = F x D: Force F lifts weight W a distance D into the air.

32.1 The woman uses force to raise weight over a pulley, O.

To calculate the amount of energy she uses, you need to know how much work she puts into her job. The amount of work is the force she uses to lift the weight, *W*, a distance, *D*. Thus, according to the definition of energy:

Energy = Work = Force × Distance

Now the weight, *W*, is a distance, *D*, off the ground. How much energy does it have? To begin with, we can think of energy as being divided into two kinds, kinetic and potential. Potential energy means just what it says. Potential energy is stored; it is not being used; it is hidden. Potential energy includes the energy stored as a result of gravity, electricity, and nuclear and chemical capabilities. Kinetic energy is the energy of action; it is dynamic and due to motion.

Let's study potential energy first. The weight gains potential energy by being raised. If the woman takes the weight and raises it, the amount of potential energy (PE) depends on how much energy she put into the weight through the work she did. In other words, the weight gained potential energy in the amount of the work energy she put into it. The potential energy can also be measured in terms of how much work the weight could do if it were dropped. If the woman put in $W = F \times D$, and if the potential energy is equivalent to that amount of work, then the potential energy of the weight is:

$$E = F \times D$$

I call that energy potential energy even though the weight is not doing anything, because it could do some work if it had to. It could do work because of its position above the ground. The higher the weight is from the ground, the more potential energy it has.

POTENTIAL ENERGY AND RANK

A position above the ground gives the weight more potential energy than the same weight ($|W|$) that is still on the ground. The weight above the ground has more ability to do work. For example, if we connected our weight to a pulley, and if we dropped our weight slowly, it might lift another weight off the ground. If you don't do anything more than raise the weight, its energy remains potential.[2]

Potential energy is like having money in the bank. If you have the money in the bank, if you want to, you can do things, although you need not do anything at all. An important psychological analogy to potential energy is social rank. If you are in a higher social position than others are, you have rank over them and more potential to do things.

Whether or not you use this rank or are even conscious of it, rank means you have the potential to do things in the world that others with less rank cannot do. In most countries, for example, men are generally paid more than women and are found more frequently in leadership positions. This is because women have less social rank. Some men will protest and say they do not have this rank. Instead, they should say that they are not using their rank, or are not able to use it in a given moment, or that they have less rank in other areas. Despite this protest, the potential ability of someone born as a man is greater than the potential ability of a woman of the same culture and race. In Western countries, people of darker skin color generally have fewer social opportunities and have to work harder to get to the same place, or "height," as people who have lighter skin color. All this is because of rank, because social status and potential are connected.

Rank is like potential energy. In any given human group, our gender, race, religion, sexual orientation, age, and the like give us more or less social rank than others.

All of us have some rank, and all of us are rarely conscious of it. Those with the most rank rarely notice it, just as the potential energy of the weight in our example is not visible. Minority groups know this well. Most of the time, no one in the mainstream notices her or his rank because, if you have rank, you are like a weight placed on a stair. A weight on a very high stair looks about the same as a weight on a lower stair. But the potential of those "privileged" to rest on higher stairs because of social status gives them opportunities not shared by others from lower places. This holds true whether or not the privileged use these opportunities. Thus, in a social field, some have more rank, that is, more potential energy to accomplish things, than others do.[3]

THE PHYSICS OF POWER AND HISTORY

In physics, power is the rate at which work is done or energy transferred. Power is defined as work rate, or energy used over time:

$$Power = Energy/Time$$

Power is the rate of using energy. It can be expressed in terms of horse-power or watts.[4] Power is "horse" or animal strength for us. It is the rate of pulling ability, the speed at which work can be done. Your electric energy bill is a bill for the work your electricity did over the past month.

Power is the speed of doing work, of using energy over time. The woman raising the weight may have used a lot of power to raise that weight—if she did it quickly. Or, if she was relaxed, she may have lifted the weight slowly and used less power. You know that, if you want to lose weight, you can burn more energy more quickly if you jog than if you walk.

Psychologically, those "in power" are able to use their potential energy to get things done faster than those without the same rank. A social activist rarely has as much power as a corporate leader. Even if a social activist has less social rank, she can still have a lot of power if she uses her rank quickly. We can calculate this mathematically: if power = rank/time or energy/time, if the time you use to do things is very rapid and very small, your power increases.

Terrorists know all about this. They may have very little social rank, but if they do things instantaneously, they can make up for their lack of rank by increasing their power through speed. With a bomb, a single person can briefly hold up an entire nation. In this way, you may have little rank but can still have a lot of power.

Thus potential energy or rank is not the only important measure of events in physics or social psychology. Power is crucial as well. We all know that power can be used against others for all sorts of purposes, both good and bad. Physics does not think about how it uses power, which is why it, too, creates bombs that can destroy as much as heal. Societies of the future need to think about the ethics around the use of both physical and psychological power.

Until now, physics has said very little about *how* to use power. The reason for this is that the Earth and its field of gravity have been assumed to be soulless. We thought we did not have to speak with it about how we use its power. It is my hope that this will change in the future, as psychology becomes an integral part of physics. Pushing and pulling, applying power, using energy for any reason, are psychological as well as physical processes requiring communication between the one applying force and the "dead weight" or people you consider to be dead weights.

KINETIC ENERGY

If you let the weight drop in a gravity field, it starts going fast. If I let go of the weight, then its potential energy transforms into action, or kinetic energy. If the weight is dropped, it moves quickly and could break something on the floor. It could self-destruct, or it could be used to make a noise and wake people up.

As the weight falls, its velocity increases. Kinetic, or action, energy, KE, is defined in terms of the velocity of the weight's mass relative to a given frame of reference. Kinetic energy = mass (m) times velocity squared (v^2), then divided by 2, (that is, KE $= mv^2/2$).[5]

This quantity for kinetic energy reminds me of Leibniz. What we call kinetic energy today, he called the "vis viva," that is, the "living force" of an object. In Chapter 10, we saw that Leibniz had an NCR concept of energy. For him, matter had its own inner life force, which manifested in its movement and ability to do things. He defined this vis viva almost the same way we define kinetic energy, namely, as mv^2 instead of as $mv^2/2$. Leibniz suspected that a living force was inherent in matter, that it had a soul, which manifested in terms of energy. I think he was intuiting the revolution of the twentieth century in which Einstein discovered that there was a sort of living force, an energy which was inherent in matter, and that matter itself was a form of energy. We will go more deeply into this revolution in the next chapter.

CONSERVATION OF ENERGY

Until now, we have been considering potential and kinetic energy, or the types of energies. Now let's think about the general rules for how energy flows between being potential, or stored, and being active, or dynamic, as when the weight is in motion, falling to the ground.

All transformations of energy are governed by a principle called the "conservation of energy." This is a general and important principle, which tells us that in all of nature, the total amount of energy of a system does not change. In the example of the weight we were discussing earlier, the total energy of the weight does not change when it falls. Instead, the energy it accrued in terms of potential energy by being raised above the ground transforms into kinetic energy when it is falling and picking up velocity. As the weight falls, all of its potential energy becomes kinetic; the form of energy changes from potential to kinetic, but the total amount remains the same. This is an example of the conservation of energy.

The potential energy the weight accrued by being raised was found from the amount of work involved, namely, $F \times D$. This stored energy becomes unpacked, so to speak, when the weight is released and falls to the ground. The potential energy is converted into kinetic energy, which, according to the law of conservation of energy, must be equal to $F \times D$. In other words, the weight's kinetic energy as it nears the ground, $mv^2/2$, is equal to $F \times D$. Physics says this is a law of nature; the total energy of the weight in that gravity field must remain the same. It cannot be created or destroyed.

When the weight finally lands on the ground, the kinetic energy seems to leave the weight and disappear. But the principle of conservation of energy forbids this. Where did the potential energy that was converted into kinetic energy go? All we notice is a crash site. We can guess from our principle (and be right in our guess) that the energy of crashing must be equal to the amount of energy needed to heat up the ground, the air, and the weight. The conservation law tells us that the heat energy amounts to the kinetic energy just before the crash! The conservation of energy law gives us a chance to predict things we might otherwise not be able to predict.

The woman who put energy into the system through lifting the weight lost energy. She burned some calories doing her work. Finally, the amount of energy she put in ended up in heating up the environment. She can't see heat energy, but she knows her work changed the world because of the conservation of energy. The world warmed up a bit. Everything we do, even if it is just walking down the street, influences the entire universe by using and transforming energy.

The conservation of energy law is amazing. It says that the form and availability of energy may change, but the total amount of energy remains constant.

PSYCHOLOGICAL ENERGY

Therapists use a lot of energy-like expressions such as, "That is an intense person!" Some therapists call themselves "energy workers." Many experience their work as following the Tao, the Ki or Chi energy, which are non-consensus experiences of vitality or the life force sometimes described as streaming or flowing. Shamans, too, speak of energy. Most native shamans speak of power, getting in touch with power, using it, generating it, and finding it.

Finding power spots, finding your own power, and feeling empowered are all linked with getting in touch with your energy or your process and feeling well and alive. A central human problem is having too much or too little energy. Many people don't have much energy; they are mildly depressed or exhausted. Some people say that they experience being depressed as being stuck and not flowing. Now, how and why do we assume a person is stuck if they have no energy? One reason is that the law of the conservation of energy is derived from an NCR sense of the spirit as a constant.

Everyone feels low at times. From your perspective in consensus reality, it may feel as if you are missing some energy, pep, vim, or intensity. You may feel you can't do anything, you hate your work. You may be depressed. But what you are saying is that energy is missing; it has become invisible. If it is missing, you suspect it must be somewhere. People do not simply believe that energy is gone. We feel that it must simply be invisible or inaccessible.

Thus, when you say you feel depressed or have no energy, you are implying that some sort of universal principle must exist which assures you that the energy is not lost, but simply gone from your grasp. Therapists, too, assume that energy is around somewhere and that the client just does not have access to it. Most people experience energy as if it were a spirit: we believe it cannot disappear but must be somewhere. We just lose track of it. It's like the sun that went behind the clouds, or dipped below the horizon and will rise tomorrow.

The energy conservation law in physics is linked to a sense of energy as spirit, which we believe exists all the time, even when it is not immediately available. The conservation of energy in the shamanic realm makes psychologists energy hunters. Even though we as individuals are anything but closed systems, the energy principle urges us to suspect that something about us cannot die, cannot end. We have many different names for this non-consensual energy experience. For example, some aboriginal groups in West Africa think your life energy, your soul, is a quantity borrowed from the tribal energy source, which returns to this source when you die. The tribe is considered a closed system where life energy is conserved. Many peoples have felt that at death, your personal life energy flows back into the tribal energy reservoir from which new people are created.

Community is a kind of closed system where the energy is a constant. We are all bits and pieces of a larger system, and the energy that creates us undergoes a steady transformation as we live and die. Energy is something we all share, pick up, transform, and give away. The belief that energy returns to some sort of pool when we die is an NCR energy conservation law. In this view, life is borrowed from the field of your community, from the field we call the universe.

Thus, when our energy leaves our conscious focus in consensus reality, it becomes unavailable to work with and has slipped away into the environment or into someone else. We need second attention to find it, a shaman to hunt it in dreaming! When psychological energy leaves, it leaves consensus reality and can, in principle, be found in dreams and in altered states. We might find our energy in our dreams in the form of someone we love or hate; they have all the intensity and vigor we do not have. These figures in our dreams represent altered states of consciousness, processes and potentials that go beyond the edge of our identities.

Jung speaks about a psychological energy law (*Collected Works* Vol. 8). He said that if energy isn't in consciousness, it is in what he called the unconscious. A more detailed restatement is that energy manifests as experience. If we have edges to an experience, if we ignore outer events, dreams, and body experiences, the energy of these experiences is not destroyed but transforms. It switches sensory channels. For example, if we dream of a bright light and ignore the dream, the energy might change from a visual channel and appear proprioceptively in the form of a headache, which is experienced as a burning light. Energy is a constant, even if it transforms from one channel to another, i.e., from being visual to becoming somatic.

I have shown in my book on body symptoms, *Working with the Dreaming Body*, that what Jung called the unconscious can be translated into the concept of the unoccupied channel, that is, a sensory channel that is not actively used. For example, a man who depended entirely on hearing himself think and who loved to dialogue with people fell into a sudden and serious depression when his beloved partner of many years suddenly died. With the death of his partner, the man, who was mainly an auditory type person, became suicidal. He said he had lost his partner forever. At first, it seemed impossible to help him. Then I realized that he was used to focusing only on his auditory channel, but not visual experience. To help him find "her" again, I showed him a picture of his wife, hoping to find her in his unoccupied visual channel. Suddenly, he had a remarkable experience. He remembered that just after her death, his wife appeared to him in a dream, beckoning him to follow her to a party. When he saw this inner picture of her, he became ecstatic. The contact with her was not lost; it had simply switched into a visual channel. When he saw her again, he decided to live.

ENERGY AND THE FUTURE OF THE HUMAN RACE

The physical principle of energy conservation tells us that the total amount of energy in a closed system remains more or less the same even when it apparently disappears, or becomes heat energy, that is, less available than ever.

We cannot really waste energy. What we can waste, instead, is the availability of energy. Once the energy gained from raising the weight is dissipated in heat energy through falling, the energy available to do work is more difficult to tap. Heat dissipates into the atmosphere and becomes less available for work.

Entropy, which measures the unavailability of energy, increases when the weight is dropped. The entropy law, sometimes called "the heat death of the universe" law, says that energy becomes increasingly unavailable in closed physical systems. Entropy is a measure of the availability of energy. When the weight is raised, it has a lot of available energy, which can be immediately used. This state of energy has very low entropy. When the weight is dropped, its energy turns into the energy of the crash, which cannot be tapped so easily for doing work. Scientists say the state of entropy is higher, even though the amount of energy is conserved.

We constantly use available energy, like gas, coal, and oil, to heat things and create the human world today. So much energy has been used that available energy resources on the planet Earth are running out. We are slowly destroying our available energy forms such as coal, gas, and wood. The entropy of our planet is going up as the energy that can be easily used goes down. The so-called first-world countries must learn to use less energy, to recycle wastes, and to truly conserve energy in other ways.

Perhaps just here, science might learn a lot from shamans and energy hunters about making unavailable energy more available. The traditional shamanic method uses the second attention to find the energy in dreamland. In other words, what science calls the entropy law stating that energy of a system remains the same but slowly becomes less available and more "entropic" may simply be a law which says that without the second attention, energy becomes less available. The increasing unavailability of energy is a kind of awareness law.

If you use your awareness to focus on unconscious, spontaneous processes, you can find energy when it seems to have disappeared. Through awareness, you can reverse the universe's so-called entropy, or heat death. Clerk Maxwell discovered the entropy law, which predicts that the energy of closed systems becomes increasingly unavailable. He predicted that the whole universe would run downhill. At the end of the nineteenth century, at the same time Maxwell formulated this law, he played with the idea that a demon—today called a Maxwell demon—could reverse that law. The demon did this by being totally aware.

Here is how. The Maxwell demon was imagined to be a tiny presence standing inside a system such as a room, at a door dividing the room into two halves. Half of the room was hot; the other half was cold.

We know that, according to the energy law, the total energy in the room must remain the same, even when hot molecules go through the door to the left and cold ones go to the hot side on the right (Figure 32.2). We know that energy transforms, eventually evening out the temperature of the whole box. Maxwell's entropy law says that the energy, although remaining basically the same, becomes more and more unavailable to do work. For example, before the evening out of temperature, the hot side could be used to move air to the cooler side. But after the overall temperature of both sides is equalized, the energy in both sides of the room is less available for moving anything around. The entropy of the system has increased.

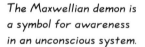

The Maxwellian demon is a symbol for awareness in an unconscious system.

32.2 Hot and cold molecules checked at the door by demon

But the entropy law would not hold if a little demon were present. Here is Clerk Maxwell's thought experiment. He imagined that the demon could use its awareness to open or close the door as it pleased. In an even-temperature system, where the temperature on both sides is equal, the tricky little demon might check every molecule that comes to the door and open it only when a warm molecule wants to go to the right and then quickly close it when a cold one wants to go to the right. Likewise, he could let the cooler molecules from the right go to the left. In this way, by using his attention and the door, he could take the even-temperature system and heat up one side, breaking every law of probability!

It would be like seeing a bowl of cool soup, for example, suddenly transform into a bowl that had frozen soup on one side and boiling soup on the other. In the physical world, such events are possible but rarely occur. I have never seen that happen to soup. However, if a Maxwellian demon existed, these things could happen all the time.

In the worlds of psychology, meditation, and shamanism, such things seem to occur more often. When you develop your sentient abilities, you become a Maxwellian demon who can enter situations where consciousness is missing. You can enter black holes and unknown areas of life and suddenly transform yourself. You can find energy where there was apparently none available. In this way, you can reverse the entropy law, the law of the heat death of the universe. Mediums, mystics, healers, and shamans do this all the time. There are many stories of how they can bring people back to life, create miracles, and create life where there was only unconsciousness and death.

Psychosomatic medicine and alternative medical procedures are based on sentient awareness practice. Just when you are about to give up on life, by going into the body, you can feel, sense, see, hear, and know what is happening, and therefore heal and create important changes in life. Awareness and the life process are connected.

In other words, the entropy law, the so-called second law of thermodynamics discovered by Maxwell, is based on a non-sentient universe. If the universe were aware of itself, as Maxwell speculated and as mediums, mystics, and shamans perceive, then the world would create the kind of order that reverses the second law of thermodynamics.

A PERSONAL EXPERIMENT: HUNTING FOR ENERGY

At this point, you may want to experiment with becoming a Maxwellian demon and finding energy. The following questions may help you find your own energy, your spirit. To do the exercise, you may want to find a quiet and relaxed position. Then try answering the following questions.

1. **What do you first notice when you awaken in the morning?** Do you see something, feel something, move in a certain direction, or hear something? Note the first channel you use upon awakening. Are you seeing, feeling, moving, or hearing? Just note this channel.

2. **Now choose another channel, one where your focus has not primarily been used in the morning.** If you were feeling, now turn to visualizations. If you see something first in the morning, try focusing on your body feelings. If you hear things in the morning, try using your body movement. The point is to use your attention and focus on a new and different channel for a few minutes. Any different channel will do.

Note and follow the experiences happening in that channel—see, hear, feel, or move—and give yourself time to let those experiences unfold in that channel. This is how to become a Maxwellian demon and use your second attention. This channel and these experiences are where your energy is.

3. **If you are able, you can now use other channels to complete your experience.** That is, see the experience, move it, feel it, and let it make sounds, talk to it, or let it speak.

4. **How does the experience you just had connect, if at all, with the peak experience you were working on in the previous chapters?**

5. **The experience you just had is where your energy has been.** Now this energy is available; it is potential and can be used and made kinetic. What would you like to do with it? Do you want to use it rapidly or slowly?

Think about how to use your energy. If you let this potential energy set things into action, if this potential energy becomes kinetic energy, what would it create for yourself or for your community or the world?

CIVILIZATIONS OF THE FUTURE

The study and use of energy are so important that many scientists and futurists measure civilizations of the future by how well they will use energy.[6] How we use energy within ourselves, on the Earth, from the sun, from our entire galaxy and universe, determines our fate. For example, the manner in which we use energy determines the future of eco-systems that sustain human life on earth. How we tap into energies of the universe may some day play a crucial role in whether or not the human race escapes the collapse of our solar system.

According to predictions of today's astronomers, in five billion years our sun will burn out. After that, our galaxy and the rest of the universe will condense and collapse. But if we learn more about how we dissipate and use energy, the future becomes unpredictable.

At present, we can say with certainty that the laws of physics are based on observers who are unconscious of the meaning or quality of events that are not part of consensus reality. The laws of physics assume that matter has no soul and is not alive, that observers have no second attention and no shamanic ability. However, what happens to the present laws of physics when human, sentient awareness becomes applied to physical events can be intuited by the story of Maxwell's demon.

Maxwell suspected that our hunt for lost energy and our ability to follow the spirit can create miracles, that is, events that reverse the entropy law, which says that energy becomes slowly lost to us forever. Most people sense the meaning of this law in personal life. When mundane reality no longer follows the irrational curves emanating from peak experiences, life is boring and dead. We lose track of energy, which reappears in dreams, symptoms, and synchronicities whose messages seem distant and obscure.

Until now, futurists focus only on consensual methods of tapping the physical energy in our universe and ignore the potential we have in using the second attention, the awareness which seeks out those special world lines, the life lines of meaning. All we know for sure is that energy transforms and, like the spirit, seems more or less constant. How energy transforms, and exactly what the future will bring for you as an individual and for your community, depends on everyone's transforming mundane, everyday life into a dreamlike, timeless and infinite path reaching back to the beginning of the universe and forward to the ends of time.

NOTES

1. Superstring theory, which we shall consider later, intends to increase the number of dimensions from 4 to 10. See Michio Kaku's *Hyperspace* for more.

2. Since the weight falls because of gravity, the force needed to lift it in the first place must have been equivalent to the force holding it down, that is, to its weight, which in physics is mg, where m is the mass of the weight and g is the acceleration of all material objects under the force of gravity.

3. Social rank is not the only form of rank. There are all sorts of potential ranks, including spiritual and psychological rank (see my *Sitting in the Fire* for more details on rank). The point is that rank is privilege.

4. One horsepower is 550 foot-pound force per second, or about 746 watts.

5. In relativity, kinetic energy must be changed from its Newtonian form, so that now, KE = $([m - m_o]v^2/2)$ where m_o is the rest mass.

6. Kaku's discussion of the future of civilizations in terms of the use of energy is down to earth and easy to understand; see the last chapters of his *Hyperspace*.

33 | Atomic Energy and Virtual Particles

By building up the spiritual body through meditation exercises, the Chinese attempted in this life to disengage the energies attached to one's ordinary body and thus to endow... the self—with a new body... In this way a field of force forms around one's psychic core.... This ego with its subtle body is no longer bound to the physical body which (according to Richard Wilhelm)... is Tao, the meaning which uniformly permeates all existence and becoming.

—M. L. von Franz in *Number and Time*

We have seen that Leibniz thought matter had a soul and energy of its own. Three hundred years after Leibniz, Einstein discovered the same idea in his special theory of relativity. According to the special theory, the energy of a piece of matter whose mass (m) is traveling at a certain velocity (v) is no longer simply $mv^2/2$, as it was in classical physics. Energy became more complex; it involved an additional factor, which had been hidden to physicists before Einstein. The total energy of a moving object was now $mv^2/2 + mc^2$. This new additional factor, mc^2, was due to the incorporation of various viewpoints, the frameworks of the observer and of the event itself.[1] For the special case of a non-moving framework (relative to the observer) in which an object of mass, m, is not moving at all, the energy of the still mass contains a sort of locked up or secret energy:

$$E = mc^2$$

Energy equals mass times the speed of light squared

where c is the speed of light. Before this formulation, the energy of an object was considered to be the sum of its potential energy, *PE*, and its kinetic energy, *KE*. If there was no potential and no kinetic energy, the object was at rest and had no energy:

$$E = PE + KE = 0$$

Einstein's new formula said that, even when there is no potential energy—for example, as a result of being in a gravity field; and even when there is no kinetic energy—because the object is not moving relative to a given observer, there is still energy latent in every piece of matter:

$$E = PE + KE + mc^2 = mc^2$$

In fact, even a little particle of matter, like an atom that is at rest and not in a gravity field, has a lot of energy locked up in its little mass. The amount of energy is large because when the mass is multiplied by the velocity of light squared, the velocity of light is so large—186,000 miles per second—that when you square that velocity, E gets enormous.

The equation $E = mc^2$ symbolizes the idea that mass and energy are essentially expressions of the *same* essence. In relativity theory, we already learned that time and space are inseparable, that is, they are of the same essence. Now, we learn that matter and energy are also inseparable. We could say that energy is locked up in matter. There is energy in mass. We can also say the opposite: there is potential mass in energy. What we call mass from one viewpoint is energy from another viewpoint. In this chapter, we will be exploring how Einstein's equation gives us permission to imagine the creation of virtual particles because energy can have material forms.

Physicists were surprised by the energy formula because, from the viewpoint of consensus reality since Leibniz, mass had been associated with inert, dead, passive objects. In contrast, energy has always had an intrinsically dynamic character. With the advent of Einstein's special theory of relativity, mass is energy. Suddenly, mass has Leibniz's living force; it seems to be coming back to life! The CR ideas of mass and energy are no longer binding. In CR, these concepts are separable. But in our feelings they are combined and intertwined. For example, in the United States, "heavy" is a slang expression for something really exciting and awesome. The reason for this is that we experience something important and exciting as weighty, or massive. Likewise, something very heavy, like a huge stone, might be called intense. In our NCR experiences the concepts of mass and energy, heavy and intense, are one.

In physics, Einstein's equation implies that loss of energy means loss of mass. Consider something familiar, such as a flashlight. If you use the energy of its batteries by turning on your flashlight, the flashlight's battery energy will be reduced and the amount of mass in that battery will be diminished as well, if ever so slightly. By how much? If E is the energy you used from the batteries in your light, the amount the mass decreased is $m = E/c^2$. Because c is so large, the amount of mass lost is very small.

That is why you never notice the change of mass, m. Nevertheless, as you use your flashlight, it loses weight!

THE ATOMIC BOMB

A more dramatic example of the conversion of mass into energy is an atomic bomb where the mass that is lost transforms into energy. The amount of energy produced from the loss of a tiny bit of mass can be very big because in the formula $E = mc^2$, the speed of light, c, is such a big number.

Relativity made physics extremely heavy, intense, and political: it gave scientists in the Second World War the concept of the atomic bomb. When the Germans first began to develop the atomic bomb, the frightened American scientists rushed forward to develop it first. The rest is not just history, but present-day politics as well. Today, almost any nation can create an atomic bomb and control the world. Atomic energy can create electric power and also destroy human life. Let's begin now to study this energy.

Here is how to calculate and tap the energy tied up in matter. Let's say that the Greek letter delta, Δ, means a change in the amount of something. According to Einstein, a change in mass means a change in energy according to the following:

$$\Delta E = \Delta m \times c^2$$

This equation shows that it takes a little mass to make a lot of energy. The same equation can be read in reverse to show that it takes a huge amount of energy, ΔE, to produce even a little bit of matter. We don't use energy to create matter today because we do not have enough energy at our disposal; it is too expensive for us at this point. But this equation shows that we could, if we had access to great amounts of energy, eventually produce matter, maybe even whole planets!

The formula $\Delta E = \Delta m \times c^2$ is the essence of the atomic bomb. To make an atomic bomb, or to release atomic energy with all its associated problems, you take a heavy atom like uranium and break it down into parts. If you bang the uranium atom with another particle, uranium breaks down into a bunch of smaller particles. However, the way in which it breaks into parts is special. It does not just break up, but also radiates and therefore loses energy in the form of radiation. The chemical equation for the breakdown of uranium is

$$Uranium = 3\ ATOMSmass + E\ (heat + radiation)$$
$$+\ 2\ neutrons$$

which means that the mass of uranium (URANIUMmass) transforms into three smaller atoms (3ATOMSmass), plus E (the energy of heat and radiation) and two *neutrons*, (2 neutrons), which fly· away. If there are other uranium atoms around, the neutrons that were let loose from the first uranium atom bang into the other uranium atoms and we have a chain reaction: one bombardment sets off others, just as one firecracker can ignite others if they are nearby. In this way, one uranium atom gives rise to other atoms, particles, and radiation. And bombarding one uranium atom with a neutron sets loose other neutrons, and a chain reaction occurs. That's what makes an atomic bomb.

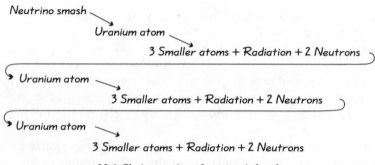

33.1 *Chain reaction of an atomic bomb*

The key to the amount of energy released in each reaction lies in the fact that the total amount of mass of the two little neutrons plus the three smaller atoms doesn't quite add up to the total mass of the original uranium atom. In other words, the mass of uranium is greater than the three smaller atoms and the two neutrons. Mass is lost during this bombardment.

The lost mass breaks out in terms of a huge amount of heat and a horrendous amount of radiation. One atom ignites the others and you've got one of the most creative, dynamic, and deadly processes in the universe.

You may wonder how a few bumps among little invisible things can make such big energy changes. If you bang wood, you only get a dent, or if you burn wood, you get a little heat and a lot of charcoal.

The answer is that the bangs to wood affect only the way in which molecules are put together in the wood, not the structure of the atoms that make up the molecules. Remember, molecules are bunches of atoms held together by their electrical attractions. The bang on the wood affects the way these molecules hold together. The bang adds energy to their arrangement, but this just heats the wood a little, or readjusts the arrangement in the form of a dent.

In contrast to chemical reactions, where matter is transformed into other material forms without losing mass, actual mass is lost during the breakdown of atoms like uranium. Chemical reactions change the arrangement of the atoms in molecules, but atomic reactions, in blasting the atoms to pieces, can lose mass.

To sum up in terms of physics, Einstein said that space-time and matter are interconnected, space and time can no longer be divorced, and that mass and energy are of the same essence as well.

PSYCHOLOGICAL ANALOGIES TO $E = MC^2$

We have all experienced "chemical" and "atomic" reactions in psychology as well. If you have a friendship with someone, you have a sort of chemical combination. You have a minus filled by their plus, and they have a few minuses that your pluses complete. If you hit that relationship with a hammer, if you pull and push on your relationship, you get lots of trouble. Lots of heat and rearrangement are possible. That is the nature of a chemical attraction.

But if you or your friend dies or "goes psychotic," if a severe trauma occurs and you or your friend is deeply injured, the very essence of one of you is shattered. It is as if something material is lost and transformed into energy that gets dissociated from you. The energy or spirit flies off into violent memories, bloody nightmares, life-threatening symptoms, or worse. That is like an atomic bomb. At any point in life, you are like a uranium atom. If something small touches you in the wrong way, you flip, and you create a powerful chain reaction around you, as anyone who has dealt with psychosis or trauma knows. Under these circumstances, a tiny bump can create a horrendous chain reaction.

HOW FIELDS BECOME PARTICLES

We are studying the ideas of physics and psychology to the point where I can explain how material particles could be created from energy. You probably remember the atomic energy equation $E = mc^2$. To build on that as we learn how energy could create matter, our next step is to explore the meaning of physical fields such as those created by electricity.

Earlier we looked at electric fields. We saw how they were connected with magnetism, but we did not really explore what a field is. One reason for this is that no one knows exactly what an electric field is. As physics unfolds, concepts such as fields also develop. You know that electric fields can be created by electric charges, which are carried by particles such as electrons or positrons. Atoms have electric charges; that is one of the ways they attract one another to form molecules. The electric fields around atoms attract particles and other atoms. The fields around atoms explain much of molecular chemistry: it's the old story of attracting and repelling one another.

Fields are fascinating but very abstract. How exactly do they work? How do things attract and repel other things at a distance? Is this magic? Even space-time fields are weird. How on earth does the curvature of space-time produce gravity fields? Many physicists were not as Taoistic or field-oriented as Einstein, and wanted to know more about the mechanics of fields. In fact, many quantum physicists who were contemporaries of Einstein (and more recent ones as well) were never totally satisfied with the idea that space-time curvature was equivalent to gravity. Matter and gravity could theoretically be replaced by curved space-time, but what does this mean? Useful and important as the concept of space-time was in explaining the nature of matter, the space-time field seems mystical and too mathematical for some physicists, who wanted to know more about how fields could manifest physical properties.

Many scientists felt that the concept of imaginary particles would be closer to everyday reality. Even if such imaginary particles could not be seen, the particle seemed closer to many people than fields. Thus began the incredible story of "virtual particles," a domain of physics where relativity theory and quantum mechanics merge.

Some of the information about virtual particles is best understood as a story. If you think of the following as a story, you might be able to accept and follow it. Otherwise, your rational mind is going to argue about it. In the following chapters, I promise to give more rational reasons for the story, but here, I will only try to make it sound reasonable.[2]

Since the 1700s, people have thought that matter had different physical fields around it—electric fields, magnetic fields, and gravitational fields. Material fields could be described in terms of math; thus they had clear definitions. But no one knew exactly what these fields really were, or how they worked in terms of mechanical analogies. How do they manage to exert forces on objects? How can a magnet influence an iron filing at a distance? Was this magic?

Einstein said that the spaces of the universe, the dimensions of space-time, were substance-like because the curvature of space-time was equivalent to the concept of gravity. He connected the ideas of matter and field. This made physicists suspect that even more tangible things, such as particles, might also be expressions of fields.

We know that an electron or a proton or any kind of charged particle has a charged electric field around it. This field radiates outward and affects other particles, even at a distance. Physicists can check on the strength of the field by finding out how much force they need to push two electrons together. When two electrons get too close, they repel one another because of the electric field between them. But what actually happens there? Here is how people answered that question.

The physicists who resisted the idea that the electric field was responsible for this repulsion said, let's explain that field in terms of mechanical particles—tiny bits of matter. These physicists did not like the idea of a field creating repulsion, having magical effects at a distance. In their minds, things repelled other things if there was a bump, not a buzz!

The connection between fields and particles is not unfamiliar to us. You probably remember the connection between fields and numbers from our earlier discussion. First, we assumed there was something like an undifferentiated field, which we called "process." We called the process that cannot be described "the Tao which cannot be said." Since the Tao which cannot be said is a field idea, difficult to imagine, it has a tendency to unfold itself in terms of things we can think about and relate to one another. To describe this Tao or process, numbers appeared. The Tao unfolded in terms of 1, 2, and 3. Numbers are parts, or particles, quantities describing the field. However, there was a lot of uncertainty around numbers because their use tends to marginalize NCR experiences. Numbers, like particles, are definitive and create a consensus reality that can be shared.

Today's physicists are engaged in a similar quandary. To describe fields, they decided to stick with the CR concept of particles, even though this concept was already made uncertain—or even invalidated—because of the measurement uncertainties in quantum theory. Nevertheless, despite the vagueness of the particle concept, physicists decided to use one unknown—the particle—to describe another unknown—a force field.

My teachers approached the attempt to explain fields in terms of particles by starting with a question: "What does explanation itself mean? How can we explain an unknown field with another unknown, an invisible particle? What does the term 'explain' mean?"

There are many different opinions on what it means to explain something. One idea is that, "Explaining means giving a description of fields in terms of experience." Another idea is that, "To explain means relating to the questioner in terms of their primary process, their consensus reality, their personal identity." A third idea is: "Explaining means using a concept that is consistent with the rest of one's experience." Many of my students agree with this third idea, saying that most people's personal experience and identity are based on having causes for things.

We can see that what explains something to one person may not explain it to another person. So far, physics has gotten away with using mainly consensus reality concepts that mean something to most people, concepts such as particle, energy, work, time, space, matter, and number. An exact exploration of these terms shows that they are not very precise; they are all interconnected and more process-oriented than fixed and separable. Still, to keep things understandable, physics has continued to use this language.

Apparently, a generally accepted explanation is one that describes events in consensus reality terms. For example, if people all agree to speak about experiences in terms of brain chemistry and dreams, I need to speak that language to understand them and to explain new things to them. I don't know what brain chemistry or dreams are about, but that does not matter as much as the fact that these experiences have meaning for some.

Collectively accepted explanations deal with consensus reality terms and concepts. At present, using extraterrestrial beings or aliens to explain what happens in our minds would not be an accepted explanation to mainstream scientists, while brain chemistry would be.

The same is true in physics. As we begin a new century, causality and particles are still more acceptable terms than fields and action at a distance. Thus, even though they don't exist, particles "explain" things to people. The concept of a particle allows us to relate to an event, and even to develop useful theories that can be tested and later used to develop technology. In another century, ghosts may play a more consensual role than particles. Then, we will speak of ghosts, or of whatever else is acceptable in consensual reality.

Preferred explanations today contain causal elements. For instance, one imaginary particle bumps into another visible particle, causing it to move. Explanations in physics must not only be formulated in collectively acceptable terms; they are also constrained by experimental results. The only acceptable explanations have something testable about them.

In the case of "virtual" particles, you can't really measure them, but you can measure other things related to the virtual particle concept. If the virtual particle concept is to be acceptable in physics, it must fit with known laws and patterns such as relativity and quantum mechanics, that is, Einstein's "energy = mass × speed of light squared" law and the uncertainty principle in quantum mechanics. In summary, an acceptable explanation in physics uses CR terms, has elements that can be tested, and fits into other known laws of physics.

QUANTUM ELECTRODYNAMICS

Physicists decided to explain fields in terms of particles because the particle explanation was acceptable in physics. Physicists explain fields with quantum electrodynamics, or QED, one of the most useful and generally accepted theories in physics. Quantum electrodynamics is a combination of quantum mechanics, relativity, and electric field theory. It explains that two charged particles, like two electrons, repel one another not because of an electric "field" between them, but because "virtual" particles are emitted from each electron and these virtual particles repel each other.

Thanks largely to Richard Feynman's work, QED beautifully explains how chemistry works, how electrons exchange virtual particles called photons. The theory is not perfect, but it is still the best in many ways.

Physics will eventually develop new ideas beyond QED (such as super-string theory), but these new theories have a long way to go before they can tell us as much about the world as QED.

The story of the development of virtual particles as imaginary expla-nations of fields is very exciting. Let's take two positively charged parti-cles of any kind, negatively charged electrons or positively charged protons. The imagined answer to why these two protons repel each other and stay apart is because virtual particles are created out of nothing. Vir-tual particles are imagined to leave one of the protons and bump into the others. On the left in Figure 33.2, we see repulsion "explained" by an elec-tric field that is replaced, on the right in the diagram, by bumps from vir-tual particles.

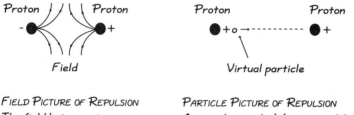

FIELD PICTURE OF REPULSION
The field between two
protons exerts a force
of repulsion.

PARTICLE PICTURE OF REPULSION
A virtual particle. 'o.' is emitted from
one proton and bangs into the other.
thereby creating the force of repulsion.

33.2 Field and particle explanation of electric fields

Charged particles in the diagram on the right have virtual particles in them, and these virtual particles bang into other charged particles, thereby causing repulsion. But where do these virtual particles come from?

In the particle picture of matter, ordinary matter like a proton is imag-ined to "contain" a bunch of virtual particles like little particles of light, which come and go from the main particle. In this picture of things, vir-tual particles such as momentarily existing photons of light, come out of a larger charged particle like the proton and get reabsorbed by it before they can be seen, measured, or weighed.

The situation of a charged particle is similar to that of a person like you or me thinking to himself, walking down the street. A comic strip picture of my situation might portray a person who has a lot of ideas and stuff coming out of and going back into his head as he walks along.

Physicists see a charged particle like such a head out of which a lot of stuff emerges and is reabsorbed. Their imagination suggests that, when two charged particles get close, the virtual particles of each don't give off charges but rather bump and bang into the other charged particle, thereby repelling it. That's the answer from quantum electrodynamics about how positive or negative charges repel one another.

Actually, quantum electrodynamics is even wilder than I have said. According to QED, the exchange particles (as virtual particles are often called) can go forward and backward in time. We can't tell which protron first popped its virtual particle to bump the other proton. We only know that in the quantum world, there are uncertainties about time and space and measurement. However, we need not even worry about measuring virtual particles, because we can't; they exist for too short a time.

How can physicists get away with such wild speculation? The explanations of QED start to sound almost psychological, because psychologists also invent imaginary dream figures to explain human behavior. You may wonder, how on earth are such psychological or physical theories allowed? The idea of virtual particles that bump into real ones is allowed because the virtual particles cannot be measured.

Virtual particles move so fast that they are protected by the uncertainty principle. They cannot be measured or seen. Real particles also cannot be seen directly. Remember quantum theory? You only see particles like electrons when they make clicks on electron counters on a screen they hit. You can also track particles in a cloud chamber by seeing the streaks they leave behind. The results of particles can be seen, but the particles themselves cannot be viewed directly.

We will never be able to hear clicks or find tracks of virtual particles, yet they are believed to exist. Why? There are several reasons. First, because, as we will see in the next chapters, they obey the laws of physics. Second, because people like the particle concept. And, third, because *the story of virtual particles is a useful thinking aid to explain the behavior of measurable, technological effects* (such as X-rays, as we will see in Chapter 34). Virtual particles give comprehensible explanations for things that can be measured.

Virtual particles are an interesting possible bridge between physical and non-physical realms. With the virtual particle concept, physicists are using their NCR imagination to explain CR phenomena. They are using one magical explanation, "virtual particles," to explain another, namely, fields. Particles are a magical explanation that depends on a worldview that believes everything is reducible to a thing—this invisible little thing creates that effect.

Virtual particles are very much based on the billiard ball model of life. Nobody has ever taken a photograph of an electron, although you can, at least, track an electron in a cloud chamber. Yet people believe that virtual photons or light particles come out of electrons, even though virtual photons cannot be tracked. We could say that this whole story or rather, theory, of subatomic physics is just a projection.

Quantum electrodynamics theory is one of the places where psychology and physics intersect. We need to project from non-consensus realities to understand our consensual world. Nature follows most of our projections because reality emerges from NCR dreaming. But, since several projections can describe the same phenomena such as fields and virtual particles, the projection or theory that is best is the one that explains the most. Projections become acceptable only as long as they fit the other rules of physics and the behavior of matter we can see, as well as the current views of consensus reality. In other words, as this consensus reality changes, our views of nature and matter will change as well.

Remember, if you don't like the concept of virtual particles, you can always come up with a better idea. You never have to understand or agree with anything in physics. If you can think of something better, just rebel against what has been taught until now, and prove your ideas. Nothing in physics is final. If something in you refuses to understand something in physics, it may be that everybody else is wrong and something is missing.

In any case, at the present time, the picture of virtual reality that goes along with consensus reality measurements of cloud chambers, X-rays, and other things, and which obeys the laws of physics, is as follows:

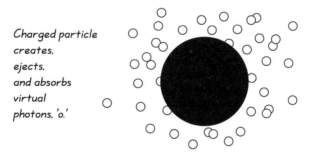

Charged particle creates, ejects, and absorbs virtual photons, 'o.'

33.3 QED picture of a charged particle

A charged particle is considered to be surrounded by a bunch of virtual particles, which make a sort of fuzz of photons. This charged particle is imagined to eject and re-absorb these photons which cannot be measured.

The story goes that these particles come from nowhere, or rather, that they come from fluctuations in energy. They are acceptable ghosts, protected by the laws of physics. According to the energy laws, if a charged particle is excited enough, a virtual photon gets so much energy that it radiates and actually leaves the charged particle. When a virtual photon gets enough juice, it leaves, which means that you can see it in the form of light! Fluctuations in energy create virtual particles, but only if they are given more energy do they turn into visible light.

VIRTUAL PARTS AND PARTICLES IN PSYCHOLOGY

It is important at this point to remember that we do a lot of things that we can't see. Psychology, like physics, is full of virtual things, parts and particles. Most psychologies speak about virtual parts such as the shadow, the animus, the inner child, channels, and energy, although no one has ever seen these things. They become real for us because, like all explanations, they help some people understand what is happening.

Virtual psychological parts are great as long as you don't believe that they are permanent and real. You can use any NCR concepts you like— gods, goddesses, self, individuation, and ego—as long as they are useful in explaining CR (real) things, such as behavior, which you can speak about. All virtual parts are complementary descriptions to field theories, like Taoism and process. Taoism, for example, is a unified theory without parts. It is a field theory out of which parts emerge, much as electromagnetic theory "produces" virtual particles, so to speak.

I love fields, but parts are fun as well. For example, the idea that there is something called an unconscious around, within, or between us made me crazy for years. It sounded like the mysterious ether people used to believe in before the discovery of relativity. I could not see the unconscious. Was it static or moving? What should I look for? Dream images? Well, they are OK. But they are not everything.

In my quandary around the unconscious, I came up with another particle theory. I call all the particles signals. Some gestures have meanings that you intend to transmit to others. These intentional signals are like the charged particles in physics. In a sense, the signals are fundamental bits we use in communication. If you get really precise, you will have trouble finding out when and where signals begin or end, but from a consensus reality viewpoint, they exist just like particles.

Other gestures are "double signals." These are sort of fuzzy, unclear, and circulate around the intended signals. We usually do not intend to send double signals and rarely notice their occurrence unless we are trained. Double signals are like virtual particles.

For example, if I am lecturing in a class, I am writing on the board and talking with students. My words and tone of voice are signals that I identify with. But at the same time, I may keep looking up while I am speaking. That is a double signal. I will have to stop speaking, be quiet for a moment, and study myself to find that I am actually looking at the clock because I do not want to rush. Yet, I also realize that I need to rush because I have to finish in a few minutes. My rush—my looking up—was a fuzzy, double signal. I was sort of flirting with the clock, or was the clock flirting with me? Who was sending which virtual double signal first?

In any case, an intentional signal is like a particle leaving tracks that you can see on videotape. A double signal is like a virtual particle, fuzz—like my looking up—which you can't quite see or comprehend. Only if you heat up that signal with awareness—like you heat up a charged particle with energy—does the virtual nature of my double signal become clear. Only if I study my double and unintended signal of looking up does it become like a normal signal. Then I know that it means my time is up.

Usually, you can't quite see the double signal. It is similar to the mermaid Melusina. If you don't approach her with love, she goes away and has no measurable mass or content! There will never be a consensus on the significance of double signals unless they are heated up, that is, cooked and unfolded. Double signals are only potentially meaningful; they are like exchange particles in quantum electrodynamics. My double signals bump into your normal signals, and vice versa, yours bump into mine—they flirt with one another. That is how we attract and repel one another. Double signals behave like virtual particles.

Double signals and virtual particles are great ideas when we want to explain how we interact with one another at a distance. You can say that we send out auras and fields, or that we emit double signals and virtual particles. Both field and particle theories are interesting, although neither is absolutely real. The point is that your mind is desperate to explain to itself the nature of the mysterious fields between objects and people.

As soon as we find an explanation, we need to remember that it is an explanation for something that may never be fully explainable. Furthermore, in the future this mysterious something may yet receive newer and better explanations. Nothing is real in an absolute sense; concepts are helpful aids in comprehending and sharing ideas about nature. Virtual particles are something physics made up to explain attraction and repulsion in a field. This amounts to an NCR explanation—something totally imagined—to explain where reality came from. In other words, physics can no longer exist without dreaming.

NOTES

1. Because the speed of motion depends on the observer, velocity is no longer absolute but is subject to the Lorentz transformation connecting space and time.

    The energy of a point of mass in relativity now must be represented by

    $$mc^2 / \sqrt{1 - v^2/c^2}$$

    which at low velocities can be approximated by $mc^2 = mv^2/2$. See Einstein's *Relativity*, page 49 and following, for a "relatively" simple derivation of this formula. He shows that the total energy of a piece of matter traveling at low velocities, v, can be written as $E = mc^2 + mv^2/2$. Notice the additional energy of matter, mc^2, which is due to relativity. The famous formula results, $E = mc^2$, when the energy of matter is measured from a framework that is moving with the piece of matter, since from this perspective v is zero. In other words, $E = mc^2$ is the energy latent in a piece of matter at rest within its own system.

2. I am especially thankful to Amy Mindell for all-night talks on this subject.

34 | Creation Out of Nothing

I am optimistic that over the next few decades there will be a great change in our world view both from the material and the spiritual perspectives.

—Fourteenth Dalai Lama

Physicists will look very seriously at any idea, such as the concept of virtual particles, which is consistent with other theories in physics and fits experimental results. In this chapter, we will explore what the term "consistent" means and how virtual particles are consistent with the principles of quantum physics and relativity, that is, how they fit into the principles of the conservation of energy, uncertainty, and energy-mass. More important, we will ponder just how science generates new theories. We will see just why one theory about existence wins approval over other theories.

Here are the main principles that virtual particles—or any new theory in physics and psychology or shamanism—must obey.

Energy Conservation. In physics, the total amount of energy (or according to relativity, mass-energy) in a closed system remains constant.

Uncertainty. According to energy conservation, the energy of a system must remain the same over time. However, from the uncertainty principles of quantum mechanics we discovered that all measurable quantities—such as energy—wobble a bit, that is, they can briefly vary in time. No measurement can be absolutely accurate or certain, since the measurement disturbs the system or object being measured.

Relativity. You probably remember that Einstein discovered that energy and mass are related through the equation, $E = mc^2$ (for measurements made of systems at rest in their own frameworks). Thus we must think that a change in energy gives rise to a change in mass, or that a little change in energy gives rise to a small amount of mass such as a particle.

I will explain these general principles with a more or less mechanical analogy. Let's pretend we have a sandbox with about one million grains of sand in it. Let's pretend further that these grains represent the energy of the box. Each grain represents a little energy. The amount of sand is more or less constant because sand cannot get out of the box, and nothing else can get in.

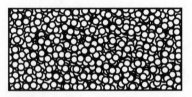

34.1 Box with 1,000,000 grains of sand represents a bit of energy.

Because of the uncertainty principle, even though nothing can enter or leave the box, we still have small deviations in energy, that is, a little uncertainty about the total number of grains of sand in the box. Whatever we do, being human, we cannot measure each particle of sand with certainty. Thus, if E is the total amount of energy or sand, then E is more or less constant because of the energy conservation law.

Let's think about uncertainty. Say you have a good pair of tweezers to count the approximately one million grains of sand in the box. If you are crazy enough to count every one of those grains, and you start tweezing away, one day you will measure 1,000,001 grains of sand. But the next day you will measure only 999,999 grains. There is uncertainty in your measurement of energy.

Again, let's pretend that the Greek letter delta, Δ, means a "little bit of something." Let's call ΔE a little bit of energy, say, the deviations in the counting; in this case ΔE is one or two grains. Small deviations ΔE in the total number of grains are bound to occur simply because there are hundreds of thousands of grains of sand and counting each one is difficult. Furthermore, some grains may be almost too small to count because they are like powder. How do you decide what is a grain and what is powder? Thus the very best measurement of the number of grains of sand in that box, the energy of the box, is always a little uncertain. Let's calls this uncertainty ΔE.[1]

Now let's think about what role time plays in our uncertainty. If there were no rush, if you had all the time in the world, your uncertainty would be less. If you are rushed, ΔE will be greater. That is, for a small amount of time, Δt, ΔE will be greater. If you have large amounts of time, the uncertainty in the grains of sand is less, so ΔE is less.

Now we can make a simple description of the uncertainty principle of quantum mechanics (for more information see Chapters 15 and 16). The Heisenberg uncertainty principle says that the uncertainty in energy multiplied by the amount of time used for an experiment must be the same as or less than a very tiny number called Planck's constant, symbolized by h.[2] Thus: $\Delta t \times \Delta E \geq h$

This means that if the time is short, energy uncertainty will be large. To reduce the amount of uncertainty in energy ΔE, that is, to make ΔE smaller, we simply take more time with the measurement.

How can quantum physicists say that there is a little deviation or uncertainty in energy? After all, according to the principle of conservation of energy, the energy of an enclosed system must be a constant. Is this not in conflict with the uncertainty principle, which says the energy can deviate?

Uncertainty is not actually in conflict with the conservation of energy because, although the number of grains must remain about the same, since E is constant, slight deviations in energy can occur because of the uncertainty principle, that is, *because we cannot check those little deviations.* The uncertainty principle says uncertainty is part of consensus reality: we can never know *exactly* how large or small something is.

The seeming contradiction between the idea that energy is basically constant and the idea that energy is uncertain for brief periods of time can be seen in our own lives as well. Take relationships. We make relationships that seem more or less constant, but then we break them for split seconds—or longer—through little quantum flirts. Both methods of relating are "principles" of human nature; one principle says, conserve the energy in your relationship, don't break it, while the other says that you can break the constancy of relationship through a quick flirt, through dreaming, because no one can prove that you did it. Both principles about relationships are simultaneous. Short deviations are allowable in nature. Long deviations break laws.

The same holds true in physics. The law of conservation of energy says, hold things basically steady, but then the uncertainty principle allows for a quick deviation that cannot be measured. For a split second, we can have a little break in energy conservation.

What you can't see in a trillionth of a second is allowed. Nature allows two seemingly opposite laws to work at the same time, as long as one has a time limit for its occurrence. The uncertainty principle does not overrule the energy conservation law—except for immeasurably short periods of time. The energy conservation law holds only over time, not for every split second, because energy cannot be measured in that split second.

Now let's return to relativity. Deviations in energy are allowed by the uncertainty principle, but according to the energy-mass law of relativity,

$E = mc^2$. This equation says that a deviation in energy means a deviation in mass. Here is where relativity and quantum mechanics overlap.

The energy-mass relationship says that the energy of mass at rest is given by $E = mc^2$. If we can get away with a little deviation in energy, then we can get away with a little deviation in mass, which can be calculated from the equation $\Delta m = \Delta E / c^2$, where Δm is the uncertainty in the measurement of the mass.

Now comes the big moment. Hold your breath. For short periods of time, if we are allowed to have small deviations in mass, we can have virtual particles created out of deviations in energy. This amounts to creating virtual particles out of nothing. Since we cannot measure the energy accurately, we can have little deviations in mass, or little particles appearing and disappearing, since no one can measure them. The uncertainty principle says you cannot measure them. If you cannot measure them, then they are "virtual," that is, they are implicit, and they are not really there.

Virtual particles are consistent with the rule of conservation of energy, with the energy-mass relationship in relativity, and with the uncertainty principle in quantum mechanics. According to the rules of physics, virtual particles are okay to think about. Although you can't see or measure them, you can consider them. Virtual particles are something like science fiction BB pellets created from the uncertainty in energy. Particles are CR concepts used in an NCR sense. Since everything has immeasurable fluctuations in energy, everything has immeasurable fluctuation in mass as long as the deviations are there only briefly. During brief time lapses, no one can check on whether this little piece of matter was really there or not. Our measuring instruments will never be that good! Thus we allow ourselves to consider the idea of virtual particles. They live in a sort of green zone, a protected zone that cannot be measured.

At this point in my lectures, an intense debate often breaks out in the classroom. Some students argue that you cannot create something out of nothing. Others say it is possible because nobody can measure the creation. Someone once said you might as well think that some goddess or god put her hand into that box of sand or energy and created virtual particles; others say it is the goddess Nun that made one charged particle flirt with another for a split second. Usually, everyone agrees that quantum flirts are protected by the basic principles of psychology and physics—for short deviations.

We have seen that we can invent whatever theories we like about fields and particles, as long as our thoughts are consistent with the rules of physics, which means they must obey the following:

I. **Energy Conservation:** Over time, the total energy must be constant, that is, E = constant.

II. **Energy-Mass Conversion:** Energy can appear as mass because $E = mc^2$.

III. **Uncertainty Principle:** Energy can briefly deviate, that is, $\Delta E \times \Delta t \geq h$.

In other words, we can disobey consensus reality laws if it is done so quickly that we are not detected.

In any case, because virtual particles are consistent with other laws, physicists allowed themselves the outrageous thought that particles that cannot be measured could be present for a split second. They allowed themselves to think that the energy fields surrounding larger, charged particles like electrons and protrons had quick deviations which amount to virtual particles coming from fluctuations in those fields. Hence, the concept of energy fields was replaced by the concept of virtual particles bumping into one another and into the larger particles, the electrons and protrons.

THE UNWRITTEN LAW OF CONSENSUS REALITY

If you really think about it, you might ask, "If something imaginary can happen, why call it a particle? Why not call it a phantom or a ghost?" In one hundred years, will physicists still explain fields in terms of particles? No one can tell. But one thing is certain. The term "particle" is used today because it has the consensus of many people. The term "ghost" does not currently get a consensus from the scientific community.

In other words, consensus reality plays an important role in formulating science. In fact, we had better put this last sentence in with our other three laws. The fourth, unwritten law in physics is that theories must find approval to be accepted. Theories must use concepts shared by the scientific community. We have a fourth principle that the virtual particles have to obey.

I.   **Energy Conservation:** Over time, energy is constant.

II. **Energy-Mass Conversion:** Energy can appear as mass
       (because $E = mc^2$).

III. **Uncertainty Principle:** $\Delta E \times \Delta t$ must be equal to or greater than h.

IV. **Community Principle:** Theories must use consensus reality
       concepts.

34.2 The rules governing accepted belief systems

Physics says that virtual particles, or any other concept that fits these laws, must be considered. Rule IV is special. It implies that if consensus reality changes in the direction of the belief in ghosts, then over short periods of time, ghosts will come and go, just as today virtual particles can appear and disappear. If you think logically, it almost seems that the concept of ghosts is better than the concept of particles because no one can see virtual particles. But the idea of ghosts does not fit Rule IV.

Theories are connected with collective trends. Some scientists who have not thought about this before might contend that theories are not bound by collective limitations. Nevertheless, we are pressed to a seemingly unavoidable conclusion. Collective belief systems are integral parts of theories. The fourth principle is one of the reasons that physicists still retain ideas such as space, time, and particle, even though the vagueness of these concepts might have made us drop them in the 1920s, after relativity and quantum mechanics were developed.

Today, personal, subjective experiences are considered non-consensual. They are not yet acceptable according to Law IV. Scientific consensus does not favor ghosts. However, if interest in altered states of consciousness increases, if the ability to use second attention becomes part of our education, the physics of the future will be formulated very differently.

VIRTUAL PARTICLES AND INNER WORK

The concept of the particle has evolved over time. The concept of a firmly contained particle of matter from four hundred years ago became the concept of a wavelike packet in quantum mechanics in the early part of the twentieth century. Now, in the newest mixture of relativity and quantum mechanics, the "particle" becomes an elementary "thing" with a bunch of fuzzy virtual things coming out of it, interacting with its neighbors. Virtual particles are relational; they are exchange particles, making connections with themselves and their neighbors.

The images of particles and of people change as consensual views of reality change. For example, in Newtonian physics, a person was seen as a machine composed of parts and particles in a clockwork universe. Around 1905, at about the same time as the special theory of relativity and the beginnings of quantum mechanics, Freud imagined that the person had a mysterious subconscious. Then came Jung's unconscious, which contained even more than the subconscious. Alfred Adler stressed the power drive, Gestalt introduced the foreground and background and made everything present in the here and now, and so forth.

In the century now passing, depth psychologists understood people as more or less independent of other people. Now, at the beginning of a new century, the person is on the verge of finding herself in relationship not only with herself but also with her neighbors and the universe. Family therapy has suggested this for years, but individual therapy has focused mainly on the individual, just as quantum mechanics focused mainly on the individual particle even though relativity has long insisted that each particle is part of a universal field. Over the next twenty years, clinical psychology is likely to be renewed by an overarching relationship ethos that integrates personal psychology with relationship and group processes.

The present view of particles in physics reminds me of the present view in psychology of how people interact with themselves. Many psychologists working with individuals see the person as a particle called a personality with fuzz around it. The image is like a comic book figure whose head is surrounded by stuff that is being constantly emitted and reabsorbed. There is a collective consensus in psychological circles about this image of the person as having a head with imaginary beings—called the shadow, the self, the parent, child, and so on—running around, coming into and going out from the head.

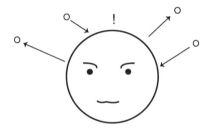

34.3 The human being as a head with signals coming and going

Relationship theory in process-oriented psychology sees these beings as the origin of signals, unconscious signals that are radiated outward into the world and absorbed from people around us. In double signal theory, these virtual processes are relational; they attract and repel us from one another, make us irresistibly attractive or repulsive. Most of the time, people do not use their second attention to make much out of the buzz from the head.

Do people really have ghosts and dream figures coming out of their heads in the form of signals? The answer depends on the governing consensus reality as well as the experimental facts. If you believe in non-consensus experiences, the fuzz is real, otherwise, the fuzz is a form of dreaming; it is subjective, unreal. To many therapists, these ideas are useful and practical because they can be used to explain people to themselves and to others.

X-RAYS

In physics, the value of an idea like virtual particles is that it explains things in more or less ordinary terms and can be imagined to be behind other things that can be tested. If someone comes up with a better idea to explain the same or more things, virtual particles will be put aside. But today, particles are on the throne (although they are being challenged by superstring theory).

For example, virtual particles can be used to imagine how x-rays are produced. X-rays were so named by W. K. Roentgen in 1895 because no one knew what they were. X-rays are beams of electromagnetic radiation (of a shorter wavelength than ultraviolet radiation) produced by bombardment of atoms by high-energy particles. When bombarded, all atoms produce their own x-ray spectrum. X-rays can pass through many forms of matter and are used medically and industrially to examine internal structures.

X-rays are part of the electromagnetic spectrum of radiation (0.005 to 5 nanometers, see diagram in note 3). X-rays result when a piece of metal made of heavy atoms is placed in a vacuum tube and bombarded by electrons in that tube. An x-ray is a form of energy that radiates from atoms when the electron shells around the atoms are excited. X-rays can then penetrate solids; they affect photographic plates and fluorescent screens. X-rays are so small that they can squeeze through many material things, as you know when you have your teeth x-rayed.

Virtual particles help to imagine x-rays. Take the atoms in a piece of metal. If you give an electron with virtual particles hovering around it in the atoms of that metal a bang from another charged particle, you knock some off the virtual ones (Figure 34.4).

In the virtual particle explanation of x-rays, when the virtual particles around an electron of an atom are bombarded, they pick up a little of the energy of the bombardment. They become super excited, so to speak. Then, the super-excited virtual particles fly off in the form of an x-ray. Although the virtual particles can not be measured, the x-ray can be. The explanation is that when the low-energy virtual particles pick up a lot of energy, they can manifest or materialize in everyday reality.

Thus, the explanation for x-rays is that if you shoot a stream of electrons into a heavy metal, some of the virtual photons hanging around the atoms of the metal get excited from the energy picked up in the bang and are shaken out of the metal in the form of x-rays.

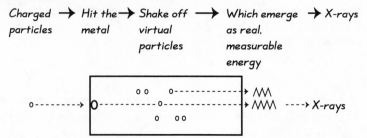

34.4 *Exchange particle explanation of x-rays*

In the past, x-rays were observed but were understood simply as emerging energy from the atoms of heavy metals. Virtual particles give the "emerging energy" explanation a sort of mechanics by explaining x-rays in CR terms of particles. You excite a charge by giving it a bang, and out of that collision the charge's virtual particles get excited and emerge as x-rays, or microwaves.

You may wonder about the difference between producing x-rays and making atomic bombs. Making x-rays is different from making atomic bombs because, to get an x-ray, you don't have to break the core of the atom into pieces; there is no measurable loss of mass. You just excite the electrons that surround the atom, and the energy they pick up from the bombardment is re-emitted in the form of an x-ray. In a bomb, a macroscopic loss of mass occurs, which transforms into huge blasts of radiation. An x-ray has only as much energy as the electron stream you shot at the metal. The amount of energy you put into the bang determines the energy that is radiated.

We should remember that our virtual particle theory was, to begin with, an attempt to give a quantum electrodynamic picture of an electric field. In this picture, a field around an electron becomes a bunch of virtual particles that are constantly being emitted and absorbed by that electron. What used to be a field that exerted forces at a distance is now thought of as a bunch of virtual particles ready and willing to do all sorts of quick bumps and bangs, exchanges which cannot be measured—unless a bang increased their energy to the point that they could be seen. Until that bang, they did not have the energy to be anything but quick, immeasurable fluctuations.

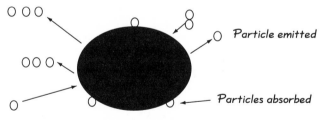

34.5 The image of a particle surrounded by its virtual particles

Similar to x-rays, the light from fires and light bulbs can be "explained" as virtual particles picking up energy, which is shaken loose as electromagnetic radiation.

The idea of virtual exchange particles has been broadly extended in physics to "explain" all force fields. The strong nuclear force in the nucleus of atoms, which sticks protons together, is thought of as the interaction among exchange particles called "mesons." There are many more exchange particles, such as "gluons," which interact with "quarks," the stuff that makes up neutrons and protons. There may even be "gravitons" which offer another explanation for the field of gravity (instead of think-ing of it as an effect of curved space-time). No one has discovered gravi-tons yet, but the name already exists, showing how strong the particle concept is.

EXPLAINING EXPLANATION

Here we reach the limits of today's physics, which is trying to explain all the forces of nature in terms of particle exchanges. Many physicists hope that elementary exchange particles or "relationship particles," as I call them, will eventually give us a unified picture of all the forces in nature.

One of the reasons to discuss virtual exchange or relationship parti-cles, is because they prompt us to ask once again, "What do we mean by explanation?" Remember the four principles mentioned earlier, which virtual particles must satisfy? They give us a few hints about what expla-nation means. Those principles were:

I.   **Energy Conservation**
     Energy over time must be constant.

II. **Energy-Mass Conversion**
     Energy can appear as mass (because $E = mc^2$).

III. **Uncertainty Principle**
     $\Delta e \times \Delta t$ must be equal or greater than Planck's constant.

IV. **CR Community Principle**
     New theories must use consensus reality concepts.

The first three theories already exist; they have been accepted because they lead to results that can be checked in consensus reality. The first three principles imply that any explanation must involve experimental, CR verification.

The fourth principle says that scientific theories must themselves be based on consensual concepts. For example, exchange particles cannot be seen—except when they are bumped up in energy—and yet the concept of particle has a consensus. People like the particle idea; it is shared in the minds of many and can be discussed. As I said before, what we call parti-cles, exchange particles, or virtual particles today, we may call strings or ghosts in the future.

Problems arise only when explanations are taken to be "The Truth." We must always bear in mind that as consensus reality changes, explana-tory concepts change as well. All this depends on the *Zeit Geist*, German words that mean, literally, "time" and "spirit," or "spirit of the times."

The Zeitgeist is a hidden variable in physics and psychology. The Zeit-geist, the spirit of the times of consensus reality, for example, allows the ideas of virtual particles and dream figures.

We know that the same Zeitgeist found as a hidden variable in physics influences psychology as well. In Chapter 27 on synchronicity, we saw that Einstein's relativity theory influenced Jung's idea of synchronicity. Freud's and Jung's notions of the unconscious reflect the particle Zeitgeist, for the unconscious was imagined to be a vast sea of potential, a sort of field, which at the same time could be imagined as the interaction between virtual parts called drives (Freud) or archetypes (Jung). Like the invisible particles coming forth from the sea of energy in physics, drives and archetypes cannot be seen. Yet today, many use drives and archetypes to explain human behavior. Indeed, elementary particles are to physics what dream figures and archetypes are to psychology.[4]

BATTLE BETWEEN WORLDS

The radical theorist rebels against the consensual Zeitgeist. The conflict between new ways of thinking and the existing Zeitgeist is a battle between worlds, between new ways of thinking and older ways, which constrain and check on the new ones. The battle does not occur in science only during periods of paradigm shifts. It occurs in all areas of human change. Indigenous traditions stress the importance of the tension between a governing Zeitgeist and new ideas. For example, an indigenous person who has had a remarkable experience during a vision quest is not automatically validated as a spiritual person, a shaman-to-be. The vision must conform to characteristics that are determined by the shamanic tradition and the entire community. In a similar way, spiritual traditions constrain the visionary person seeking new horizons.

The history of science and religion is full of painful stories about such conflicts. Gallileo was imprisoned until the end of his life because his views were so different from the governing religious traditions of his day. Many constraints are hurtful, and many seem unnecessary because they are so traditional and dogmatic. Yet, the tension that arises between CR and NCR, between a collective Zeitgeist and an individual or "subjective" experience, is a crucial tension: it can be a creative battle between worlds.

Both worlds, all worlds, are needed to check on one another. The conflict presses new NCR ideas to be practical, useful, and comprehensible. The conflict between worlds nudges those possessed by the older CR to become more flexible than they feel necessary.

New theories arise in shamanism, psychology, and physics from the battle between the worlds, from new experiences, and from doubting these new experiences. The ever-changing face of culture and community arises from the fourth principle, the collision between CR and NCR.

Judging from what has already been said, and remembering the conflict between the ruling spirits and new ideas which lies behind theories, we can predict that future discoveries in physics will follow changes in the general psychology of the cosmopolitan mainstream. Each physical theory is a product of a given Zeitgeist and describes a form of psychology. Furthermore, new physical theory must have an existing psychological counterpart.

For example, within psychology, the rebirth of interest in native cultures and new-age belief systems surrounding Mother Earth and dreamtime predicts unification of psychology, theology, and physics in the future. In particular, I predict that we will see a merging of psychological concepts such as dream figures and physical concepts such as virtual particles, of psychological fields such as the Tao with the invisible spatial and energetic fields of physics, and of Native and Western sciences.

We have seen that Australian Aborigines thought of the universe as part of a great Dreaming, ancient Chinese called it the Tao, and spiritual traditions identified the universe as a god or goddess with consciousness. Today's physicists speak of virtual particles appearing where there were energetic fields; the Africans spoke of mathematically perfect forms coming from the sea goddess Nun. Instead of Nun, modern physicists talk about consciousness in the universe and speak of the earth as a goddess (since Lovelock's Gaia hypothesis).

The times are constantly changing. In the light of these reflections on the future of science, our present discussion occurs in the midst of the battle between the worlds, of known laws and new explanations for hitherto inexplicable events. For example, the voice of the physicist inside me is disgruntled. Some of my new ideas initially evoke disbelief in the Zeitgeist of this physicist because I have been emphasizing the importance of examining NCR experience in order to understand the nature of reality and answer the question, "Where does consciousness enter physics?"

That Zeitgeist is uncomfortable with my use of dreaming because this concept has not been part of physics for three hundred years. I gladly entertain such disbelief because it presses me to stay close to mainstream, proven ways of thinking and empirical reasoning. However, just as virtual particles help us understand x-rays, dreaming helps us comprehend the quantum wave function, Einstein's space-time and Hawking's imaginary time. Moreover, unlike virtual particles, everyone can experience dreaming. Therefore, I will speculate that, since dreaming satisfies given laws of physics and explains consciousness, it will eventually become widely acceptable.

The battle between the worlds also evokes dissatisfaction in the therapist and shaman inside me. They insist that there is too much emphasis on physics. However, the ideas we have been discussing produce explanations not only for hitherto unexplained phenomena in physics but also for mysterious elements in psychology. Since these explanations include older concepts in psychology, psychology in its present form is likely to eventually expand to become part of a new science, the emerging unification of the physical sciences and shamanism.

NOTES

1. Using the everyday or "classical" analogy of particles will hopefully give the reader a sense of uncertainty, the kind due to our inability to count everything. Uncertainty in quantum mechanics is an inherent quality of describing our interactions with matter and it is something that will exist no matter how precise measurements become.

2. Planck's constant, h, is defined as the ratio of a quantum of energy to the frequency of that energy and is 6.626176×10^{-34} joule-seconds.

3. Visible light has a specific wavelength, which is a small part of a very large family or spectrum of waves including radio and TV waves, visible light, and x-rays. This spectrum is called the electromagnetic spectrum.

1000 Meters   *10 Trillionths of a Meter*

10^3 10^{-11}

|----|----|----|----|----|----|----|----|----|----|----|----|----|----|----

10^3 10^2 10^1 10 10^{-1} 10^{-2} 10^{-3} 10^{-4} 10^{-5} 10^{-6} 10^{-7} 10^{-8} 10^{-9} 10^{-10}

AM   FM   UHF   Micro-   Infra-   Visible   Ultra-   X   Gamma
radio   radio   radio   wave   red   light   violet   rays   rays

Radio   Light

34.6 (1000 Meters to 10 trillionths of a meters long (logarithmic scale)

4. In his study of the archetypes in "The Archetypal Hypothesis of Jung and Pauli and Its Relevance to Physics and Epistemology," University of Victoria physicist Charles Card proposes that elementary particles are the archetypes of physics.

35 | Process Theory in Physics

But I do believe that this is precisely the point where our present way of thinking does need to be amended, perhaps by a bit of blood-transfusion from Eastern thought.

—Irwin Schroedinger, originator of wave mechanics

We have discovered that, to date, most physicists feel that virtual particles are the most satisfactory explanation of force fields. However, there are competing theories, which are very different. For example, instead of thinking about the area around particles as an interactional space where virtual particles bump into one another, physicists have also considered the area around a particle such as an electron to be a mysterious "matrix" in which interactions take place. The word matrix is connected to the word "mother" and implies an area that is womb-like, a place where things come to fruition.

S-matrix theory (S stands for scattering) developed after quantum electrodynamics (QED) attempted to grasp the details of what happens when electrons and other elementary particles interact. S-matrix theory thinks of the area around particles as womb-like. While QED tried to imagine the mechanical details of the relationships between particles—details such as virtual particles with paths going forward and backward in time,[1] S-matrix theory attempted to avoid the contradictions of particle theory by describing the overall scattering process.

Developed in the 1960s, S-matrix theory is a process-oriented approach to physics. Instead of trying to find out which particle did what, it studies the overall results of particle collisions. In the late

1990s, new ideas such as string theory and its challenger, the ten-dimensional theory of the universe, have been born from S-matrix theory. These newer ideas also portray the overall nature of events and are strongly based on S-matrix thinking and its philosophy, as well as on quantum mechanics and relativity.[2]

In contrast to process-oriented approaches, particle theory is reductionistic: it attempts to comprehend the nature of events in terms of elementary parts and states. To understand the difference between virtual particle and S-matrix thinking, that is, between state and process thinking, let's consider two different medical approaches to illness. To understand illness, reductionistic medicine looks at the body as a machine that can be understood in terms of its parts. In this approach, you study the body's elementary particles, so to speak, its atoms, molecules, organs, and systems, the bits and pieces that make up the cells and the whole of the body.

To understand the same illness, an S-matrix approach would notice what the body does, what it eats, when it sleeps, how it interacts with others, and the like. The illness process is studied in terms of these overall interaction patterns and behavior, not so much in terms of the individual parts within the body.

In this analogy, the body is a matrix, that is, a container for processes and interactions with the world. You can't separate body parts as you might be able to separate a gas gauge in a car from its gas tank, because body parts are more interdependent. Likewise, we cannot pull one particle out of an interaction without totally disturbing the entire interaction.

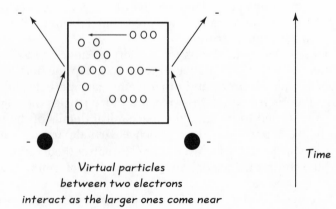

Virtual particles
between two electrons
interact as the larger ones come near

35.1 State-oriented, particle view of electrons interacting

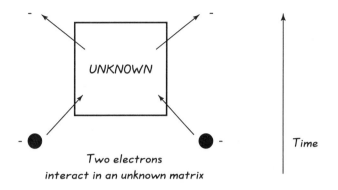

35.2 *Process-oriented, S-matrix approach to electron interchange*

Instead of dealing with the speculated virtual particles, S-matrix thinking says, forget parts we can't see, they are not fundamental. Instead, the overall process is fundamental. The S-matrix theory attempts to reflect the irreducible wholeness of events, in contrast to reductionistic theories that analyze the whole in terms of its separate entities and reduce the subatomic reactions to bits and pieces. In terms of the above example of the body, the S-matrix approach reflects the overall life process of an individual, instead of understanding that process in terms of the liver, gallbladder, and so forth.

S-matrix theory asks how the overall scattering pattern of the electrons appears before and after they interact with one another. This pattern is considered more important than the mechanics of what the particles do to one another during the interaction. S-matrix theory says that since we cannot track virtual interactions, we won't use them. All we know is that the area around an electron is a matrix for scattering to take place.

Again, in terms of the human body, S-matrix theory does not study the individual parts of the body but instead assumes that the human body is only a channel in which reactions take place when disturbed by outside influences. Likewise, instead of talking about the inexplicable mass and energy of individual virtual particles, S-matrix philosophy focuses on the outcome of interactional processes. In this theory, there are only processes and events. There are particles before and after interactions, but during these interactions there is simply their relationship matrix. We can measure the situation beforehand and afterwards, but what happened in the middle can't be measured or known in CR terms.

In S-matrix theory, virtual particle and exchange interactions in quantum field theory are understood as process events. Force fields, which were explained in terms of interacting virtual particles in quantum field theories, are once again unexplained fields in S-matrix theory.

IN QUANTUM FIELD THEORY	IN S-MATRIX THEORY
Force fields due to virtual particle exchanges	Process potentials
Particle	Reaction channel

35.3 Comparison of particle and S-matrix concepts

PROCESS AND STATE ORIENTATIONS IN PHYSICS

State-oriented concepts such as particle, space, and time inevitably convey fixedness and immutability; they are useful for consensus reality approximations of nature. While these concepts are common and useful to us in everyday reality, there are many problems associated with them in physics. For example, the particle concept implies a tiny point in space, which is treated as an object. Yet space cannot be dissected indefinitely because, when you get down to a certain point, you run into the uncertainty principle of quantum physics. Furthermore, the ordinary, linear (CR) significance of time is almost meaningless in the subatomic world because events go forward and backward in time. What is more, relativity has taken the separability out of concepts such as time and space, energy and matter. Even the CR concept of the "present" is vague. If time moves along in a continuous fashion, there can be no present, no absolutely still, fixed point!

Physics has always operated in two realms. One is the realm of consensus reality where events are discussed in terms of state-oriented ideas such as time and space, matter and energy. The other realm is process, where overall patterns, rather than individual details, are studied. We saw in our exploration of calculus how physics made a transition from studying events at a point to studying continuous flow. In S-matrix theory, as we have just seen, particles are processes rather than things.

PROCESS AND STATES IN PSYCHOLOGY

Psychology also works with parts and processes. If we use particle thinking, so to speak, the archetypes are named in terms of their images, such as the Great Mother or the Divine Child. These are more like entities and states than processes. Yet, in altered states of consciousness, dreaming, and meditation, the archetypes flow together, and as they intermix, separability becomes impossible. The particle concept of the archetype has more to do with our state-oriented viewpoint from consensus reality than it does with our experience of dreaming.

A state-oriented approach to understanding a person in relationship might be to examine his dreams. There you find various experiences, parts that may be important for that person to think about. These parts may be thought of as differentiable images that express aspects of his behavior in relationship. This particle viewpoint can be helpful and bring great insights showing new aspects and feelings that were unconscious before. When two people get together in relationship, then, you can think of their virtual parts as interacting with one another. Jungians often speak of his anima (often his feelings) and her animus (frequently her opinions) as interacting with one another. This is a virtual particle theory.

Most of the time, most people are virtual particle–oriented in relationships. Before, during, and after relationships, you probably think of yourself and the other as having been good or bad, as having done this or that, and you try to explain everything in terms of childhood events and the like.

A process-oriented view focuses on your overall behavior in relationship. This view sees you as a reaction channel, an interaction matrix, or an area where typical interactions take place. During a meeting with your partner, all you can say about yourself is that you are in a relationship matrix or process. Certain overall relationship patterns emerge, again and again, when others interact with you or your partner.

For example, in a conflict, many people first get angry, then try to put the other down, later behave righteously, and finally may be self-critical. Others get depressed and self-critical, then are sweet and refer to love as the solution to all things. Some are kind over long periods of time during the conflict, then suddenly flip and get angry, then later try to see everyone as a winner, and so on. In the terms of S-matrix thinking, these patterns are characteristic of your "process potential."

Most people have more virtual particle knowledge of themselves (in terms of history and the like) than process knowledge (overall picture of relationship behavior). Particle thinking analyzes your relationship interactions in a moment-to-moment way, breaking them down into a series of given exchanges. A particle-oriented relationship therapist might stop the overall flow of process to focus on actions and reactions, on who causes what and who is responsible for doing what to whom. A process-oriented view focuses on the overall patterns while explaining them. In a conflict, such a therapist brings awareness to patterns that are occurring, and might say, "Now this is the time when this pattern is happening, now this is the time for another pattern."

In the process view of relationships, the dance we do together cannot be explained in terms of the steps needed by the people dancing together; the actual dance is beyond the steps and is inhibited by breaking it up. Both process and particle views are complementary and may be significant in psychology at one moment or another.

You may remember a similar situation from when we discussed calculus. The state-oriented approach to calculus understood it as a measure of infinitesimally small parts or steps. The process orientation appeared when Newton developed the concept of pure flow, of the fluxion, which could no longer be reduced to the infinitesimal steps (see Chapter 11).

Whether we view things as parts or steps is a matter of viewpoint. Both particles and process are real, depending on your frame of reference and the world you come from. You can use reductionistic thinking and try to understand life as particles as long as you don't mind a lot of hypothetical ghosts and uncertainties. Reductionistic details can be satisfying, but a total explanation also needs the overall process view. Complete process orientation theoretically includes both elementary particle and S-matrix thinking, awareness of both the state-oriented and the flow-oriented views.

A more complete process orientation in physics will integrate virtual particle views of entities going backward and forward in time, aliens, and superluminal beings moving faster than the speed of light. It will also include the process view that any momentary situation is mysterious: only the overall pattern can be known. A complete process view makes no firm statement about the ultimate reality of nature, but sees Her as a shifting collage of interacting viewpoints.

In psychology, the process viewpoint is based on the discovery that when awareness is present, process has its own wisdom, which, if honored and followed, produces remarkable results. This viewpoint extends the applications of psychology to comatose states, psychotic conditions, and individual and large-group processes, where verbal and nonverbal interactions take place. The limits of its application are not yet known.[3]

Some physicists, who say the basic stuff of the universe is process, have attempted a complete process view. Physicists such as David Finkelstein say there are no particles: there is nothing but process.[4] Finkelstein means that there are processes beyond what we think of as the parameters of time and space, processes that can be experienced but cannot be described or measured in terms of consensus reality.

David Bohm's theory of unfolding and of unbroken wholeness is another process-oriented view of quantum mechanics. Niels Bohr, originator of the theory of complementarity and one of the fathers of quantum mechanics, was also an ardent process thinker. I heard a story that Bohr, on his sixtieth birthday, asked only for a necklace containing the central process symbol—the Chinese figure of the Tai Chi, a circle that contains the swirling interaction energies of the yin and yang.

35.4 Tai Chi

Bohr was intuiting that the crucial thing in physics, and perhaps mysticism, was process—the eternal change, impermanence, and constant flow. While process is crucial, from the perspective of dimensions it is simply one of the hyperspaces, a fourth dimension compensating the one-sidedness and fixed-state orientations of the other three. Process is part of the big picture. Yet without fixed states, the great revolution of the Tao that cannot be said would have no meaning.

We saw in Chapter 34 that the future of science depends on the tensions between CR and NCR views. Today, process is on the non-consensus side of things, and state-oriented thinking is favored. At some point in the future, I imagine we will move toward a larger process view that incorporates and appreciates state-oriented thinking as the state of mind many people are in most of the time.

PARTICLE OR PROCESS: A PERSONAL EXPERIMENT

If you would like to sense the difference between the particle and process viewpoints, you may want to try the following experiment. If you do this experiment with someone else, it is important that you both do it simultaneously.

1. **Take a few seconds and sense the atmosphere or the field around you.** This statement is meant to be vague. Just sense the atmosphere, the field, and the world space, in any way that you can. Use your inner imagination to pick up what's happening in the field around you. Just sense it. What is the atmosphere like in your room, your street, your city, or the environment—wherever you are?

2. **When you are ready, use your second attention and let the field speak to you in the form of one word.** Listen to the first word (or couple of words) you hear coming from the field. If you are not an "auditory" type of person, you may, as an alternative, catch the first images you see. Notice the word or image and focus on it.

   Listen to or see its message. Remember the very first words or pictures that come before you. Catch them!

   Are the words or images meaningful to you? What do they mean for you personally?

3. **When you are ready, ask yourself if you can feel this message.** Can you feel that information also as a force that works on you somehow? Can you feel the information you got somehow as a force that's working on your body? How does that force feel?

4. **Check in with yourself again.** Ask yourself if what you just experienced was your personal psychology, or was this the field that you were receiving and transmitting? Just guess at this answer.

5. **Finally, if you were doing this with someone else, share your answer.** If you were doing this alone, note the time of the experience and, later on, ask other people in your neighborhood what they experienced during the time you were doing this experiment. What did they experience? Compare your experiences.

When I asked you in question 2 to sense what the field was expressing, in essence, I was asking you to experience the field around you as if it had virtual particles, bits of information that bump into you. The field around you was sending you virtual messages.

Then in question 3, I asked you to experience the field as a scattering force. The field becomes something like a force field, which affects you in a non-specific manner. The area around you, your environment, is then a relationship matrix, a mysterious area pressing you to react, to flow or move in a certain way. The field told you something by scattering particles, so to speak.

If you think about it, you may find elements of what you heard from the field in terms of your personal psychology. On the other hand, when you checked with your neighbor, you may have discovered that what she heard from the field was connected with your experience. In other words, what we call the world around us is also a relationship matrix, a process that affects all that are near in a similar way. Thus, you, the environment, and I are all channels for reactions to take place. We are individual entities who can be described in terms of the interactions we leave behind us.

For example, Peter, a student in my class who had done this experiment, stood up in an excited manner and said, "I heard the field telling me to dance like a maniac. And my partner Angela said it told her to heat up the world, to get particles dancing! Was the field telling her how to deal with me?"

Their experiences of the field were virtual, non-consensual because the two of them heard the same thing. The field was informing Angela about Peter as much as it was speaking about its own "wildness." The field wanted her to heat things up, and it wanted him to dance. In a non-consensual way, the two were relating through the field as if it were a third party in their relationship.

From the particle viewpoint the field is telling people what to do, and from the process viewpoint we can only tell that it "scattered," that is, it heated up Angela and made Peter dance. From the process viewpoint, the field and everything else is a reaction channel scattering things that come near it.

From the viewpoint of personal psychology, the field around us informs us about ourselves, as we imagine messages, information, and suggestions applying to ourselves. From the process perspective, our personalities, as well as the environment, are mysterious reaction channels moving one another about.

From one viewpoint, you have dreams, body parts, and a personality, while from another, you are a mystery that makes things around you move in certain ways. From the particle view you are composed of a personality with specific complexes, dreams, and other features. From this view, you have an ego, a particular culture, and a unique history. From the process viewpoint, you are a matrix, a womb for experiences.

MATRIX THEORY, PROCESS, AND SPIRITUALITY

If we extrapolate the process idea about ourselves, we might look at life as a scattering diagram. This means that we would see our biography in terms of the trail of interactions we have left behind us. While from the particle viewpoint, you or others might seek to explain your behavior in terms of your culture, gender, sexual orientation, religion, and personal history, from the process viewpoint, you are a mystery that can never be explained in anything but NCR terms.

It is amazing how many NCR viewpoints we can have about a human being. Recently, I read several autobiographies of C.G. Jung. One author explained Jung's work in terms of his being crazy; another accused him of being Swiss; a third said that Jung did what he did because his father was a Christian minister. Still another author said that Jung should not have slept with this or that person. All these NCR viewpoints are virtual particle explanations of Jung's life. But when all is said and done, the only thing we can say for sure is that Jung left behind a trail of relationship interactions. He had a certain effect on his community and the human race, he came up with the concepts of the archetypes and synchronicity, and so forth.

In a way, the ancient Book of Changes, the Chinese *I Ching*, is correct: a person can be measured only by the effect she has had on others and on the environment around her. The *I Ching* has an S-matrix view and sees each of us as essentially inexplicable, a mystery, an unknown that has scattered, interacted, and touched the world around us.

While you and I may have our personal, individual NCR sentient experiences and explanations for what we do, nothing can be said in consensus reality about us except what has occurred in our vicinities. This view is similar to the view of quantum mechanics applied to human beings. We are essentially sentient NCR experiences, wave functions, mysteries that appear in CR as you and me, but whose ultimate truth can never be known. Each "real" object is finally based on a self-reflective process which itself is non-consensual. We can agree only on what we did, on the outer aspect of our biographies, but not on how we experienced life, knew it, hated and loved.

Like the *I Ching*, Buddhism also speaks about your personality in a process-oriented manner. It detaches from self-descriptions or investigations of your personality and suggests that you let go of yourself, your ambitions, your health, and your age and open up to the flow of states, the impermanence of life. In the Buddhist view, life is about noticing and dropping your personal explanation of what goes through you and letting it go. You are awareness of the flow.

If you ask who you are from the process viewpoint, you do not appear as an entity with given inner parts, but as a reaction channel, a way of interacting with others. Whenever someone speaks about you, they are speaking about a particular manner in which events are processed. How or why you do this is a matter of NCR opinions.

While the goal from one view is to individuate, to know your different parts, the goal of another viewpoint is to notice the effect you have on others. Developing as a reaction channel instead of an individual with parts means knowing your overall effect in relationship instead of focusing only on what you did and why.[5] It means seeing your life as an inexplicable secret whose overall effects can be seen, but whose exact nature can never be known.

NOTES

1. Richard Feynman in "The Theory of Positrons" (1949) uses consensus reality concepts such as particle, and moving backward in time, concepts that cannot be directly tested. For example, consider the positron, that is, the antimatter equivalent of an electron. According to the mathematics of quantum mechanics, a positron going forward in time could just as well become an electron going backward in time! To date, no one knows how to measure something going backward in time.

2. Michio Kaku discusses the evolution of S-matrix theory in his *Hyperspace*, page 325 and following. String theory is an attempt to ground S-matrix theory and replaces the idea of pointlike particles by vibrating lines, loops, or closed strings.

3. I discuss nonverbal interactions in *City Shadows* and *Coma*.

4. David Finkelstein's process view of physics can be found in his "Quantum Physics and Process Metaphysics."

5. Einstein sees life similarly: "A human being is a part of the whole, called by us the 'Universe,' a part limited in time and space. He experiences himself,

his thoughts and feelings, as something separated from the rest—a kind of optical delusion of his consciousness. This delusion is a kind of prison for us, restricting us to our personal desires and to affection for a few persons nearest us. Our task must be to free ourselves from this prison by widening our circle of compassion to embrace all living creatures and the whole of nature in its beauty." This quote comes from Debbora Duda's *Coming Home* (1984), page 95.

36 | The Self-reflecting Universe

Nothing can stay long removed from God, nor long divorced from that Ground of Being outside of which nothing exists....

—Ken Wilber in *Up From Eden*

The father of quantum or wave mechanics, Erwin Schroedinger, said that nature, in her effort to understand herself, could only do so at first by excluding human consciousness from this understanding. In other words, instead of participants, at first we became observers in physics. In Schroedinger's words:

> Mind has erected the objective outside world of the natural philosopher out of its own stuff. Mind could not cope with the gigantic task otherwise than by the simplifying device of excluding itself... withdrawing from its conception.[1]

If Schroedinger had participated in our exploration thus far, he might rephrase his statement to say, "The Mind of nature is smarter than we knew, because it fooled us into thinking that it excluded itself from our formulation of the universe."

Schroedinger might agree that mind secretly encoded itself in the overall picture we have of the universe through the vehicle of complex numbers, which, until now, have not been interpreted. Mind hid itself in those complex numbers, which have the amazing ability to disappear in the final, consensus reality formulation of things. Nevertheless, the code for the consciousness of this Mind is in those complex numbers, waiting to be used.

In this chapter, we will explore the code or pattern of Schroedinger's universal mind as seen in physics, psychology, and mythology, and will investigate what this Mind says about its own consciousness.

Uncertainty

In Chapter 1, we heard the story of two monks from different schools of Zen meeting on a bridge over a river. When one asks how deep the water is, the other throws him in. To know that math encodes "mind" in the formulation of the physical universe, the physicist must get into the water, so to speak, into the sentient background encoded in complex numbers, to experience the significance of non-consensus events such as dreaming.

Without this experience, the interpretation of quantum mechanics and relativity suffers from one-sided views of a two-sided math that deals with consensus and non-consensus reality. Using the framework of consensus reality to understand this math is non-relativistic if the non-consensual world of complex world and dreaming is considered irrelevant. Consensus reality becomes the "one and only" framework, denying the essential contribution of relativity, which demonstrated that no one framework is absolute.

Like everyone else, the physicist lives in both frameworks. By marginalizing how she participates with her feelings in the world surrounding her observations, the physicist inadvertently treats herself merely as a recording instrument and makes herself into a one-sided observer. A more holistic interpretation of physics that encompasses the various realities in the mathematics of complex numbers understands them as patterns for the "mind's" presence in events as the sentient experience, the dreamlike seeds preceding consensus reality.

The one-sided, CR viewpoint of the observer in physics is also found in mainstream attitudes everywhere, including in psychology and medicine. In psychology, for example, therapists strive to be "objective" and not to get caught up in the emotional flow connecting them to the events within themselves and their clients. In medicine, we find the doctor working with a patient's body—which is viewed as a system of parts that are largely independent of what the patient or doctor is experiencing. The doctor strives to remain objective and is rarely heard asking the patient about her emotional life.

In physics, psychology, and medicine, relationships between observer and the observed are as "objective" as possible. Observers, trying to keep themselves divorced from the observed, attempt to maintain a state-oriented view of life that can be divided into parts, although sentient, dreamlike experience indicates that such divisions are one-sided.

DOMAIN/OBSERVER	CONSENSUS REALITY	NON-CONSENSUS REALITY
	Object of Observation	**Subject of Observation**
Physics/Physicist	Particle	Virtual particles, wave functions
Psychology/ Therapist	Client, inner life	Dreams, fantasies, sentient feelings
Medicine/Doctor	Body illness	Psychosomatic pain, feelings, imaginations

36.1 CR and NCR in physics, psychology, and medicine

In each of these domains—physics, psychology, and medicine—the classical or CR observers are inextricably linked with uncertainties. The relationship between the physicist and the particle is governed by the Heisenberg uncertainty principle, which says, in essence, that there is a limit to how much you can know about a particle in terms of consensus reality. This principle allows for all sorts of imaginary objects—such as virtual particles—none of which can be measurable.

In a similar fashion, the therapist is forever uncertain about the client's future or moods, which cannot be completely controlled or predicted. Without entering the dreaming process, the therapist can only know that part of the client which manifests in consensus reality.

In medicine, too, the effects of causal interventions such as surgery are not completely predictable because healing involves many non-mechanical factors that are beyond conscious control.

As they now stand, physics, psychology, and medicine are characterized by a classical, state-oriented description of an observer and observed which relate to one another as if they are separable. Uncertainties result from marginalizing the non-consensus experiences of the observer.

Remaining in the CR framework creates uncertainty about the influence of NCR events in everyday life. Uncertainty principles are needed in any CR formulation of nature. Rather than denying the pervasive presence of uncertainty, it should be included in every consensus reality and state-oriented description of events.

Domain/ Observer	U = UNCERTAINTY		
	Consensus Object of Observation	U	Non-Consensus Subject of Observation
Physics/Physicist	Particle	U	Virtual particles, wave function
Psychology/ Therapist	Person, inner life	U	Dreams, fantasies, sentient feelings
Medicine/Doctor	Body illness	U	Psychosomatic pain, feelings, imaginations

36.2 Uncertainty in physics, psychology, and medicine

This diagram shows that, for the observer in the framework of consensus reality, uncertainty about the "observed" must exist, since NCR experiences are not taken into consideration.

In a more process-oriented framework, which begins with awareness of non-consensual sentient experience such as deep feelings and intuitions that cannot be expressed in words, the sense of separation between observer and observed disappears. With the disappearance of this separation, relationship between observer and observed is created. This relationship diminishes the isolation, lack of control, and sense of uncertainty about nature.

The traditional shaman is a prototype of a new kind of observer who worships the observed, relates to her, and dives into the sentient realm to find knowledge where uncertainty previously reigned supreme. The traditional shaman deals not only with events on this Earth or within individuals, but also with the entire cosmos.

UNCERTAINTY ABOUT THE UNIVERSE

Now let's add the domain of the entire universe to the above scheme. The scientific observer of the universe is called the cosmologist. Remember space-time separation? In relativity, this is the measure of events that is common to all observers in all frameworks. It is the consensual measurement of events in the universe.

In the foregoing chapters, we discussed how space-time separation becomes imaginary, that is, non-consensual, when events seem connected at velocities greater than the speed of light. This happens in moments when the future seems to influence the present, when you seem to move backward or out of time, and when there was no space in the first moment of creation when the universe began. Remember how Stephen Hawking described the beginning of the universe with imaginary numbers and imaginary time? Just as non-consensual, non-observable events are contained in the imaginary numbers of the quantum wave functions for particles, these same kind of events are allowed by Einstein's formula for relativity.

If we add the domain of the universe and the observing cosmologist to our scheme, we find the following:

U = Uncertainty			
Domain/ Observer	**Consensus Object of Observation**	U	**Non-Consensus Subject of Observation**
Physics/Physicist	Particle	U	Virtual particles, wave function
Psychology/ Therapist	Person, inner life	U	Dreams, fantasies, sentient feelings
Medicine/Doctor	Body illness	U	Psychosomatic pain, feelings, imaginations
Universe/ Cosmologist	Universe, space-time separation	U	Space-time ($v > c$), wave function

36.3 Uncertainty in cosmology, physics, psychology, and medicine

From the above diagram, we can say by analogy that uncertainty about the universe is due in part to lack of shamanic involvement in dreamtime, in the non-consensual experiences of creation, such as those you intuit from your peak experiences.

THE UNIVERSE'S WAVE FUNCTION

Most physicists today do not incorporate shamanic views into their concepts of the universe, yet people like Stephen Hawking are closing the gap between the worlds by considering the universe as if it were a particle with a wave function. Let's see how his consideration works and what it means for us.

Like all physicists, cosmologists expect the whole universe, including all known and unknown galaxies, future and past spaces, and vast, as-yet-to-be-observed events, to obey the same laws of physics we observe here on Earth. For example, if the universe obeys the same laws as those we experience on Earth, then the universe must be characterized by a quantum wave function, since every object has such a wave function, whether the object is a particle, a planet, or a universe.

Quantum cosmologists like Stephen Hawking view the entire universe much as particle physicists view small quantum objects. Hawking has speculated that the universe must have a wave function just as each particle does.

From our discussion in Chapters 14 through 17, you will recall that the wave function is a complex number, part real and part imaginary. Although physicists do not yet interpret complex numbers in terms of non-consensus events such as quantum flirts, we saw that such interpretations give quantum mechanics a basis that does not presently exist. Without the new interpretations of the wave functions, they are best seen as what Heisenberg called "tendencies" to find the system in a certain location at a certain time. I called these tendencies sentient experiences that catch our attention before we actually turn to observe an object.

The interpretation of wave functions as sentient experiences or as Heisenberg's tendencies cannot be measured because tendencies are complex numbers, $(a + ib)$. However, the real number resulting from conjugation of reflecting tendencies is a measurable probability of finding the quantum object at a certain place and time.[2]

To understand the wave function of the universe, let's try to understand tendencies the way a physicist might. The wave function of a large piece of matter, such as a planet, can be thought of as the wave function or tendency of something we are all familiar with, like the tendency of a large group of people in a city.

You will probably agree that the tendency of a crowd to gather in the center of a city is usually greater than the tendency of a crowd to gather at the outskirts of the city. To figure out what the chances are of finding a crowd anywhere, you need to know where people live, how many live in the center, how many live farther out, and so on.

The wave function for the crowd is the tendency for people to be in a certain place at a certain time. Likewise, the wave function for a group of planets is their tendency to congregate in a certain section of the universe. In the same way, the chance of finding an electron located at a certain place, in the midst of its own nebulous territory such as an atom, can be found by considering how it "populates" the areas around where we expect it to be. The description of its tendency to be in a certain place at a certain time is the wave function. Although the particle's wave function is spread throughout this nebulous area, it has the largest numbers where it is expected to be.

In the same manner, the chance of finding a person like me typing at a computer can be found if you know my dreams or my wave function, which theoretically spreads out all over space even to the ends of the universe. Like the particle, my wave function will be largest where you usually find me. If I live in Portland, Oregon, then my wave function will be smaller in other places and just about zero on the moon.

The wave function, or tendency for a certain occurrence to exist in CR, when conjugated, tells us where we are most likely to find the CR properties of an object, person, electron, planet, or crowd. Stephen Hawking made an intellectual leap by replacing the word "particle" with "universe." Instead of thinking about a particle whose wave function is all over the universe, he thought about our universe whose wave function is spread out all over. Spread over what? Over an infinite number of parallel universes! In his thinking, the universe is a quantum object, and the spaces it occupies must be other universes![3]

There are unsolved mathematical and philosophical problems with Hawking's speculative new theory, such as proving that the wave function for any universe other than our own is very small. After all, if the wave function were not minimal in other universes, we would be constantly finding ourselves in other universes, spaces and times radically different from our own. Shamans, of course, would argue that we do, indeed, occasionally switch universes; by and large, however, this is rare, and such switching cannot be measured in consensus reality.

THE GODS ARE OBSERVERS

If we assume, with Hawking, that there is a wave function for our entire universe, then by analogy with the wave function or tendency for a particle, the universe must be a tendency for itself to exist, a tendency that is not always quite here! Only because it is capable of self-reflection, of flirting with itself, flirting with us and everything else, does the universe achieve reality in the sense of CR.

Now comes a big question. For the universe to exist in CR as it does, with all its marvelous microscopic and cosmological beings, with all its stones, planets and galaxies, something dreamed it into being from its original dream, or tendency, state. Who did that? Who was the first observer capable of observing the universe, conjugating its wave function, reflecting its sentient essence, transforming its tendency into a reality? When it was created, none of us, not even the rest of the present consensus reality universe, was around.

One answer to this question is that the universe is curious. It is a sentient, dreaming universe capable of reflecting upon itself, dreaming itself into consensus reality as it expands. Our universe must be capable of self-reflection. Without this conclusion, physics, psychology, and our universe itself could not exist today.

While physicists will forever be checking out this answer, we can recall that the most ancient answer is that our universe is a goddess or god, watched over by itself. In Chapter 26 on sacred geometry, we saw how the gods reflected upon themselves to know themselves, thereby creating the world. This is similar to how we wake up in the morning wondering who we are. Curiosity brings us to a mirror, and there we reflect or see our reflections and become the person we are in consensus reality.

Likewise, according to myths, our universe is its own self-observer and self-creator. The universe is sentient. It experiences its own tendencies, and because it is curious, reflects upon them to create itself.

For example, the Zuni Native American creator, Awanawilona, conceived himself through thought. Awanawilona "conceived in himself the thought and the thought took shape and got out into space, and through this it stepped out into the void, into outer space and from this came nebulae of growth and mist, full of power and growth."[4]

Likewise, the Indian god Purusha divided himself into male and female and the two halves of a couple and created the rest of the universe accordingly. In Eskimo myths, Father Raven and his double, the "little sparrow," are co-creators of the universe. Reflecting parts of the universe were imagined by the Greeks as a split cosmic egg; the Japanese saw Heaven and Earth as a split egg; the Jews, Chinese, Maoris, and many others saws this cosmic reflection as the source of creation.[5] The Ngadju Dyak saw the clashing of two mountains as the force of creation. A Navajo sand painting shows the conjoint opposites of the sky and the earth creating the world. In the replica of that painting which follows, notice how the deities are equal but opposite! [6]

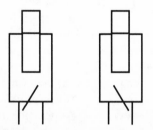

36.4 Simplified schematic representation of conjoint opposites
in conjugation: Father Sky and Mother Earth

This cosmological mythic diagram has a pattern like that of the wave equation with real and imaginary features, that is, $a + ib$. When this pattern meets its reflection or conjugate, that is, $a - ib$, the two numbers conjugate or are multiplied and generate reality.

The Navajos must have been experiencing what mathematics calls conjugation. The conjugation pattern we find in quantum cosmology is a universe conjugating itself by its reflection. This same pattern is seen in the mythological cosmology and ancient theories as the conjugation of our foreparent who broke into two. In other words, the reflection pattern found in the math of the universe contains similar features to the patterns we find in aboriginal creation myths and the sand paintings. [7]

The belief that reality is based on twinship patterns is very widespread. In Tsimshian myths life itself is seen as a pair of twin spirits looking with equal but opposite eyes. These First Nation people from the west coast of Canada describe their most ancient masks—apparently thirty centuries old—which are of twins, etched in stone, looking at one another with equal but opposite eyes:

> Life is a pair of twin stone masks which are the very same but have opposite eyes... They are with full self-consciousness, a paradox... about self-recognition.[8]

Scientists have tried since the sixteenth century to avoid projecting human forms onto the universe. Much of the outer success of physics came from its basis in testable hypotheses instead of in beliefs and feelings. But this success has not helped us understand the "things nearest and dearest to our hearts," to quote Schroedinger.

Although science has tried to avoid anthropomorphizing the universe, all our concepts are nevertheless "human." As we have seen, the formulation of any explanation in physics depends on the spirit of the times, the Zeitgeist. There is no way that we can have a truly objective universe. Every statement, every number, depends on an anthropomorphization of the universe because, as we saw early on in our journey, the very use of numbers is linked to our personal and community psychologies.

We cannot get around the suspicion that mythic anthropomorphizations explaining how the universe arises—such as we find in Navajo diagrams—represent the same reality as complex numbers in math. Mythic figures mirror the math and geometry of reflection.

The "anthropic principle" says that a human-like description of the universe is inevitable. A weak statement of the anthropic principle is that the universe is human in the sense that our concepts describe it well enough to create clocks, do surgery, understand dreams, and land on the moon.[9]

Therefore you are like the universe, or its logic is like yours. In other words, you understand the mind of God because in some ways, your mind is God's. From this, you must conclude, like many peoples before you, that your mind is like the mind of every other sentient being.[10]

Based on the conclusion that you are God, what you think and feel is what God thinks and feels. Thus, to reduce your uncertainty about the everyday world and about the whole universe, you need to go back to your sentient experience of what you are looking at. Your uncertainty is then reduced by rediscovering that what you are looking at is an aspect of yourself. The people and events around you are aspects of you; the universe, as well, is one of your faces. If you want to know who you are before life and after death, take your experiences seriously. This helps the universe take its own NCR events seriously. In other words, be the universe, as you experience it.

RETHINKING CONSCIOUSNESS

We have learned that the Australian Aborigines always believed that all objects have a sentient power to flirt with us, to bring about observations. The NCR experience of reflection is basic to our survival. It allows us to know things without being able to prove them—such as how we know to take a safer rather than a more dangerous path in the forest. All paths in life "flirt" with us, so to speak.

The prime element found in all myths is that sentient awareness is already present in the process of dreaming, an awareness that can reflect upon itself. The universe reflects upon itself, notices its own path, and creates reality.

From the viewpoint of non-consensus reality, in quantum mechanics, the real world arises through an "object" flirting with an "observer." This is how sentient experience or tendencies realize themselves. By analogy, then, the universe arises through flirting with itself; something like awareness of our CR selves arises when we catch sight of ourselves looking into a pool of water or in any other kind of mirror.

Thus, consciousness arises through the self-reflection and consists of the following:

1. **Tendencies, sentient, dreaming processes** that you subliminally experience as if they originated in you. Symbols of this sentience are found in the wave functions of physics and the deities of mythology.

2. **Sentient, flash-like signals, experienced subliminally as if they came from another person or object.** Symbols of these flirts are found in the complex conjugates of quantum mechanics and twin gods or conjugal deities flirting with one another in mythology.

3. **Conjugation, the process in which a sentient, dreaming process reflects upon itself, generating everyday, CR reality and consciousness.** Symbols of this process can be found in quantum mechanics where complex numbers are multiplied, producing real numbers and in mythology when a god unites with herself, creating the world as we know it.

Consciousness is based on sentient, NCR quantum flashes of perception, flirts reflecting upon one another. Consciousness involves the transition between two realms, between sentient NCR experience and CR.

According to quantum physics as well as mythology, the universe has the same tendency to mirror itself, to reflect upon itself. If we use the terms of our discussion thus far, we can say that the gods created this world by conjugation: they unfolded the universe through focusing on their own self-reflections. A universe that reflects upon its sentient self and creates consensus reality is a curious sentient being. It participates in itself, as we might when we become curious about, reflect upon, and unfold our own NCR processes.

The idea that the universe is sentient is found among Native peoples who feel that each species and object has NCR awareness characteristics. For example, a human being can transform into a salmon, but a salmon can also transform into a human or a leaf falling into the river in which the salmon is swimming.[11] In other words, what we consider to be a human activity called sensory awareness belongs to all beings and all things.

You might conclude that reality, that is, consensus reality, comes into being through the interaction of everything with everything else at the sentient level of awareness. Our bodies exist because of the manner in which their parts reflect upon one another; communities are created through our NCR signal exchanges. Likewise, the whole universe exists through the interlinking flirts of all Her parts. These conclusions are based on and consistent with what we know about physics, psychology, and mythology.

While the idea of a self-reflecting universe may be new to some, Mircea Eliade pointed out in *The Myth of the Eternal Return* that many early peoples believed that every act on this Earth was a reflection of its mirror image in the heavens where all patterns originate. People have always thought that the universe creates "reality" through reflecting or conjugating itself.

PEOPLE ARE NOT CENTRAL

How central are we humans in the universe? The answer to this question depends on how we define what we mean by human. If we exist only as CR observers, the answer is no, we are not central. But if we allow for our NCR awareness of quantum flirts, the definition of the human being must extend to all objects you are capable of seeing. In this case, "human" means widespread, non-local sentient awareness. Such an NCR "human" awareness is central and implicit in all the theories of the universe mentioned so far, and belongs to everything in the universe.

The fact that ordinary human consciousness is not central to the story of creation and reality may be why the stories and pictures of the creators in mythology contain only gods and goddesses and not real, living people. Mythology and math do not contain explicit descriptions of human beings because the human element is sentience, NCR, spirit- or god-like. We only see complex numbers or mythic goddesses and gods. Another way of saying all this is that our self-definition of being human should not be limited to the human form, or that the universe has an NCR human-like nature.

We can notice the absence of an explicit, CR human form in the following religious statements, which all show reality as created without a human form per se[12]:

Sikh Adi Granth: One Word, and the whole Universe throbbed into being.

Old Testament: In the beginning was the Word, and the Word was with God, and the Word was God... And God said, "Let there be light," and there was light.

Islamic Koran: Creator of the heavens and the earth from nothingness, He has only to say when He wills a thing "Be," and it is.

Taoist Tao Te Ching: The nameless is the beginning of heaven and earth. The named is the mother of ten thousand things.

Hindu Upanishads: Accordingly, with the Word, with that Self, he brought forth this whole universe, everything that exists.

The mystic and shaman's NCR view of the universe that we have been exploring differs from that of today's physics, where the physicist plays the central role in creation. At the present in quantum physics, the physicist's decision to create an experiment determines its outcome. From the shaman's NCR viewpoint, however, reality is not the result of objective observers, but of participatory interconnections between sentient beings.

If we ask where this sentience is located, where the roots of consciousness and reality are, we can only answer that *according to the math of quantum physics and the stories of mythology, the roots of consciousness are tendencies found everywhere, at all times.* In other words, the roots of consciousness characterize our universe.

CREATION AND ANNIHILATION

From the foregoing discussion, we can conclude that in order to know ourselves, we need to know the universe. Furthermore, according to the anthropic principle, to know the universe, you need to know yourself.

The anthropic principle offers a few hints about the possible evolution of the universe. If you think about yourself, you know from the foregoing chapters that in a way, you are a dreamline, a quantum wave function, and a tendency to manifest the messages of a big bang or peak experience that you have had.

Our lives can be seen as trying to unfold according to the lines of the dream from the big bangs, or peak experiences. When we marginalize or do not recognize the NCR paths of meaning we are traveling on, we tend to feel cut off from some ground. We can become purely CR oriented, and no longer self-reflect. This marginalization of NCR experiences can leave us feeling partly dead. On the other hand, if we notice the potential significance of our dream lines, we reflect and recognize ourselves unfolding in consensus reality. Our identities then change from being normal everyday people to being a dream, having a life myth connected with the rest of the cosmos. When we live as a dream trying to happen, we feel closer to NCR and are liberated, free of our CR forms.

Regardless of whether we live our lives marginalizing or realizing our true natures, near death, even the most devout atheist seems to sense the return of that marginalized non-consensual reality, the ground of all being, and knows the potentially conscious universe firsthand.

All of us, like Aboriginal people and physicists, theorize about how God's Mind works. From our exploration of math and shamanism, and from the anthropic principle, we can guess that Her mind dreams, and unfolds from a big bang. She adds, She subtracts, and everything She experiences happens in one world, that is, She has "closure." Her awareness is non-local. She is curious and tends to self-reflect, thereby recreating Herself.

Using the anthropic principle, we can create a theory of evolution. We could say that before the universe originated and appeared in Her present CR form, She was dreaming; She was a tendency to exist. At some point, She reflected and unfolded into what we call the present phase of expansion. Her reflection generates CR and our present universe.

As the universe expands, there are two possible experiences. Either Her self-reflection and CR world lead Her to recognizing Her own dreaming Self, or, She marginalizes this Self. One way or another, Her CR aspect disappears or is annihilated. Like the anthropos figures of Pan Ku and Wotan, She collapses and becomes a black hole and dreams in a world of tendencies. In Her dreaming, curiosity returns. She self-reflects and recreates the CR universe. She conjugates what Stephen Hawking called "imaginary time" and creates the expanding universe as we know it today.

In other words, the universe goes through phases of creation and annihilation, self-knowledge and marginalization. This theory, which unifies the math of physics with mythology and psychological experience, implies that the present state of our universe is but one small moment in an infinite, cyclical history of the process of creation and annihilation.

NOTES

1. *Mind and Matter*, page 276.
2. The interpretation of the wave function's probability follows from taking the "absolute square," that is, multiplying the wave function by its conjugate $(a + ib) \times (a - ib) = a^2 + b^2$, which is a real number.

3.   Hawking's idea of parallel universes is like Everett's and DeWitt's, which we discussed in Chapter 17, except for one point. Hawking views interconnections among the universes via "worm hole tubes," whereas Einstein's equations pointed to discontinuities. In the Everett and DeWitt scheme of things, the parallel worlds were not connected.

4.   David Maclagan reports on Native American stories in his *Creation Myths,* page 15.

5.   *Ibid.,* page 15. She thinks, "How can he embrace me after having reproduced me from himself? I shall hide myself." And so she transformed into various animals, through each of which the couple procreates.

6.   *Ibid.*

7.   *Ibid.,* page 43.

8.   This quote comes from Wilson Dunn's *Images Stone B.C.: Thirty Centuries of Northwest Coast Indian Sculpture* (1975). I first saw this information in Marjorie Halpin's "'Seeing' in Stone: Masking and the Twin Stone Masks" in *The Tsimshian: Images of the Past, Views for the Present,* edited by Margaret Seguin (1993).

9.   A stronger principle would receive less attention from physicists today if it claimed there was an executive board of gods who determined things such as the distance of the Earth from the sun and the speed of light. See Brian Hines's *God's Whisper: Creation's Thunder, Echoes of Ultimate Reality in the New Physics,* page 62.

10. The Tsimshian, for example, believed that the human mind was in every way like that of any other sentient being. See note 8.

11. See Marie-Francoise Guerdon's article, "An Introduction to Tsimshian Worldview and its Practitioners," in *The Tsimshian: Images of the Past, Views for the Present,* edited by Margaret Seguin (1993), page 141 and following. "The Tsimshian… have worked out their own version of the universal network: If one is to follow the main myths, for the human being the world looks like a human community surrounded by a spiritual realm, including an animal kingdom with all beings coming and going according to their kinds and interfering with each others' lives. However, if one were to go and become an animal, a salmon for instance, one would discover that salmon people are to themselves, as human beings are to us, and that to them, we human beings, might look like 'naxnoq,' bears feeding on their salmon." In other words, all beings are the same in their communication qualities. Elaboration of this thesis can be found in Halpin, op. cit.

12. See Brian Hines, op.cit., page 62.

IV

PSYCHOLOGY IS
SENTIENT PHYSICS

37 | Symmetry and Consciousness

In the 1950s, Wolfgang Pauli, a Nobel Prize–winning physicist, and Carl Jung, a well-known depth psychologist, wrote a book that brought psychology and physics closer together. Shortly after the publication of that book, both men died, Pauli in 1958 and Jung in 1961. Their work was speculative and courageous and left us with many challenges. This final section of our journey together is a step toward meeting the challenge formulated by Pauli in his work with Jung:

> To us... the only acceptable point of view appears to be the one that recognizes both sides of reality—the quantitative and the qualitative, the physical and the psychic—as compatible with each other, and which can embrace them simultaneously... It would be most satisfactory of all if physics and psyche (i.e., matter and mind) could be seen as complementary aspects of the same reality.[1]

In this chapter, we will be discussing a viewpoint that embraces the physical and the psychic, and which sees matter and mind not only as "complementary" but also as symmetrical.

The viewpoint that has been developing from our previous discussion is that, in order to know yourself, you must understand the universe, and to know the universe, you must understand yourself.

In this and later chapters, using the physics and math we have studied, we will develop this viewpoint and show its significance for psychology.

SHORT REVIEW

Before going forward, let's briefly review our explorations thus far. Early on, we saw that counting in terms of numbers appeared as a largely unconscious process that occurred through marginalizing some of the experiences behind counting. Number systems are derived from accepted linguistic patterns based on the human body.

You probably remember that while an adult may count stones, a child sees the stones in terms of two brown and three black ones. The process of counting an event creates uncertainty through discounting the way in which we choose what to count. The resulting uncertainty occurs whether we are speaking about sheep leaving a pasture, dreams from the night before, or quantum objects in a cloud chamber. Counting maps out certain consensual aspects of unfolding processes but marginalizes the psychology of the observer.

Uncertainty also occurs in calculus. In our discussion of Newton's fluxion (or differential, as it is called today), we discovered that uncertainty arose because you can never measure infinitesimally small increments of what you are counting, which is suggested by the formalism of calculus.[2] Calculus represents the shift that takes place when you move from the world of physical measurement in consensus reality into the domain of fluxion, that is, direct experience of flow and process.

In Chapters 7 and 8, we saw that complex numbers consist of both real and imaginary numbers. The imaginary number i is the square root of minus one, $\sqrt{-1}$. Imaginary numbers are needed to increase the scope and applicability of mathematics, but they also bring a new kind of uncertainty into the mathematics that describes real events. The reason for this uncertainty is that the imaginary number cannot be directly measured. Since the square root of any negative real number is not immediately measurable, its quantitative and CR significance remains obscure. Imaginary numbers add a new, immeasurable dimension to reality.

COMPLEX NUMBERS IN QUANTUM PHYSICS

Physicists use imaginary numbers to describe many aspects of nature, including the wave function in quantum mechanics and space-time in relativity. Since an imaginary number times itself becomes a real number, imaginary or complex numbers have the wonderful characteristic of becoming real when they are conjugated. And real numbers can be measured. Although imaginary and complex numbers are very useful, physicists do not speculate about what these numbers might refer to because they cannot be directly measured. They simply conform to abstract mathematical reasoning.

Since physics uses imaginary numbers to describe the basic wave equation of quantum mechanics and space-time in relativity, the exact meaning of these equations has remained obscure. In our journey together, we have discovered some solutions to a basic question that has previously remained unanswered in physics: How does consciousness enter physics?

We have seen that consciousness enters quantum mechanics during the process of conjugation in the form of the reflection of quantum flirts; these reduce or "collapse" the wave function that was all over space into one locality, thereby creating an observation.

By ignoring the significance of complex numbers and by conjugating them to arrive at "real" numbers, physics "works" effectively enough in reality without understanding its own roots.[3] Physics uses the mathematical rules for complex numbers in quantum mechanics and relativity without knowing exactly what these rules mean.[4] Until now, there has been no known physical principle that explained the use of conjugation in computing what happens in reality.

I suggested in earlier chapters that conjugation, that is, multiplying an imaginary number by its mirror image, represents our sentient, self-reflective tendency, which precedes consciousness and observations.

You may wonder how something as unknown as an imaginary number could be so central to comprehending the patterns and laws of physical reality. My answer is that we do many things based on assumptions we do not fully understand. For example, therapists work with dreams to understand the everyday behavior of people, yet no one knows for sure what dreams are. Likewise, we don't understand imaginary numbers, yet they help to describe the behavior of observable, physical processes.

Just as many physicists, including Einstein, wondered about what he called the "unreasonable effectiveness" of mathematics in physics, many therapists wonder about the unreasonable effectiveness of dreams in understanding people. My thesis is that this "unreasonable effectiveness" exists because it reflects simply or mysteriously what math and dreaming really are—holistic and total representations of reality. This holistic reality is encoded in imaginary numbers whose characteristics are similar to dreaming experiences.[5] Dreaming, too, contains both real and imaginary phenomena, and dreaming, like complex numbers, when reflected upon, produces realizable insights, actions, and results. Dreaming is sentient; that is, it comes from a level of awareness in which subliminal perceptions, hunches, intuitions, and preverbal feelings occur.

Thus imaginary numbers, which play a central role in quantum physics and relativity, resemble the awareness experience, self-reflection, and the psychology behind the physics of observation.

Let's take an example from psychology. Let's consider pain, which is both a CR and an NCR experience. Pain is a form of dreaming and is similar to a complex number. For instance, pain from a tumor can be traced to "real" things, such as the pressure the tumor creates on the surrounding tissue. But other aspects of pain cannot be traced. You can't measure the feeling which can only be approximated by the statement, "That feels like hell!" Sentient experiences such as pain resemble complex numbers. Pain has both real and imaginary characteristics, symbolized by the combination of a real and an imaginary number, such as $(a + ib)$. The "real" component is linked to the pressure from the tumor. But the "imaginary" "hell" of the pain is a non-consensual, subjective feeling. That is why even when some tumors are removed, the sense of pain remains although there is no "physical" reason for this.

Only real numbers are crucial to the results of physics, which has marginalized the significance of imaginary numbers until now. However, psychology cannot get along without understanding the complex realm. In physics, only CR or "real" experiences are given credence; imaginary experiences have not been considered relevant. Medicine is the same. We ignore the significance of hell, and focus mainly on the tumor.

In Chapter 16, we discussed Heisenberg's uncertainty principle in quantum mechanics, which says there is a limit to what you can know about a quantum object in CR. You cannot track its path in CR without completely disturbing that path. However, I suggested that you can know its path through dreaming and experiencing it in NCR.

When we discussed relativity, we spoke not only about the relativity of the framework of our perceptions, but also about the non-relativity of the speed of light and that special measure called space-time separation, which is constant in all frameworks. Space-time is a metaphor for the common ground that we experience in synchronicities and in the coming together of groups.

In events with velocities greater than the speed of light, you land in the realm of imaginary numbers and NCR once again. In this realm, the math for space-time allows for NCR interpretations of events in terms of synchronicity, projections, dreams, and movement that goes forward, backward, and out of time.[6]

CONSCIOUSNESS

The perspectives of NCR experiences, psychology, and traditional shamanism help physics find its basis. To understand more about physics, we need to understand more about NCR experiences in psychology and shamanism. Let's explore how to differentiate the everyday phenomena of psychology such as perception, self-reflection, and consciousness in terms of mathematics. The meaning of these terms and their connection to the wave function are examined in the Appendix. The following is a summary of these connections.

1. **Wave Function and Dreaming.** The wave function is to physics as dreaming is to shamanism and psychology. The wave function describes basic, elementary NCR processes behind material reality and is the tendency for events to occur.

   From the viewpoint of consensus realty, dreaming is the tendency for things to happen. For example, we cannot measure the pain that is connected with the pressure from a tumor and to "hell," yet we can apprehend this experience in NCR as a tendency for pain to occur and unfold itself in everyday reality.

2. **Consensus Reality and Conjugation.** Consensus reality is generated in quantum physics though observation, through the mathematics of conjugation, which I have interpreted as noticing, unfolding, and reflecting quantum flirts.

   In physics, the process of observation begins in NCR through flirts between the observer and the observed. In psychology, these flirts may occur, for example, between our everyday attention and body sensations. For instance, we can notice the feeling of "hell" in a tumor and unfold or generate it through reflecting upon it. If we do this consciously, the hellish "tendency" may unfold as a fiery heat, then as a passion. By living this passion in CR, the bodily sensation of "hell" in the sentient realm can disappear. Conjugation "collapses" the wave function.

   While the conjugation behind reality occurs automatically and unconsciously in physics, in psychology and shamanism the observer becomes a participant and can co-create and change everyday reality. We will discover how to do this in the following chapters.

3. **Consciousness and Observation.** While the process of observation appears in the math of physics as automatic and involuntary (in conjugating the wave function), according to what I have just said, observation can be tracked in a voluntary or an involuntary manner. When it is voluntary, we can choose to pay attention and reflect upon the subtle NCR flirts—such as pain—thereby participating in creating reality.

   What the physicist calls observation is analogous to what the psychologist calls consciousness. Once observation or consciousness occurs through conjugation, the observer can choose to marginalize NCR experiences or unfold and track them further.

   Thus observation is experienced as a superficial act or as a very deep event based on sentient experience. When you conjugate with awareness, you notice you are constantly participating in quantum flirting in the NCR domain. This means that what you call consensus reality and consciousness is not a fundamental reality but more like a platform supported above the ground by NCR experiences such as the sentient, interactional processes between people and objects.

Remember Hawking's view of the universe. Just as there are wave functions for all objects, the universe has a wave function as well. Based on our foregoing discussion, we have to consider that the universe is dreaming and creates CR through its own self-reflection. The universe creates itself, so to speak, through tracking and reflecting its experience. This implies that all of its parts are involved in mutual, NCR interactions in quantum reflections. The universe is like a curious person with a tendency toward self-awareness.

DIVERSE NCR PATHS TO CONSCIOUSNESS

Now that we have reviewed some of our learning, let's see what we can reveal about psychology from the foregoing physics and math. The math of physics predicts that conjugation can take place in many different ways, analogous to the many different ways in which you and I can reflect upon a situation and create observations and consciousness.[7] To understand the significance of what the math of physics predicts, let's examine some of the diverse psychological or NCR paths that create everyday reality.

Consider the communication between you and me. Let's pretend we are reflecting together on our feelings about one another. Say you decide to speak to me first about your experiences. Talking to me is a consensual interconnection between you and me and can be sketched as follows.

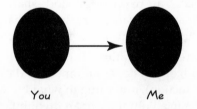

You   Me

37.1 Consensus reality: You speak to me first.

Various types of NCR interactions may occur before you speak to me. We could call these interactions by various names, including dreaming, flirting, sentient awareness, conjugation, projection, and dreaming up. Regardless of what we call these NCR interactions, they all have the following characteristics predicted by the math of physics (see the Appendix for details):

Non-locality, no space. In NCR, the CR ideas of here and there, you and me, become disrupted. We do not know where your or my awareness is located in space. Part of our communication is based on a shared mind, so to speak.

Non-temporality, no time direction. Though we may be clear that our CR communication was initiated by you, in NCR we cannot separate you from me in time because an NCR experience of a signal from me to you could just as well be the echo of an NCR signal originating in me. There is no way of being certain about the direction of time in NCR; we cannot tell who did what first. The CR question about time, "Did you flirt with me or I with you?" cannot be answered.

Non-personality, no inner or outer. Did you send me an NCR signal or are you a part of me, trying to connect with the rest of me? The differentiation of who you and I are becomes blurred with the world around us.

Thus an NCR picture of you and me might be something like the Tai Chi, a rotating circle in which the concepts of you and me are impermanent.

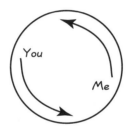

37.2 NCR version of you and me as a whole: The boundaries between us as NCR communicators are not visible.

From the viewpoint of consensus reality, no one can tell for sure whether we are dreaming, self-reflecting, conjugating, flirting, projecting, or dreaming one another up to do certain things because all these NCR processes are subjective and undifferentiatable to outer observers. Were you projecting, or did I evoke your reaction? Was flirting involved? Who reflected upon what to create our situation? You and I will surely have our own NCR experiences of these events, but from the outside, all or any of these various processes could have occurred. Any one of them could have led to where we are in relationship.

To use an analogy of how various NCR experiences may be either singularly or collectively equivalent to a CR situation, and how any or all of these interactions can be considered to have created any observation in consensus reality, think about going from home to work.

You can walk through the park, take a cab, use a bus, jog, have a friend pick you up, or take a helicopter. But as far as your boss at work is concerned, all she notices is that you are coming through the door of your office. If you don't tell her, she will not be able to tell which path you took. In a way, all paths are equivalent for her, since what matters is only your arrival at work.

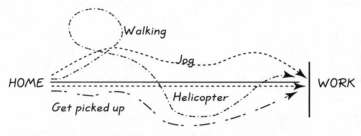

37.3 The various paths to work

For you, however, the paths are not equivalent: some paths feel better than others do. Analogously, some NCR paths to reality feel better than others do.

In the example where you speak to me first, projection may be less useful than self-reflection. Your statement may be based on what you project upon me, instead of on how you reflected about what part of yourself you projected onto me.

Psychology deals with the various ways of going to work, so to speak. There are myriad NCR ways of being present in the world. Some ways make life miserable; others make it more enjoyable. The path you take to arrive where you are is a non-consensus activity because it depends on your individuality and your relationship to your dreaming.

From the framework of CR, NCR paths are difficult to distinguish. You and I, however, feel that our various experiences occur simultaneously, separately, and move forward or backward in time, slower or faster than the speed of light.

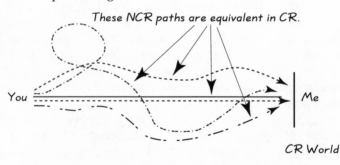

37.4 Various NCR paths behind reality are equivalent for the CR world.

You and I have choices; we can marginalize or notice which path we are on. We can project, dream one another up, reflect our own dreaming, reflect flirts from one another, conjugate our experiences, and track the innermost experience behind our CR interaction.

Here is a list of possible CR names for NCR interactions that are patterned by the rules of quantum mechanics described in the Appendix.

1. **Measuring or Interpreting.** In quantum physics, measuring or interpreting occurs by taking the absolute square in mathematics. Measuring or interpreting in psychology occurs when an observer focuses only on consensual reality, making observations through measurements and interpretations of tendencies in a way that marginalizes their imaginary aspects. Notice how you marginalize aspects of what you observe.

2. **Reflection or Conjugation.** You can voluntarily or involuntarily reflect upon a dreamlike, sentient experience and conjugate or unfold it. If this reflection is done voluntarily, shamans call it lucid dreaming.

3. **Flirting and Dreaming Together.** You and I can create reality through flirting with one another. When we notice these flirts, we co-create reality.

4. **Projecting and Dreaming Up.** In projection, you confuse your NCR experience with CR. You believe your dreaming is consensus reality, whereas on closer inspection, you notice your dreaming is an aspect of yourself.

   In dreaming up, you do not realize that your CR behavior can be seen as having been evoked by signals from me. I dream you up, so to speak. Your behavior comes from signals that seem to be originating only in me. In both projection and dreaming up, you marginalize your NCR role in events, the quantum flirts between us.

CR is created in great part by marginalizing the experiences of reflection, dreaming up, flirting, interpreting, and measuring. None of these paths to reality can be clearly differentiated in CR according to the math of quantum mechanics, yet they are all crucial to psychology.

INDIVIDUATION AND COLLECTIVE CONSCIOUSNESS

The non-locality and non-temporality of these various paths mean that you participate and reflect in dreaming with whatever or whomever catches your attention. For example, think about a man, John, who may be very rough but marginalizes his own rough behavior—he just doesn't see it. When you reflect this to him, he begins to sees how rough he has been.

However, your ability to reflect his behavior depends on your having this behavior in yourself. In short, in NCR, there is roughness without specific locality or time. Everyone who notices roughness participates in it, though in the end, John may be the one who says he became conscious of his unconscious behavior. *Consciousness has location and timing, but the flirting which gave rise to it was shared by all sentient beings involved.*

Thus, in a way, personal growth is really personal only in CR; in NCR it depends on everything and everyone participating in flirting and creating consciousness. We should broaden the concept of consciousness so that it does not only belong to one person but includes everything we notice as part of its roots.

Similarly, what physics refers to as an observer could be seen as someone who is unaware of her NCR interactions with the objects she observes. The classical observer marginalizes the fact that what she looks at is a reflection of herself. During observation, objects become partners in dreaming.

Whatever you observe in consensus reality—be it an electron, an animal, the universe or another person—becomes inseparable from you in the domain of dreaming. In CR, you cannot say where the quantum flirt originated—whether from you or me. This indistinguishability appears in the math of physics as symmetry.

The result of comparing the math of physics with psychology is simple: *In NCR dreaming, what we call you could just as well be called me.*[8]

INTEGRATION AND WAVE FUNCTION COLLAPSE

Psychology is based on personal growth that occurs through "integration" of dreaming. The analogy to integration in physics is called "collapsing the wave function." Let me explain.

Dreaming is a non-local experience—that is, its location is unknown and sentient. The location of dreaming is nowhere and everywhere at once. This non-locality is similar to that of the wave function, which is located throughout the universe as a tendency or pre-observation state. At the moment of observation in physics, the wave function mysteriously collapses into being a particle with a more or less specific location.

The process of collapsing a wave function through observation is analogous to integrating a piece of unconscious content. For the dreamer, integration means reflecting and experiencing a figure in a dream that carries qualities that have been "in the air" as a potential part of the dreamer's own personality located in a certain time and place. In the moment of such reflection, integration occurs. Integration consists of the realization that a piece of the environment—a dream figure or someone onto whom something was projected—is a mirror image of an aspect of one's own behavior.

In other words, integration collapses the non-locality of dreaming into a specific place. In psychology, consciousness, or the process of integration, begins when you focus on NCR dreaming experiences, which may seem to be anywhere, and ends when you locate the dream as a reality in yourself. Likewise, observation collapses wave functions in physics. Observation begins with a tendency for an object's wave function to be all over space and time and ends by locating it in one spot.

Thus consciousness and integration are to psychology as observation and the collapse of the wave function are to physics. However, integration and the collapse of the wave function are not just similar in the metaphorical sense. In NCR, they are one and the same phenomenon. Parapsychological phenomena such as the following seem to support this hypothesis.

Some years ago, when I worked in Switzerland, I was amazed at how integration resolved a parapsychological problem. A family brought their twelve-year-old daughter to see me because she was regularly visited by poltergeists, spooks banging on the window of the living room each time the family sat down to dinner. Her family asked for my help, each attesting dramatically to the noise made by the poltergeist. They were frightened by the spook and said it banged on the window only when the twelve-year-old was there.

I asked the girl to play a game with me. I suggested that the girl, who had been very quiet until that point, make noise and bang on the floor of my office. I remembered that the German word "Poltern" means "banging." She was shy at first but after making some noise and enjoying herself in my practice, said she would try that at home as well. I asked her to bang the table at home and to express herself loudly, especially when the poltergeist was near.

The girl followed my suggestions and "integrated" the poltergeist. She not only reflected its behavior in my office but at home as well. To her family's surprise, instead of remaining the quiet girl she had been until then, she became quite rowdy at dinner. The otherwise quiet family was thrilled, however, with the obstreperous child, because as soon she banged on the table at dinner, the poltergeist disappeared and never returned.

What happened? You could say that the poltergeist is like a wave function, that is, it is partially real—everyone heard it—and partially imaginary, since it was never caught on film. It was like a complex number, an NCR reality for that family. Like a wave function, the poltergeist collapsed when it was reflected by the girl who banged on her family table.

From one viewpoint you could say that the girl integrated the poltergeist by giving it a specific and permanent location in her own behavior. Before that, its locality, its home, was unknown. Before the twelve-year-old did her banging, the family said it was somewhere around in the atmosphere of their house.

From another viewpoint, the girl dreamed up the poltergeist. In a way she provoked nature by being so quiet. Or perhaps she had been flirting with it without telling anyone. Still another explanation is that the poltergeist, like the wave function, was an aspect of dreaming, part of the whole environment in central Europe and, of course, part of my psychology as well.

All of these explanations are theoretically equivalent, since we cannot test which is the one and only correct one. The child would say that a part of her had been projected onto that poltergeist spirit, a boisterous part that she had been too shy to play out in everyday life.

However, you could just as well argue that the poltergeist spirit did not belong to the girl at all, but to her whole family. She was simply the "identified patient" of the family, which, as a unit, had a problem being noisy. Other schools of psychology or parapsychology will have other theories about what happened. Some will say that she had repressed her sexuality, or that an archetype was constellated, or that an alien being from another planet had arrived, or that a long-dead ghost had come back to life.

All of these interpretations are like virtual particle interpretations. Depending on the state of consciousness of the people involved, all such interpretations can be useful. As far as the event of the poltergeist itself is concerned, all interpretations are equivalent and cannot be differentiated from one another. You could say that the poltergeist event had many different sides, and that the view from each side is equivalent from the CR viewpoint, since each leads to the final collapse of the wave function, the disappearance of the poltergeist, or its integration. Each view is valuable, and each is equivalent from the final viewpoint.

Answers to questions such as how or why the banging on shutters occurred without wind or known causes and why the banging stopped after the girl banged cannot be tested. Since CR has no means of measurement of NCR experience, a CR observer can call this luck, although a shaman or therapist might speak about having tapped spiritual powers.

Here we see the difference and similarity between integration and observation. The two concepts are similar in collapsing a tendency into a psychological or physical fact. Yet they are also different. In the case of integration, the observer picks up NCR tendencies and becomes them. All dreamlike events become potentially meaningful. In the case of physics, however, non-consensual events have no meaning, since meaning is an NCR quality and observers do not attempt to benefit psychologically from what they see. Instead, they marginalize the feelings and personal experiences connected to their observations.

In the collapse of the wave function and the integration of flirting, dreamlike material, we see how psychology and physics may eventually become one science. Pauli hoped for such a unification, saying, "it would be most satisfactory of all if physics and psyche (i.e., matter and mind) could be seen as complementary aspects of the same reality." Indeed, our discussion of the math that describes NCR realities gives us a hint about what the shared reality must be. The common ground of physics and psychology is the preverbal, NCR reality of dreaming expressed in the math of physics as complex numbers and as dreamlike and mythic figures in psychology. To use Pauli's words, "physics and psyche" are "complementary aspects of the same reality."

What appears in CR to be psyche or matter is impossible to distinguish in NCR. Whether events were material or psychological, you or me, object or observer, personal, collective, meaningful, or meaningless is a matter of perspective.

While consensus reality observers remain either awestruck or distrustful of the apparent non-locality and symmetrical behavior of NCR events, both the traditional shamanic warrior and the modern shaman en route to self-knowledge know that the purpose of existence is to get beyond the reality of everyday life by living and moving through the world of dreaming.

The girl in the poltergeist story demonstrates the basic difference between physics and shamanism. In physics, as in everyday life, observers remain in CR, gazing through consensual lenses at the dreaming world, in our case, the poltergeist. In shamanism, the warrior "on the path of self-knowledge" "stops the world," steps out of CR to investigate dreaming.[9]

Although stepping out of time is a speculation in today's physics, tomorrow's science will be different. Dreaming will be seen as the universe's background process, as an ancient shamanic path. In the newly emerging worldview, the modern shaman will be able to move beyond consensus reality's stultifying identification of her. As far as observers in consensus reality are concerned, she will become an unpredictable spirit, an enigmatic sentient being, part of a symmetrical universe where space, time, and consensus reality are not as important as immediate, direct experience.

The modern shaman enters dreaming, meets poltergeists and whatever else presents itself, shape-shifts and becomes them. In time, her identity as an ordinary person transforms as she realizes she is awareness, a non-local entity that CR observers can no longer understand. As she frees herself from the concepts of locality and time, the consensual views of what it means to be a person no longer bind her. For her, the math and symmetry principles of physics are but a pale description of the experience of her total Self. For her, psychological explanations seem pale in comparison with the colorful experience of dreaming.

NOTES

1. From *The Interpretation of Nature and the Psyche,* by C.G. Jung and W. Pauli, pages 208 to 210.

2. The fluxion or differential is ds/dt in calculus. The level that can be measured was denoted by $\Delta s / \Delta t$ as Δt approaches zero. These symbols indicate making very rapid measurements of distances, Δs, which take only short times, Δt.

3. This means that only the real number solutions are given significance; the imaginary solutions to problems are marginalized as insignificant. For example, the equations used to describe the amplitude of a pendulum's swing may have real and imaginary components. Only the real ones, however, have any "sense," to quote Richard Feynman, in his *Lectures on Physics.*

4. To repeat, if a complex number has the general form $a + ib$, where a and b are real, the complex conjugate or reflection of $a + ib$ is $a - ib$. While $a + ib$ itself cannot be measured or discussed in consensus reality, the result of conjugation—also called "taking the absolute square"—is a real number and can be measured. That is, $(a + ib) \times (a - ib) = a^2 + b^2$, which is a "real," consensus measurable number. See the Appendix for the way in which these mathematical definitions fit quantum mechanical rules.

5. Pauli and Jung, op. cit., noted that numbers describe a unitary realm that is both psyche and matter, as we can see in quantum mechanics and relativity.

6. As we see below, the Lorentz transformation for space, x, and time, t, becomes imaginary if v is larger than c (see Chapter 24), since the value of the numbers under the square root signs becomes negative and the square root of a negative number is imaginary:

$$x' = \frac{x - vt}{\sqrt{1 - v^2/c^2}} \quad \text{and} \quad t' = \frac{t - vx/c^2}{\sqrt{1 - v^2/c^2}}$$

7. See the Appendix for how the math of physics predicts that conjugation can happen in many different ways.

8. In other words, the CR results of psychology remain unaltered if we switch our CR identities of "me" with "not me." We cannot differentiate in NCR between you and me. The consensus reality observer cannot differentiate locality in dreaming. We can say that the mathematical formalism behind quantum physics is symmetrical as to a and b. Remember the wave function, appearing in the form a + ib. Consensus reality occurs through conjugation, namely, $(a + ib) \times (a - ib) = a^2 + b^2$. Consensus reality does not change if we reverse a and b. In other words, what we call ourselves and the other are reversible.

9. In *The Shaman's Body* I talk about methods for stopping the world of consensus reality and following dreaming.

38 | Dreambody: Two Kinds of Death

> *We may well now ask whether the close analogy*
> *between quantum process and our inner experiences*
> *and thought processes is mere coincidence... the*
> *remarkable point-by-point analogy between thought*
> *processes and quantum processes would suggest that a*
> *hypothesis relating these two may well turn out to be*
> *fruitful. If such a hypothesis could ever be verified, it*
> *would explain in a natural way a great many features of*
> *our thinking.*

—David Bohm in *Quantum Theory*

We are now moving into the training ground of modern shamanism. Shamans travel in and out of consensus reality time as they move through non-consensual worlds. To learn how to step in and out of time, we can follow the teachings of the shaman don Juan, the psychologist C.G. Jung, or the space-time diagrams of the physicist Richard Feynman. Studying the shamanistic powers, psychological complexes, and creation and annihilation diagrams in space-time will give us new insights into the nature of death.

Disturbances in your ordinary attention give you immediate access to the appearance of dreaming during times of consensus reality orientation. These disturbances may occur as slight flickering in your attention, sudden slips of the tongue, fleeting fantasies, or as more permanent processes such as persistent altered states or comatose conditions resulting, for example, from brain injury.

There are two methods to deal with dreaming: one is to remain in CR and to understand the disturbances, incorporating their messages into your everyday life. The other is to switch realities, taking the disturbance in attention as an invitation to altered states and altered identities. The first is the interpretative method of the therapist, the second, the shaman's way. Both are valuable, though very different, as we shall see shortly.

THE ANALYST'S METHOD

Jung called complexes "disturbances of attention" and originally thought that their etiology was traumatic, that is, that they were caused by painful events in the past.[1] He said that complexes manifested as "split off experiences, splinter psyches" (such as the poltergeist in Chapter 37) and that they were "the architect of dreams." In his "Review of the Complex Theory" Jung says, "the etiology of complexes is frequently a so-called trauma, a shock or some such thing, that's split off a bit from the psyche." Later Jung realized that complexes did not arise only from traumatic, shocking experiences but may have had no ostensible origin at all, that they were simply "archetypal."

In any case, a complex is the process arising when a body feeling, movement, word, or memory disturbs your attention, whether or not the origin of the emotional experience can be found in your past. Jung noticed that when people were "in a complex," the electrical conductivity of their skin changed. It was from this observation that the lie detector test was developed. Lie detector machines measure changes in the electrical characteristics of the skin when a subject lies, or is in a complex.

Just as wave functions are the patterns of particles, dreams show the patterns of complexes. Both complexes and particles can be measured, but you cannot see dreams or wave functions; they are NCR patterns that cannot be measured in consensus reality. To work on complexes and disturbances of attention, you need access to dreaming.

THE CR APPEARANCE OF COMPLEXES

To measure complexes, Jung developed the complex association experiment by asking the "test person" to report the first word that came to mind in connection with each specific word Jung mentioned. Jung created a diagram with different words and measured the time it took a person to respond to each of them. The words that produced the longest response times indicated that a complex was present. If the test subject took a longer time to associate to the word "forest" than to the other words, Jung would say, "You have a 'forest' complex." Let's say it took a second to respond to the test word "mother" with the response "father" but then more than a whole second to respond with "beautiful" to "forest." This makes "forest" a complex. In the terms of the preceding work on physics, we might say there are two processes happening at the same time, which interfere with one another in connection with the word "forest."

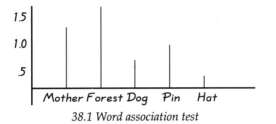

38.1 Word association test

Jung discovered that dreams seemed to be constructed around complexes because identifying a person's complexes via the word association test allowed him to reliably predict the content of their dreams. For example, the person in the above experiment might dream about a forest, or meeting a bear in a forest.

Complexes are multi-channeled; that is, they manifest in both dreams and body phenomena—although in his practice Jung mainly focused on how they appeared in dreams. We know today that dreaming and NCR experiences appear in everyday life in the form of body symptoms, relationship signals, and addictions, as well as in disturbances of attention, slips of the tongue, and fantasies.

SHAMANS WITH COMPLEXES

While a therapist might see a complex as an invitation to knowing herself better, a modern shaman sees the disturbance of attention as another world knocking on the door of consensus reality. While most of us keep that door shut to repress or analyze the other world, the shaman opens that door to meet the unknown. What happens when we open that door to dreaming is unpredictable.

In Chapter 5, we saw that the first edge in dreaming is the edge to getting into it. This edge occurs each time that a complex disturbs your attention. How you deal with the phenomena that disturb your attention determines the kind of life you lead. Sometimes analyzing the dreamlike experience or integrating it by adjusting everyday attitudes is sufficient. But frequently, nothing resolves a disturbance besides going through that door of reality and entering directly into the river of dreaming.

Fear of the unknown meets you at the door to dreaming, fear of freedom from your old identity. At the point where dreaming disturbs your focus, your identity and CR framework are challenged, shaken, or destroyed, depending on the strength of the dreaming process. The meeting between dreaming and your CR identity is represented in Figure 38.2.

In Figure 38.2, your process over time can be seen as a more or less continuous line starting from the left and moving upward. As you first meet a complex, you experience it as a sort of force field that disturbs your focus. Let's call the normal identity, which is shaken by complexes, your "primary process" and the content of the dreaming—such as a scary forest—a "secondary process." In the following diagram, you move along in time to the right until you meet your secondary process, an unknown that goes by the label "forest." At this moment, you meet your edge and become split.

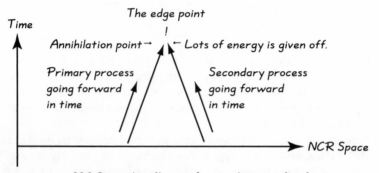

38.2 Space-time diagram for experiences at the edge

Let's imagine a possible real experience and say that you are actually taking a hike, either alone or with a friend, and come to a forest. The appearance of a forest sets you into a terrible complex. You fear a bear might be in there.

There are now two processes going on at the same time. You are still your ordinary self and, at the same time, you begin to fear and fantasize about what is in that forest. At the edge, you come face to face with that mysterious forest. At this moment, your primary process falters; you can no longer go on as you have been, and a sort of annihilation takes place in which your primary identity becomes temporarily interrupted.

On the left side of the "hill" in the above diagram, you see your primary process, your normal self, and on the right side of the hill are your secondary processes—the mysterious forest and bear, which plummet you into an altered and disturbed state of consciousness. The electric characteristics of your body change; your movements become hesitant, your mouth dry, and you may seem dazed or just quiet to your hiking companion.

At the top of the diagram is the edge where the primary and secondary processes are divided. That is the border between the worlds. Lots of energy and excitement occur here. This is the point where you feel as if your path will be upset or annihilated, where your consciousness is taken over by complexes.

Let's pretend you normally identify with being a very sober and clear person. This is your primary process. For you, being afraid, getting dizzy, or having trance-like feelings is a secondary process. You tend to marginalize, or disidentify with, these trance-like states.

What happens when you actually enter a forest can be seen in the above diagram. Since you are normally clear and sober and fear the trance-like states associated with the forest, you tend to avoid it. Now imagine you are facing the forest. For you, this is like entering an electric field, and everything that happens is magical and numinous. While walking into that forest, you feel dizzy and unwell, your attention is disturbed, and lots of extra energy and sweat are radiated into the universe! You struggle to remain with your old identity but change is impending. At the edge, you feel scared, uncertain, and confused, but also excited. You ask yourself and your hiking companion whether you should stop... or should you go into the feelings you are having? Should you detach from your old identity and move with the flow of feelings into your secondary process, or sit down because you feel ill?

ANTIMATTER AND SECONDARY PROCESSES

Let's stop here for a moment. Before discussing what you are going to do in that forest and with that bear, let's discuss the analogy to this situation in physics: the scattering diagram for a charged particle in a strong field. This diagram (see Figures 38.4 and 38.5) was originally developed by Richard Feynman to explain what happens to a piece of matter like an electron when its direction is changed by a field.[2] This diagram introduces a new concept, antimatter, which is simply ordinary matter with an opposite charge.

The antimatter positron is the same as an electron but has a positive instead of a negative charge. By analogy we could say that the bear is to you as antimatter is to matter. The bear is, in short, your own antimatter double, your bearlike personality, which is the same as you in many ways but has an opposite charge! For example, you may be exhausted, but the bear is full of energy. Similarly, antimatter is like matter but has an opposite charge.

Richard Feynman was largely responsible for developing quantum electrodynamics, or QED, the theory that uses virtual particles to explain electric fields. Feynman's diagram (see Figures 38.4 and 38.5) explains what happens to an electron that moves through an electric field in terms of the creation and annihilation of the short-lived, virtual particles, the electron and positron pair on the bottom right of the diagram. You may remember from Chapter 34 that no one can actually measure those particles or prove that they get created, yet the rules of physics allow us to think the particles could be there. They are created out of fluctuations in the electric field.

Feynman's original electron is analogous to what I have been calling the primary process, the way in which we normally identify ourselves. Furthermore, what Feynman refers to as antimatter, I have been calling secondary processes. In this analogy, the feelings of being pulled and pushed by what you experience near the edge in a complex field are similar to what happens to an electron in an electric field in physics. The creation of a fantasy about the bear and your relationship to it is analogous to the creation of a virtual electron/positron pair. Your fantasy cannot be proven to actually exist in CR, yet you surely feel it!

The analogies we will be discussing are shown below.

PSYCHOLOGY	PHYSICS
Field created by complex	Electric field
Primary process, being clear	Matter, like an electron
Secondary process, the bear	Antimatter, like a positron
Edge	Annihilation point

38.3 Analogies between complexes and electric fields

Feynman did not speak of complexes or primary or secondary processes but described how a piece of matter such as an electron behaves in an electric field that pulls and pushes or "scatters" the electron. He did this by reinterpreting the math of quantum mechanics (a mathematical "formalism" developed by Paul Dirac), much as we have been reinterpreting quantum mechanics to understand conjugation.[3]

In Feynman's reinterpretation, a scattered electron in a field can be seen in two ways. In the first view, portrayed in Figure 38.4, the electron moves forward in time where it meets a field, temporarily creating an electron/positron pair (lower right in the diagram), and is eventually annihilated by the antimatter particle of that pair. Finally, the electron of that pair reemerges, deflected in a new direction.

Feynman's second interpretation (Figure 38.5) shows a surprising *backward* movement in time. At first, the electron moves forward and then backward in time; no electron/positron pair creations or antimatter annihilations occur.

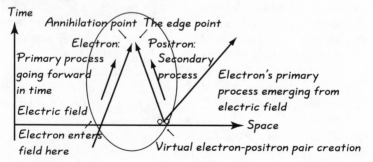

38.4 Electron scattering in an electric field involving the creation of a positron

Now let's consider the connections with psychology. The electron meeting the charge field, which deflects it, is a metaphor for your sober, primary process, which is altered by the forest. What happens at the edge in the forest can be understood in two ways.

Annihilation. The first possibility is that you, or by analogy, the electron, continue to hold on to your identity and go forward in time. When you meet the field of the forest, a virtual pair is created analogously to the positron and the other electron in Figure 38.4. This creation occurs in your fantasy where you meet a bear. Just as the electron gets annihilated by its antimatter positron, you get dazed, "knocked unconscious" by the effect of that forest fantasy. A while later, you awaken and reemerge from the forest; your path was changed, but you barely know why.

The Fluid Self. In Figure 38.5, we see a second possibility for Feynman's electron, which follows a continuous path (physicists call this a "world line" in space-time) that goes first up and then down, that is, forward and then backward in time. This electron is immortal; it simply steps out of time and reverses its own direction instead of being annihilated by the positron. This is how it avoids annihilation and death.

In Feynman's words, the path of the electron is like a road through life. "It is as though a bombardier flying low over a road suddenly sees three roads and it is only when two of them come together and disappear again that he realizes that he has simply passed over a long switchback in a single road...."[4]

In Figure 38.5, I represent the Feynman theory of how an electron is bumped about in a field and its psychological analogy, a tense situation like getting into a complex. I equate the original electron with the primary process and the positron, which is a virtual antimatter aspect of the electron matter, with secondary processes such as the bear in the forest. In other words, it is as if matter has two aspects: one is the way we normally identify it, and the other is its antimatter, or secondary aspect.

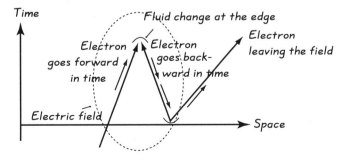

38.5 Electron's time reversal in an electric field

Normally, you rarely think about the details of what happens to you in a complex. You simply enter places like the forest and reemerge from such troubled areas of life as if they were blanks (see Figure 38.6).

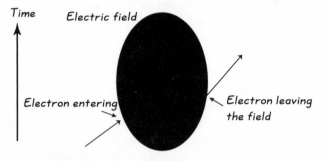

38.6 What happens in the electric field is a mystery.

Physicists realize as well that what happens to an electron in this electric field is a blank, that is, non-consensual. That is why Feynman decided to imagine the virtual particle interactions that occurred within this field. Likewise, shamans realized that what happens when you get into a complex is non-consensual. Traditional shamans (and modern ones too) realize that such moments are the chance of a lifetime. Traditional shamanism has explored the different paths a shaman-warrior might take through NCR.

Feynman's second possibility of going forward and backward in time uses an overall space-time viewpoint. In this view, the forward movement of time and the imaginary positron are abandoned. Instead you find yourself in a world where continuous flow in a non-consensus reality is possible, where you can go backward or "out of time," so to speak.

Feynman found that both views are permitted by the math of physics, although physics will never be able to track in CR the path of the electron and prove, once and for all, whether it was annihilated by its opposite or whether it fluidly stepped out of time and went backward into history before reemerging from the field. No one knows how to reverse time in a laboratory to measure such events. Feynman's theory is an attempt to explain the overall observed phenomena—the great egg into and out of which things enter and emerge.

Now let's return to psychology. The analogy to the Feynman diagrams can be understood with the help of the story we began earlier. Imagine two scenarios of the scene in the forest.

Annihilation. In one scene, analogous to the first Feynman diagram (Figure 38.4), you move forward in time, enter the forest, and become uncomfortable. You fear losing your cool, clear head and suddenly can no longer pay attention or remember what is happening. You imagine meeting a bear. Your attention and focus are disturbed. You cannot follow what is being said, you get into a complex. As you move forward in time, you become more and more upset and finally go into a dazed, altered state of consciousness. At the edge, your fantasy of the bear "annihilates" you, so to speak. While you are "tranced out," you fantasize the forest, its magical powers, and the bear standing on its hind legs. A few minutes later, you come out of your trance feeling normal again. It is as if you were "knocked out" for a few minutes.

Immortality. An alternative scene (the second Feynman diagram, Figure 38.5) is one in which your identity is more fluid. You enter the forest, feel uncomfortable, and sense a kind of knock on the door from the world of dreaming. You are a shaman and, using your well-developed second attention and your courage, you realize that the fantasy of the bear in the forest is inviting you to let go of your clear, cool mind. You go over your edge, let go of your self temporarily, and go into an altered state. You reverse your path, becoming the bear on its hind legs. Your hiking companion may not believe what she is seeing. There you are, standing like a bear, having hypnotic, magical powers. You shape-shift into the bear form, and your body dances and sings. You reverse yourself and totally lose track of time, which for you is no longer binding.

You were clear before, but now you are singing and dancing in ecstasy. In a way, you move counterclockwise, that is, counter to your normal direction in life. You become your double. You lose track of time in CR, enter into "your own world" and let your dreaming process articulate and express itself. It is as if you "stopped the world," to use don Juan's term. You go through intense excitement and activity and, some minutes later, walk out of the forest, your old self again. Your path in life is changed. You decide to be closer to those ecstatic bear energies and not act only like your old self.

In the first scenario, you were annihilated by your secondary process, fell into a daze, and awakened again. In the second scene, you were more fluid and went through the door to dreaming, temporarily becoming your secondary process, and later reemerging with your old identity. You were your self the whole time, fluid and unpredictable.

Feynman would have said it this way: The electron meeting a field can either be annihilated by its antimatter opposite, the positron, and reawaken as an electron again, or the electron can step out of normal forward-moving time, go briefly backward, and emerge as a more awakened and changed electron.

We could use process language instead of physics to understand the physics involved here. We could just as well say that the electron develops a secondary process when it meets a field of change. The secondary process is a reflection of the electron with a negative sign in front of its charge.

The secondary process is to the primary one as antimatter is to matter. Just as antimatter is matter with an opposite charge, the secondary process, which has a negative sign in front of it, so to speak, is a projection, something borrowed from nature, from the bear.

STOPPING THE WORLD

These explanations are consistent with psychology and quantum physics, that is, with the mathematical equations of quantum physics and the psychology of disturbances of attention. You could say that Feynman's physics, and physics in general, is patterned after two different psychologies.

In one scenario your fluidity is inhibited by an edge, by your identity and in the other, you notice the edge coming and move freely through it. Like the girl who, with some support, became the poltergeist, you, too, can become the mysterious forest when you meet it.

The door is the edge to timelessness, to "stopping the world," as the shaman don Juan would say. You sense strong emotional fields, step out of time and space and into a new identity. In the first scenario, you stay behind the edge, marginalize your experiences, and feel that the world is disturbing you. You feel as if you are being hurt by what you inadvertently split off, by secondary processes, and this makes you feel ill or dissociated. Then you project onto others and have conflicts with people who are more ecstatic and less sober than you, or you feel impinged upon by states of confusion; perhaps you fear a wild, powerful illness or get addicted to substances that alter your everyday reality. In any case, the world seems like a problem, instead of like an opportunity to continuously change.

When you are fluid with your identity, any disturbance of attention is seen as an invitation to go through the door into the world of dreaming, into new forms of NCR behavior. In the first scenario you have a complex and remain ordinary "matter." In the second, you become a "fluid warrior," to use the words of the shaman don Juan.

Richard Feynman was a wild and wonderful teacher. He himself was very fluid and unpredictable. He played when he should have been working, and worked during his playtime. I remember hearing stories about his working on top-secret projects and spending time tricking the guards who kept spies away from such projects. He was a lot of fun.

But Feynman did not speak about the psychology of his physics. If he were alive today I am sure he would agree that his diagrams show that stepping out of forward-moving time or being annihilated by a given situation is not just determined by your individual abilities but is linked to the power of the field you find yourself in.

This field provides the energy to "surf" its powers, to move with life either clockwise or counterclockwise, in and out of identities.

The NCR path we take in life is indistinguishable for an observer in consensus reality. All paths are the same for this observer, whether we take the route of projection, dreaming each other up to be like our dreams, experience double signals and symptoms, interpret and analyze, or become fluid warriors who know complexes are doors to dreaming. But these paths do not feel the same for us. In fact, the way we travel and the path we take are a matter of life and death.

REAL AND PHANTOM PEOPLE

Physics says that all routes are possible but does not tell you which route to take. What determines the route you are on?

To answer this, we must turn to shamanism, which also has special terms for the two scenes above. Don Juan called the field the nagual. This nagual gives us the option to be a "phantom" who lives in ordinary consensus reality and is periodically annihilated by the unknown, or a "real" person who steps out of time and space by shape-shifting identities.[5] Don Juan suggests that we transform our normal identity as a particular person, in a particular society, and that we become free spirits moving independent of time and space.

Don Juan's idea of being a real person is exactly the opposite of what we normally think of as being "real." For him, a real person is someone who moves with dreaming and can go backward in time. Real people are part of the community of sentient beings who use their second attention and their courage to live their full potential.

Don Juan's group of shamans gives consensus to dreaming as being real—just the opposite of the rest of the world, which considers consensus reality as real. Don Juan's "phantom" is exactly what everyone else calls a real, normal, everyday person. To use his terms, when you are a phantom, you have personal psychology and dream figures, which you view as if they were not quite you. As a real person, you are a changing dream figure yourself. Don Juan's real person is neither herself nor is she one of things she dreams of: she is anything that catches her attention and excites her. She has a fluid identity and therefore is whatever imagination, movement, mood, fantasy, or feeling disturbs her. To use spiritual language, she is the vastness working on itself. Taking Feynman's thoughts to their logical conclusion reveals similar thoughts about the vastness of the connection of the individual to the whole universe.[6]

WHAT DETERMINES WHETHER YOU (OR THE ELECTRON) GO OVER THE EDGE?

Physics speaks mainly about the phantom but includes the patterns for being a real person. Physics does not say how to choose which path to be on, but only reveals that electric force fields present us with the opportunity to choose.

What determines whether or not you go over an edge and become a fluid warrior? The timing and existence of a complex or field are important. Other factors are the nature and strength of the field you encounter, the rigidity of your own identity, and your ability to use your second attention.

Another factor is who is around you in the field. For example, if the person you are with is very open to irrational behavior, you are more likely to go through the door to dreaming and will be less afraid of being misunderstood. This is why you can make changes when you are around certain artists or therapists but stay blocked with people who are more rational. In psychology, the outcomes of events in NCR depend on the development of all involved. You cannot become a bear at any time, but you can if you have enough support from the environment.

Is the same true in physics? When will an electron's path in NCR be annihilated by antimatter and when will it instead demonstrate fluidity and oscillate in time? Since there are no objective measurements to prove whether events go forward or backward in time, we can speculate about the answer based on experiences with NCR realities in shamanism and psychology.

As we have seen, the observer's psychology influences the NCR path of quantum events. My hypothesis is that the fluidity and edges of the observer influence the behavior of quantum objects, determining whether they create a CR or an unusual NCR reality. In other words, whether or not parapsychological phenomena such as poltergeists occur depends on the edges and fluidity of everyone who observes those phenomena. Whether your body or the world around you behaves normally or in a highly unpredictable manner depends in part on everyone's fluidity. The chance of matter behaving as if it stepped out of time or is moving backward in time is greater if the observer and all who are involved are open to NCR events and are prepared to go through the door to dreaming. That is why, around certain people and places, you experience yourself having past lives, while around others, you will feel as if this life is the one and only.

Jung said that as long as he was excited and open to parapsychological events, they occurred. When he was less excited, they did not occur. Although interactions between the observer and quantum objects will always be hard to prove in CR, physicists experience parapsychological phenomena as well. During the 1960s, while I was a student at the ETH in Zurich, I heard stories about Wolfgang Pauli, who had died in 1958. His colleagues were still talking about the "Pauli effect," namely, the parapsychological influence he seemed to have had on matter. For example, experimental physicists from Munich told me that they knew Pauli must have been traveling through their city one day when the bottles in their laboratory suddenly exploded for no apparent causal reason. When Pauli was around, matter no longer behaved like itself.

Similarly, you know that the psychology of observers who are looking at you influences your body—you can feel it. If individuals can affect you, then families, towns, whole environments, even the world and the universe influence your body as well. This means that if your family, your culture, or your universe has certain edges, you get more stuck more readily than in an atmosphere that is freer. In an open-minded environment, you have an easier time being fluid. In this way, your individual psychology is connected with where you live as well as with the rest of the universe.

Likewise, the behavior of matter depends on the nature of culture and of the universe. Changes in your attitude change the material world, and changes in the universe also influence your psychology.

I can imagine a future test of this thinking which could check on the amount of antimatter in the universe. In the moment, there is more matter than antimatter. But this proportion might be reversed in a world where consensus reality encouraged people to be real and step out of time, instead of encouraging them to be phantoms who avoid the river of experience.

Another test would notice the connection between physical illness and social tension. The openness of communities to dreaming and the number of physical ailments at a given time must be interconnected.

THE DREAMBODY

Let's call the NCR connection between dreams and body experiences the "dreambody" (see my book by that name.) The dreambody is to your ordinary experience of the body as the antimatter particle is to the ordinary particle. The dreambody is your bodily sense of another world. Most people pay attention to this sense only when it has become a strong symptom they fear will annihilate them. The dreambody is the body experience shamans use to travel between the worlds.

The dreambody begins with a subtle feeling or sentient experience, which manifests in the body in terms of symptoms and uncontrolled movements, in dreams, in synchronicities, and the like. In fact, you could say that the dreaming body, that is, your sense of the ongoing dreambody process, is interpreted by your visual abilities in terms of CR concepts such as dream figures; by your proprioceptive sense in terms of pressures, temperatures, pains, happiness, and so forth; in terms of relationships as the other person; in terms of movement as disturbances of movement, and so on. Yet the dreambody is no one of these. Rather, it is your personal, individual experience of the Tao that cannot be said in consensual terms. Dreams and body experiences are like the Tao that can be said.

The dreambody is analogous to the quantum wave function in physics. Just as the quantum wave function cannot be seen in consensus reality but can be understood as a tendency for things to happen, the dreambody is an NCR, sentient, pre-signal experience manifesting in terms of symptoms and unpredictable motions.

To explain the dreambody briefly, let's pretend that you are my therapist and I say, "I had a dream about a hammer." At that moment, you notice that I am standing up and tapping my foot on the floor. Instead of focusing on my dream of the hammer, you might follow my overall dreaming process and follow the tapping of my foot. You might reflect my foot moving and ask me to drop my normal identity and move into its movement. Assuming that I had no edges, with your help, I might move through the door to dreaming and begin to conjugate the tapping of my foot. Imagine me stomping on the floor. Say I go into an altered state and enjoy that stomping, and dance about, and start to yell.

After this state has subsided, I realize the meaning of my hammer dream, which is now revealing itself in the pounding of my foot. My dream means that I should be taking more of a stand, putting my foot down, using the power of the hammer in my everyday life.

In this experience, I drop my normal viewpoint, enter dreaming, come back out again, and understand that my dreaming body was an invitation for me to change. In CR terms, the dreambody manifests as the dream of the hammer and the tapping of my foot, yet it has sentient roots in the almost indescribable experience of excitement. The dreambody manifests during dreaming, complexes, and symptoms, but exists all the time as an NCR experience you can step into when you go through the door of dreaming.

THE DREAMBODY IN PHYSICS AND OCCULT PRACTICES

We have seen that the dreambody appears in physics as the wave function. In *Dreambody* (pages 14-16), I discuss how dreaming is like the quantum wave function and shows a "tendency for something," a "potential" in the body. Physicist Fred Wolf, in *The Dreaming Universe* (page 214 and following), continues with my definition of the dreambody, saying that it has the same relationship to the body as the quantum wave function has to particles:

> The dreambody can be related to the physical body in much the same way that the quantum wave function that gives the probability of a particle's state can be related to the particle's physical state.

Wolf seems to agree that the key to the physical body is its wave function, its real and imaginary numbers, the dreambody. You could also say that the key to experiencing wave functions is the dreambody. While your CR identity is who you are in everyday reality, your NCR identity is your dreambody, your wave function, a fluid and changing essence of whatever catches your attention.

Not only does the dreambody appear in physics in terms of the quantum wave function, it has always been seen in the sacred sciences as a tendency toward fieldlike or wavelike phenomena. Dreambody experiences have been variously described worldwide in connection with fields, waves, and lights. Dreambody experience was called Shakti or Kundalini in India, Mercury in ancient Rome, Chi in Japan. The shaman don Juan gave dreambody experience various names, such as personal power, the dance which can hold up death, and the double. These latter names refer to special NCR physical abilities and powers beyond our ordinary view of our bodies.

The Chinese diamond body, the West African Tshi Kra or group spirit, the Egyptian Ka, Hindu subtle bodies, Tibetan shadow reality, and Western etheric and astral bodies and doubles are some of the many names used for dreambody experiences.[7] In Africa, China, India, Europe, and the Americas, near or at death the dreambody has been experienced as a flux, a process, a melting in with the rest of the universe

The dreambody has been thought of as a subtle substance not directly apparent to our ordinary senses. It has been visualized as serpentine, shocking, electric, and magnetic or fluid. Sometimes it is seen as a ghost or an angel, images that indicate our sense of the dreambody as a piece of human-like intelligence and communication ability inherent in all of nature. In all these cases, the dreambody was a second body, universally thought of as an intelligent source of life, part of the river or the continuum of existence in death.

Since the beginning of history, people have believed that when we step into dreaming, we experience our body as a dreambody, a non-local, non-temporal form or tendency only weakly attached to our CR bodies. If we learn to follow the body's dreaming, we can develop the shamanic subtle body, the most ancient method to freedom.

NOTES ON DEATH

Stepping into the dreambody has been compared worldwide to dying, to leaving the physical or CR aspect of ourselves. The dreambody seems to be an immortal, thanatic body, that is, an experience that goes through death to emerge on other side. The dreambody is a master shape-shifter.

Let's now use dreambody concepts as the ancients have, to understand death. In ordinary life, you can step out of time and into the dreaming body, becoming a "real person," as don Juan would say. To do this, you temporarily leave your CR identity and go into the hitherto marginalized dreaming process which conjugated itself, finally appearing as your CR identity as well as its symptoms, complexes, and troubles. Stepping into the dreambody, you step out of CR reality and relate to the wave function that is behind reality. Instead of identifying with yourself, you identify with the sensations you marginalized, and finally with the dreaming process, which was previously experienced as a knock at the door of your consensus reality, a disturbance of your attention.

If we extrapolate from these practical methods of identifying with your dreaming body for short periods in everyday life, we can say that at the moment of physical death, consensus reality "unconjugates" itself, so to speak. That is, you identify once again with your dreaming process, with your wave function, your original home or self. You no longer identify with your CR identity, and you become the dreaming process, which is non-local, non-temporal, and neither "you" as you have known yourself, nor "not you."

The many ancient descriptions of death make me suspect that death is similar to this experience of the dreambody you can have in life; death is like being identified with your wave function, your basic patterns, matrix, or nature. You become the complex numbers, the unconjugated elements of consensus reality, and the dreaming ground of everyday life, implied by the mathematics that presides over quantum reality before measurement.[8]

As long as you identify with being an ordinary person living in CR, you are a phantom who must fear death. As a "real person," you become a warrior-shaman, training your second attention and shape-shifting into whatever you experience. In this way, you develop your awareness of your dreaming body. Once you loosen your attachment to your CR identity and learn to step into dreaming, you realize that your dreaming body is not one fixed thing, not just the opposite of your everyday identity, but a fluid experience, an awareness of whatever catches your attention. Similarly, in death, you become all those people and things that flirted with you, that conjugated you into reality; you become the dreaming core of what you are now.

Benjamin Walker collected myths about death from around the world. These stories describe you as a river running into the sea, as an individual whose process flows into a universal process.[9]

In a Zoroastrian hymn (ca. 800 BC) the dreambody is connected to Lord Mazda:

O Lord Mazda, grant that we may catch sight of thee, may approach thee, may be united with thee.

The ancient Greek Euripides (480-406 BC) spoke about himself at death joining the gods:

I shall go soaring to the firmament of heaven, to be made one with Zeus.

A similar view is held by Virgil (70-19 BC), who stressed the immortality of the dreambody:

The enfranchised soul tends to God. He is her home, her author and her end. No death is hers; when earthly eyes grow dark, she soars, and godlike melts in high.

The Sufi Jalaluddin Rumi (1207-73) sounds almost like a Taoist when he says:

When I have surrendered my soul I shall become what no mind ever conceived. O let me cease to exist, for Non-Existence only means that I shall return to Him.

In the Mundaka *Upanishads* (ca. 650 BC) we find the idea of the dreambody as a river flowing into the ocean, an image which reminds me of the communal vessel containing all souls found in the African Tshi Kra[8]:

As the flowing river disappears into the ocean, quitting form and name, so the wise man goes into the heavenly Being, higher than the high.

The Taoist Lao Tse (450-375 BC) said the final stage of human development is to become one with the Tao, that is:

The course of our progress, when our nature has been developed to the full, ends in our return to the source, in "Not-Being."

The Egyptian burial ceremony (Wallis 1974, pages 158 to 173) stresses reincarnation in the same body and tries to preserve the real body so that the Ba soul can revivify it upon return. A man was buried:

...so that his soul Ba, and his intelligence, Xu, when they returned some thousands of years hence to seek his body in the tomb, might find his "ka" or "genius" there waiting, and that all three might enter into the body once more, and revive it, and live with it forever in the kingdom of Osiris.

In all these traditions, we find the shamanic message; freedom from consensus reality and knowledge of the dreaming body is the mystic purpose of life. This may be why, since earliest times, yogis practiced "dissolving the earth element" to become "subtle," to become a "dead man in life."[10]

These conclusions are consistent with what we know from physics and psychology. Your ordinary self may shudder at the very possibility of considering what happens at death, just as you probably wondered at the possibility of considering the origins of the universe. Yet, we all need to make an honest attempt at formulating our views of life and death. In a way, that is what psychology, theoretical physics, and spiritual traditions are all about.

If we carry these considerations to their conclusions, there must be at least two kinds of death. One kind is dying in the sense of being annihilated by something marginalized, something secondary. In that case, you are overwhelmed by your secondary process and lose track of who you are. You become comatose, so to speak.

In the other kind of death, you switch identities, shape-shift and surf the dreaming experience. You step out of time, moving with whatever is occurring to you. In this kind of death, you free yourself from time and the idea of one fixed identity. Instead, you mirror the dreaming path emanating from your peak experiences. Your path merges with that of the universe.

In the first kind of death, you experience yourself as endangered, threatened, and annihilated. After that death you return to life. You reincarnate, so to speak, as if you were an electron emerging from an intense electromagnetic field at another point in space and time. This experience of death and rebirth may be the NCR pattern behind the custom of naming children after a recently deceased relative or an important person.

In the other kind of death, you do not experience annihilation but fluidly step out of time and become your sentient self, the perennial immortal, one with all things. While no one can track in CR exactly which path you take through complexes, illness, and death, you know from your own experience of the dreaming body that not only your death, but life as well, depends on your overall fluidity and courage in following what at first appeared to be incomprehensible fantasies, feelings, and movements.

NOTES

1. In his 1920s article, "A Review of Complex Theory" (*Collected Works*, Volume 8, page 92), Jung thought about how abuse issues are connected with complexes. His ideas were not independent of Freud's, who claimed that most of our problems come from abuse issues. Later, Freud retracted his belief and suspected that abuse stories must have been mistaken.

2. See Feynman's article, "The Theory of Positrons," page 167.

3. Not much was known about antimatter until the 1930s, when Paul Dirac predicted its existence by studying the equations of quantum mechanics. He found that the equations for an electron described not only the electron, but also its reflection, which he could not understand. He speculated that the reflection must also be a piece of matter which had not yet been discovered and which had the same characteristics as the electron except for charge. He boldly speculated that positrons existed before they were discovered. Sure enough, a couple of years later, positrons were discovered and, shortly thereafter, many other antimatter particles as well.

4. Richard Feynman, op.cit.

5. Carlos Castaneda's don Juan speaks at length about phantoms and real peo-
    ple in *The Teachings of Don Juan*. I elucidate the implications of these terms in
    The Shaman's Body.

6. The idea of vastness is not as far out as it may seem. Feynman's diagram
    leads to the possibility that the electron moving forward and backward in
    time is, because of its reversibility and interconnection with other electrons,
    the only electron in the entire universe! Thus, according to this theory, we are
    all one or several pieces of matter consisting of neutrons, protons, and elec-
    trons. There is only one of each particle in the universe, and we are it! Hence,
    in his model of reality, we are the vastness, working on itself. It turns out that
    the Feynman model predicts that there is as much matter as antimatter in the
    universe, a fact yet to be experimentally confirmed.

7. Benjamin Walker's (1977) *The Subtle Body; The Human Double and the Astral
    Planes* is a virtual encyclopedia of information on the double and the subtle
    bodies.
    The European Double: Europeans called the dreamlike body form outside
    of the real body the "Double." It conforms to the person's thought, character,
    and feeling and separates out in sleep, trance, and death. It coexists with the
    real body.
    The Australian Churinga: Australian Aborigines believe that your dream-
    ing self, your soul, resides in Churinga, that is, in a piece of wood or stone
    with a geometrical pattern. This material harbors your individual or family
    spirit. Here the dreambody is associated with a symmetrical aspect of the
    environment.
    The African Tshi Kra or group spirit: On the west coast of Africa the Tshi
    group venerates the spirit of the individual, called "Kra." It existed before
    birth as part of tribal substance and served all the ancestors and will serve
    descendants to come. When you die, your individual Kra merges with the
    tribal Kra, which is a container for the souls for the people who will be born.
    It continues from generation to generation. Here the dreambody appears
    linked to the field of a particular culture; the individual spirit merges with a
    collective one, which provides energy for new dreambody pictures. Your dre-
    ambody belongs to the history and future of your tribe. The individual soul is
    borrowed, in a way, from the collective soul. Another way of looking at this is
    to say that you are an aspect of your group field. In turn, the group dream-
    body, the "corporation" (from "corpus" or "body"), consists of all the spirits
    of the living and the dead.
    The Egyptian Ka, or wave function: Egyptians speak of the "ka," a dupli-
    cate of the body, a "fluidic spirit," which remains with the body during life
    and after death. Egyptologist Gaston Maspero, working with hieroglyphic
    texts, describes the ka as a "less dense copy of the body" capable of reproduc-
    ing every part of the organism. The Ka stays in the tomb and survives as long
    as the embalmed physical body stays intact. This view of the dreambody
    reminds us of the double, the reflection of the body pattern of a given consen-
    sus reality body. It is analogous to the complex wave pattern which gives rise
    to the real body.

Chinese Diamond Body: According to Chinese Taoists, the subtle body is a "diamond body," seen as multiple pictures of yourself emerging from the top of the head during meditation. Meditating on space between the eyes can also activate it. When it is exteriorized, it leaves by the head, while the physical body remains in a trance. The meditator then becomes clairvoyant and clairaudiant and can see and hear things that would be impossible with normal senses. This sounds like a theory of a non-local self. The psychological analogy to this process is to become detached from yourself. The detached dreambody is symmetrical; regardless of which angle or channel you look through, you see the same essence. Thus its analogy is the symmetrical crystal, the diamond.

Christian Resurrection Body: The dreambody also appears in Christian views as capable of leaving the body at death and of resurrection on another plane. Here the dreambody again becomes non-local.

Hindu Causal and Subtle Bodies: In the Hindu view we have three bodies, the physical, the subtle, and the causal body or soul. The subtle includes the five senses, faculties of actions, five forces, and lower and higher minds, and the causal is created by the past and makes us individual. In other words, the dreambody is our sensory-grounded experience of the present together with experiences created in past lives. That is, our body experience is created or "caused" in part by our past unconscious actions the day, the week, or a lifetime before this one.

The Tibetan Shadow Reality: In Tibetan thinking, everything, living and non-living, has a double, or a shadow reality. Lamas, moving out during sleep or in meditative practices, can see doubles. Death, however, destroys this double. This theory is similar to the Egyptian concept of the "ka" insofar as the dreaming field is linked with the consensus reality body.

Western astral body: Western astral body theory appears in hermetic treatises from about 150 BC. For example, the Gnostic teacher St. Paul spoke of a "divine spark which was in man." This was an "Augoeides," from the Greek meaning "dawn." The neo-Platonists in the 1600s imagined an immortal and eternal soul enveloped in a shining garment, a starlike vehicle that was subject to astrological influences. Paracelsus and alchemists thought the subtle body was a seed that must be transmuted. Here the dreambody appears as a divine spark, as light, as a seed. The dreambody has light, perhaps some rudimentary form of consciousness associated with it. It is a seed, the potential of something which is to be unfolded.

Over the past two hundred years, many experiments have been carried out to measure the dreambody's weight, since human beings are believed to lose weight at the moment of death. To my knowledge, no one has yet measured this apparently non-consensus experience. Some visionaries see dreambody attached by a cord to the living body.

8. Mathematically speaking, at the moment of physical death, the CR aspect of our dreambody, namely, $|(a + ib)|^2$ reduces back to the wave function as a tendency for consensus reality, namely, $(a + ib)$.

9. Walker collects these views on the behavior of the dreambody at death (op. cit., page 294), showing the dreambody at death to be connected to God.

10. See Mircea Eliade, in *Yoga, Immortality and Freedom,* page 272: "...the yogin... witnesses the reabsorption of these cosmic elements into their respective matrices, a process set in motion at the instant of death and continuing during the first stages of existence beyond the world."

39 | Dreamwork: The Heart as Dream Guide

*The dream is the small hidden door in the deepest and
most intimate sanctum of the soul, which opens into
that primeval cosmic night that was soul long before
there was a conscious ego and will be soul far beyond
what a conscious ego could ever reach.*

—C.G. Jung

Psychology and shamanism are needed to augment the scientific
worldview that mainly focuses on consensus reality, thus marginalizing experiences that are close to our hearts. Erwin Schroedinger, one of the parents of quantum mechanics, put it this way:

> The scientific picture of the real world around me is very defi-
> cient. It gives me a lot of factual information, puts all our
> experience in a magnificently consistent order, but is ghastly
> silent about all and sundry that is really dear to our heart, that
> really matters to us.[1]

Physicists feel that they have discovered a lot of facts and worlds
such as quantum mechanics and relativity, which you and I no longer
experience. But we have seen that physicists feel this way only
because they have marginalized the significance of the NCR patterns
in the mathematics of physics. By marginalizing these patterns, physics neglects dreaming, neglects "all and sundry that is really dear to
our heart, that really matters to us."

To understand how to travel through the dreaming realm, physics
must look to shamanism and psychology. In this chapter, we will
leave the CR aspects of reality to focus on dreaming and the manner
in which the heart guides us through the nebulous, moody, ghostlike
figments of our reverie and imagination.

PATH OF HEART

Shamans know that, from the viewpoint or framework of consensus reality, all NCR paths seem indistinguishable. Although these non-consensual paths may be indistinguishable, they are not equivalent. The shaman don Juan Matus tells his apprentice, Carlos Castaneda, who asks for a formula to live by, that "all paths are equal." He means that any particular path "is only one of many" as far as consensus reality is concerned. Therefore the warrior follows the path of heart, the path which brings him happiness with life:

> Keep in mind that a path is only a path; if you feel you should not follow it... drop it if that is what your heart tells you... All paths... lead nowhere... but one has a heart, the other doesn't.[2]

The shaman says that the heart is our guide through the various CR and NCR paths in dreaming. If the compass, measuring stick, and clock help us negotiate CR, the heart helps us deal with NCR experiences. Clocks, measuring sticks, and compasses do not help you much in dreaming. Without the heart, you have only an objective relationship to what you observe. Without the heart, you do not feel what you are looking at. You are merely an observer who, like a physicist, has no awareness of how you are transformed by the observed.[3]

In contrast to physics, where the observer is not significantly changed (at least in CR) by observations, as a dreamer, you can be totally transformed by connection to what you experience. Remaining in CR and observing dreaming is one kind of physics and psychology. Going through the door to dreaming by relating to it is another physics and psychology altogether. The first kind of physics/psychology stays in CR by measuring and interpreting NCR events such as dreams, intuitions, alterations in consciousness, and fantasies. The second kind steps into, mirrors, tracks, and relates to the generating process. Here the observer becomes a relational partner with the dreaming world.

INTERPRETING AND CONJUGATING

Let's look at these two methods. Interpreting in psychology and taking the real value in conjugation are similar kinds of observation. You examine NCR processes such as the wave function, a pain, or a fantasy about a bear, but you remain in the CR framework. To maintain the CR viewpoint in psychology, you interpret NCR phenomena by adding what you know about the dreamer's identity together with what you know about symbols and their relationship to everyday reality. You can "take the real value of dreams," by asking the dreamer what a dream image or experience is associated with in everyday reality. Let's say you associate the word "Berserk" with "Bear." You might then interpret a fantasy about a bear as meaning the wild, berserk, or boisterous part of the personality.

This procedure notices the association or image made by the dream in your everyday behavior, much as observation in physics sees the image an electron makes on a screen during measurement and calls that an "electron." Like electrons hitting a screen, associations "pop up" from a dreaming realm that is analogous to the physicist's quantum wave function.

Besides the association method, there are many effective methods of connecting to dreams.[4] The advantage of interpreting, that is, taking the absolute value, is that you get an immediate value in consensus reality of what has been missing in everyday life. The disadvantage is that you think of CR as the basic ground of life and forget that consensus reality is only a dock, a landing place floating in the water.

Although the association method is helpful as long as you remain in CR, it does not help you when you are stuck in the water, moody, unhappy—when you unable to be an objective CR observer. A further difficulty that arises from associating and interpreting is that you focus only on dream statements and not on the dreaming process happening in the moment. As a result, your identity develops in a stepwise fashion from day to day rather than in a continuous fashion through constant contact with NCR processes.

If you would like to experience the transition from being an observer of dreaming to becoming a participant, a shaman on the path of heart, you may want to try the following experiment.

PERSONAL EXPERIMENT: FROM OBSERVER TO SHAMAN

1. **Remember and jot down a recent dream or fantasy.**

2. **Choose an image or a couple of images from your dream.** After you have the image(s), ask yourself, "What is the first word I associate to that image?" Tell a little story about that association, where it came from, what happened with that figure or similar figures.

3. **Attempt to explain your dream as best you can by considering your associations to your dream image.** Your explanation or interpretation does not have to be "the right one." Just try to interpret for the purpose of the experiment. Write down your interpretation.

4. Now put your paper aside and take a moment to ask yourself, **"What is happening to me in the moment that cannot yet be expressed in words?"** or "What am I actually experiencing but have not yet put into words?"

5. **Now try opening your heart and relating to your momentary experience.** Just try to follow it, feel it, see it, watch it, hear it, reflect it by

moving—in other words, dream it on in NCR. Use your attention, be patient, stay with it until it completes itself. If you are feeling something, express that in images and movement. If you are seeing something, feel it and let it express itself in movement, and so forth.

6. When you have done that for some time, write down a few notes about what you just experienced. **Ask yourself, "How does this dreaming process relate, if at all, to my dream?"** Is the dream an aspect, a picture of your inner dreaming process? What is the same, and what is different about, analyzing your dream and experiencing dreaming?

7. **Now ask yourself, "What sort of body sensations or problems have I been pondering recently?"** Are there any you have not been able to cure or ameliorate with medicine? How does your dreaming process relate to your body process, if at all? How are the two experiences, that is, your dreaming and your body process, connected?

Once you are finished, you may want to ask yourself what, if anything, you learned from this experiment. Try to explain in your own words what the connection is between following your dreaming process with heart and interpreting your dreams. This is the difference between observing the world from the framework of CR and participating in the NCR experiences in the background of CR.

The shaman don Juan calls a person who is learning about following dreaming a "hunter," probably because at one time, following NCR experiences was a matter of survival. If you are an aboriginal hunter who has to live from the woods, you need dreaming as well as observation to know the woods.

KLAUS

Hunting is something you can learn either alone, following your dreams, or with a teacher. A personal story about a teacher of mine, an aboriginal hunter, comes to mind. Such stories tend to teach lessons of the heart better than more cognitive discussion.

When I was in my early twenties, bored with my studies in Zurich, my best friend was an old hermit, a mountain man in his seventies who lived in the Swiss Mountains. I visited Klaus regularly on weekends, in his shack at the end of a road, about a half-mile into the forest, behind a brook and some waterfalls.

I loved Klaus dearly. He had a great sense of humor and was always laughing. Spending an evening with that unusual man was an ecstatic experience. We used to drink a beverage he made from plums and get into altered states together. It was in one of these altered states of consciousness that he once told me that he was a hunter.

"How do you hunt?" I asked. He mumbled in an unusually depressed tone, "The law forbids me from using a rifle because I don't want to spend the money for a license, so I have to use other means of hunting. I wait for dreams."

He didn't know I was a student of Jungian psychology at the time—he would not have known what that was—and so he did not realize how interested I was in dreams. I said naively, "Are you waiting now for a dream?" "Yes," he blurted out impatiently. "I'm waiting for the winter season." I said, "It's winter now, so what kind of game are you looking for?" He said the winter announced itself in dreams and that he was hoping for a fox. I suggested that we look for a fox now in the woods but he insisted that we would have to wait for a dream.

To make the story short, we talked a while and then fell asleep on his tattered old stuffed sofas in that broken-down mountain hut. We woke up some time later and he mumbled, half asleep, "A fox is in the woods now." I said, "How do you know?" He said, "I dreamed it!" I was excited and wanted to go look for it, but again he said we had to wait for the next morning.

The next morning, it seemed to me that we waited for hours until he felt it was time to move. He told me where the fox would be from his dream of the fox in the woods. We went right to that spot and there it was, a real flesh-and-blood fox!

Klaus developed his own special method of hunting by dreaming, by using his second attention and "stopping the world." Since he couldn't afford a license for a rifle, he did not have firearms for catching game. So he developed a method of hunting by screaming. He slithered toward the fox, which did not notice us coming, then, after waiting for it to move to a certain spot, he seemed to transform into another person. He began to scream loudly, totally shocking both the fox and me. The fox, which had been standing near a cliff, jumped in fright right over the edge. We quickly climbed down the cliff and picked up the dead animal. Klaus pulled out his knife and, in a second, took out its liver, which we ate raw on the spot.

Everything from beginning to end was shocking. I had never hunted before, much less eaten the liver of an animal that had been alive minutes before. I have to admit it was a terrifying but also a tasty experience! This method of hunting is not for everybody. Most hunters in Switzerland don't use their dreams or this screech-and-jump method. In any case, we ate what we needed and took the rest back to his house to preserve for the winter.

Klaus was hungry and impoverished, yet he loved the ragged clothes he wore; he was proud not to look like someone from the city. He always acted like a happy and somehow wealthy man of leisure, though he had to work hard to keep his small farm operating. He followed his dreams, his sense of humor, and his love for the unknown. When he was hungry, he would hunt.

When you are hungry, you don't necessarily worry about the life or death of the animal you are hunting. You become part of an NCR process and all events somehow fit together. Your hunger, the death of the animal, the winter, and the dreaming seem part of an experience beyond the boundaries of your ordinary consensus reality.

Klaus admired and loved the animals around him, yet this feeling did not conflict with his hunting. I can't explain it. If you only hunt for what you need to eat, death is part of the process. In this way, hunting is part of nature.

I am not interested in hunting animals myself. But I do know that whatever occurs in a dreaming process is beyond life and death. The reason is that the events that occur are part of that mysterious path of heart. The path that "feels right" is dreaming. The path of heart is the path of least effort, most excitement, and a sense of careful abandonment.

If you follow the path of heart, there is no longer "that ghastly silence about all... that is really dear to our heart, that really matters to us." Relating to NCR processes with the heart moves us beyond the world of the observer, beyond life and death, into the domain of the quantum wave function and dreaming.

HUNTING CIGARETTES IN PSYCHOLOGY

Hunting, that is, following sentient, non-consensus experiences, is something you can learn best from hermits, shamans, and therapists. Hunting is difficult to formulate theoretically in words. Perhaps that is why Jung wrote very little about dream theory; he said that there was no theory about dreams that would work over a long period of time.[5]

Jung's *Collected Works,* Volume 8, had a strong influence on the Jungian community. Although Jung said that there would be no single method of dreamwork, over time, many Jungian therapists developed a style of working with dreams. In this style, a dreamer reports the dream, and then the dream-worker asks about the symbols and associations to the images. The dream is considered a compensation for everyday life.[6] This kind of dream work has become well known today and has spread all over the world. People do not often give Jung credit for this non-pathological attitude toward dreams, but he was its originator.[7]

Barbara Hannah, one of Jung's students, did not follow any particular method of working with dreams. She once told me that Jung told her to follow her own method, which for her meant, "following the unconscious." That was her way. She was an English lady in her late seventies when I first met her, and she was the most radical therapist with whom I have studied. For example, she loved to say, "I am a Jungian, though I don't understand dreams." She said, "If you want to know what a dream means, ask someone else." In a community where so much focus is placed upon the dream, that was a radical statement!

Barbara taught me about the value of what I am now calling "following the heart" through the dreaming process. She would jump out of her seat and say something if she felt like it; she was a very real woman and a sorceress of the best and most ancient style. When I worked with other therapists, I could usually tell you afterwards what had happened. After the session I could understand myself better. But after I worked with Barbara Hannah, I was absolutely baffled and could not figure out how she discovered things I never, ever wanted to reveal.

The second time I saw her for a therapy session in Zurich, she was sitting in a dignified English setting that looked to me as if it came directly from early seventeenth-century England, at about the time of Isaac Newton. Her room was decorated as if we were living 300 years ago. She seemed like an old woman to me at the time; I was in my early twenties. Remember that I had just graduated from MIT in Boston and was full of rational thinking. I thought, "Oh no, this is going to be a very stiff situation."

I sat down for analysis, preparing for the worst. She sat down properly, right next to me, and we began to speak together. There was a small, insignificant ashtray in her office, and in that ashtray was a half-smoked cigarette with lipstick on it. I chatted away about myself, and just to pass the time, I said, "Oh! It looks like somebody was smoking here."

"Ah ha!" She blurted out—using her second attention and expecting incorrectly that I could use mine—"so *you* are interested in *that* cigarette!"

"No, not really" I said defensively, marginalizing the fact that the cigarette had, indeed, caught my attention for a flicker of a moment. She pounced on that cigarette like a hunter cornering a fox. "And just exactly what do *you* see in *that* cigarette?"

What could I say? I gasped for breath and muttered defensively, "Well, I see a little lipstick." In my mind, this whole conversation had gone much too far and I needed an exit. I was looking for the door.

She saw my head turn toward the door and pounced on that damn cigarette like a cat after a rat. She spewed forth, "So what is happening with *your* sex life?" She went on like a wildcat, shocking my young, white, naive, male, heterosexual, American sensibilities. Noticing my shock, she marched relentlessly forward, "Well, what are you afraid of?"

I was shaken to the bone. Any attempt to remain above it all collapsed inwardly, and I found myself whimpering as if for mercy, "Well, I have a dream to talk about." I had scarcely completed that sentence when she pulled out what seemed like my last life support, right from under me. Decisively, she pronounced my fate: "We *must* stay with that cigarette!"

Actually, I don't want to go into more details about that cigarette today, any more than I did at that time in her office, but let me say that I got a lot out of that lousy cigarette. It was a really good cigarette! At the time, my sex life was less than thrilling, and with her help, improved immensely.

I thought I was a bright young scientist, but here I met my match in the form of a warrior-shaman. She knew how to hold to NCR processes that I considered insignificant. She used her heart to guide her into my dreaming and through my resistance and my edges. She threw open the door to dreaming—though we used no such terms in those days. She focused on just the information that was "flirting" with me at the boundary of how I identified myself, in this case, the lipstick on the cigarette. She knew that my dreaming had to do with relationships and with a fantasy woman I had not yet discovered.

Barbara developed this system of dreaming more or less by herself; it was her "style." She rarely talked about dreams, but she could really produce change by following the dreaming process. That cigarette with lipstick on it, which began as a "Tao which had not been said" or in my case, the Tao which had not been focused on, became, through her conjugating and unfolding, a major insight into my inner lipstick, inner woman, my interests in sexuality, and a life of feelings which I had feared to know. From her I learned that NCR processes and quantum wave functions create new universes.

TEACHER OF NON-LOCALITY

Another one of my analysts was Dr. Franz Ricklin, Jr. He was also free from rules about how therapists should behave and rarely looked up when working on anything, including dreams. He spent most of the time brooding with his hands over his eyes, dealing with his bushy eyebrows. I did not see his face for some time. He talked mainly to himself about himself. What a therapist!

Although I told him dreams, he never analyzed them in a linear way. He would draw inward and mumble things like, "That dream... that dream... my wife..." I would ask, "Your wife, what does she have to do with my dream?"

Without answering, he would go on. "My wife... we had this amazing scene last Friday night... why am I telling you this? Why should you have to hear this?" I would say, "I don't know, I really don't know. You tell me!" He never did tell me why he did the things he did. He was detached from consensus reality in my presence; he stopped the world again and again.

If you're wondering if he ever interpreted dreams or found connections between my dreams and personal issues, the answer is never. He spoke frequently about relationships but never defined them as such. He was the most confusing person I had ever met. I never understood anything about myself or about him. And yet I was always healed of something I could not define. I was inspired.

Ricklin taught me about non-locality. I learned that whatever was on my mind was on his mind as well. Following the non-consensual inner events that occurred to him became, for me, an experience of non-locality. Whatever I thought of as my process, he acted on as if it were his. The lack of boundaries between us made him the friend I had always looked for. We did not do "therapy" together; we did absolutely nothing! Yet it was everything.

He gave me back something that had been taken away by my Western education. He gave me imagination, the nagual, as Castaneda called the dreaming process. When I was around him, I knew that non-consensus events were real. After I had been with him, I knew that following nonsensical, non-consensual events was the path of heart.

Ricklin was very popular because he was always in his dreaming process; indeed, he taught by modeling dreaming. He taught me about focusing on what is happening in the dreaming process, about "controlled abandon," about not marginalizing my own sentient experiences when working with others. He taught me how to close my therapy practice before I even opened it, and to understand my work with people as awareness work, as dreaming.

I learned from Ricklin that it was okay to move with the unknown, to follow the heart. I found out that life itself was always startling and that one could live like a madman and get away with it. In many ways Ricklin was just a regular guy. He was a psychiatrist who taught other doctors, a major in the Swiss army, the president of the Jung Institute, and so forth. Jung was his uncle.

I honor my teachers who lived and demonstrated a process-oriented lifestyle that fostered essence rather than content. They taught me to trust my sentient capacities, because without them, reality is sterile.

THE BREAD DREAM

I am telling personal experiences about dreaming amidst our discussion of mainstream and sacred sciences because non-consensus reality is very personal and intimate. Stories tell you something about the awesomeness and passion involved in non-consensus experiences, which are difficult to relate in any other way. I don't know how to speak about "heart" without stories.

To show you various heartfelt methods of approaching NCR processes, I want to give an example of how my different therapists dealt with the same dream! In my dream I was selling bread. That is the whole dream.

One of my therapists, Marie Louise von Franz, was brilliant with personal and collective associations. She asked me what I associated with the bread. I said, "Bread is something that you need to eat." "That's a definition," she said, "not an association!"

A definition is a recall of known, impersonal information. An association is a spontaneous "pop up," or feeling connection to a word.[8] It is often difficult to get to true associations because we have edges against the information.

"Well, you know," I said, "I like Swiss bread, and I hate American bread." Von Franz said, "So, it is Switzerland and Europe which you are eating and which challenge you." That produced an "ah ha" reaction in me, a physiological response showing that through the process of taking the real value in consensus reality of an NCR process, I got what I needed. A new piece of reality emerged for me in consensus reality. I was no longer just American. My dream showed that my identity was becoming European!

When I told Barbara Hannah the same dream about the bread, she promptly changed the subject. She responded by asking me why I was wearing the shoes that I had on when I came to see her. The interesting thing about those shoes (which must have flirted with her) was that they were the first pair of shoes I had bought in Europe. My shoes were new and shiny, though the rest of my clothes were rather tattered and old. The pointed toes on those Italian shoes enthralled me.

We got into a discussion about the shoes and came to the same final conclusion: I was becoming European. We never went into the dream! Barbara taught me that the dreaming process is multi-channeled; it does not appear only in dreams, but in everything you do that flirts with you or with others. And she taught that the dreaming process itself interprets dreams.

When I began telling Ricklin the dream about the bread, he also changed the subject. He said that he "...had some problems on my mind... what were they? Relationship problems!" Suddenly, he began to speak about his relationships again. This time I realized that one of the problems I was having at that time was connected with a specific relationship of mine. I blurted out that I needed a new style of relating. He said that he knew nothing about relationships and could never help me with that. I admitted I knew nothing either. I asked him how he and his friends developed relationships, and he spoke a lot about romantic scenes and affairs, and all of that. This sounded like my cigarette butt experience. I got a lot out of that session. I realized at that time that the American culture I had grown up in was more puritanical about relationships than the more open-minded, European world. It was Swiss bread I wanted to buy and sell in my dream!

Ricklin's focus on himself and his own relationships led us to a discussion about the differences in culture, and the ways in which I was changing. From him, I experienced the NCR reality of which my dream was a part. I learned how dreaming shows that we are entangled, interconnected, in the same way that quantum objects are entangled, interconnected, and non-local.

One of the associations I had to bread, which I never told him, was that bread was the Body of Christ, that is, the body of love. That association was so deep that I could barely admit it to myself. I know I had that association at that time because I wrote it down in my dream journal. Thus my bread contained something deeply spiritual and, for me, European, about relationships.

My learning from these three therapists was different, but the information about the dream's content was the same. They gave me different angles to experience the same process. I learned CR information, which reinforced my sense of identity. I was leaving my American identity. I also learned that direct experience of non-consensual reality, which happened when I was helped over my edges, brought me more than I had hoped for: it showed me the path of heart.

Schroedinger said that the scientific view of the world gives us factual information and orders our experiences but does not address what is closest to the human heart. Science is incredible, and I love it dearly! Science points a finger to the mysterious, and describes its CR effects admirably. But its worldview stops at the end of the finger. The scientific worldview does not belong only to science. It is the view you probably follow most of the time, a view that stands on a bridge and points to the river of sentient experience, to dreams and the quantum realm of imaginary numbers. This view sees water but stays clear of it.

To know that river, you must get off the bridge and jump in, swim, spin and whirl about. Then you realize that the ideas of the conscious and unconscious, observer and particle, physics and psychology, therapist and dream, indeed, all CR terms, are descriptions that can keep you from living. There are no words for the world of that magical cigarette butt, my Italian shoes, Barbara's lucidity about quantum flirts, or Klaus's scream, which brought him food for the winter. When you connect to that NCR world, you sense that you are dealing with dreaming, the basic substance of the universe. Without this connection, the material world feels as if it has no life of its own.

There are many skills for swimming in the water, being in the dreaming universe.[9] Working with dreaming is a shamanic art and science in constant need of updating. Yet, beneath those many psychological and shamanic skills lies the wisdom of the heart, which embraces the sentient world that flirts with your attention. The path of heart, dreaming, is the direct experience of the quantum wave function, your death in life. When you are on this path, you have a sense of timelessness and freedom.

In contrast, CR paths are full of information, yet they can leave you numb or make you curse existence. The path of heart is instantaneous; it makes you feel that every day is the most remarkable one, every second, all day long.

NOTES

1.   Erwin Schroedinger, in Ken Wilber's *Quantum Questions*, page 81.

2.   Carlos Castaneda, *The Teachings of Don Juan*, pages 106 to 107. I discuss this statement in greater detail in *The Shaman's Body*, page 140 and following.

3.   Pauli (1964) alluded to the limits of science in the following, previously quoted in Chapter 38: "The pure perception of a dream, if one may say so, has already changed the state of consciousness and thereby created a new phenomenon analogous to measuring observation in quantum physics. The conscious reflection of a dream then has to have a more extensive effect on the unconscious as a result, for which there are no more direct analogies in physics."

4.   Gayle Delaney has done a marvelous job putting together the work of dream work theorists with her own very grounded and fundamental manner of working with dreams in her *Breakthrough Dreaming*.

5.   See Jung's, "Review of the Complex Theory," page 92.

6.   Jung describes compensation, complementarity, and symbolism in his *Collected Works*, Volume 8, pages 253, 287 to 288, and following. In "General Aspects of Dream Psychology" Jung said that compensation was a generalization of the "complementary principle," and a means of balancing and comparing different data or points of view so as to produce an adjustment or a rectification. He meant that dreams compensate or balance what is missing in everyday reality. If you are following your inner life, then your dreams mirror where you are. Then you wake up and feel, "Yeah, that's pretty close to where I'm at," that is, your primary process is close to your momentary secondary one. If your everyday mind and identity are far from secondary processes, dreams bring up what is missing.

7.   Jung took the content of dreams empirically, like the physicist looking at elementary particles. He took parts of the dream out of the dreaming world and studied each dream in connection with the dreamer's reality.

8.   According to Jung, each dream symbol such as a circle has both personal and collective meanings. For example, a circle might be connected through your personal associations with a circular shape in your garden, but a circle could also have a general or collective meaning of being complete. In the language of our present discussion, all NCR experiences such as dreams have not only personal and collective meanings and verbalizable CR associations but also non-verbalizable NCR associations. For example, in the case of a circle, an

NCR association might be a sensation of dizziness since circles make some people dizzy, while a CR association would be a "circle of friends" etc.

9. See Amy Mindell's *Metaskills,* a study of the feeling skills necessary to work with the dreaming process.

40 | Bodywork: Between Illness and Ecstasy

According to the perennial philosophy, then, one's real self or Buddha Nature is not everlasting and death defying; it is rather timeless and transcendent.

—Ken Wilber in *Up From Eden*

You may not be able to convince others that your experiences of your body are real in a consensual sense, and you may never be able to photograph your dreambody, but that doesn't make much difference to you when it hurts. To you, pain is as real as can be. This next piece of our exploration shows how, when physics and medicine don't help with the reality of pain, going over your edge through the door of dreaming and into secondary processes does.

Whether you experience body problems as agony or as a spiritual adventure depends on how you approach the sensations involved in your discomfort. If you can approach them with the attitude of, "Oh, how difficult but how potentially important," then the worst of the suffering—its meaninglessness—is ameliorated. If you have pain, constantly going against it and marginalizing the experience makes it worse. On the other hand, if you can interact with your pain by discovering the subtle, sentient essence behind it, the pain will eventually diminish or become tolerable. The greatest pain may be due to marginalizing the NCR processes that are trying to unfold.

I remember working with a man who had a cancerous tumor on his heart wall; he felt stabbing pains in his chest each time his heart beat. He was body shy, and so at first we focused on a dream he had in which he saw "peaceful water." He speculated that "something is wrong with the water, though I don't know what." I saw him scratching his scalp as he spoke to me about his dream, so I suggested to him to see what was knocking at the door to dreaming in that "itch" and try to embrace the scalp process.

He had come to see me because his doctor thought it might be good for him; he knew nothing about my work. So he asked me why he should focus on scratching his scalp. I did not know what to say to him, so I just said the truth, that, it might be a path of heart and could be more interesting than the pain from his tumor. He focused on the scratching motion and found himself experiencing his scratching fingernails as daggers attacking what he called his "peaceful" partner. I soon discovered that he, too, wanted to be peaceful all the time, and that he resisted all sorts of conflict. His dream about peaceful water that he thought was somehow amiss was a dream about the inadequacy of his own peacefulness in dealing with conflict.

Apparently he projected onto his partner his own tendency to avoid conflict, and his nails were that part of himself angry about his peacefulness and resistance to conflict. As soon as he discovered that he was angry with himself, as soon as he felt upset with himself instead of his partner, the stabbing pain in his heart subsided. On his own, he said that the peaceful water in his dream, which had something wrong with it, was too peaceful.

From the framework of CR, the body is described by its anatomy, blood type, weight, age, tumors, and so on. The marginalized, dreamlike body sensation of his "symptoms" was a "stabbing" pain, his own self-anger with his peacefulness.

We cannot always locate dreambody experience in the physical CR body. I remember meeting a woman who lived on the West Coast of the United States. She told me that she felt a pain in her breast that no one could explain. The next time I saw her, she told me that her sister, who lived on the other side of the country and with whom she had ceased to communicate some years earlier, had called and told her that she had discovered several months earlier that she had breast cancer. My client told me that her sister discovered her cancer the same day the pains in my client's breast had begun.

Non-local aspects of the dreambody are probably why localized prescriptions do not always work. You can't always heal a problem in the body by working on the body. The non-locality of the dreambody requires dreamlike communication methods. Working with my client included working non-locally, not working on her pain directly but working on the relationship between her and her sister. During a facilitated telephone conference call, I encouraged them both to become a "pain" for one another. After a hesitant beginning, they said some "painful" things to one another, got very angry, and the pain in the chest of my client improved, as well as the relationship between the two women. The two sisters ended up being friends.

You may be wondering if the sister's cancer disappeared. The answer to this question depends on what you mean by cancer. If you refer to the NCR gnawing feelings eating at both women, the answer is yes. If you mean the CR breast cancer, the answer is also yes. The sister chose to undergo surgery for her condition and improved. As far as I know to date, it did not recur.

Another question you may have is "What healed the woman and her sister?" This again depends on what we mean by healing. Was the sister of my client ill in the first place? Illness is a CR concept. She was ill only from a CR perspective. From the viewpoint of NCR, both sisters were in the midst of working with painful issues. We saw in Chapter 21 that illness and healing exist only in a CR framework. That is why most people do not dream they are ill—because from the NCR viewpoint, they are simply dreaming up new aspects of themselves.

THE PSYCHOLOGY OF ILLNESS

Every chronic body problem is a war zone between who you thought you were in CR and infinity. Part of the psychology of body problems is that you are faced with the fact that your primary process is under attack. When you become ill, you enter into a dramatic situation.

Life is relatively painless when you get a short-term illness such as a cold or flu, but when you get a really serious illness, you see time rushing by you. In agony, you think you did something wrong and are being punished. Perhaps you should have done more of this or less of that. You think that your life was too stressful or too dull, or whatever. Christianity symbolizes this situation in the image of Christ on the cross, praying, "Father, if it be possible, let this cup pass from me."

It is indeed difficult to bear that cup of pain. In illness, your body goes through abuse of major proportions against which you cannot defend yourself. If you have a serious illness, you feel yourself being crushed by the universe, by the gods, by the illness. It is as if you have been imprisoned without justification.

Those of us who are not ill must remember to appreciate the mythic dimensions of this conflict for those who are. Being very sick is like losing your life, though you are still alive. You are forced to dream and step out of consensus reality, whether or not you want to do this.

In some cases, no medicine exists that overcomes the disease; it becomes an impossible Tao for which there is no cure. A revolutionary process is created by chronic symptoms. Frequently, perhaps always, they first appear as flickering secondary processes. Then they amplify themselves, begin to scare us, come again, and this time we cannot help but notice them as body sensations.

What was, at first, a split-second flirt becomes a permanent bombing. Bit by bit we become shell-shocked, forced to submit and adjust to the "enemy's" power, the symptoms, especially when they become chronic. We become a "patient" with little patience.

Some people, either because of luck or aging near the end of their lives, dis-identify with who they are and become fluid in dealing with NCR processes. At this point they drop the victim identity of being an ill person, go through the door of dreaming, step out of time, and become what they have always dreamed.

I recall with sadness and amazement a friend of mine who died of AIDS. In the beginning of his suffering, he dreamed that Christ wanted to speak with him. He suffered a great deal over the ensuing years, but then, near the end of his life, he started to reflect the processes that the world called AIDS. Every time he was disturbed by his AIDS-related agonies, he picked up the flirt and conjugated it. I saw him one day suffering from tremor, shaking like a leaf. Courageously, he picked up the process and started to shake himself with awareness instead of just being its victim. He gently shook me as well. "For God's sake," he said to me as if I were him, "Let go, let go, let go of everything and become me!" I acted like I thought I might, and asked him, "Who are you?"

His answer was, "I am the God." Immediately, he stopped shaking and tears came to his eyes. "God," I responded, trying to act like my friend in his normal state of consciousness, "Speak to me. What is this all about?" God answered after a moment's pause. "It's about shaking up life, loosening up and believing that this shaking is Me, and not your disease."

I thought I should continue arguing for his normal state of consciousness and insisted, "This is all too much for me." But God answered abruptly, "You are doing this for others." At this point my friend stepped out of his role as God, turned to me, his old self again, and said, "Arny I am suffering for you, because you are not speaking of your suffering. I speak constantly of my suffering because no one else speaks of theirs."

I did my best to speak about troubles I had been having, and we embraced. I felt better and, for that moment, my friend did not experience himself as being ill. Best yet, his shaking subsided when I began speaking about my inner pain, which had been bothering me. I told my friend that I had forgotten what I had learned from Franz Ricklin, my old teacher, that dreaming belongs to no one, it is non-local.

For a week afterward, my friend had no pain, and no shaking from his AIDS-related neurological symptoms. He was suffering for all of us. He became, in his own way, Jesus on the cross, and counseled others to see him as suffering for them, reminding them of pain they had forgotten.

During the last weeks of his life, my friend was God. Life pressed him to move through the door to dreaming. In its own way, illness can be a healing, not just for those who suffer physically, but for everyone lucky enough to be around them.

INTERACTING WITH PAIN

Painkillers are wonderful. They can often make life bearable. In my experience, when they don't work, it is often because the person has an "allopathic" psychology that views disease only as an opponent. As we know from Chapter 10, allopathic medical thinking reflects the philosophy of Newtonian physics, which sees the ill person as a broken machine. Since the 1600s, Western medical thinking has held the view that if there is a disease, there must be a cause.

Process thinking extends this CR belief system with teleology, that is, it assumes that all experiences also have NCR significance for the individual. A comparison of the two methods of thinking is given below.

ALLOPATHY	PROCESS THINKING
Body problem	Body experience
Your body is sick	Your body is dreaming
Healthy/sick	Experience and new experience
Pain	Altered states

40.1 Comparison of allopathic and process concepts

In medicine's allopathic psychology, you are either sick or well. You have a body problem, or your psychology is wrong. In the past, people may have said you did not pray enough. Today they suggest that your problem is heredity, carcinogens, too much fat, or not enough vitamins. Dualism reigns supreme when you are not feeling well. Then, to make things worse, you may feel worse because of dualistic thinking; when you are well, you think of yourself as successful. Others say, "You look so well today."

But when you feel ill, they imply that you look like hell, like you are failing at something. When you are full of arthritis or have had a stroke and are drooling from the corner of your mouth, people say "Ugh! You don't look well." Those comments hurt. Culture is against your having a dreambody; it is against the quantum wave function, against your dreaming. The culture wants you to get medicine to eradicate your new Tao. Put on a white shirt and clean your dreaming face!

People don't look at you now and say, "What an opportunity, you are dreaming with arthritis! Now you are in another phase of your human process." Collective negativity toward illness is why people who are ill often don't like talking about it. Dualism hurts their feelings by splitting their experiences into parts, into biology and feeling, healthy and ill, good and bad. Dualism is about success and failure, not about process. It is about short and long life, not about awareness.

If your life is going to be shortened by a disease, a good-natured allopath either tries to hide the fact, or informs you that your condition is described statistically as if you are a loser. You feel your life has become a gamble, and that the only possibilities left are to be a loser or a winner. If your illness continues, then not only you, but also medicine, is failing because it does not know enough, no one can help, your time is up. The medical system tried to be helpful but is "heartless" in the sense that its paradigm sees you as a victim in need of help. That CR view, which is implicit in all the sciences, adds to your pain. Imagine a hospital staff trained to look at you and say, "Wow, far out, you are into having an incredible process." You would probably be a bit less upset about your "condition."

A non-dualistic paradigm of illness would see your body experiences not only as a local, physical difficulty, but also as a global dreaming process. Illness is not only terrible; from an NCR viewpoint, it is the chance for liberation, freedom from a rigid identity.

One of the things I've experienced many times in my practice and in the seminars I have given with Amy is that people with body problems have enriching experiences and feel better after going through the door of dreaming. This is due in part to a new, positive, attitude toward NCR experiences or, in the case of working with people in an open clinical setting, to the attitude of everyone who is present.

We have seen that our ease and sense of freedom in going over edges and into dreaming depend in part on the environment. An open-minded clinic is healing in the greatest sense, since it makes life easier. In this open atmosphere, even the most fearful person has an easier time becoming more flexible and stepping into dreaming.

When we were discussing the Feynman diagrams, we spoke about the possibility that an electron can step out of time and that this occurrence may depend on the edges of the observer. The same may be true in psychology. The chance for someone who is ill to become one with their dreaming body may depend on the freedom of the whole community. The reverse may be true as well. An uptight observer fearful of dreaming may, like an observer of quantum mechanics, be disturbing to the unfolding of dream and body experiences, just as they are disturbing to the way an electron unfolds its fate in time. The unrelated viewpoint of an observer hurts in ways we can feel but cannot easily measure.

I recall working with a woman who was on the brink of death. She was so ill that she could not stand and had to be wheeled around in a special vehicle. Her pain was immense. When I asked her to explore her silence for a moment and feel what was happening in her body sitting in that special wheelchair, to her great surprise and mine, she said, "Lightness. How can that be possible? This is the heaviest, worst place in my life!"

Instead of arguing with her CR "heavy" body evaluation, I opened up to my own experience and found myself, against my better judgment, getting into a light-hearted mood. The more light-hearted I became, the more she began to smile. Suddenly, she blurted out, "What's the sense of acting ill all the time?" She promptly got up out of her wheelchair and, teetering on her weak legs without help, walked straight ahead. At first, she hesitated, but then she became almost light on her feet. It was a spontaneous transformation! She laughed and laughed. Everyone around her was shocked. In a state of delighted detachment, she laughed all day long and maintained that laughter all the way to her death two weeks later. Sometimes I think she is still giggling today.

You may ask, "Was she denying her pain? How could she make everyone laugh at taking life so seriously?" I have no certain answers to these questions. But if the lightness were just my process, she probably would have stopped laughing after our interaction, which was not the case. By opening up to dreaming, all of us helped ourselves and her go over the edge, over the CR thought that life is short and the end is usually painful. We were light-hearted because we, too, know we are going to die, and we knew somehow that we were her. In a way, it was a collective discovery. If you know you are going to die, you can let go and enjoy things because there is nothing more to hold on to.

According to Buddha, suffering is due to attachment to identity, to consensus reality. If you hold on to who you are, you suffer from the impermanence of things, from the delusion of being an individual, from self-existence. For Buddha, the medicine for suffering was the Dharma, his teaching. According to Buddha, what hinders us from being on track is personal history, which is composed of all sorts of mental and emotional obscurations, habitual reactive complexes, and confusion, that is, attachment to what you like and aversion to what you detest. The worst problems are due to a CR attitude, to subject-object dualism, to holding to the idea of a separate self. The cause of illness in Buddhism is identity, our ignorance of our true identity-lessness.[1]

In Buddhism, the CR world and its creatures are an illusion attributable to thinking that you are only your CR identity. As we saw earlier in the shamanism of don Juan, those who identify with CR attitudes are phantoms. The real person moves on the path with heart, on the path of dreaming.

Thus the *real alternative* to the medical system is not an alternative medical system but *an alternative way of thinking,* another way of looking at the person altogether. The alternative to the medical system is seeing the ill person as a warrior en route to dreaming.

ANCIENT HEALING PRACTICES

Anthropologist Mircea Eliade collected stories showing that indigenous people healed one another through dreaming, through becoming warriors en route to dreaming. While they were reciting myths and tales, they entered into a state of dreaming by feeling once again the power of the images they were talking about. According to Eliade:

> Every magical chant must be preceded by an incantation telling the origin of the remedy used, otherwise it does not act... For the remedy of the healing chant to have its effect it is necessary to know the origin of the plant, the manner in which the first woman gave birth to it.[2]

Native medicine is sentient dreaming, participation in the process story of existence. You can test this theory with children. If you tell them a story about how a placebo does fascinating things and invite the "sick" child to help embellish the story, "healings" often happen because the child was opened up to dreaming.

I once worked with a child who had severe asthma attacks that almost killed him. One day, while we were working together in my office, he had such an attack. I gave him a placebo, telling him that it did magical things for people. He listened carefully to what I had to say, choked, coughed, and asked if it also could make windows larger. Although I did not know what he was talking about, I said, "Yes, but only wizards know how." I asked the child how he knew that the pill could widen windows. He smiled secretively and said he did not know. I was lost about what to do next, but had a flickering thought of getting him to open my windows. I challenged him to climb up on my windows and "widen them." He jumped at the opportunity, and as he pushed open one of the heavy windows in my office, his asthma attack subsided. He never took the placebo.

He got better because he entered into dreaming through my healing story and his addition that the pill could make windows larger. He experienced those asthma attacks as enclosing him, pressing down on his lungs so that he could hardly breathe. The CR term "asthma" was patterned by the dreaming he was in the midst of, his body's reaction to feeling enclosed. My placebo story gave him a chance to gain access to his dreaming, which is why he asked whether the magical pill could widen windows. In a way, we were Eliade's indigenous people reciting myths and tales. What seemed like asthma in consensus reality was the river of dreaming in non-consensus reality, a heavy window being opened by a wizard.

He not only opened one of my office windows, but also made windows larger in the mythic sense and enlarged his CR cramped lungs. We went on to find a way to fight the cramped condition of his depressed family as well. Indigenous medicine is a path of heart: it is connected to dreaming.

DREAMBODY WORK

Normally, in the course of a day, you sense many small body flickers that disturb your attention. Your body flirts with you. In the dreambody experiment that follows, I will suggest taking one of those flirts seriously by becoming a partner of the process. You need your second attention to follow body processes. If you like, as you follow your body process, you can imagine that your job is to become a flower that follows the sun as it moves across the sky. The sun sometimes goes behind a cloud, but then the flower waits for it to reappear. Follow your own process like the flower follows the sun as it moves in the heavens.

At first you might be shy about doing this; perhaps, to begin with, you simply want to read about it. This work requires courage and training in the use of your attention. By using the second attention, you are breaking a cardinal rule of consensus reality. The rule is to repress your NCR experiences and stick to interpretations. The cardinal rule says that you are a person with a given identity instead of a dream being dreamed.

If you like, you can experiment now with the possibility of going into dreamtime.

BODY DREAM TRAINING EXERCISE

1. **Let a dream come to mind.** You might ask yourself about some associations to images in the dream. Jot down this information.

2. **Choose a symptom to work on, either a past symptom or one you have been feeling recently.** Choose just one symptom. Try to explain that symptom to yourself in terms of consensual reality, in terms of heredity, aging, and eating habits.

3. **Now try dreaming. Watch for flirts; watch what catches your attention from that symptom.** Notice the strongest aspect of the symptom, and hold it in your attention, that is, in your second attention. For example, say you are working on a small pain, a "burning pain." Hold the burning sensation.

4. **Now unfold the flirt.** Let go of your normal identity, and drop into the NCR dreaming process. Let it create what it wants, be poetic, go

into movement, let your fantasy unravel.

For example, if you are working on burning, you might feel burning, you might see a fire, dance fire, and make up poetry about fire. Take the freedom to become a poet, a singer, and a dancer of spontaneous movements. Let yourself dramatize the situation, "shape-shift" as you did while studying relativity.

5. **When you can go no further, and you have tried to go on, check to see if you just need encouragement to go further.** Are you at an edge? Which edge? Knowing your edges may help you.

Were you stuck at the door to dreaming, attached to your ordinary identity?

Were the images, motions, or sound expressions that emerged too far from how you identify yourself?

Do you think you are creating all these images and experiences and therefore they are not "true"?

Are you hesitant to live your process with those closest to you or in your outer life?

If there has been some sort of completion in your experiment, then it is time to notice how your process automatically unfolds into the world, how the "virtual" or personal realities you have been unfolding tend to renew and recreate your everyday life.

6. **Use your attention and notice which CR thoughts you focus on first as you come out of your dreaming. Follow them, and notice whether your process is trying to renew and recreate reality in some way.** Imagine doing with yourself and others in everyday life what you are now thinking of. Remember that there may be an edge to the world. Perhaps you may need to explain to people around you what you are planning to do next!

For example, one of my clients had been working on the experience of a stomach ulcer. She followed the burning flirt, focused on it, saw herself being consumed by a hot, white light, a bright fiery light, and wrote a poem about becoming the sun, one that brightened the world.

Then the fantasy would go no further. As she came back to CR, she noticed she was fantasizing about the religious community she was part of and how "burned up" she was with them because of their lack of interest in diversity issues. So she called them and asked her minister to make certain changes. His response was, "How enlightening."

What she called an ulcer turned out to be an NCR burning light, a sort of wave function that was trying to be conjugated into creating or recreating reality. In a way, all symptoms are wave functions which, like dreams, need to be taken more seriously.

In any case, before her inner work her pain made her feel ill. Afterwards, she was ecstatic that her process seemed to connect to the world around her. What she had thought of as her body and her mind, was, in her NCR experience, a synchronicity: it was a non-local field spread around her community.

Just as psychologists can learn a great deal from physics, physicists (and all of us when we are in a scientific frame of mind) can discover new worlds from dreambody work. You can learn about the necessity of getting off the bridge and into the water, about experiencing your dreambody as non-local, dreamlike wave functions. You can go through the experience of shape-shifting between vastly different frameworks, from your consensus reality selves to your non-consensus dreaming body. You can learn that beneath the CR description of material symptoms lies a sentient, almost indescribable sensation, an awareness of dreaming that was there before the symptom. As you unfold the sentient experience, you find it leading you into a dreamland flow that re-creates reality.

When a doctor diagnoses you as a body with an illness whose outcome is unpredictable, you can imagine what matter must feel like when it is called a particle with uncertainty. You need to remind your CR self that in dreamtime, you and all of the material world are neither a body nor an illness with a statistical outcome, neither a particle nor an uncertainty, but a dramatic world myth, unfolding.

In a way, the body is your best physics lab, your personal sentient experience of the universe, trying to conjugate and unfold itself. Like the wave function of quantum physics, the dreambody is non-local; it is all over, everywhere at a given moment. In NCR there is no uncertainty that we are, like the woman whose stomach ulcer was a light for her minister, simply pieces of the world unfolding.

NOTES

1. The first teaching of Buddha's "four noble truths" contains a core point. In Zen and Pure Land Buddhism, Hinayana and Mahayana Buddhism, in Ceylon, China, and Tibet, this first teaching says that we suffer from conditioned existence and must remember that consensus reality passes on. We suffer from birth, sickness, old age, and death, not getting what we want, not wanting what we get, being separated from whomever or whatever is dear to us, being connected to people we do not like.

2. In his *Myth and Reality*, page 16, Eliade quotes anthropologist Erland Nordenskiold.

41 | Worldwork: How to Change History

When a person rediscovers that his deepest Nature is one with the All, he is relieved of the burdens of time, of anxiety, of worry; he is released from the chains of alienation and separate-self existence. Seeing that the self and other are one, he is released from the fear of life..."

—Ken Wilber in *Up From Eden*

At this point in our journey, we will move into the implications of the physics of non-locality and symmetry for relationship and large-group work.

Only from your CR, primary viewpoint do you have a mind of your own. From the viewpoint of dreaming, what you may call your mind is a shared phenomenon. The brain is a consensus reality term with a location in the head, but the location of the mind is an NCR experience, like a wave function, governed by uncertainty as far as locality is concerned. From the CR viewpoint, we can only say that those flickering secondary thoughts you normally marginalize are coming from everything, everywhere, at every time, that is, they are shared with the environment.

Physics and psychology both deal with flickering signal exchanges. The locations and senders of CR signals from two people or objects can be separated from one another, but the flickering, original origins of these signals are entangled quantum objects. In Chapter 19, we discussed the surprising results of Bell's theorem and the experimental verification of Alain Aspect in 1982; we discovered the entangled nature of twin photons traveling to LA and Moscow. Since Aspect's experiment, physicists are in general agreement about non-locality. The experiment showed that entangled photons give the impression of coming from a background of unbroken wholeness.

This surprised some of us because we tend to marginalize our sense of interconnectedness.

David Bohm suggested the concept of unbroken wholeness to explain non-locality and the mysterious connections between entangled quantum objects. He said, "The essential new quality implied by the quantum theory is non-locality; i.e. that a system cannot be analyzed into parts whose basic properties do not depend on the... whole system... This leads to the radically new notion of unbroken wholeness of the entire universe."[1]

Bohm hoped the idea of unbroken wholeness could be used to renew the conceptual foundations of physics, which had been based on the idea of the separability of individual particles. His unifying theory was a way of putting the world, which had been broken apart, back together again.

This world of parts is described by myths of the death of great anthropos figures such as Pan Ku in China and Ymir in Germany (see Chapter 19). When these figures die, our sense of the world around us goes to pieces. These myths describe today's CR world of separateness as the result of a death, as a system gone to pieces, resulting in a broken sense of interconnectedness. According to these myths, our inability to get along with diversity comes from living in the phase of a universe whose elements have been blasted apart by something not unlike the Big Bang.[2] The resulting world, the deceased anthropos we live in, is an NCR picture of today's cosmopolitan CR. Bell's theorem, the Aspect experiment, and Bohm's theory of unbroken wholeness seek to revive the original sense of unbroken wholeness.

We saw in Chapter 19 that a video study of two people communicating together can indicate the origin of primary, or intentional, signals in one person or the other. In this case you can speak of signal exchanges, since one signal can be seen to come before another. However, in other situations, when we examine the origin of secondary, or unintentional, signals, it is often impossible to tell which signals came first.

In the first case, you may agree that there are two separate people. But how do you interpret the second case, in which it is impossible to say which signal came first? One possibility is that one system is manifesting in two separate, entangled people. There is no clear you or the other except in your subjective experience. There is no CR separability, no clear demarcation or locality.

We have seen non-locality in terms of symptoms, which are normally associated with a given person and locality. You probably remember the woman's chest pain (see Chapter 40), which occurred when her sister discovered breast cancer. The generalization of this example is that relationships normally associated with the locality of two separable people are essentially non-local. Relationship is anywhere, anytime, as the following example shows.

Non-Locality in Relationship

I was on the Oregon coast, writing this chapter, when Amy and I had an amazing experience. While eating breakfast one morning, out of the clear blue sky, I told Amy that I had the intuition that someone wanted to break in somewhere. I caught my flickering intuition (an example of using my second attention) and, with Amy's support, fantasized about a criminal who needed money. We both wondered about this fantasy because, at that time, we were earning enough to give some away to others. We then discussed how we sometimes get needy ourselves when our finances go through fluctuating lows.

Amy pointed out that although I was not momentarily low on finances, I did not realize I was low on the need for psychological "credit," that is, I needed encouragement for my work. At this moment, Amy suddenly remembered a dream she had forgotten from the night before. In her dream, someone from a developing country wanted to break in! She, too, needed support in what she was doing. That was a relationship field between us.

Our conversation was interrupted by a telephone call. A security agency in Portland, which had set up a burglar alarm in our office there, told us that the burglar alarm went off. The security company said the police were sent to our Portland office to investigate. Amy and I were shocked by the call. We decided to climb aboard our fantasies and dream together. Amy and I played cops and robbers. First I was the burglar, then Amy. She said she was from a country with less financial power than the United States. When I played that role, I was a poor person from the States. In that role, we both said, "Give me money." We both tried to take this information internally but also considered whether we could do more than we are presently doing for others.

From the NCR viewpoint, this process is a combination of my intuition that someone would break in, Amy's dream, and the call about someone actually breaking in. Is this a synchronicity? For us, indeed, it was.

But things did not stop there. When Amy called the police, she learned that when the police went to investigate the burglar alarm, they discovered that a friend of ours had entered our office in Portland to bring us something and had inadvertently set off the alarm. Which friend of ours was this? A friend from a so-called developing country!

The CR description of events included Amy, me, the police, the burglar alarm, our friend in Portland, and so forth. Individuals and localities are separable. You can ask CR questions, namely, did Amy dream up this situation, or did I? You would have to answer "yes" to both these questions. Amy and I learned a lot from that sort of consensual thinking. I expressed some of my needs, which I had marginalized until then. Perhaps our friend needed financial help? Indeed, that turned out to be very true, and we gave help there as well.

So far, the physics and psychology of this situation are based on assumptions about separability. But what about the non-local nature of events? Causality cannot be located with any particular person, time, or place. While there seem to be separate events—Amy's dream, my intuition, the burglar alarm and the arrival of our friend in Portland—there is also a non-local environment between the seacoast and the city connecting us.

In the spirit of unbroken wholeness, you could say that the atmosphere, the universe, was an anthropos manifesting through the non-locality of apparent parts. The anthropos had an "inner" conflict. It was working on itself, on the problem between the rich and the poor, on class-consciousness, on inner love and understanding among all parts of itself. From this viewpoint, there is only non-local awareness shared by Amy, me, the cops, and our friend. What we call people or objects are like roles in a drama, roles in the field of the anthropos. Going further with the theory of unbroken wholeness, we could say that we are, at one time or another, shuffled, or switched from one role into another. One role has the money, while another has none. There is one field with roles and a bunch of apparently separate people to fill them.

Roles are CR names like objects, or observables, in physics. From the NCR viewpoint, CR objects do not exist; all that exists are quantum wave functions for these objects. Likewise, from the viewpoint of unbroken wholeness, roles do not really exist in a field; only the NCR feelings that create these roles exist. Like wave functions, these feelings are shared by everyone. We live in an entangled web of interconnections and are like virtual particles moving into and out of CR roles.

The atmosphere or the field in which we live is like an electromagnetic field. If you want to imagine that field, imagine putting iron filings on a piece of paper and holding a magnet beneath the paper. The result is that the filings appear organized in oval forms around the magnetic poles. These poles represent the field, which can be described by the polarity of the magnetic poles beneath the paper, or by the apparent forces and tensions manifesting in the organization of iron filings on the paper's surface. The magnetic field creates roles. Likewise, fields polarize group life. In the example above, the roles of the rich, the poor, and the cops describe the overall situation.

At any one moment, Amy, our friend, and I can feel like or be in any one of these roles. None of us are any one of these roles, although our CR identities are usually associated with one or the other. We all have mixed blood, or mixed psyches. We are entangled. Therefore, a crucial aspect of individual and group work is role switching, discovering the various aspects of yourself that you may have marginalized.

In our discussion in Chapter 38, we saw the quantum electrodynamic description of what happens to us in a strong field. You may remember that this description gives you a choice of either being annihilated by your antimatter opposite or of reversing your own position and stepping out of your CR identity.

In the above example, Amy and I felt the field and opted for reversing our directions by becoming the antimatter role, that is, the role attacking us in our fantasies, the role of the one breaking in. We used the field to shuffle between roles, between who we were and the "other" in the field. If we had had the opportunity, we would have invited our friend from Portland and the cops into our role-shuffling process.

ROLE-SHUFFLING INVARIANCE

When roles remain the same but the people filling them change, a shuffling invariance occurs. Invariance means no variation. Even though the roles are shuffled, the structure of the system as a whole remains the same. You can switch roles when you sentiently experience another form of behavior impinging upon you. A shaman would say that you shapeshift when you do this.

Most frequently, this sentient experience is marginalized. When you sense that you share the viewpoint of the other and then leave your own viewpoint temporarily and share the other viewpoint, you have shuffled or switched roles. Since all roles still remain, the system is invariant. That is what is meant by shuffling invariance. The system remains the same. In the diagrams below, big, round circles represent the roles A and B, and the people filling them are smaller, dark circles.

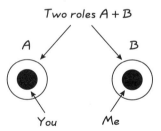

41.1 A system or field with two roles, a and b, and two people, you and me, in those roles

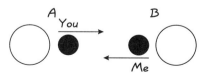

*41.2 Two people, you and me, switching roles, yet the role structure
of the system remains the same*

The shuffling invariance principle allows you to work on a relationship or group process by switching roles. A relationship is then composed of two or more people and a bunch of roles in the field.

Shuffling invariance and shape-shifting allow you the possibility of taking all the NCR phenomena you experience as your own. For example, the dreams and body gestures of the "other" can be seen as your own, as long as their dreams and gestures interest or flirt with you! In Chapter 17, we first came across the possibility that everything that fascinates you belongs to the NCR field between you and the object or person that caught your attention. What you remember is as much you as it is the other. That is why your partner may recall a dream or experience you had and then forgot. Your experience belongs to the other as much as it does to you. At the sentient level, you are your partner.

Relationship and group work depend on someone noticing when new, virtual roles arise. For example, when you or your partner are gossiping about a third person, the third person is another role, let's call it C. You can work on yourself and your relationships or group by dreaming into this third person. There are three roles in the field: you, your partner, and the "third person," who is a sort of ghost role or virtual particle bouncing between the two of you. In our example above, at first, before the phone call, the "person from the developing country" was a virtual or ghost role in our field, a role that was soon to become real!

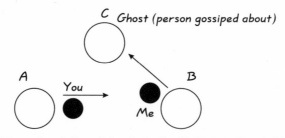

41.3 Three roles, A, B, and the ghost, C, with two people switching roles

In working with couples or larger groups, the facilitator herself is a role in the field, the part overseeing what is happening. The facilitator is a "dreaming eye," the eye of the field itself. From the perspective of this eye, everything we notice, including ourselves, is part of the dream we are unfolding! If you or another does not fill this facilitator role, relationship work and group work feel like a pot of stew without a cook. No one is there to add the right spicing to the various parts or to turn off the flame when the cooking is done. The facilitator knows that people are not roles, and that almost anyone can fill the roles. Any one person is too whole to be only one role. Everyone is responsible for every role, including the role of the facilitator.

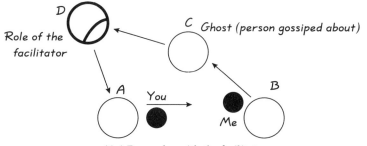

41.4 Four roles with the facilitator

In consensus reality, we are people with given identities filling roles linked to those identities. But from the viewpoint of non-consensus reality, roles come first and dream us into being. You are more complex than any role, including the role of yourself! Your most honest identity, if you have one, would be that you are all roles and the interactional processes between them.

Being a field reminds me of the African group described by Jack Kornfield. In this group, the birth of a child occurs when its mother first hears the child's song. After she hears the child's song, she searches and finds the husband-to-be. They come together and the child appears in the flesh nine months later. In the experience of this group, the song precedes the individual or relationship, and the song draws the parents together. The song is like the quantum wave function, the flirt that precedes reality. In other words, you were originally a song, a field connecting people.[3]

I remember a Native American telling me that every couple in her group had to make a choice about whether their child was to live to be 80 or 800 years old. Couples must discover whether they are meant to have a real child who will live to be 80, or whether they are to create a new song for the community, which is seen to live approximately 800 years.

These stories, which come from cultures whose consensus reality was not yet broken into bits, indicate that people and relationships were thought of as manifestations of a field that sounds like a song, or appears as a dream or vision. Each of these songs or dreams is connected with a task that is important to the community as a whole. The task might be to have a child or to create a new song or way of life for the culture.

Unlike the fields in physics, the NCR fields in mythology have tasks. The song's field creates us and our friendships to complete its task. Our individual song or dreamlike task is simultaneously a community field, a field of unbroken wholeness, and a deep pattern that draws us together. Our relationships are determined by the community's song, which is channeled through us.

From the viewpoint of dreaming, it is not the details of the relationship that are crucial, not our individual psychologies, but the song connecting us, the community mind trying to manifest through us and our relationships. The song is sometimes cacophonous, dissonant, but it is still a song.

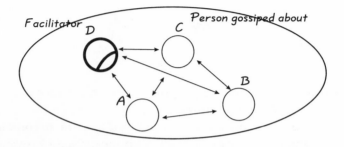

41.5 You as a field: You have four or more roles within you, including who you used to be and who I used to be.

COMMUNITY SYMMETRIES

I have often been mesmerized by the beautiful artwork and various types of symmetry communities create in the sacred objects placed at their center. These highly symmetrical and balanced objects, which are found all over the world, seem to indicate that the field in which we live is structured by symmetry principles.

In Chapter 36, we saw how Native peoples see the creation of community arising from conjugated opposites that combine and coalesce into harmonious existence. For example, the Native American Delaware people express the time after creation when all creatures were friendly with one another with a diagram (after Maclagon 1977, page 79)[4]:

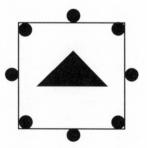

41.6 Time when all creatures were friendly with one another

The sketch of community above shows the kind of mirror symmetry we found in the mathematical idea of conjugation. When you look at the diagram, you will find a horizontal symmetry (right to left), not a vertical (up and down) symmetry. If you turned the book around in your hands and looked through the page, you would see the same diagram from the back side. But if you turned this book upside down, it would not be symmetrical: the top of the triangle would be on the bottom, and the bottom on the top.

Figure 41.6 gives us the impression that the patterns for community well-being and individual awareness are similar to the mathematical scheme for observation in physics, since complex numbers are also symmetrical with respect to one direction and asymmetrical in the other. The diagrams in Chapter 7 show that the complex number, $a + ib$, becomes its conjugate, $a - ib$, if rotated in one direction but not in the other, that is, only if turned upside down, not when rotated right to left.

Community among the many Native peoples is based on the equality and symmetry of all human, animal, and plant beings, while simultaneously supporting clear and central differentiations around authority and rank. You will remember from Chapter 32 that rank is potential energy, symbolized by a weight raised above the ground. In Figure 41.6, higher and lower rank seem to be symbolized by the triangle which clearly makes a difference between above and below.

In other words, harmony in community depends in part on social rank being central and clear, in contrast to being hidden and secretive. Harmony also depends simultaneously on the basic equality of all beings.

SHUFFLING SYMMETRY IN COMMUNITY

Birds, fish, turtles, wild beasts, monsters, flies, and mosquitoes are all very different animals. Yet, in Figure 41.6, we see a big square and little circles. Thus, only the roles or positions in a field are important, not their individual natures. This lack of differentiation in the individual nature of each position indicates that a shuffling symmetry lies behind a community field of diverse beings such as birds, trees, people, and rocks.

Let's look more closely at this shuffling symmetry. Consider, for example, four balls being tossed and caught by a master juggler whose hands are constantly moving. The balls have a shuffling symmetry: each ball can be substituted for another, but the overall pattern remains the same. The only thing that differentiates one ball from another is its momentary position in the air or in the juggler's hands. A shuffling symmetry is a dynamic invariance process happening over time.

According to Native myths, not just couples, but large groups of people, in fact, all beings, show an underlying shuffling symmetry over time. Shuffling symmetries, from the human and individual viewpoint, have their origin in the dynamic wholeness of each individual. While you are a significant individual coming from a specific background and group, and while you are needed by the larger whole to play the role you do with your present identity, you are attracted to and tend to play all the possible roles in your community over time. In other words, you shuffle about in these roles. Anyone, everyone, shares each and every role. At a deep level, we are reflections of one another and have the need to experience ourselves as the "other."

For example, let's pretend that one position of Figure 41.6 represents the chief while another represents the children. At one time the designated chief may be in the role of leader, but at another point in time she played the role of the child in the field relative to her chief. Moreover, a child can be in the child role, but at another point in time may be the chief. When children play at being mom, dad, and chief, they are practicing shape-shifting, shuffling between roles.

Shuffling symmetry comes about in part because of the tendency over time for each individual to be whole, to be all the parts in herself. From another viewpoint, shuffling symmetry comes about because community wholeness and equality depend on having all community roles occupied by someone. From yet another viewpoint, shuffling symmetry exists because of an underlying sense of unbroken wholeness and cooperation in flirting and creation.

In any case, the dynamics of a community are based on shuffling symmetry in groups as well as in individuals. The community remains its unique self as we individuals shuffle among its various roles. In this way, from the viewpoint of consensus reality, we are all very different and, at the same time, we are identical in NCR because each of us is a whole with all parts in herself. Furthermore, each whole is the same whole. At a given moment we are different but also the same.

Whoever is oppressor or victim today becomes victim or oppressor tomorrow. Until now, this shuffling has directed world history, constantly recasting the same roles with new figures. From the viewpoint of mythic stories, community symmetries come from universal anthropos figures such as Purusha, Shiva, Christ, and Nun. The gods are mathematicians, geometers creating and recreating themselves. In Chapter 26, we discussed how the structure of the universe is the body of the gods manifesting in terms of mathematical structures. Like today's scientists, earlier peoples believed that the universe was not haphazard, but structured, geometrical.

RANK BALANCING

In Figure 41.6, the triangle creates a sense of difference and a direction. Pyramids are asymmetrical from top to bottom. In the social domain, such top-bottom dichotomies are related to differentiation and rank, asymmetry and imbalance. In any given community there are many kinds of rank difference; some people are better at some things than others, some are older, some younger, some part of the powerful clans and groups, others part of less powerful clans and subgroups. There are dichotomies around race, gender, age, religion, sexual orientation, health, social power, spiritual power, wealth, and so on.

As a result, some people have higher rank and are higher up on the social scale. They have more power than others do. Rank is never absolute, but relative to others. You remember from Chapter 32 that rank, like potential energy, can be used or not, and usually those who have it don't realize they have it. All rocks of the same kind look the same when placed as a group of steps going from one floor to another in a building. But the rocks higher up have more potential energy than the lower ones.

In community life, rank imbalance creates polarization. Those with less social rank in a community inevitably strain to come forward to demand recognition. In time, if those on the bottom are forbidden access to the top, struggles ensue. Rank imbalance evokes group process as an attempt to equalize power distribution. Whoever wants to be on top is eventually balanced by those on the bottom. Each side is balanced by the other. Rank imbalance in all communities acts as a great provocation, a great equalizer, even if this principle takes years or centuries to complete itself.

Global tensions are due in part to the fact that you and I insist on being equal. We refuse to be marginalized. Each of us wants recognition. If one person or group in a community gets more recognition than other groups, the process of equalization begins. Then, it is only a matter of time until we either pull each other down or build each other up.

The equalizing principle tends to decrease those stuck in rankful positions and increase those who are marginalized into lower-ranking positions. The drive moves from asymmetry and imbalance toward balance. This tendency toward symmetry shows itself not only in the balancing tendency which occurs over time, but in how we reflect one another instantaneously, generating our community consciousness about its own nature. This reflection helps everyone realize that those with higher rank are less conscious of that rank than those below. This explains why those on top always stress that we are all equal, and are forever upset with those of lower rank for upsetting the apparent peace based on unequal rank.[5]

COMMUNITY CONSCIOUSNESS: HOW TO CHANGE HISTORY

Community awakening depends on rank awareness—the sense of difference—and shuffling ability—the sense that we are all everything. Consciousness depends on being aware of and standing for your rank, noticing how it marginalizes the issues of those with lower social status. Consciousness also depends on knowing you are the other, a seamless dreaming entity. If you get stuck in the spiritual NCR of the equality of all beings, you are likely to marginalize real, social issues. Similarly, if you fight only for rank consciousness, you easily marginalize spirituality and love. As an individual, you need both a Newtonian CR awareness of the push and pull of reality and the quantum physicist's awareness of unbroken wholeness.

History will change when you and I have awareness of diversity and sameness, when social change is accompanied by recognition of rank imbalance and NCR equality. Gaining awareness of both processes simultaneously takes patience and can only be developed with the help of an entire community. My closest friends and worst enemies have been great teachers. This consciousness does not occur in me sitting alone in meditation.

I remember recently taking part in the process of an academic institution where some of the students, who had long been silent about diversity issues, came forward to awaken their peers and teachers about the pain of being repressed. I think of one amazing interaction that demonstrates what I mean by community consciousness.

The students and faculty of this large Western institution gathered in a big, impersonal auditorium. After both students and faculty presented the issues, no one spoke. Eventually, several teachers spoke about how they thought their institution should change. The students remained quiet. Then, suddenly, speaking from the rear, several students vehemently brought forth an invective, accusing the teachers of ignoring diversity issues in the institution. The students raged about the fact that no one mentioned gender, race, religion, or sexual orientation. The teachers became terrified, fell silent, and inadvertently switched roles.

Revenge! At this moment in time, the students were in power and the teachers felt threatened. Almost everyone was stunned. Some were confused, and many were numb: who was the oppressed and who was the oppressor?

Ignoring the role-switching tendency and unconsciously using her rank as a powerful speaker, one teacher insisted that the students not get out of hand. This comment was like a match that lit the fire. Breaking the decorum, one student yelled about her hatred for the teachers. Again, everyone froze, fearing the end of the institution was near.

To everyone's surprise, one wide-awake student used her courage, awareness and ability to shuffle roles. She stood up and said that the roles had been switched, and that no one was playing the role of the teacher. So she was going to do just that. Acting out the role of the teacher, she proclaimed, "I am on my knees, begging you students for mercy. Dear screaming student, do not behead me on the spot for my unconsciousness, but show me a better world than the one we live in now."

The student who had screamed at the teachers now stumbled forward toward the woman who had just spoken in the role of the teacher. They stood face to face for a moment, then, weeping, both students embraced. The role of the unconscious-teacher-turned-beggar and the role of the revolutionary-student-now-humbled melted. It was an awesome moment, one in which rank awareness and shuffling symmetry melted into that special consciousness called community.

What happened? Well, a lot happened after this interaction. The institution survived and transformed. Everyone began speaking with one another, learning about diversity, the pain of the marginalized, and also the difficulties of being a teacher. The institution changed. But for our purposes here, let's study the details of the student-teacher interaction.

The student who spoke in the teacher role knew that the community was defined in CR by its roles of student and teacher. She knew that she was a student, but also that she was one of the teachers. Her knowledge resulted in role switching, shape-shifting. She reminded everyone of power differences and the deep equality at an NCR level. Although she was a student, she knew that she was also a teacher, and as one of the teachers she could experience the sense of being victimized by the students, just as they felt hurt by the ignorance of the teachers. She knew that the students had become what they had projected onto the teachers. The oppressed had unwittingly become oppressors, and vice versa. She helped community consciousness by showing how the teachers are unconscious of their rank, but also how to become a humble learner.

I have focused until now on this wise student who was the "heroine" of the day. But to do justice to the overall interaction, you must remember that she was part of a field. Everyone in that auditorium contributed to what occurred; everyone was polarized by it. Everyone suffered from and finally celebrated that field. Her work could not have occurred without the help of her revolutionary student colleagues or her unconscious teachers. From the NCR viewpoint, they were all equally important; in fact, they are all the same.

SYMMETRY IN THE UNIVERSE

When communities work on themselves and consciousness occurs, in time an underlying feeling of unity, which does not marginalize anyone, emerges. In such moments, people often say that the community is like a goddess and her body is a great place to be.

The Delaware Indians symbolize such harmonious experiences as the Great Manitou, creator of the world. This god is symbolized by a symmetrical geometry, a round circle almost covering a square, with a dot in the middle.[6]

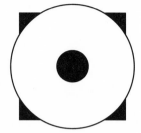

The Great Manitou

41.7 "In the beginning, for ever, lost in space, was the Great Manitou."

The symmetry found in the creator is mirrored by or analogous to the symmetries found in physics.[7] In Chapter 36, we learned about Stephen Hawking's theory that a wave function and a purely imaginary time characterized the very beginning of the universe. To make sense of this theory, we needed the idea that the universe is self-reflecting. This idea coincides with aboriginal concepts that the universe is a self-reflecting being. In physics, self-reflection at the NCR level results in conjugating the wave function, thereby generating the real world.

The idea of a purely imaginary universe, a non-spatial beginning to our universe, is consistent with the Delaware idea that, "In the beginning, for ever, lost in space," was the great symmetrical, self-reflecting Manitou.

In group processes, when you and others argue, wail, battle, and laugh, the symmetry of a self-reflecting creator manifests in your tendency to switch roles. When you reflect the rank imbalance in community processes, shuffling symmetry, the timeless, one-world experience occurs. In Figure 41.8, you can see how shuffling processes in the student-teacher interaction led to the experience of this timeless, symmetrical world.

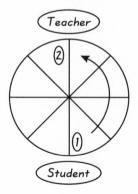

41.8 Through shuffling, rank imbalance leads to a dynamic harmony. (While the roles of teacher and student remain relatively fixed, people such as 1 and 2 switch roles.)

CONSCIOUS COMMUNITY PROCESS

Consciousness in group processes is a "miracle," one I have seen during conflicts between African and European Americans, during a group process in Kenya, with the Haida community (Native Americans on Canada's west coast), and in open city forums elsewhere. I have seen this circle occur after severe conflicts among the Koreans, Japanese, and Chinese and also between Latinos and Anglos. During such moments, I have the sense of being part of the mind of nature, the mind of god.

But I wish to stress that, attractive as such moments are, they do not occur without having first struggled through the sense of diversity and the inequality between roles, which leads us to shuffling. You and I need to remember that tolerance is needed to sit through the tension of diversity, especially when multi-cultural situations are involved.

THE GROUP'S UNIVERSAL INTELLIGENCE

Group experiences inevitably connect both directly and indirectly to the world around them. I have been part of many group processes that were connected with radical changes in the environment. I remember working in Tel Aviv, where a peaceful ending to a group process coincided with a settlement between conflicting parties on the political level. I remember a heated conflict in Vancouver, British Columbia, which coincided with the assassination in Israel of Rabin, one of the world's great peacemakers. I have been through awesome experiences in San Francisco and Tokyo, where groups coming together manifested dramatic improvements in the environment. In note 8, I discuss details of several group processes in Japan, the United States, and China, where community transformation was inextricably linked with changes in the environment.

Each group process is linked to changes both in the immediate community and in the entire environment. In a way, the process of any given group does not belong only to that group, culture, or environment alone, but is an aspect of the world field. In a group process, not just your group, but the planet Earth and theoretically the entire universe, are involved with all the stars, galaxies, solar systems, and even other potential universes in real and imaginary space-time.

In any group process, before you make a CR observation about me, or I make a comment about you, we merge with one another, flirting in NCR. Our lives are sentient, interconnected, and non-local. As if we were entangled photons in the Bell experiment, whatever touches you affects me as well. From this NCR level, we know that what we call our CR selves are merely roles. When you or I marginalize this sense of interconnectedness, the CR world comes into being, and we feel absolutely clear about the fact that the roles we play are the people we are. At that moment we are separate and distinct.

However, during moments of consciousness, you or I notice both aspects of the universe, the NCR world of entanglement and the CR world of social issues. This gives us a chance to shuffle, mirroring the physics of the universe.

These are the implicit teachings of relativity, quantum mechanics, and the spirituality of our aboriginal ancestors. These teachings connect individual, relationship, political, and cosmic processes. If we can pick up what catches our attention, switch roles, and use the awareness of shape-shifting like shamans of all times, each moment in time becomes a chance to experience the reenactment of the creation of the universe. You recreate by becoming curious and reflecting upon your community's dream, its field of entangled, interconnected roles.

Your choice is to forget NCR and remain in CR where people are roles, or to remember your awareness of being the other. If you use your awareness, you know that most of the time we all forget our whole selves and identify with the roles we play. However, if you use your awareness, you awaken us by shuffling between roles in personal and community life. In other words, you can either marginalize your experiences or become aware of them to create consciousness. If you choose to use awareness in the typical, ongoing conflicts and occasional resolutions of everyday life, you participate in the universe's self-renewal. That's how to change world history and the course of time.

NOTES

1. David Bohm, in his 1975 paper with Basil Hiley, page 94. Quantum objects are said to be "quantum entangled," meaning they appear to connect at speeds greater than the speed of light. Quantum entanglement implies that if there are connections, they have to be non-consensus ones.

2. In Persian myths, the world is formed after a great female goddess, Taimat, is slain. In India, the whole universe in the form of Purusha was cut up; his head became the sky, his navel the air, his feet the earth. From his mind springs the moon, from his eyes the sun, and from his breath the wind. In China, when Pan Ku dies as the world dies, his parts become the world. See my earlier work, *The Year I* (pages 49 to 53), for further details.

3. Jack Kornfield, *A Path With Heart: A Guide Through the Perils and Promises of Spiritual Life*, Bantam Doubleday Dell, Pub. 1993.

4. See also *Creation Myths* (page 79) by David Maclagan.

5. In my *Leader As Martial Artist* and *Sitting in the Fire*, I speak about the details of creating harmony through diversity.

6. Maclagan, op. cit., page 78.

7. Symmetries are basic to all NCR fields in mythology, psychology, and physics. Physicists speak of God when they speak of the symmetries behind physics.

Richard Feynman (in his *Lectures on Physics,* Chapter 17, pages 1 to 8) gives the mathematically oriented reader a general overview of some of the more important conservation laws and their connections with symmetry principles. Symmetry with respect to space implies, for example, conservation of momentum with respect to a given direction in space; symmetry with respect to rotation around a spatial axis describes conservation of angular moment; symmetry with respect to reflection deals with conservation of parity, and symmetry with respect to electron exchange. Every conservation law implies a symmetry.

The mathematical laws of physics are symmetrical or nearly symmetrical. Symmetry in time, for example, means that when we substitute +t for -t (that is, time going forward for time going backward) in the mathematical expression of a law, if the law does not change, it is symmetrical with respect to time. It does not vary. The technical expression is that it is "time invariant."

You saw symmetries with respect to moving forward and backward in time related to the switch for an individual from a primary process to a secondary one in the Feynman diagrams of Chapter 38. This switch was initiated through an NCR awareness of quantum flirts and is based on our NCR sentient experience that we are the "other."

In group process this shuffling happens when people switch roles; they step out of time, "stop the world," or make time irrelevant to history.

Many symmetries in physics can be related to the complex number plane, which has its own type of symmetry. For example, the number $|a + ib|^2$, which is the absolute square of $a + ib$, remains the same if you switch a and b.

Here is how. If you multiply each number on the complex plane by i, for example, if you multiply the complex number $3 + 5i$ by i, you get $3i - 5$ since $i \times i = i^2 = -1$. If all numbers are multiplied in the same way, the general formula is:

$$i \times (a + ib) = ia - b \text{ or } -b + ia$$

It is a fascinating fact that

$$|-b + ia|^2 = (-b + ia)(-b - ia) = |a + ib|^2 = a^2 + b^2$$

Thus the absolute square of $a + ib$ is symmetrical if the real and the imaginary are reversed. This means that from the viewpoint of CR, CR and NCR properties are reversible, or that there is no one absolute reality. This is another kind of relativity principle.

Consider the difference between $a + ib$ and $-b + ia$ geometrically. If $a + ib$ is multiplied by i, the sign in front of a and b is reversed, and what was real is now imaginary. It is as if every number were rotated counterclockwise by 90 degrees. See Figures 41.9 and 41.10.

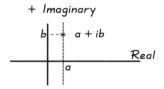

41.9 a+ib *before multiplication by i.*

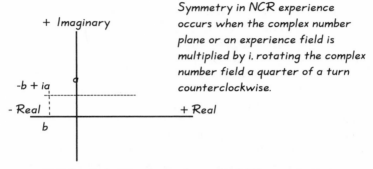

41.10 Result of rotating the complex number field by a quarter turn

At the level of non-consensus experience, at the level of the complex plane, if you reverse what is real with what is imaginary, you switch a non-consensus experience with consensual one. You shape-shift. You become a "real" person, to use the words of don Juan, instead of a "phantom." You experience a radical shift. However, from the CR world outside, you look the same. That is because of the underlying symmetry between the real and the imaginary.

Inwardly, how you deal with non-consensual realities is a matter of life and death, though this matter cannot be noticed at the CR level.

8. I think of an incredible interaction that occurred in Japan, which strongly influenced the environment. An example of shuffling and rank equalization occurred while we were working recently in Tokyo. When we arrived in Japan to do a group work seminar, we found that there had been a long, hard drought. To conserve water, people were not allowed to use water for sixteen hours a day. It seemed to the group as if it succeeded in creating rain. Here is how the story went.

    The first evening we spun a pen in the middle of the large circle of participants, and it pointed to a particular man who said he was suffering from chronic muscular spasms and tension. We said, since it was "chance" that selected him, he might be an expression of the Tao—that is, of the group field or mind. To make the story short, we worked with him in the center, and asked him to describe his spasms. He said they were cramping experiences and agreed to show us what they were like by acting like one of his tense muscles. He contracted like the muscle, curled up and withdrew inwardly. We acted like the man's ordinary identity and gently tugged on him to unwind and relax, saying things like, "Come on dear muscle, just relax."

    Suddenly he said that he recalled an experience from childhood in which people were "pulling at him" to go out, be more sociable. Amy and I acted like these people. We played the society and continued to tug at him in his curled-up position, saying, "Come out, come out and be sociable." He resisted and pulled inward and finally said being sociable was OK, but society would have to have more respect for the individual. Only then would the muscles relax, he said. His body was the stage for a cultural conflict between individual values and collective adaptation.

In this example you see how social tensions expressed themselves in body symptoms. I could give hundreds of examples from all over the world, but let this simple example represent, for the moment, the generalization mentioned in Chapter 38: world tensions manifest in our bodies. Our bodies are expressions of the NCR world field. His body was carrying the tensions of his culture. Thus individual work alone cannot "cure" someone.

Next we needed to also bring the whole group in. This was not difficult to do because as soon as he said that the culture would have to become more tolerant of the individual who wants to introvert, a muffled debate ensued in the group. People were whispering to one another. We asked what they were speaking about and they said the question was whether or not people would be allowed to be individual.

Some members of the group got up and pulled on one side of the man in the middle, saying, "We want to follow our own rhythm and not follow others." Other members of the group pulled on the other side of the man, saying, "You must respect the group. If you follow yourself as an individual, the community will not last!" A group struggle ensued, and it was evident that we could not clearly distinguish between the conflicted personal inner roles and the conflicting social roles in the community.

After the man with muscular spasms thanked all for the insights into his body problems, the group continued its process. The question was, would being an individual not disturb the wholeness and wellness of the group and culture? Students in our large-group open forum said they had long been silent, and asked to be listened to as individuals. They wanted to be considered important. The great Equalizer! They said they needed to be involved in every decision around their education, they wanted respect from their teachers. They felt it was one-sided to only respect the teacher. An emotional debate ensued.

In the midst of this, some women said the problem was not just the teachers. The women said they felt oppressed by men. The whole group joined in this debate. Some men said they no longer agreed with keeping women in inferior social positions. Amy and I asked if anyone knew what to do about this. After a long, dry, and strained silence, one person after another began hesitantly to speak. At first they said they were afraid to speak. Then they began to role-play and someone played the governing social order. He was the oppressor, a "ghost role" personifying the invisible social law. As a mighty ruler who kept everyone silent, he said "Respect your elders, obey me!" This seemed to be the central polarization, the central pyramid.

Men and women struggled to defend themselves against him. Someone complained that, since 1945, Japanese men had lost their spiritual warrior-ship and had become economic champions instead. The ancient spirits of justice and chivalry, the Samurai, were gone. Where were the Samurai? Suddenly one Japanese man sprang forth and attacked the "Oppressor" who was making both women and men subservient. The heroic "Samurai" spoke forcefully, and though he was half the size of the man playing the "Oppressor," the larger man began to shake.

The Japanese taboo against speaking forcefully in public against authorities was being tested! A hero had created a forum of social action. Now many people felt freer. Women and men spoke about how they wanted to resolve the women's issues and relationships between men and women. What an amazing, authentic interaction! Women spoke about being dominated and men spoke of their fear of powerful women. Everyone felt repressed by the social system. After the dialogue, there were personal resolutions and many deep insights and feelings. There had been a great shuffling symmetry, and a huge party ensued.

Many people had never witnessed anything like this before. It was an evening to remember. It had been the hottest, driest summer in the history of Japan. After working for three days with the large group on their individual and social issues, it poured so hard the roads flooded. We almost missed our plane the day after the seminar because the train lines to the airport were flooded as well.

This story reminds me of the Rainmaker, a story told by Richard Wilhelm and reported by Jung. In the early 1900s, a village suffering from drought invited a Chinese Taoist to help them make rain. He noticed that the community was "out of Tao" and decided to work on that by getting himself back in Tao. So he withdrew to the mountains for three days and on the fourth day it rained and rained. When Wilhelm asked him how he had "created" rain in China, the rainmaker said, "By getting into Tao."

There was no causality involved in this rainmaking; causality is a consensus reality concept. Instead, the rainmaker entered the non-consensus realm of the Tao. He worked on himself, and in that way he worked on the field of the entire village. In the case of the Japanese community with which we were working, entering the Tao was connected with awareness of positions in the field, rank imbalances, and shuffling symmetry. Everyone wanted social rank to be dealt with by using greater awareness and sensitivity. Everyone was a social oppressor in upholding ancient forms; everyone was a hero in breaking these forms.

This was the second time we have seen large-group processes around social issues break through the aridity of long-standing tension and bring rain. The first was at Esalen, in Big Sur, California, some years before. (See Amy's and my *Riding the Horse Backward,* for more on that story.) Groups entering the fire of social change seem to make water flow again when the blockade of long-standing cultural conflict is melted. The group becomes a rainmaker.

What was the problem? Was there a problem? Yes, from the CR viewpoint—a problem of cultural and individual psychology. The situation was lopsided. And no, there was no problem from the NCR viewpoint. We just landed in the midst of a Tao of dryness and no rain, no flow. The Tai Chi's momentary imbalance and diversity needed to be reflected so that it could shuffle along, rotating the eternal wheel.

42 | Planetwork: The Sixth Great Extinction

It all depends on you and me. If we see the world as a living organism of which we are a part—not the owner, nor the tenant; not even a passenger—we could have a long time ahead of us and our species might survive for its "allotted span."

—James Lovelock in *The Ages of Gaia*

In Chapter 32, we discussed Maxwell's second law of thermodynamics, which says that the energy in closed systems deteriorates in time into a less useable form and eventually cannot be tapped for use. Maxwell said that the whole universe was subject to this fate but also fantasized about a Maxwellian demon, an awareness potential in a closed system which, if it existed, could reverse that law and bring order out of chaos.

Is it true that, instead of lurching forward in time toward the ultimate chaos predicted by the second law of thermodynamics, the universe can produce order from its images of symmetry, self-reflect, and re-create itself? Is there an ordering tendency that will balance the entropy principle's doomsday forecast, which predicted that closed systems and perhaps our Earth would end in the heat death called thermal equilibrium? Most scientists believe that, with or without recycling, our own eco-system is condemned to death. At this stage of our journey together, let's look at how the shuffling symmetries we have been discussing can contribute answers to these ominous problems.

TIME

The seeming unidirectionality of time appears only in consensus reality. From the perspective of dreaming, time is reversible or irrelevant, as we have seen in quantum mechanics. You may remember from our discussion of antimatter in Chapter 37 that physics, psychology, and shamanism have processes that mirror time reversibility.

We have seen that whenever a complex arises, you can resist it and have your attention annihilated, or you can use your second attention and reflect, thus becoming the disturbing observation. In this way, you always have the choice of stepping out of time into dreaming. The shaman don Juan refers to this act as "stopping the world."

In group work, practicing role switching stops the world. If you are sufficiently fluid, you notice which roles attract or disturb you and can shuffle between roles, reversing your opinions. In this way, the whole world stops, for a moment at least, and unity experiences can arise. In that moment, the pattern of history, that eternal battle of opposites, is reversed, and time comes to a halt.

Thus our CR experience of the unidirectionality of time can be compensated for by stepping into complexes or by noticing the moment for role switches. In this way, tensions from complexes or from community problems lead to a sense of community and become a blessing instead of a curse. The model of such facilitation is found in the Maxwellian demon, whose awareness can turn the madhouse of particle and chemical reactions into a time-reversible universe.

THE SIXTH GREAT EXTINCTION

Without a wise presence such as the Maxwellian demon, our social and physical universes are predicted to end in ecological catastrophe, that unmitigated, violent conclusion characterizing the current period of planetary history.

Biologists refer to our current period of history as the beginning of the sixth great extinction. They tell us that, in the previous five extinctions, all animals and plant life were destroyed. If we look at the history of our planet, it seems that every 26 million years or so there is a mass extinction. For example, in one of these extinctions 65 million years ago, most dinosaurs were killed off. In another extinction 35 million years ago, many land mammals were extinguished.[1]

The present extinction process will be the sixth, the first annihilation caused mainly by humans. In ecological visions of this apocalypse, humans are going to die because of overpopulation and toxic waste, not because the Earth, solar system, galaxy, or universe is burning out. We don't need human beings to create an ecological annihilation, but this time, humans are contributing to such a cataclysmic event. How might increases in awareness and consciousness influence this dismal outcome? We know that individual, group, and environmental events seem intimately connected (see note 8 in Chapter 41).

Physics and psychology, personal and community processes are entangled with environmental processes. We have spoken of this entanglement in many ways, with various terms:

- In terms of the non-consensus, subjective interactions hidden in the process of counting and the creation of numbers 1, 2, and 3.
- In terms of the mathematics of quantum mechanics: observation requires a quantum flirt between the observer and the observed in non-consensus reality.
- In terms of the mathematics of relativity, where time becomes an imaginary quantity with non-consensual characteristics.

We are inextricably linked with everything we observe. Yet, most of us focus on consensual, classical, Newtonian connections with the environment that are clearly causal. It's important and easy to recognize that the environment's sixth great extinction is only hastened by toxic waste. If the amount of toxins killing our eco-systems depends on how much we recycle, why not recycle?

The problem is that not everyone feels included in the "we" that would recycle. Most environmentalists place far less emphasis on how to create a community than on the Newtonian physics and chemistry involved in destroying plants and animals.

Working through environmental problems would be easy if we knew as much about getting along with one another as we know about getting to the moon or recycling paper. Space exploration, elementary particles, and recycling get more emphasis in the news than shamanic acts and discoveries about large-group processes. It may well be that marginalization of human relationship problems is a key contribution to the sixth great extinction. Immediate, physical, causal, Newtonian interventions are essential, but they do not solve the background issues, that is, the sentient relationship problems we have with one another and with Mother Earth.

ECO-PSYCHOLOGY

To be complete, environmental ecology needs to deal with eco-psychology, which integrates Native spiritual beliefs just as it deals with Newtonian, causal solutions. Arne Naess, an elder of the eco-psychology movement, made a distinction between shallow and deep ecology. He said superficial ecology was survival environmentalism; it focuses mainly on the issues of human survival. This shallow ecology is anthropocentric: it focuses on pollution, resource depletion, health, and affluence in developed countries. Naess's "deep, long-range ecology" speaks about the need for humans to identify with non-humans and the need for a nonviolent environmental activism coming from a more total view.[2]

To do this, we need to consider the essential point that we have been discussing thus far: that we have the potential to be modern shamans who can influence the world on all levels. We have the potential to facilitate NCR connections, quantum flirts, and dreams as well as local, causal signal exchanges between the observer and the observed. We need to feel ourselves holding hands with the Earth as well as recycling real garbage.

However, for the average person, CR is the crucial reality. The idea that matter may share awareness or have an awareness of its own is untenable. How can She flirt with us? Most people today doubt that their environment is a sentient being and pay only lip service to the spirit of matter. Remember, whether or not a rock is alive and conscious depends on the state of consciousness you are in—in short, on relativity.

In the NCR experience of observation, everything is alive in the sense of interacting through quantum flirts with everything else, thus creating the solidity we experience in CR as matter. The mathematical patterns of quantum mechanics reveal the process of conjugation behind observer-object interactions. Sentient experiences of the "material" world are constantly occurring. Symmetries and interconnections are behind what we call "looking," behind observation and consciousness.

In psychology, personal well-being is determined in part by how we facilitate our own self-reflective processes. Reflection is not only basic to psychology and physics but also to ancient principles found in the Taoist Tai Chi, sacred geometries, and aboriginal mythologies.

From the viewpoint of the consensus reality of indigenous peoples, everything in the environment is a living being whose awareness process is similar to that of humans. In this view, it is natural to consider that a tree participates in our observing her and to think she calls to us to observe her. To use Western CR terms, the tree looks at me at the same time I look at it. Such aboriginal thinking is needed to make sense of quantum mechanics.[3] The mutual flirting process can be experienced by anyone at any time, but it may not be testable in terms of consensus reality, which marginalizes imaginary qualities of "real" observations.

In the math of physics and in aboriginal thinking, the tree exists in part because of the quantum flirts needed to observe it. If two of us observe that tree, its existence is based on additional interactions. In other words, the existence in consensus reality of an observed tree—or of a person, or any object—depends on everything and everyone interacting with it in NCR.

You are not emotionally or physically separable from anything you observe, be it a particle, a tree, or another person. The sense of separateness arises from marginalizing the non-consensus aspects of sensory-grounded perception. Every observation in CR is based on non-consensual, participatory exchanges in dreaming. From the NCR viewpoint in quantum mechanics, it is no longer clear exactly who is the observer and who is the observed. Both flirt with one another in NCR. You are on safer ground if you say that, from the viewpoint of NCR, each so-called human observation consists of a piece of nature looking at herself.

A clinical psychologist's view is that I see you because you reflect a part of me. An Aboriginal Australian shaman would say that people and objects "catch my attention," they "grab me." The things you pay attention to are paying attention to you in the non-consensual dimensions of quantum mechanics; everything you think about is thinking about you. Only in consensus reality can we separate the human being from the environment, the logger from the tree. In dreaming, the logger and the tree are two parts of the same interaction.

The European Renaissance, in the voice of Francis Bacon, proclaimed naively that nature was a slave whose secrets could be tortured out of her. Today, these ideas need updating. Nature cannot be enslaved. Because you, Bacon, and I all participate in nature, you are Her. What you call nature is a reflection, in dreaming, of yourself. In NCR, you can only do something to nature if She is involved in it in dreaming.

The conclusion is that everything you do is, from another viewpoint, nature's doing! The only way to separate yourself from Her is to ignore NCR experiences, to marginalize sentient, dreaming interactions. Such separation is neither relativistic nor ecological.

A more relativistic view includes both CR and NCR realities, namely, that on the one hand, you need to protect nature and, on the other, you need to be aware that nature Herself creates and destroys parts of Herself through your behavior. From the CR viewpoint, you are responsible for life on Earth. But from the NCR viewpoint, nature creates and destroys Herself and "our" ecosystem.

This does not mean that She cannot change; after all, you and I are a part of Her and we can change. It simply means that our experiences and acts are not just ours. For example, the tendency to marginalize is a natural tendency in the sense that we all do it all the time, in the same way an imaginary number times itself produces a real one. After all, $i \times i = -1$, which means that the imaginary number, i, can be forgotten in the final accounting. Of course, you don't have to forget. You can always remember to notice that every real observation is the result of an imaginary conjugation, an imagination realizing itself. But the nature of mathematics makes it possible to forget and to marginalize the imaginary, just as the nature of our psychology allows us to marginalize experience.

Marginalization of NCR processes is part of nature. It is a part of psychology, math, and physics. It can even be useful to marginalize. After all, when you are crossing a street and suddenly think you see a ring in the middle of the road, you can marginalize that flickering fantasy and cross the road to avoid getting hit by an oncoming car.

Many good things have come from this marginalization of the spirit in matter. How can I be totally against Francis Bacon's wish to enslave nature when I enjoy the labor-saving devices of my own computer? My point is that nature marginalizes nature.

It is "normal" and important to focus in CR on the effect of toxic wastes and to promote useful social action to stop producing such wastes. But it is helpful to remember as well that nature hurts herself by marginalizing sentience and the unity of all beings. In this way she participates in her own death.

Both CR and NCR realities depend on one anther. Although you may marginalize the spirit of the material environment, the vis viva,[4] or soul of matter that moves it from within, that soul is still there.[5] The moral of all this is that you and I need to learn to shuffle between CR and NCR viewpoints of nature. It's not that hard. Try viewing yourself and the things around you as solid and real, and then, after a moment, try also to view yourself and your environment as created by dreaming.

WHAT IS A TREE?

Future science will have greater awareness of both NCR and CR realities. When this happens, new questions arise. You can guess that when cultures relearn to see NCR experiences as real, new problems will occur. For example, if you can intimately communicate with the "inorganic" world around you, with, for example, a tree, what happens if several people look at a tree and each person says that the tree communicates something different to her? Who is right?

To be more specific, what if an environmentalist says, "The tree is sad and does not want to be cut down," while a logger says, "The tree is happy to offer itself so that I can earn a living." Who has the right view of the tree? Who hears its "true" voice?

From the CR viewpoint, all observers are hallucinating. If you live in a CR, democratic country, you would take a vote about whether to cut the tree down or not, and the answer would depend on the results of that vote.

42.1 Comments about the tree

From the CR viewpoint, everyone projects himself or herself onto the tree. The CR viewpoint insists that we are all separate individuals, that what we say about trees is either pure fantasy or rational fact. Therefore no one is correct about the tree. Only its physical characteristics and measurements are "objective," "real," and "correct."

However, from the viewpoint of NCR, we are all participants who hear the voice of the tree. We participate in a shared mind. From the NCR viewpoint of dreaming, from the foregoing interpretations of quantum physics and relativity, whatever you observe about the tree is an aspect of both your and its mind. This shared mind is a sentient experience of a shared intelligence, a kind of field in space-time, a common ground which each of us normally sees from her own individual viewpoint.

In NCR, the tree is a shared field that is apprehended through dreaming together, through processing our experiences of her. From this viewpoint, everyone who observes the tree is a channel for her. The tree thinks through us. We are her parts, just as you find a part of yourself in her. By the same reasoning which makes you partly a tree, she is partly human. Your behavior is partly reflected in her motions, and her mind is partly reflected in your thoughts.

In a "tree-centric" world, all of us are parts of her personality, just as much as, from the human-centered viewpoint, everything you think the tree "says" is part of your personality.

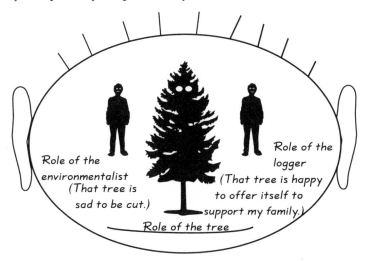

42.2 *The tree's mind in a tree-centric world*
"Hmm, I have some inner conflicts."

In other words, if two of us are talking about a tree, *the two of us and the one tree are all roles in the tree's personality,* roles in a tree field of which we take part.

All viewpoints are simultaneously relevant as parts of the tree in a tree-centric world. In other words, one part of her acts as if she is happy to be cut down to feed the logger's family, while another side of her is sad about being killed.

From a universal viewpoint, the logger, the environmentalist, the tree, you, and I are all parts of Nature's dreaming. Nature is in conflict about using herself to support other parts of herself, like the logger who earns a living off the environment.

The entire conflict you and I experience between our environment and ourselves is global, planetary, cosmic, and also very human and mundane. Our conflict is Hers as well. But Hers is ours. Think about the last time you used your own body, neglected it, almost cut it down to earn a living or to do something else that you deemed humanely necessary? You, too, sacrifice one part of life for another.

Each conflict about the environment is a conflict in each of us; each decision about the environment is global. In this sentient view, you are a part of Nature's mind, and she is a part of yours. The quantum reason for this kind of relativistic thinking is that we are all entangled. What we call "you" and what we call "the tree" are, at best, CR coordinates, state-oriented approximations of dreaming experiences in NCR, which are connected with uncertainties in CR. We know only that we are all entangled at the quantum level.

Before CR observation, the dreamer experiences herself and everything else as being anywhere, at any time. Non-locality is crucial to dreaming and quantum wave functions. In principle, the same holds true for the tree. She, too, is all over at any moment. The tree's mind consists in part of feelings and thoughts of those whose attention she has caught. From the viewpoint of CR psychology, we are as much products of the tree's psychology as she is a product of ours. In other words, what she decides to do with herself is reflected not only in what we decide to do with her, but also in how we treat ourselves, as well as in how the whole universe treats itself.

PLANETWORK

The CR perspective that we do not mirror the basic sentient qualities of nature in NCR and that we are responsible for ruining our ecosystem is not only anthropocentric—it is naive and only one side of the picture. This perspective makes you think you have the power to dominate nature. It's an important view, because you can change such domination: you can contribute to preserve the environment.

However, a more relativistic view would be to say that what appears in consensus reality to be the domination of nature by the human race, is, in dreaming, an interaction in the community of all beings. Think of the

Delaware symbols for community and a group process involving issues of rank with roles for rocks, plants, animals, people, and spirits of all kinds. From this perspective, each role is crucial, and each is involved in interacting with the others.

When there was conflict in the NCR world of sentient beings in the past, communities called in their shamans to set things in order. Traditional shamans were worldwork facilitators. Just as an individual needs individual work, and a human community needs worldwork, the community of all beings needs facilitators to do planetwork. Planetwork requires shamanic facilitators, dreamworkers, to handle negotiations in the community of all beings. Until now, only traditional shamans have done planetwork, teaching us that, to live together, we must notice and facilitate situations in nature where humans abused the spirits of the environment, or where the spirits of the environment hurt people. Shamans knew that whenever they worked with individuals or communities, the planetwork being done influenced all beings. Healing a community healed an individual; working with an individual healed the whole community and even the environment.

The NCR view of our being aspects of nature broadens our self-definition, a central goal of eco-psychology. According to Sara Conn:

> …an ecologically responsible construction of the self will require what Arne Naess calls, an "ecological self" which includes not only growth and human relationships… but a broadening of the self through identification of the self with all beings… As Naess points out, if we "broaden and deepen" our end of self, then the Earth flows through us, and we can naturally care for it.[6]

In a way, Conn and Naess are ahead of the physicists. In caring for nature, none of us can wait for the hard sciences to catch up with the shamans. Truly caring for Mother Nature requires becoming sentient, becoming aware of non-consensual experience. Since nature cannot be differentiated from perception, which is a two-way project involving the observer and the observed, marginalization of any NCR experience of nature not only represses a part of Her, but a part of yourself as well.

THINKING ABOUT THE FUTURE

Although marginalization is natural, it creates dissonance. We cannot predict how the relationship between the human and the apparently non-human realm will evolve, but today the ecosystem on our planet looks like it is heading toward the sixth great extinction. We saw hints of this in the tale of Melusina in Chapter 16. Remember Melusina and the man who doubted her? The mermaid suffered misunderstanding from her partner's doubts. She symbolizes the NCR experiences of nature marginalized by the CR observer.

In a way, the sixth great extinction occurs every moment that you ignore the NCR reality of the environment. Whenever you marginalize any of your sentient NCR feelings, you injure Nature.

Although the fairy tale of Melusina ends with her disappearing forever, extinction can also be reversed. The metaphorical extinction that marginalizes one-time events and experiences can be reversed by valuing them as much as you value the causal world of locality and separability. You can start by communicating with your fantasies, your feelings, and your pots and pans, chairs and tables, computers and motors, and the rocks, plants, and animals around you.

This attitude will revitalize politics, physics, and psychology. Since Marx's communism, Ghandi's nonviolent protests, Freud's unconscious and Jung's collective unconscious, since Heisenberg's uncertainty principle and Einstein's theory of relativity, investigations of the central issues of politics, psychology, and physics have been slowed in part by keeping them separate. New impulses in politics, physics, and psychology come from bringing them together, from activists and physicists studying nonconsensus experiences, from therapists realizing that dreaming connects with matter and forms your awareness of the CR and NCR dimensions of what you see.

Asking what objects have to say about their own future will eventually be part of city politics. In this deeper democracy, everything will have a voice and a vote!

It seems to me that a new phase of math and physics is imminent. By considering awareness in counting and observing matter, this new phase will include sentient awareness as the fundamental "stuff" that is ontologically prior to number, time, psyche, and matter. Sentient awareness is non-local; it is not contained in a material place such as the human brain. Sentient awareness is the ground of consciousness and everyday reality; it lies behind observation, which becomes nature's general tendency to self-reflect. In this new development of science, complex numbers become to science as the alphabet is to language: fundamental particles of the way we perceive and communicate.

In recent years the new kinds of mathematical thinking used in physics seem to reflect what I see as the future development of science. As the story of elementary and virtual particles unfolds, some theorists are using new, multi-dimensional, "hyperspaces" to unify relativity and quantum mechanics. These spaces promise to be more fundamental than either particles or matter.[7]

This unification through math reminds me of the central nature of dreamtime, whose imaginary spaces were also meant to be a theory of everything. The new math is a rebirth of aboriginal dreamtime.[8]

In part, physics too seems to be centering itself around the use of imaginary numbers. I think especially of Cramer's echo theory interpretation of the wave function, mentioned in Chapter 17, of Hawking's imaginary time in relativity, mentioned in Chapter 31, and of Roger Penrose's recent "twister" theory, which uses complex space to unify quantum mechanics and relativity. His space has eight dimensions, a real and an imaginary one for each of the four dimensions of space-time.

As a new century begins, physics is heading toward invisible spaces and forces, a track originating in the early part of the century now passing, when quantum mechanics and relativity used imaginary domains to describe the world.

Some scientists may frown on the unification of shamanism, psychology, and physics now impending. Other readers may resist a change in worldview in which NCR experience is considered to be the fundamental stuff of the universe. Yet, this change must be considered, since the interpretations of math are consistent with the existing laws of psychology and the ideas of physics. Furthermore, these interpretations make sense of phenomena like parapsychology, which, until now, have averted understanding. Remember the striking similarity pointed out in Chapter 37 between the psychological concept of "integration," the physicist's concept of the collapse of the wave function, and the phenomenon of the poltergeist.

Most scientists today are busier with applications and less interested in the basic philosophy of physics. Richard Feynman spent hours reducing philosophical discussions down to "brass tacks." I remember myself as a student at MIT, laughing with my peers at older scientists going off on tangents into the spiritual blue yonder, following thoughts that could not be tied down to material reality.

I am still one of those students. Being pragmatic is important to me. But I think that a most down-to-earth and realistic view requires facing the fact that the mathematical laws of physics are incomplete. Their foundations are unknown. Physics is an experimental procedure described by an incomprehensible mathematics.

I think that the foundation of this mathematics and of the physical world is dreaming. To understand the real world, we must look to shamanism and psychology, sentient flirts and perceptual flashes between the observer and the observed environment. The direction I am suggesting will undoubtedly lead to breakthroughs in technology, neurosciences, psychiatry, and parapsychology. There will be applications to the NCR aspects of medicine. We shall better understand the interconnection between diseases such as cancer and our dreams, between quantum mechanics and sentient awareness.

Best yet, as the foundations of physics expand, our relationship and interaction with the environment will improve. Then it will be clear that the central problems of today's theoretical physics and of today's damaged environment are due to one and the same event: marginalizing the dreaming, NCR background of the universe.

REVERSING THE SIXTH GREAT EXTINCTION

Recent developments in physics validate what the Melusina fairy tale indicates: The CR observer's state of consciousness disturbs quantum processes. This disturbance is implied by the recent work of Mistra and Sudarshan, which indicates that observation of the decay of an unstable particle, such as a radioactive nucleus, can be suppressed by the act of such observation.[9] Such "quantum eraser" experiments suggest that particles even react to the possibility that they will be observed at a later date!

In other words, just planning to look at yourself in the future can erase experiences today. If we take the future to be your present secondary and unconscious process, then these "eraser" experiments imply that how you unconsciously see yourself now influences your physical body.

Physics is rediscovering what aboriginal people always knew: creation and annihilation occur in dreamtime. While scientists try to prove through CR testing whether or not the state of consciousness influences life on Earth or destroys our ecology, aboriginal thinking sets about to heal this hurt. Shamans intervene in dreamtime to prevent Nature's various parts from destroying themselves.

The planetwork of shamans takes non-consensus experience seriously, transforming the universe from a fact into an interactive process. Those who feel most at ease with this universe have something shamanic about them and interact with Her on many levels. When you interact holistically both as a Newtonian observer and a dreamer, you experience how fate depends on facilitating the consensual and non-consensual signal exchanges in the community of all beings.

A new worldview is upon us, one in which you still identify yourself as you do now, as an observer separated from other observers and "objects," and in which you also identity with everything that catches your attention. Shamans have achieved this expanded identity through being regular people, working every day at whatever they did in CR, and honoring nature, shape-shifting at night, catching reflections and becoming the natural forces they observed.

We find the pattern for the new worldview and expanded identity in many places. Zen speaks of such an expanded identity in terms of enlightenment. According to Zen master Maurine Stuart, enlightenment entails "seeing clearly." This enlightenment:

> ...doesn't mean that you look at something and analyze it, noting all its composite parts; no. When you see clearly, when you look at a flower and really see it, the flower sees you. It's not that the flower has eyes, of course. It's that the flower is no longer just a flower, and you are no longer just you. Flower and you are dissolved into something way beyond what we can even say, but we

can experience this... Meister Eckhart, a thirteenth-century Christian mystic who really understood this, said, "The eye with which I see God is the same eye with which god sees me."...Realizing we are a part of the whole universe, not separate, our minds become as clear as crystal, and all the Dharma is revealed. So let us see clearly....[10]

The awareness acts this wise Zen master calls enlightenment are the non-consensual foundation to quantum physics, relativity, and all of reality.

From the viewpoint of Zen, aboriginal thinking, and non-consensus reality, planetary destruction is not the next or the sixth great extinction, but the seventh. The sixth occurred when we all but wiped out the aboriginal peoples and their shamanistic worldview. In other words, the sixth extinction of our eco-sphere is not happening as a result of dumping toxic wastes on all that lives on Earth. The sixth huge catastrophe occurs every time you denounce your non-consensual experience as irrelevant.

To reverse the sixth great extinction, use your attention in closed, hopeless, material systems. Take any personal, family, world or universal situation. Become the metaphorical demon imagined by Maxwell. The shamanic consciousness of that demon may or may not save the universe, effecting a CR reversal of the heat death imagined by Maxwell, but such consciousness will surely add zest to existence.

Remember the Feynman diagrams and the fate of electrons in electromagnetic fields. Recall don Juan's "real people," who greet fields, complexes, and trouble as a chance to stop the world and step out of time. Enter into a closed field and remember that whatever you and I think is part of "its" mind. Whether it lives or dies depends in part upon how we deal with one another. There is no longer a universal situation or planetary ecology independent of how we feel towards one another. When the field is tense, notice the role you are in and shape-shift into another. Help the planetary mind to become more fluid by moving lucidly between the role of the tree, the environmentalist, the logger, and whatever else is present.

Your attention to non-consensual dreaming upholds state-oriented, fixed conceptions, such as success, failure, life, and death. The great problems that threaten are a chance to shape-shift and transform devastating energy into incredible life forces. Doing this, you reverse the sense of the sixth great extinction. With the unrestrained intensity coming from this planetwork, you create a new world, and make the seventh extinction irrelevant.

NOTES

1. See Michio Kaku's *Hyperspace*, pages 290 to 296. One theory is that large asteroids hitting the Earth caused these extinctions.

2. In *Deep Ecology for the 21st Century*, edited by George Sessions, work on ecology is traced in part to the ideas of Henry David Thoreau, John Muir, D.H. Lawrence, and Aldous Huxley. The connections between ecology and social action can be found in the works of George Orwell and, more recently, in Theodore Roszak's *Ecopsychology*. He points out that deeper roots go further back to all Native peoples and to Taoism, which encompasses human and nonhuman life in one. St. Francis of Assisi, the romantics, countercultural movements in the nineteenth century, the hippies in the 1960s, Zen, Alan Watts, and Gary Snyder all spoke of the equality of all beings. Roszak points out that Lynn White also connects ecological problems of nature with views from mainstream religions that see humans as better than animals and plants. Francis of Assisi was different: he preached "the equality of all creatures."

3. The reader can review the discussion about the quantum flirt in Chapter 17.

4. Leibniz's "vis viva" was mv^2 where m is mass and v is velocity. Today's kinetic energy is $(mv^2/2)$. See Chapter 10 for more.

5. In other words, what we call energy or matter today was once believed to have a soul. See Fred Wolf's *The Spiritual Universe* (1996), for the beginning of a rebirth of soulful physics.

6. In George Sessions's work, op. cit., we find deep ecologist Sara Conn's words in her "Eco-psychology," pages 163 to 165. We also find Arne Naess's ideas in "Deep, Long-Range Ecology." Joanna Macy, John Seed, and many others who were instrumental in connecting ecological philosophy to the teachings of Buddhism can also be found in Sessions's work.

7. If we follow the development of quantum electrodynamics into what is called quantum chromodynamics, electroweakdynamics, Guts, and superstring theory, it almost seems as if the concept of mathematical space will overtake the idea of particles. Kaku agrees; op. cit., page 313.

8. Hyperspace theories of superstrings may bring the various natural forces under one theory. See Kaku, op. cit., page 165. The evolving theories of particles (and their newest reformulation in terms of strings, twisters, and stretched and foamy space-time) can be understood as discovering or describing new detail about the structure of awareness. Simplifications of particle theory found in the work of David Gross and others see the four basic forces in nature (the electromagnetic, the strong nuclear force, the weak nuclear force, and the gravitational force) as a single, unified force that existed at the beginning of the universe. This sounds like indigenous mythology, where in the beginning there was the force of awareness, which reflected and created everything we see today.

9. See Darling's *Zen Physics*, page 135, on Raymond Chiao's work in 1992.

10. See Stuart's *Subtle Sound: The Zen Teachings of Maurine Stuart* (1996).

43 | Answer to a Prayer

From the viewpoint of the fairy tale *Alice in Wonderland*, the real world is above ground and full of people and things—like the tree trunk. The tree's roots symbolize non-consensual reality below the ground. Using the metaphor of the tree, the CR observer sees the trunk, while the sentient experiencer notices the roots.

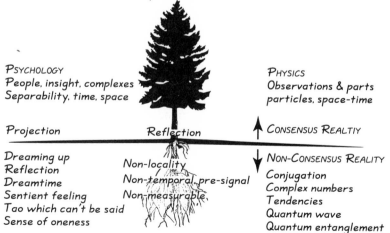

World of duality, the Tao which can be said

PSYCHOLOGY
People, insight, complexes
Separability, time, space

PHYSICS
Observations & parts
particles, space-time

Projection   Reflection   ↑ CONSENSUS REALTIY

Dreaming up
Reflection   Non-locality   ↓ NON-CONSENSUS REALITY
Dreamtime   Non-temporal, pre-signal
Sentient feeling   Non-measurable.   Conjugation
Tao which can't be said   Complex numbers
Sense of oneness   Tendencies
                                             Quantum wave
                                             Quantum entanglement

43.1 The world as a tree spanning two realities

Sentient knowing in non-consensual reality is marked by your capacity to perceive things not generally recognized. Sentience is that special state of oneness that cannot differentiate between your looking at something and its looking at you. When you are not lucid about your sentient perceptions, you marginalize them and the world becomes not only terrestrial and mundane, but also incomprehensible and meaningless.

Marginalization of sentient experience made physicists think they discovered new worlds in quantum mechanics and relativity, worlds we do not experience. Actually, Alice discovered these worlds long ago. In her story, she and the rabbit she is chasing are aware that the roots of reality lie in the NCR communication between all sentient beings. In Alice's world, doorknobs speak and everything is alive.

Until now, physics has focused mainly on the trunk and branches of the tree. The roots below, which are described by an incomprehensible mathematics, represent the land of fairy tales and imaginary spaces, the domain of sentient experience. In this mathematics, just as in Zen and aboriginal tradition, you can see only because you are seen. You are in a steady state of constantly being attracted by yourself.

In mythic terms, the world comes into being through divine powers reflecting upon themselves. You experience this as wondering about yourself and everyone else as well. In the terms of our discussion, self-love comes from taking your perceptions seriously, accepting your wondering, noticing it as the beginning of a conjugal act, a heartfelt relationship process. I have tried to show that embracing your experience and following whatever flirts with you is the path of heart, a modern shaman's guide through life, death, dreaming, and the universe.

Until now, physics has had trouble understanding the significance of its mathematics and apparently superluminal interactions between particles. Likewise, psychology has had problems comprehending the origins of dreams and synchronicities and strongly altered or comatose states of consciousness. These problems were created in physics by treating the observer as an irrelevant, soulless being and then, later, discovering that consciousness was still, somewhere, implicit in the math. Psychology's problems arise from assuming the observer is the ego—again, a basically CR observer localized in a body—instead of assuming a state of non-locality and unbroken wholeness from the beginning.

My viewpoint is that subliminal awareness is groundwork, the alpha and omega of science, and the first principle, which creates the others. This awareness notices that the basic world substance is dreaming. The observer, the observed, and everything else in CR arise through marginalizing non-local entanglements. Assuming this first principle allows the mathematical foundations of physics to be more complete.

In the new physics and psychology, the fundamental process is not elementary particles or parts of the personality such as ego or Self, but dreaming. This fundamental dreaming process reminds me of Richard Feynman's seminal text on particle physics, *The Theory of Fundamental Processes*. His title stresses that the particles themselves are not the roots of physical reality; instead, the true roots are the interactions, invisible relationship processes between particles.

As we near the end of our journey together, our explorations have led to a similar view. We have seen that dreaming processes are the roots of physics and psychology. The basic stuff of the universe is an interactional relationship process between everything involved in observation. This process is mirrored in the mathematics of quantum mechanics and relativity. That math is a metaphor for the dynamic, dreamlike interaction in complex hyperspaces with the "other," which is the object of observation. In non-consensual, dreamlike reality, you are not an individual object or person, but a composite relationship with everything that is seen.

In other words, dreaming is pre-material. Dreaming no longer means only dreams, pictures from the night. Dreaming now refers to all sentient NCR experiences, such as the feelings you have in sleep, your fantasies, intuitions, and unexpected body feelings, as well as partially observed objects that fleetingly catch your attention. These are the pre-material origins of the world.

Pre-material dreaming is trying to generate itself through you into reality. In NCR, what you are looking at is a momentary aspect of yourself, that part of you trying to unfold into reality. In general, every "real" thing you see has a real and also a dreamlike nature. The universe is a material substance consisting of planets and solar systems, quasars and black holes, and a dreaming substance consisting of everything you feel.

Without sentient awareness, not only does observation lose its soul—you do as well. Since the sixteenth century, physics has based its experiments on consensual reality, which marginalizes non-consensual experience. To be more complete, physics needs your help to include non-consensus reality experiments, that is, subjective impressions.

Thé border between psychology and physics remains only for the CR observer who marginalizes sentient experience. As you relearn to use your awareness, at first, sentient experience seems weird or abnormal. As you continue learning, the old consensus reality will probably appear one-sided.

Remember the lesson of relativity: no framework is real in the absolute sense. No perception or level of perception is everything. There is no *one* reality. Awareness itself is a moving ground which, like a searchlight, moves back and forth between NCR sentient experience and CR observation.

The more you use your attention, the more the world becomes a composite reality based as much on concrete as it is on fairy tales. The world shimmers, it regains the luster it had when you were a child. Life seems remarkable again, fascinating, a place for liberated, playful artists.

Being impressionable to things that are like you gives you a new identity. Normally, you feel different from others; the world is full of diversity, packed with foreign, wonderful or frightening events. This CR viewpoint isolates you from events you must defend yourself against.

However, from the sentient viewpoint, the most potentially devastating or fantastic thing you will ever meet on your awesome path is yourself, your interconnectedness, your own reflection. In a way, you can only be attracted to and repelled by yourself. There is something basically homoerotic (from *homo*, meaning "the same") behind everything you look at.

In today's language, basic physics and psychology are queer physics and psychology. Only CR physics is heterosexual (from *hetero*, meaning "other"), since it is based on marginalizing the sense of sameness and assumes that the observer is different from the observed.

From the viewpoint of sentient physics, self-reflection is the origin of all symmetry principles. It creates time symmetry, that is, the ability to travel forward, backward, and out of time in the world of quantum events. Self-reflection is the essence of non-locality, the irrelevance of spatial separation during NCR events. Self-reflection manifests in your ability to shape-shift and, in a group process, to experience shuffling symmetry and the sense of liberation from yourself while the outer system remains the same. When you are able to do this, you know that the world was not wrong; the difficulty came from the state of being like an elementary particle in that world, separate, permanently fixed, unable to vibrate and change states.

Symmetries appear in the relativity of all viewpoints and in the geometry of mythic figures that created the universe, in Nun, Purusha, and Christ. The Self-reflection used by the gods to know themselves created the world. The universe is a curious person. Your own tendency to be reflective, to wonder about yourself, comes in from this curious universe. Finally, the more you know yourself, the more you know the mind of the universe, the swirling Tai Chi, and the shaman's double.

ENTANGLEMENT IN RELATIONSHIP

From the viewpoint of NCR, there is only one relationship problem: getting to know yourself. In NCR, you are relationship, a song about you and me, a song searching for the right people to fill your stanzas. From the NCR viewpoint, the only process is dreaming together. Some call this view creativity, others enlightenment, or love.

Yet marginalization is also part of nature's mind. Catch yourself at the edge, marginalizing sentient experience that you refuse to admit has anything to do with yourself. Marginalizing others around you makes trouble. Then, you feel that everyone and all things, people and objects, no longer flirt but invade your life—especially when you insist they are not you. The sounds, sights, and feelings you marginalized in the day reverberate as echoes and dreams in the night. Everyone and everything you discounted returns as a chronic problem.

Since marginalizing happens unconsciously, you generally notice only how others marginalize you. You know what it is like to be overlooked—it hurts. Marginalization creates time; it represses your own NCR perceptions and generates the future from the past by inspiring you to awaken those who marginalized you. Marginalization makes you dream of revenge.

Since most of us identify with being marginalized, the world seems full of oppressors who always seem to get away with it. But in this CR world, everyone passes over everyone else, failing to see the significance of the other. As marginalizers, we are all basically unconscious oppressors. As a result of not noticing our own tendency to marginalize others, they always seem unnecessarily angry, while we seem to them to be sleepers in need of awakening.

Your tendency to marginalize events is based on a subtle selectivity, on the assumption that you are more or less significant than what you experience. Your identity is the all-important thing, a fragile essence you must constantly protect from the people and events you marginalized. Marginalization is a painful but natural process that makes time go forward. It creates the sense of difference and the inevitability of history, and provokes you through the cycle of revenge to learn what you once knew, that is, how to self-reflect and shuffle roles, realizing you are different from and also the same as the "other."

SYMMETRICAL LIVING: A PERSONAL EXPERIMENT

If you are interested in experimenting with the entangled nature of relationship and the interconnections behind marginalization, you may want to try the following:

Consider someone you feel does not like you. What is their opinion of you? In what way have you unconsciously ranked them as being better or worse than you are? In what way, if any, is their revenge an attempt to awaken you to your unconscious ranking that put them down (or up)? Do you marginalize their opinion in yourself?

Now, try to shape-shift, be the other, and see yourself through their eyes. Try dropping your momentary identity and consider the possibility that you are neither yourself nor the other, but a song about the two of you.

With insight, encouragement, and experience, you can learn to shuffle and live symmetrically. By taking all your perceptions as equally important, a deeper, more practical and immediate democracy becomes possible.

WHO ARE YOU?

From the viewpoint of CR, you are a person, an identity that plays an insignificant or important role in a social field. You are a body that was born and will one day die. You look different, however, from the viewpoint of NCR. There, you are a group process, the interactions between all sentient beings, a system of co-dreamers, fundamental pre-material interactions that reflect on themselves and create the world.

Personal identity in CR arises from marginalizing all your NCR experiences. Becoming material through reflection and marginalizing reflection, you unconsciously consent to forget the fairy tale behind you, temporarily thinking that being a person is the central experience. But being a person without a divine counterpart means that something is always missing. You are constantly plagued by fear of the enemy or of death. Near sleep, you remember what you forgot, the community of self-reflecting interactions that marginalizes parts of itself.

From one perspective life is a turmoil in which we are the victims of shifting and relentless fates. This position is difficult for everyone, yet it is neither preordained nor unalterable. From another perspective, time no longer exists. In fact, you were never born and are not the one who will die. Instead you are the sum of all of us together, a cosmos of relationships, a virtual and changing wonderland. While you normally think of yourself as a body that lives and dies, your NCR self rises and sets, cycling around CR like the moon around the Earth.

Being a person includes both a celestial self and its negation, forgetting you ever dreamed. Like Cinderella returning from an enchanted evening, you leave your magic shoes at midnight, abandoning your whole self to work like hell, trying to survive the hastiness of everyday life. You go back to cleaning what seem like someone else's ashes, and struggle to succeed in the confines of consensual reality.

ANSWER TO A PRAYER

If we do not have solid footing in magical spaces, we seek protection in the impermanence of everyday reality. Uncertainty and sometimes loneliness make us tremble. While battling to survive and accomplish something, we lose ourselves in details, subtly longing for a message about some infinite task or reassurance that in this world, there will be justice and freedom from suffering.

During the most ungodly days, distracted by daydreams, you somehow recall that abandoned enchanted state. Help occurs when you ask, "Where are my magic shoes?" "Where is that foothold in the infinite that makes this world bearable?"

THE MODERN SHAMAN'S DREAMING

The answer to our questions from above lies in the moment. If you like, you can try now.

1. **Look around you and notice what is flirting with you in the moment.** What do you notice, what catches your attention? Just notice it, look or listen. What does it seem like, what is it doing, what does it look like or sound like? How does it feel? Pretend it has semi-human face and imagine what its message must be. Remember what it was that flirted with you.

2. **Now pretend there is a divine being. Call it by whatever name seems right for you.** If you don't believe in such things, pretend you do, at least for a moment. Allow yourself to pray for something, anything, perhaps the solution to a problem that has been bothering you. Whatever it is, experiment with prayer. Ask a divine presence for something important to you, perhaps something you barely admit to needing. Take a moment, feel your deepest need and write down your prayer. Remember it.

3. **Now, recall whatever flirted with you in the first part of this experiment.** Ask yourself how that flirt is the answer to your prayer. In what way is the content or experience of that flirt the answer you were looking for? Try taking the message of that flirt seriously; let it change your present world. Feel that change trying to happen now.

Your own awareness shows that your deepest, almost unconscious prayers are organized by the things that catch your attention, by connections to the infinite, the mind of nature. Your mind is entangled with that of God. Bringing these prayers and the flirts connected with them to consciousness informs you about what Einstein called "God's thoughts" in his famous statement, "I want to know God's thoughts... all the rest are details."

Remember Pauli's dream about the magic ring with the letter "i" on it? Remember that "master" who spoke from the center of that ring. That mastermind is always speaking with you, all the time, through the "quantum mind."

The quantum mind is non-consensual, non-local, not-temporal, sentient experience. In that world are the magic shoes and the answers to your prayers. Being realistic means recognizing the infinite is not in the distant yonder but is the very ground of reality, flickering in your present experience. Always there, ready to support you, the stars in heaven are closer than you realized.

At the end of our journey, we find ourselves with a new answer to those intermittent questions about why we are here. The implication is that "you" are not here; there is only dreaming. From this dreaming worldview, this quantum mind, you and I are not just ourselves, but the whole universe. In other words, we were always here.

I have tried to consistently show that not only physics, but medicine, psychology and politics are also at the edge of a new kind of awareness. Understanding and becoming lucid that we are non-local essences of the dreaming, quantum mind, as well as real people with limited bodies, allows us to appreciate and also step out of consensus reality. We can shape-shift into that quantum mind, becoming whatever we notice. I predict that this shape-shifting will not only relieve the body of its most unfathomable problems, but also have ameliorating effects upon world history, through realizing that the "other" is not me, and—at the same time—really me.

I predict that this dual awareness will create a new kind of social movement, certainly as dramatic as the concept of a new millennium. Just as the essence of a person cannot be found only in a name or a role that is played in life, the essence of every material object is not the object but the quantum mind everywhere. At present, our world is at an edge. The world we live in believes people are material objects with finite lives, people who must live and die. From this viewpoint, it is clear that we have personalities, belong to given families, cultures, and traditions. We need clarity about and appreciation of our differences. Such clarity is urgently needed.

However, the diversity issues and conflicts of this world will never be solved with such clarity alone, any more than the problems of Newtonian physics could be solved without quantum thinking. In the new millennium, as physics, psychology, medicine, and politics go over the edge that split material reality from the quantum mind, people will be freer to be their whole selves, both real and imaginary. In that moment, the world we have always prayed for and dreamed of will be closer to reality.

Appendix: Mathematical Patterns of Consciousness

T his appendix discusses mathematical patterns of quantum physics as metaphors for psychological processes. The material in the appendix will be easiest for the mathematically oriented reader interested in remembering wave theory and pondering its connections with psychology. The non-mathematical reader will find the applications and results of this appendix in Chapter 37.

In my analysis of the math behind physics in this appendix, I show that the indistinguishability in consensus reality (CR) of specific non-consensus reality (NCR) processes is represented by the math and principles of quantum mechanics.

ABOUT WAVES

Let's begin with a brief review of wave theory. Light, electricity, and magnetism travel as waves, which can interfere and cancel themselves out. Sound interference results in beats.

We know about many kinds of waves. Sound waves create echoes when the sound is confined. Changes in the gravitation pull from the moon result in the tides. The sea has long waves or swells and smaller ripples resulting from the surface tension of water. Earthquakes send compression waves along the surface of the Earth, as well as oscillations in the Earth's surface, going up and down.

Quantum mechanics deals with the invisible quantum waves, sometimes called "matter waves," probability waves, or tendencies. Their probability amplitude is proportional to their frequency and energy.

In general, if a wave is moving outward in the direction of the positive x-axis at time t, and at a velocity c, then $x = ct$ at the front of the wave, as with a light wave. The wave's amplitude is a function of the mathematical expression, $x - ct$. The echo going toward decreasing x would be a function of $x + ct$, since in this case, $x = -ct$.

For a wave moving between an observer and a reflector, we have a superposition of waves, one going forward, the other backward along x. Since

$$x = -ct = c(-t)$$

the reflected wave could be understood as going backward in time.

When superposition of two waves occurs, they amplify or interfere at any given x. When we amplify waves of the same velocity but of opposite phase (that is, 180 degrees out of phase), they interfere and can cancel each other out. If they arrive in phase, they add themselves, and the wave is stronger (e.g., the sound is louder, or many electrons arrive at the same place). In short:

Waves in phase amplify.

Waves out of phase interfere or cancel, creating an apparent emptiness, a loss of signal.

In general, for two sources of different frequencies, the result is an oscillation with slowly pulsating intensity.

PIGGYBACKING

The amplitudes of secondary or higher frequencies perturb or "piggyback" on the primary wave.

To confine a wave within a boundary (as occurs when the light you use to look at something bounces off it and back to you), you have the case of reflection of waves. For example, if a string is confined at $x = 0$, we have waves traveling from it and to it in the form

$$y = F(x - ct) + G(x + ct), \text{ or } y = F(x - ct) - G(x - ct)$$

since at $x = 0, y = 0$.

If a wave reaches a fixed point, this arrival at a fixed point is reflected with a change in sign, so it travels in the opposite direction. Waves reaching a fixed end point can also be understood as coming out, upside down, from beyond the fixed point.

Complex numbers simplify the description of waves because of the properties of these numbers, namely,

$$x + iy = e^{+i\omega t}, \text{ and } x - iy = Ae^{-i\omega t}$$

where i is the imaginary number. Furthermore,

$$A^2 = x^2 + y^2 = (x + iy) \times (x - iy)$$

Complex numbers have real and imaginary parts, or geometrical representations with a magnitude r and a phase angle Θ. Thus they describe oscillations and wavelike phenomena.

Waves can be written in exponential form:

$$F(x - ct) = Ae^{i\omega t(t - x/c)} \quad \text{and} \quad F(-x - ct) = Ae^{i\omega t(t + x/c)}$$

The wave displacement has nodes or standing waves. Nodes are sinusoidal points with the same, or "natural," frequencies.

Any motion at all can be analyzed by assuming that it is the sum of the motions of all the different nodes, combined with appropriate amplitudes and phases.

QUANTUM MECHANICS AND WAVE AMPLITUDES

Quantum mechanics depends on the assumption that there is an amplitude, Ψ, for every event, such as a particle at position x and time t. This amplitude can be written as $\Psi(x,t)$. Thus,

$$\Psi(x,t) = amplitude\ of\ (x,t)$$

In this instance, amplitude, which is sometimes called the tendency, is the tendency to find that particle at different places and times in consensus reality.

The probability of finding a particle is proportional to the absolute square of the amplitude, that is,

$$|\Psi|^2$$

What is the difference between Ψ and $|\Psi|^2$? The difference is that Ψ still contains imaginary numbers. In Chapters 15 to 17, we saw that Ψ symbolizes non-consensus perceptions, which cannot be verified in consensus reality. Ψ represents perceptions that are dreamlike. Ψ, the amplitude of quantum mechanics, is a composition of real and imaginary values.

PRINCIPLES IN QUANTUM MECHANICS

The following is a quantum mechanical description of a particle in a simple field. It follows the general scheme given by Richard Feynman in Chapter 3 of his *Lectures on Physics,* Volume III.

Ψ for simple situations is wavelike; it is proportional to $e^{i(\omega t - kr)}$, which means that the amplitude varies periodically in space and time, and r is the vector position from some origin in a complex number space.

Ψ is the wave amplitude.

t is time.

ω is frequency.

k, the wave number, comes from the momentum, which equals $\hbar k$ (the energy of a particle $= \hbar\omega$, where $\hbar$ is Planck's constant).

Principle I. Ψ, the probability amplitude of a particle arriving at x leaving from source s, is given by the wave function. In the Dirac notation, or language of quantum mechanics, the amplitude is $<x\,|\,s>$. Thus

$<x\,|\,s>$ means <particle arrives at $x\,|$ particle leaves $s>$

Principle II. If a particle can reach a given state by two possible routes, the total amplitude of the process is the sum of the amplitudes for the two routes considered separately. Thus, if there are two paths open through which particles go (i.e., openings 1 and 2), then a particle's amplitude is the sum of the descriptions of its going through both slits, or openings, namely,

$$<x\,|\,s>_{both\ routes} = <x\,|\,s>_{route\ 1} + <x\,|\,s>_{route\ 2}$$

Principle III. If a particle can go by a particular path, such as from s to 1 to x, then the amplitude can be written as a product of the amplitudes for the sections of the path:

$$<x\,|\,1><1\,|\,s>$$

Thus

$<x\,|\,s>$ through both possible paths 1 and 2 $= <x\,|\,1><1\,|\,s> + <x\,|\,2><2\,|\,s>$

Principle IV. Furthermore, from the laws for complex numbers it turns out that

$$<x\,|\,s> = <s\,|\,x>^* \text{ and } <s\,|\,x> = <x\,|\,s>^*$$

That is, the amplitude to get directly from one state to another is the complex conjugate of the reverse situation.

Thus symmetries in space and time in quantum mechanics come from the world of complex numbers and the definitions of wave functions.

Principle V. The probability for an electron starting at x and arriving at s can be given by

$$|<s|x>|$$

which is the product of a wave for something going from s to x multiplied by its reflection, namely, a wave going from x to s.

PSYCHOLOGICAL EXPERIENCES PATTERNED BY MATHEMATICS

If we take the math behind observation as a metaphor for sentient experiences behind conscious realizations, interesting patterns emerge, such as equivalencies and paradoxes, all or most of which are known by therapists dealing with altered states of consciousness. (The readers should consider the following as a first attempt to connect sentient experience with mathematical formalism.)

For example, the mathematical expression $<x|s>$ represents the statement, "I am dreaming and, in that dreaming a signal from me is going to you in dreamtime."

$<x|s>^*$ represents the statement, "I am reflecting or tracking: I am sending you an NCR signal which is reversed in time, that is, I am sending you a signal where I have changed the sign on the imaginary number, having noticed and reflected upon it." This may also be understood as a reflection signal of something you send me. And this may also be understood as my reflecting or tracking what I am sending you.

$<s|x>$ represents your dreaming: you are emitting a dreamlike signal to me.

$<s|x>^*$ represents your reflecting or tracking a signal from you to me, where you have reflected and reversed the value on the imaginary, that is, where you have reversed what is called time in CR. This is a metaphor for your reflecting the situation, you tracking the signal from me to you.

However, because

$$<x|s> = <s|x>^* \text{ and } <s|x> = <x|s>^*$$

my signals to you are equivalent to your noticing and tracking or reflection of my signals. You can be tracking me.

The laws and rules of quantum physics sound bizarre and incomprehensible to the physicists because all of these sentient experiences are marginalized. However, all of us know that in moments such as synchronicities, we cannot tell who did what first or second.

In other words, in quantum mechanics, the ideas of "you and me" in a given locality and time become disrupted, just as future and past are indistinguishable at the sentient level. In this way, in physics, we will never be certain whether the electron signaled its existence to the observer or the idea of the electron occurred to the observer before observation took place.

Quantum physics gives us a basis for the consideration that, in NCR, there is no localized you or me; there is only a signal from me which simultaneously could be a recognition signal from you to me. Furthermore, your awareness of your signals to me originating from you is equivalent to my awareness of them coming from you.

FROM QUANTUM PHYSICS TO DREAMING

Thus the wave function, Ψ, or the amplitude of the wave function, is a metaphor for a sentient experience, implying NCR movement or projection between what we experience in NCR as localities and differences. Whether these localities and differences are there, however, cannot be proven in CR.

My sentient dreaming of you and your reflecting upon me or tracking of me as a result of your recognizing me are indistinguishably the same.

In NCR, my unconscious behavior is the same as your reflecting upon it as if it were yours. Likewise, your unconscious behavior is the same as my recognizing it.

For example, let's say you blow a whistle in your home. The next day I call you. Without knowing about your whistle blowing, I intuitively sense it and say to you that you should stop blowing your whistle in your home. This means that my sentient feedback or reflection on what (I am suspecting) you did is the "same" as your having done it in the first place. In NCR, your whistling is indistinguishable from my reflecting on it, or my reflecting on it is the same as your whistling.

Here "the same " means that in NCR, we cannot tell whether your whistling originated with you yesterday or with me today, intuiting what happened yesterday! In other words, we could say that I blew the whistle today in dreaming, just as much as you did yesterday. Or we could say that I was whistling through you yesterday, or you were pondering your whistling through me today after having done it yesterday. All this thinking warps our CR concepts of time and locality.

In dreaming there is an equivalence of the information about doing something and someone else reflecting on that later without knowing about it occurring earlier.

Perhaps a simpler way of saying all this is that in NCR, there is no firm, localizable, you or I. There is a you or an I only in CR. In NCR, we have a sense of non-locality, non-temporality, and unbroken wholeness.

CONSENSUS REALITY

Now, going on with physics as a metaphor for NCR experience, Principle V says that to arrive at consensus reality (CR), we conjugate the wave function. In doing this, there are several possibilities, including the following:

1. Working Alone

   The probability that a signal from me gets to you is $|<x|s>|$, or $<x|s><x|s>^*$. This may be understood as, "I am working on this scene, reflecting by myself, alone." For example, I dream of you and reflect upon that as well, thereby creating insight and reality. I track my own fantasies and can discuss them.

2. Lucid Dreaming Together

   $<s|x>^*<x|s>^*$ is a pattern for dreaming together; here, you and I sentiently and simultaneously reflect on each other. We are both conjugating or unfolding, lucidly dreaming together; we co-create reality.

3. Projecting Together

   $<x|s><s|x>$ represents how I send a signal to you and you send it back to me in dreaming. This could be called co-projecting, or projecting onto one another. In this way, we bring something from dreaming to consciousness.

4. Lucid Dreaming Alone

   $<s|x>^*<s|x>$ can be understood as you lucidly dreaming alone. You are working on the above scene by yourself, alone.

5. Marginalization

   None of these sentient awareness experiences can be measured in CR. Thus they are equivalent to multiplying the wave function by its conjugate. In other words, everyday reality can be arrived at by entirely negating non-consensus reality experiences.

   For example, a Zen painting can be understood as having taken a sixty-year-old painter sixty years of life to have created, or you can negate those sixty years and say he or she made that painting in twenty seconds.

   Whether reality is created by lucid dreaming or is just there in CR cannot be decided alone from the viewpoint of consensus reality. Because of mathematical equivalencies, the creation by consciousness is equivalent to the existence of the world without sentient dreaming: in consensus reality both are equivalent and cannot be differentiated.

CONSCIOUSNESS: A GENERAL PRINCIPLE

I have taken the conjugation of the wave function to be a general reflective tendency toward consciousness in nature. Quantum physics is a specific aspect of this principle. This general tendency of sentient experience to generate everyday reality and consciousness is the creation of what today's physics and psychology identify as "reality." From the viewpoint of NCR, this creation occurs in the world of complex numbers as reflection or lucid dreaming. Observation and consciousness are the result of lucid dreaming.

In spiritual and paradoxical terms, the Tao which cannot be said tracks itself. Thus, by reflection upon itself, the Tao creates reality, the Tao which can be said.

Why should it do this? I have said that physics needs an additional principle, which assumes that the universe is curious and not only wants to know itself through reflection but wants to become conscious. We experience this principle in terms of our own curiosity about ourselves.

All observable events in the so-called real world are, from the viewpoint of non-consensus reality, a result of this tendency to become conscious.

There are many paths to consciousness, and as far as the results in CR are concerned, all paths are equal. From the viewpoint of consensus reality, this appears as an equivalency of all NCR paths.

For example, assume something has a value of 12. There are many ways to arrive at 12, such as $1 + 11$, $2 + 10$, $2 \times (5 + 1)$, and $(20 - 9) + 1$. Quantitatively speaking, as far as measurements in CR are concerned, all have the result of 12 and all are equivalent.

This is like the example from Chapter 37 in which you go from home to work. You can take many paths: go through the park, meet someone, meet no one, you can fall down, get hurt, go to the hospital, then go to work, and so on. As far as the people at work are concerned, when you arrive, they consider you present. That is all the "boss" cares about in consensus reality.

For psychology, however, the various paths you use in getting from one point to another are crucial. You can move alone on the NCR path and reflect lucidly what you are doing; you can dream up the world to reflect you; you can live in various ways. The point is that sentient experience tends to reflect itself, to create consensus reality and consciousness. Although you cannot differentiate these NCR paths in CR, how you travel your paths can make the difference between enjoying or detesting life.

The math of quantum mechanics patterns various conclusions, which sound like perennial wisdom:

1. Every day is potentially a great day as far as consciousness is concerned, because every day the universe uses all your perceptions to discover herself.

2. Everything and anything that happens is everything striving to see itself.

3. Every day, together with everything else, you are involved in creating the world through reflecting sentient experiences.

4. Becoming a whole person within yourself is a specific application of the tendency for consciousness, but this tendency is not individual, it is universal. You cannot become whole as an individual by your CR self alone. You become conscious in connection with everything else participating in this act. Everything together enables the creation of reality and consciousness.

This philosophy is optimistic. It means that all your experiences are important and meaningful. Because there is no clear you or me in dreaming, we co-create consciousness and everyday reality together.

Bibliography

Aspect, Alain, P. J. Dalibard, and G. Roger. 1982. *Physics Review* 49: 1804 (letter).

Aung, S. Z. *Compendium of Philosophy.* Revised and edited by Mrs. C.A.F. Rhys-Davids. 1910. London: Pauli Text Society, 1972.

Auyang, Sunny. *How Is Quantum Field Theory Possible?* New York: Oxford University Press, 1995.

Aziz, Robert. C. G. *Jung's Psychology of Religion and Synchronicity.* Albany, NY: State University of New York, 1990.

Bass, L. A. "A Quantum Mechanical Mind-Body Interaction." *Foundations of Physics* 5: 150-172, (1975).

Bell, John Stewart. "On the Einstein Podolsky Rosen Paradox." *Physics* 1: 95-200, (1964).

———. "On the Problem of Hidden Variables in Quantum Mechanics." *Reviews of Modern Physics* 38: 447, (1966).

———. *Speakable and Unspeakable in Quantum Mechanics.* Cambridge, England: Cambridge University Press, 1987.

Bernstein, J. "I Am This Whole World: Erwin Schroedinger." In *Project Physics Reader.* Vol. 5 (1968-69). New York: Holt, Rinehart and Winston.

Bohm, David. *Quantum Theory.* Englewood Cliffs, NJ: Prentice Hall, 1951.

―――. *Wholeness and the Implicate Order.* Boston: Routledge and Kegan Paul, 1980.

―――. *Unfolding Meaning: A Weekend of Dialogue With David Bohm.* London: Routledge, 1985.

Bohm, David, and Y. Aharanov. "Discussion of Experimental Proof for the Paradox of Einstein, Rosen, and Podolsky." *Physical Review* 108: 1070, (1945).

Bohm, David, and Basil Hiley. "On the Unitive Understanding of Nonlocality as Implied by Quantum Theory." *Foundations of Physics* 5: 93-109, issue 1, (1975).

Bohm, David, and D. Peat. *Science, Order and Creativity.* New York: Bantam, 1987.

Bohr, Niels. *Atomic Theory and the Description of Nature.* Cambridge, England: Cambridge University Press, 1934.

―――. *The Philosophy of Niels Bohr,* edited by A. P. French and P. J. Kennedy. Cambridge, MA.: Harvard University Press, 1985.

Born, Max. *Natural Philosophy of Cause and Chance.* London: Oxford University Press, 1949.

Boyer, Carl B. *The History of the Calculus and Its Conceptual Development.* New York: Dover, 1959.

Boyer, Carl B. *A History of Mathematics.* 2nd ed. Revised by Uta Merzbach. New York: John Wiley and Sons, 1991.

Capra, Fritjof. *The Tao of Physics.* New York: Fontana/Collins, 1978.

―――. *The Web of Life.* New York: Anchor-Doubleday, 1996.

Card, Charles R. "The Archetypal Hypothesis of Jung and Pauli and Its Relevance to Physics and Epistemology." Paper presented at the First International Conference on the Study of Consciousness within Science, Bhaktivedanta Institute, San Francisco, CA, 1991.

Castaneda, Carlos. *The Teachings of Don Juan: A Yaqui Way of Knowledge.* New York: Penguin, 1968.

―――. *The Art of Dreaming.* New York: HarperCollins, 1993.

Chen, Ellen. *The Tao Te Ching.* A new translation with commentary. New York: Paragon House, 1989.

Churchill, Rule. *Complex Variables and Applications.* New York: McGraw-Hill, 1960.

Close, Edward R. *Infinite Continuity.* Los Alamitos, CA: C&C Publishers, 1990.

Cramer, John G. "An Overview of the Transactional Interpretation of Quantum Mechanics." *International Journal of Theoreticl Physics* 27(2): 227-236, (1988).

Crosland, M. P., ed. *The Science of Matter.* New York: Penguin, 1971.

Cushing, James T. *Quantum Mechanics, History Contingency and the Copenhagen Hegemony.* Chicago: University of Chicago Press, 1994.

Dalai Lama. *Sleeping, Dreaming and Dying*, edited by Francisco Varela. Boston: Wisdom Publications , 1997.

Darling David. *Zen Physics.* New York: HarperCollins, 1996.

Dante [Alighieri, Dante]. Inferno. *In The Divine Comedy of Dante Alighieri.* With an introduction by Alan Mandelbaum. New York: Bantam, 1982.

Davies, Paul. *About Time; Einstein's Unfinished Revolution.* Simon & Schuster, 1995.

de Vesme, Caesar. *Peoples of Antiquity.* Translated by F. Fothwell. London: Rider, 1931.

Delaney, Gayle. *Breakthrough Dreaming: How To Tap the Power of Your 24-Hour Mind.* New York: Bantam, 1990.

DeWitt, Bryce, and N. Graham, eds. *The Many-Worlds Interpretation of Quantum Mechanics.* With papers by Hugh Everett. Princeton, NJ: Princeton University Press, 1973.

Duda, Deborah. *Coming Home.* Sante Fe, NM: John Muir Publisher, 1984.

Dunn, Wilson. *Images Stone BC: Thirty Centuries of Northwest Coast Indian Sculpture.* Sannichton, Canada: Hancock House, 1975.

Eliade, Mircea. *Myth and Reality.* New York: Harper, 1963.

———. *Yoga, Immortality and Freedom.* Translated from the French by Willard R Trask. Bollingen Series, LVI. Princeton, NJ: Princeton University Press, 1970.

———. *The Myth of the Eternal Return: Cosmos and History.* Bollingen Series, XLVI. Princeton, NJ: Princeton University Press, 1974.

Einstein, Albert. *Relativity, the Special and General Theory.* Translated by Robert W. Lawson. New York: Bonaza Books, 1961.

———. *The Meaning of Relativity.* Princeton, NJ: Princeton University Press, 1955.

Einstein, Albert, with H. A. Lorentz, H. Weyl, and H. Minkowski. *The Principle of Relativity.* New York: Dover, 1923.

Einstein, Albert, B. Podolsky, and N. Rosen. "Can Quantum Mechanical Description of Physical Reality Be Considered Complete?" *Physical Review* (1935) 47: 777.

———. *A. Einstein; How I see the World.* PBS Home Video, Distributed by Pacific Arts, 1997, shown on "Nova," Oregon Public Broadcasting.

Ellis, Jean A. *From the Dreamtime; Australian Aboriginal Legends.* New York: Harper Collins, 1992.

Eves, Howard. *History of Mathematics*. New York: Holt, Rinehart and Winston, 1969.

Feinberg, G. "Possibility of Faster Than Light Particles." *Physical Review* (1989) 159:1067.

Feynman, Richard. "The Theory of Positrons." *Physical Review* 76:6 (1949).

———. *Theory of Fundamental Processes*. New York: Addison-Wesley Pub. Co., 1961.

———. Probability and Uncertainty: The Quantum Mechanical View of Nature. In *The Character of Physical Law*. Cambridge, MA: Massachusetts Institute of Technology Press, 1965.

Feynman, Richard, R. Leighton, and M. Sands. *The Feynman Lectures on Physics*. Vol. 1. Read, MA: Addison and Co., 1965.

———. *The Feynman Lectures on Physics*. Vol. 2. Read, MA: Addison and Co., 1965.

Finkelstein, David. "Quantum Physics and Process Metaphysics." In *Physical Reality and Mathematical Description*, edited by Charles P. Enz and Jagdish Mehra. Dordrecht, Holland, Boston, MA: D. Reidel Pub. Co., 1974.

———. "Primitive Concept of Process." In *Physical Reality and Mathematical Description*, edited by Charles P. Enz and Jagdish Mehra. Dordrecht, Holland, Boston, MA: D. Reidel Pub. Co., 1974.

Gamow, George. *One Two Three ... Infinity, Facts and Speculations of Science*. New York: New American Library, 1960.

Gell-Mann, Murray. "Questions for the Future." In *The Nature of Matter*, edited by J. H. Mulvey. Oxford: Oxford University Press, 1981.

Gibilisco, Stan. *Understanding Einstein's Theories of Relativity*. New York: Dover, 1983.

Globus, Gordeon G. "Self, Cognition, Qualia and World in Quantum Brain Dynamics." *Journal of Consciousness Studies,* Vol. 5, No. 1, (1988), pp. 34-52.

Goedel, Kurt. "On Formally Undecidable Propositions of Principia Mathematica and Related Systems." Reprinted in English in *From Frege to Goedel: A Source Book in Mathematical Logic*, 1879-1931, edited by Jean van Heijenoort. Cambridge, MA: Harvard University Press, 1967.

Gonnick, Larry and Art Huffman. *The Cartoon Guide to Physics*. New York: Harper Perennial, 1990.

Goodbread, Joseph. *Radical Intercourse*. Portland, OR: Lao Tse Press, 1997.

Goswami, Amit, with Richard Reed and Maggie Goswami. *The Self-Aware Universe: How Consciousness Creates the Material World*. New York: Tarcher, 1995.

Govinda, Lama Anagarika. *Foundations of Tibetan Mysticism, According to the Esoteric Teachings of the Great Mantra, Ocm Mani Padme H-ucm.* New York: Samuel Weiser 1974.

Gribbin, John. *Schroedinger's Kittens and the Search for Reality: Solving the Quantum Mysteries.* Boston, MA: Little, Brown and Company, 1995.

Halpin, Marjorie. "Seeing in Stone: Masking and the Twin Stone Masks." In *The Tsimshian: Images of the Past, Views for the Present,* edited by Margaret Seguin. Vancouver, BC: UBC Press, 1993.

Hannah, Barbara. *Active Imagination.* Boston: Sigo Press, 1981.

Harman, Willis. "The Scientific Exploration of Consciousness: Towards an Adequate Epistemology." *Journal of Consciousness Studies* (1994) 1(1): 140.

Hawking, Stephen. *Black Holes and Baby Universes, and Other Essays.* New York: Bantam Books, 1993.

Heisenberg, Werner. *Physics and Philosophy.* New York: Harper & Row, 1958.

———. *Physics and Beyond.* New York: Harper & Row, 1971.

Herbert, Nick. *Quantum Reality.* New York: Doubleday, 1985.

Hines, Brian. *God's Whisper, Creation's Thunder: Echoes of Ultimate Reality in the New Physics.* Brattleborough, VT: Threshold Books, 1996.

Huxley, Aldous. *The Doors of Perception and Heaven and Hell.* New York: Harper & Row, 1990.

I Ching, or *Book of Changes.* Translated by Richard Wilhelm. Bollingen Series. Princeton, NJ: Princeton University Press, 1981.

Jibu, Mari, and Kunio Yasue. *Quantum Brain Dynamics and Consciousness.* New York: John Benjamin Publisher, 1995.

Jung, C. G. *The Collected Works of C. G. Jung.* Translated by R. F. C. Hull, edited by Gerhard Adler, Michael Fordham, and Herbert Read. Bollingen Foundation. Princeton, NJ: Princeton University Press. 1969-1980.

———. 1966. Structure and Dynamics of the Psyche. Vol. 8, *Collected Works.*

———. 1974. Letters. Vols. 1 and 2, *Collected Works.*

———.Synchronicity: 1956. An Acausal Connecting Principle. Vol. 8, *Collected Works.*

———. 1969. Mysterium Conjunctionis. Vol. 14, *Collected Works.*

———.1980. Psychology and Alchemy. Vol. 13, *Collected Works.*

———. 1971. *The Portable Jung,* edited by Joseph Campbell. New York: Viking.

Jung, C. G., and Wolfgang Pauli. 1955. *The Interpretation of Nature and the Psyche*. Princeton, NJ: Pantheon. In German, *Naturerklaerung und Psyche*. 1952. Zurich: Rascher Verlag.

Kafatos, Menas, and Robert Nadeau. *Conscious Universe: Part and Whole in Modern Physical Theory*. New York: Springer Verlag, 1990.

Kaku, Michio. *Hyperspace: A Scientific Odyssey Through Parallel Universes, Time Warps, and the Tenth Dimension*. New York: Anchor Books, Doubleday, 1994.

Kalf, Dora. *Sandplay: A Psychotherapeutic Approach to the Psyche*. Boston: Sigo Press, 1990.

Kant, Immanuel. *Critique of Judgment*. Translated by Werer S. Pluhar. Indianapolis, IN: Hacked, 1987.

Keepin, William. "Lifework of David Bohm: River of Truth." *Revision* (1993) 16(1): 32-48.

Keynes, John. "Newton, the Man." In *The World of Mathematics*, edited by James Roy Newman. Vol. 1. New York: Simon and Schuster, 1956. (More recently republished by Microsoft Press 1988.)

Kornfield, Jack. *A Path With Heart: A Guide Through the Perils and Promises of Spiritual Life*. New York, Bantam Doubleday Dell, 1993.

LaBerge, Stephen, and Howard Rheingold. *Exploring the World of Lucid Dreaming*. New York: Ballantine Books, 1990.

Lahti, Kakka, and Peter Mittelstadt, eds. *Symposium on the Foundation of Modern Physics*. River Edge, NJ: World Scientific Publishing, 1991.

——— *Quantum Theory of Measurement and Related Philosophical Problems*. River Edge, NJ: World Scientific Publishing, 1990.

Lamy, Lucie. *Egyptian Mysteries: New Light on Ancient Knowledge*. London: Thames and Hudson, 1981.

Lancaster, B. L. "Towards a Synthesis of Cognitive Science and the Buddhist Abhidhamma Tradition." *Journal of Consciousness Studies* (1997) 4(2).

Laurikainen, K.V. *Beyond the Atom: The Philosophical Thought of Wolfgang Pauli*. Berlin: Germany, Springer Verlag, 1959.

Lawlor, Robert. *Voices of the First Day: Inner Traditions*. Rochester, VT: Inner Traditions, 1991.

———. *Sacred Geometry*. London: Thames and Hudson, 1982.

Lederman, Leon, with Dick Teresi. *The God Particle: If the Universe Is the Answer, What Is the Question*. New York: Delta Publishing, 1994.

Libet, B. E., W. Wright, B. Feinstein, and Dennis Pearl. 1979. "Subjective Referral of the Timing for a Conscious Sensory Experience: A Functional Role for the Somatosensory Specific Projection System in Man." *Brain* No. 102 (Part 1), 193-224, 1979.

Lovelock, James. *The Ages of Gaia: A Biography of Our Living Earth*. New York: Bantam Books, 1990.

Maclagan, David. *Creation Myths: Man's Introduction to the World*. London: Thames and Hudson, 1977.

Macy, Joanna. *The Soul of Nature: Celebrating the Spirit of the Earth*, Plume, New York, 1996.

Macy, Joanna, J. Fleming, and A. Naess. *In Thinking Like a Mountain: Towards a Council of All Beings*, edited by John Seed. Philadelphia: New Society Publishers, 1988.

Macy, Joanna, and J. Seed. In *The Green Reader: Essays Toward a Sustainable Society*, edited by Andrew Dobson. Mercury House, 1991.

Mansfield, Victor. *Synchronicity, Science and Soul-Making: Understanding Jungian Synchronicity Through Physics, Buddhism, and Philosophy*. La Salle, IN: Open Court Pub., 1995.

Mansfield, Victor, and J. M. Spiegelman. "Quantum Mechanics and Jungian Psychology: Building a Bridge." *Journal of Analytical Psychology* (1989) 34: 17, pages 3-31, issue 1.

Mehra, J. "Quantum Mechanics and the Explanation of Life." *American Scientist* (1973) 61: 722-728.

Merchant, Carolyn. *The Death of Nature*. New York: Harper and Row, 1980.

Merzbach, Ute and Carl Boyer. *A History of Mathematics*. New York: John Wiley and Sons, 1991

Mindell, Amy. *Metaskills: The Spiritual Art of Therapy*. Tempe, AZ: New Falcon Press, 1995.

———. *Coma, a Healing Journey: A Guide for Family, Friends and Helpers*. Portland, OR: Lao Tse Press, 1999.

Amy Mindell, with Arnold Mindell. *Riding the Horse Backwards*. New York: Penguin, 1985.

Mindell, Arnold. *Working With the Dreaming Body*. London: Penguin-Arkana, 1984.

———. *River's Way: The Process Science of the Dreambody*. London: Penguin, 1986.

———. *The Dreambody in Relationships*. New York: Penguin, 1987.

———. *City Shadows: Psychological Interventions in Psychiatry*. New York: Penguin, 1988.

———. *The Year I: Global Process Work With Planetary Tensions*. New York: Penguin-Arkana, 1989.

———. *Working on Yourself Alone: Inner Dreambody Work*. New York: Penguin, 1990.

————. *The Leader as Martial Artist: An Introduction to Deep Democracy-Techniques and Strategies for Resolving Conflict and Creating Community.* San Francisco: HarperCollins, 1992.

————. *The Shaman's Body: A New Shamanism for Health, Relationships, and Community.* San Francisco: HarperCollins, 1993.

————. *Coma, Key to Awakening: Working with the Dreambody near Death.* New York: Penguin-Arkana, 1995.

————. *Sitting in the Fire: Large Group Transformation Through Diversity and Conflict.* Portland, OR: Lao Tse Press, 1995.

————. *Dreambody: The Body's Role in Revealing the Self.* 2nd ed. Portland, OR: Lao Tse Press, 1998.

Mindell, Arnold, with Amy Mindell. *Riding the Horse Backwards: Process Work in Theory and Practice.* New York: Penguin, 1992.

Needham, Joseph. *Science and Civilization in China.* Vols. 1-3. Cambridge, England: Cambridge University Press, 1959.

Neihardt, John G. *Black Elk Speaks: Being the Life Story of a Holy Man of the Oglala Sioux.* Told through John G. Neihardt. New York: Washington Square Press of Pocketbooks and New York: Simon and Schuster, 1972.

Osserman, Robert. 1995. *Poetry of the Universe: A Mathematical Exploration of the Cosmos.* New York: Anchor Books.

Oteri, L, ed. "Quantum Physics and Parapsychology," Parts 1 and 2. Proceedings of an international conference, Geneva, Switzerland. New York: Parapsychology Foundation, 1974.

Parker, Barry. *Einstein's Dream.* New York: Plenum Press, 1988.

Pauli, Wolfgang. *The Theory of Relativity.* New York: Dover, 1958.

————. "Naturwissenschaftlicher und Erkenntnistheoretische Aspekte der Ideen vom Umbewussten." In *The Collected Scientific Papers of Wolfgang Pauli,* edited by R. Kronig and V. Weisskopf. New York: Interscience Publishers, 1964.

————. Letters. ETH (Eidgenoische Technische Hochschule) Collection no. WHS. Hs 176-52. Hs 1056:30867. Zurich, Switzerland: ETH.

Pauli, Wolfgang, and C. G. Jung. *The Interpretation of Nature and the Psyche.* Princeton, NJ: Pantheon, 1955. In German, *Naturerklaerung Und Psyche.* 1952. Zurich: Rascher Verlag.

Peat, David, F. *Einstein's Moon.* Chicago: Contemporary Books, 1990.

————. *Synchronicity: The Bridge Between Matter and Mind.* New York: Bantam, 1987.

Penrose, Roger. *Shadows of the Mind: The Search for the Missing Science of Consciousness.* Oxford: Oxford University Press, 1994.

————. *Shadows of the Mind.* London: Oxford University Press, 1994.

————. *The Emperor's New Mind.* London: Oxford University Press, 1989.

Penrose, Roger, and Stuart Hameroff. "Conscious Events As Orchestrated Space-time Selections." *Journal of Consciousness Studies* (1996) 3(1): 36-53.

Picard, Barbara Leonie, Joan Kiddell-Monroe (Illustrator). *French Legends, Tales, and Fairy Stories.* Oxford Myths and Legends, Oxford University Press, 1992.

Pouley, Jim. *The Secret of Dreaming.* Templestowe, Australia: Red Hen Enterprises, 1988.

Rawson, Philip and Laszlo Legeza. *Tao: The Chinese Philosophy of Time and Change.* London: Thames and Hudson, 1979.

Rinpoche, Sogyal. *The Tibetan Book of Living and Dying.* San Francisco: HarperCollins, 1992.

Roszak, Theodore, ed. *Ecopsychology: Restoring the Earth, Healing the Mind.* San Francisco: Sierra Club Books, 1995.

Rhys, Davids, C. A. F. *Buddhist Psychology: An Inquiry into the Analysis and Theory of Mind in Pali Literature.* London: G. Bell and Sons, Ltd., 1914.

Satori, Jessika. "Synchronisitic Experiences of Entrepreneurs in the Creation of a Socially Responsible Business Venture: A Delphi Study." Doctoral thesis, Seattle, WA: Seattle University, 1996.

Schroedinger, Erwin. "Discussions of Probability Relationship Between Separated Systems." *Proceedings of the Cambridge Philosophical Society* 31: 555, 1935.

————. *Mind and Matter.* Cambridge, England: Cambridge University Press, 1958.

————. *What Is Life?* Cambridge, England: Cambridge University Press, 1964.

Schwarz, Salome. "Shifting the Assemblage Point: Transformation in Therapy and Everyday Life." Doctoral thesis, Union Institute, 1996.

Schwerdtfeger, Hans. *Geometry of Complex Numbers.* New York: Dover.

Sessions, George, ed. *Deep Ecology for the 21st Century.* Boston: Shambhala, 1995.

Sheldrake, Rupert. *A New Science of Life: The Hypothesis of Morphic Resonance.* London, Inner Traditions Intl., 1995.

Shiva, Shahram T. *Rending the Veil: Literal and Poetic Translations of Rumi.* Prescott, AZ: Hohm Press, 1995.

Singh, Jagjit. *Great Ideas of Modern Mathematics: Their Nature and Use.* New York: Dover, 1959.

Spencer-Brown, G. *Laws of Form.* New York: Dutton, 1979.

Stapp, Henry. "Mind, Matter and Quantum Mechanics." A talk given at the Joint Psychology, Philosophy and Physics Colloquium, University of Nevada, Reno, October 20, 1967.

———. The Copenhagen Interpretation and the Nature of Space-time. *American Journal of Physics* 40: 1098-1116, 1972.

Stuart, Maurine. *Subtle Sound: The Zen Teachings of Maurine Stuart.* Boston: Shambhala, 1996.

Sutton, Peter, ed. *Dreamings: The Art of Aboriginal Australia.* Victoria, BC: Penguin Books, 1988.

Suzuki, Daisetz T. *Zen and Japanese Culture.* Bollingen Series, LXIV, Princeton, NJ: Princeton University Press, 1973.

———. *The Zen Doctrine of No Mind.* London: Rider, 1986.

———. *The Awakening of Zen.* Boston: Shambhala, 1987.

Swetz, Frank J, ed. *From Five Fingers to Infinity: A Journey Through the History of Mathematics.* Chicago: Open Court Publishing, 1994.

Talbot, Michael. *The Holographic Universe.* New York, Harper Collins, 1991.

Tart, Charles. *Altered States of Consciousness.* New York. John Wiley and Sons, Inc. 1969.

Teller, Paul. *An Interpretive Introduction to Quantum Field Theory.* Princeton, NJ: Princeton University Press, 1995.

Van Erkelens, Herbert. "Wolfgang Pauli and the Spirit of Matter." In Kakka Lahti and Peter Middelstadt, eds. *Symposium on the Foundation of Modern Physics, 1990; Quantum Theory of Measurement and Related Philosophical Problems.* River Edge, NJ: World Scientific Publishing Co. 1991.

Venkataraman, G. *What Is Reality?* London: Sangam Books, 1994.

von Bekesy, George. *Sensory Inhibition.* Princeton, NJ: Princeton University Press, 1967.

von Franz, Marie-Louise. *Creation Myths.* Dallas, TX: Spring Publications, 1970.

———. *Number and Time: Reflections Leading Toward a Unification of Depth Psychology and Physics.* Translated from the German by Andrea Dykes. Evanston, Ill: Northwestern University Press, 1974.

———. *Time, Rhythm and Repose.* London: Thames and Hudson, 1978.

von Neuman, John. *Mathematical Foundations of Quantum Mechanics.* Princeton, NJ: Princeton University Press, 1932, 1955.

Walker, Benjamin. *Body, the Human Double and the Astral Planes.* London: Routledge and Kegan Paul. 1974.

Wallis, E.A. *The Mummy, Secrets of Ancient Egypt's Funereal Amulets and Scarabs, Idols and Mummy Making, and How To Read Hieroglyphics.* London: Collier Books, 1974.

Wheeler, John A. *At Home in the Universe.* Woodbury NY: The American Institute of Physics, 1994.

———. "Beyond the Black Hole: Some Strangeness in the Proportion." In *A Centennial Symposium To Celebrate the Achievements of Albert Einstein,* edited by H. Wolf. New York: Addison-Wesley, 1980.

Wigner, Eugene. "Remarks on the Mind-Body Problems." In *The Scientist Speculates,* edited by I. J. Good. London: Heineman, 1961.

———. *Symmetries and Reflections: Scientific Essays of Eugene P. Wigner.* Cambridge, MA: MIT Press, (Page 280) 1970.

———. "The Problem of Measurement." *American Journal of Physics* 31: 6, 1963.

Wilber, Ken, ed. *Quantum Questions.* Boulder, CO: New Science Library, 1984.

———. *Up From Eden: A Transpersonal View of Human Evolution.* Wheaton, IL: Theosophical Publishing House, 1996.

Wilhelm, Richard, trans. *The Lao Tzu, Tao Teh Ching.* London: Penguin-Arkana, 1985.

———. *The I Ching,* or *Book of Changes.* English translation by Cary F. Baynes. Princeton NJ: Princeton University Press, 1990.

Wolf, Fred Alan. *Taking the Quantum Leap: The New Physics for Nonscientists.* Revised edition. San Francisco: Harper & Row, 1989.

———. *The Dreaming Universe: A Mind Expanding Journey into the Realm Where Psyche and Physics Meet.* New York: Simon and Schuster, 1994.

———. *The Eagle's Quest.* London: Mandala Press, 1991.

———. *The Spiritual Universe: How Quantum Physics Proves the Existence of the Soul.* New York: Simon and Schuster, 1996.

———. *Star Wave: Mind, Consciousness, and Quantum Physics.* New York: Macmillan, 1984.

Wright, Alan, and Hilary Wright. *At the Edge of the Universe.* New York: John Wiley and Sons, 1989.

Yutang, Lin. *The Wisdom of Lao Tse.* New York: Random House Modern Library, 1948.

Zohar, Donah with I.N. Marshall. *Quantum Society.* New York: Quill, William Morrow, 1990.

For More Information about Mindell Seminars, Process Work or the Lao Tse Press, please contact, Process Work Center of Portland, 2049 NW Hoyt, Portland Oregon, 97209, USA, or E-Mail pwcp@igc.apc.org Phone 503 223-8188, fax 503 227-7003.

Index

Coma: A Healing Journey

A Guide for Family, Friends and Helpers

Amy Mindell

BRIDGE TO A NEW WORLD

Coma, A Healing Journey is the first practical guide to non-intrusive treatment of coma patients. Step-by-step exercises show family members and caregivers how to communicate with and care for patients thought lost to coma while furthering their meaningful personal journeys. Dr. Mindell's heartful approach bridges the chasm between the coma patient and concerned family, friends, and health care professionals. The deep relationship that comes from caring for and communicating with the person in coma makes healing part of the caregiver's as well as the patient's journey.

Contains:

- Step-by-step exercises for communicating with people in coma
- Advanced training for health-care providers
- Help in understanding the comatose person's experience
- Tips for families in crisis due to coma
- Over 80 illustrations of hands-on technique
- Examples of connecting with people in coma
- "First steps" A guide for getting essential information for working with the patient

"A consummate Guide for reconnecting with, and caring properly for, those we may consider 'lost to coma.' An absolute must for committed care givers." —Ondrea and Stephen Levine authors of *Embracing the Beloved* and *Healing into Life and Death*

289 pages
ISBN 1-887078-05-3
Price: $26.95
Illustrations by Robert King

Lao Tse Press
Call toll free: 888 526-8731

Sitting in the Fire

Large Group Transformation Using Conflict and Diversity

Arnold Mindell

Behind the world's most difficult problems are people—groups of people who don't get along together. You can blame crime, war, drugs, greed, poverty, capitalism or the collective unconscious. The bottom line is that people cause our problems.

Many teachers told me to avoid large groups: they are unruly and dangerous. The only way work can be done, they maintain, is in small groups where law and order prevail. But the world is not composed of docile little groups. Enforcing law and order can't be our only strategy for resolving problems.

Many of us shudder at violence. We want to insist on peaceful behavior: Line up here, single file. Follow *Robert's Rules of Order*. One person speak at a time. Finish one subject before moving on to the next.

Yet enforcing order does not stop riots, hinder war or reduce world problems. It may even kindle the fire of group chaos. If we don't permit hostilities a legitimate outlet, they are bound to take illegitimate routes.

This book demonstrates that engaging in heated conflict instead of running away from it is one of the best ways to resolve the divisiveness that prevails on every level of society—in personal relationships, business and the world...

The fire that burns in the social, psychological and spiritual dimensions of humanity can ruin the world or this fire can transform trouble into community. It's up to us. We can avoid contention, or we can fearlessly sit in the fire, intervene and prevent world history's most painful errors from being repeated.

272 pages
ISBN 1-887078-00-2
Price: $15.95

Lao Tse Press
Call toll free: 888 526-8731

Books and Publications from Lao Tse Press

Quantum Mind	Arnold Mindell	*$26.95*
Sitting in the Fire	Arnold Mindell	$15.95
Dreambody (2nd Ed.)	Arnold Mindell	$16.00
Radical Intercourse	Joseph Goodbread	$14.00
Dreambody Toolkit (2nd Ed.)	Joseph Goodbread	$14.00
Coma: A Healing Journey	Amy Mindell	$26.95
The Leader as Martial Artist	Arnold Mindell	Forthcoming
The Journal of Process Oriented Psychology		$12.00

All books published by Lao Tse Press Ltd. are available at your local bookstore, or can be ordered directly from the publisher:

Phone Orders: (888) 526-8731

Mail Orders: P.O. Box 8898, Portland, OR 97207-8898
To order by mail, please enclose a check in US funds drawn on a US bank made payable to Lao Tse Press for the cover price plus the following for postage and handling: North American destinations, add $4 for the first book and $2 for each additional book. Outside of North America, add $14 for the first book and $4 for each additional book. Allow 3-7 weeks for delivery. Prices and availability subject to change without notice.

Order online: www.laotse.com.

Write for catalog: Lao Tse Press, P.O. Box 8898, Portland, OR 97207-8898 or visit our website at: www.laotse.com